THE

ANTE-NICENE FATHERS

TRANSLATIONS OF

The Writings of the Fathers down to A.D. 325

ORIGINAL SUPPLEMENT TO THE AMERICAN EDITION

A. CLEVELAND COXE, D.D.,

EDITOR

VOLUME IX

I.

BIBLIOGRAPHICAL SYNOPSIS
BY ERNEST C. RICHARDSON, M.A.

II.

GENERAL INDEX
BY BERNHARD PICK, PH.D.

WM. B. EERDMANS PUBLISHING COMPANY
GRAND RAPIDS   MICHIGAN

Reprinted, September 1971

ISBN 0-8028-8095-9

Reprinted, October 1975

PHOTOLITHOPRINTED BY CUSHING - MALLOY, INC.
ANN ARBOR, MICHIGAN, UNITED STATES OF AMERICA

GENERAL PREFACE

TO provide the student of the Ante-Nicene Literature with a copious General Index was necessary to the work which, in eight volumes, comprises the original twenty-four and not a little additional material. But the General Editor felt, at every step of his own undertaking, the need of a systematized Bibliography, to which scholars intolerant of merely superficial attainment might be referred for the entire mastery of any particular subject. It is not unlikely that our countrymen are about to enter on such studies as require the aid of the Ante-Nicene Fathers, in the spirit of honest and very earnest research, and it is cheering to observe that patient industry and unwearied continuous effort in the investigation of great questions is no longer to be considered impossible in our hurried and hasty American modes of life. He, then, who means to understand these volumes thoroughly, and to use them for the benefit of others, must have the keys of knowledge at hand. To supply such keys is of itself the task of none other than a specialist and an expert. The introductory notice of the Rev. Dr. Riddle will inform the reader that I am indebted to him for committing to Professor Richardson the labour of compiling the Bibliography which I had proposed, and which, in my opinion, has been so admirably performed. His work, though it falls below his own standard of all that could be desired, is practically exhaustive, and I rejoice to present it to American scholars as honourable to our literature, and especially to its author. It is most creditable to the Theological Seminary at Hartford that such a work has been completed within its walls, and largely by the aid of its library, which must be especially rich in a collection of rare works, indispensable to a performance of this description. May I venture to say, in behalf of the Commonwealth of Letters and the interests of Learning in America, that I have reason to believe that for this wealth of resources we are all debtors to the enlightened munificence of NEWTON CASE, Esq., of Hartford.

I have felt it due to my sense of obligation to those who have added such an important supplement to my own work on the Ante-Nicene Fathers not only to express in this way my warmest thanks, but to add in a note,[1] brief biographical *data*, which will record here their previous labours in behalf of learning and of Christianity.

A. C. C.

AUGUST 2, 1887.

BIOGRAPHICAL NOTICES.

1. RIDDLE, Matthew Brown, D.D., was born in Pittsburg, Penn., Oct. 17, 1836; B. A. (Jefferson Coll., Penn.), 1852; theological education at New Brunswick, N.J., 1859; Chaplain New Jersey Regiment, 1861; at Hoboken, N.J., Pastorate (Reformed), 1862–65, and at Newark, N.J., 1865–69; studied in Europe, 1869–71. Since then, Professor of New Testament Exegesis in the Hartford Theo-

---

[1] For which I am chiefly indebted to the *Schaff-Herzog Encyclopædia of Living Divines* (Supplement). New York, 1887.

logical Seminary. Elected to a corresponding professorship in the "Western Theological Seminary," at Allegheny, Penn., Feb. 15, 1887, he is about to enter upon his new duties at that place, in the immediate vicinity of his native town. For a list of Dr. Riddle's learned and valuable contributions to Theological Literature, see the Schaff-Herzog Supplement, p. 180. His important contributions to this series will be found in the seventh and eighth volumes. He was conspicuous as a member of the New Testament company of the American revisers in the recent Bible revision.

2. PICK, Bernhard, Ph.D., was born at Kempen. Prussia, Dec. 19, 1842; educated at Breslau and Berlin, and in the "Union Theological Seminary," New York, 1868. Engaged in pastoral duties in New York and elsewhere (Lutheran) from 1868 till 1881, and now in Allegheny, Penn. Member of the German Oriental Society (Halle-Leipzig), 1877, and of the American Society of Biblical Literature and Exegesis, 1881. His literary and theological works are noted, as above, p. 168. In compiling Indexes to later volumes of this series, as well as in the authorship of the General Index, he has rendered most valuable service.

4. RICHARDSON, Ernest Cushing, born at Woburn, Mass., Feb. 9, 1860; B. A. at Amherst, 1880; theological education (Congregationalist), at the Hartford Theological Seminary, 1882-4. Since 1884 he has conferred great services upon his Alma Mater, as Librarian of that Seminary, a position for which his eminent qualifications may be inferred from the Bibliography here subjoined. His publications are enumerated in the Schaff-Herzog Supplement, p. 179. He is announced to edit Eusebius' "Life of Constantine," and to translate the "Lives of Illustrious Men" of Jerome and Gennadius for the "Post-Nicene Fathers," edited by Dr. Schaff, and now in course of publication. He has had, since 1884, a prominent position as Assistant Secretary to the "American Library Association," and is one of the Lecturers in the Columbia College "School of Library Economy."

BIBLIOGRAPHICAL SYNOPSIS

BY

ERNEST C. RICHARDSON, M.A.,

Librarian of Hartford Theological Seminary, and Assistant Secretary of the American Library Association.

WITH AN INTRODUCTORY NOTE

By Matthew B. Riddle, D.D.

INTRODUCTORY NOTE

THE General Editor of the American Edition of the "Ante-Nicene Fathers" was kind enough to commit to me the task of preparing a Bibliography of the entire series. A plan of arrangement was, after conference, agreed upon; being substantially that adopted in this volume. The original design was to include this new matter in volume viii. The exacting labors connected with the preparation of other matter, published in vols. vii and viii, made it necessary to call upon some expert for assistance. The Rev. Mr. RICHARDSON, the librarian of Hartford Theological Seminary, was close at hand, and had, as I knew, gathered material adapted for the purpose in view. It soon became apparent to me that he could do the work much more satisfactorily, both to himself and to the public, if it were entrusted almost entirely to his skill and patience. The proposal to issue a supplementary volume gave time for better results, and Mr. RICHARDSON gladly availed himself of this opportunity for perfecting the work. In view of what he has done, it is simple honesty to allow his name to appear on the title-page as author. My duty to the public is fulfilled when I have made this explanation.

Mr. RICHARDSON, in his Preface, gives a statement of his method. It seems proper that I should here express my cordial appreciation of his fidelity, persistence, and unwearied efforts to render the various lists as complete as possible. Only those who have attempted a similar task can fully understand how much it costs to secure fulness and accuracy in such a bibliography. Having witnessed throughout the scholarly spirit in which Mr. RICHARDSON has ungrudgingly given himself to this task, I cannot refrain from bearing testimony to it in this Introductory Notice. May others be stimulated to more successful labour by the abundant helps he has here indicated to them.

M. B. RIDDLE.

HARTFORD, July, 1887.

PREFACE

THE plan of this work, as suggested by the General Editor, through Dr. Riddle, was a "complete synopsis" of the literature relating to the works included in THE ANTE-NICENE FATHERS. Its purpose is to furnish a guide to a farther critical study for those who have been stimulated by the present quickened interest in the study of the Church Fathers in America, and especially to open the field of modern German critical scholarship. This latter idea was a design particularly cherished by the Editor-in-Chief.

The treatment is one which the author's own method of study, and eleven years' experience in furnishing tools for College and Seminary students and professors, suggests as, on the whole, the most practical: 1. Monographic; 2. By (*a.*) Editions chronologically arranged; (*b.*) Translations, ancient and modern, each language chronologically arranged; (*c.*) Literature alphabetically arranged.

A full method would include also a synopsis of: (1.) Manuscripts; (2.) Sources. Toward these the author had made some collections, but found it impossible to complete in the limited time at disposal. The references to the "Veterum testimonia" in Migne, Galland, and elsewhere, partially supply the place of a synopsis of sources, and the author hopes to carry out his design, formed some years since, and publish in some shape, within a few years, a synopsis of mss. of Ante-Nicene Literature with references to published descriptions where any exist.

The alphabetical arrangement has been adopted under *Literature*, Gebhardt and Harnock's capital monographs to the contrary notwithstanding, as, on the whole, furnishing more easily the information for which men consult such a work. Experience shows that most students use such a bibliography by authors: (1.) One comes soon to know what shade or weight of scholarship, Harnack, or Zahn, or Funk, Lightfoot, or Schaff, and so on, represent, according to their various scholarship or *tendence*, and his first use of a list is to see who have written on the subject, and where their results can be found. (2.) The views of some one are referred to, and one consults such a list to verify the reference and find where those views are expressed. For this latter use a special effort has been made to supply page-references, as a time-saving device.

The first aim of the work is *exhaustiveness*. This is peculiarly necessary in the use of American students in order that the scanty and heterogeneous collections on which American scholars must depend for tools may yield all that they have on the subject. It is a constant embarrassment that there is *not a single adequate theological library in America*, and the student has to use every device to cull what he can from secondary sources. The American student thus works at an immense disadvantage, and must do so until there is somewhere a library which will compare, *e.g.*, with what medical men have in the Library of the Surgeon-General's office.

Literal exhaustiveness is, of course, even more undesirable than impossible. The author has at hand, for example, a very large number of Encyclopædias, Histories of

Popes, Councils, Doctrine, Life, N. T. Introductions, works on Archæology, etc., etc., etc., which have more or less patristic matter, while his notes of general histories of the Ante-Nicene period alone number about five hundred. The greater part of these add absolutely nothing for critical study, and little even to the most accessible of the sources indicated, so that the criterion has been *everything that has fairly entered into the critical discussion of a work* judged largely in the following: —

Method. (1.) The examination and direct analysis of such standard works and periodicals as were available. (2.) The exhausting of such monographs as could be obtained, *e.g.*, those in Gebhardt u. Harnack's Patres apost. (3.) The exhausting of (*a.*) the the general bibliographies of Chevalier, Englemann, Hofmann, Oettinger, Winer, Poole, Graesse, Brunet, etc. (*b.*) The patrologies of Walch, (Caillau), (Clarke), Busse, Permaneder, Alzog, Nirschl, (Schmid). (*c.*) The articles in the Encyclopædias of Herzog-Plitt-Hauck, Schaff-Herzog, Lichtenberger, Wetzer u. Welte (first edition), M'Clintock and Strong, Ersch u. Gruber and the Britannica, and the dictionaries of Smith, Smith and Wace, Hoefer and Michaud. (*d.*) The literary histories of Teuffel, (Ebert), Schönemann and Reuss. (*e.*) The church histories of Schaff, Kurtz, Hergenröther, (Hase), (Hagenbach), (Bapheides). (*f.*) The foot-notes of various monographs, and general works, *e.g.*, "Supernatural Religion."

In addition to these all the minor sources available have been used, especially in the vexatious and difficult matter of the Editions and Translations. In the matter of the later literature the most fruitful source has been the periodical literature, especially the twelve volumes of the Theol. Literaturzeitung.

Purely bibliographical references (*i.e.*, to Graesse, etc.) are in general omitted. Chevalier and Darling are no exception to this rule, since they contain brief notices of the authors. A few works of very little critical value have been admitted, either because they are in English, where there is scanty English literature, or because of some subject where there is little literature, or for some other reason, *e.g.*, Waite, Stowe, Blackburn, etc.

The *fulness and accuracy* of titles are limited by the necessity of doing so much of the work from secondary sources. The author has verified and enlarged as far as time and tools would permit, and, while regretting defects which must exist, can only say that most of the titles are the result of the collation of several references, and embody the corrections of innumerable mis-citations.

Abbreviations. The abbreviations adopted are those of the references themselves, or such as have become the familiar forms. The forms of English periodicals are usually those of Poole's Index, although in many cases these are lengthened for readier recognition. The citation of German periodicals is very various, but a guide is given by cross-references in the list in the Appendix.

The *Appendix* includes supplemental matter introductory to the study of Patrology or aiding in the use of the foregoing *Synopsis;* (1.) A full list of works on Patoology, in which a special effort has been made to straighten the editions of the earlier modern works, — a bibliographical Chinese puzzle. (2.) A very limited list of works quoted in the *Synopsis* which seemed to need enlarged titles or descriptions, and especially where the edition which is quoted is not the latest, as in the case of Wetzer u. Welte, Hergenröther, and Westcott's Canon. (3.) A full list of periodicals referred to in the *Synopsis*. This is included, although it falls very far short of the ideal symmetry which the author would like, and which might be secured with time, 1. Because of the need of such a list in the lack of uniform reference, 2. As a contribution in one of the most deficient fields of theological literature, — the bibliography of theological periodicals.

The author has worked with the very practical purpose of furnishing just what he found desirable in his own method, and, recognizing the limitations of the work, can only say that he has spared no pains nor effort to make the work as complete and exact as time and tools would permit. If it shall prove as useful to others as he expects it to be to himself, he will not regret the time which he has somewhat reluctantly spared from more direct critical work.

May the very practical and direct results of modern, critical patristic scholarship stimulate those who love Him who is the Truth, to a more eager, unwearied, unremitting, humble, unprejudiced study, in His Spirit, of every circumstance which confirms and illumines the story of His life on earth, to the glory of His name.

The author takes this opportunity to express his thanks to the Rev. Messrs. Ropes and Gillett of the Andover and the Union (New York) Theological Seminary Libraries, to Mr. Whitney of the Boston Public Library, and very particularly and warmly to Mr. Cutter of the Boston Athenaeum Library, for special favors in the use of works of reference, and to the various helpers whose interest in the work has contributed to increased accuracy.

ERNEST C. RICHARDSON.

HOSMER HALL, HARTFORD, July, 1887.

TABLE OF CONTENTS

BIBLIOGRAPHICAL SYNOPSIS

NOTE. — For fuller titles, editions, and criticisms of various analyzed works, see Appendix.

VOLUME I.

I. ST. CLEMENT. EPISTLE TO THE CORINTHIANS, ETC.

I. *Editions.*

JUNIUS, PATR. (Patrick Young) Gr. lat. *Oxon.* 1633. 4°; 1637. 4°. [Conjectures in red ink. Generally followed until Wotton.]

MADERUS, JOACH. J. Gr. lat. *Helmst.* 1654. 4°.

FELL, JO. Gr. lat. *Oxon.* 1669. 12° [1 ep. only]; 1677. 12° [2 ep. added].

LABBE ET COSSART. Gr. lat. In: Collect. conc. *Par.* 1671. f°. I. 116–. [Lat. by Vendelini.]

COTELERIUS, J. B. Gr. lat. In his: Patr. ap. *Par.* 1672. f°. I. 143–. [The Latin translation often followed.]

COLOMESIUS, PAUL. Gr. lat. *Lond.* 1687. 12°; 1694. 12°.

CLERICUS, J. . Gr. lat. In: Patr. apost. *Amst.* 1698. f°; 1724. f°. [Ed. of Cotelerius. Patr. ap. Quoted under both names.]

ITTIG, TH. Gr. lat. In: Bibl. patr. *Lips.* 1699. 8°.

WOTTON, HENRY. Gr. lat. *Cantab.* 1718. 8°. [New recension. Generally followed by later eds., except Coustant.]

COUSTANT. In his: Ep. Rom. Pont. *Par.* 1721. f°. I.

FREY, J. L. Gr. lat. In: Epist. ss. patr. ap. *Bas.* 1742. 8°.

RUSSELL, RICH. Gr. lat. In: Patr. ap. *Lond.* 1746. 8°. I.

GALLANDIUS. Gr. lat. In: Bibl. patr. *Venet.* 1765. f°. I. 1–47.

EBERTHUS, CONR. *Fuldae*, 1788. 8°.

SCHOENEMANN, C. T. G. Gr. lat. In: Epist. pontif. Rom. *Goetting.* 1796. 8°.

HORNEMANN, C. F. Gr. lat. In: Scr. patr. ap. *Hafn.* 1828 (9?) 4°. [New transl.]

Patr. ap. gr. *Lugd. Bat.* 1831. I. (?)

HEFELE, C. J. In: Patr. ap. *Tüb.* 1834. 8°; 1842. 8°; 1847. 8°; 1855. 8°. pp. 52–133.

JACOBSON, GUL. Gr. lat. In: Patr. ap. *Oxon.* 1838. 8°. I. 1–203; 1840. 8°; 1847. 8°; 4th, 1863. 8°. I. 1–217. [Text followed by Hefele, Dressel, Hilgenfeld, etc. Cf. Apx.]

BÉTANT. *Genev.* 1843 [?].

REITHMAYR, FR. X. In: Patr. ap. *Monach.* 1844. 12°.

GRENFELL, A. Gr. In: Ap. fath. *Lond.* 1844[–3?]. 8°. [Hefele's text.]

MURALT, ED. DE. Codex N. T. *Turici,* 1847.

MADDEN, F. Gr. *Lond.* 1856. 4°. [Photo. fac-simile.]

DRESSEL, A. R. M. Gr. lat. In: Patr. ap. *Lips.* 1856(57). 8°; repr. 1863. 8°. 46–105.

MIGNE. In: Patrol. gr. I. (1857) 31–198 [Prooemia on Clement], 199–328 [" Ep. 1. Gr. et lat. et notae." Text= Galland, degenerate.]

HILGENFELD. In: N. T. extra canon Rec. *Lips.* 1866. 8°; 1876. 8°. [Entirely new ed.]

TISCHENDORF. Gr. In: App. Cod. Sinait. Vat. Alex. *Lips.* 1867; separately, *Leipz.* 1873. 4°.

LIGHTFOOT, J. B. Gr. Engl. *Cambr.* 1869–1877. 2 v. 8°. [Scholarly, exhaustive. A real thesaurus.]

LAURENT, J. C. M. *Lips.* 1870. 8°; (New title-page) 1873. 8°. [After Tisch. Cf. Apx.]

BRYENNIOS, PHILOTH. *Constantinop.* 1875. 8°. [Based on new ms. The foundation of all later.]

GEBHARDT U. HARNACK. Gr. lat. In: Gebhardt, H. & Z. Patr. ap. I. 1. (*Lips.* 1876) 1–110; Ed. min. 1877. 8°. [1 ed. 1875, " Post Dressel, III." Cf. Apx.]

FUNK, F. X. Gr. lat. In: Patr. ap. *Tüb.* 1878. 8°; 1881. 8°. I. 60–144. [Post Hefel. Cf. Apx.]

II. *Translations.*

Syriac.

[Ms. in Cambridge Univ. Lib. Ed. by Bensly, announced by Lightfoot (1877).]

Latin.

See under editions. In general only translations without text are included here, and so throughout.

ROUS, FR. In: Mella patr. *Lond.* 1650. 8°.

HOGELIUS. *Erfurt,* 1667 [I. Clem. 58–63. II. Clem. 12, 5.]

LEGRAS, ANT. In: Livr. apocr. *Par.* 1717. f°; 1742. 2 v. 12°.

Dutch.

Amst. 1646. 12°. *Amst.* 1656. 4°.

English.

BURTON, WM. *Lond.* 1647. 4°; Repr. 1652. 4°.

WAKE. *Lond.* 1693. 8°, 3–21, 1–78; *Lond.* 1710. 8° [Greatly improved]; *Lond.* 1719. 8°, 5–17, (2) 1–47; 1737. 8°; 5th ed. 1818 [7?]; *Hartford,* 1834. 8°, 13–78; *Lond.* 1842 [3?], 8° [Revised]; *Lond.* 1846. 8°; 1860. 8°; *Phila.* 1846. 8°; also, *Manccina,* 1799, and in: Bickersteth Chr. Fath. 1838. 12°.

Aberdeen, 1768. 18°. [Scarce.]

HONE, W. In: Apocr. N.T. 1820; 1821; 1832; 1836; *Phila.* 1820. 12°. p. 142–79; *Phila.* Gebbie, n. d. 8°. p. 112–139.

CHEVALLIER. *Lond.* 1833. 8°; 1851. 8°; also in: Whittingham. Ap. fath. *N. Y.* 1830. [Based on Wake.]

COWPER, B. H. *Lond.* 1867.

ROBERTS & DONALDSON. In: Ante-Nic. Lib. I. (1868) 7–49. Ed. COXE. I. (1885) 5–21.

HOOLE. *Lond.* 1872.

LIGHTFOOT. In: St. Clement. App. (*Cambr.* 1877.) 345–79.

French.

TEISSIER, ANT. [Cousin?] *Avignon,* 1684. 8°.

LEGRAS (Grassius), ANT. In: Livr. apocr. *Paris,* 1717. f°; 1742. 12°. Also in his: Ouvr. d. s. Pères. *Par.* 1717. 12°.

RUCHAT, ABR. In: Pères ap. *Leyde,* 1738. 8°. II; 1741. 2 v. 12°.

GENOUDE [? ?]. In: Pères de l'égl. *Par.* 1837-43. 8⁰.
FELIX. *Par.* 1837. [? ?]

German.

ARNOLD, GF. *Frf.* 1695. [6?] 12⁰; 1718. 8⁰.
Bibliorum Pentapl. *Schiffbec.* 1710.
N.T. *Schifbecae prope Hamburgum,* 1711. 12⁰; 1717. 4⁰.
GLÜSING, J. O. In: Br. u. Schr. d. ap. Män. *Hamb.* 1723. 8⁰.
GRYNAEUS. In: Werke. apost. Männer. *Basil.* 1772. 8⁰; also ed. Mösl. *Aug. Vind.* 1774. 8⁰.
UNTERKIRCHER, K. In: Ap. V. *Innsbruck,* 1817. 8⁰.
HERZOG. *Bresl.* 1825. 8⁰.
WOCHER. In: Ap. Vät. *Tüb.* 1830. 8⁰.
KARKER. In: Ap. Vät. *Bresl.* 1847.
SCHOLZ. Ap. Vät. *Gutersl.* 1865. 8⁰.
MAYER. Ap. Vät. In: Reithmayr. Bibl. *Kempten,* 1869.
WAGENMANN. In: Jahrb. f. deut. Theol. XXI. (1876) 163-.

Italian.

GALLICIOLLI, GIO. BAT. *Venezia,* 1798. 8⁰.
GRAZIANI, A. L. *Roma,* 1832. 8⁰.

Russian.

In: Christijanskoje Tschtenije. *Petrop.* 1824.
In: Christijanskoje Tschtenije. *Petrop.* 1842.
PREOBRAZENSKIJ. *Mosc.* 1862.

III. *Literature.*

ABBOTT, E. A. Gospels. In: Encycl. Brit. (9th. ed.) X. 814.
Account of Clemens Romanus. In: Chr. Obs. I. (1802) 689, 761 (Am. ed. 692-4, 764-6). II. (1803) 1-2.
ALZOG. Patrol. (1876-8) 21-30.
ANASTASIUS BIBLIOTHECARIUS. Hist. eccl. In: Migne. Patrol. lat. CXXVII. 1077-1114.
ANGER. Synopsis. (1852) XX-. [" de epp. Clem. et evv. can."]
ARDENNA, JACOB DE. Conjectura circa επινομην Cl. R. etc. *Lond.* 1683. 4⁰.
AUBÉ. Hist. des persécut. *Paris.* (1875) 126-; 167-.
BARATERIUS, JO. PH. De Clementis R. ab apostolis ordinatione. In: Success. Episc. RR. p. 32.
BARONIUS. Annal. (1589) 102, 1-23; cf. Pagi. Crit. (1689), 2-12.
BAUMGARTEN-CRUSIUS. Dogmenges. (1832) 84 [v. I].
BAUR, F. C. Urspr. d. Episcopats. (1838) 53; 61-, 95-.
— Ignat. Br. (*Tüb.* 1848) 125-.
— Lehrb. d. Dogmengesch. (1858) 82, note.
— Kirchenges. 3 e. J. (1863) 133-4, 261-3, 275-83, et pass.
— Dogmengesch. I. (1865) 155, 249, etc.
— Paulus. Edit. II. (1866) I. 245-.
ΒΑΦΕΙΔΗΣ. 'Εκκλ. ίστ. I. (1884) 146.
BELLARMIN-LABBE. Script. eccl. (1728) 22'-'4.
BIANCHI, G. A. In: Zaccaria. Raccolt. di diss. (1793) IV. 179-88.
BIGONIUS, HIER. Epistola ad H. Grotium. In: Migne. Patr. gr. I. 47-8, 49-50.
BIRRUS, ANT. Animadv. in Cl. epistolas. *Basil.* 1744. 4⁰.
BLEEK-MANGOLD. Einl. in d. N. T. (1875) 541-; 590-; 752-.
BOWER. Hist. of Popes. I. (1749) 14-20.
BROCHMAND, CASPAR ERASMUS. Dissertatio de Clemente Romano. *Hafniae,* 1637. 4⁰.
BRÜLL, A. Ursprung u. Verfasser des Briefes des Clemens v. Rom. In: Theol. Quartalschr. LVIII. (1876) 252-.
— Clemens von Rom. und der Hirt. von Hermas. In: Theol. Quartalschr. LX. (1878) 44-52.
— Ueb. d. Ursprung d. I. Cl. u. s. w. In: Theol. Quartalschr. LXIV. (1882) 201-5.
— Der erste Br. d. Klemens von R. u. s. geschichtl. Bedeutung. *Freib.* 1883. 8⁰. (VII. 66 p.) [" Nothing new." Harnack. *i.e.* nothing not in 3 preceding nos.]
BRYENNIOS. Prolegomena. 169 pp. s. u. eds.

BUDDEUS, J. F. Clementem Romanum atque Irenaeum non favere missae pontificae. *Jenae,* 1705. 4⁰.
BUNSEN. Ignatius. (1847) 95-, 189-.
— Hippolytus. (1854) I. 44-7.
BURTON. Div'ty of Christ. (1829) 4-12.
BUSSE. Chr. Lit. (1828-9) I. 1-2.
CAILLAU. Introd. in ss. Patr. (1825) 27-29.
CASPARI. Quellen zur Gesch. d. Taufsymb. u. s. w. III. (1875) 157-, 293-, 426.
CAVE. Scr. eccl. hist. lit. (1740-) I. 28-30. II. IV. 1(-17.
— Lives. (1840) I. 147-63. Abr. in: Wake. Ap. :ath. *Hartf.* 1834. 8⁰. 475-8.
CEILLIER. Hist. aut. sac. I. (1729) 598-620. I. (1358) 339-62.
CHAPUIS, P. Un nouv. manuscrit des épîtres de Clément R. In: Rev. de théol. et de philos. (1877) 558-571.
CHARTERIS. Canonicity. (1880) viii-xviii, 104-6, 142-3, 155, 170-1, 196, 209, 215-6, 222-3, 233, 238, 243, 251, 255-6, 266, 272-4, 292-3, 302.
CHEVALIER. Rép. d. sources hist. (1877-86) 465-6.
CLARKE. Sacred lit. (1830-1) I. 91.
CLEMENTINE RECOGNITIONS, HOMILIES and EPITOME. See under these heads.
CLINTON. Fasti Rom. (1845-50) 11, 399.
COFFIN. Clemens R. In his: Lives of fath. (1846) 75-84.
Congregational Mag. XXV. (1833) 682.
CONRINGIUS, HERM. Ep. ad Maderum. 1654. In: Migne. Patr. gr. I. 49-54.
COTELERIUS. Judicium de priore ep. S. Clementis. In: Patr. ap. (1672); also in: Migne. Patr. gr. I. 67-70.
COTTA. Kirchen-Hist. (1768-73) §§ 358-60.
COTTON, G. E. L. In: Smith. Gr. and Rom. Biog. (1859) I. 788-9.
COUSTANT, P. Epist. S. Cl. In: Ep. Rom. pont. (1721); also in: Migne. Patr. Gr. I. 75-84.
COWPER, B. H. What the first bishops of Rome taught. The ep. of Cl. of R. to the Corinthians. With an introd. and Notes. The trans. by B. H. C. *Lond.* 1867. 8⁰.
CREDNER. Beiträge u. s. w. (1832) I. 13-, 27-.
— Gesch. d. N. T. Kanon. (1860) 49-, 120-, etc.
CUNNINGHAM. Hist. theol. (1870) I. 97-104.
— Churches of Asia. (1880) passim.
DAEHNE. D. Christuspartei i. d. ap. k. z. Korinth. (1841) 107.
DAMASUS (Pope). Note fr. Pontifical. In: Mansi, Concil. I. 83; also in: Migne. Patrol. gr. I. (1857) 31-2.
DARLING. Cyclop. bibl. (1854) 697-8.
DAVIDSON. Introduction. (1868) I. 211; II. 112, 269.
DELITZSCH, J. De inspiratione S. S. (1870) 30-, 58-.
DESPORTES. In: Biog. Univ. (Michaud.) (1842-65) VIII. 391.
DONALDSON, J. Hist. Chr. Lit. (1864-6) I. 90-153.
— Apost. Fath. (1874) 113-190.
— The New ms. of Cl. In: Theol. Rev. (1877) 35.
— In: Encycl. Brit. (9th ed.) II. 195-6.
DORNER. Person Chr. (1841) I. 135-. Tr. Engl. I. (1864) 96-101, 356-7.
DOUHET. Dict. d. légend. (1855) 298-306, 1248-51.
Dublin Rev. XLVI. (1859) 42.
Dublin Univ. Rev. XC. (1877) 245.
DUMONT, Ed. In: Ann. de Philos. chrét. (1872). F, III. 405-18.
DUPIN, L. Bibl. aut. eccl. (1698-) I. 12-28, 674.
EBEDJESU. Catal. scr. eccl. In: Assemani. Bibl. orient. III. I. 13-14.
EKKER, E. De Cl. R. epist. priore. *Traj.* 1854.
EPHRAIM CHERSON. Homilia de miraculo, quod in puero factum est a S. Clemente sacro martyre. In: Cotelerius, Patr. ap. (1672) I. 837-44. In: Clericus (1698) I. 811-16. In: Migne. Patrol. gr. II. 633-46.
ERBES, CARL. Flavius Clemens von Rom. und das älteste Päpstverzeichniss. In: Jahrb. f. prot. Theol. (1878) 690-750. [?]

EWALD. Gesch. d. Volkes Israel. (1868) VII. 296–.
FABRICIUS. Bibl. Gr. (1708–22) III. 175–7; V. 31–38;
IX. 67, 410, 414–5; XI. 10–2. "2ª. IV. 828–31; VII.
21–32; X. 211–212, 711, 715; XII. 155–7."
— Verit. rel. christ. (1725) 40–2.
— Bib. Lat. med. et inf. aet. (1734) I. 1101; (1754–)
I. 393.
FARRAR. Interpretation. (1886) 166–7.
FLEURY. Hist. eccl. (1691–) I. 223–4, 240–53, 299–
300.
FRANKE, C. E. Die Lehre d. C. In: Ztschr. f. Luth.
Theol. II. (1841) 73–109.
FRITZSCHE, JUDITH. In: Schenkel. Bibellex. (1871)
III. 452. [Date of Ep.]
FUNK. In: Theol. Quartalschr. LVIII. (1876) 286. [The
Bryennios ms.]
— Die syrische Uebersetzung d. Clemensbriefe. In:
Theol. Quartalschr. LIX. (1877) 477–498.
— In: Theol. Quartalschr. LXVI. (1884) 122–3.
GALLAND. Bibl. vet. patr. (1765) I. XI; also in: Migne.
Patrol. gr. I. 85–122.
GEBHARDT. Z. Textkritik d. neuen Clemensstücke. In:
Zeitschr. f. Kirchenges. I. (1876) 305–.
GIESELER. Church. Hist. (1868–) I. 107–9.
GILSE, JAN VAN. In his: De patr. ap. doct. mor. (1833)
GRABE. Spicil. patr. (1700) I. 254–288. [De scriptis
genuinis et suppositiis.]
GRAETZ. Gesch. d. Juden. u. s. w. (1866) 112; 435–.
GROTIUS, HUGO. Epistola ad H. Bigonium. In: Migne.
Patr. gr. I. 47–50.
GUNDERT. D. I. Br. d. Clem. R. In: Ztschr. f. luth.
Theol. XIV. (1853) 638–658; XV. (1854) 29–63,
450–85.
HACKENSCHMIDT. Die Anfänge d. cathol. Kirchen-
begriffs. (1874) 46–.
HAGENBACH. Hist. of Doct. I. (1850) 56, etc.
— Kirchenges. (1885) I. 105–6.
HAMMOND, HENRY. In: Works. (1684) IV. 824.
HANARD. In: Schulthess theol. Nachr. II. 286.
HARNACK, A. In: Theol. Ltzng. I. (1876) 97–105.
[Rev. of Bryennios.]
— In: Ztschr. f. Kirchenges. I. (1877) 264–283, 329–
365.
HASE. Kirchenges. (1885–) I. 163, 170, 194–5.
HASSARD, J. R. G. In: Cath. World, VI. (1867) 93.
HAUSRATH. NTliche Ztgesch. (1874) III. 99 n. 5;
298–. [Date.]
HEFELE, C. J. In Wetzer u. W. Kirch-Lex. (1847–
54) II. 580–90.
— De duabus ep. Cl. R. In: Patr. apost. (1853)
Proleg. xvii-xviii; also [From ed. of 1842] in: Migne.
Patr. gr. I. 183–98.
HELLWAG. Die Vorstellung v. d. Präexistenz Chr. u. s. w.
In: Theol. Jahrbb. II. (1848) 233–, 254–.
HERGENROETHER. Kirchenges. (1879–80) I. 197–8, III.
91–2.
HEYNS. De patr. ap. doct. mor. (1833)
HIERONYMUS. De vir. ill. 15. (ed. Herdinger 1879)
19–20.
HILGENFELD, A. Apost. Vät. (1853) 85–92.
— In: Ztschr. f. w. Theol. IV. (1858) 572–.
— In: Ztschr. f. w. Theol. (1858) 247–. [Against Volk-
mar.]
— In: Ztschr. f. w. Theol. (1873) 302. [Rev. of Tischen-
dorf's ed.]
— Einl. in d. N. T. (1875) 156–, 348–, 621–.
— Die Br. d. C. u. ihre syrische Uebersetzung. In:
Ztschr. f. wiss. Theol. XX. (1877) 549–562.
— In: Ztschr. f. wiss. Theol. XXIII. (1880) 383, 384.
[I. Cl. c. 44.]
HITZIG. Ueb. Joh. Marcus u. s. Schriften. (1843) 165–.
HOEFLING. D. Lehre d. Ap. Vät. v. Opfer im Chr.
Cultus. Erlangen, 1841. 8º.
HOEKSTRA. In: Theol. Tijdschrift. II. (1868) 650.

v. HOFMANN. D. h. Schrift N. T.'s (1873) V. 4–.
[I. Clem. 5.]
HOLTZMANN. D. Ansiedelung d. Chr. in Rom. In: Mo-
natsblätter f. innere Ztgesch. (1869) 301.
— Kritik d. Eph. u. Kol. briefe. (1872) 276–285, 317–.
[Ep. Clem. and ep. to Ephes. and Coloss.]
— Nero u. d. Christen. In: Sybel. Histor. Zeitschr.
(1874) II. 1–. [I. Clem. 6.]
— In: Prot.-Kirchenz. (1874) No. 36. [Date.]
— D. Stellung d. Cl.-br. in d. Gesch. d. N. T. Kanons.
In: Ztschr. f. wiss. Theol. XX. (1877) 387–403.
— Einl. in d. N. T. (1886) 110–1, etc., 550.
HONORIUS. De scr. eccl. 1.15. Ed. Fabricius (1718) [II.]
74.
HORNE. Introduction, ed. Tregelles. (1869) IV. 322–.
ISAMBERT. In: Nouv. Biog. Gen. (Hoefer) X. (1863)
749–59.
ITTIG. Hist. eccl. (1709) I. 46–50, 62–5, 179–208.
JACKSON. Ap. fath. (1879) 23–61.
JACOBI, J. L. Die beiden Br. d. C. In: Stud. u. Krit.
XLIX. (1876) 707–18.
JACOBSON, GUL. De S. Clementis Rom. vita et scriptis.
In: Patr. ap. (1838) I. vii-xxi. (1863) I. ix-xvii.
JACOBUS DE VORAGINE. Legenda aurea (1846) 777–88.
[Cf. Apx.]
JAFFÉ. Reg. pont. Rom. (1851) 1–2, 917–8. 2 Aufl.
(1883–85).
Judgment of the Fathers concerning the doctrine of the
Trinity, The. Lond. 1695. 4º. p. 29–32.
JUNIUS, F. J. J. A. De patr. ap. doct. mor. (1833).
JUNIUS, PATR. Praef. [See ed.]; also in: Migne. Patr.
gr. I. 43–8.
KAYSER. In: Revue de Théol. II. (1851) 85–.
KEIM. Gesch. Jesu (1867) I. 141, 147–. [C. and Gosp. of Jo.]
— Clemens. In: Schenkel. Bibbellex. (1869) I. 545.
KESTNER. Die Agape u. s. w. Jena, 1819. [" Nur ein
Roman."]
KILLEN. Ancient Church (1859) 186–7.
KIRCHHOFER. Quellensammlung u. s. w. (1844) 79–.
KNOEDEL. Hist. Analekt. a. d. I. Br. d. Clem. R. an d.
Cor. In: Stud. u. Krit. XXIV. (1862) 764–. [State ot
Church at Corinth.]
KONTOGONES. Φιλολ. και κριτ. ιστ. των αγ — πατέρων.
'Εν 'Αθήναις. (1851) I. 13–.
KOESTLIN. Zur Gesch. d. Urchristenthums. In: Theol.
Jahrbb. (1850) 28–, 243–.
KRAUS. Roma sotterranea. (1872) 18–, 41–, 79.
— In: Theol. Lit.-Bl. (1873) 414–.
KURTZ. Kirchenges. (1885–) I. 103–4.
LA BARRE, L. DE. Hist. christ. vet. patr. (1583) 47–8.
LAMBECIUS. De codicibus op. Cl. R. In his: Commen-
tar. in Bibl. Vindobon. VIII. p. 601–4, 606–607. Cf. Ban-
dini, Catal. Mss. graec. I. 92, 99.
LANGE. Ap. Zeitalt. (1854) II. 476–.
LARDNER, NATH. In his: Credibility. pt. II. Vol. I. Lond.
1748. p. 48–108. In his: Works (1831) II. 29–57.
[Hist. of C. and 2nd Ep.]
LAURENT, J. C. M. Zur Kritik d. Clemens von Rom.
In: Zeitschr. f. luth. Theol. XXIV. (1863) 416–425.
— — In: Stud. u. Krit. XLI. (1868) 380–4.
[Rev. of Tischendorf's App.]
— — XLIII. (1870) 135–46. [" Tischendorf's Nachbil-
dung d. alex. Handschr. d. C."]
LECHLER. Ap. u. Nachap. Z-A. (1885) 593–99; Eng. tr.
(1886) II. 340–8.
LEFORT, L. Les récentes découvertes dans la catacomb de
Domitille près Rome. (1875) Rev. Archéol. (1874) VI.
353, 372; VIII. 128; (1875) I. 20; III. 198; VII. 39.
LESKIEN, A. Zur Kritik der kürzeren Legende vom h.
Clemens. In: Archiv f. slav. Philol. III. 1, 379–83. [?]
LIGHTFOOT, J. B. Philippians. III. (1873) 74, 95, 166,
201–221, 247–; Galatians. (1874) 323–, 326, 341–.
— — In: The Academy (1876) May 20. [The new ms.]
— — In: Acad. (1876) July 29.

LIPSIUS. In: Gersdorf. Repertorium. III. (1854) II. 65–.
— De Clementis Rom. Epistola ad Corinth. priore dis-
  quisitio. *Lips*. 1855. 8⁰. (VIII. 188.) [“The most im-
  portant.” *Lightfoot*, 1869.]
— Chronol. d. röm Bischöfe (1869) 145–, 166–.
— In: Academy (1870) July 9. 255–.
— Urspr. d. Christennamen. *Jena*. (1873) 20 not. [Date.]
— In: Jenaer Litzng. (1877) Jan. 13. [Rev.]
LÜBKERT. D. Theol. d. Ap. vät. In: Ztschr. f. d. Hist.
  Theol. IV. (1854) 589–.
LUMPER. Hist. ss. patrum. (1783–91) I. 11–97 (=Migne.
  Patr. gr. I. 121–82.) VIII. 300–3.
LUTTERBECK. D. NTlichen Lehrbegriffe. (1852) II. 54–.
MACK. In: Theol. Quartalschr. III. (1838) 385. [“De
  ratione inter ep. ad Hebr. et ep. Clem. intercedente.” *Geb-
  hardt*.]
M'CLINTOCK and S. Cycl. (1874–) II. 376–8.
MADER. Praefatio. Also in: Migne. Patr. gr. I. 53–62.
MAISTRE, L'ABBE.   Saint-Clément de Rome. *Paris*,
  1883–4. 2 v. 8⁰. [Seems honest and naïve. Critical?
  Judge. Speaking of *all* the Cl. writings, “Leur authenticité
  est manifest. Un autre que S. Clément n'eut jamais accom-
  pli un travail aussi parfait,” etc., etc. If a satire, then
  admirable.]
MANGOLD. D. Römerbrief u. s. w. (1866) 167–.
MARTINOV. Ann. Eccl. gr.-slav. (1864) 57–8, 288.
MAURICE. Eccl. Hist. (1854) 243–8.
MELLIERIUS, LUCAS. Fides prim. Chri. ex Barnaba,
  Herma et Cl. R. demonstrata. *Lond*. 1697. 8⁰. [Agst.
  Bull.]
MÖHLER. Patrol. (1840) 52–85.
MOMBRITIUS, BONIN. Sanctuarium (c.1479) I. clxxxxiii–v.
MULLOOLY, JAS. St. Clement Pope and Martyr, and his
  Basilica in Rome. *Roma*, 1869. 8⁰. (lii, 341 p.) 2d
  ed. 1873. 8⁰. [“Does not discuss his works.”]
MUENSCHER. Dogmenges. (1817–8) I. 113–4, etc.
NEANDER. Hist. of dogmas. (1858) 216 [v. 1] [8 ll.]
— Ch. hist. (1872) 1. 658–660, etc.
NIRSCHL. Patrol. (1881) I. 66–80.
NITZSCH. Dogmengesch. I. (1870) 96–8, etc.
NODIER. Bib. sacr. (1826) 146–7.
NOLTE. Ein Wort über sog. Fragmente des Clem. v.
  Rom. In: Theol. Quartalschr. (1859) 276–; (1861)
  443; (1862) 647. [?]
NORTON. Genuineness of Gosp. I. (1846) 4, etc.
ORSI. Ist eccl. (1746–) I. 288–94; (1749–) I. 407–15.
OUDIN. Script. eccl. (1722) I. 19–48.
PERMANEDER. Bibl. patrist. (1842) I. 411–12: II. 22–
  35; 941–2.
PFLEIDERER. Paulinismus. (1873) 405–. (Tr. Engl.)
  II. 135. [Doctrine of C.]
PHOTIUS. Bibliotheca. 113 and 126.
PLANCK. Judenth. u. Urchristenth. In: Theol. Jahrbb.
  (1847) 487–.
PRESSENSÉ, E. DE. In: Lichtenberger. Encycl. (1877–82)
  III. 205–8.
— Chr. life. (1878) 525–8.
— Martyrs. (1879) 217–23, 629–30.
PROBST. D. Br. d. röm. Clem. u. d. Tod d. Ap. Petr. u.
  Paul. In: d. Katholik (1870) Dec.
RENAN. D. Antichrist. (1873) xiii, xix, 21, 24–, 82–, 120–
  168, 437–. [I Clem. 5-6.]
— In: Jour. d. Savants (1877) 13–. [?]
— Evangiles et la 2 génération chr. p. 311.
REUCHLIN, F. JAC. Clem. R. doctrina. *Arg*. 1738.
REUSS. Hist. de la théol. chrét. II. (1864) 318–.
— Gesch. N. T. (1874) I. 243–5; Tr. Eng. (1884) 244–6
  [v. 1].
RÉVILLE. Essais de critiques religieuses. (1860) 62–.
RIDDLE. Introd. note. In: Ante-Nic. Fath. Ed. Coxe.
  I. (1885).
RINCK. In: Stud. u. Krit. (1839) 1002–. [Agst. Mack.]
RITSCHL. Altkath. Kirche. (1850) 283–; (1857) 274–284.
  [2ed. omits pp. 282-7 of 1850 ed.]

RITSCHL. In: Theol. Jahrbb. (1851) 495–. [“de ep. Clem.
  et evv.”]
ROBERTS & DONALDSON. Introd. note. In: Ante-Nic.
  Lib. I. (1868) 3–5; Ed. Coxe. I. (1885) 1–3.
ROBERTSON. Hist. of Church. (1875–) I. 9–10.
ROHRBACKER. Hist. universelle de l'église catholique.
  (1868) II. 627–, 649–.
ROLLER. St. Clément à Rome. In: Rev. archéolog.
  n. s. XXV. (1873) 289–.
RONDININI, PHIL. De s. Cl., papa et mart., ejusque ba-
  silica in urbe Roma, libri II. *Romae*, 1706 [4?]. 4⁰.
ROPES, C. J. H. The new ms. of Cl. of R. In: Presb.
  Q. and Princeton Rev. (1877) 325-343.
ROSENMÜLLER. Hist. interp. I. (1795) 114–6.
ROSSI, DE. Bullettino di Archeologia Cristiana. (1875)
  I. § 5; II. §§ 4, 5. [“de sepulchris Flavianis”]; Revue
  Archéologique (1876) III. 167–174.
ROESSLER. Bibl. d. K.-V. I. (1776) 45–66 [1 a. 2 ep.]
ROTHE. D. Anfänge d. christl. Kirche u. s. w. (1837)
  374–. [“De numere eccl.”]
RUSSELL, C. W. In : Acad. (1876) May 6 and 13.
  [New ms.]
S., L. In : Evang. Kirchztg. (1877) 228–232. [The
  Bryennios ms.]
SALMON, G. In: Smith and Wace. Dict. I. 554–9.
SANDAY. Gosp. in 2 cent. (1876) 26–31, 58–70, 269.
SCHAFF. Hist. * * Church, II. (1886) 636–48.
SCHENKEL. De eccl. Corinthia primaeva factionibus tur-
  bata. *Basil*. 1838. 8⁰. 77–.
— In: Stud. u. Krit. I. (1841) 53–87. [The second im-
  prisonment of Paul.]
SCHILLER. Gesch. d. röm Kaiserreichs unter Nero.
  (1873) 453–; 583–.
SCHLIEMANN. Die Clementinen. (1844) 118–24, etc.
SCHOLTEN. D. ältesten Zeugnisse u. s. w. (1867) 4–.
SCHRAM. Anal. ss. patr. (1780–) I. 54–71. [Ep. 1.]
SCHROECKH. Kirchenges. (1772) II. 267–72.
SCHWEGLER. Nachap. Zeitalt. (1846) II. 125–33.
SHEDD. Hist. of doct. 3d. ed. (1865–) II. 209–11.
SHEPHERD. Hist. of Cl. of Rome (1851) 8–9.
SEYERLEN. Entsteh. d. Christengemeinde zu Rom. *Tübin-
  gen* (1874). [I. Cl. 5 & 6.]
SIMON, D. W. In: Bib. Sac. XXII. (1865) 353.
SPRINZL. Theol. d. apost. Vät. (1880) 21 sq., 57 sq.
STAP. Études sur les origines du Chr. (1866) 232–.
STOLLE. Ueber Clemens. In his: Nachricht. v. d. Leben
  der Kirchenv. Cap. 2. p. 14–28.
STRAATMAN, J. W. Clemens en de οἱ ἐκ τῆς καισαρος οἰκιας
  van den brief aan de Filipiers. In: Theol. Tidjschr.
  (1881) p. 429–438.
Supernatural Religion. (1875–) I. 215–32, III. 3–7.
SURIUS. Vitae ss. (1618) XI. 484–5.
SYMEON METAPHR. Martyrium S. Clementis. In: Cote-
  lerius. Patr. ap. (1672) I. 828–36. In : Clericus. (1698)
  I. 804–10. In: Migne. Patrol. gr. II. 617–32; CXVI,
  179–84. In: Funk. Patr. ap. (1881) II. 28–45.
THIERSCH. Kirche im Ap. Zeitalt. (1858) 347–50.
THOENISSEN. Zwei theolog. Abhandlung. (1841). [I.
  Authent. u. Integrität d. 1 Br. d. Cl.]
TILLEMONT. Mém. hist. eccl. (1694) II. 149–66, 545–68.
TIRABOSCHI. Storia let. ital. (1806) II. 11. 367–8.
TISCHENDORF. Wann wurden uns. Evv. verf. (1866) 20–,
  92–.
TRITHEMIUS. De scr. eccl. 1.
UEBERWEG. Hist. philos. (1876) 274–6.
UHLHORN, G. In: Ztschr. f. die hist. Theol. (1851) 322–.
  [“de faction. Corinth. et temp. ep. Clem.”]
— In: Ztschr. f. d. hist. Theol. (1866) 33. [Date.]
— In: Herzog. Real.-Enc. (1877–) III. 248–57. (Abr.
  in: Schaff-Herz. I. 492–4.)
VALLINGS, J. F. In: The Monthly Interpreter (1885)
  21–39. [C. and Chr- doct.]
— St. Peter and St. Clement of Rome. In: The Monthly
  Interpreter (1885) 443-444.

VENDELINI, GODEF. De Clementis et ejus epistolarum tempore divinatio. In: Migne. Patr. gr. I. 61–68.

Veterum Testimonia de s. Clem. epp. In: Cotelerius. Patr. ap. *Amst.* 1724. f°; also in: Migne. Patrol. gr. I. (1857) 31–44.

VINCENTIUS BEL. Spect. hist. XI. 12, 52–4.

VOIGT. In: Ersch u. Gruber. I. XVIII. (1828) 13–4.

VOLKMAR. D. Ev. Marcion's. (1852) 176–. ["de factionibus Corinth."]

— Ueb. Cl. von R. u. d. nächste Folgezeit. In: Theol. Jahrb. (1856) III. 287–. [Date.]

— Religion Jesu. (1857) 391–.

— Urspr. uns. Evv. (1866) 64.

WAITE. Hist. Chr. Rel. (1881) 37–43 et pass.

WAGENMANN. In: Jahrb. f. deut. Theol. (1876) 161–70. [Rev. of Bryennios.]

WALCH, J. G. Bibl. Patrist. (1834) 19–20, 278–82, 367.

— In his: Hist. eccl. N. T. p. 322–336.

WEINGARTEN. Rothe's Vorlesungen üb. Kirchenges. (1875) I. 96.

WEISMANN. Clem. R. de justif. per fidem. *Tüb.* 1732.

WEISS, AD. G. In: Theol. Lit.-Bl. (1870) 779–. [Rev. of Laurent's ed.]

WEISS, B. In: Stud. u. Krit. I. (1859) 159–. ["de Clem. ep. et Petri ep."]

WESTCOTT. Canon (1875) 22–7, and 507–8.

— Bible in the Church (1877) 74–6.

WHITNEY, S. W. In: Univ. Q. XXIX. (1872) 24.

WIESELER, K. Chronol. d. apost. Ztalt. (1848) 521–. [I. Clem. 5.]

— Untersuch. üb. d. Hebr.-br. (1861) I. 3–. [Date.]

— In: Jahrb. f. deut. Theol. XXII. (1877) 353–406.

WINDISCHMANN. Vindiciae Petrinae. *Ratisbon.* 1836. [I. Clem. 5.]

ZAHN, TH. D. Hirt des Hermas. (1868) 41–69, 94, 96–, 117, 132, 160, 226, 293, 476–.

— Cl. v. R. im ältest. Märtyrerverzeichn. In: Ztschr. f. d. hist. Theol. (1869) 627–.

— In: Jahrb. f. deutsche Theologie. (1872) 158. [Rev. of Laurent's ed.]

— Ignatius v. Antioch. (1873) 79, 125–, 616–. ["de epp. Ign. Polyc. et Clem."]

— In: Gött. gel. Anz. (1876) 1409–, 1430–.

ZELLER. Z. NTlichen Christologie. In: Theol. Jahrbb. (1842) 62–.

— In: Theol. Jahrbb. (1847) 72–; (1848) 530–.

— Apostelgesch. (1854) 7–9.

    See also, and throughout, the editions, for prolegomena and notes. In general prolegomena are omitted from *Literature*, excepting when printed apart from text.

II. MATHETES. EPISTLE TO DIOGNETUS.

I. *Editions.*

STEPHENS, HENR. Gr. lat. *Par.* 1592. 4°; 1671. 4°.

SYLBURG, F. Gr. lat. In: Justini opera. *Heidelb.* 1593. f°.

MORELLI (?). Gr. lat. In: Justini opera. *Par.* 1615. f°; *Par.* 1636. f°; *Colon.* 1685 [6 or *Viteb.* 1687?]. f°.

MARANUS. Gr. lat. In: Justini opera. *Par.* 1742. f°; *Venet.* 1747 [6?]. f°. [Benedictin.]

GALLANDIUS. *Venet.* 1765. f°. I. 320–.

OBERTHÜR. Gr. lat. *Wirceb.* 1779 [7?]. 8°. In his: Justini opera. III. 2–.

OLSHAUSEN, HERM. In: Hist. eccl. vet. mon. *Berol.* 1822. 8°. I. II, 171–184. ["Vitiose."]

BÖHL, GEO. In: Opusc. patr. select. *Berol.* 1826. 8°. I. 124–74.

HEFELE. Gr. lat. In his: Patr. apost. *Tüb.* 1839. 8°. 125–. *Tüb.* 1842. 223–. *Tüb.* 1847. 300–. *Tüb.* 1855. 296–.

OTTO. Gr. lat. In his: Justini opera. II. (1843. 8°.) 464–507. II. (1849. 8°.) 156–207, and II. (1879. 8°.); also separately. *Lips.* 1852. 8°.

GRENFELL, ALGERN. *Lond.* 1844. 8°. 147–161. [Hefele's Text.]

HOFFMANN. Gr. Ger. *Neisse,* 1851. 4°. (II. 26 p.)

BUNSEN. Gr. Engl. In his: Hippolytus. I. (*Lond.* 1852) 188–. Also: Gr. Ger. I. (*Lips.* 1852) 139–. [Ch XI. and XII. only.]

HOLLENBERG, W. A. Gr. Ger. *Berlin,* 1853 (1851?). 8°.

BUNSEN. In his: Christianity and Mankind. V. (= Analecta Ante-Nic. I. 1854) 101–121.

LINDNER, GUIL. B. In his: Bibl. patr. eccl. sel. I. *Lips.* 1857. 12°. 5–14.

MIGNE. Gr. lat. In: Patrol. gr. II. (1857) 1167–1186 (= Galland.)

CREDNER. Gr. Ger. In his: Gesch. d. Kanon. *Berol.* 1860. 59–61. [Ch. 11 and 12 only.]

KRENKEL, E. M. Gr. lat. *Lips.* 1860. 8°.

HURTER. H. Opusc. ss. patr. XV. *Innsb.* (1871).

STELKENS, AD. Gr. lat. *Recklingh.* 1871. 4°. [I contains c. 1–6. II not published.]

GEBHARDT U. HARNACK. In: Gebhardt, H. & Z. Patr. ap. I. (1875) 216–226. I. II. (1878) 154–64. Ed. minor. (1877) 78–86.

GILDERSLEEVE, BASIL L. In his: Apol. of Justin Martyr, etc. *N.Y.* 1877. 12°. 83–94.

FUNK. Patr. ap. *Tüb.* 1878. 8°; also 1881. 8°. I. 310–333.

II. *Translations.*

Latin.

ROUS. In: Mella Patrum. *Lond.* 1650. 8°. p. 21–66.

LEGRAS. Livr. apocr. *Par.* 1717. f°; 1742. 12°.

HURTER, H. In his: SS. patr. opusc. XI. (*Oeniponti,* 1871. 16°.) 182–200.

Danish.

MUUS, C. H. *Kjoebenhavn,* 1836. 8°.

Dutch.

POOLMAN, W. R. In: Kalender voor de Protestanten in Nederland (Moll). VI. (*Amst.* 1861) p. 39–54. [Omits ch. 11 and 12.]

DUKER, A. C. and MANEN, W. C. VAN. In their: Oud Chr. Letterkunde. Apost. vad. II. (*Amst.* 1871. 8°.) 222–247.

English.

WHISTON, W. In: Sacr. Hist. *Lond.* 1746. 8°. V. p. 346–73.

BICKERSTETH. In: Chr. fathers. *Lond.* 1838. 8°.

C., W. S. *Bost.* 1844. In: Chr. R. IX. 280–290.

COOPER, BASIL. In his: The free church of ancient Christendom. *Lond.* 1852. 12°; 2d ed. *Lond.* 1852.

BUNSEN. In his: Hippolytus. I. (*Lond.* 1852) 188–. [Chs. 11 and 12 only.] In his: Christianity and Mankind. I. (*Lond.* 1854) 174–181, 415–6.

C[OWPER], B. H. In: Kitto's Jour. of Sac. Lit. II. (*Lond.* 1852.) [So quoted but rather by Cooper. See above.]

Phila. 1853. In: Princ. R. XXV. 54–64. [Cf. Lit.]

ROBERTS and DONALDSON. In: Ante-Nic. Lib. I. (1868) 303–316. Ed. Coxe. I. (1885) 25–30.

French.

LEGRAS, ANT. In his: Livr. apocr. *Par.* 1717. f°; 1742. 12°.

— Epître à Diognète. Traduite du grec. *Par.* 1725. 12°.

GENOUDE, [EUG.] DE. *Paris,* 1837 [8?]. 8°. II.

KAYSER, AUG. In: Rev. de Théol. et phil. XIII. (*Par.* 1856) 266–. [Chs. VII.-X.]

German.

GLÜSING, J. OTTO. In his: Briefe u. Schr. d. Apost. Männer. *Hamb.* 1723. 8°. 425–463.

GEHLE, AUGUSTUS GABRIEL. In: Brem. u. Verdische Bibl. *Hamb.* 1753. 8°. I. II. p. 221–39.

SAILER, J. M. In his: Briefe aus alle Jahrh. I. (*Monac.* 1800. 8º.) 37–56.
ZEIGLER. In: Sämmtl. Werke d. K. V. *Kempten*, 1830. I. 126–138. [?]
KARKER, FR. XAV. Ap. Väter. *Vratisb.* 1847. 8º. 103–.
HOFFMANN. *Neisse*, 1851. 4º.
BUNSEN. Hippolytus. I. (*Lips*, 1852) 139–. [Ch. 11 and 12 only.]
HOLLENBERG. *Berl.* 1853. 8º. [?]
CREDNER. Gesch. d. Kanon. *Berol.* 1860. p. 59–61.
SCHOLZ, HERM. Apost. Väter. *Gütersl.* 1865. p. 167–178.
MAYER, J. C. Apost. Väter. *Kempten*, 1869. 16º. 422–440. [Reithmayr's Bibl. d. K. V.]
Protestantische Kirchenz. *Berol.* 1872. 309–315. [Omits ch. 11 and 12.]
BENDIXEN. In: Beweis d. Glaubens (1884) 201–211.

Greek, Modern.

Κομποθεκρᾱ, Δ. I. In his: Ὁ ἀληθὴς Βίος τοῦ Ἰησοῦ Χριστοῦ. Ἀθήνῃσι, 1866.

Russian.

SCHAFRANOFF. 1783.
CHRISTIJANSKOJE TSCHTENIJE. XX. (*Petrop.* 1825) 143–.
PREOBRAZENSKIJ. *Mosc.* 1863. IV. 13–26.

III. Literature.

ALZOG. Patrol. (1869) 45–49; (1876) 53–60.
BARATIUS. De success. ant. episc. Rom. (1740) 76–. [By Apollos.]
BASNAGE. Annal. An. 165.
BAUDOUIN, FR. L'épitre à Diognète. Thèse, *Strasb.* 1860.
BAUR. Kirche d. 3 ersten Jahrh. (1863) 373.
— Dogmengesch. I. (1865) 638–9, etc.
ΒΑΦΕΙΔΟΣ. Ἐκκλ. ἱστ. I. (1884) 148–9.
BIRKS, E. B. In: Smith and Wace. Dict. II. 162–7. [Ambrosius author.]
BUNSEN. Anal. Antenic. 1, 103 seq.
— Hippolytus. (1854) I. 170–173. (*Lpz.* 1852) I. 138–.
CAVE. Scr. eccl. hist. lit. I. (1740) 62–3.
CEILLIER. Hist. gén. aut. sac. (1730) II. 38–42; I. (1858) 428–30.
CHARTERIS. Canonicity (1880) 65, 127, 179–80, 198, 217–18, 226, 230–1, 234, 245, 257, 306, 321.
CLARKE. Sacred lit. (1830–1) I. 100–1.
COTTERILL. Peregrinus Proteus. 1879.
CREDNER. Beiträge (1832) I. 150.
— Ges. d. N. T. Kanon (1860) 58–.
CUNNINGHAM. Hist. theol. (1870) I. 106–8.
— Churches of Asia (1880) passim.
CURETON. Spicil. Syr. *Lond.* 1854.
DAVIDSON. Introd. to N. T. "1868. II. 270–399. I. 101."
DONALDSON. Hist. Chr. Lit. (1864–6) II. 126–142.
DORNER. Person Chr. I. (1845) 409–; Tr. Engl. I. (1864) 260–4.
DOULCET, H. In: Rév. d. quest. hist. (*Par.* 1880) 601.
DRÄSEKE, J. Der Brief an Diognetos. In: Jahrbb. f. prot. Theol. (1881) 213–283; 414–484.
— Der Brief an Diogn., nebst Beitr. zur Gesch. d. Lebens u. d. Schr. d. Gregorios v. Neocæsarea. *Leipzig*, 1881. 8º. (VIII, 207). [Perhaps by Apelles.]
Epistle to Diognetus. In: Princeton Rev. XXV. (1853) 44–66.
EWALD. Gesch. Volk. Isr. (1868) VII. 250–.
FESSLER. Inst. patrol. (1850–2) I. 193–.
FUNK. Zu Ep. ad D. 10, 6. In: Theol. Quartalschr. LXIII. (1881) 146–8.
GALLAND. Vet. patr. bibl. *Venet.* 1765. I. lxviii–; also in: Migne. Patrol. gr. II. (1857) 1159–68. [By Cl. of R.]
GASS. In: Zeitschr. f. wiss. Theol. (1874) 474–8.
GRABE. Spicil. patr. (1700) II. 165–6.

GROSSHEIM, C. A. De ep. ad Diogn. *Lips.* 1828.
HAGENBACH. Kirchenges. (1885) I. 298–9.
HALLOIX. Ill. eccl. orient. scr. II. 281.
HASE. Kirchenges. (1885–) I. 249–251, 318.
HEFELE. In: Wetzer u. W. Kirch-Lex. (1847–54) III. 156–9.
— In: Theol. Quartalschr. (1864) 460–470.
HILGENFELD. Ap. Väter. (1853) I. 9–.
— In: Zeitschr. f. wiss. Theol. (1873) 270–286.
HOFFMANN. Ueber Justinus des M. Brief an Diognet. *Neisse.* 1851.
HOLLENBERG, W. A. D. Brief an Diogn. *Berlin*, 1853. 8º.
HOLTZMANN. Einl. in d. N. T. (1886) 131.
HORT, F. J. A. Letter in: Academy. (1877) May 12.
JACKSON. Ap. fath. (1879) 128–140.
JORTIN, J. In his: Remarks on Eccl. Hist. *Lond.* 1751. 8º. I. 342–.
Justin Martyr's Epistle to Diognetus and the Oration to the Gentiles. In: Church Q. (1877). Apr.
KAYSER, A. La lettre à Diognète. In: Rev. de Théol. (1856) 265.
KEIM. In: Prot. Kirchenz. (1873) nos. 13, 14.
— Celsus Wahres Wort. (1873) 272–.
— Geschichte Jesu. (1875) 375–.
— Rom u. d. Christhum. 460–468.
KESTNER. Die Agape. (1819) 394–.
KIHN, HEINR. Der Ursprung des Briefes an Diognet. *Freib. i. B.* 1882. 8º.
KILLEN. Ancient Church (1859) 367.
KIRCHHOFER. Quellensamml. 36 anm. 1.
KRENKEL. Epist. ad Diogn. *Lips.* 1860.
KURTZ. Kirchenges. (1885–) I. 108–9.
LARDNER. Credibility. Works. (1831) II. 140–4.
LECHLER. Ap. u. Nachap. Z.-A. (1885) 613–5. Engl. tr. (1886) 363–5.
LENOURRY. Appar. bibl. patr. (1703) I. 445.
LIPSIUS. In: Lit. Centralbl. (1873) no. 40.
LUMPER. Hist. ss. patr. I. (1783) 183–201.
LUTHARDT. Urspr. d. viert. Ev. (1874) 67–. Tr. Engl. (1875) 67.
MOEHLER. In: Theol. Quartalschr. (1825) 444–.
— Schriften. I. (1839) 19–31.
— Patrol. I. (1840) 164.
MUENSCHER. Chr. Littenlehre in d. ersten 2. In: Henke. N. Magazin. I. 337.
— Dogmenges. (1817–18) II. 212.
NEANDER. Hist. of dogmas. (1858) 212–13. [v. 11.]
— Church Hist. (1872) I. 69–70, 670–1. [Justin.]
NEUMANN, K. J. In: Ztschr. f. Kirchengesch. IV. (1880) 284–7. [Tübinginen ms. of.]
NIRSCHL. Patrol. (1881–). I. 131–7.
NITZSCH. Dogmengesch. I. (1870) 108–9, etc.
NODIER. Bib. sacr. (1826) 144–5.
NOLTE. In: Zeitschr. f. Kath. Theol. *Wien*, 1854. 130–7. In: Migne. Patrol. gr. II. (1857) 1301–4. [Conjecturae, emend. etc.]
ORSI. Ist. eccl. (1746–) I. 268–71. (1749–) I. 378–83.
OTTO. De Justini scriptis. *Jena*, 1841. 8º.
— In: Ztschr. f. hist. Theol. (1842) 41–.
— De Ep. ad Diogn. *Jen.* 1845 [4º] 8º; 2. Aufl. 1852. [?]
OUDIN. Scr. eccl. (1722) I. 212.
[OVERBECK.] In: The Academy (1874) 64.
OVERBECK, F. Ueber den pseudojustinischen Brief an Diognet. *Basel*, 1872. [Post-Constantine.]
— Studien z. Gesch. d. alt. K. I. (1875) p. 1–92.
PERMANEDER. Bibl. Patrist. (1841–2) I. 414. II. 51–8.
PRESSENSÉ, E. de. Hist. 3 prem. siecles. IV. 509–; V. 254–; Engl. tr. *N.Y.* Heresy (n. d.) 221–7.
— In: Lichtenberger. Encycl. (1877–82) III. 761–3.
Protest. Kirchenzeitung. (1872) No. 15.
REUSS. Gesch. N.T. (1874) II. 16. Tr. Eng. (1884) 299. [v. 2.]
RIGGENBACH. D. Zeugnisse f. d. Ev. Joh. (1866) 139–.

RITTER. Chr. philos. (1841) I. 290–295.
ROBERTS and DONALDSON. Introd. note. In: Ante-Nic. Lib. I. (1868) 301–2. Ed. Coxe. I. (1885) 23–4.
ROSSI, DE. "Bulletino, 1866. pp. 86, 95."
SCHAFF. In: M'Clintock and S. Cycl. (1874–) 807–8.
— Hist. * * Church. II. (1886) 698–703, et pass.
SCHEIBE. In: Theol. Stud. u. Krit. (1862) 576–.
SCHMID. Patrol. (1879); (1886) 35–6.
SCHOLTEN. Die älteste Zeugnisse. (1867) 101.
SCHRŒCKH. Kirchenges. (1772–) III. 45.
SEMISCH. Justin Mart. I. (1840) 172–. Tr. Engl. I. 84–, 193–.
— In: Herzog. Real.-Enc. (1877–) III. 611–15 (Abr. in: Schaff-Herz. I. 641).
SHEDD. Hist. of doct. 3d ed. (1865–) II. 218–9.
SNOECK, GUIL. P. I. Specimen theol. exhibens introductionem in Ep. ad Diogn. Lugd. Bat. 1861.
STAEUDLIN. De scr. patr. ap. Goett. 1800. 4°.
— Sittenlehre Jesu. II. 7–.
STELKENS. U. d. Br. an Diognet. Progr. Recklingh. 1860.
Supernatural Religion (1875) II. 38–40, 354–370, etc.
TILLEMONT. Mém. hist. eccl. II. (1732) 73, 371–2, 493–4.
TISCHENDORF. Wann wurden u. s. w. (1866) 40–.
TZSCHIRNER. Fall des Heidenthums. (1829) I. 217–.
Ueber den Brief an Diognetos. In: Theol. Quartalschr. (1825) 444–.
UEBERWEG. Hist. philos. (1876) 279–80.
WAITE. Hist. Chr. Rel. (1881) 238.
WALCH. Bibl. patrist. (1834) 287, 654–5.
WERNER. Gesch. d. apol. Lit. Schaffh. 1861. I. 126–.
WESCOTT. Canon (1875) 85–92.
WHISTON, W. An ep. to D. . . . . , and proved to be genuine. In his: Sacr. Hist. Lond. 1746. 8°. V. 346–73.
WITTICHEN. Der gesch. Charakter d. Ev. Joh. (1868) 105.
WORDSWORTH. Church Hist. (1881) 104–9.
ZAHN. In: Gött. Geleh. Anz. (1873) 106–116.
ZELLER, ED. In: Theol. Jahrb. (1845) 619–.
— Apostelgesch. (1854) 50–1.
Compare editions and literature under Justin Martyr.
　Note. Ceiller, Hoffmann, Otto (in early eds.), etc., make Justin the Author; Gallandius suggests Clement of R.; Baraterius, Apollos; Bunsen, Marcion; and Birks insists on Ambrosius; Möhler, Permaneder, Hefele, Fessler and Alzog put it ab. the year 100; Funk, later, as Tillemont, Dorner, and others earlier, Bunsen in 134-5, Birks in 3d cent. Overbeck, Donaldson, at first, and Cotterhill make it Post-Constantine. This view is conclusively opposed by Dræseke, Lipsius, Hilgenfeld, and many others.

III. POLYCARP. EPISTLE TO THE PHILIPPIANS.

I. Editions.

HALLOIX. Gr. lat. Duaci, 1632 (3?). f°. I. 525–532. In his: Ill. eccl. orient. scr.
USSERIUS. Epist. [With Ignatian epistles.] Oxon. 1644. 4°. [Not. Lond. 1647. 4°. "Mistake of Fabricius." Means.]
MADER, J. J. Helmst. 1653. 4°.
COTELERIUS, J. B. Gr. lat. In: Patr. apost. 1672. f°; Ed. Clericus. 1698. f°. II. 1. 184–; 1724. f°. II. 186–9.
LE MOYNE, Steph. Gr. lat. In his: Varia sacra. Lugd. Bat. 1685. 4°. I. 1–10, II. 1–524; 1694. 4°.
CLERICUS. 1698 and 1724, s. u. Cotelerius.
ITTIG, TH. Gr. lat. In his: Bibl. Patr. apost. Lips. 1699. f°. 370–390.
ALDRICH, C. (Ignatius and). Oxon., 1708. 8°. [100 cops. only printed.]
SMITH, TH. (Ignatius and). Gr. lat. Oxon. 1709. 4°. [New collation.]
FREY. Patr. ap. II. (1741) 141–64, 335–8.

RUSSELL, RICH. Gr. lat. In his: SS. patr. apost. Lond. 1746. 8°. v. II.
GALLANDIUS. Gr. lat. Venet. 1765. f°. In his: Bibl. patr. I. 305–.
DANZ, J. L. Jena, 1818. 4°.
HORNEMANN. Hafn. 1828 (9?). 4°.
ROUTH. Scr. eccl. op. Oxon. 1832. 8°. I.; 1840. I.; 1858. I. 1–31.
JACOBSON. Gr. lat. Oxon. 1838; 1840; 1847; 1863. 8°. 521–56. s. u. Clement of R.
HEFELE. Tüb. 1839. 8°; 1842; 1847; 1855. 256–73. s. u. Clement.
REITHMAYR. Monach. 1844. 12°.
DRESSEL, A. R. M. Gr. lat. In: Patr. ap. Lips. 1857. 8°; 1863. 376–90.
MIGNE. Gr. lat. In: Patrol. gr. V. (1857) 1005–16.
ZAHN. Gr. lat. In: Gebhardt, H. & Z. Patr. ap. II. (1876) xlii–viii, 109–33. [Cf. Apx. Reconstructs the gr. text of missing portions, from the lat.]
FUNK. Patr. ap. (Tüb. 1881.) 266–282.
PLEZIOTES, CONST. Athens, 1883. In: Δελτίον τῆς ἱστορικῆς και ἐθν. ἑταιρίας της Ἑλλάδος. I. 209–. [P. and Barnab. Transcr. from ms. in Monastery in Andros.]
LIGHTFOOT. Ap. fathers. II. (1885) II. 895–934. [pt. ii.]

II. Translations.

Latin. Ancient.

(Dionysius Areop. and) Par. 1498. f°.
(Dionysius Areop., etc., and) Venet. 1502. f°.
(Dionysius Areop., etc., and) Argentine, 1502. f°.
(Dionysius Areop., etc., and) Argent. 1507. f°.
(Dionysius Areop., etc., and) Par. 1515. f°.
(Ignatius and) Basil. 1520. 4°. Argentor. 1527. 8°. Colon. 1536.
(Ignatius —, etc.) Antv. 1540. 8°.
(Ignatius —, etc.) Venet. 1546. 8°.
(Clementina and) Aureatum? 1546. 4°.
In: Μικροπρεσβύτικον. Basil. 1550 (?) p. 27–.
In: Orthodoxographa (Heroldus). Basil. 1555. f°. p. 95–.
(Dion. Areop. and) Colon. 1557.
In: Orthodoxographa. (Grynaeus). Basil. 1569. f°. I. II. 4–.
In: Bibl. patr. (De la Bigne) 1575; Paris, 1610. f°; 1624. f°; 1644. f°.
In Cotelerius. Patr. ap. Amst. 1724. f°. I. 190–. Also in Migne. Patrol. gr. V. (1857) 1015–22.
FREY. Patr. ap. II. (1741) 153–64.
And in various eds.

ROUS, FR. [Ed.] In his: Mella patr. 1659. 8°. [?]
LEGRAS. In his: Livr. apocr. Par. 1717. f°; 1742. 12°. [?]

Fragments.

　Note. The fragments published first by Feuardent (Irenaeus) from works of Victor of Capua, and afterwards by Halloix, Usher, Mader, Cotelerius, Ittig, Galland, Pitra, Migne, Zahn, Lightfoot, etc., are, rather, Victor's own.

English.

ELBOROWE, THOM. Lond. 1668. 12°.
CAVE, W. In his: Apostolici. Lond. 1677. f°. I. 126–; Lond. 1682. f°; 1716. f°; 1733. f°.
WAKE. Lond. 1693. 8°. 22–39, 79–98; Lond. 1710. 8° [Greatly improved]; Lond. 1719. 8°. 18–29, (2) 48–59; 1737. 8°; 5th ed. 1818 [7?]; Hartford, 1834. 8°. 79–100; Lond. 1842 [3?] 8° [Revised]; Lond. 1846. 8°; 1860. 8°; Phila. 1846. 8°.
CLEMENTSON, W. K. Brighton, 1827.
CHEVALLIER. Lond. 1833. 8°.
STOWE. Books of the Bible. (1867) 433–40.
ROBERTS & DONALDSON. In: Ante-Nic. Lib. I. (1868) 69–77. Ed. Coxe. I. (1885) 33–6.
LIGHTFOOT. Ap. fathers. II. (1885) II. 1051–6. [pt. ii.]

French.

LEGRAS, ANT. In his: Livr. apocr. *Par.* 1717. f⁰; 1742. 12⁰. Also in his: Ouvr. d. s. pères. *Par.* 1717. 12⁰; also in DESPREZ, Bible. 1717.

RUCHAT. In: Pères ap. *Leyde*, 1738. 8⁰; 1741. 12⁰.

GENOUDE? In: Pères de l'égl. *Par.* 1837-43. 8⁰.

German.

MOELLERUS, MART. *Görlitz*, 1578. 8⁰; 1592.

ARNOLD, GOTTFR. (?) In his: Sendschreiben der Alten. *Frf.* 1700. 8⁰. p. 1–.

Brem. 1701. 4⁰.

GLÜSING, J. O. [Ep. et mart.] In his: Briefe u. schr. d. Apost. män. *Hamb.* 1723. 8⁰. p. 387–.

GRYNAEUS. *Basil.* 1772; Ed. Mösl. *Aug. Vind.* 1744. 8⁰.

UNTERKIRCHER. Ap. V. *Innsbr.* 1817. 8⁰.

HERZOG. *Bresl.* 1825. 8⁰.

Italian.

GALLICIOLLI. *Venez.* 1799. 8⁰.

GRAZIANI. *Roma*, 1833. 8⁰.

III. Literature.

ABBOTT, E. A. Gospels. In: Encycl. Brit. (9th ed.) X. 815, 822.

ADENEY, W. F. In: Brit. Q. LXXXII. (1886) 31–67.

ALZOG. Patrol. (1876) 44–46.

ANGER. Synops. Ev. xxiii.

ARMACHANUS, JAC. Dissertationes de epistolis ss. Ignatii et Polycarpi. In: Cotelerius. Patr. apost. *Antv.* 1698; *Amst.* 1724. f⁰.

ARUNDEL. Discov. in Asia Minor. 11. 397.

AUBÉ. Hist. d. perséc. (1875) 325–, etc.

— La polémique chr. (1883) 103.

BACKHOUSE, J. H. Curious blunders in several eds. of Polycarp. Letter. In: The Academy (1881) 394ª–395ᵇ.

— Eds. of P. and Barnabas. In: The Academy (1881) 435ᵇ–436ª.

— Mader's editions of Polycarp and Barnabas. In: The Academy (1881) 32ᶜ.

BALTHAZAR, J. H. Doct. P. de praecipuis Chr. fidei capitibus. *Jenae*, 1738. 8⁰.

BARATIER. De success. ant. episc. Rom. (1740) 201.

BARONIUS. Annal. (1689) 167, 8–10; 169, 2–20: cf. Pagi. Crit. (1689) 167, 5; 169, 4–5.

BAUMGARTEN–CRUSIUS. Dogmenges. (1832) 84 [v. 1].

BAUR. Dogmengesch. I. (1865) 252–3, 260–1.

ΒΑΦΕΙΔΗΣ 'Εκκλ. ἱστ. I. (1884) 147–8.

BELLARMIN–LABBE. Script. eccl. (1728) 26.

BERTHOLDT. Dogmenges. (1822–3) I. 31, etc.

BING, JUST. Dissertatio de P. *Hafn.* 1740. 4⁰.

BLACKBURN. Hist. of Church. (1879) 29–30.

BLEEK. Einl. N. T. 234.

BOEHRINGER. Kirchenges. (1873–) I. 1.

BORGHESI. Iscrizioni di Sepino (1852); also in Oeuvres. V. 345–.

BUCHERUS. Tract. de Pasch. Cycl. Jud. 8.

BULLIALDUS, ISMAEL. Dissertatio de S. Benigno Divionensi, qua fabulam de Benigno hoc, per Polycarpum in Galliam misso, refellit. *Paris*, 1657. 8⁰.

BUNSEN. Ignatius. (1847) 107–.

— Hippolytus. (1854) I. 223–8.

BURTON. Trinity. (1831) 4–6 (–15).

BUSSE. Chr. Lit. (1828–9) I. 4–5.

CAILLAU. Introd. in ss. Patr. (1825) 39–46.

CAVE. Hist. lit. (1740–) I. 44–47.

— Lives (1840) I. 192–218. Abr. in: Wake. Ap. fath. *Hart.* 1834. p. 479–83.

CEILLIER; Hist. gén. d. aut. sac. (1729) I. 672–83; I. (1858) 392–8.

CENTURIATORES MAGDEB. Cent. II. c. 10.

CHARTERIS. Canonicity. (1880) xxxiii.-xl., 112, 197, 216, 225, 230, 233–4, 239–40, 244, 253, 257, 262–3, 275, 304–5, 320–1, 328, 331.

CHEVALIER. Rép. d. sources hist. (1877–86) 1857.

CLARKE. Sacred lit. (1830–1) I. 43–4.

CLEMENS ALEXANDR. In: Liber quis dives, etc.

CLINTON. Fasti Rom. (1845–50) I. Ann. 150, 166; II. 401.

COETLOSQUET. Vie de s. Ignace et de s. Polycarpe. *Metz*, 1852. 12⁰.

COFFIN. Lives of fath. (1846) 117–126.

COTTA. § 275–282.

CRUCIGERUS, CASP. Oratio de Polycarpi vita. *Wittebergae*, 1543. 8⁰. Repr. in: Declamationes Melanchthonis. *Argent.* 1558. 8⁰. II. 336–.

CUNNINGHAM, WM. Hist. theol. (1870) I. 105–6.

— Churches of Asia. (1880) passim.

DALLAEUS. De scr. Dionysii Areop. et Ignatii. 426–.

DARLING. Cyclop. bibliog. 2414–5, 2979.

DAVIDSON. Introd. N. T. II. 512.

DENZINGER. In: Theol. Quartalschr. (1851) 399–409.

De ss. mart. Smyrn. Polycarpo et aliis XII. In: Acta ss. Bolland (1643) Jan. II. 691–5 (3. III. 306–10.)

DONALDSON, J. Hist. Chr. L. 1864–6. I. 154–200.

— Apost. fathers. (1874) 191–242.

— In: Encycl. Brit. (9th ed.) II. 197.

DORNER. Person of Christ. I. (1864) 116–9, 371–4.

DOUHET. Dict. d. légend. (1855) 1308.

DUPIN. Nouv. bibl. aut. eccl. (1698) I. 80–91.

EGLI, E. D. Mart. d. P. In: Ztschr. f. wiss. Theol. XXV. (1882) 227–.

— Lucian u. P. In: Ztschr. f. wiss. Theol. XXVI. (1883) 166–80.

— Zum Todesjahr, P. In: Ztschr. f. wiss. Theol. XXVII. (1884) 216–9.

EICHHORN. Einl. N. T. I. 151.

EUSEBIUS. Hist. eccl. IV. c. 15.

EWALD. Gesch. d. V. Israel. VII. 310.

FABRICIUS. Bibl. Gr. (1712) V. 47–51; IX. 414–5 (2. VII. 47–52; X. 315, 715).

FISHER. Beginnings. (1877) 321–, 552–.

F[ISQUET?], H. In: Nouv. Biog. Gen. (Hoefer) XL. (1862) 670–1.

FLEURY. Hist. eccl. (1691–) I. 372–6, 432–4.

FRIEDLÄNDER. Sittengeschichte Roms. III. 440, 442, 654.

GALLAND. Vet. patr. bibl. *Venet.* 1765. f⁰. I. lxv–; also in: Migne. Patrol. gr. V. (1857) 1021–4.

GEBHARDT. In: Ztschr. f. wiss. Theol. (1875) 377–395.

GIESELER. Church Hist. (1868–) I. 110.

GLEY. In: Biog. Univ. (Michaud) (1842–65) XXXIII. 674–5.

GRODDECK, GABR. De anno et die passionis s. Polycarpi. *Gedani*, 1704. 4⁰. [Groddeck = Zitzschär, Frid?]

HAGENBACH. Hist. of Doct. I. (1850) 57, etc.

— Kirchenges. (1885) I. 139–42.

HALLOIX. Eccl. orient. script. (1633) I. 470–598.

HARNACK, A. In: Encycl. Brit. (9th ed.) XIX. 414–6.

— In: Theol. Ltzng. (1882).

— In: Expositor (1885) 401–14; (1886) 9–22, 175–92. [Rev. of Lightfoot.]

HASE. Kirchenges. (1885–) I. 227–9, 290–1, 393–4.

HEFELE. In: Theol. Quartalschr. (1843) 143–.

— In: Wetzer u. W. Kirch-Lex. (1847–54) VIII. 572–5.

— Patr. ap. opera. ed. 3. *Tub.* 1847. 8⁰; also in: Migne. Patrol. gr. V. (1857) 995–1002.

HERGENROETHER. Kirchenges. (1879–80) I. 89–90; III. 38.

HEUMANNUS, CHRIST. AUG. Examen fabulae de columba ex Polycarpi rogo evolante. In: Bibl. hist.-phil.-theol. (*Bremae*, 1720) III. 429–38.

HIERONYMUS. De vir. ill. 17.

HILGENFELD. Apost. Vät. 271–4.

HILGENFELD. In: Ztschr. f. wiss. Theol. (1861) 290–; (1870) 203; (1874) 199–, etc., 310–, 342–.
— D. Mart. In: Ztschr. f. wiss. Theol. XXII. (1879) 145–170.
— D. Br. d. P. an d. Phil. In: Ztschr. f. wiss. Theol. XXIX. (1886) 180–206.
HOFMANN. Heil. Schr. N. T. V. 27–.
HOLTZMANN, H. L. D. Verhältniss d. Johannes zu Ign. u. P. In: Ztschr. f. wiss. Theol. XX. (1877) 187–214.
— Einl. in d. N. T. (1886) 124–5, etc.
ITTIG. Hist. eccl. (1709) II. 4–6, 194–204.
JACKSON. Ap. fath. (1879) 77–87.
JORTIN, J. Mart. of P. In his: Remarks on Eccl. Hist. *Lond.* 1752. 8°. II. 101–, 373–, 416–.
JUNIUS, PATR. In P. ep. Notulae crit.
KEIM. Aus d. Urchristenthum. (1878) 90–133.
— Celsus' Wahres Wort. (1873) 145.
— Gesch. Jesu. (1867) I. 162–.
— Rom u. d. Christenth. 586–.
KILLEN. Anc. Church. (1859) 293–4, 365.
KURTZ. Kirchenges. (1885–) I. 107–8.
LARDNER. Credibility. *Lond.* 1748. 8°. II. 1. 189–; also in: Works (1831) II. 94–111.
LE BLANT, EDM. Mém. sur les supplices. In: Mém. Acad. Inscript. XXVIII. (1874).
LECHLER. Ap. u. Nachap. Z–A. (1885) 607–8. Engl. tr. (1886) II. 356–8.
LE MOYNE, ST. In his: Varia Sacr. *Lugd. Bat.* 1685. 4°. I. Proleg.
LE NOURRY, NIC. De Epist. Polycarpi. In his: Appar. ad Bibl. Patr. (1703) col. 161–66.
LESSIUS. Ueber Polycarps Brief. In his: Wahrh. d. chr. Rel. p. 47–.
LETRONNE. Recherches sur l'Égypte. (1823) 253.
Life of P. *Lond.* 1847. 32°.
LIGHTFOOT, J. B. In: Contemp. XXV. (1874) 827–.
— Apost. fathers. II. (1885) I. 417–702.
LIPSIUS. 3 syr. Briefe d. Ignat. (1859) 14–.
— Chron. d. röm. Bisch. (1869) 189–, 263.
— In: Ztschr. f. wiss. Theol. (1874) 188–214.
— Das Todesjahr Polycarps. In: Jahrbb. f. prot. Theol. (1878) 751–768.
— Z. Mart. Polycarps. In: Jahrbb. f. prot. Theol. (1881), 574–576.
LONGUERUE, L. DUF. DE. De P. ann. mart. In his: Diss. de var. epochis ... vett. Orientt. *Lips.* 1750. 4°. p. 17.
LUCHINI. Atti sinceri. (1777) I. 293–310.
LUMPER. Hist. ss. patrum. (1783) I. 333–359.
LUTHARDT. St. John the Author of the Fourth Gospel. (1875) 69–73, 126.
M'CLINTOCK and S. Cycl. (1874–) VIII. 360–3.
MARQUADT. Röm. Staatsverwaltung. I. (1873) 375.
MASSON. In: Jebb's Aristides (*Oxon.* 1722); also in: Dindorf. Aristides. (1829) p. lxxxviii–.
MAURICE. Eccl. Hist. (1854) 185–193.
MEANS, J. C. In: Smith. Gr. and Rom. Biog. (1859) III. 450–3.
Memoirs of Polycarp. In: Meth. M. XXXII. (1809) 313–.
MILMAN. Hist. of Chr. II. ch. 7.
MOMBRITIUS, BONIN. Sanctuarium. (c. 1479) II. ccxi.
MOSHEIM. De Rebus Chr. 161.
MUIR, A. F. In: Brit. & For. R. XXXV. (1886) 298–325.
MUENSCHER. Dogmenges. (1817–8) I. 114.
NEANDER. Church Hist. (1872) I. 299, 465, 661, 677.
NIRSCHL. Patrol. (1881–) I. 121–131.
NITZSCH. Dogmengesch. I. (1870) 107–8, etc.
NODIER. Bib. sacr. (1826) 148.
NORIS. De anno Maced. I.
— In: Op. (*Veron.* 1729) II. 30.
NORTON. Genuineness of Gosp. I. (1846) 4, etc.
OLSHAUSEN. Monum. hist. eccles. I. (1870).
ORSI. Ist. eccl. (1746–) I. 351–3. II. 48–51, 121–4.
(1749–) I. 497–9. II. 69–74, 175–80.

PEARSON, J. De anno mart. P. In his: De scr. et success. prim. Romae Epp. *Lond.* 1687. 4°. II. 276.
PERMANEDER. Bibl. patrist. (1842) I. 413–4; II. 64–70.
PIONIUS. Vita S. Polycarpi. In: Acta ss. *Antv.* Jun. II. 691–; In: Tenzelius, Gui. E. Exercitationes selectae. I. 73; Ed. Duchesne. *Par.* 1881; also in: Funk. Patr. ap. *Tüb.* 1881. liv.-lviii. 315–357; Zahn; Lightfoot. Ap. F. *Lond.* 1885. II. ii. 1005–47, 1068–86 [Gr. and Engl.] [4th or 5th cent. *Funk.* "Worthless." *Harnack.*]
PITRA. Spicil. Solesm. (1852) I. 266.
PRESSENSÉ. Martyrs. (1879) 232–6.
RANDELL, T. The date of Polycarp's martyrdom. In: Studia Biblica. *Oxford,* 1885. 175–207.
REINACH, S. Saint P. et les juifs de Smyrne. In: Revue des études juives. (1885) p. 235–238.
RENAN. Antichrist. 1873.
— In: Jour. d. savants. (1874) 46–.
— L'église chrét. (1879) 437–466, etc.
— Les évangiles. xxviii–. 486–, 494–.
— Marc-Aurèle. 417–.
RÉVILLE, JO. De Anno Dieque quibus Polycarpus Smyrnæ martyrium tulit. *Genx.* 1880. 8°. (65 p.)
RITSCHL. Entsteh. d. altkath. Kirche. (1857) 584–600.
ROBERTS and DONALDSON. Introd. note. In: Ante-Nic. Lib. I. (1868) 65–8. Ed. Coxe. I. (1885) 31–32.
ROBERTSON. Hist. of Church. (1875–) I. 40–4.
ROSENMÜLLER. Hist. interp. I. (1795) 114–6.
RÖSSLER. Bibl. d. K. V. I. (1776) 93–100.
ROVERS, M. A. A. De Marteldood van Polycarpus. In: Theol. Tijdschr. (1881) 450–464.
SANDAY. Gosp. in 2 cent. (1876) 36, 82–7, 276–8.
St. Polycarp. In: Chr. Obs. III. (1804) 521–; 585–.
SCHAFF. Hist. * * Church. II. (1886) 50–52, 664–70.
SCHILLER, H. Gesch. d. Röm. Kaiserzeit. I. ii. (1883) 684.
SCHLIEMANN. Clementinen. (1884) 418–21.
SCHMID. Patrol. (1879); (1886) 33–4.
SCHOLTEN. Die ält. Zeugnisse. (1867) 41.
SCHRAM. Anal. ss. patr. (1780) I. 105–9.
SCHROECKH. Kirchenges. (1772–) III. 56–7, 108–14.
SCHÜRER. In: Ztschr. f. hist. Theol. (1870) 202–204.
SCHWEGLER. Nachap. Zcitalt. (1846) II. 154–9.
SCULTETUS, ABR. De P. vita et scr. In his: Medullae theol. patr. synt. *Francof.* 1634. 4°. I. 350–.
SEMLER. Zu Baumgarten's Unters. Theol. Streitigk. II. 36–.
SHEDD. Hist. of doct. 3d ed. (1865–) II. 208.
STEITZ. In: Jabrb. f. deut. Theol. (1861) 126–133.
STIEREN. In: Ztschr. f. hist. Theol. (1842).
STRAUSS, V. Polykarpus. *Heidelb.* 1859 (60?) 8°.
STRŒHLIN, E. In: Lichtenberger. Encycl. (1877–82) X. 673–6.
Supernatural Religion. (1875–) I. 274–82; II. 267–71; III. 13–5.
SURIUS. Vitae ss. (1618) I. 431–4.
TENTZELIUS, W. E. Comment. de P. *Vitemb.* 1684. 8°; also in his: Exercitat. sel. I. 73–.
TILLEMONT. Mémoirs. (1694) II. 327–44, 632–41.
TISCHENDORF. Reise i. d. Orient. II. 248.
— Wann wurden u. s. w. 23.
UEBERWEG. Hist. philos. (1876) 278–9.
UHLHORN, G. In: Herzog. Real.-Encl. (1877) XII. 103–7. (Abr. in: Schaff.-Herz. III. 1863–4.)
ULLMANN. D. zweite Br. Petri. 3 anm.
USSERIUS. Ign. et Polyc. mart. 1647.
VALESIUS. Not. in Euseb. h. e. IV. c. 15.
VINCENTIUS BELVAC. Spec. hist. XI. 96.
VOLKMAR. In: Jenaer Ltzng. (1874) 291.
— Religion Jesu. 505.
— Urspr. uns. Evv. 38–.
WADDINGTON. Aristide. In: Mém. de l'Institut. XXVL (1867) 203–, 232–.

WADDINGTON. Fastes des prov. asiatiques. *Par.* 1872.
I. 219–.
WAITE. Hist. of Chr. Rel. (1881) 50–55.
WALCH. Bibl. patrist. (1834) 22–4.
WESTCOTT. Canon. (1875) 36–40.
— Bible in the Church (1877) 79–80.
WIESELER. Das Martyrium Polykarp's und dessen Chronologie. In his: Christenverfolgungen. (1878) 34–87.
WIESELER, K. Das Todesjanr P. In: Stud. u. Krit. LIII. (1880) 141–65.
WORDSWORTH. Church Hist. (1881) 157–171.
YONGE. Pupils of St. John. (1878) 179–200.
ZAHN. In: Gött. gel. Anz. (1882).
— Ignatius v. A. 494–511.
ZELLER. Apostelgesch. (1854) 52–3.
For Literature, see also under Martyrdom of Polycarp and under Ignatius.

Note 1. Date of Polycarp's death. 147 A.D., Pearson, Galland, Dodwell; 155, Borghesi, Cavedoni, Mozzoni, Douhet, Marquardt, Schiller, Friedländer, WADDINGTON, Holtzmann, Aubé, Renan, Egli, Zahn, Funk, etc.; 155 or 6, Harnack; 156, Lipsius, Hilgenfeld, Gebhardt; 160, Hase, Réville (perhaps 166); 161, Stieren; 163, Chronicon Paschale; 166, Eusebius (?), Tillemont, Noris, Clinton, Masson, Keim, Wieseler, Uhlhorn, Nirschl, Wordsworth, Kurtz; 167, Eusebius (?), Hieronymus, Scaliger, Le Moyne, Cave, Valesius, Killen; 169, Usher, Pagi, Bucherus, Bollandus.

Note 2. Genuineness, etc., of the Epistle. For: Pearson, Mosheim, Tillemont, Ittig, Hefele, Gieseler, Neander, Möhler, Lardner, Ewald, Bleek, Tischendorf, Schliemann, Strauss, Uhlhorn, Harnack, Zahn, Lightfoot. *Against:* Magdeb. centur., Semler, Rössler, Schwegler, Keim, Scholten, Zeller, Lipsius, Eichhorn, Hilgenfeld, Tayler. *Interpolated:* Daillé, Bunsen, Ueberweg, Ritschl, Scholten, Volkmar, Böhringer, Donaldson, Lipsius.

MARTYRDOM.

I. *Editions.*

USSERIUS. *Lond.* 1647. 4°. In: Ap. Ign.
COTELERIUS. *Antw.* 1672. f°; Ed. Clericus. 1698. f°; 1724. f°.
RUINART. Act. mart. *Par.* 1689. 4°.
CLERICUS. 1698; 1724. s. u. Cotelerius.
ITTIG. Patr. ap. *Lips.* 1699. f°. 392–431.
SMITH. *Oxon.* 1709. 4°. s. u. Ep.
FREY. Patr. ap. II. (1741) 165–202, 339–44.
RUSSEL. *Lond.* 1746. s. u. Ep.
GALLAND. *Ven.* 1765. s. u. Ep.
JACOBSON. Gr. lat. 1838; 1840; 1847; 1863. 8°. II. 603–659.
HEFELE. *Tüb.* 1839; 1842; 1847; 1855. 8°. 272–95.
MIGNE. Gr. lat. In: Patrol. gr. V. (1857) 1029–46.
DRESSEL, A. R. M. Gr. lat. In: Patr. ap. (*Lips.* 1863). 391–407.
ZAHN. Gr. lat. In: Gebhardt, H. & Z. Patr. ap. II. (1876) 132–72.
FUNK. Patr. ap. (*Tüb.* 1881.) I. 282–309.
LIGHTFOOT. Ap. Fathers. II. (1885) II. 935–98 [pt. ii.].

II. *Translations.*

Ancient Latin.

FREY. Patr. ap. II. (1741) 191–202, and often in eds.

English.

WAKE. *Lond.* 1693. 8°. 73–87, 231–52; *Lond.* 1710. 8° [Greatly improved]; *Lond.* 1719. 8°. 51–60, (2) 138–53; 1737. 8°; 5th ed. 1818 [7?]; *Hartford,* 1834. 8°. 182–206; *Lond.* 1842 [3?] 8° [Revised]; *Lond.* 1846. 8°; 1860. 8°; *Phila.* 1846. 8°.
DALRYMPLE. *Edini.* 1776. 8°. In: Remains of Chr. Ant.
ROBERTS & DONALDSON. In: Ante-Nic. Lib. I. (1868) 83–96. Ed. Coxe. I. (1885) 39–44.
CUNNINGHAM. In: Churches of Asia (1880) 259–72.
LIGHTFOOT. Ap. fathers. II. (1885) II. 1057–67 [pt. ii.].

German.

ARNOLD. *Frf.* 1700. 8°.
GLÜSING. *Hamb.* 1723. 8°.

III. *Literature.*

ALZOG. Patrol. (1876) 47–52.
BURTON. Trinity (1831) 6–15.
BUSSE. Chr. Lit. (1828–9) I. 5–6.
CHARTERIS. Canonicity. (1880) xxxiii., xl., 113, 174, 197, 217, 225, 244.
COFFIN. Lives of fath. (1846) 137–150.
DONALDSON. Apost. fathers (1874) 198–224.
FLEURY. Hist. eccl. (1691–) I. 446–56.
HARNACK, A. Zeit d. Ignat. *Lpz.* 1877. [" Verbreitung d. Passio Polyc."]
— Zu Eusebius Hist. eccl. IV. 15, 37. In: Ztschr. f. Kirchengesch. II. (1877) 291–296.
HEFELE. Patr. ap. opera. Ed. 3. *Tüb.* 1847. 8°, also in: Migne. Patrol. gr. V. (1857) 1001–4.
ITTIG. Hist. eccl. (1709) II. 47.
LUMPER. Hist. ss. patr. II. (1784) 450–61.
NEANDER. Church Hist. (1872) I. 109–11, 335.
NIRSCHL. Patrol. (1881–) I. 129–31.
ORSI. Ist. eccl. (1746–) II. 146–58; (1749–) II. 212–28.
ROBERTS & DONALDSON. Introd. note. In: Ante-Nic. Lib. I. (1868) 79–81. Ed. Coxe. I. (1885) 37–8.
ZAHN. In: Gebhardt, H. & Z. Patr. ap. xlviii.-cv. See above. Many of the numbers treat of the Martyrium.

Note. Genuineness of the Martyrium. For: Renan, Hilgenfeld, Lightfoot. *Against:* Schürer, Keim (260–282), Lipsius, (250), so Gebhardt. *Interpolated:* Steitz, Zahn, Funk, Donaldson.

IV. IGNATIUS. EPISTLES.

I. *Editions.*

PACEUS, VALENT. (12 ep.) *Par.* 1557. 4° [Rare. *Par.* 1558, often given as the first]; 1558. 8° [Improved]; 1562. 8°. [1558 and 1562 ed. Morellus?]
GESNER. (12 ep.) Gr. lat. *Tigur.* 1559. f°. [Tr. Bunnerus.]
Gr. lat. *Antv. Plautus,* 1566. 8°; 1572. 8°; also in: Grynaeus. Orthodoxographia. *Basil.* 1569. f°. I. 5–70. [Lat. of Vairlenius.]
MAESTRAEUS, MARTIALIS. Gr. lat. *Paris,* 1608. 8°.
VEDELIUS, NIC. Gr. lat. *Genev.* 1623. 4°. [Lat. of Maestraeus. 7 genuine, 5 spur.]
DUCAEUS, FREUT. Gr. lat. (With scholia of Vairlenius and Maestraeus.) In his: Auct. bibl. patr. *Paris,* 1624. f°.
USSERIUS. (12 Gr. 11 lat.) *Oxon.* 1644. 4°; 1647. 4°.
VOSSIUS. Gr. lat. *Amst.* 1646. 4°; *Lond.* 1680. 4°. [1 ed. of shorter Gr. form of 6 eps. Romans in longer.]
COTELERIUS. (15) Gr. lat. In his: Patr. ap. *Paris,* 1672. f°; Ed. Clericus. *Antw.* (or *Amst.*) 1698. f°; *Amst.* 1724. f°. III. 11–120. [Improved ed. of Voss; in 1724 ed. Text of Rom. and Mart. improved.]
RUINART. Gr. lat. *Par.* 1689. 4°. [Rom.]
ITTIG, TH. (Genuine, spur. ep. and Acta.) Gr. lat. In his: Bibl. patr. ap. *Lips.* 1699. 8°. 95–431.
GRABE, J. E. Ep. ad Rom. et fragm. In his: Spicil. ss. patr. *Oxon.* 1700. 8°; p. 1 sq.; 1714.
ALDRICH, C. Gr. lat. *Oxon.* 1708. 8°. [100 copies only. Cf. Schelhorn. Acta Erud. *Lips.* 1713, p. 399.]
SMITH, THOMAS. (7 shorter.) Gr. lat. *Lond.* 1709. 4°.
WHISTON, W. (Both forms.) Gr. Eng. In his: Primitive Christianity. *Lond.* 1711. 8°. I. 1–391. [Text is that of Smith.]
FREY, J. L. (Ep. gen. et mart.) In his: Ep. ss. patr. apost. *Basil.* 1741. 8°. a–112, 205–329.
RUSSEL, RICH. (Ep. gen. et mart.) Gr. lat. In his: Patr. apost. *Lond.* 1746. 8°. Vol. I.
GALLANDIUS. (Ep. gen. et mart.) In his: Bibl. patr. *Venet.* 1765. f°. 243–303.

THILO, J. C. (Ep.) *Hal.* 1821 (2?) 8⁰. [After Voss.]

HORNEMANN. (Rom. Polyc. Eph. Smyr. Trall.) *Hafn.* 1829. 4⁰.

JACOBSON. *Oxon.* 1838; 1840; 1847; 1863. 8⁰. 269–519. s. u. Clement R.

HEFELE. *Tüb.* 1839; 1842; 1847; 1855. s. u. Clement R.

GRENFELL. *Rugby*, 1844. 8⁰.

REITHMAYR. *Monach.* 1844. 12⁰.

CURETON (3). *Lond.* 1845; also (Long, Short, Syriac and trs.) in: Corp. Ign. *Lond.* 1849.

BUNSEN, C. C. J. (7 ep.) *Hamb.* 1847.

PETERMANN, J. H. (Gr. lat. syr. armen. etc.) *Lips.* 1849.

BUNSEN. Analect. antenic. (1854.) I. 41–3. [Polyc. Eph. Rom.]

LIPSIUS. 1859.

Migne. Gr. lat. In: Patrol. gr. V. (1857) 643–728. [Short recension. Hefele's text.]

Migne. Gr. lat. In: Patrol. gr. V. (1857) 729–948. [Longer recen. Text of Cotelerius.]

Migne. Patrol. gr. V. (1857) 947–60. [Fragments. From Galland.]

DRESSEL. Gr. lat. In: Patr. Ap. *Lips.* 1857; also, 1863. 118–349.

MÖSINGER. In: Suppl. Corp. Ign. a Cureton ed. *Oenipont.* 1872.

ZAHN, TH. In: Gebhardt, Harnack u. Zahn. Patr. ap. *Lpz.* III. II. (1876) v.-xlii. 1–107, 173–300.

FUNK. Patr. ap. (*Tüb.* 1881.) 172–253.

— (Long recen.) Patr. ap. (*Tüb.* 1881.) II. 46–213.

LIGHTFOOT. (Short rec. 7 ep.) Apost. Fathers. II. (1885) II. 15–360. [pt. i.]

— (13 ep. Long recen.) Ap. Fathers. II. (1885) II. 708–857. [pt. ii.]

II. *Translations.*

Latin.

(6) *Colon.* 1478. [Doubtful.]

(3) *Parisiis*, 1495. 4⁰.

Ed. J. Faber. (11) *Parhis.* 1498. f⁰; (With Dionysius Areop. Opera.) –1502. f⁰; (do.) –(11) *Argentine*, 1502. f⁰. (do.)

Argentinae, 1503. f⁰; –1507. f⁰; 1515. f⁰. [All with Dionysius Areop.]

(15) *Paris*, 1516. 4⁰. [With Antonius Magnus. Ed. Champerus? Cureton has 1536, but Ch. died 1533.]

(Polycarp and.) *Basil.* 1520. 4⁰.

(Trallians.) *Colon.* 1526. 4⁰. In: Epist. Clementis, etc.

(Polycarp and.) [11 ep.] *Argent.* 1527. 8⁰.

(9) *Daventriae*, 1529. 8⁰.

(Dionys. Areop. and.) *Colon.* 1536. f⁰.

(Polyc. etc., and.) *Antw.* 1540. 8⁰.

Complut. 1541. 8⁰.

(Polyc., etc., and.) *Venet.* 1546. 8⁰.

(12) *Basil.* 1550. f⁰. In: Mikropresbyticum. p. 1–27.

(12) *Basil.* 1555. f⁰. In: Orthodoxographa.

(Clemens, R., etc.) *Col. Agr.* 1570 (not 1569). f⁰.

(15) *Paris*, 1575. f⁰; *Paris*, 1586. f⁰. In: Bibl. patr. I.

Colon. 1618. f⁰. In: Bibl. patr. II.

Oxon. 1642. 4⁰.

(6) *Lond.* 1650. 8⁰. In: Rous, Fr. Mella patrum. 18–21.

(12) *Lugd.* 1677. f⁰. In: Bibl. max. patr. II. 1. 73–104.

Par. 1654. f⁰. In: Bibl. patr. III.

LEGRAS. In his: Livr. apocr. *Par.* 1717. f⁰; 1742. 12⁰.

Paris, 1731. f⁰. In: Biblia sácra.

FREY. Patr. ap. II. (1741) 75–112.

FUNK. Patr. ap. (*Tüb.* 1881.) II. 214–7.

LAGARDE, P. DE. D. lat übers. d. I. hrsg. [Aus: Abhandlgn. d. k. Gesellsch. d. Wiss. zu Göttingen.] *Götting.* 1882. 8⁰.

LIGHTFOOT. Ap. Fathers. II. (1885) II. 597–656. [pt. ii.]

Arabic.

WRIGHT, W. In: Lightfoot. Ap. Fathers. II. (1885) II. 833–90. [pt. ii.]

Armenian.

Const. 1783; also in: Petermann. *Lips.* 1849. [With transl.]

Coptic.

LIGHTFOOT. Ap. Fathers. II. (1885) II. 859–64. [pt. ii.]

Syriac.

CURETON. (Polyc. Eph. Rom.) *Lond.* 1845.

— *Lond.* 1849. In: Corpus Ign.

WRIGHT, W. (3 eps.) In: Lightfoot. Ap. Fathers. II. (1885) II. 657–76. [pt. ii.]

— (Frgm.) In: Lightfoot. Ap. Fathers. II. (1885) II. 677–87. [pt. ii.]

CURETON. (Tr. Lat.) In: Corpus Ignat. (1849); also in: Migne. Patrol. gr. V. (1857) 961–8.

ROBERTS & DONALDSON (Tr. Engl.). In: Ante-Nic. Lib. I. (1868) 273–85. Ed. Coxe. I. (1885) 99–104.

Bohemian.

BENNESON, MATTH. a. s. a. et l. 4⁰.

English.

WAKE. *Lond.* 1693. 8⁰. 40–57, 99–216; *Lond.* 1710. 8⁰ [Greatly improved]; *Lond.* 1719. 8⁰. 30–41, (2) 60–128; 1737. 8⁰; 5th ed. 1818 [7?]; *Hartford*, 1834. 8⁰. 101–65; *Lond.* 1842 [3?]. 8⁰ [Revised]; *Lond.* 1846. 8⁰; 1860. 8⁰; *Phila.* 1846. 8⁰.

CALDER, ROB. *Edini.* 1708. 8⁰.

WHISTON, W. In his: Primitive Christianity. *Lond.* 1711. 8⁰. p. 1.

APOCR. N. T. (1825) 215–247; (*Phila.* n. d.) 166–192. [Eph. Magn. Trall. Rom. Phil. Smyr. Polyc.]

CLEMENTSON, W. K. *Brighton*, 1827.

CHEVALLIER. *Lond.* 1833. 8⁰; 1851 (2?). 8⁰.

BUNSEN. (3) Hippolytus. (1854) I. 92–8.

STOWE. (1 ep.) Books of the Bible. (1867) 424–32.

ROBERTS & DONALDSON. (Gen. ep.) In: Ante-Nic. Lib. I. (1868) 145–267. Ed. Coxe. I. (1885) 49–96.

— (Pseud. ep.) In: Ante-Nic. Lib. I. (1868) 455–93. Ed. Coxe. I. (1885) 107–26.

CUNNINGHAM. (Trall.) Churches of Asia. (1880) 228–33.

LIGHTFOOT. Ap. Fathers. II. (1885) II. 537–70. [pt. i.]

French.

Paris, 1500. 8⁰.

MOREL, GUIL. *Paris*, 1562. 8⁰; — 1612. 8⁰.

EUDEMAIR. *Rothomag.* 1615. 8⁰.

LEGRAS, ANT. In his: Livres apocr. *Par.* 1717. f⁰; 1742. 12⁰; also in his: Ouvr. d. s. pères. *Par.* 1717. 12⁰.

RUCHAT. *Lugd. Bat.* 1738. 8⁰.

GENOUDE [? ?]. In: Pères de l'égl. *Par.* 1837–43. 8⁰.

German.

MÖLLER, MART. *Görlitz*, 1578. 8⁰.

ARNOLD, GOTTFR. (7) In his: Sendschreiben der Alten. *Frf. u. Lpz.* 1700. 8⁰. p. 28–106. [Also 1696?]

Schifbecae prope Hamburgum. 1711. 12⁰.

GRYNAEUS, SAM. *Basel*, 1722. 8⁰.

GLÜSING, J. OTTO. (7) In his: Briefe u. Schr. d apost. MÄNNER. *Hamb.* 1723. 8⁰. p. 305–74.

UNTERKIRCHER. *Innsbr.* 1817. 8⁰.

Münst. 1826. 8⁰.

GENELLI, CHR. *Münster*, 1828. 8⁰.

WOCHER. *Tüb.* 1829. 8⁰.

NIRSCHL, J. *Passau*, 1870. 8⁰.

Italian.

GALLICIOLI. *Venet.* 1798 [9?]. 8⁰.

GRAZIANI. *Romae*, 1833. 8⁰. [7 eps.]

Russian.

SERTIS–KAMENSKJ, A. *Mosk.* 1772.

Note. History of the Eds. In 1495 the 3 lat. epp. and the Ep. of the Virgin; 1498, ed. Faber, 11 epp. longer form not including Mary of C.; 1516, ed. Symphorianus Champerus, these 14 with Mary of C. added; 1557, the first Gr. ed. 12 epp. by Paceus, longer form; 1644 (rather 1642), ed. Usher, first gave shorter form of 11 epp. Latin; 1646, Voss first brought to light the shorter form in Greek, giving 6 epp. in this form with Romans in the longer; 1689, Ruinart published Rom. in the shorter form; 1783, Armenian Transl. publ. at Constantinople; 1845, Cureton published the Syr. version of Polyc. Rom. and Eph.

III. *Literature.*

ABBOTT, E. A. Gospels. In: Encycl. Brit. (9th ed.) X. 815, 822.

ABULPHARAGIUS. Hist. dynast. Ed. Pocock. *Oxon.* 1663. VII. 75.

ADENEY, W. F. In: Brit. Q. LXXXIII. (1886) 31–67.

ALEXANDER, NATALIS. Hist. eccles. (1778) III. 232–43.

Allgem. ev.-luth. Kirchenz. (1873) 596.

ALZOG. Patrol. (1876) 37–44.

American Church Review. XXI. (1870) 563–.

Am. Presb. R. XVI. (1867) 137–.

ANGER. Synops. Ev. (1852).

ARNDT. Ueb. d. Echtheit d. Br. d. Ign. In: Stud. u. Krit. XII. (1839) 136–86.

BACKHOUSE, J. H. A forgotten ed. of I. In: Academy (1881) 263–4. [Champier, 1516. But mentioned by Hoffmann (1839) and Means in: Smith. Dict. (1859).]

BARATERIUS, J. P. De Ign. mart. In his: De success. antiqq. episcc. RR. 87–.

BARONIUS. Ann. (1589) 109, 5–36; 110, 1–7; 438, 13. Cf. Pagi, Crit. (1689) 109, 3–5, 7; 438, 3.

BAUMGARTEN–CRUSIUS. Dogmenges. (1832) 83 [v. 1].

BAUR, F. C. In: Ztschr. f. hist. Theol. VIII. (1836) 199–.

— In: Ztschr. f. hist. Theol. X. (*Tüb.* 1838) 148.

— Urspr. d. Episcopats. 1838.

— D. Ign. Br. u. ihr neueste Kritiker. . . gegen Bunsen. *Tübing.* 1848. 8°.

— Kirchenges. 3 e. J. (1863) 275–83.

— Dogmengesch. I. (1865) 252, etc.

— D. sog. Pastoral-briefe.

ΒΑΦΕΙΛΗΣ. Ἐκκλ. ἰστ. I. (1884) 147.

BEAUSOBRE. Hist. de Manichée. (1734) I.

BELLARMIN–LABBE. Script. eccl. (1728) 24–6.

BEYER, CHR. de Ign. Dissert. II. *Lips.,* 1722. 4°.

Bibl. ges. deutsch. Nat. Liter. (1852) A. XXXII. 161–8.

BLACKBURN. Hist. of Church. (1879) 27–8.

BLEEK. Einl. N. T. (1862) 142.

BOEHRINGER. Kirchenges. (1873–) I. I.

BOSIA, A. In: Ann. de philos. chrét. (1872) F. IV. 245–63.

BOSIUS, J. A. Exerc. in 2 Tim. II. 22. In his: Opusc. hist. *Jena,* 1723. 8°. 428–.

BRETSCHNEIDER. Probabilia.

Brit. & For. R. XXXIII. 640–.

BRÜLL, A. In: Theol. Quartalschr. LXII. (1880) 686–9. [Rev of Nirschl.]

— D. Episkopat u. die ignatianischen Briefe. In: Theol. Quartalschr. 61 : 247–257.

BUNSEN, C. C. J. VON. Ign. v. A. u. s. Zeit. Sendschr. an Dr. Neander. *Hamb.* 1847. 4°.

BUNSEN. Hippolytus. (1854) I. 88–103.

BURTON. Divinity of Christ. (1829) 14–32.

— Trinity. (1831) 1–4.

BUSSE. Chr. Lit. (1828–9) I. 3–4.

CAILLAU. Introd. in ss. Patr. (1825) 33–8.

CAVE. Hist. lit. (1740–) I. 41–3.

— Lives (1840) I. 176–91. Abr. in: Wake. Ap. fath. *Hartf.* 1834. p. 485–94.

CEILLIER. Hist. gén. d. aut. sac. (1729) I. 620–67. I. (1858) 362–88.

CHARTERIS. Canonicity. (1880) xxvi–xxxiii, 42–3, 110–2, 171–2, 196, 216, 224–5, 239, 243, 251, 256, 262, 320, 338, 451.

CHEVALIER. Rép. d. sources hist. (1877–86) 1107–8.

CHRYSOSTOM. In: S. Ignat. Homilia.

[CIACCIO, GIAC.] Vita di s. Ignazio, vescovo e martire. *Palermo,* 1678. 12°.

CLARKE. Sacred lit. (1830–1) I. 92–3.

CLERICUS. De epistolis Ignatianis. In: Cotelerius, Patr. Apost. (1724) II. II. 501–.

CLINTON. Fasti Rom. (1845–50) I. 95, 101; II. 401.

COËTLOSQUET. Vie de S. Ignace et de S. Polycarpe. *Metz,* 1862. 12°.

COFFIN. Lives of fath. (1846) 107–115.

COLEMAN. Anc. Christianity. p. 197–200.

COTELERIUS. Patr. ap. *Amst.* 1724. f°. II. 9–; also in: Migne. Patrol. gr. V. (1857) 33–6.

CREDNER. Einl. N. T. I. I.

CRUSE, C. F. Syriac Version of the Epistles of Ignatius. In: Am. Church R. I. (1848) 566–.

CUNNINGHAM. Hist. theol. (1870) I. 108–20.

— Churches of Asia. (1880) passim.

CURETON. Vindiciæ Ignatianæ. *Lond.* 1846.

— Corpus Ign. (1849) Introd. (lxxxvii p.)

Cureton's Corpus Ignatianum. In: Chr. Obs. XLIX (1849) 681–.

Cureton's Vindiciæ Ignatianæ. In: Bib. R. I. (1846) 443–.

DALLAEUS, J. De scr. quae sub Dionysii Areop. et Ign. nominibus circumferuntur libri II. *Genev.* 1666. 4°.

DARLING. Cyclop. Bibliog. (1854) I. 603–4; 2979, 3176.

DAVIDSON. Introd. N. T.

DELITZSCH, Jo. In: Ztschr. f. luth. Theol. (1874) 305.

DENZINGER. In: Theol. Quartalschr. (1851) 389–.

— Ueb. d. Aechtheit d. Textes d. I. *Würzb.* 1849. 8°. In: Migne. Patrol. gr. V. (1857) 601–24. [Integrity of text. Agst. Cureton.]

DIETELMAIER, J. A. Erkl. d. Stelle aus Ign. ep. ad Trall. v. d. Höllenfahrt Christi. In: Hamburgische vern. Bibl. III. I. 78–85.

DONALDSON, J. In: Encycl. Brit. (9th ed.) II. 196–7.

DORNER. Person of Christ. I. (1864) 102–13, 358–70.

D. 3 ersten gr. Ausg. d. längeren Rec. d. Ign. Briefe u. ihre handschriftliche Grundlage. In: Theol. Quartalschr. LXI. 610–628.

DOUHET. Dict. d. mystér. (1854) 421–34.

— Dict. d. légend. (1855) 647–51.

DREHER, T. S. Ignatii Ep. Antioch. de Christo doctrina. Gymnasialprogramm. *Hedingen,* 1877. 4°.

DUPIN. Bibl. aut. eccl. (1698) I. 42–79.

DÜSTERDIEK. De I. ep. authent. *Goett.* 1843. 4°.

DU VERDIER. Bibl. Franç. (1773) IV. 533.

EBEDJESU. Catal. script. eccl. 9 (Assemani Bibl. orient. III. I. 16).

EDWARDS, J. Brief Observations and Reflections on Mr. Whiston's Primitive Christianity. *Lond.* 1712. 8°.

Epistles of Ignatius. In: New York R. I. (1837) 367–; Kitto. V. (1850) 339–; Brit. Q. XXXIV. (1856) 422–; Dub. R. XLIV (1857) 412–; LXXIII. (1868) 349–; Ed. R. XC. (1849) 155–; Quar. LXXXVIII. (1850) 69–; Church Q. R. XXI. (1886) 356–89.

ERNESTI. N. Theol. Bibl. II. (1761).

EWALD. Gesch. d. V. Israel. VII. (1859) 281–.

FABRICIUS. Bibl. gr. (1712) V. 38–45 (VII. 32–44; X. 254).

FLEURY. Hist. eccl. (1691–) I. 342–72.

FORSYTH, J. Ignatius and his Times. In: Princ. XXI (1849) 378–.

FOERTSCHIUS, M. Oratio de partu Mariae, etc. [Ign. in Ep. to Eph·] In his: Decade Dissertat. Theolog. (*Tübing.* 1704. 4°.) p. 439–453.

FRANCKE, C. E. Lehre d. Ign. In: Ztschr. f. luth. Theol. 42.

Martyrium Ignatii. See below.

MAURICE. Eccl. Hist. (1854) 171–8.

MAYERHOFF. Einl. petr. schr.

MEANS, J. C. In: Smith. Gr. and Rom. Biog. (1859) II. 563–7.

MEBES, A. M. De I. nonnullis locis ad praeexist. Christi pertinent etc. disput. II. *Francquerae*, 1733.

Meditations of Ignatius. In: Brownson, XIX. (1862) 360–.

MEIER, F. K. Ueb. d. doppelte Recen. u. s. w. In: Stud. u. Krit. IX. (1836) 340–82.

MERX, A. Meletemata Ignatiana. Critica de ep. ignat. versione syriaca commentatio. *Halle*, 1861. 8°. [Cf. Land, in: Ztschr. f. wiss. Theol. 1868, IV.]

MEYER. Apostelgesch. (1870).

MICHEL, FRANC. Théat. franç. 1839, p. 265.

MILMAN. Hist. of Chr. II. (1863) 102.

— Lat. Chr. I. 53–.

MILTON. Prose Works. (Bohn) II. 426–8.

MOMBRITIUS, BONIN. Sanctuarium (c. 1479) II. XXII–III.

MORINUS, J. Comment. de sacris ordinationibus. *Par.* 1680. III.

MOSHEIM. De rebus Chr.

MUENSCHER. Dogmenges. (1817–8) I. 114, etc.

MUIR, A. F. In: Brit. & For. R. XXXV. (1886) 298–325.

MURDOCK, J. In: New Eng. VII. (1849) 501–.

— Syriac Version of the Epistles of Ignatius. In: Am. Church R. II. (1850) 194–.

NEALE. Eastern Ch. Antioch. (1873) 11–21.

NEANDER. Hist. of dogmas. (1858) 74–6, 211 (v. 1).

— Church hist. (1872) I. 100, 191–2, 660–1.

NETZ, G. C. Brief d. Ign. an Polykarp. In: Stud. u. Krit. VIII. (1835) 881–906.

NEUDECKER. Einl. N.T.

NEVE, FÉLIX. In: Rev. cathol. (*Louv.*) (= Le Correspondent (1852) XXIX. 656–65.)

NEWMAN, J. H. Essays. I. *Lond.* 1877. 8°. 186–261.

NIEDNER. Gesch. Chr. K.

NIEMEYER, H. A. Ueb. einige Stellen in Brr. Ign. In: Fries et A. Oppositionsschr. I. 2.

NIRSCHL. Das Todesjahr des heil. Ignatius von Antiochien und die drei orientalischen Feldzüge des Kaisers Trajan. *Passau*, 1869. 8°. (IV. 84 p.)

— Einl. In his: Briefe u. Mart. 1870.

— D. Theologie d. heil. Ignatius. *Mainz*, 1880. 8°. [" To be heartily recommended." *Brüll*.]

— Patrol. (1881–) I. 95–121.

— D. Mart. d. Ignatius. In: Hist.-polit. Blätt. 84, 89–102; 193–206. [" Gegen Zahn."]

NITZSCH. Dogmengesch. I. (1870) 104–7, etc.

NODIER. Bib. sacr. (1826) 147–8.

NORTON. Genuineness of Gosp. I. (1846) 4, etc.

OBSERVATIO de θεοδρυμοις Ignatii, in Ep. ad Philadelphenos. In: Acta Erudit. *Lips.* a. 1731. 455–461.

ORSI. Ist eccl. (1746–) II. 20–47; (1749–) II. 29–69.

OUDIN. Scr. eccl. (1722) I. 71–142.

O[VERBECK], F. In: Lit. Centralbl. (1874) No. 1.

OWEN, J. Enquiry into orig. nature evang. ch. In: Works. Ed. Russel. 1826. XX. 147.

PALTINIERI, IGNAZ. (Lazarelli, Mauro Aless.) Vita di s. Ignazio, vescoco di Ant. *Modena*, 1696. 16°.

PEARSON, JOHN. Vindiciae epistolarum s. Ignatii, acc. Is. Vossii epistolae 11 adv. Dav. Blondellum. *Cantabrigiae*, 1672. 4°; *Oxf.* 1852. 2 v. 8°; also in: Cotelerius. Patr. ap. *Amst.* 1724. f°. II. 252–; in: Migne. Patrol. gr. V. (1857) 37–472.

PERMANEDER. Bibl. Patrist. (1841–3) I. 412–3; II. 35–50.

PETERMANN, H. In: Verhndlgn. d. d. Orient. (*Dresden*, 1846) 198–204.

— S. Ign. Epist. *Lips.* 1849. [" Rich coll. especially regarding Orient. versions."]

PFLEIDERER. Paulinismus. Eng. tr. *Lond.* 1877. II. 214–.

PITRA. Nouvelles controverses sur l'authenticité des épitres de St. Ignace. In: L'Auxil. cathol. (1845–6) II. 234; III. 81, 220, 272; IV. 244, 302.

PRESSENSÉ. Trois prem. sièc. de chr. (*Par.* 1858.) II. 505–; (1863) II. 102; Tr. Engl. Mart. (1879) 223–32, 630–4.

RENAN. In: Jour. d. savants. (1874) 38.

— Les Évangiles. (*Par.* 1877.) xv–.

RÉVILLE. In: Le Lien. (1856) nos. 18–22.

RITSCHL. D. Enst. d. altkath. Kirche. *Bonn.* 1850. 577–.

ROBERTS and DONALDSON. Introd. note. In: Ante-Nic. Lib. I. (1868) 137–44, 269–71, 449–53. Ed. Coxe. I. (1885) 45–8, 97, 105–6.

ROBERTSON. Hist. of Church. (1875) I. 20–6.

ROSENMÜLLER. Hist. interp. I. (1795) 114–6.

ROESSLER. Bibl. d. K–V. I. (1776) 67–100.

RÖTHE, R. Beilage über d. Echtheit d. Ign. Br. In his: Anfänge d. christl. Kirche. (1837) I. 739.

RUINART. Acta sinc. (1689) 9–11, 695–6.

RUMPF. In: N. Rev. de Théol. (1867) 8–.

SANDAY. Gosp. in 2 cent. (1876) 36, 76–82, 274–6.

SAVIO, NIC. Vita di s. Ignazio . . . . *Palermo*, 1761. 18°.

SCHAFF. Hist. . . . Church. II. (1886) 47–, 149–, 651–664.

SCHLIEMANN. Clementinen. (1844) 421, etc.

SCHMID. Patrol. (1879); (1886) 31–3.

SCHMIDT, J. E. CH. Bibl. für kritik und Exegese des N. T. I. 463–.

— D. gedoppelte Recens. d. Br. d. Ign. In: Henke's Magazin für Religionsphilos. u. Kirchengesch. III. (*Helmst.* 1795. 8°.) 91–.

SCHOLTEN. Die ält. Zeugnisse.

SCHRAM. Anal. ss. patr. (1780) I. 77–105.

SCHROECKH. Kirchenges. (1772) II. 336–47.

SCHWEGLER. Nachap. Zeitalt. (1846) II. 159–79.

SEMLER. Paraphr. in II. Pet. (1784) Praef.

SEVESTRE. Dict. patrol. (1854) III. 504–22.

SHEDD. Hist. of doct. 3d ed. (1865–) I. 265–8; II. 208–9.

SKWORZOW. Patrol. Untersuch. (*Lpz.* 1875) 55–97.

"SMECTYMNUUS." Answer to the book entitled " An Humble Remonstrance." *Lond.* 1641. [Answer of 5 Presb. clergymen to Hall.]

SMITH, R. T. In: Smith and Wace. Dict. III. 209–23.

SMITH, THOM., and LEDYARD, JOH. In: Hearne. Script. hist. Anglic. XXI. (*Oxon.* 1726) 459–89.

SPRINTZL. Theol. d. Apost. Väter. *Wien*, 1880.

STOLLE, GTL. Nachr. v. d. Leben d. Kirchenväter, p. 32–.

Supernatural Religion. (1875–) 258–74; II. 260–7; III. xxxiii–lxxx, 10–13.

SURIUS. Vitae ss. (1618) II. 1–4.

SYMEON METAPHRAST. In: Migne. Patrol gr. CXIV. 1269–86.

TAYLER, J. J. Fourth Gosp. (1867).

TAYLOR, JER. Episcopacy. In: Works. ed. Heber. 1822. VII. 3–.

Testimony of Ignatius to Christianity. In: Brit. Q. LXIII. (1876) 341–.

TENTZELIUS, W. E. Schediasma historico criticum de Apophthegmate Ignatii: Ό ἐμος ἐρος ἐσαυρωται. *Witteb.* 1683. 4°.

— In: Fiebig. Corp. diss. theol. 12267.

THIERSCH. D. K. im ap. Ztalt.

THWING, C. F. In: Meth. Q. XL. (1880) 31–.

TILLEMONT. Mémoires. (1694) II. 190–212, 576–83.

TISCHENDORF. Wann wurden u. s. w.

TOLA. Uom. ill. Sardegna (1838) II. 167–71.

TRITHEMIUS. Scr. eccl. 8.

UHLHORN. In: Ztschr. f. hist. Theol. XXV. (1851); Tr. Engl. by H. Browne in Theol. Critic (1852). [Relation of shorter Greek to the Syr.]
— In: Herzog. Real.-Enc. (1877) VI. 688–94 (Abr. in: Schaff-Herz. III. 1058–60).
Untersuchung d. Stelle d. Ignatius von der Höllenfahrt Christi. In: Hamb. verm. Bibl. II. v. p. 778–785.
USSHER. Diss. de Ign. et Polycarpo. 1644. In: Works. ed. Elrington. VII. 87–295.
— Appendix Ignatiana. Londini, 1647. 4°.
VAUCHER. Recherches crit. sur les lettres d'I. Genève, 1856.
VERPOORTENNUS, A. M. Diss. ad Ignatii Ep. ad Philadelphum c. VIII. rub.: Ἐμοι ἀρχεια ἐστιν Ἰησος Χριστος. In his: Fascic. Dissertationum. (Coburgi, 1739. 8°.) 151–.
Veterum Testimonia. In: Galland. Patr. bibl. Venet. 1765. f°. I. 245–; also in: Migne. Patrol. gr. V. (1857) 9–32. [A full collection of " Quotations and references " in Lightfoot I. 127–221; also in Cureton. Corp. Ign.]
VINCENTIUS BELVAC. Spec. hist. XI. 56–7.
VOLKMAR. Einl. in die Apokryphen. I. (1860) 121–7.
— Urspr. Evv. (1866) 51–.
— Evangelien. (1870) 636–.
— In: Jenaer Literaturz. (1874) 290.
VÖLTER, D. "Die Lösung der Ignatianischen Frage." In: Theol. Tijdschr. (1886) Jan. 114–136.
VOSS. Praef. in ep. Ign. Amst. 1646. 4°; also in Migne. Patrol. gr. V. (1857) 31–4.
WAITE. Hist. Chr. Rel. (1881) 43–50, et pass.
[WALCH, C. W. FR.] Num Ignatius Christum post resurrectionem in carne viderit. Goettingae, 1772. 4°.
WALCH, J. G. Bibl. patrist. (1834) 20–2, 283–5, 367–9.
— In his: Hist. eccles. p. 578–.
WEISMANN. Memorab. Eccles. (1745).
WEISS. In: Reuter's Repertorium (1852) 169–.
— In Biog. Univ. Michaud. 1842–65. XX. 302–3.
WEIZSÄCKER. Unters. evang. gesch.
WERNSDORF, E. F. In: Fiebig. Corp. diss. theol. 13394.
WESTCOTT. Canon. (1875) 28–36.
— Bible in the Church. (1877) 76–9.
WETTE, DE. Einl. N.T.
WHISTON, W. An Essay upon the Epistles of Ign. Lond. 1710. 8°; rep. in his: Works. I. (Lond. 1711. 8°.) p. 79–.
WIESELER. D. Christenverfolgerungen. (1878) 125–.
WINSCHEMIUS, S. T. Oratio de Ign. In: Orationes scriptae et recitatae in Acad. Witteb. a. 1568. (Witteb. 1571. 8°.) VI.
WINTER, V. In: Gesch. d. ältesten Zeugen. 212–.
WORDSWORTH. In: English Rev. (1845) no. VIII.
— Church Hist. (1881) 126–47.
WOTTON. Præf Clem. R. Epp. (1718).
YONGE. Pupils of St. John (1878) 103–53.
ZAHN, THEOD. Ignatius von Antiochien. Gotha, 1873 8°. (XVI, 631.) ["The best vindication." Schaff. Cf. Renan, Ernst. In: Journ. d. Savants (1874) 34–50.]
Ztschr. f. Kirchenges. I. (1876) 121; II. 73, 80.
ZELLER. Apostelgesch. (1854) 51–2.
ZIEGLER. Gesch. kirchl. Verfassungs-formen. (1798).

Note 1. Death of Ignatius. 105–117, Zahn, R. T. Smith; 107, Zahn, Ruinart, Tillemont, Ceillier, Gallandi, Busse, Wieseler, Möhler, Funk, Roberts and D., Schmid; 114, Borghesi, (cf. u. Polycarp); 115, Chronicon Paschale, Volkmar, Ueberweg, Kurtz; 115–6, Lloyd, Pagi, Grabe, Smith, Routh, Gieseler; 116, Pearson; 138, (?) Harnack.
Note 2. Genuineness of the Epistles. For all, Baronius, Halloix, Whiston, Meier; twelve gen., Paceus, Baronius, Bellarmin, Whitgift, Hooker, Andrewes (cf. their works); nine gen., Maestraeus; seven genuine (long or short), Usher, Grotius, Bull, Hall, Bentley, Waterland, (short) Pearson, Gieseler, Arndt, Huther, Möhler, Rothe, Düsterdieck, Dorner, Jacobson, Hefele, Denzinger, Petermann, Wordsworth, Uhlhorn, Zahn, Wieseler, Funk, Lipsius, Smith, Lightfoot, Schaff; six gen., Usher (Polyc. spur.) Syriac form, Cureton, Lee, Bunsen, Baur (?), Ritschl, Weiss, Pressensé, Ewald, Milman, Bleek, Chastel, Böhringer and Lipsius, and Lightfoot at first; one gen. (Rom.) Renan; all spurious, Calvin, Magdeb. cent., Salmasius, Blondel, Dallaeus, Basnage,

Oudin, Aubertin, Heumann, Ernesti, Semler (?) Tentzel (?), Killen, Baur, Volkmar (" kein Iota ist ächt") Schwegler, Hilgenfeld; much interpolated, Lardner, Petavius, Scultet, Vedelius, Semler (?) Tentzel (?), Neander, Schmidt, Netz, Hase.

MARTYRDOM.

I. Editions.

USHER. Lat. (Antioch. and Bolland in part.) Lond. 1644; Lond. 1647.
RUINART. (Antioch.) Gr. Acta mart. Par. 1689. App.
FREY. Gr. Patr. ap. II. (1741) 113–40, 330–4.
— Anc. Lat. Patr. ap. II. (1741) 135–40.
GALLAND. Anc. Lat. In: Vet. patr. bibl. Venet. 1765. f°. I. 299–; also in: Migne. Patrol. gr. V. (1857) 987–90.
AUCHER, J. B. (Armenian.) Ven. 1810–14.
JACOBSON. 1838.
HEFELE. 1839.
PETERMANN. (Armen.) 1849. 496–.
CURETON. (Antioch.) Syr. Corp. Ign. 1849. [In part.]
MIGNE. Gr. lat. In: Patrol. gr. V. (1857) 979–88. [From Hefele, ed. 3.]
DRESSEL. (Roman) Gr. lat. In: Patr. ap. 1857; also Lips. 1863. xxxii–iv, 350–375.
MÖSINGER. (Antioch) Syr. Suppl. Cureton Corp. Ign. 1872. 7–. (Short lat.) 18–.
ZAHN. Gr. lat. In: Gebhardt, H. & Z. Patr. ap. II. (1876) lv–lvi, 301–25.
FUNK. Patr. ap. (Tüb. 1881.) I. 254–265.
— (Roman) Gr. Patr. ap. (Tüb. 1881.) II. 218–245.
— (Metaphrastes) Gr. Patr. ap. (Tüb. 1881.) II. 246–258.
— Lat. Patr. ap. (Tüb. 1881.) II. 259–275.
LIGHTFOOT, J. B. Apost. fathers. II. (1885) II. 361–536. [pt. i.] [Ant. acts. 473–491. Roman. 492–536.]
WRIGHT, W. (Antioch.) Syr. In: Lightfoot. Ap. fathers. II. (1885) II. 687–708. [pt. ii.]
LIGHTFOOT. (Roman) Copt. In: Ap. fathers. II. (1885) II. 865–82. [pt. ii.]

II. Translations.

English.

WAKE. Lond. 1693. 8°. 58–72, 217–29; Lond. 1710. 8° [Greatly improved]; Lond. 1719. 8°. 42–51, (2) 129–37; 1737. 8°; 5th ed. 1818 [7?]; Hartford, 1834, 8°. 166–81; Lond. 1842 [3?] 8° [Revised]; Lond. 1846. 8°; 1860. 8°; Phila. 1846.
ROBERTS and DONALDSON. In: Ante-Nic. Lib. I. (1868) 291–7. Ed. Coxe. I. (1885) 129–31.
LIGHTFOOT. Ap. fathers. II. (1885) II. 571–84. [pt. i.]
Note. Lightfoot distinguishes five forms of the Mart. 1. Antiochene. (1) Greek. (2) Latin. (3) Syriac. 2. Roman. (1) Greek. (2) Coptic. 3. Bollandists-latin. 4. Armenian. 5. Acts of the Metaphrast. Besides above eds. the mart. is found in various eds. and trs. of I. and of Simon Metaphr.

III. Literature.

BRÜLL, A. Ueb. d. Echtheit d. Marterakten d. Ign. In: Theol. Quartalschr. (1884) 607–620.
CEILLIER. Hist. gén. aut. sacr. I. (1858) 389–92.
HEFELE. Praef. Patr. ap. opera. Ed. 3. Tüb. 1847. 8°; also in: Migne. Patrol. gr. V. (1857) 639–42.
HOLLENBERG, W. In: Stud. u. Krit. LIV. (1881) 311–3. [2te. Martyrium.]
ITTIG. Hist. eccl. (1709) II. 46–7.
LUMPER. Hist. S. Patr. II. (1784) 428–35.
NIRSCHL. Patrol. (1881–) I. 117–21.
ROBERTS and DONALDSON. Introd. note. In: Ante-Nic. Lib. I. (1868) 287–90. Ed. Coxe. I. (1885) 127–8.
WAITE. Hist. Chr. Rel. (1881) 50.
See above for literature.

V. BARNABAS. Epistle.

I. *Editions*.

USSERIUS. Gr. lat. *Oxon.* 1643. 4⁰. [1st ed. All copies burned in fire, 1644.]

MENARD, HUGO. Gr. lat. *Paris*, 1645. 4⁰. [Posthumous. Ed. D'Achery.]

VOSS, ISAAC. (Ign. and) Gr. lat. *Amst.* 1646. 4⁰; *Lond.* 1680. 8⁰. p. 207-254.

MADER, J. J. Gr. lat. *Helmst.* 1655. 4⁰.

COTELERIUS. Gr. lat. *Par.* 1672. f⁰; Ed. Clericus. *Antv.* 1698. f⁰; *Amst.* 1724. f⁰.

[FELL.] (Hermas and) Gr. lat. *Oxon.* 1685. 12⁰. [Not by Bernard, but his notes are included.]

LE MOYNE. Gr. lat. *Lugd. Bat.* 1685. 4⁰. In : Var. sacr.

CLERICUS. 1698 ; 1724. s. u. Cotelerius.

RUSSEL, RICH. Gr. lat. *Lond.* 1746. 8⁰.

GALLANDIUS. Gr. lat. 1765. f⁰. In : Bibl. patr. I.

Patr. ap. gr. *Lugd. Bat.* 1831. [?]

HEFELE. *Tüb.* 1839; 1842; 1847; 1855. s. u. Clement of R.

SIMONIDES. *Smyrna*, 1843. [Sinait. Text.]

GRENFELL. *Rugby*, 1844. 8⁰.

REITHMAYR. Patr. ap. *Monach.* 1844.

MURALT. Codex N. T. etc. *Turici*, 1847. I.

DRESSEL. Patr. ap. *Lips.* 1857; 1863. 1-45.

MIGNE. Patrol gr. II. (1857) 727-82.

TISCHENDORF. (Sinaitic.) Gr. *Petrop.* 1862. IV. 135-141; *Lips.* 1863. 4⁰; 1865. 8⁰. [?]

VOLKMAR. Mon. vet. chr. *Turici*, 1864. [Ch. 1-v.]

HILGENFELD. (N.T. extra canon rec.) 1866; Ed. 2, 1877.

MÜLLER. Gr. lat. *Lpz.* 1869. 8⁰. In : De Wette. Exeg. Handb. N. T.

GEBHARDT U. HARNACK. Gr. lat. In : Gebhardt, H. & Z. Patr. ap. *Lips.* 1875. 8⁰; also (with Constantinople readings in regard) Ed. Minor. 1877; and new ed. 1878. I. II. 1-83.

CUNNINGHAM. Gr. lat. engl. *Lond.* 1877. 8⁰. [Gebhardt H. & Z's. text.]

HILGENFELD. Gr. lat. *Lips.* 1877. 8⁰.

SHARPE, S. Gr. engl. *Lond.* 1880.

FUNK. Patr. ap. (*Tüb.* 1881.) I. 3-59.

II. *Translations*.

Latin.

LEGRAS. In his : Livr. apocr. 1717. f⁰; 1742. 12⁰.

English.

WAKE. *Lond.* 1693. 8⁰. 87-111, 257-314; *Lond.* 1710. 8⁰ [Greatly improved]; *Lond.* 1719. 8⁰. 60-77, (2) 157-95; 1737. 8⁰; 5th ed. 1818 [7?]; *Hartford*, 1834. 8⁰. 207-62; *Lond.* 1842 [3?]. 8⁰ [Revised]; *Lond.* 1846. 8⁰; 1860. 8⁰; *Phila.* 1846. 8⁰.

Apocr. N. T. (1825) 187-215 (*Phila.* n. d.) 145-165.

Jour. of Sacr. Lit. N. S. IV. V. *Lond.* 1864.

ROBERTS and DONALDSON. In : Ante-Nic. Lib. I. (1868) 101-35. Ed. Coxe. I. (1885) 137-49.

HOOLE. Apost. fath. *Lond.* 1872.

RENDALL, G. H. *Lond.* 1877. [Cf. Cunningham.]

French.

Bibl. *Antverp.* (1717) II.

LEGRAS, ANT. In his : Livr. apocr. *Par.* 1717. f⁰; 1742. 2 v. 12⁰; also in his : Ouvr. d. s. Pères. *Par.* 1717. 12⁰.

GENOUDE [??] In : Péres de l'égl. *Par.* 1837-43. 8⁰.

German.

"M. G. A. A. M." [Arnold?] 1695 (Not 1696) 12⁰.

[ARNOLD?] [REITZ?] In : Bibl. pentapl. *Wandsbeck.* 1710; also in N. T. *Schiffbec*, 1711. 12⁰; also in N. T. Apocr. *Bading*, 1723. 8⁰.

Apocr. N. T. In : Bibl. *Schiffbec*, 1717. 4⁰. I. 1. ed. 2.

GLÜSING. (Br. u. Schr.) *Hamb.* 1723. 8⁰. 1-43.

ARNOLD, GOTTFR. *Halle*, 1738. 8⁰. In : Gottfried Arnold's Erstes Marterthum, etc., p. 184-.

GRYNAEUS. Werke apost. Män. *Basil*, 1772; ed. Moesl. *Aug. Vind.* 1774.

RÖSSLER. 1776.

UNTERKIRCHER. Schr. ap. Vät. *Œnip.* 1817.

Sämmt. Werke d. Kirchenv. I. (*Kempten*, 1830.)

HEFELE. *Tüb.* 1840. 8⁰.

KARKER, FR. X. Ap. Vät. *Ratisb.* 1847.

SCHOLZ. Apost. Vät. *Gutersl.* 1865.

MAYER, J. C. Ap. Vät. In : Reithmayr's Bibl. d. Kirchenv. I. (*Kempten*, 1869.)

RIGGENBACH. *Basil.* 1873.

Italian.

GALLICCIOLI, GIO. BAT. *Venez.* 1797. 8⁰.

Russian.

In : Christijanskoje Tschtenije (1830).

PREOBRAZENSKIJ. *Moscow*, 1862.

III. *Literature*.

ABBOTT, E. A. Gospels. In : Encycl. Brit. (9th ed.) X. 815.

ALEXANDER, Natal. Hist. Eccles.Sec. 1, c. 12.

ALFORD, H. In : Smith. Bible dict. I. (1879) 247-8.

ALZOG. Patrol. (1876) 30-7.

ANGER. Synopsis. 1852. p. xx.

ARISIUS. Cremona liter. (1702) I. 39-40.

ARNOLD, K. F. Quaest. de comp. et fontibus Barnabae epp. capita nonnulla. *Königsb.* 1886.

BACKHOUSE, J. H. Eds. of Polyc. and Barnabas. Letter. In : Academy. (1881) 435ᵇ-436ᵃ.

— Letter. In : Academy. (1882) 213. [Punctuation.]

Barnabas from Cod. Sin. In : Am. Presb. R. XIII. (1864), 29-, 440-.

BARONIUS, ANN. (1588) 51, 54-5; 485, 4-14. Cf. Pagi. Crit. (1689) 51, 4; 485, 2.

BASNAGE. Hist. de l'Égl.

BAUMGARTEN. (Ausz. d. Kirchenges. *Halle ?*) 1743-, 62.

BAUMGARTEN-CRUSIUS. Dogmenges. (1832) 83. [v. 1.]

BAUR. Lehrb. d. Dogmengesch. (1858) 80-.

— D. Christenth. u. d. K. der. 3 ersten Jahrh. edit. II. (1863) 131-.

— Dogmengesch. I. (1865) 248-9.

ΒΑΦΕΙΔΟΣ. 'Εκκλ. ἱστ. I. (1884) 145.

BERTHOLDT. Einl. in A. u. N. T. VI. (1819) 2900-.

BLEEK. Einl. i. d. Br. an d. Hebr. (1828) 415-.

BLEEK-MANGOLD. Einl. i. d. N. T. (1875) 740, 279-.

BLOM, A. H. Paulus en Barnabas. In : Theol. Tijdschr. (1882) 186-199.

BRAUNSBERGER, O. In : Der Katholik. (1875) 251-, 449.

— D. Apostel B. *Mainz*, 1876. 8⁰.

BREHME, E. G. Schediasma historicum de J. Barsaba s. Barnaba. *Leucopetrae*, 1735. 4⁰.

BRETSCHNEIDER. Pietismus. *Lpz.* 1833. 8⁰.

BULL. Works. *Oxf.* 1843. 8⁰. V. 41; VI. 246.

BUNSEN. Hippolytus. (1854) I. 53-7.

— Bibelwerk (1866) VIII.

BURTON. Divinity of Christ. (1829) 1-3.

BUSSE. Chr. Lit. (1828-9) I. 2.

CAILLAU. Introd. in ss. Patr. (1825) 19-24. (1830) I. 19-24.

CALOV. Confessio mart. *Viteb.* 1658. I. 1.

— Biblia illustrata. *Frf.* 1672.

CAVE. Hist. lit. s. e. I. (1740) 18-21.

— Lives. (1840) I. 90-105. Abr. In : Wake. Ap. fath. *Hart.* 1834. 495-503.

CEILLIER. Hist. gén. aut. sac. (1729) I. 498-505; (1858) 281-5.

CHARTERIS. Canonicity. (1880) i–vii, 102–4, 142, 154, 168–70, 196, 215, 222, 233, 237, 248, 253, 255, 262, 272, 319.
CHEVALIER. Rép. d. sources hist. (1877–86) 223.
CLARKE. Sacred lit. (1830–1) I. 90–1.
COFFIN. Lives of fath. (1846) 169–174.
COTELERIUS. Patr. ap. *Amst.* 1724. I. 5–; also in: Migne. Patrol. gr. II. (1857) 651–60.
CREDNER. Einl. i. d. bibl. Schr. I. (1829) 11, 78–.
CREDNER–VOLKMAR. Gesch. d. NTlich. Kanon (1860) 119–.
CUNNINGHAM, W. Hist. theol. (1870) I. 95–6.
— The Ep. of B. a dissertation. *Lond.* 1877. 8º.
— Churches of Asia. (1880) pass.
DALLÆUS. De scr. Ign. *Gen.* 1666. 4º.
DANZ. Kirchenges. *Jena*, 1818. 8º.
DAVIDSON. Introd. N. T. I. (1868) 216, 268, 513–.
DELITZSCH, IOH. De inspirat. S. S. quid statuerunt PP. App. et apologetae sec. saec. *Lips.* (1872) 60–.
Dissert sur la lettre de S. B. In: Dissert. melées. (*Amst.* 1740. 8º) II. 37–56.
DONALDSON, J. Hist. Chr. Lit. (1864–6) I. 201–54.
— Apost. fath. (1874) 248–317.
— Recent edd. of Barnabas. In: Theo. R. XVI. (1879) 113–.
— In: Encycl. Brit. (9th ed.) II. 197.
DORNER. Person of Christ. I. (1864) 113–6.
"DU PIN. Bibl. des auteurs. I." [?]
EBRARD. Krit. d. ev. Gesch. *Frf. a. M.* 1868. 8º. p. 1076.
EICHHORN. Einl. N. T. I. (1827).
ENGELHARDT. D. Christenth. Justin d. M. (1878) 375–394.
EUSEBIUS. Hist. eccl. III. 26; VI. 14.
EWALD. Die joh. Schriften. II. (1862) 394–.
— Gesch. d. Volkes Israel. VII. (1868) 155–.
FABRICIUS. Bibl. gr. (1708–12–9) III. 173–5; V. 3; IX. 61. (2ª, IV. 826–8; VII, 5–6; X, 204.)
— Cod. Apocr. (1719) 781–2, etc.
FARRAR. Life of S. Paul. I. ch. xiii.
— Interpretation (1886). 167–70.
FLEURY. Hist. eccl. (1691–) I. 325–33.
FRANCKE, C. E. Lehre d. B. In: Ztschr. f. luth. Theol. I. (1840) II. 67–92.
FUNK. In Theol Quartalschr. (1878) 156–.
— Der Codex Vaticanus gr. 859 [Barnabas-brief] und seine Descendenten. In: Theol. Quartalschr. LXII. (1880) 629–637.
— In: Theol. Quartalschr. LXVI. (1884) 3–33.
GAAB. Dogmengeschichte. *Jena*, 1790. 8º.
GALLAND. Bibl. vet. patr. (1765) I. xxix–; also in: Migne. Patrol. gr. II. (1857) 685–706.
GEBHARDT U. H. s. u. eds.
GFRÖRER. Allg. K. G. I.
— Das Jahrh. des Heils. II.
GIESELER. Church Hist. (1868–) I. 108–9.
GÜDEMANN, M. Zur Erkl. d. B. In: Religionsgesch. Stud. [Schr. d. Israel. Lit. Vereins.] II. (*Lpz.* 1876) 99–131.
GUERICKE. Kirchenges.
HACKENSCHMIDT. D. Anfänge. d. cathol. Kirchenbegriffs. (1874) 47–.
HAGENBACH. Hist. of Doct. I. (1850) 55, etc.
HAMMOND. Dissertations. *Lond.* 1651. 4º.
HÄNLEIN. Einl. in N. T. *Erlang.* 1801.
HARNACK, AD. In: Herzog. Real.-Enc. (1877) II. 101–5. (Abr. in: Schaff-Herz. III. 214–5.)
HASE. Kirchenges. (1885–) I. 192–4.
HAUSRATH. NTliche Ztgesch. III. (1874) 522–. 2. Aufl. (1875).
HEBERLE. Ueb. d. Leser d. Br. B. In: Stud. d. ev. Geistlichkeit Würtembergs. I. (1846) 32.
— In: Herzog. Encykl. I. Aufl.

HEFELE, K. J. In. Theol. Quartalschr. I. (1839) 50–.
— D. Sendschr. d. Ap. Barnabas aufs neue untersucht, übersetzt u. erklärt. *Tüb.* 1840. 8º.
— Patr. ap. opera. *Tüb.* 1842. 8º. vii–; also in: Migne. Patrol. gr. II. (1857) 719–26; s. u. eds.
— In: Wetzer u. W. Kirch-Lex. (1847–54) I. 619–23.
HELLWAG. Präexist. Chr. i. d. ältest. K. In: Tüb. Theol. Jahrbb. II. (1848) 252–.
HEMSEN. Ev. Joh. *Schleswig*, 1823. 8º.
HENKE, E. De Epist. B. authent. *Jenae*, 1827. 8º.
HEYDECKE. Dissertat., qua B. epistola interpolata demonstretur. *Brunsv.* 1874. 8º.
HEYNS, IUNIUS ET VAN GILSE. De PP. App. doctrina morali. *Lugd. Bat.*, 1833.
HIERONYMUS. De vir. ill. c. 6.
HILGENFELD. Die App. VV. (1853) 11–.
— D. Urchristenth. (1855) 77–.
— Ztschr. f. wiss. Theol. (1858) 282, 569–; (1860) 328, 334; (1861) 221–.
— Die Propheten Esra und Daniel (1863) 7, 70–.
— D. Kanon u. d. Kritik d. N. T. (1863) 235–.
— Zeitschr. f. wiss. Theol. (1868) 214–; (1870) 115–; (1871) 262–.
— Einl. i. d. N. T. (1875) 544–.
— Zeitschr. f. wiss. Theol. XVIII. (1875) 596–; XIX. (1876) 438–; XX. (1877) 278–, 417–.
— In: Ztschr. f. wiss. Theol. XXI. (1878) 150, 295–.
HOEFLING. D. Lehre d App. VV. v. Opfer im christl. cultus. *Erlangen* (1841) 3–.
HOLTZMANN. Barnabas u Joh. In: Ztschr. f. wiss. Theol. (1871) 336–.
— Einl. in d. N. T. (1886) III. etc., 550.
HORNE. Introduction to the N. T. ed. Tregelles. IV. (1869) 333–.
HUG. In: Freiburger Ztschr. II. 138.
ITTIG. Hist. eccl. (1709) I. 20–4, 121–54, 477–8.
— Utrum B. ad Gnosticos respexerit. In his: De Haeresiarchis. *Lips.* 1703. 4º. 180–.
— Hist. sec. primi. 121–.
JACKSON. Ap. fath. (1879) 87–99.
JACOBUS DE VORAGINE. Legenda aurea. 81. (1846) 346–9.
JANNING. In: Acta ss. Bolland (1715) June. VI. 95. ("3ª II. 35–6.")
JONES. Canon N. T. (1798) II. 412–462.
JORTIN. Remarks on Eccl. Hist. (*Lond.* 1751.) I. 329–336.
KAYSER. In: Revue de théol. II. (1851) 202–.
— Ueber den sogen. Barnabasbrief. *Paderborn*, 1866.
KEIM. Gesch. Jesu v. Nazara. I. (1867) 141–3. [B. and the doct. of the Logos.]
KELLE. Barnabae epist., etc. *Fribergae*, 1822.
KILLEN. Ancient Church (1859) 367–8.
KIRCHHOFER. Quellensammlung u. s. w. (1844) 77–.
Kitto. XXXII. (1863) 66–; XXXIII. (1864) 103–.
KOESTLIN. D. Urspr. d. synopt. Evv. (1852)121–.
KONTOGONES. Φιλολ. κ. κριτ. ἱστορία τ . . . ἁγ. πατέρων. Ἐν Ἀθήναις, I. (1851) 73–.
KRUEGER. In: Theol. Quartalschr. IV. (1852) 615–. [de capp. VII. et VIII.]
KURTZ. Kirchenges. (1885–) I. 105.
LANGE. Gesch. d. Dogmen. (*Leipz.* 1795. 8º.) I. 58.
LARDNER. Credibility. Works (1831) II. 17–28.
LECHLER. Ap. u. Nachap. Z–A. (1885) 601–4. Engl. tr. (1886) II. 349–53.
LEE. Inspiration of Scripture. (1860) 415–8.
LE MOYNE, St. In his: Varia Sacra. Proleg. 72–.
LENOURRY. Appar. ad bibl. max. vet. Patr. *Par.* 1703. fº. 38–; also in: Migne. Patrol. gr. II. (1857) 673–86.
LESS, G. [Religionstheorie?] *Götting.* 1789.
LICHTENBERGER. Encycl. (1877–82) II. 85–6.
LIPSIUS. In Lpz. Repertorium. XII. (1854) 67–.
— De Clementis R. ep. I. *Lips.* (1855) 49–.
— In: Schehkel's Bibl.-Lexicon. I. (1869) 359–373.

LIPSIUS. In: Jenaer Literaturz. (1875) 491-.

LUEBKERT. D. Theol. d. app. VV. In: Zeitschr. f. d. hist. Theol. IV. (1854) 589-.

LUECKE. Einl. i. d. Offenb. Joh. I. (1852) 151, 318-.

LUMPER. Hist. ss. patr. *Aug. Vind.* 1783. 8°. I. 149-82; also in: Migne. Patrol. gr. II. (1857) 705-20.

LUTHARDT. Urspr. d. 4 Ev. (1874) 75-; Tr. Engl. (1875) 76-7.

M'CLINTOCK and S. CYCL. (1874) I. 670-2.

MACKENZIE, J. M. In: Smith. Gr. and Rom. Biog. (1859) I. 463-4.

MANEN, W. C. VAN. Een vraagteeken bij het geboortjaar van Barnabas' brief. — Loman, A. D. Een vraagteeken bij Dr. van Manen's kritiek. In: Theol. Tijdschr. (1884) 552-581.

MARSHALL, J. C. In: Expositor. XVI. (1882) 63-77. [B. and the Jewish ritual.]

MAZOCHIUS. Comm. in vet. Marmor. Neap. Ecclesiae Calend. *Neap.* 1763. 570-.

MELLIERIUS. s. u. Clement.

MENARDUS. Praef. in ed. Dacherii. 1645; also in: Migne. Patrol. gr. II. (1857) 659-64.

MENARD, HUG. Jud. de Barnab. et ejus epist. *Par.* 1645. 4°.

MICHAELIS. Einl. N. T. II.

MILLIGAN, W. In: Smith and Wace. Dict. I. 260-5.

MOEHLER. Patrologie ed. Reithmayr. (1840) 84-.

MOMBRITIUS BONIN. Sanctuarium. (c. 1479) I. lxviiii-xxii.

MOSHEIM. Kirchengeschichte.

MUELLER. Erkl. d. Barnabasbr. (1869) s. u. eds.

MUENSCHER. Dogmenges. (1817-8) I. 110-2, 389-90.

MURALT, ED. DE. In: Bull. acad. sciences St. Pétersbourg, Hist.-phil. (1848) V. 209-18.

MYNSTER. In: Stud. u. Krit. II. (1829) 323-.

NÄBE. Hist. eccl. *Lips.* 1832. 8°.

NEANDER. Church Hist. (1872) I. 657-8, et pass.

— Planting and Training. I. 196-.

NEUDECKER. Einl. N. T.

NIRSCHL. In: Der Katholik. (1881) 425-433. ["Todesjahr."]

— Patrol. (1881-) I. 51-66.

NITZSCH. Dogmengesch. I. (1870) 100-4, etc.

NODIER. Bib. sacr. (1826) 143-4.

NORTON. Genuineness of Gosp. I. (1846) 4, etc.

Nouv. Biog. Gen. (Hoefer). IV. (1853) 524-5.

ORELLI. Selecta Patr. (1820).

ORSI. Ist. eccl. (1746-) I. 96-8; (1749) I. 136-8.

OTTO, J. K. TH. v. Haben Barnabas, Justinus u. Irenäus d. 2. Petrnsbrief (3, 8) benützt? In: Ztschr. f. wiss. Theol. (1877) 525-529.

OUDIN. Scr. eccl. (1722) I. 8-15.

— Suppl. Bellarm. (1728) 20.

PAPEBROCH. Comment. praev. In: Acta ss. Bolland. (1698) Jun. II. 421-3 (3ᵃ, 415-7); analecta, 453-60 (3ᵃ, 448-54), fig; embolismus, 425-31 (3ᵃ, 420-5).

PERMANEDER. Bibl. patr. (184-) I. 409-10; II. 2-12, 941.

PERTSCH. (Kirchenhistorie.) *Wolfenb.* 1736-40. 4°.

PFLEIDERER. D. Paulinismus. (1873) 390-. [Doctrine of B.]

PUCCINELLI, PLACIDO. Vita di S. Barnaba. apostolo. *Milano,* 1649. 4°; 1718. 4°.

REDSLOB, G. F. Doctrina fidei quam expos. P. P. ap. *Arg.* 1829.

REUSS. Hist. de la théol. chrét. II. (1864) 305-; Eng. tr. II. 276.

— Gesch. N. T. (1874) I. 56, 242-3; Tr. Eng. (1884) 57-8, 242-4. [V. I.]

RIGGENBACH, C. J. D. Zeugnisse f. d. Joh. Ev. *Basel.* (1866) 84-.

— Der sogenannte Brief des Barnabas. *Basle,* 1873. 4°.

RITSCHL. Entsteh. d. altkath. K. (1857) 294-.

RITSCHL. In: Theod. Stud. n. Krit. (1865).

RIVETUS. Crit. sacri.

ROBERTS AND DONALDSON. Introd. note. In: Ante-Nic. Lib. I. (1868) 97-100. Ed. Coxe. I. (1885) 133-5.

ROERDAM, I. C. De authent. ep. Barn. *Hafn.* 1827 [8?]. 8°.

ROESSLER. Bibl. d. K.-V. I. (1776) 1-20.

ROSENMÜLLER, J. G. Hist. interpr. I. (1795) 42-.

ROTHE-WEINGARTEN. Kirchengesch. I. (1875) 96-.

RUMPF. In: N. Rev. de Théologie. (1867).

RYSEWYK. De Barnaba. *Arnh.* 1835. 8°.

SANDAY. Gosp. in 2 cent. (1876) 31-6, 71-6, 270-3.

SAXIUS, J. A. Archiep. Mediol. series. (1755) I. i-xcv. 4-.

SCHAFF. Hist. . . Church. II. (1886) 671-8.

SCHENKEL, D. In: Stud. u. Krit. X. (1837) 652-86.

SCHLIEMANN. Clementinen. (1844) 414-8, etc.

SCHMID. Patrol. (1879); (1886) 30-31.

SCHMIDT, J. E. C. Kirchenges. (1801) I. 437-.

SCHNECKENBURGER. In: Theol. Stud. u. Krit. (1855) [In: Krit. d. Apostelges.]

SCHOLTEN. Die ältesten Zeugnisse. (1867) 7-.

SCHRAM. Anal. ss. patr. (1780-) I. 1-18.

SCHROECKH. Kirchenges. (1772-) II. 272-3.

SCHULTHESS. In: Neuest. Theol. Annal. (1829) 943-.

SCHUERER. Lehrb. d. NTichlen Ztgesch. (1874) 355.

SCHWEGLER. Nachap. Zeitalt. (1846) II. 240-2.

SEMISCH. Justin M. *Bresl.* 1842. 8°.

SEMLER. Einl. In: Baumgarten. Unters. Theol. Streitigk. II. (1763) 2-.

SHEDD. Hist. of doct. 3d ed. (1865-) I. 267; II. 209.

SIEGFRIED. Philo. v. Alex. (1875) 330-.

SKWORZOW. Patrol. Untersuchungen. *Leipzig,* 1875.

SORMANI, N. Orig. apost. chiesa. *Milan,* 1754. 293-302.

SPANHEIM. Ann.

SPRINZL. Theol. d. ap. Vät. *Wien,* 1880.

STARKE. Gesch. chr. K. *Berlin,* 1779-80. [?]

STÄUDLIN. (Sittenlehre Jesu?) 1802.

STEIGER, W. Mélanges. I. 1.

STOLLE. Kirchenvät. *Jena,* 1733. 4°.

STRAUSS. Das Leben Jesu.

STRŒHLIN, E. In: Lichtenberger. Encycl. (1877-82) II. 83-5. (85-66 p., Anon.)

Supernatural Religion. (1875-) I. 232-56; II. 251-3; III. 7.

TABARAUD. In: Biog. Univ. Michaud. 1842-65. III. 109-10.

TENZELIUS. Florum sparsio ad Hier. catal. (1703) 17-.

THIERSCH. Die Kirche im ap. Zeit.

THILO. In: Ersch u. Gruber. I. VII. (1821) 404-5.

TILLEMONT. Mém. (1732) I. 408-15, 655-60; XVI. 379-80, 766-7.

TISCHENDORF. In: Augsb. allg. Ztng. (1857) 2253.

— Notitia edit. cod. bibl. Sinait. (1860) 13-.

— Wann wurden uns Evv. u. s. w. (1866) 92-.

TOBLER. In: Zeitschr. wiss. Theol. (1860).

UEBERWEG. Hist. philos. (1876) 278.

ULLMANN. Indentität d. Barn. u. Barsabas. In: Stud. u. Krit. I. (1828) 377-399. [Also Letter of B. and B. as author of Ep. to Hebrews.]

Veterum Testimonia de S. Barn. et ejus ep. In: Galland. Vet. Patr. Bibl. I. *Venet.* 1765. f°. 113-; also in: Migne. Patrol. gr. II. (1857) 647-50.

VOLKMAR. D. Ev. Marcion's. (1852) 176-.

— Ueb. Clemens v. Rom. . . . . mit bes. Bezieh. auf den Barn. 1856.

— Brief in: Theol. Jahrbb. (1856) 350-.

— Religion Jesu. (1857) 392.

— In: Zeitschr. der deutschen morgenländischen Gesellsch. I. (1860) 100 not. 296-.

— In: Zeitschr. f. wiss. Theol. (1861) 115, 433-.

VOLKMAR. Comment. Apok. Joh. (1862) 12–.
— Handbuch d. Apokr. II. (1863) 24, 376–.
— Monumentum vetust. Christ. ineditum. 1864.
— In: Rhein. Mus. f. Philol. (1865) 265–.
— In: Ztschr. f. wiss. Theol. (1865) 445–.
— Ursp. uns. Evang. (1866) 65, 140–.
— Die Evang. (1870) 361–.
VINCENTIUS BELVAC. Speculum hist. XXI. 103.
VOSS. Epist. s. Barn. *Amst.* 1646. Praef.; also in: Migne. Patrol. gr. II. (1857) 663–6; Praef. ed. *Oxon.* 1680; also in: Migne. Patrol. gr. II. (1857) 665–74.
WAITE. Hist. Chr. Rel. (1881) 226–7, et pass.
WALCH. Bibl. patrist. (1834) 24–5, 282–3, 367.
WEISS. In: Theol. Stud. u. Krit. (1864).
WEIZSAECKER. Z. Kritik. d. Barnab.-Briefes aus dem Cod. Sinait. *Tüb.* 1863.
— In: Jahrb. f. deut. Theol. (1865) 391–3.
WESTCOTT. Canon. (1875) 40–46.
— Bible in the church. (1877) 80–1.
WETTE, DE. 1841.
WIESELER. Unters. üb. d. Hebräerbrief. I. (1861).
WIESELER, K. Ursprung u. Verf. In: Jahb. f. deut. Theol. XV. (1870) 603–14.
— In: Am. Presb. R. XX. (1871) 625–.
WINER. Bibl. Reallex. I. (1847) 138–.
WINTER, V. Krit. Gesch. d. ältest. Zeugen u. Lehrer d. Christenthums. 1814. 8⁰. 245.
WITTCHEN. D. gesch. Character d. Ev. Joh. (1869) 103–.
ZAHN. Ignatius v. Antiochien. (1873) 397, 455–.
ZELLER. Apostelgeschichte. (1854) 17–8.
Zur älteren Geschichte des Barnabasbriefes. In: Katholik, 1875. Nov.

Note 1. Genuineness, etc. For: Origen, Clement of A., Eusebius, Hieron., Apost. const., Voss, Hammond, Pearson, Bull, Cave, Du Pin, Grynaeus, Wake, Lardner, Fleury, Le Nourry, Russel, Galland, Less, Rosenmüller, Muenscher, Stäudlin, Danz, Bertholdt, Hemsen, Schmidt, Henke, Bleek, Rördam, Gieseler, Näbe, Credner, Bretschneider, Guericke, Francke, Gfrörer, Möhler, Baumgarten - Crusius, De Wette(?), Rysewyk, Schneckenburger, Sprinzl, Alzog, Nirschl, Sharpe. *Against:* Rivet, Usher, Menard, Daillé, Papebroch, Calmet, Cotelerius, Le Moyne, Tenzel, Natalis Alex., Ittig, Spanheim, Tillemont, Basnage, Oudin, Ceillier, Stolle, Pertsch, Baumgarten, Walch, Mosheim, Semler, Schroekh, Rössler, Starke, Lumper, Michaelis, Gaab, Lange, Hänlein, Winter, Neander, Ullmann, Mynster, Hug, Baur, Winer, Hase, Ebrard, Semisch, Kayser, Reithmayr, Hefele, MacKenzie, Lipsius, Weizäcker, Donaldson, Roberts and D., Riggenbach, Westcott, Braunsberger, Cunningham, Funk, Alford. *Interpolated.* Schenkel, Heydecke.
Note 2. Date. Reign of Vespasian, Menardus, Ewald, Weizsäcker, Milligan; 71–73, Galland; 70–100, Tischendorf (at first); reign of Domitian, Wieseler, Hilgenfeld, Riggenbach. Donaldson, Reuss, Ewald, Dressel, and Ritschl, also put it in the first century. Papebroch pronounces for some time later than 97, Hefele for 107–20, Volkmar, Tischendorf (later), Baur, and others, for 119; Tentzel for the reign of Trajan; and Hug, Ullmann, Lücke, Neander, Winer, Zeller, and Köstlin for some time early in the 2d century, while Heydecke distinguishes into a genuine B., 70–71, and an interpolator, 119–121.

VI. PAPIAS. FRAGMENTS.

I. *Editions.*

HALLOIX. In: Ill. orient. scr. *Duaci*, 1633. f⁰.
GRABE. Gr. lat. In: Spicil. patr. (1700) II. 26–35.
GALLAND. Bibl. patr. vet. *Ven.* 1765. f⁰. I. 316–420.
MÜNTER. In: Fragm. patr. gr. *Hafn.* 1788. 8⁰. I. 13–.
ROUTH. Rel. sacr. (*Oxon.* 1846–8) I. 1–44.
MIGNE. Gr. lat. In: Patrol. gr. V. (1857) 1255–62.
GEBHARDT U. HARNACK. In: Gebhardt, H. & Z. Patr. ap. *Lips.* 1875. 8⁰; I. 180–196, 248. *Lips.* 1878. I. 1. 87–104.
FUNK. Patr. ap. (*Tüb.* 1881) II. 276–300.

For sources of text of individual fragments see Gebhardt u. Harnack (1878).

II. *Translations.*

English.

ROBERTS and DONALDSON. In: Ante-Nic. Lib. I. (1868) 441–8. Ed. Coxe. I. (1885) 153–5.

For other translations, complete or partial, see late editions of the apostolical fathers and works on the Canon and the Fourth Gospel.

III. *Literature.*

ABBOTT, E. A. Gospels. In: Encycl. Brit. (9th ed.) X. 815–6, 820–1; XVIII. 228.
ABERLE. In: Theol. Quartalschr. (1864) 1–.
ALFORD. Greek Test. (1868) Proleg. I.
ALZOG. Patrol. (1876) 52–3.
ANGER. Synops. Evv. (1852).
BARONIUS. Ann. (1589), 118, 2–6. Cf. Pagi, Crit. (1689) 3–5.
BAUMGARTEN–CRUSIUS. Dogmenges. (1832) 85. [v. 1.]
BÄUMLEIN. D. Nachricht d. P. ü. d. Marcusev. In: Stud. u. Krit. XXXVI. (1863) 111–3.
BAUR. Unters. kan. Evv. (1847).
— Das Markus Evang. (1851).
— Dogmengesch. I. (1865) 371–2, etc.
ΒΑΦΕΙΔΗΣ. Ἐκκλ. ἱστ. I. (1884) 148.
BERTHOLDT. Dogmenges. (1822–3) I. 67, etc.
— Einl. A. u. N. T. III.
BICKELL. In: Ztschr. f. kath. Th. (1879) 799–803.
BLEEK–MANGOLD. Einl. N. T. (1875) 113–.
BUSSE. Chr. lit. (1828–9) I. 4.
CAVE. Scr. eccl. hist. lit. (1740–3) I. 47–9.
CEILLIER. Hist. gén. aut. sacr. (1729) I. 683–7; (1858) 398–401.
CHARTERIS. Canonicity. (1880) xli-xlvi, 53–9, 114, 141–2, 167–8, 197, 305, 321, 338–9.
CHEVALIER. Rép. d. sources hist. (1877–86) 1717.
Christian Rem. (1853) 218–.
CLARKE. Sacred lit. (1830–1) I. 95.
CLINTON. Fasti Rom. (1845–50) I. 87. II. 401–2.
CREDNER. Beiträge. I. (1832).
— Gesch. N. T. Kanon. (1860).
CUNNINGHAM. Churches of Asia. (1880) pass.
DAVIDSON. Introd. N. T. (1848–) passim, especially I. 425–7.
— In: Theol. Rev. IV. (1867).
DELITZSCH. Unters. Entst. Matth. Ev. (1853).
DONALDSON. Hist. Chr. Lit. 1864–6. I. 312–9.
— Apost. fath. (1874) 393–402.
DORNER. Person of Christ. I. (1864) 135–7, 399–400.
DUPIN. Nouv. bibl. d. aut. eccl. (1698 seq.) I. 91.
EBRARD. Krit. ev. Gesch. (1868) 964–79, 1130–1, etc.
EICHHORN. Einl. N. T. II. (1824).
EUSEBIUS. Hist. eccl. III. 39.
EWALD. In: Jahrb. bibl. Wiss. (1849).
— Die Joh. Schriften. II. (1862) 371–, 392–, 400, etc.
— Gesch. d. V. Isr. VII. (1868).
— In: Gött. gel. Anz. (1875) 103–.
FABRICIUS. Bibl. gr. (1712) V. 185–6. ("2ᵃ, 151–3, 176.")
FEILMOSER. Einl. N. T. 2 Ausg. (1830).
FLEURY. Hist. eccl. (1691–) I. 377–8.
FROMMANN. In: Th. Stud. u. Krit. (1840).
GALLAND. Vet. patr. bibl. *Venet.* 1765. f⁰. I. lxvi–; also in: Migne. Patrol. gr. V. (1857) 1251–4.
GFRÖRER. Urchristenthum II. 1. (1838).
— Allg. K. G. (1841) I.
GIESELER. Church Hist. (1868) I. 110–1.
— Entst. Schr. Evv. (1818).
GODET. Comment. s. S. Jean. (1876) I. 1. 58–66. Tr. Engl. I. (1879) 48–54.
GRATZ, N. Entst. d. 3 erst. Evv. (1812).
GRIESBACH. Comment. qua Marci Evang. totum e Matth. et Lúc. Comm. decerpt. esse demonstratur.

GRIMM. In: Ztschr. f. wiss. Th. (1874) 122.

GROOT, HOFSTEELE DE. Basilides. Tr. Ger. (1868) 111-.

GUERICKE. Gesammtgesch. N. T. (1854).

— H'buch Kirchengesch. Tr. Engl. (1867) 149–195.

HAGENBACH. Hist. of Doct. I. (1850) 57, etc.

HALLOIX. Eccl. orient. scr. (1633) I. 635–67.· [637-45. Vita S. P. "Purely imaginary."— *Schaff.*]

HARLESS. Lucubr. Evang. can. spect. pars I. (1841).

HASE. Kirchenges. (1885–) I. 291–3.

HAUSRATH. Neutestl. Ztgesch. " 111. 59." [?]

HENGSTENBERG. Die Offenbarung Joh. II. (1862) 383–93.

HENSCHENIUS. Comment. histor. in: Acta ss. Bolland. (1658) Feb. III. 285–7. (" 3ᵃ, 289–92.")

HERGENROETHER. Kirchenges. (1879–80) I. 15; III. 8.

HIERONYMUS. De vir. ill. 18 (Honor. August. I. 19).

HILGENFELD, A. Die Evangelien. (1854).

— Kanon. (1863) 13–.

— In: Ztschr. f. wiss. Theol. (1865) 78–.

— In: Zeitschr. f. wiss. Theol. X. (1867) 179–.

— Papias von Hierapolis. Ztschr. wiss. Theol. 1875. S. 231–270.

— Einl. in das N. T. 1875. S. 52 ff. 396 ff.

— Papias über Marcus u. Matthaus. Ztschr. f. wiss. Theol. XXII. (1879) S. 1–18. [Agst. Weiffenbach.]

— P. u. d. neueste Evangelienforschung. In: Ztschr. f. wiss. Theol. XXIX. (1886) 257–91.

HOLTZMANN. Die synopt. Evv. (1863).

— Joh. d. Presbyter. In: Schenkel. Bibel.-Lex. III. (1871) 352–60.

— Epheser. u. Col.-Br. (1872) 322?

— P. u. Johannes. In: Ztschr. f. wiss. Theol. XXIII. (1880) 64–77.

— Einl. in d. N. T. (1886) 114–8, etc.

HORNE. Introd. H.S. (1869) IV.

HUG. Einl. N. T. I. (1847).

IRENAEUS. V. 33.

ITTIG. Hist. eccl. (1709) II. 48–9, 243–4.

JACKSON. Ap. fath. (1879) 119–121.

KAYSER, A. Rev. de Théol. (1854).

KEIM. Gesch. Jesu. 1867. I. 161–. Dritte Bearb. 2 Aufl. 41 f. 378 ff. 1875.

KERN. Tübing. Zeitschr. f. Theol. (1834) 2.

KIENLEN, H. W. Zeugniss. d. Papias f. unser Markusev. In: Stud. v. Krit. XVI. (1843) 423–9.

KILLEN. Ancient Church. (1859) 369.

KLENER. De. Authen. Ev. Matth. (1832).

KLOSTERMANN. Das Markusevang. (1867) 326–.

KÖSTLIN. Urspr. synopt. Evv. (1853).

KUHN, J. Leben Jesu. I. (1838).

KURTZ. Kirchenges. (1885–) I. 108.

LACHMANN. In: Th. Studien u. Krit. (1835) 577–.

LANGE, J. P. Bibelwerk. N. T. I. (1857–8).

LARDNER. Credibility. Works. (1831) II. 116–125.

LEIMBACH, C. L. D. Papiasfragment. Exeget. Untersuch. d. Fragmentes [Eusebius Hist. eccl. III. 39, 3–4.] u. Kritik d. gleichmam. Schrift. v. Lic. Dr. Weiffenbach. Gotha, 1875. 8⁰.

LEUSCHNER. Ev. St. Joh. (1873) 72–.

LIGHTFOOT, J. B. In: Contemp. V. (1867) 397–.

— In: Contemp. R. (1875) 377–403, 828–856. [Agst. "Supernatural Religion."]

LIPSIUS. In: Jen. Litzng. I. (1874) No. 38.

LOMAN, A. Het Getuigenis van Papias, etc. In: Theol. Tijdschrift. IX. (1875) 125–154.

LÜCKE. Einl. in Offenb. (1852) 524–.

— In: Stud. u. Krit. (1833) 499–.

LÜDEMANN, H. Zur Erklärung des Papiasfragments bei Euseb. hist. eccl. III. 39. § 3, 4. In: Jahrbb. f. prot. Theol. (1879) 365–384.

LUMPER. Hist. ss. patr. I. (1783) 360–73.

LUTHARDT. De Compos. Evv. Matth. (1861).

— Der johanneische Urspr. d. vierten Evang. (1874) 71–73, 104–114. Tr. Engl. (1875) 126–39.

LÜTZELBERGER. Tradition üb. ap. Joh. (1840).

M'CLINTOCK and S. Cycl. (1874–) VII. 638.

MARTENS. Papias als exegeet van logia des heeren. *Amsterdam*, 1875. 8⁰. (116).

MAURICE. Eccl. Hist. (1854) 200–1.

MEANS, J. C. In: Smith. Gr. and Rom. Biog. (1859) III. 116–7.

Meth. Q. R. XIII. (1853) 487–; XXVI. (1866) 605–.

MEYER. Kr. ex. H'buch Ev. Matth. (1864) 4–5; Mk. u. Lk. (1867) 3–6; Joh. (1862) 5–6, etc. etc.

MILLIGAN, John the Presbyter. In: Jour. of sacr. lit. (1867) 106–.

MIRAEUS. Scr. eccl. 8.

MÖHLER. Patrologie. (1840) 175–9.

MUENSCHER. Dogmenges. (1817–8) I. 269, II. 417–8.

NEANDER. Church Hist. (1872) I. 513, 650–1.

NEUDECKER. Einl. N. T. (1840).

NICOLAS. Études crit. N. T. (1863).

NIEMEYER. Recens. Schott's Isagoge. In: Haller Litt. Zeitung. (1832) No. 57.

NIRSCHL. Patrol. (1881–) I. 138–9.

NORTON. Genuineness of Gosp. I. (1846) 59–60, etc.

OLSHAUSEN. Apost. Ev. Matth. origo defenditur. (1835).

ORSI. Ise. eccl. (1746–) II. 51–5. (1749–) II. 74–80.

OVERBECK. In: Ztschr. f. wiss. Th. (1867) 39–.

PAULUS. Exeg. Conserv. I. (1842).

PERMANEDER. Bibl. patrist. (1842) II. 58–61.

PHOTIUS. Codex. 232.

PICOT. In: Biog. Univ. Michaud. (1842–65) XXXII. 94.

PITRA. Spicil. Solesm. (1852) I. iv–vi.

REISCHL. Chiliasmus. In: Theol. Monatschr. (1850) März.

REITHMAYR. Einl. can. Bücher. N. B. (1852).

RENAN. Vie de Jésus. 15 ed. (1876) li–.

RETTIG, H. C. M. In: Stud. v. Krit. IV. (1831) 734–76. [P. and the N. T. Canon.]

REUSS. Gesch. N. T. (1874) I. 183–5. Tr. Eng. (1884) 184–6. [y. 1.]

RÉVILLE. Ét. crit. sur. l' Ev. selon S. Matth. (1862).

RIGGENBACH. Die Zeugn. f. das Ev. Johann. (1866).

— Joh. d. Ap. u. d. Presb. In: Jahrb. f. deut. Theol. (1868) 319–.

— In: Jahrb. f. deut. Theol. XIV. (1869) 138. [Agst. Steitz.]

ROBERTS and DONALDSON. Introd. note. In: Ante-Nic. Lib. I. (1868) 437–9. Ed. Coxe. I. (1885) 151–2.

ROTHE. Anfänge. (1837).

RUMPF. In: Rev. de Théol. (1867).

SANDAY. Gosp. in 2 cent. (1876) 145–60.

SAUNIER. Ueb. Quell. des. Ev. Marci. (1825).

SCHAFF. Hist. . . Church. II. (1886) 693–8.

SCHENKEL. Das Charakterbild Jesu. (1864).

SCHERER. In: Rev. de Théol. (1859).

SCHLEIERMACHER, F. P. u. ans. beiden ersten Evv. In: Stud. v. Krit. V. (1832) 735–68.

SCHLIEMANN. Clementinen. (1884) 427–8.

SCHMID. Patrol. (1879) 34.

SCHNECKENBURGER. Urspr. erst. kan. Evang. (1834).

SCHOLTEN. Apost. Joh. in Kleinasien. Tr. Spiegel (1872) 21–.

— Het. Ev. naar Joh. (1864) 7–.

SCHOTT. Authen. d. kan. Ev. n. Matth. (1837).

SCHROECKH. Kirchenges. (1772–) II. 345–7.

SCHWEGLER. Nachap. Zeitalt. (1846) I. 304–7.

SEMLER. Zusätze zu Townson's Abh. üb. 4 Ev. I.

SIEFFERT. Urspr. erst. kan. Ev. (1832).

STEITZ, G. E. In: Stud. v. Krit. XLI. (1868) 63–95.

— (Karl L. Leimbach). In: Herzog. Real.-Enc. (1877–) XI. 194–206. (Abr. in: Schaff-Herz. III. 1738–9.)

STEMLER. Is het Papias-fragment zuiver exegetisch verklaard? In: "Studiën II. 2."

STORR. Zweck. d. ev. Gesch. u. Br. Joh.

STRAATMAN. Nog eens het Papias-fragment I. In Theol. Tijdschr. (1876) Maart; II. in: do. Mei.

STRAUSS. Das Leben Jesu. (1864).

STRŒHLIN, E. In: Lichtenberger. Encycl. (1877–82) X. 171–5.

Stud. u. Krit. 1870, 1875.

Supernatural Religion. (1875–) I. 444–85, II. 320–36, III. xxi–xxiii, 19–21.

THEILE. Winer's n. kr. Journal. (1824) I.

— Zur Biographie Jesu.

Theol. Ecl. R. III. (1867) 241–.

THIERSCH. Versuch z. Herst. hist. Standp. d. krit. N. T. Schr. (1845).

— Die Kirche im ap. Zeit. (1858).

THOLUCK. Glaubw. d. ev. Gesch.

TILLEMONT. Mém. (1732) II. 296–300, 620–3.

TISCHENDORF. Wenn wurden u. s. w. 118–.

TRITHEMIUS. Scr. eccl. 9.

VOLKMAR. Der Ursprung. (1866).

— Die Evangelien. (1870).

WAITE. Hist. Chr. Rel. (1881) 235–8 et pass.

WEIFFENBACH, WILH. Das Papias-Fragment bei Euse-bius H. E. III. 39, 3–4. *Giessen*, 1874. 8º.

— Rückblick auf d. neuesten Papias-Verhandlungen. In: Jahrbb. f. prot. Theol. (1877) 323–379, 405–468.

— Die Papias-Fragmente ub. Marcus u. Matthaus. Zug-leich e. Beitrag. zur synopt. Frage. *Berlin*, 1878. 8º.

— Rplik auf d. 'Erklärung' d. Herrn Dr. B. Weiss. In: Jahrbb. f. prot. Theol. 1884, 2, S. 320–325 [λογια in Papias.]

WEIHENMAIER. Dissert. de Papia Hier. in Asia episcop. antiq. *Wittenb.* 1694. 4º.

WEISS. In: Jahrb. deutsche Theol. (1865) II.

WEISSE. Evangelienfrage.

WEIZSÄCKER. Unters. üb. d. evang. Gesch.

WESTCOTT. Canon (1875) 68–79.

— Bible in the Church (1879) 95–7.

WETTE, DE. Einl. N. T.

WETZER u. W. Kirch-Lex. (1847–54) VIII. 90–1.

WIESELER. Chronol. Synops. d. 4 Evv. (1843).

WILCKE. Tradition und Mythe. (1837).

WILKE. Die Urevangelist. (1838).

WITTICHEN. In. Prot. Kirchenz. (1871) 794.

Y. In: Nouv. Biog. Gen. (Hoefer) XXXIX. (1865) 160.

YONGE. Pupils of St. John (1878) 201–5.

ZAHN, T. In: Stud. u. Krit. XXXIX. (1866) 649–96. [" s. gesch. Stellung, s. Werk, u. s. Zeugn. ü. d. Ev."]

— In: Theol. Stud. u. Krit. XL. (1867) 539–42. [Sup-plementary to his art. in (1866)].

ZELLER. In: Theol. Jahrb. (1845), (1847).

— Apostelgesch. (1854) 10–11.

ZYRO, FERD. FR. Neue Beleuchtung d. Papiasstelle in der Kirchenges. d. Eusebius. III. 39. *Darmstadt*, 1869. 8º.

See also all works on the authorship of the fourth gospel, and the history of Millenarianism.

Note. Presbyter John. Same as Apostle John, Irenaeus (?), Hieronymus, Guericke, Lange, Hengstenberg, Milligan, Riggenbach, ZAHN, Leimbach, Schaff, Nirschl. *Some one else*, Eusebius, Steitz, Tischendorf, Keim, Weiffenbach, Lüde-mann, Donaldson, Davidson, Credner, Wieseler, Ebrard, Holtzmann, Westcott, Lightfoot.

VII. JUSTIN MARTYR. VARIOUS WORKS.

I. *Editions.*

(Admonit. ad Gentes.) *Paris*, 1539. 8º.

STEPHANUS, ROB. (Opera.) *Paris*, 1551. fº.

(Fragm. liturg.) *Par*. 1560. fº. In: Liturgiae ss. patr. Jacobi, Basilii, etc. *Paris*.

STEPHANUS, HENR. (Epist. ad Diogn. and Oratio.) Gr. lat. *Paris*, 1571. 4º; do. 1592. 4º; 1595. ??

BRUNELLUS, HIER. (Cohortatio.) *Romae*, 1586. 8º. In: SS. patr. orat. et epist. sel. I. 1–.

SYLBURGIUS, FRID. (Opera.) Gr. lat. *Heidelb*. 1593. fº.

MORELLUS, FEDER. (Opera.) Gr. lat. *Par*. 1615. fº; 1636. fº; also ["Vitiose"] *Colon*. 1686. fº.

HALLOIX, PETR. (De resurrectione.) Gr. lat. In his: Justini vita. *Duaci*, 1622. fº; also in his: Ill. eccl. orient. scr. *Duaci*, 1636. fº. 299–329.

GRABE. (Apol. I. etc.) Gr. lat. *Oxon*. 1700. 8º.

KOCH, C. (Dialogue.) *Kil*. 1700. 8º.

HUTCHIN. (Apol. 2, Oratio cohort., Oratio ad Gr. et Lib. de Monarchia.) Gr. lat. *Oxon*. 1703. 8º.

LEQUIEN, MICH. (De resurrectione.) Gr. lat. In: Joannis Damasc. opera. II. (*Par*. 1712. fº.) 756–. [Humphreys. (Resurrect.) *Lond*. 1714. 8º, often quoted, is an error. "With the original Greek" applies only to frag-ments from Josephus, etc. s. u. Translations.]

JEBB, SAM. (Dialogue.) Gr. lat. *Lond*. 1719. 8º.

THIRLBIUS. (Apoll. duae. et Dial. c. Tr.) Gr. lat. *Lond*. 1722. fº. [Really by Markland?]

MARANUS, PRUD. (Opera.) Gr. lat. *Par*. 1742. fº; repr. *Venet*. 1747. fº. [Benedictin.]

THALEMANNUS. (Apologiae.) Gr. *Lips*. 1755. 8º.

TELLERUS, GU. ALB. (Resurrectione.) *Helmst*. 1764 [6?]. 4º.

GALLANDIUS. (Apol. dialogue, fragm.) *Venet*. 1765. fº. In his: Bibl. patr. I. 411–.

ASHTON. (Apologiae.) *Cantab*. 1768. 8º.

OBERTHÜR. (Opera.) Gr. lat. *Wirceb*. 1777. 8º; 1794. 8º.

GOETZ, J. AD. (2d Apol., etc.) Gr. ger. *Nürnb*. 1796. 8º.

AUGUSTI. (De resurrectione.) Gr. lat. In his: Chrest. patrist. I. (*Lips*. 1812. 8º.) 3–.

HORNEMANN, C. F. (Dial. c. Tryph.) In his: Patr. apost. *Havn*. 1829. 4º.

BRAUNIUS, J. W. J. *Bonn*, 1830. 8º; *Bonn*, 1860. 8º.

OTTO, J. C. T. (Opera.) *Jen*. 1842–8. 3 v. 8º; 1847–50. 8º; 1876–81. 5 v. 8º. [All works, genuine and spurious. Full.]

TROLLOPE, W. (Apol. and Dial.) *Camb*. and *Lond*. 1845 –7. 3 v. 8º. [Otto's text.]

MIGNE. Patrol. gr. VI. (1857) (Genuine works) 227–800, (Pseudo-Justin) 1181–1564, (Fragments) 1571–1600. [After Maranus.]

GILDERSLEEVE, B. L. (Apologies.) *N. Y.* 1877. 12º.

GUTBERLET, C. (Apologiae.) *Lips*. 1883. 8º. ["Braunius. ed. iii."]

II. *Translations.*

Latin.

PICUS, JO. FR. (Admonitio) 1506. fº; also in his: Op. *Argent*. 1506 (7?). fº; *Basil*, 1601. fº; in Champerus. De tripl. discipl. *Lugd*. 1508. 8º; Sichard, J. Antido-tum contra haereses. *Basil*. 1528. fº, 112–121; Micro-presbyticum (*Basil*. 1550. fº), 31–47; in: Monumenta Orthodoxogr. PP. *Basil*. 1555. fº, 98–; *Basil*. 1569. fº. H. VII. 1947–1966; also separately. *Par*. 1538. 4º.

POSTELLUS, GUIL. In: Evers. fals. dogm. *Par*. 1552. 16º.

PERIONIUS, JOACH. *Par*. 1554. fº; also in: Bibl. patr. *Colon*. 1618. fº. II.

GELENIUS, SIGISM. (Op.) *Basil*. 1555. fº.

(Excerpta liturgica.) *Antv*. 1562. 8º. In: Liturgiae s. Missae ss. patr.

LANGIUS, JO. (Op.) *Basil*. 1565. fº. 3 v. in 1; *Par*. 1575. 16º (with Hippolytus); also in: Bibl. patr. *Lug-dun*. 1677. fº. II. 1–.

BILLIUS, JAC. (De resurrectione.) In his: Damasceni Opera. *Par*. 1619. fº.

ROUS, FR. (Various) In his: Meller patr. *Lond*. 1650. 8º. 21–26.

CHANTELOS, CLAUDIUS. [?] (Ep. de vita chr.) *Par*. 1661. 4º. In his: Bibl. patr. ascet. I. 1–.

PRILESZKY, J. B. *Cassov*. 1765. 4º. [Maranus version.]

CAILLAU and GUILLON. *Par*. and *Brux*. 1829. 8º; *Mediol*. 1830. 8º.

Danish.

MUUS, C. H. *Kjoebenh.* 1836. 8⁰.

English.

REEVES, WM. (I. Apol.) *Lond.* 1709. 2 v. 8⁰; repr. 1716.
2 v. 8⁰. [Poor.]
HUMPHREYS, DAV. (Resur.) *Lond.* 1714. 8⁰. In his:
Athenagoras.
BROWN, H. (Dialogue.) *Lond.* 1755. 2 v. 8⁰; 1846. 8⁰.
["Literal and faithful."]
MOSES, TH. (Exh. to Gent.) *Lond.* 1757. 8⁰. ["Free."]
DALRYMPLE, D. *Edinb.* 1778. 12⁰. [?]
CHEVALLIER. *Camb.* 1833.
Library of the Fathers. XL. *Lond.* 1861. 8⁰.
DODS, REITH, and ROBERTS. In: Ante-Nic. Lib. II.
(1868) 7–361. Ed. Coxe. I. (1885) 163–302.

French.

MAUMONT, JEAN DE. (Oeuvres) *Par.* 1554. f⁰; 2 éd.
Par. 1559. f⁰.
DUPIN, MARTIN. Cohortatio. *Par.* 1580. 8⁰.
FONDET, PIERRE. (2d Apol.) *Par.* 1670. 12⁰; *Par.* 1686.
12⁰. [Really by Chanut. *Caillau.*]
GENOUDE [??] In: Pères de l'égl. *Par.* 1837–43. 8⁰.

German.

HEDIUS, D.(?) CASPAR. (Cohortatio.) *Strasb.* 1529. f⁰.
In: Chronica, etc.
GLÜSING, J. OTTO. (Diognet. zenam.) *Hamb.* 1723. 8⁰.
In his: Briefe u. Schr. d. Ap. Männer. p. 443–.
DENIS, M. (I. Apol.) In: Denkmale aus allen Jahrhh.
I. 1. *Vindob.* 1795. 8⁰. 21–; 1830. 16–.
GÖTZ, JO. A. (De monarchia.) *Norimb.* 1796.
KESTNER, AUG. (Orat. ad gent.) In his: Die Agape.
(*Jenae*, 1819. 8⁰.) 333–7.
BRUN, N. DE. (Dialogue.) *Basil*, 1822. 8⁰.
DECKERS. (I. Apol.) In: Kath. Monatsschr. III.
(1828.)
WAIZMANN, J. S. In: Sämmtl. Werke d. K. V. *Kempten*, 1830. 8⁰. II. [?]
RICHARD, P. A. *Kempten*, 1870. 16⁰. [The Reithmayer-Thalhofer Bibl.]

Italian.

GALLICCIOLI, GIOV. BAPT. *Venezia*, 1799. 8⁰.

Russian.

METODIJ, JER. (De monarchio.) *Mosc.* 1783. 73–80.
SMIRNOW, M. (Selections.) *Mosk.* 1783. 8⁰.
CLEMENTJEWSKJ, I. (Dialogue.) *St. Petersb.* 1797. 8⁰.
(I. Apol.) In: Christijanskoje Tschtenije. 1825. (2d
Apol.) 1840.
PREOBRAZENSKIJ. *Moscov.* 1862–3.

III. *Literature.*

ABBOTT, E. A. Gospels. In: Encycl. Brit. (9th ed.) X.
816–8, 821–2.
— J. and the fourth Gosp. In: Modern Rev. (1882)
559–88, 716–56.
ALEXANDER, NATAL. Hist. eccl. (1778) III. 363–7.
ALZOG. Patrol. (1876) 72–82.
Anal. juris pontif. (1874) XIII. 631–2, 889–91.
ANGER. Synops. Evan. (1852).
Anthropologie Just. d. M. In: Der Katholik, N. F.
I. (1859) 423–43, 574–91.
ARENDT. Kr. Untersuch. ueb. d. schr. Justins d. M. In:
Theol. Quartalschr. XVI. (1834) 256–95.
AUBÉ, B. In: Nouv. Biog. Gen. (Hoefer) XXVII.
(1861) 292–303.
AUBÉ, BARTH. St. Justin, philosophe et martyr, these
. . . *Paris*, 1861. 8⁰. (lxxvi. 370); *Paris*, 1875. 8⁰.
(lxxvi. 366); ("*Paris*, 1874. 8⁰." *Lorenz*).

BALLOU, H., 2D. Justin Martyr, or the Orthodox Faith,
A.D. 150–165. In: Univ. Q. III. (1846) 272–.
BARATERIUS, J. P. Success. ant. episc. Rom. (1740) 95–.
BARONIUS. Ann. (1589) 130, 5–9; 142, 13; 143, 1–2;
150, 1–7; 164, 10, 12–23; 165, 1–11. Cf. Pagi. Crit.
(1689) 150, 3–7; 164, 2–7; 165, 3–4.
BARRINGTON, D. Tomb of Justin Martyr. In: Archae-
ologia. V. (1784) 143–.
BAUMGARTEN–CRUSIUS. Dogmenges. (1832) 171–3.
[v. 1.]
BAUR. In: Theol. Jahrb. (1857).
— Dogmengesch. I. (1865) 253–6.
ΒΑΦΕΙΔΗΣ.'Εκκλ. ἱστ. I. (1884) 151–2.
BEAUSOBRE. Hist. d. Manich. I. (1734) 288.
BEHM, H. M. T. D. Christenthum J. In: Ztschr. f.
kirchl. Wiss u. Leben. III. (1882) 478–91, 627–36.
Bekehrung Justin's. In: Allg. Ev. Luth. Kirchztg. (1878)
409–13, 433–8.
BELLAMIN–LABBE. Scr. eccl. (1728) 32–4.
BERTHOLDT. Einl. A. u. N. T. (1813) 111.
— Dogmenges. (1822–3) I. 57 sc.
BINDEMANN, E. In: Stud. u. Krit. XV. (1842) 355–
482. [Gospels used by J. M. Critique of Credner.]
BLACKBURN. Hist. of Church. [1879] 34–6.
BLEEK. Beiträge zur. E. Krit. (1846).
BLEEK–MANGOLD. Einl. N. T. (1875).
BLESSIG, J. L. De Just. M. N. T. citandi methodo. In
his: Animadv. ad Voltarii de relig. chr. orig. asserta.
Argent. 1786. p. 84.
BOEHRINGER. Kirchenges. (1864) I. 1. 97–270; (1873–)
I. 1.
BOLL. Verhaltn. d. beiden App. J. zu einander. In:
Zeitschr. f. d. hist. Theol. (1842) III. 3–. Cf. Ztschr.
f. Phil. u. kathol. Theol. (1841) 171–.
BONIFAS, SAM. E. Des Evangiles employés par Justin
Martyr, thèse. 1850. 8⁰. (92 p.)
BONNETY, A. In: Vies des saint. *Par.* 1845.
BORNEMANN, W. Das Taufsymbol Justin's d. Märtyrers.
In: Ztschr. f. Kirchengesch. (1879) 1–27.
BOURGON. In: Biog. Univ. (Michaud) (1842–65) XXI.
363–5.
BRETSCHNEIDER. Probabilia de Ev. et Ep. Joan. Apost.
(1820).
BROWN, J. A. In: Evang. R. VI. (1855) 151–.
BRUCKER. Hist. crit. phil. (1766–7) III. 367–78; VI.
534–6.
[BRYANT, JAMES.] Observations on a controverted pas-
sage in J., p. 47, ed. Bened. *Lond.* 1793. 4⁰.
BULL, G. De celebri loco J. in Dialogo cum Tryph. dis-
seritur. In his: Judicium eccl. cath. (*Oxon.* 1694.
8⁰.) 164–192; also in: Works. VI. (*Oxf.* 1846) 187–
235.
BUNSEN. Hippolytus. (1854) I. 216–24.
BURTON. Divinity of Christ (1829) 32–61.
— Trinity (1831) 15–27.
BUSSE. Chr. Lit. (1828–9) I. 10–11.
CAILLAU. Introd. in ss. Patr. (1825) 47–52.
CALOGERAS, N. 'Ιουστῖνος ὁ φιλόσοφος καὶ μαρτύς. In:
'Αθήναιον. II. (1873) 359–80.
CAVE. Scr. eccl. hist. lit. (1740–43) I. 60–65.
— Lives (1840) I. 228–57.
CEILLIER. Hist. gén. d. aut. sac. (1730) II. 1–73;
(1858) I. 408–48.
CHARPENTIER. Études sur les Pères de l'Égl. II. (1853).
CHARTERIS. Canonicity (1880) liii-lxiii, 59–64, 114–27,
143–5, 156–8, 176–9, 198, 217, 225–6, 234, 244–5, 248–
9, 253, 258, 267, 275, 314, 321, 339.
CHASTEL. St. J., son sentiment sur la valeur de la raison
humaine. In: Le Correspondent. "1863 (5?) A.
xxxi, 189–206."
CHEVALIER. Rép. d. sources hist. (1877–86) 1323–5.
CHISHULL. Some Testimonies of J. . . . concerning
the immortality of the soul. . . . *Lond.*, 1708. 8⁰.

Christian Observer. III. (1804) 649–; 717–.
CLARKE. Sacred lit. (1830–1) I. 95–100.
CLERICUS, J. In: Bibl. Univ.; also in: Lebensbeschrr. einige Kirchenväter. (Halle, 1721) 1–21.
CLINTON. Fasti Rom. (1845–50) I. 131, 139; II. 409.
COFFIN. Lives of fath. (1846) 183–196.
v. CÖLLN. In: Allgem. Hall. Lit. Ztng. (1828) 391.
CORRODI. Versuch Beleucht. d. jüd. u. chr. Bibel Kanons. (1792) II.
COTTA, F. Dissert. de memorabilibus Justini M. historicis atque dogmaticis. *Tubingae*, 1766. 4°.
COTTA. Kirchen.-Hist. (1768–73) §§ 284–90.
CREDNER. De libr. N. T. inspiratione, etc. I. (*Jen.* 1828) 53–.
— Beiträge. z. Einl. e. d. bibl. Schr. Halle. I. (1832) 92–267; (1838) 17–98, 104–133, 157–311.
CREDNER–VOLCKMAR. Gesch. d. Canon. 7–.
CUNNINGHAM. Hist. theol. (1870) I. 134–9.
— Churches of Asia (1880) passim.
CYPRIAN, E. SA. Diss. de Cl. R. . . . et Justini M. doctrina evang. *Coburg.* 1701. 4°.
DANZIUS, J. A. Oratio de Tryphone, habita a. 1708. In: Parerga Gotting. (*Gotting.* 1738. 8°.) I. IV. 80–91.
DARLING. Cyclop. bibliog. (1855) 1699–701.
Darstellung d. ältesten Christenthums aus d. Schr. d. J. u. s. w. In: Beyträge zur Beförderung des ältesten Christenthums u. d. neuesten Philos. (*Ulm*, 1791. 8°.)
DAVIDSON. Introd. N. T. (1848) I. 124, etc., etc.
DELITZSCH. Neue Unters. Entst. Kan. Evv. (1853).
DIECKHOFF, A. W. Just., Augustin, Bernhard, u. Luth. Entwickelungsgang chr. Wahrheitserfassung. *Lpz.* 1882.
DODS, M. Introd. note. In: Ante-Nic. Lib. II. (1865) 1–5, 363–5. Ed. Coxe. I. (1885) 157–61, 303.
DODWELL, H. Natural mortality of human souls. *Lond.* 1708. 8°.
— Dissert. in Irenaeum. (1689) p. 256. [?]
DONALDSON. Hist. Chr. Lit. (1864–6) II. 62–344.
DORNER. Person of Christ. I. (1864) 264–79, 458–61.
DRÄSEKE, J. Abfassungsz. d. pseudoj. ΕΚΘΕΣΙΣ. In: Ztschr. f. wiss. Theol. XXVI. (1883) 481–96.
— Apollinarios von Laodien Verf. d. echten Bestandteile d. pseudojust. Schrift ἔκθεσις, etc. In: Ztschr. f. Kirchengesch. (1884) 503–549.
— D. doppel. Fassung d. pseudojust. Εκθεσις, etc. In: Ztschr. f. Kirchenges. VI. (1884) 1–45.
— Zu den . . . . . . christologischen Bruchstücken. In: Jahrbb. f. prot. Theol. (1884) 347–52.
— Der Verfasser des falschlich Justinus beigelegten Λόγος παραινετιχὸς πρὸς ῾Ελληνας. In: Ztschr. f. Kirchengesch. VII. (1885) 257–302.
DRUMMOND, J. Justin Martyr on the New Birth. In: Theo. R. XII. (1875) 471–.
— Justin Martyr and the Fourth Gospel. In: Theological Rev. XIV. (1877) 155.
— Engelhardt on Justin Martyr. In: Theological Rev. XVI. (1879) 365–.
DUNCKER. Apologett. 2. saec. de essentialibus naturae humanae, etc. *Goetting.* 1844. 4°. I.
— D. Legoslehre Justin's d. Märt. Abgedr. aus d. Göttinger Studien, 1847. *Göttingen*, 1848. 8°. (39).
DUPIN. Nouv. bibl. d. aut. eccl. (1698) I. 104–33.
ECKERMANN. Theol. Beiträge. (1796) V. 2.
EICHHORN. Einl. N. T. II. (1827).
EISENLOHR. Comment. de argumentis apol. saec. 2. *Tub.* 1797; repr. in: Pott et Ruperti. Sylloge comment. theol. II. 114–202.
EMMERICH, F. C. T. De evangel. secund. Ebr. Aegypt. atque Justini Martyris. *Argent.* 1807. 4°.
ENGELHARDT, J. G. Dogmenges. I. (1839) 226, etc.
ENGELHARDT, W. D. Abendmahlslehre d. J. M. In: Ztschr. f. luth. Theol. XXXI. (1870) 230–52.
ENGELHARDT, Moritz v. In: Herzog. Real.-Enc. (1877–) vii. 318–327. (Abr. in Schaff-Herz. II. 1219–20.)

ENGELHARDT. D. Christenthum Justin's d. M. *Dorpat*, 1878. 8°.
EUSEBIUS, H. E. IV. 16. Chron. Pasch. A.D. 165.
EWALD. Jahrb. bibl. Wiss. (1853–54).
— Gesch. d. Volkes Isr. VI. (1868).
FABRICIUS. Bibl. gr. (1712) V. 51–65; IX. 414; 12°. VII. 52–75; X. 714–5.
— De verit. rel. chr. (1725) 42–50, 158.
FARRAR. Interpretation. (1886) 172–4.
FEILMOSER. Einl. N. T. 2 aufl. (1830).
FELDE, ALB. a. Epist. de dialogo Justini Martyris cum Tryphone Judæo. *Sleswici*, 1700. 8°.
— Demonst. invictæ, dialogum in Tryphone esse verum Justini foetum. *Hamb.* 1707. 8°.
FISHER. Supernatural origin of Chr. (1866) 46–56.
FLEURY. Hist. eccl. (1691–) I. 413–31, 458–80.
FRATECELLI, G. B.: [Moreni, Bibl. Tosc., I. 399].
FREPPEL. Les Apolog. chrét. au 11e siècle: St. Justin. III. ed. *Paris*, 1886. 8°.
FUNK. In: Theol. Quartalschr. LXII. (1880) 480–7. [Rev. of Engelhardt.]
GAAB. In his: Abhandl. dogmengesch. d. ältesten gr. Kirche. (*Jen.* 1790. 8°.) 58–.
GASS. Die unter Justin's Schr. befindl. Fragen an d. Rechtgläubigen. In: Ztschr. f. d. hist. Theol. (1842) 35–.
GEORGII. Lehre v. heil. Geiste bei J. In: Stirm's Studien d. ev. Geistlichkeit Würtembergs. X. (1838) II. 100–.
GERKENIUS, C. Ch. Dissert. de Just. M. ad. rel. chr. conversione admodum memorabili. *Lips.* 1753. 4°.
GFRÖRER. Gesch. des Urchristenthums. (1835) I. 1.
GIESELER. Church Hist. (1868–) I. 145–6, 148.
— Entst. Schr. Evv. (1818).
GOETZ, J. Ad. Leben, Schr. u. Lehr. J. (1796) s. u. eds.
GRABE. Spicileg. ss. patr. (1699) I. 133–203.
GRATIANUS, P. C. Dissert. de memorabilibus Justini Mart. hist. atque dogmat. *Tub.* 1766. 4°.
GRATZ. Krit. Untersuchungen über Justin's apost. Denkwürdigkeiten. *Stuttg.* 1814. 4°.
GRIMM, W. D. apost. Denkwürdigkeiten Justinus. In: Stud. v. Krit. XXIV. (1851) 669–702.
GRUBE, K. Die hermeneutische Grundsätze Justin's des Mart. In: Der Katholik (1880) 1–42.
GUNDLINGIUS, M. N. Hier. In: [Buddeus] Observ. sel. litter. (1700) II. 89–113, 170–99.
GUERICKE. Gessammtgesch. N. T. (1854).
GÜSSMAN, F. Tryphon. u. Justinus. *Wien*, 1785. 8°.
HAGEN, J. A. Beiträge z. Erkl. d. J apol. In: Ztschr. f. Philos. u. Kath. Theol. N. F. IX. (1848) 35–67.
HAGENBACH. Hist. of Doct. I. (1850) 58–9, etc.
— Kirchenges. (1885) I. 150–6.
HAHN, J. E. De Platonismo vet. eccl. doct. *Vit.* 1733.
HALLOIX, P. Vita et documenta S. Justini. *Duaci*, 1622. 8°; also in his: Eccl. orient. script. (1636) II. 151–401; Acta ss. Bolland. (1675) Apr. II. 108–19.
HARLES. Introd. in hist. ling. gr. II. 2, 191. Suppl. II. 198.
HARNACK. z. Quellenkrit. d. Ges. d. Gnost. 1873.
— In: Texte, etc. I. (1882) 130–195.
— Dogmenges. I. (1886) 223–5, 380–6, 415–9.
HASE. Kirchenges. (1885–) I. 157–8, 247–9, 271.
HASSELBACH. Ueb. d. Stelle in J. d. M. Ap. I. p. 56. In: Stud. v. Krit. XII. (1839) 329–92.
HEFELE. In: Theol. Quartalschr. (1843) 143–.
— In: Wetzer u. W. Kirch-Lex. (1847–54) V. 935–47.
HEISCHKEIL, Ch. Ob. J. keine spur. zeigt. dass er evang. Schriften ein ausschliessendes Ansehn beigelegt habe. In: Augusti's Neue theol. Bibl. I. II. 49–56.
HENGSTENBERG. Offenbarung Joh. (1861) 393–6.
HEPP, J. Gesch. d. chr. K. (*Mainz*, 1851) 76–.
HERBIG. Chr. E. Comm. de scr. quae sub nom. J. circumferuntur. *Vratisl.* 1833. 8°.

HERGENROETHER. Kirchenges. (1879–80) I. 104–6; III. 37–8, 41–2.

HESS, J. J. In: Bibl. der. heil. Geschichte. (*Zürich*, 1791. 8°.) I. no. 4.

HEUMANN, Ch. A. Symbola critica ad J. In: Miscellan. Lipsiens. nov. (*Lips.* 1744. 8°). III. 222–.

HICKES, G. A. A passage in J.'s first (commonly called his second) apology vindicated against . . . Whiston. S. his discourse in Grabe's: Some instances of the defects and omissions in Mr. Whiston's collection of testimonies. (*Lond.* 1712. 8°.) xxxiv–li.

HIERONYMUS. De vir ill. 23 (*Honor. August.* I. 24).

HILGENFELD. In: Tüb. Jahrbb. (1850) Heft, 3 u. 4.

HILGENFELD, ADOLF. Krit. Untersuchungen über d. Evangelien Justin's, u. s. w. *Halle*, 1850. 8°.

— Die Evangelien. (1854).

— Kanon. u. Krit. N. T. (*Halle*, 1863) 24–8, etc., etc.

— In: Zeitschr. wiss. Theol. (1865).

— In: Zeitschr. wiss. Theol. (1871).

— Die Ap. Gesch. u. der M. Just. In: Zeitschr. f. wiss. Theol. (1872) 495–509.

— In: Zeitschr. f. wiss. Theol. XXII. (1879) 492–516. [Response to Engelhardt.]

— In: Zeitschr. f. wiss. Theol. XXIV. (1881) 251–6. [Rev. of Stählin.]

— Ketzergesch. (1884) 3–4, 21–30, 70–3, 162–341.

HÖFLING, J. W. F. Die Lehre J. vom Opfer. *Erlang.* 1839; repr. in his: Lehre d. ält. Kirche u. s. w. *Erlang.* 1851. p. 43–.

HOLLAND, H. S. In: Smith and Wace. Dict. III. 560–87.

HOLSTEN. In: Zeitschr. wiss. Theol. (1861).

HOLTZMANN. Die Synopt. Evv. (1863).

— Einl. in d. N. T. (1886) 118–21, etc.

HORT, F. J. A. On the date of Justin M. In: Journ. of class. and sacr. philol. III. (1856) [7?] 155–193.

HOVEN, J. D. ab. De aet. Minuaii F. et ordine apol. Justini M. *Campis*, 1762. 4°.

HUBER. Philos. d. K.–V. (1859) 11–20.

HUG. Einl. N. T. (1821) 11.

HUGONIN. Des motifs qui ont déterminé St. J. à abandonner le Platonisme. In: Ann. de phil. chrét. (1851) D. III. 459–71.

ITTIG. Hist. eccl. (1709) II. 6–15, 204–12.

JACKSON. Ap. fath. (1879) 140–186.

JEREMIE. Hist. church (1852) 81–3.

JÖCHER. Allgem. Gelehrten Lex. (1750–51).

JORTIN. Charakter and writings of J. M. In: Remarks in Eccl. Hist. II. (1751) 155–.

— In his: "Tracts, philo., crit. and misc. (*Lond.* 1790. 8°.) II. 102–116.

JUNIUS, F. J. J. A. Dissertatio de Justino Mart. Apologeta adv. Ethnicos. *Lugd. Bat.* 1836. 8°.

Justin Martyr's testimony on Baptism. In: Chr. R. VI. (1841) 302.

KAYE, JOHN. Some account of the writings and opinions of J. M. *Cambr.* 1829. 8°; 2d ed. revised. *Lond.* 1836. 8°; 3d revised. *Cambr.* 1845. 8°; also *Lond.* 1853. 8°.

KAYSER, AUGUST. De Justini Martyris doctrina dissertatio histor. *Argentorati*, 1850. 8°.

KEIM. Jesu v. Nazara. (1875) passim.

— Rom. u. d. Christenth. (1881).

KESTNER. Die Agape (1819).

KIHN. In: Theol. Quartalschr. LXVI. (1884) 497–500. [Rev. of Gutberlet's Braun's ed. III.]

KILLEN. Ancient Church (1859) 365–7.

KIRCHHOFER. Quellens. N. T. Can. (1844).

KOCH, CH. GLI. Dial. J. M. cum Tryphone examinatus. *Kilonii*, 1700. 8°.

KONTOGENES. Ἰστ. τῶν πατέρων. (1851).

KORTHOLT, CH. Comment. in Just. Mart. Athenagoram, Theophilum Antioch. et Tatianum. *Francof. & Lips.* 1686. f°.

KÖSTLIN. Der Ursprung synopt. Evv. (1852).

KROME, HERM. I. De authent. dial. J. M. cum Tryphone. *Medioburgi*, 1788. 8°; Ed. II. *Ultraj.* 1792. 8°.

KURTZ. Kirchenges. (1885–) I. 112–3.

LA CROZE, M. V. Dissert. qua ostenditur scriptorem Quaestionum ad Orthodoxos, Diodorum esse Tarsensem. In: Bibl. Bremensis. V. IV. p. 656–669.

LAMSON, A. In: Chr. Exam. VII. (1825) 141–, 303–.

LANGE, J. P. Das Evang. Nach. Markus. (1868).

LANGE, LOBEG. In: Röhr's Krit. Prediger-biblioth. XXV. (1844) 982–.

LANGE, S. G. Ausf. Gesch. d. Dogmen. (1796) I. 91–189. [2 Apologies and Dialogue. Rejects Dial.]

LANGIUS, J. Comm. in Just. M. *Basil.* 1565. f°.

LANSSELIUS, PETR. Dispunctio calumniarum quae St. Justino Martyri inuruntur ab Is. Casaubono. *Paris*, 1615. f°.

LARDNER. Credibility. Works (1831) II. 125–140.

LECHLER. Ap. u. Nachap. Z–A. (1885) 610–13. Engl. tr. (1886) 360–3.

LE CLERC, J. Bibl. univ. (1687) VII. 15–31; also in: Lebensbeschr. Kirchenväter (1711) 1–.

— Bibl. choisie (1703–4) II. 328–; III. 372–.

LEIBES, FR. (Praes. Oberthür) Dissert. S. Just. de praecipuis rel. dogmat. sententiam. *Wirceb.* 1777. 8°.

LELONG. Bibl. sac. II. 811.

LE NOURRY. Appar. bibl. patr. (1703) I. 350.

Life and Writings of Justin Martyr. In: Kitto. V. (1850) 253–; Chr. R. XV. (1850) 353–; Ecl. R. LXXXI. (1844) 186–.

LINDSAY, T. M. In: Encycl. Brit. (9th ed.) XIII. 790–ᵗ.

LIPSIUS. Zur Quellenkr. des Epiphanius (1865).

— In: Zeitschr. wiss. Theol. (1867).

— Quell. d. Ketzerges. (1875) 21, 22.

[LIRON.] Singul. histor. (1739) III. 8–16.

Locus Justini Mart. emendatur (Apol. I. p. II. ed. Thirlby.) In: Bibl. Litter., being a Collection of Inscriptions, Medals, Dissertations, etc. An. 1722. (*Lond.* 1724. 4°.) VIII. 1–28.

LONGUERUE, L. DUFOUR DE. Dissertations . . . de vita s. Justini M., de Athenagora, etc. *Lipsiae*, 1751. 4°.

LUCHINI. Atti sinceri (1777) I. 362–6.

LUMPER. Hist. ss. patrum. II. (1784) 48–316, 461–81; X. (1793) 514–41.

LUTHARDT. St. John the Author of the Fourth Gospel. (1875) 52–66, 139.

LÜTZELBERGER. Die kirchl. Tradition üb. Ap. Joh. u. s. w. (1849).

MARANUS, PRUD. S. Justini op. omnia (1742) i–cxxviii; also in: Sprenger. Thes. rei patr. II. 1–; also in: Migne. Patrol. gr. VI. (1857) 9–206.

MARTINOV. Ann. eccl. gr.-slav. (1864) 144.

Martyrium Justini. S. u. Martyrdom.

MATTES. Zur Lehre Justin's von der Erbsünde. In: Theol. Quartalschr. (*Tüb.* 1859.)

MAURICE. Eccl. Hist. (1854) 170, 207–16.

MAYERHOFF. Einl. petr. Schr. (1835) passim.

MAZOCHIUS, ALEX. SYMON. In: Galland. Bib. vet. patr. (1765) I. 709.

MEANS, J. C. In: Smith. Gr. and Rom. Biog. (1859) II. 682–6.

Methodist Magazine. XXXII. (1809) 3–.

MEYER. Kr.-ex. H'buch. [Various vols.]

MICHAELIS. Einl. N. B. (1788) I.

MILMAN. Hist. of Christianity. II. (1875).

MÖHLER. In: Theol. Quartalschr. XV. (1833).

— Gesammt. Schriften. (1839) II. 49–60.

MÖLLER, W. Kosmologie in d. griech. K. (1860) 112–88.

MÖSINGER. Monumenta syriaca. II. (1878) 251–65.

[MÜNSCHER, GU.] Progr. an dial. cum Tryphone Justino M. recte adscribatur. *Marb.* 1799. 4°.

MUENSCHER, W. Dogmenges. (1817–8) I. 139–41, etc.

MYNSTER. Theolog. Schriften. (1825).

— Justin u. s. evang. In: Credner. Beiträge. *Halle,* 1831. I. 92–267.

NEANDER, A. In: Stud. v. Krit. VI. (1833) 772–6. [Apolog. I: 6. Reply to Möhler.]

— Hist. of dogmas. (1858) 61–2, 95, 140–2, 172–3, 186–7, 200–1, 213–4, 233, 238–40. [v. I.]

— Church Hist. (1872) I. 661–71, et pass.

NEUDECKER. Einl. N. T. (1840).

NICOLAS, M. Études crit. sur la Bible: N. T. (1864).

NIEDNER. Kirchengeschichte. (1866) 263, 286.

NIRSCHL. Patrol. (1881–) I. 141–58.

NITZSCH. Dogmengesch. I. (1870) 116–8, etc.

NODIER. Bib. sacr. (1826) 149–50.

NOLTE. Conjecturae et emend. In: Migne. Patrol. gr. VI. (1857) 1705–38, 1763–1802.

NORTON. Genuineness of Gosp. I. (1846) 7–9, etc.

OBERTHÜR. S. u. Leibes.

Observationes in Justini M. Apol. I. et Dial. cum Tryph. ed. Thirlby. In: Miscellaneae Obss. (*Amst.* 1732. 8º.) I. 363–72.

OLSHAUSEN. Ueb. d. von J. gebrauchte Evang. In his: Die Aechtheit d. vier canon. Evv. (1823) 331–.

ORSI. Ist eccl. (1746–) 81, 89–95, 102–13, 126–37, 163–5, 168–72; (1749–) II. 129–39, 148–64, 183–99, 233–5, 239–45.

OTTO, JOHANN KARL THEODOR. Dissertatio de Justini martyris scriptis et doctrina. *Jenae.* 1841. 8º.

OTTO. In: Illgen's Ztschr. 1841, 1842, 1843.

— In: Corp. apologet. christ. (1842–) I. xxxi–. (= Migne. Patrol. gr. VI. 205–26); do. (1847). Cf. Hase. In: Journ. d. Savants (1852) 619–30; (1853) 182–8, 363–70.

— Zur Characteristik des heil. J. In: Sitzungsber. Akad. Wissensch. (1852) VIII. 164–81. *Wien,* 1852. 8º.

— In: Ersch u. Gruber. II. (1853) 39–76.

— Die Zeit J. In: Theol. Jahrb. (1855) III.

— S. u. eds.

OUDIN. Scr. eccl. (1722) I. 179–203.

PAPEBROCHIUS. Comment. praev. In: Acta ss. Bolland., Apr. II. 104–8. (3ª. 105–9.)

PAUL, L. Ueb. d. Logoslehre bei Justinus M. In: Jahrbb. f. prot. Theol. (1886) 661–690.

PAULUS, H. E. G. Ob d. Ev. Justins d. Ev. nach d. Hebräern sey? In his: Exegetisch-kritische Abhandl. *Tübing.* 1784. 8º.

PERIONIUS, JOACH. In: Surius Vitae ss. (1618) IV. 151–2.

PERMANEDER. Bibl. patrist. (1842) I. 414–5; II. 98–149, 309–13, 943.

PETAVIUS. De doctr. tempp. II. (*Par.* 1627) 629.

PFLEIDERER. In: Zeitschr. wiss. Theol. (1869).

PHOTIUS. Bibl. Cod. 48, 125, 232, 234.

PRESSENSÉ. Hist. 3 prem. sièc. III. 201–; IV. 169; V. 262; Tr. Engl., Heresy (n. d.) 227–49, Chr. life (1878) 23–32, 266–71, Martyrs (1879) 127–9, 243–51, 531–40.

— In: Lichtenberger. Encycl. (1877–82) VII. 576–83.

PRILESZKY, J. B. Acta et scripta s. Justini, philosophi et martyris. *Cassoviae,* 1765. 8º.

PUISEAU, H. W. DE. [Christology of Justin.] *Leyden,* 1864.

RAU, J. J. Diatribe de philosophia ss. Patrum Justini martyris et Athenagorae. *Jenae,* 1733. 4º.

REHLING. S. u. Wokenius.

Remarques sur la I. Apologie de S. Justin M. In: Bibl. choisie. II. 328–52; III. 372–94.

RENAN. L'égl. chr. (1879) 364–89, 480–.

RETTIG. Das ält. Zeugn. p. 59.

REUCHLIN. Dissertationes III. de doctrina Justini martyris. *Argent.* 1747. 4º.

REUSS. Gesch. N. T. (1874) II. 15–6, 251–2. Tr. Eng. (1884) 299, 531. [v. 2.]

RÉVILLE. Hist. du Dogme de la Div. de J. C. (1869).

RHODE, C. V. Justini Martyris de Theopneustia libror. sacr. judicium. *Lundini,* 1830. 8º.

RIGGENBACH. D. Zeugnisse f. d. Ev. Joh. (1866).

RITSCHL. Altkath. Kirche (1850) 316–; (1857) 298–312.

— In: Theol. Jahrbb. (*Tüb.* 1851) 482–.

RITTER, H. Chr. philos. (1841) I. 295–308.

RITTER, J. J. Animadv. in primam S. Justini Mart. Apol. *Vratisl.* 1836. 4º,

ROBERTSON. Hist. of Church. (1875–) I. 30–5.

ROESSLER. Bibl. d. K.-V. I. (1776) 101–181.

ROSENMÜLLER. Hist. interp. I. (1795) 148–93.

ROW, T. Difficulty in Justin M. in the Oratio ad Græcos explained; Critique on Thirlby's J.; Illustration of a disputed passage in J. by E. Haiwood; A controverted passage in J. In: Gentleman's Mag. (1783) 551–, 750–, 831–, 904–; (1786) 570–.

RUDELBACH. Christl. Biographie. I. (*Lpz.* 1849.)

RUGGIERI, E. Vita e dottrina di S. Giustino, filosofo martire. *Roma,* 1863. 8º; cf. Civiltà cattol., E, VI, 335–9.

RUINART. Acta sincer. (1689) 38–.

SANDAY. Gosp. in 2 cent. (1876) 39–48, 88–137, 278–87.

SCHAFF. Hist. . . Church. II. (1886) 710–26.

SCHALLER, L. Les deux Apologies de Justin M. au point de vue dogmatique. *Strasb.* 1861.

SCHARFFENBERG, G. H., and D. Comment. academ. de Justino, Tertulliano, et Cypriano adv. Judæos disputantibus. *Lund. Goth.* 1820. 4º. (20 p.)

SCHERER. In: Rev. de Théologie (1855).

SCHICK, A. H. Ueb. d. εὐχὴ λόγου bei J. · In: Ztschr. f. d. ges. luth. Theol. u. K. XVIII. (1857) 76–107.

SCHLEIERMACHER. Sämmtl. Werke. (1840) XI.

SCHLIEMANN. Clementinen. (1844) 441–2, etc.

SCHMID. Patrol. (1879) 38–40.

SCHMIDT, J. A. De Justini Martyris theologia moralii. programma. *Helmstadtii,* 1698. 4º.

SCHMIDT, J. G. C. Hist. crit. Einl. N. T. (1804).

SCHNECKENBURGER. Vorles ü. N. T. Zeitgesch. ed. Löhlein. (1862).

SCHOLTEN. Het Ev. n. Johann. (1864) 8º.

— Die ält. Zeugnisse (1867).

SCHOTT. Isagoge Hist. Crit. in lib. N. Foed. (1830).

SCHRAM. Anal. ss. patr. (1780–) I. 295–524.

SCHROECKH. Kirchenges. (1772–) III. 17–51, 106–8.

SCHÜTZ, D. F. De Ev. Justini M. In his: Dissert. de Evangiliis, quae ante Ev. canon. in usu eccles. christ. fuisse dicuntur. (*Regiom.* 1812.) II. 1–.

SCHWEGLER. Nachap. Zeitalt. (1846) I. 216–33, 359–63.

SCULTETUS, Abr. De vita, scriptis et doctrina Justini M. In: Medullæ theol. I. 1. 1–45.

SEIBERT, C. G. Justinus, d. Vertheidiger d. Christenthums vor dem Thron. d. Cæsaren. *Elberf.* 1859.

SEILER, G. F. Christologia Justini martyris. *Erlang.* 1775. 4º.

SEMISCH, Carl. Ueb. d. Todesjahr Justins d. M. In: Stud. u. Krit. VIII. (1835) 907–52.

— Justin der Märtyrer eine kirchen- und dogmengeschichtliche Monographie. *Bres.* 1840–2. 2 Th. 8º. Tr. English by J. E. Ryland. *Edinb.* 1843. 2 v. 8º. [Cf. Reithmayr, Fr. X., in Archiv. f. theol. Liter. (1842) I. 321–35, 632–62.] 2 Aufl. 1859.

— Die Apostolischen Denkwürdigkeiten d. Märtyrers Justinus. *Hamburg-Gotha,* 1848. 8º.

SEMLER. Gesch. d. chr. Glaubenslehre vor Baumgartens Untersuchung. (1763) II. 42, 70.

SEVESTRE. Dict. patrol. (1854) III. 965–99.

SHEDD. Hist. of doct. 3d ed. (1865–) I. 268–74; II. 28.

STÄHLIN, A. Justin d. Martyrer u. sein neuester Beurtheiler. *Leipzig,* 1880. 8º. (iv, 67 p.) [From: Alleg. Ev. Luth. Kirchenz (1879) No. 47.]

STÄUDLIN. Moral J. d. M. In: Sittenlehre Jesu. (*Götting.* 1802.) II. 93–121.

STIEREN. In: Ztschr. f. hist. Theol. (1842) 225.

STORR. Zweck d. Evang. Gesch. u. Br. Joh. (1786).

STOWE, C. E. In: Bib. Sac. IX. (1852) 821–30.

— Books of the Bible. (1867) 245–9.

STROTH. Fragm. d. Evang. n. d. Hebräern aus Just. Märt. In: Repert. f. bibl. u. morgenl. Litt. (1771) I.

Supernatural Religion. (1875–) I. 283–428; II. 271–316; III. 15–7.

SURIUS. Vit. ss. 13 Apr. 151–.

SYMEON METAPHR. In: Surius. Vitae ss. (1618) II. 182–3.

TAMBURINI, PIETRO. Analisi delle apologie di S. Giustino martire, etc. *Pavia*, 1792. 8⁰.

TENNEMANN. Gesch. d. Philos. VII. 140–.

TENTZEL, W. E. Exercitat. Select. P. I. (1692) 165–99.

THOLUCK. Glaubwürdigkeit d. evang. Gesch. (1838).

THOMA. In: Ztschr. f. wiss. Theol. (1875).

THÜMER. Ueber d. Platonismus d. Justinus Martyr. Realschulprogramm. *Glauchau.* 1880. 4⁰.

TILLEMONT. Mém. (1732) II. 344–404, 642–62.

TISCHENDORF. Wann wurden, u. s. w. (1866).

TOBLER. In: Theol. Jahrb. (1860).

Tracts for the times. (1840) I. Rec.

TREGELLES. Canon Murat. (1867) 70–3, 84, etc.

TRITHEMIUS. Scr. eccl. 11.

TZSCHIRNER. Gesch. d. Apologet. (1805) 1.

— Fall d. Heidenth. (1829) I. 204–.

UEBERWEG. Hist. philos. (1876) 290–4.

VACHEROT. Hist. de l'École d'Alexandrie. I.

VINCENTIUS BELVAC. Spec. hist. XI. 94.

VOLKMAR. In: Theol. Jahrb. (1850).

— Das Evangelium Marcion's, Text u. Kritik, mit Rücksicht auf d. Evangelien d. Märt. Justin, d. Clementinen u. d. apost. Väter. *Lpz.* 1852. 8⁰.

— Über Justin den Märtyrer u. sein Verhältniss zu unsern Evv. Programm. *Zürich*, 1853. 8⁰.

— Die Zeit Justin's d. Mart. kritisch untersucht. In: Theol. Jahrb. (1855) II. 227–, 412–.

— In: Zeitschr. wiss. Theol. (1860).

— In: Theol. Jahrb. (1865).

— Urspr. uns. Evangelien. (1866).

VÖLTER, D. Pseudojust. Cohortatio ad Gr. In: Ztschr. f. wiss. Theol. XXVI. (1883) 180–215.

VOLZ, W. L. Krit. Bemerk. zu. J. Apol. I. 66. In: Stud. u. Krit. XLVII. (1874) 354–7.

WAITE. Hist. Chr. Rel. (1881) 267–79.

WEBER, C. F. Ueber d. Evangelium J. In his: Beyträge zur Gesch. d. N. T. Canons. (1791. 8⁰.) 105–.

WEGSCHEIDER. Einl. in d. Ev. d. Joh. (1806). .

WEIZSÄCKER, C. D. Theologie d. J. In: Jahrb. f. deut. Theol. XII. (1867) 60–119.

WESTCOTT. Canon. (1875) 95–177.

— Bible in the Church. (1877) 97–105.

WETSTEIN. Proleg. N. T. I. 66.

WETTE, DE. Einl. N. T. (1860).

WILCKE. Tradition u. Mythe. (1837).

WILLINK, H. D. TJEENK. Justinus Martyr in zijne verhandling tot Paulus. *Zwolle*, 1868. 8⁰.

WINER, G. B. Dissert. qua Justinum M. Evangeliis canonicis usum fuisse ostenditur. *Lipsiae*, 1819. 4⁰. (32 p.) (= Rosenmüller. Commentatt. (1825) I. 221–.)

WINTER. Gesch. d. ältesten Zeugen. p. 265.

WOKENIUS, F. [Rehling, J.] Dissert. crit. de Samaritanismo et Hebraismo Justini M. *Vitemb.* 1729. 4⁰.

WORDSWORTH. Church Hist. (1881) 73, 150–7.

WORMAN, J. H. In: M'Clintock and S. Cycl. (1874–) IV. 1104–10.

Worship of Angels. *Lond.* 1795. 4⁰. [Cf. Lowndes.]

"Woskresnoe Tschenie." (1849) No. 33–.

WURM. Apol. v. J., Tatian, Athenag., Theoph., and Hermias. In: Stud. d. evang. Geistl. Würt. (1828) I. II. 1–34.

ZAHN, T. In: Ztschr. f. Kirchenges. VIII. (1885) 1–84.

ZASTRAU, D. F. De Justini Martyris biblicis studiis. *Vratisl.* 1831–2. 8⁰. (52 p.)

ZELLER. Apostelgesch. (1854) 26–50.

Compare also literature under Mathetes. Epistle to Diognetus.

> *Note 1.* The judgment of Holland as to Justin's works may be taken as the general view : *genuine*, the two Apologies and the Dialogue ; *very doubtful*, the Oratio, Cohortatio, De resur., Monarchia ; *spurious*, all the rest. Yet the Oratio has been defended by Cave, Tillemont, Ceillier, Maranus, De Wette, Baumgarten-Crusius and Otto ; the Cohortatio by Maranus, Semisch, and Otto, and almost every one has a champion, if no one else then Kestner at least !
>
> *Note 2.* *Date of first Apol.* 138–9 : Scaliger, Petau, Dodwell, Pagi, Longuerue, Tentzel, Clericus, Galland, Lumper, Winter, Rettig, Neander, Möhler, Otto, Semisch. 140 : Koch, Augusti. 141 : Eusebius. 147–50 : Volkmar, Baur, Engelhardt, Hort, Donaldson, Holland. 150 : Halloix, Le Nourry, Maranus, Grabe, Tillemont, Ceillier, Fleury, Gerkenius, Ritter, Lipsius, Renan. 160 : Keim, Aubé.
>
> *Note 3.* *Date of Justin's death.* *Before* 161 : Valois, Mozzoni. 161–2 : Stieren, Ritter. 163 : Petavius. 165 [6?] : Chronicon Paschale, Tillemont (?), Baronius, Pagi, Grabe, Otto. 166 : Dupin, Semisch, Schaff. 167 : Fleury, Ruinart. 166–7 : "the majority" (so Hergenröther). 168 : Tillemont, Maran. 171 : Papebroch.

MARTYRDOM.

I. *Editions.*

PAPEBROCHIUS. In: Acta sanctorum. I. (*Antv.* 1695. f⁰.) 20–.

GALLANDIUS. In: Bibl. vet. patr. *Venet.* 1765. f⁰. I. 19.

MIGNE. Gr. lat. In: Patrol. gr. VI. (1857) 1563–72.

See also the editions of Maranus, Otto, and others.

II. *Translations.*

Latin.

SIRLETUS, GUIL. (Acta mart. Justini.) In: Łipomanus, Al. Vitae ss. patr. VII. II. (*Rom.* 1558. 4⁰.) 184–; also in: Surius Laur. Sanct. vit. (*Colon. Agr.* 1618. f⁰.) 182–; in: Baronius. Annal. II. (*Colon. Agr.* 1685. f⁰.) 163–; in: Halloix. Justini vita. (1622) 181–; in: Ruinart. Acta mart. (*Amst.* 1713. f⁰.) 58–; (*Aug. Vind.* 1802) 129–; and in: Jebb, Sam. Dial. c. Trypho. *Lond.* 1719.

English.

DODS, M. In: Ante-Nic. Lib. II. (1868) 367–70. Ed. Coxe. I. (1885) 305–6.

Other translations among the works above.

> *Note. Genuineness of the Martyrdom. For* : Tillemont, Ruinart, Papebroch, Galland, Mazochius, Semisch. *Against* : many.

VIII. IRENAEUS.

I. *Editions.*

ERASMUS. (Adv. haer. Lat. only.) *Basil*, 1526. f⁰; 1528. f⁰; 1534. f⁰; *Par.* 1545. 8⁰; *Basil*, 1545. f⁰ [? ?]; *Basil*, 1548. f⁰; *Basil*, 1554; *Basil*, 1560. f⁰; *Paris*, 1563. 8⁰; *Basil*, 1566; *Paris*, 1567. 8⁰.

GALLASIUS, NIC. (Opera.) *Genev.* 1570. f⁰. [1st ed. of fragments of the Greek.]

GRYNAEUS, J. J. (Adv. haer.) *Basil*, 1571. 8⁰. [" Worthless."]

FEUARDENT, FR. (Opera.) *Par.* 1575–6. f⁰. [?]; *Colon.* 1596. f⁰; *Colon.* 1625. f⁰ [Improved]; *Par.* 1639. f⁰; *Par.* 1675. f⁰; also in: Bibl. patr. *Lugd.* 1677. f⁰.

HALLOIX. (Fragments.) Gr. lat. In his: Ill. eccl. orient. scr. *Duaci*, 1636. f⁰. p. 480–507.

Rous, Fr. (Adv. haer. and De pace.) In his: Mella patrum. *Lond.* 1650. 8⁰. p. 75–123.

Combefisius. (Fragments.) Gr. lat. In his: Auct. nov. Bibl. patr. 1672. f⁰. I. 298–.

Grabe, J. E. (Adv. haer.) Gr. lat. *Oxon.* 1702. f⁰.

Massuet, R. (Opera.) Gr. lat. *Par.* 1712. f⁰; *Venet.* 1734. 2 v. f⁰. [Enlarged.]

Pfaffius. (Fragments.) Gr. lat. *La Haye*, 1715. 8⁰ (with new title). *Lugd. Bat.* 1743. 8⁰; first publ. in: Giornale de' Letterati d' Italia. T. XVI. p. 228–45. [1714]; also in: Pfaff. syntagma dissert. theol. *Stuttg.* 1720. 8⁰. p. 573–724; and Hippolytus. Opera. *Hamb.* 1718. f⁰. II. 64–.

Münter, F. (Fragments.) Gr. lat. In his: Fragm. patr. gr. *Hafniae*, 1788. 8⁰. I. p. 25–.

Routh. (Fragments.) *Oxon.* 1814. 8⁰. I. 389–; (Frgm. from Haer.) In: Scr. eccl. op. (1858) II. 209–16; (Ad Flor.) In: Scr. eccl. op. (1858) I. 33–41.

Olshausen. (Ep. ad Fl.) In: Monumenta. (1822) I.

Beaven, J. *Lond.* 1838. 2 v. 8⁰.

Migne. Gr. lat! In: Patrol. gr. VII. (1857) 433–1322. [Repr. of Massuet.]

Harvey, W. W. Gr. lat. arm., etc. *Camb.* 1857. 2 v. 8⁰; 1859. 8⁰. [Still in print.]

Stieren, A. (Opera.) Gr. lat. *Lips.* 1848–9–53. 2 v. 8⁰.

Deane, H. (Haer. Bk. III.) *Oxford.* 1874. 8⁰.
Note. As the Adv. Haer., excepting fragments of the Greek and of Syriac and Armenian translations, exists only in the Latin translation, this has been classed under editions.

II. *Translations.*

English.

Whiston, W. ("Some passages.") In his: Primitive Christ. *Lond* 1736. 8⁰. p. 24–26, 49–52.

Roberts and Rambaut In: Ante-Nic. Lib. V. (1868) 1–480; IX. (1869) 1–187. Ed. Coxe. I. (1885) 315–578.

Keble. In: Library of the Fathers. *Oxf.* 1872. 8⁰.

French.

Genoude [? ?] In: Pères de l'égl. *Par.* 1837–43. 8⁰.

German.

Ziegler. In: Werke d. K.-V. III., IV. (*Kempten,* 1831.)

Hayd, H. *Kempten,* 1872–3. 16⁰. [The Reithmayer-Thalhofer Bibl.]

III. *Literature.*

Alexander, John. The primitive doctrine of Christ's divinity, etc., in an essay on Irenæus. *Lond.* 1727.

Alexander, Natalis. Hist. eccl. (1778) III. 367–71.

Alzog. Patrol. (1876) 100–11.

Ampère. Hist. lit. France. (1839) I. 166–91.

Aubé, B. In: Nouv. Biog. Gen. (Hoefer). XXV. (1858) 943–8.

Augusti. Dogmengesch. I., II.

Baronius. Ann. (1589) 179, 52–4; 180, 1–18; 205, 28–30.

Baumgarten. Untersuchung theol. Streitigkeiten. II. 86, 104, 131.

Baumgarten–Crusius. Dogmenges. (1832) 187–8. [v 1.]

Baur. Christliche Gnosis. (*Tüb.* 1835.) 460–.
— Kirchenges. 3 e. J. (1863) 253–6.
— Dogmengesch. I. (1865) 260–2, etc.
— Geschichte der Trinitaetslehre.
— Gesch. d. Lehre von d. Versoehnung.

ΒΑΦΕΙΔΗΣ. Ἐκκλ. ἱστ. I. (1884) 154–5.

Beaven, James. Life and writings of St. Irenæus. *London,* 1841. 8⁰.

Bellarmin–Labbe. Scr. eccl. (1728) 37–8.

Bertholdt. Dogmenges. (1822–3) I. 58, etc.

Bill, J. In: Migne. Patrol. gr. VII. (1857) 1339–40.

Blackburn. Hist. of Church. (1879) 36–8.

Boehringer. Kirchenges. (1873–) I. II. (= p, 271–612).

Brit. & For. R. 1869. Jan.

Brucker. Hist. crit. phil. (1766–7) III. 408–10; VI. 538–9.

Buddeus. Dissert. in qua evincitur Cl. R. atq. Iren. non favere Missae pontif.

Bulletin Théolog. (1869) 319–.

Bunsen. Hippolytus. (1854) I. 246–50.

Burton. Divinity of Christ. (1829) 68–111.
— Trinity. (1881) 47–54.

Busse. Chr. Lit. (1828–9) I. 16–7.

Caillau. Introd. in ss. Patr. (1825) 61–5.

Castellus, H. S. Erkl. e. bey dem Irenaeo Lib. I. Cap. 18. p. 90 edit. Grab. befindl. Syrisehen Gebets-Formel d. Marcosier. In: Teutsche Acta Eruditor. (*Leipz.* 1712. 8⁰.) I. VI. 482.

Cave. Scr. eccl. hist. lit. (1740–3) I. 66–9.
— Lives. (1840) I. 258–72.

Ceillier. Hist. gén. aut. sac. (1730) II. 135–96; (1858) I. 495–531.

Charteris. Canonicity. (1880) 45–6, 66–70, 129–31, 145, 159–62, 182–3, 200–2, 219, 229, 231, 235, 240, 245, 249, 252, 253–4, 259, 263, 266, 276, 295–6, 307, 315, 322, 328, 340–2.

Chemnitius. Orat. de lectione patr. 5–.

Chevalier. Rép. d. sources hist. (1877–86) 1118–9.

Chladen, M. Irenaei Elpistii de elig. relig. commenta excut. *Wittebergae*, 1719.

Christian Obs. IV. (1805) 1–, 65–, 129–.

Christian Rem. (1853) 226–.

Clarke. Sacred lit. (1830–1) I. 105–8.

Clinton. Fasti Rom. (1845–50) I. 175, 181, 183, 201; II. 412.

Coffin. Lives of fath. (1846) 227–239.

Collombet. Ss. dioc. Lyon. (1835) 55–72, 379–80.

Colonia. Hist. lit. Lyon. (1728) I. II. 51–110.

Croï, Jean de. Specimen conject. et obs. in quaedam Origenis, Irenaei et Tertulliani loca. *Genev.* 1632. 4⁰.

Cunningham. Hist. theol. (1870) I. 139–46.
— Churches of Asia. (1880) passim.

Darling. Cycl. bibl. (1854) 1610–1, 2979.

Deyling, Sal. S. Irenaeus a Renati Massueti pravis explicationibus vindicatus. *Lips.* 1717. 4⁰; 2 Ed. auct. et emend. 1721. 4⁰; also in his Observat. sac. (1757) IV. (V.) 1–116.

Dietelmaier, J. A. In: Hamb. verm. bibl. (1743) I. 2, 144.

Dissert. sur la vie et sur les ouvrages de St. Irénée. In: Mém. de Trévoux (1703) 344–; Tr. Ital. In: Zaccaria, Racc. di dissert. (1794) VI. 59–70.

Dodwell, Henry. Dissertationes in Irenaeum. *Oxon.* 1689. 8⁰. Cf. Acta erudit. (1690) 547–61; also Le Clerc. Bibl. univ. (1690–1) XVIII. 230; XX. 95.

Dorner. Person of Christ. I. (1864) 303–26, 462–7.

Douhet. Dict. d. lég. 656.

Duncker, L. Des Heil. Irenaeus Christologie. *Göttingen,* 1843. 8⁰. (VIII. 262.)

Dupin. Nouv. bibl. d. aut. eccl. (1698) I. 160–78.

Duysing, Henr. Otto. Disputatio de textu Irenaei graeco. *Marpurgi Cattor.* 1747. 4⁰.
— Disputatio de versione Irenaei latina. *Marpurgi Cattor.* 1747. 4⁰.

Eichhorn. Bibl. I. 620.

Engelhardt. Dogmenges. I. (1839) 66.

Erasmus. In: Migne. Patrol. gr. VII. (1857) 1321–30.

Erbkam, H. W. De princ. eth. S. Irenaei. *Regiomenti,* 1856.

FABRICIUS. Bibl. gr. (1712) V. 66–74; IX. 413 (2ª VI.); 75–87; X. 713–4.
— Cod. apocr. N. T. (1719) 382–6.
— Bibl. med. aev. (1735) IV. 528–9 (2ª 180).
FARRAR. Interpretation. (1886) 174–75.
FEUARDENT, F. Vita Iren. *Par.* 1576. f°; also in: Migne. Patrol. gr. VII. (1857) 1339–52.
FEUERLEIN, J. W. De sententia Iren. de divinitate Sp. S. *Gött.* 1738. 4°.
— De nostr. ignorantia aetern. generat. Chr. in loc. Iren. *Gött.* 1750. 4°.
FLEURY. Hist. eccl. (1691–) I. 528–31, 540–57, 599–601; II. 39–40.
[FLORUS.] In: Spicil. Solesmense. *Par.* 1852. I. 8–; also in: Migne. Patrol. gr. VII. (1857) 431–2.
FREPPEL. St. Irénée et l'éloquence chrét. dans la Gaule pend. l. deux prem. siècles. *Paris,* 1861. 8°; 3 éd. *Paris,* 1886. 8°.
FROMMANN, E. A. Interpret. N. T. ex Irenaeo, dissert. I. II. *Coburgi,* 1766. 4°.
GALLASIUS, N. In: Migne. Patrol. gr. VII. (1857) 1329–34.
GEBHARDT. In: Ztschr. f. hist. Theol. (1875) 369–.
[GERVAISE, FR. DRM.] La vie de S. Irénée. *Paris,* (3 éd.) 1723. 2 v. 12°. ["Quelques bibliographes attribuent cet ouvrage au libraire-éditeur Barois."]
GIESELER. Church Hist. (1868–) I. 148–9, 156, 197.
Gnosticism and the rule of faith in S. Irenaeus. In: Dubl. Rev. XXIV. (1875) 56–113.
GORINI. Défense de l'Eglise. (1866) I. 12–63.
GOUILLOUD, ANDRÉ. St. Irénée et son temps. *Lyon,* 1876. 8°. (XVI. 519.)
GRABE, J. E. De vita et scr. I. In: Migne. Patrol. gr. VII. (1857) 1351–64.
GRAUL, K. D. chr. K. a. d. Schwelle d. Iren. Ztalters. *Lpz.* 1860.
GRIESBACH, J. J. De potentiore Eccl. Rom. principalitate ad loc. Irenaei. III. 5. *Jena,* 1780. 4°; also in his: Opusc. I.
GRYNAEUS, J. J. In: Migne. Patrol. gr. VII. (1857) 1333–40.
HACKENSCHMIDT. Die Anfänge des kath. Kirchenbegriffs. I. (1874) 83–.
HAGENBACH. Hist. of Doct. I. (1850) 60, etc.
— Kirchenges. (1885) I. 162–8.
HALLOIX. Eccl. orient. script. (1636) II. 402–694.
HARLES. Introd. II. 2, 203.
HARNACK. In: Ztschr. f. hist. Th. (1874) 174–, 211–.
— Dogmenges. I. (1886) 226–7, 263–4, 303–5, 422–500, 648–9.
HARRISON. Whose are the fathers?
HASE. Kirchenges. (1885–) I. 158, 163, 298, 336–7, 434.
HEISCHKEIL, D. C. Ueb einige Stellen Iren. In: Augusti N. theol. Blätt. II. 3, 73.
HENGSTENBERG. Einl. Offenb. Jo. (1861) 406–8.
HERGENROETHER. Kirchenges. (1879–80) I. 168; III. 73.
HEUMANN, C. A. Exercitium artis criticae in Irenaeo. In: Hamburg. verm. Bibl. (1743) I. II. 144–.
HIERONYMUS. De vir. ill. 35.
HILGENFELD. In: Ztschr. f. wiss. Theol. (1879) 319–.
— Ketzergesch. (1884) 5–9, 46–58, 73–4, 342–449.
Hist. lit. France. (1733) I. I, 324–52.
HÖFLING. Lehre d. ältest. K. vom Opfer. (1854) 71–107.
HOLTZMANN. Einl. in d. N. T. (1886) 50, etc.
HOPFENMÜLLER, LAUR. St. Irenaeus de Eucharistia. Dissert. inaug. *Bambergae,* 1867. 8°. Cf. Kraus, J. B., in: Theol. Lit.-blatt. (1868) III. 466–71.
HUBER. Philos. d. K.-V. (1859) 77–93.
JÖCHER. Allgem. Gelehrten-Lex. (1750–51).
Irenaeus and Gnosticism. In: Dub. R. LXXVI. (1874) 56–.
ITTIG. Hist. eccl. (1709) II. 20–9, 212–23.
JANNIGUS. In: Acta ss. Bolland (1715) Jun. VI. 263–72. ("3ª. VII. 698–704.")
JEREMIE. Hist. church (1852) 86–7.
JORTIN, J. Ir. of miracles. In his: Eccl. Hist. (*Lond.* 1752. 8°.) II. 206–375.
KAYSER, A. In: Lichtenberger. Encycl. (1877–82) VII. 1–6.
— L'opinion d'Ireneé sur le siècle apostolique. Rev. d. Théol. VI. 321.
KILLEN. Ancient church. (1859) 368–9.
KIRCHNER, M. D. Eschatologie. d. Iren. In: Stud. u. Krit. XXXVI. (1863) 315–58.
KLING. In: Herzog. Real-Encyclop. s. v.
KOELER, I. D. Testim. S. Ir. de Germanis christianis in saec. II. p. Chr. nat. *Gotting.* 1742–47. 4°.
KOERBER, JOA. S. Irenaeus de gratia sanctificante, Dissert. inaug. *Bambergae,* 1866. 8°.
[KÖRNER, GER.] Explicat. loc. Iren. adv. haer. v. 19. *Lips.* 1781. 4°.
KURTZ. Kirchenges. (1885–) I. 115–6.
LABOUDERIE. In Biog. Univ. Michaud. 1842–65. XX. 362–3.
LANGE, S. GLI. Gesch. d. Dogmen. I. (*Lpz.* 1796) 286–.
LARDNER. Credibility. (*Lond.* 1748. 8°) I. I. 343–. Works (1831) II. 165–193.
LEIMBACH. Wann ist I. geboren? In: Ztschr. f. luth. Theol. XXXIV. (1873) 614–29. [Before 120.]
LEIMBACH, C. L. In: Ztschr. f. luth. Theol. XXXVIII. (1877) 244–9. [1 and 2 Peter.]
LE NOURRY. Appar. bibl. vet. patr. (1703) I. 559–.
LIGHTFOOT, J. B. The Churches of Gaul. In: Contemp. Rev. XXIX. (1876) 405–.
LINDSAY, T. M. In: Encycl. Brit. (9th ed.) XIII. 273–4.
LIPSIUS, R. A. Die Zeit d. Ir. u. d. Enstehung d. altkath. Kirche. In: Sybel Histor. Zeitschr. XXVIII. (*München,* 1872) 241–95.
— Quellen d. ält. Ketzergesch. (1875) 36–.
— Quellenkritik d. Epiphanios. 161–, 168–.
— In: Smith and Wace. Dict. III. 253–79.
LUMBY. History of the Creeds. p. 14.
LUMPER. Hist. ss. patr. III. (1784) 188–628; X. (1794) 568–774.
LUTHARDT. St. John the author of the Fourth Gospel. (1875) 45–8, 141–7.
MAFFEI, SCIP. In: Giorn. de' Letter. (1713–16) XVI. 245–; XXVI. 53–; Tr. Ger. In: Neue Bibl. u. s. w. LVIII. 597–. [Rev. of Pfaff's fragments.]
MANSEL. Gnostic Heresies. *Lond.* 1875.
MASSUET, REN. S. Irenaei contra haereses lib. V. (1710) dissert. III.; also in: Migne. Patrol. gr. VII. 9–382.
MATTER. Hist. crit. du Gnost. II.
MAURICE. Eccl. Hist. (1854) 260–8.
MÖHLER. Patrologie. (*Regensburg,* 1840.) 330–394.
MÖLLER, W. D. Kosmologie in d. gr. K. (1860) 474–506.
MONTET, E. La Légende d'Irénée et l'introduction du christianisme à Lyon. *Genève,* 1880. 8°.
MOSHEIM. De reb. chr. ante Const.
MUENSCHER. Dogmenges. (1817–8) I. 143–5, etc.
NEANDER. Hist. of dogmas. (1858) 50–1, 77–9, etc.
— Church Hist. (1872) I. 215, 299–300, 677–82, et pass.
NIRSCHL. Patrol. (1881–) I. 182–200.
NITZSCH. Dogmengesch. I. (1870) 120–1, etc.
NODIER. Bib. sacr. (1826) 154–5.
NORTON. Genuineness of Gosp. I. (1846) 39, etc.
ORSI. Ist. eccl. (1746) II. 233–5, 283–302, 449–50; (1749) II. 333–7, 406–31, 649–50.
OUDIN. Scr. eccl. (1722) I. 206–9.
PAPEBROCHIUS. Comment. histor. In: Acta ss. Bolland. (1709) Jun. V. 335–42. ("3ª. VII, 303–9.")

PERMANEDER. Bibl. patrist (1842) I. 416–7, II. 219–68.

PFAFF, C. M. Dissert. apol. de frgmm. Iren. . . . adv. Maffeium. *Tübing*. 1718. 4°.

PISANSKY, G. C. De errore Iren. in determ. aet. Christi. *Regiom*. 1778. 8°.

PITRA. Spicil. Solesm. (1852) I. vi–xi, 565.

POWERS, W. R. Irenaeus and Infant Baptism. In: Am. Presb. R. XVI. (1867) 239–.

PRAT, J. M. Histoire de S. Irénée. *Paris* (1843). 8°; tr. Ger. by J. N. Oischinger. Regensb. 1846. 8°. [" But what a confused, poverty-stricken work this is." —*Rudelbach*.]

PRESSENSÉ. Chr. life. (1878) 98–9, 271–3.
— Martyrs. (1879) 252–60.
— Heresy. (N.Y.) 375–404.

PRILESZKY, J. B. Acta et scripta S. Irenaei episcopo et mart. *Cassoviae*, 1765. 8°.

QUARRY, J. Ir. and early Christianity. In: British Qt. LXX. (1879) 96–; 311–. (Am. ed. 51–68; 165–83.)

RAMBOUILLET. St. Irénée et l'infaillibilité . . . *Paris*, 1870. 18°.

Remarks upon St. Ir. by one of the authors of the Acta Eruditorum. In: Memoirs of Literature. (*Lond.* 1712. 4°.) II. 267–9.

REUSCH. In: Wetzer u. W. Kirch-Lex. (1847–54) V. 818–21.

REUSS. Gesch. N. T. (1874) II. 19, 258–9; Tr. Eng. (1884) 302, 538. [v. 2.]

RÉVILLE, Albert. St. Irénée et les Gnostiques de son temps. In: Rev. d. deux Mondes, H. LV. (1865) 998–1032. Cf. Desjardins, E. G. In: Rev. d. scien. eccl. B. II. (1865) 238–40.

Revue d. scien. eccl. (1861) IV. 397–423.

RITTER. Chr. philos. (1841) I. 345–362.

RITSCHL. Entst. d. altkath. K. (1857) 312–339–.

RITTER. Gesch. christl. Philos. (1841) I. 345–62.

ROBERTS and RAMBAUT. Introd. note. In: Ante-Nic. Lib. V. (1868) xv–xx. Ed. Coxe. I. (1885) 307–13.

ROBERTSON. Hist. of Church. (1875) I. 100–2.

ROPES, C. J. H. In: Bib. Sac. XXXIV. (1877) 284–334. [Agt. Harvey. Iren. of Greek origin.]

ROSENMÜLLER. De Theologiae Chr. origine. (1786) 75–.
— Hist. interp. II. (1798) 185–228.

ROESSLER. Bibl. d. K.-V. I. (1776) 262–384.

RUINART. Acta sinc. (1689) 59, 708.

SANDAY. Gosp. in 2 cent. (1876) 49–57, 315–7, 326, 329–33.

SCHAFF. In: Deutsche Kirchenfreund. V. (1852).
— Creeds of Christendom. II. (1877) 12–16.
— Hist. . . Church. II. (1886) 746–57.

SCHLIEMANN. Clementinen. (1884) 120 et pass.

SCHMID. Patrol. (1879); (1886) 44–5.

SCHMIDT, J. Etude sur. S. Irenée et les Gnostiques. *Brux*. (*Louvain?*) 1855. 8°. In: Rev. Cathol. (1855) D. II. 390–; E. I. 558–72, 622–34, 688–93, 736–43.

SCHNEEMANN, GERARD. S. Ir. de eccl. Romanae pricipatu testimonium. commentatum et defensum. *Frieb. i. Br*. 1870. 4°. (xxxiv. p.)

SCHRAM. Anal. ss. patr. (1780) II. 1–403.

SCHROECKH. Kirchenges. (1772–) III. 192–237; IX. 96–7, 146.

SCULTETUS. Medull. theolog. patr. 83–.

SEMLER, I. LAL. Prolusio . . . ad corrigendas quasd. Irenaei et Tertulliani sententias. *Halae*, 1772. 4°.
— Comment. ad Ir. locum de nomine Iesu hebraico. In: Acta soc. lat. Jenens. I. 68–.

SEVESTRE. Dict. patrol. (1854) III. 566–91.

SHEDD. Hist. of doct. 3d ed. (1865–) I. 282–5; II. 392–3, 432–3.

SMITH, P. In: Smith. Gr. and Rom. Biog. (1859) II. 620.

Sopra la vita e le opere di S. Ereneo. In: Zaccaria. Raccolt. (1794) VI. 59–. [Fm. Mémoirs de Trévoux.]

STIEBNITZ (?). Widerlegung e. Irrth. d. Iren. In: Wöchentl. Hallische. Anz. (1751) 81–.

STIEREN, A. De Irenaei adv. haer. operis fontibus, indole, doctrina et dignitate. Comment. hist.-crit. praemio ornata. *Götting*. 1836. 4°.
— In: Ersch. u. Gruber. II. XXIII. (1844) 357–86.
— De cod. Vossano seu Burelliano quo continentur Irenaei. libri V. *Lipsiae*, 1847. 4°.
— Prolegg. in: Opp. Irenaei. *Lips*. 1853. 2 v. 8°; also (Excerpts) in: Migne. Patrol. gr. VII. (1857) 405–20.

STOLL, G. Nachr. d. Kirchenv. 87–.

SÜSKIND. Aus welchen Gründen nahm Ir. d. Aechtheit Uns. Evv. an? In Bezieh. auf Eckermann's theol. Beyträge. V. II. In: Flatt's Magazin f. christl. Moral, etc. (*Tüb*. 1800. 8°.) VI. IV.

TAUST, J. G. Summa probabil. hypothes. S. Irenaei de num. Apocalyps DCLXVI. argum. str. *Halae*, 1769.

THIERSCH. Lehre d. Ir. von d. Eucharistie. In: Zeitschr. f. luth. Theol. (1841) 40–.

TILLEMONT. Mém. II. (1695) 97–99, 619–29; III. (1732) 77–99, 619–29 et pass.

TRITHEMIUS. Scr. eccl. 21.

TULLOCH, J. Irenæus. In: Good Words. II. (1861) 388–.

UEBERWEG. Hist. philos. (1876) 299–301.

Veterum Testimonia. In: Migne. Patrol. gr. VII. (1857) 419–30.

VINCENTIUS BELVAC. Spec. hist. XI. 124.

WAITE. Hist. Chr. Rel. (1881) 6, etc.

WALCH, C. G. F. In: Nov. Comment. Soc. Reg. Scient. Gotting. V. (1775. 4°); II. 3–36; also in: Migne. Patrol. gr. VII. (1857) 381–404. [Authent. of the Adv. haer.]

WALCH, J. G. Bibl. patrist. (1834) 31–2, 704–7, et pass.

WERNSDORF, C. F. De Irenaei testimonio pro paedobapt. *Lipsiae*, 1775.

WESTCOTT. Canon. (1875) 334–7, 379–80.
— Bible in the church. (1877) 121–3.

Witness of Irenaeus to Catholic Doctrine. In: Dub. R. LXXIX. (= XXVII.) (1876) 117–55.

WOLFF, L. Die Lehre. d. Irenaeus von d. Trad. u. d. Natur d. Menschen. In: Ztschr. f. d. ges. Luth. Theol. (1842) IV. 1–28.

WORDSWORTH. Church Hist. (1881) 213–233.

Works of Irenaeus. In: Chr. Rem. XXXV. (1857) 402–; Ecl. R. c. (1854) 257–; Chr. Obs. LXVIII. (1868) 262–.

WORMAN, J. H. In: McClintock and S. Cycl. (1874–) IV. 647–53.

YONGE. Pupils of St. John. (1878) 235–49.

ZAHN, TH. Marcellus v. Anc. (1867) 234–245.
— In: Ztschr. f. hist. Th. (1875) 72–.
— In: Herzog. Real.-Enc. (1877–) VII. 129–40. (Abr. in: Schaff-Herz. II. 1116–8.)
— D. gr. Irenäus u. d. ganze Hegesipp im 16. Jahrh. In: Ztschr. f. Kirchengesch. II. (1880) 288–291.

ZELLER. Apostelgesch. (1854) 69–70.

ZIEGLER, HEINRICH. Des Irenäus Lehre von d. Autorität d. Schrift, d. Tradition u. d. Kirche. *Berlin*, 1868. 4°. [Progr.]
— Irenaeus d. Bischof von Lyon. Ein Beitrag zur Entstehungsgesch. der altkath. K. *Berlin*, 1871. 8°.

Note 1. Mentions of Ir. are frequent in various works on Gnosticism, Montanism, Epiphanius, Heresies, Creeds, in Introductions, Commentaries, etc.

Note 2. Birth of Irenaeus. 97–8, Dodwell; 100–120, Busse; 108, Grabe; 115, Zahn; 115–125, Schaff; 120, Tillemont, Lightfoot; 125–130, Lipsius; 126, Ropes, Leimbach, Hilgenfeld; 125–30, Gebhardt; 130, Harvey; 140, Dupin, Massuet, Kling, Böhringer, and others; 147 (?) Ziegler.

VOLUME II.

I. THE PASTOR OF HERMAS.

I. *Editions.*

BARTHIUS. (Fragments.) In his: Mamerti de Statu Animae. *Cygn.* 1655.

MONTFAUCON, BERN. DE. (Fragments.) In his ed. of Athanasius. 1698. f°.

FABRICIUS. (Fragments.) In his: Bibl. gr. 1712. 4°. 2–29.

GALLANDIUS. (Fragments.) Bibl. patr. 1788. f°. I. 49–.

HEFELE. (Fragments.) Patr. ap. *Tüb.* 1839; (1855) 329–397, passim.

ANGER and DINDORF. *Lipsiae,* 1856.

TISCHENEDORF. *Lips.* 1856; also in: Dressel. Patr. ap. (1856–7); 1863. 8°. 408–637.

SIMONIDES. In: Ορθοδόξων Ἑλλήνων θεολ γραφαι. *Lond.* 1859; also (ed. Draeseke) in: Zeitschr. f. wiss. Theol. XXX. (1887) 177–84. [Dr. has the "hitherto un-known Greek" conclusion only.]

Codex Sinaiticus. Petrop. 1862. IV. 142–148; also in: Dressel. Proleg. (1863) lxxviii–xlvi.

HILGENFELD. *Lipsiae,* 1866. In: N. T. extra canon rec.

GEBHARDT and HARNACK. Gr. lat. In: Gebhardt, H. & Z. Patr. ap. III. (1877) 1–271–.

FUNK. Patr. ap. (*Tub.* 1881.) I. 334–563.

HILGENFELD. Gr. *Leipzig,* 1881. 8°.

II. *Translations.*

Latin.

FABRUS, JAC. (Pastor.) In his: Liber trium vir., etc. *Paris,* 1513. f°.

GERBELIUS, NICOL. *Argentor.* 1522. 4°.

HEROLDUS. (Pastor.) In his: Orthodoxographi. *Basil,* 1555. f°.

(Pastor.) In: Monumentu patr. orthodoxographa. *Basil,* 1569. f°. II. 599–643.

In: Bibliotheca patrum. *Paris,* 1575. f°; 1589; 1610; 1644; 1654; *Colon.* 1618. I.; and *Lugd.* 1677. I. 11. 22–.

BARTHIUS, CASP. (Pastor.) In: Claudiani Mamerti libri III. de statu animae. Cygneae. 1655. 8°. p. 675–.

COTELERIUS. (Pastor.) In his: Patr. apost. *Par.* 1672. f°.

FELL. (Pastor.) *Oxon.* 1685. 12°. [Barnabas and —.]

CLERICUS, J. (Pastor.) In his: Ed. of Cotelerius. Patr. apost. *Amst.* 1698. f°; 1724. f°.

GRABE, J. E. (Pastor.) In his: Spicil. ss. patr. *Oxon.* 1698; 1700; 1714. 8°. I.

LEGRAS. Livr. apocr. *Par.* 1717. f°; 1742. 12°.

RUSSELL, R. Patr. ap. *Lond.* 1746. 8°. I.

HILGENFELD. *Leipzig,* 1873. 8°. [Best of "Vulgata."]

And in various other editions of the Apostolical fath-ers. For the "Palatina" version cf. especially Gebhardt and Harnack. 1877.

Ethiopic.

ABBADIE, D'. Eth. lat. In: Abh. d. deut. morgenl. Gesellsch. II. 1.; also separately. *Lpz.* 1860. f°.

Dutch.

(Pastor.) *Amst.* 1687. 8°.

English.

WAKE. *Lond.* 1693. 8°. 112–24, 315–530; *Lond.* 1710. 8° [Greatly improved]; *Lond.* 1719. 8°. 77–85, (2) 196–346; 1737. 8°; 5th ed. 1818 [7?]; *Hartford,* 1834. 8°. 279–428; *Lond.* 1842 [3?]. 8° [Revised]; *Lond.* 1846. 8°; 1860. 8°; *Phila.* 1846. 8°.

(HONE.) Apocr. N. T. (1825) 258–357 (*Phila.* n. d.) 197–268.

BUNSEN. Hippolytus. (1854) I. 185–208. [?]

CROMBIE, F. In: Ante-Nic. Lib. I. (1868) 323–435. Ed. Coxe. II. (1885) 9–55.

HOOLE. *Lond., Oxf.* and *Cambr.* 1870.

CUNNINGHAM. (Extracts) In: Churches of Asia. (1880) 234–44.

French.

BIBLE. (Desprez.) *Par.* 1715. f°. IV.

LEGRAS, ANT. In his: Livr. apocr. *Par.* 1717. f°; 1742. 12°; also in his: Ouvr. d. s. pères. *Par.* 1717. 12°.

GENOUDE [? ?]. In: Pères de l'égl. *Par.* 1837–43. 8°.

German.

KOBIAN, VALENT. [? ?] *Hagenauw.* 1539.

GLÜSING, J. O. (Pastor.) In his: Briefe u. Schriften d. Apost. Männer. *Hamburg,* 1718. 44–226.

NEHRINGEN, J. C. *Halle,* 1718.

Also the various modern translations of the ap. fath. Cf. u. Clement of R. and Apx.

Italian.

GALLICIOLLI. *Venez.* 1796.

Russian.

PREOBRASKENSKJ. *Mosk.* 1862.

Note. Hermas was first published in the "vulgata" Latin form by J. Faber in 1513. The Greek text from the Mt. Athos ms. was first published by Anger in 1856, the "Palatina" Latin version first by Dressel in 1857, the Ethiopic trans-lation by Abbadie in 1860, and the Greek text with the use of the Sinaitic ms. first by Tischendorf in the Sinaitic facsimile and in Dressel's Patr. ap. The missing Greek conclusion, published by Simonides. and republished by Dräseke, is re-ceived, though guardedly, by Hilgenfeld, but rejected by Har-nack as a demonstrated forgery.

III. *Literature.*

ABBOTT, E. A. Gospels. In: Encycl. Brit. (9th ed.) X. 815.

ALZOG. Patrol. (1876) 60–70.

Acta ss. Bolland. 1680 (9?) Maii. II. 36. (" 3ª. 357–8.")

ANGER, RUD., and DINDORF, WILH. Nachträgliche Bemerkungen zu Hermas. In: Gersdorf's Repertorium (1856) III. (1857) 1; (1858) IV. 65–. *Leipzig,* 1856–7–8. 3 Th. 8°.

— Synopsis (1852).

BARATERIUS. Disq. chron. (1740) III. § 3, 39–.

BARONIUS, ANN. (1589) 159, 5–8.

BAUMGARTEN–CRUSIUS. Dogmenges. (1832) 84. [v. 1.]

BAUR. Urspr. d. Episcopats. (1838) 75. [de Vis. 11,4.]

— Christenth. d. 3 Ersten Jahrh. (1853) 296; (1863) 134, 265, 294.

— Dogmengesch. I. (1865) 251–2, etc.

ΒΑΦΕΙΔΗΣ. Ἐκκλ. ἱστ. I. (1884) 146–7.

BEHM, HEINR. M. TH. Ueber d. Verfasser d. Schrift. welche d. Titel. "Hist." führt. *Rostock,* 1876 [7?]. 8°. [" Gekrönte Preisschrift."]

— In: Theol. Literaturbl. (1887) 6–7. [Rev. of Link.]

BELLARMIN–LABBE. Scr. eccl. (1728) 20–1.

BELLERMANN. Ueb. d. ält. chr. Begräbnissstätten u. bes. die Katakomben z. Neapel. *Hamb.* 1839. 77–.

BERTHOLDT. Dogmenges. (1822–3) I. 29–30, etc.

BLEEK–MANGOLD. Einleit. (1875) 752–, 787.

BOISSIER. Les origines de la poésie chrétienne. In: Revue des deux mondes. (1875) July. I. 84.

BRUELL. In: Theol. Quartalschr. (1878) 44–52. [Cl. of R. and Herm.]

BRÜLL, A. In: Theol. Quartalschr. LXII. (1880) 681–6. [Rev. of Nirschl.]

— Ueb. d. Urspr. d. I. Cl. u. d. H. In: Theol. Quart-alschr. LXIV. (1882) 201–5.

— Der Hirt des Hermas Nach Ursprung und Inhalt untersucht. *Freiburg i. B.* 1882. 8°.

BUNSEN. Hippolytus. (1854) I. 182–215.
BURTON. Divinity of Christ (1829) 12–14.
BUSSE. Chr. Lit. (1828–9) I. 2–3.
CAILLAU. Introd. in ss. Patr. (1825) 24–5.
CALKINS. Citations from the N. T. by the Ap. fath. In: Bibl. Sac. XXIII. (1866) 593.
CASPARI. Taufsymbols. III. (1875) 297–.
CAVE. Scr. eccl. hist. lit. (1740–3) I. 30–32.
CEILLIER. Hist. gén. d. aut. sac. (1729) I. 582–97; (1858) 330–9.
CHAMPAGNY. Les Antonins. *Par.* 1863. I. 134 not 1; II. 347 not 3; I. (1875) 144–.
CHARTERIS. Canonicity. (1880) XXIV–VI. 108–10, 155–6, 174–6, 196, 224, 238–9, 275, 293–5, 303–4, 313, 336–8.
CHEVALIER. Rép. d. sources hist. (1877–86) 1050.
CLARKE. Sacred. lit. (1830–1) I. 92.
CLINTON. Fasti Rom. (1845–50) I. 125; II. 408.
COFFIN. Lives of fath. (1846) 174–6.
COTELERIUS. Patr. ap. *Amst.* 1724. f°. I. 73–; also in: Migne. Patrol. gr. II. (1857) 859–64.
COTTA. Historia eccles. I. 647–655.
CREDNER. Z. Gesch. d. Kanons. (1847) 76–.
CREDNER–VOLKMAR. Gesch. d. NTlichen Kanon. (1860) 37–.
CUNNINGHAM. Hist. theol. (1870) I. 96–7.
— Churches of Asia. (1880) passim.
DARLING. Cyclop. bibliog. 1448.
DAVIDSON. Canon. (*London,* 1877) 273–.
DILLMANN. Bemerkungen zu d. äthiop. H. In: Ztschr. f. d. Morgenl. Gesells. 1861.
DONALDSON. Hist. Chr. Lit. (1864–6) I. 254–311.
— Apost. fathers. (1874) 318–392.
— In: Theological Rev. (1877) Oct.
— In: Encycl. Brit. (9th ed.) II. 197–8.
DORNER. Person Christi. (1845) 190–205; tr. Engl. I. (1864) 123–35, 380–98.
DRÄSEKE, J. In: Ztschr. f. wiss. Theol. XXX. (1887) 172–84. [The Greek conclusion of H.]
DUPIN. Nouv. bibl. d. aut. eccl. (1698–) I. 1–12.
ENGELHARDT. Dogmenges. I. (1839) 249, etc.
— In: Ztschr. f. d. hist. Theol. (1852) 103.
— Justin d. M. 410–27.
EWALD. Gesch. d. Volkes Israel. VII. (1868) 302; 335–.
FABRICIUS. Bibl. gr. (1712) V. 7–31.
— Cod. apocr. N. T. (1719) 966–70.
— Bibl. med. aev. (1735) III. 719–20.
FLEURY. Hist. eccl. (1691–) I. 278–99.
FONTANINI. Histor. literar. Aquilejens. II. 1. 53–.
FUNK. In: Theol. Quartalschr. LXVI. (1884) 119–22. [Rev. of Brüll. 1882.]
— Zur Versio Palatina des Pastor Hermä. In: Ztschr. f. d. österr. Gymn. 1885. 4°. 245–249.
GAÂB, ERNST. D. Hirte. d. Hermas. Ein Beitrag zur Patristik. Basel, 1866. 8°.
GALLAND. Bibl. vet. patr. (1765) I. xxvi–; also in: Migne. Patrol. gr. II. (1857) 863–72.
GARRUCCI. Storia della arte Christiana. *Prato.* II. (1873) 112–114.
GIESELER. Church Hist. (1868–) I. 109, 111–2.
GRATZ, ALOYS. Disquisitiones in Pastorem Hermae. I. *Bonnae,* 1820. 4°.
GUERANGER. S. Cecile et la société Romaine aux deux premiers siècles. *Paris,* 1874. 132–, 197–.
HACKENSCHMIDT. D. Anfänge d. cathol. Kbegriffs. (1874) 67–.
HAGEMANN. In: Theol. Quartalschr. (*Tüb.* 1860) 3–40.
— In: Tüb. Theol. Quartalschr. (1861) 509–. [H. and 2d Clement.]
— D. röm Kirche i. d. ersten 3 Jahrh. (1864) 48–, 81, 86, 112, 124, 605, 673.

HAGENBACH. Hist. of Doct. I. (1850) 56, etc.
HARNACK. In: Theol. Ltzng. (1877) 58–9. [Rev. of Schodde.]
— In: Theol. Ltzng. XII. (1887) 147–51. [A vigorous exposé of the so-called Greek Hermas of Simonides republished in the Ztschr. f. wiss. Theol. "Dieser griechische Hermas ist allerdings ein 'höchst gelungenes' Machwerk." Cf. u. Dräseke and Hilgenfeld.]
HASE. Kirchenges. (1885–) II. 195–9.
HAUSLEITER, J. Text krit. Bem. z. palat. Uebers. d. H. In: Ztschr. f. wiss Theol. XXVI. (1883) 345–56.
— De versionibus pastoris Hermae latinis. Pars prior. Diss. inaug. Erlangae, 1884. 8°. (XLIX. 262 S.) 6–.
HEFELE. In: Theol. Quartalschr. (1839) 169–.
— In: Wetzer u. W. Kirch-Lex. (1847–54) V. 119–23.
HELLWAG. D. Vorstell. v. d. Präexist. Chr. i. d. ältest. K. In: Theol. Jahrbb. (1848) 227–.
HESSE. D. Murat. Fragment. (1873) 263–.
HEYNE, GUST. Quo tempore Hermae Pastor scriptus sit. Regimonti, 1872.
HEYNS, JUNIUS, et v. GILSE, de P.P. App. doctr. morali, 1833.
HIERONYMUS. De vir. ill. 10.
HILGENFELD. Apost. Vät. (1853) 125–, 179. [?]
— D. Urchristenth. u. s. neuest. Bearbeit. In: Ztschr. f. wiss. Theol. I. (1858) 423–.
— D. Kanon u. d. Kritik d. N. T. (1863) 43.
— In: Ztschr. f. wiss. Theol. (1866) 240. ["de H. et libro Elxai."]
— In: Ztschr. f. wiss. Theol. (1868) 217. [Hermas and Gosp. of John.]
— In: Ztschr. f. wiss. Theol. (1869) II. [Date.]
— In: Ztschr. f. wiss. Theol. (1872) 560–; (1874) 214. [Muratorian fragment.]
— Einleit. i. d. N. T. (1875) 80, 85–, 115–, 126–.
— In: Ztschr. f. wiss. Theol. XXVII. (1883) 507–12. [Rev. of Hausleiter. De vers. lat.]
— In: Ztschr. f. wiss. Theol. XXVIII. (1885) 254–6, [Paris ms. of lat. version.]
— Zwei Bemerkungen zu d. H. d. H. In: Ztschr. f. wiss. Theol. XXVIII. (1885) 384.
— In: Ztschr. f. wiss. Theol. XXX. (1887) 109–14. [Rev. of Link. Christi Person u. Werk i. H.]
— Z. d. gr. Schlusse d. H. In: Ztschr. f. wiss. Theol. XXX. (1887) 185–6. [Probably *not* a fabrication of Simonides.]
HOFSTEDE DE GROOT. Basilides u. s. w. (1868) 108–.
HOLLENBERG, WILH. De Hermae Pastoris codice Lipsiensi. *Berolini,* 1856. 8°. (32 p.)
— Herm. Past. emendavit, indicem verborum addidit Guil. H. *Saarbrüchen,* 1868. 4°. (Progr.)
HOLTZMANN. Einl. in d. N. T. (1886) 111–2, etc., 552.
— Hermas u. Johannes. In: Ztschr. f. wiss. Theol. (1875) 40–.
HOOLE, CHARLES H. The Shepherd of Hermas translated into English, with an Introduction and Notes. *Lond., Oxf. and Cambr.* 1870.
HÜCKSTÄDT, E. Ueb. d. pseudotertul. Gedicht adv. Marcionem. (1875.)
HUIDEKOPER. The belief . . . concerning Christ's mission to the underworld. *New-York,* 1876. 11–, 52–.
ITTIG. Dissert. de patr. ap. p. 184–206.
— Hist. eccl. (1709) I. 65–66, 155–79.
JACHMANN, C. REINH. Der Hirte des Hermas. *Königsberg,* 1835. 8°.
JACKSON. Ap. fath. (1879) 100–119.
JALLABERT. Hermas et Simonidès. Étude sur la controverse récemment soulevée en Allemagne par la découverte d'un ms. grec. *Paris,* 1858. 8°.
J[OUBERT], L. In: Nouv. Biog. Gen. (Hoefer) XXIV. (1858) 371–3.
KAYSER. In: Revue de théolog. XIV. (1857) 239–.
KEIM. Gesch. Jesu. I. (1867) 143 [H. and Joh.]
KIKÜM. Glaubenslehre und Orthodoxie des Pastor Hermae. *Clev.* 1863.

KILLEN. Ancient Church. (1859) 368.
KIRCHHOFER. Quellensammlung. (1844) 80–, 143.
KONTOGONES. Φιλολ. κ. κριτ. ἱστορία τ . . . ἁγ. πατέρων. Ἐν᾽Ἀθήναις. (1851) 50–.
KÖSTLIN, Z. Gesch. d. Urchrist. In: Theol. Jahrbb. (1850) 54.
— Urspr. u. Composition d. synopt. Evv. (1853) 374–.
KRÜGER, G. In: Theol. Ltzng. XI. (1886) 586–88. [Rev. of Link.]
KURTZ. Kirchenges. (1885–) I. 105–7.
LANGE, L. In: Ersch u. Gruber. II. VI. (1829) 290–3.
— Hist. dogm. I. 75–84.
LARDNER. Credibility. Works. (1881) II. 57–73.
LECHLER. Ap. v. Nachap. Z–A. (1885) 608–10; Engl. tr. (1886) II. 358–60.
LÉCUY. In: Biog. Univ. (Michaud) (1842–65) XIX. 288–9.
LEDRAIN. Deux apocr. du 2 sièc. avec une ét. sur la date du pasteur d' H. Paris, 1871.
LE NOURRY. Appar. ad bibl. max. 47–; also in: Migne. Patrol. gr. II. (1857) 833–60.
LIGHTFOOT. Philippians. (1873) 166–, 217–, 221.
— Galatians. (1874) 324–.
LINK, ADF. Christi Person u. Werk im Hirten. d. H. Marb. 1886. 8°. ["besonders dankenswerth." Behm.]
LIPSIUS. De Clemente R. ep. ad Cor. priore. (1855) 171–, 179–.
— In: Ztschr. f. wiss. Theol. VIII. (1865) 266–308; IX. (1866) 27–81; XII. (1869) 249–311.
— In: Schenkel. Bibellex. III. (1871) 20–25.
LÜBKERT, D. Theol. d. App. Vät. In: Ztschr. f. d. hist. Theol. (1854) 589–.
LÜCKE. Comment. z. Ev. Joh. I. (1840) 44.
— Vers. einer vollst. Einl. i. d. Offenb. d. Joh. I. (1852) 337–.
LUMPER. Hist. ss. patr. (1783) I. 98–148; also (extract) in: Migne. Patrol. gr. II. (1857) 871–92.
LUTHARDT. D. joh. Urspr. d. 4. Ev. (1874) 69; tr. Engl. (1875) 68–9.
M., C. [? C., M.] Le pasteur d'Hermas: Analyse accompagnée d'une notice d'extraits et de notes. Paris, 1880.
M'CLINTOCK and S. Cycl. (1874) IV. 204–5.
MAYER. Ap. Vät. (1869) 255–72.
MELLIERIUS. (1697) S. u. Clement, R.
MÖHLER. Patrologie. (1840) 96–160.
MOSHEIM. Inst. hist. eccl. (1755) 51.
— Comment. de reb. chr. I. 208–9.
MUENSCHER. Dogmenges (1817–8) I. 112–3, etc.
NEANDER. Hist. of dogmas. (1858) 113, 235. [v. 1.]
— Church Hist. (1872) I. 660, et pass.
NIRSCHL, J. Der Hirt. d. Hermas. Passau, 1879.
— Patrol. (1881–) I. 80–95.
NITZSCH. Dogmengesch. I. (1870) 111–3, etc.
NODIER. Bib. sacr. (1826) 145–6.
NOLTE. In: Scheiner. Ztschr. VIII. (Wien, 1860) 107–134.
NORTON. Genuineness of Gosp. I. (1846) 6, etc.
ORSI. Ist. eccl. (1746–) I. 294–6; (1749–) I. 415–8.
PERMANEDER. Bibl. patrist. (1842) I. 410; II. 12–22.
PETERS. In: Theol. Literaturbl. (1869) 854–.
REINKENS, J. H. Hirtenbrief. Bonn. 1873. 8°.
— Hirtenbrief von 20. Febr. 1875. Bonn. 1875. 8°.
REITHMAYR. Einl. in. d. Büch. d. N. B. Regensb. 1852. p. 65.
RENAN. D. Antichrist. (1873) XXX .
REUSS. Gesch. N. T. (1874) I. 283–4; II. 16. Tr. Eng. (1884) 281–2 [v. 1], 299–300 [v. 2].
RIGAULT, H. In: Jour. d. Débats. (1857) Oct. 13–15.
RIGGENBACH. D. Zeugnisse f. d. Ev. Joh. (1866) 98.
RITSCHL. Entsteh. d. altkath. K. (1851) 546–; edit. II. (1857) 243–, 288–.

ROBERTS and DONALDSON. Introd. note. In: Ante-Nic. Lib. I. (1868) 317–21. Ed. Coxe. II. (1885) 1–8. [Also additional notes. pp. 56–8.]
ROHRBACHER. Hist. univers. de l'église catholique. II. (1868) 627, 661–.
ROESSLER. Bibl. d. K.–V. I. (1776) 21–44.
ROSENMÜLLER. De Christianae theol. origine. 28–.
ROTHE. Anfänge d. christl. K. (1837) 407, 577–.
SABATIER, A. In: Lichtenberger. Encycl. (1877–82) VI. 206–10.
SALMON, G. In: Smith and Wace. Dict. II. 912–21.
SANDAY. Gosp. in 2 cent. (1876) 273–4.
SCHAFF. Hist. . . Church. II. (1886) 678–92.
SCHENK, R. Z. Lehre d. H. vom überschüssigen Verdienst. In: Ztschr. f. kirchl. Wiss. (1885) 407–413.
— Zum ethischen Lehrbegriff d. Hermas. Progr. d. Realgymm. Aschersleben, 1886. 4°.
SCHLIEMANN. Clementinen. (1844) 421–5.
SCHMID. Patrol. (1879); (1886) 436–7.
SCHMIDT. Christl. Kirch. Gesch. I. 442.
SCHMITZ, P. In: Smith. Gr. and Rom. Biog. (1859) II. 409–10.
SCHODDE, G. H. Hêrmâ nabî, the Ethiopic version of Pastor Hermae examined. A dissertation. Leipzig, 1876. 8°.
SCHOLTEN. D. ältest. Zeugnisse (1867) 6–.
SCHRAM. Anal. ss. patr. (1780–) I. 18–54.
SCHULTZE, V. D. Katakomben v. S. Gennaro d. Pov. i. Neapel. (1877) 33–.
SCHWEGLER. Montanismus. (1841) 94, 104, 114, 159, 230.
— Nachap. Zeitalt. (1846) I. 328–42; II. 217–8.
SEMLER, J. SAL. Prolegom. ad Baumgartenii. theol. polem. II. 7–.
Shepherd of Hermas, The. In: Dub. R. LI. (   ) 133–.
SIMONIDÈS, CONST. "Essays on the Pastoral writings of Hermas the apostolic father." (In Greek.) Moscow, 1853. 4°.
SKWORZOW. Patrologische Untersuch. (1875) 15–.
STARCK. Gesch. d. christl. Kirche. II. 563, 564.
STOWE. Books of the Bible. (1867) 440–67.
Supernatural religion. (1875–) I. 256–7; II. 256–60; III. 8–10.
THIERSCH. Vers. z. Herstell. d. hist. Standpunkts u. s. w. (1845) 381–.
— D. K. i. apost. Ztalter. (1858) 350–.
THOMASIUS. Dogmengesch. I. (1874) 34–.
TILLEMONT. Mémoirs. (1694) II. 111–7, 519–22.
TISCHENDORF. De Herma graeco Lipsiensi. In: Dressel. Patr. ap. (1863) Proleg. xliv–lv.
TORELL. Placita quaedam Herm. Lund. 1825.
TREGELLES. Canon Murat. (1867) 58–64.
UEBERWEG. Hist. philos. (1876) 277–8.
UHLHORN, G. Ueb. die ethischen Auschauungen d. H. In: Ztschr. v. Lücke u. Wieseler. N. F. II. (1850) 227–.
— In: Herzog. Real.-Enc. (1877–) VI. 9–13. (Abr. in. Schaff-Herz. II. 977.)
Veterum Testimonia d. s. Herma. In: Galland. Vet. patr. bibl. I. Venet. 1765. f°. 51–; also in: Migne. Patrol. gr. II. (1857) 819–34.
VOLKMAR. D. 4. Buch Esra. (1863) 291–.
— D. Urspr. uns Evv. (1866) 64–.
WAITE. Hist. Chr. Rel. (1881) 232–3 et pass.
WALCH. Bibl. patr. (1834) 25, 329, 549.
WEINGARTEN. In: Rothe's Vorless. üb. Kirchengesch. I. (1875) 96.
WEINRICH, FR. Disquisit. in doctrinam moralem ab Herma in Pastore propositam. Wirceburgi, 1804. 8°.
WESTCOTT. Canon. (1875) 190–202.
— Bible in the church. (1875) 108.
ZAHN, THEOD. Hermae pastor e novo testamento illustratus. I. Dissertatio. Gottingen, 1867. 8°.

ZAHN. Der Hirt. d. Hermas untersucht. *Gotha*, 1868. 8⁰.
— In: Stud. u. Krit. XLI. (1868) 319–49. [Rev. of Gaâb.]
— Ignat. u. Antioch. (1873) 313, 315, 333, 514–, 585, 616–.
— In: Jahrbb. f. deutsche Theol. (1874) 144–. [H. and Muratorian fragm.]
ZELLER. Apostelgesch. (1854) 9–10.
ZIMMERMANN, J. J. Disquisitio histor. et theol. de visionibus. In his: Opusculis. I. v. 668–.

> *Note.* Hermas is, 1) (*a*) *Hermas of the N. T.*, Le Nourry, Tillemont, Bellarmin, Ceillier, Cotelerius, Dupin, Galland, Lumper, Möhler, Jachmann, Gaâb, Zahn, Mayer, Nirschl (who argues that the later H. translated the earlier into Latin), (*b*) *The companion of Clemens R.*, Dodwell, Wake, Gaâb, Caspari, Alzog, ZAHN. 2) *The brother of Pius I.* (139–154), Canon Muratori, Hefele (?), Tregelles, Heyne, Brüll, Lipsius, Alzog, Gebhardt, Sabatier (139–40), Harnack, Funk, Coxe (160). 3) *A later writer who assumed the name of the earlier* H., Ewald, Behm, Credner, Ritschl, Hefele (?), Dorner, Hagenmann; also Schwegler, Lechler, Hilgenfeld, Gratz, Donaldson, and Lange. Thiersch thinks the original work early, but that it was interpolated in the time of Pius. The Ethiopic transl. makes Hermas St. Paul.

II. TATIAN.

I. *Editions.*

(*Oratio.*)

FRISIUS, J. Tigur. 1546. f⁰. [With emendations by Gesner.]
HEROLDUS. Orthodoxographa. *Basel.* 1555. f⁰.
(JUSTIN M. and) *Paris.* 1616. 4⁰; 1636. 4⁰.
DUCAEUS. *Par.* 1624. f⁰. In: Auct.
(JUSTIN M. and) Colon. (*Witteb.*) 1686. [With notes by Kortholt.]
WORTH, WILH. Gr. lat. *Oxon.* 1700. 8⁰.
MARANUS, PRUD. (Justin M. and) *Par.* 1742. f⁰.
GALLAND. Bibl. vet. patr. *Venet.* 1765. f⁰. I.
SS. patr. opera polem. *Wirceb.* 1777. 8⁰.
OTTO. In his: Corp. Apol. VI. *Jena*, 1851. 8⁰.
Adv. Graecos. Migne. Gr. lat. In: Patrol. gr. VI. (1857) 801–88. [Maranus.]
HARNACK. In: Texte, etc. I. II. 196–231.

(*Diatessaron.*)

The remains of the Diatessaron have been gathered by ZAHN in his: Forschungen z. Gesch. d. N. T. Kanons I. *Erlangen*, 1881. 8⁰. The source is the Armenian translation of Ephraem Syrus commentary published in the works of Ephraem, *Venice*, 1836, 8⁰, and translated into Latin by Aucher, which translation revised was published by Mösinger, *Venet.* 1876, 8⁰ (pp. xii, 292). Cf. also, Harnack in: Gebhardt u. Texte u. s. w. *Leipz.* 1883. 8⁰. I. 137–153; and in: Ztschr. f. Kirchenges. (1880) 471–505.

II. *Translations.*

Latin. (*Oratio.*)

GESNER. (Oratio.) *Tiguri*, 1546. f⁰. And in various editions.

(*Diatessaron.*)

LUSCINIUS (NACHTIGAL), OTTOMAR. *August. Vind.* 1523. 4⁰; ed. Brusch. *Erfurt.* 1544. 8⁰; in: Μικροπρεσβυτικον. *Basil.* 1569. f⁰. p. 615–; in: Mon. patr. orthodox. *Basil.* I. II. 22–: in: Bibl. patr. *Lugd.* 1677. f⁰. III. 265–; also tr. Ger. by Nachtigal. *Augsb.* 1524. 8⁰.
VICTOR OF CAPUA. *Mogunt.* 1524. 8⁰; ed. Memler. *Colon.* 1532. 8⁰; in: Monum. patr. orthodox. *Basil.* 1569. f⁰. I. II. 59–; in: Bibl. patr. max. *Lugd*, 1677. f⁰. II. II. 203–; in: Bibl. patr. *Par.* 1690. f⁰; in: Schilters. Thes. *Ulm.* 1727. f⁰. (Tatian) 1–100; in: Galland. 1765. f⁰; ed. Semisch. *Vratisl.* 1856. An old German version supposed to have been translated from this was published by Palthenius. *Greifswald*, 1706. 4⁰; in: Schilter's Thesaurus (Tatian). *Ulm.* 1727. f⁰. (supplementary fragments) in: Hess. Bibl. d.

heil. Gesch. II. 543–570; also (under Ammonius) by Schmeller. *Viennae*, 1841. 8⁰; and by Sievers. *Paderborn*, 1872. 8⁰.

> *Note.* The *authenticity* of the above works, which have been assigned now to Tatian and now to Ammonius of Alexandria, has been generally denied, and, by the Aucher-Mösinger-Harnack-Zahn investigations, fully disproved.

English.

RYLAND, J. E. [not Pratten, B. P.] (Oratio.) In: Ante-Nic. Lib. III. (1868) 5–48. Ed. Coxe. II. (1885) 65–83. [The translation is ascribed to Pratten on the title-page of the Edinb. ed., but is corrected in a note in vol. XX. II. p. 4.]

French.

GENOUDE. [? ?] (Oratio.) In: Pères de l'égl. *Par.* 1837–43. 8⁰.

German.

ZIEGLER. (Oratio.) In: Werke d. K.–V. II. (*Kempten*, 1830.)
GRÖUE, V. (Oratio.) *Kempten*, 1872. 16⁰. [The Reithmayer-Thalhofer Bibl.]

III. *Literature.*

ABBOT, EZRA. Fourth Gospel. *Bost.* 1880. 8⁰. 52–56.
ALZOG. Patrol. (1876) 82–6.
ANGER. Synops. Ev. Proleg.
ARTAUD. In: Dict. scien. philos. (1875) 1704.
ASSEMANI, J. S. Bibl. Orient. II.
AUBÉ, B. In: Nouv. Biog. Gen. (Hoefer) XLIV. (1865) 927–9.
— S. u. Justin M.
BARONIUS, ANN. (1589) 165, 12–4; 174, 1–14. Cf. Pagi. Crit. (1689) 3.
BAR-SALIBI, DIONYSIUS. Cf. Assemani. Biblioth. Orient. II. 158–.
BAUMGARTEN–CRUSIUS. Dogmenges. (1832) 148–9, 173. [v. I.]
BAUR. Dogmengesch. I. (1865) 256–7, etc.
— Unters. kan. Evv.
ΒΑΦΕΙΔΟΣ. Ἐκκλ. ἱστ. I. (1884) 152–3.
BEAUSOBRE. Hist. du Manichéisme. I.
BELLARMIN–LABBE. s. v. (1728) 36.
BINDEMANN. In: Th. Stud. u. Krit. 1842.
BLEEK. Einl. N. T.
BLÜMNER, H. Ueb. d. Glaubwürdigkeit d. kunsthistorischen Nachrichten d. Tatian. In: Archaeolog. Zeitung. XXVIII. (1871) 86–89.
BRETSCHNEIDER. Probabilia.
BRUCKER. Hist. crit. philos. (1766–7) III. 378–96; VI. 536–8.
BULL. Defens. Fid. Nic. III. VI. In: Works. V. I. (*Oxf.* 1846) 567–580.
BUNSEN. Bibelwerk. VIII.
BURTON. Divinity of Christ (1829) 61–2.
BUSSE. Chr. Lit. (1828–9) I. 12.
CACHEUX. In: Mémor. catholiq. (1862) B. III. 80–6.
CAVE. Scr. eccl. hist. lit. (1740–3) I. 75–7; and, under Ammonius, 109–.
CEILLIER. Hist. gén. d. aut. sac. (1730) II. 123–31; (1858) I. 488–92.
CELÉRIER. Essai d'une Introd. N. T.
CHARTERIS. Canonicity. (1880) 72–3, 129, 162, 180–1, 202, 210, 219, 227–8, 234–5, 249.
CHEVALIER. Rép. d. sources hist. (1877–86) 2150.
CIASCA, A. De Tatiani Diatessaron Arabica versione. *Paris*, 1883. 8⁰.
CLARKE. Sacred lit. (1830–1) I. 101–3.
CLINTON. Fasti Rom. (1845–50) I. 169, 199; II. 410.
COFFIN. Lives of fath. (1846) 197–203.
CREDNER. Beiträge. I. (1832) 437–51.
— Gesch. N. T. Kanons.
DANIEL, H. A. Commentationes de Tatiano apologeta specimen, Dissert. inaug. *Halis*, 1835. 8⁰.

DANIEL, H. A. Tatianus der Apologet. Ein Beitrag zur Dogmengeschichte. *Halle*, 1837. 8°. ["Contains a complete account of the older literature." *Möller*.]

DARLING. Cyclop. bibl. 2904.

DELITZSCH. Urspr. Mt. Ev.

DEMBOWSKI, HERM. Die Quellen d. chr. Apologetik d. 2. Jahrh. I. Die Apologie Tatian's. *Leipzig*, 1878. 8°.

DONALDSON. Hist. Chr. lit. (1864–6) III. 3–62.

DORNER. Person of Christ. I. (1864) 280–2.

DUNCKER. Apologet. saec. de Essentiae naturae hum. partibus placita. *Gött.* 1850. pt. II.

DUPIN. Nouv. bibl. d. aut. eccl. (1698–) I. 137, 859.

EBEDJESU. Catal. scr. eccl. 3 (Assemani Bibl. orient. III. I, 12.)

EICHHORN. Einl. N. T. I.

ENGELHARDT. Dogmenges. I. (1839) 48–9.

EPHRAEM SYRUS. (Commentary on Tatian.) s. u. Mösinger.

FABRICIUS. Bibl. gr. (1712) III. 212; V. 81–5, 97–102; IV. 881; V. 714; VII. 87–95, 116–9.
— Cod. apocr. N. T. (1719) 377–9–.
— De verit. rel. Chr. (1725) 50–1, 159.

FEILMOSER. Einl. N. B.

FLEURY. Hist. eccl. (1691) I. 498–504.

FREPPEL. Les apologistes chrét. au deux. sièc. 1860.

FUNK. Zur Chronologie Tatian's. In: Theol. Quartalsch. LXV. (1883) 219–33.

GEBHARDT U. HARNACK. Texte u. Untersuch. I. (*Lpz.* 1883) I. II. 1–24, 90–97, 196–131; III. 137–153.

GIESELER. Entst. schr. Evv.

GRATZ. Kr. Unters. Justin's Denkw.

GUERICKE. Gesammtgesch. N. T.

HAGENBACH. Hist. of Doct. I. (1850) 59, etc.

HARNACK, A. T.'s Diatessaron im Murator. Frgm. In: Ztschr. f. luth. Theol. XXXV. (1874) 276–88.
— T.'s Diatessaron . . bei Ephraem Syrus. In: Ztschr. f. Kirchengesch. IV. (1880) 471–505.
— Dogmenges. I. (1886) 388–91.

HASE. Kirchenges. (1885–) I. 249, 323.

HAUPT, M. Varia. In: Hermes. IV. (1870) 28–29; also in his: Opuscula. III. 2 (1876) 446–. [Tatian, c.46.]

HERGENROETHER. Kirchenges. (1879–80) I. 104–6, 137; III. 41–2, 59.

HIERONYMUS. De vir. ill. 29. (Honor. August. 1, 31.)

HILGENFELD. Ketzergesch. (1884) 384–397.
— In: Ztschr. f. wiss. Theol. XXVI. (1883) 111–24.

HOLTZMANN. Einl. in d. N. T. (1886) 129, etc.

HUBER. Philos. d. K.–V. (1859) 20–22.

HUG. Einl. N. T. I.

ITTIG. Hist. eccl. (1709) II. 15–20, 225–7.

JÖCHER. Allgem. Gelehrt. Lex. (1750–51).

JONES. Canon N. T. 1798. I. 387–90.

KEIM. Jesu v. Nazara. I.

KIRCHHOFER. Quellensamml.

KORTHOLT. S. u. Justin M.

KURTZ. Kirchenges. (1885–) I. 113–4.

LANGE. Hist. dogmatum. I. 223, etc.

LARDNER. Credibility. Works. (1831) II. 147–152.
— Credibility. Works. (1831) II. 442–54.

LELONG. Bibl. sac. (1723) II. 981.

LENOURRY. Appar. bibl. patr. (1703) I.

LIGHTFOOT, J. B. Tatian's Diatessaron. In: Contemp. XXIX. (1877) 1132–43.

[LONGUERUE, LOUIS DUFOUR DE.] Dissertatio (of 27 pp.). In: Oratio. ed. Worth (1700); also in: Voigt. Bibl. haeres. *Hamb.* 1723–9. 8°. I. 2, 201.

LUMPER. Hist. ss. patr. (1784) II. 317–76.

LUTHARDT. St. John the Author of the Fourth Gospel. (1875) 50–1.

MARTIN. De T. Diatessaron arabica versione. In: Patr. Anal. Sacr. *Par.* 1883. p. 465, 487.

M'CLINTOCK and S. Cycl. (1874–) X. 223–4.

MATTER. Hist. du Christianisme. 2 ed. I.

MATTES. In: Wetzer u. W. Kirch-Lex. (1847–54) X. 644–61.

MEANS, J. C. In: Smith. Gr. and Rom. Biog. (1859) III. 980–3.

Mém. de Trévoux (1714) 1453–61.

MEYER. Ex.-Krit. Handbuch. passim.

MICHAELIS. Einl. N. T. II.

MIRAEUS. Scr. Eccl. 12.

MÖHLER. Patrologie (1840).

MÖLLER, W. In: Herzog. Real.-Enc. (1877) XV. 208–15. (Abr. in: Schaff-Herz. III. 2302.)
— Kosmologie d. gr. K. (1860) 168–.

MUENSCHER. Dogmenges. (1817–8) I. 142, etc.

NAUCK, A. Zur Kritik des Tatian πρὸς Ἑλληνας. In: Philologus. IX. (1854) 370–372.

NEANDER. Hist. of dogmas. (1858) 142–3, 187, 202. [v.1.]
— Church Hist. (1872) I. 456–8, 672–3, et pass.

NEUDECKER. Lehrb. Einl. N. T.

NICOLAS. Ét. sur les Ev. apocr.

NIRSCHL. Patrol. (1881–) I. 158–64.

NITZSCH. Dogmengesch. I. (1870) 118–9, etc.

NODIER. Bib. sacr. (1826) 150–1.

NOLTE. Conjecturae et emend. In: Migne. Patrol. gr. VI. (1857) 1737–44; 1801–8.

NORTON. Genuineness of Gosp. I. (1846) 52–3, etc.

OBERTHÜR, F. Disp. exposuit quorundam ex patr. gr. apolog. Justini, Tat., Athenag., Theoph. Aut., et Hermiae de praecipuis relig. christ. dogmatis sententiam. *Wirceb.* 1778. 8°.

OLSHAUSEN. Echth. vier can. Evv.

ORSI. Ist. eccl. (1746–) II. 172–83. (1749–) II. 245–61.

OUDIN. Scr. eccl. (1722) I. 209–12.

OVERBECK. In: Theol. Litzng. VII. (1882) 102–109. [Rev. of Zahn.]

PAULUS. Conserv. I. 121.

PEARSON. Conjecturae. In: ed. Worth.

PERMANEDER. Bibl. patrist. (1841) I. 415–6; II. 163–75.

RYLAND, J. E. [Pratten, B. P.?] Introd. note. In: Ante-Nic. Lib. III. (1868) 1–4. Ed. Coxe. II. (1885) 59–63.

PRESSENSÉ. Heresy. (*N. Y.*) 253–4.

RENAN. Marc Aurèle. *Par.* 1882.

REUSS. Gesch. N. T. (1874) I. 201; II. 14, 200. Tr. Eng. (1884) 202 [v. 1], 298, 479–80. [v. 2.]

RITTER. Chr. philos. (1841) I. 328–341[4].

ROESSLER. Bibl. d. K.–V. I. (1776) 253–261; IV. (1777) 365.

ROSENMÜLLER. Hist. interp. I. (1795) 203–8.

SANDAY. Gosp. in 2 cent. (1876) 238–42, 303–6.

SCHAFF. Hist. . . Church. II. (1886) 493–6, 726–30

SCHMID. Patrol. (1879); (1886) 40–1.

SCHMIDT. Einl. N. T. I.

SCHOLTEN. Die ält. Zeugnisse. (1867).

SCHRAM. Anal. ss. patr. (1780–) I. 525–563.

SCHROECKH. Kirchenges. (1772–) III. 158–67.

SEILER, G. F. Christologia Tat., Athenag., et Théoph. Ant. *Erlang.* 1775. 4°.

SIMON. Hist. Crit. N. T.

SPRENGER. Thesaurus rei patr. II. 76–.

STÖCKL. Gesch. d. philos. i. d. patr. zeit. (1859) 148–.

STOWE. Books of the Bible. (1867) 249–50.

STROEHLIN, E. In Lichtenbergr. Encycl. (1877–82) XII. 7–9.

Supernatural Religion. (1875) II. 148–63, 373–9; III. 22–3.

TENTZELIUS. Exercit. sel. *Lips.* 1692. 4°.

TILLEMONT. Mém. (1694) II. 410–4, 665.

TISCHENDORF. Wann wurden u. s. w. (1866).

TRAVASA, GAET. MAR. Stor. eresiarchi (17 . .) III. 93. (= Zaccaria, Racc. di dissert. (1794) VI. 102–41.)

TRITHEMIUS. Scr. eccl. 18.

UEBERWEG. Hist. philos. (1876) 294–6.
VOLKMAR. Ursprung. u. s. w. (1866).
WACE, H. In: Expos. (1881) 1–11, 128–37, 193–205.
— Zahn on T.'s Diatessaron. In: Expos. XVI. (1882) 161–71, 294–312.
WAITE. Hist. Chr. Rel. (1881) 284–6 et pass.
WALCH. Bibl. patrist. (1834) 34, 394–5.
WEISS. In Biog. Univ. (Michaud) (1842–65) XLI. 76–7.
WESTCOTT. Canon. (1875) 315–22.
WETTE, DE. Einl. A. T. 1852.
WILCKE. Tradition u. Mythe.
WURM. Apol. v. Justin, Tat., Athenag., Theoph. und Hermias. In: Stud. d. evang. Geistl. Würt. (1828) I. II. 1–34.
ZAHN. Ztschr. f. kirchl. wiss. u. Leben. (1884) 617–26.
— Forschungen zur Geschichte d. neutest. Kanons. u. d. altk. Lit. I. Tatian's Diatessaron. Erlangen, 1881. 8º. II. 286–299. Cf. Duchesne, L. In: Bull. critique (1881) II. 243–9.
— In: Keil's Analekten. II. 1. 165–.
ZELLER. Apostelgesch. (1854) 69.

Note. The Diatessaron was used by Aphraates and the author of the Doctrine of Addai, as well as by Ephraem Syrus. For literature, therefore, consult the articles on these authors in Smith and Wace, etc., etc., and especially literature under VIII. VII. (Syriac documents) of this series.

III. THEOPHILUS OF ANTIOCH.

I. Editions.

Ad Autolicum.

GESNER, CONR. Gr. Tiguri, 1546. fº.
CLAUSERUS, CONR. Gr. lat. Orthodoxographa. Basil, 1556. fº; 285–350; 1559. fº.
(JUSTIN. Op. and) Gr. lat. Par. 1615. fº; 1636. fº; 1686. fº.
DUCAEUS. Gr. lat. Paris, 1624. fº. In: Auct. Bibl. patr.
FELL, J. Gr. lat. Oxon. 1684. 12º.
MARANUS, PRUD. Par. 1742. fº; Par. 1747. fº.
WOLFIUS, JO. CHR. Gr. lat. Hamburgi, 1724. 8º.
GALLAND. Bibl. vet. patr. Venet. 1765. II. no. 4.
OBERTHÜR. Gr. lat. Wirceb. 1777. 8º.
HUMPHRY, W. G. Camb. 1852. 8º.
MIGNE. Gr. lat. In: Patrol. gr. VI. (1857) 1023–1168. [Maranus.]
OTTO. Corp. Apol. VIII. Jena, 1861.

Commentaries.

MIGNE. (Frgmts.) Gr. lat. In: Patrol. gr. VI. (1857) 1603–4.
GRABE. (Fragm.) Gr. lat. In: Spicil. patr. (1700) II. 218–24.
See Latin translations.

II. Translations.

Latin.

(Opera.) In: Bibl. patr. V. (1575) 1589; 1609; 1618; 1644; 1677. fº.
CLAUSERUS, C. Ad Autol. Zurich, 1546.
ROUS, Fr. (Ad Autol.) Lond. 1650. 8º. In his: Mella patr. p. 124–33.
OTTO. (Comment.) Corpus apol. VIII. (Jen. 1861) 278–324.
ZAHN. (Comment.) In: Forsch. z. Ges. d. N. T. Kanons. II. (1883); III. (1884) 198–278.

English.

BETTY, JOSEPH. (Tertullian's Prescription and.) Oxf. 1722, 8º.

Lond. 1860. 8º.
DODS, M. In: Ante-Nic. Lib. III. (1868) 53–133. Ed. Coxe. II. (1885) 89–121.

French.

GENOUDE. [? ?] In: Pères de l'égl. Par. 1837–43. 8º.

German.

WOLF. 1724.
HOSMANN, GUST. CHR. Hamb. 1729. 8º.
THIENMANN, W. F. Lpz. 1834. 8º.
LEITL, J. Kempten, 1872.' 16º. [The Raithmayer-Thalhofer. Bibl.]

Russian.

KRASSOWSKJ, J. J. (Autol.) (In: Proceedings of the Acad. of Sciences.)

III. Literature.

ALZOG. Patrol. (1876) 91–95.
ANGER. Synops. evv. (1852) xxxiii.
AUBÉ, B. St. Justin, etc. Par. 1861. 8º; 1874. 8º.
— In: Nouv. Biog. Gén. (Hoefer) XLV. (1866) 99–101
BARONIUS. Ann. (1589) 170, 7–10; 182, 6.
BAUMGARTEN–CRUSIUS. Dogmenges. (1832) 173. [v. 1.] (7 ll.)
BAUR. Dogmengesch. I. (1865) 258, etc.
ΒΑΦΕΙΔΟΣ. 'Εκκλ. ἱστ. I. (1884) 153.
BELLARMIN–LABBE. Scr. eccl. (1728) 35.
BERTHOLDT. Dogmenges. (1822–3) I. 54, etc.
BRUCKER. Hist. crit. phil. (1766–7) III. 399–401; VI. 538.
BUENS. Comment. praev. In: Acta ss. Bolland. (1814) Oct. VI. 168–80.
BULL, G. Defens. fid. Nic. II. IV. 72; III. VII. 214.
BURTON. Trinity. (1831) 33–47.
BUSSE. Chr. Lit. (1828–9) I. 14–5.
CACHEUX. In: Mémor. catholiq. (1862) B. III. 159–64.
CAILLAU. Introd. in ss. Patr. (1825) 54–5.
CAVE. Scr. eccl. hist. lit. (1740–3) I. 69–71.
— Lives. (1840) I. 273–79.
CEILLIER. Hist. gén. d. aut. sac. II. (1730) 103–12; (1858) I. 475–80.
CENTURIATOR. MAGDEB. II. IV. 43; X. 132.
CHARTERIS. Canonicity. (1880) 73–4, 132, 162, 182, 220, 229, 231, 240, 245–6, 249–50, 259, 267, 315, 342.
CHEVALIER. Rép. d. sources hist. (1877–86) 2185.
CLARKE. Sacred lit. [1830–1] I. 111–15.
CLINTON. Fasti Rom. (1845–50) I. 165, 181; II. 410.
COTTA. Kirchen-hist. (1768–73) §312–7.
DARLING. Cyclop. bibl. 2931.
DODS, M. Introd. note. In: Ante-Nic. Lib. III. (1868) 49–52. Ed. Coxe. II. (1885) 83–8.
DONALDSON. Hist. Chr. Lit. 1864–6. III. 63–106.
DORNER. Person of Christ. I. (1864) 279–80.
DUPIN. Nouv. bibl. d. aut. eccl. (1698–) I. 144.
Ep. ad Heumann. In: Bibl. Lubecens. II. 217–40.
ERBES. In: Jahrb. f. prot. Theol. (1879) 483. [Against the Ad Autol.]
FABRICIUS. Bibl. gr. (1712) III. 213; V. 91–4, 99–102; XII. 654–5; IV. 881; VII. 101–6, 116–9.
— De verit. rel. Christ. (1725) 55–7.
FARRAR. Interpretation. (1886) 171.
FLEURY. Hist. eccl. (1691–) I. 534–9.
FREPPEL. Apolog. chrét. au deux. siècle.
GLEY and BRUNET. In: Biog. Univ. Michaud. 1842–65, XLI. 293.
GRABE. 1700. S. u. eds.
GRABENER, GOTTLIEB. Dissertatio de Theophilo, episcopo Antiocheno. Dresd. 1744. 4º.
GRÄSSE, J. G. TH. Lehrbuch e. litterargesch. Dresd. 1838. I. 944.
HAGENBACH. Hist. of Doct. I. (1850) 59, etc.
— Kirchenges. (1885) I. 275–6.

HALLOIX. Eccl. orient. scr. (1636) II. 735–65. (= Acta ss. Bolland. (1814) Oct. VI. 180–6.)

HARLES. Introd. II. 2, 206.

HARNACK. Zeit. d. Ignatius. (1878) 42–.

— In: Gebhardt u. H. Texte u. Untersuchungen. I. II. 282–298; IV. (1883) 97–175.

— In: Theol. Litzng. VIII. (1883) 487–9.

— Dogmenges. I. (1886) 285.

HASE. Kirchenges. (1885–.) I. 251–2.

HAUCK. In: Herzog. Real.-Enc. (1877–) XV. 542–4.

— Zur Theophilusfrage. In: Ztschr. f. kirchl. Wiss. u. Leben. (1884) 561–8. [Commentary. 200 A.D. at earliest.]

HENGSTENBERG. Offenb. Joh. (1861) 408.

HERGENROETHER. Kirchenges. (1879–80) I. 104–6; III. 41–2.

HEUMANN, C. A. In his: Poecile. I. 505; III. 203–.

HIERONYMUS. De vir. ill. 25.

HOLTZMANN. Einl. in d. N. T. (1886) 130–1, etc.

HUBER. Philos. d. K.–V. (1859) 23–4.

HUET. Origeniana. III. II. i, §1.

ITTIG. Hist. eccl. (1709) II. 29–34, 229.

JEREMIE. Hist. Church. (1852) 85–6.

JÖCHER. Allgem. Gelehrt. Lex. (1750–51.)

JÖRTIN, J. Theophilus to Autol. In his: Remarks on Eccl. Hist. (London, 1752. 8º.) II. 169–206.

KORTHOLT. S. u. Justin M.

KURTZ. Kirchenges. (1885–) I. 114.

LANGE, S. G. Gesch. d. Dogmen. I. 261–.

LARDNER. Credibility. Works. (1881) II. 203–15.

LELONG. Bibl. sac. II. 986.

LE NOURRY. Appar. bibl. patr. (1703) I. 497–522.

LICHTENBERGER. Encycl. (1877–82) XII. 100.

LUMPER. . Hist. ss. patr. (1784) III. 127–87.

LUTHARDT. St. John the Author of the Fourth Gospel. (1875) 43–.

M'CLINTOCK and S. Cycl. (1874–) X. 335.

MÖHLER. Patrol. (1840) I.

MOSHEIM. Eccles. Hist.

MUENSCHER. Dogmenges. (1817–8) I. 141–2, etc.

NEALE. Eastern Ch. Antioch. (1873) 25–9.

NEANDER. Hist. of dogmas. (1858) 143, 173, 188. [v. 1.]

— Church Hist. (1872) I. 559, 674, et pass.

NIRSCHL. Patrol. (1881–) I. 171–77.

NITZSCH. Dogmengesch. I. (1870) 120, etc.

NODIER. Bib. sacr. (1826) 153.

NOLTE. Conjecturae et emend. In: Migne. Patrol. gr. VI. (1857) 1759–62.

NORTON. Genuineness of Gosp. I. (1846) 136–7, etc.

OBERTHÜR, F. 1778. S. u. Tatian.

OELRICHS, J. G. A. De Theophilo ejusque ingenio. In his: Comment. de rat. verbi cum patre. (Gotting. 1787. 4º.) 30–.

ORSI. Ist. eccl. (1746–) II. 262–73; (1749–) II. 375–91.

OTTO, J. C. TH. In: Ztschr. f. hist. Theol. (1859) IV.

PAUL, LUDW. Zu Theophilus Antiochenos. In: Jahrb. f. class. Philol. 113 Bd. (1876) p. 114–116.

PEARSON. Vind. Ignat. (1672) I. p. 4, 5.

PERMANEDER. Bibl. patrist. (184–) I. 416; II. 191–206.

PRESSENSÉ. Hist. des trois prem. sièc. II. 395; tr. Engl. Heresy. (N.Y.) 251–3.

PRILESZKY, JOH. BAPT. Acta et scripta S. Theophili Ant. et M. Minutii Felicis. Viennae et Tyrnaviae 1764. 8º; Tyrnaviae, 1766. 8º.

RENAN. Marc. Aur. 386–.

REUSCH. In: Wetzer u. W. Kirch-Lex. (1847–54) X. 891–2.

REUSS. Gesch. N. T. (1874) II. 19. Tr. Eng. (1884) 302. [v. 2.]

RITTER. Chr. philos. (1841) I. 322–328.

ROESSLER. Bibl. d. K.–V. I. (1776) 218–252.

ROSENMÜLLER. Hist. interp. I. (1795) 198–203.

SANDAY, W. A commentary on the Gospels attributed to Theophilus of Antioch. In: Studia Biblica (Oxford, 1885) 89–101.

SCHAFF. Hist. . . Church. II. (1886) 732–5.

SCHMID. Patrol. (1879); (1886) 42.

SCHRAM. Anal. ss. patr. (1780–) I. 637–709.

SCHROECKH. Kirchenges. (1772–) III. 138–44.

SCULTETUS. Medull. theol. patr. 97–.

SEILER, G. F. S. u. Tatian.

SIMON. Hist. crit. N. T. (Rott. 1693) 4–8.

SMITH, P. In: Smith. Gr. and Rom. Biog. (1859) III. 1084–5.

SOUCIET, ÉTIEN. In: Mém. de Trévoux (1708) 603–21 (695–?) (= his: Rec. de dissert. (1715. 4º.) I.

TENTZELIUS. Exercit. select. Lips. 1692. 4º.

TRITHEMIUS. Scr. eccl. 15.

TILLEMONT. Mémoires. (1698) III. 49–53, 611–3.

TZSCHIRNER. Fall d. Heidenthums. p. 217–.

UEBERWEG. Hist. philos. (1876) 294–8.

WAITE. Hist. Chr. Rel. (1881) pass.

WALCH. Bibl. patrist. (1834) 34–5, 370–1.

WALPURGER, JOHANN GOTTLIEB. Theophilus Antiochenus boni pastoris in ecclesia typus. Chemnioü, 1735. 4º.

WESTCOTT. Canon. (1875) 225–6, 585.

— Bible in the Church. (1877) 131.

WURM. S. u. Justin M.

YONGE. Pupils of St. John. (1878) 210–3.

ZAHN, TH. Der Evangelien-commentar des Theophilus von Antiochen. Erlangen, 1883. 8º. In: Forschungen z. Gesch. d. NTlichen Kanons. II.; also a reply to Harnack ["Leidenschaftl. Replik." Kurtz] in: Forsch. III. (1884) 198–277.

— In: Ztschr. f. kirchl. wiss. u. Leben. (1884) 626–8.

ZELLER. Apostelgesch. (1854) 69.

Note. Authenticity of the Commentary. Zahn maintains the Comment. to be authentic, and the work of Theoph. Harnack denies both authenticity and genuineness, dating it not earlier than the second half of the fifth century, and Kurtz agrees. Hauck maintains the authenticity, but denies that it can be the work of Theophilus.

IV. ATHENAGORAS.

I. *Editions.*

NANNIUS, PETR. (De res.) Gr. lat. Lovan. 1541. 4º; Par. 1541. 4º; repr. in: Micropresbyticon. Basil, 1550. p. 471–94; and in: Orthodoxographi. Basil, 1555. fº. p. 351–376.

(Legatio.) Gr. Basil. 1551. [? ?]

GESNER, CONR. (Legatio.) Gr. lat. Tiguri, 1557. 8º. Basil, 1558.

STEPHANUS, H. Gr. lat. Par. 1557. 8º. [Trans. by Conr. Gesner]; also in: θεολογων διαφορων συγγραμματα παλαια και ορθοδοξα. Tiguri, 1559. fº.

(De res.) Lugd. Bat. Plantin. 1588. 8º.

DUCAEUS, FRONTO. In his: Auct. bibl. patr. Paris, 1624. fº.

MORELL.? Gr. lat. Par. 1636. fº; also: Colon. 1686. fº.

FELL, JOH. Oxon. 1682. 8º.

RECHENBERGIUS, A. Gr. lat. Lips. 1684–5. 2 v. 8º.

DECHAIR, ED. Gr. lat. Oxon. 1706. 8º.

MARANUS. Gr. lat. Par. 1742. fº. [Benedictin.]

GALLANDUS. Gr. lat. In his: Bibl. patr. Venet. fº. II. (1766) 3–.

LINDNER, J. G. (Legatio.) Gr. Longosalissae, 1774. 8º.

OBERTHÜR, FR. Gr. lat. Wirceb. 1779. 8º.

PAUL, L. (Legat.) Gr. lat. Halle, 1856. 8º.

MIGNE. Gr. lat. Patrol. gr. VI. (1857) 889–1024. [Maranus.]

OTTO. Gr. lat. Jena, 1857. 8º.

MARCH, F. A. Gr. N.Y. 1876. 12º. [March, not Owen. Otto's text. Notes by W. B. Owen.]

II. *Translations.*

Latin.

FICINUS, MARSILIUS. (Res.) *Par.* 1498. 4⁰. [Lat. tr. of Geo. Valla.]

LANGUS. *Basil.* 1565.

PETRUS, SUFFRIDUS. (Legat.) *Colon.* 1567. 8⁰.

ROUS. Mella patr. 1650. 8⁰. p. 134–148.

English.

PORDER, RICHARD. *Lond.* 1573. 8⁰.

HUMPHREYS, DAV. *Lond.* 1714. 8⁰.

PRATTEN, B. P. In: Ante-Nic. Lib. III. (1868) 375–456. Ed. Coxe. II. (1885) 129–62.

French.

FLAMIGNON, (?) GAY GAUSSART. (Legat.) *Par.* 1574. 8⁰.

FERRIER, ARNAUD DE. *Bordeaux*, 1577. 4⁰.

RENIER, L. (Res.) *Breslau*, 1753. 8⁰.

GENOUDE [? ?] In: Pères de l'égl. *Par.* 1837–43. 8⁰.

German.

ZIEGLER. In: Werke d. K.–V. II. (*Kempten*, 1830.)

BIERINGER, A. *Kempten*, 1875. 16⁰. [The Reithmayer-Thalhofer Bibl.]

Italian.

FALETI, GIROLAMO. *Venet.* 1556. 4⁰; also: *Venet.* [1735] 4⁰.

GALLICCIOLI, GIOV. BATTISTA. *Venez.* 1801. 8⁰.

GOZZI, G. *Ven.* 1806. 8⁰.

Russian.

KRASSOWSKJ, J. J. (In: Proceedings of the Acad. of Sciences.)

Note. The work entitled, "Du vray et parfait Amour." *Par.* 1599. 12⁰; do. 1612. 12⁰, is Apocryphal (Henri). "Composée par Fumée de Genillé." Compare Huet. Origine des romans. *Par.* 1693. 12⁰. p. 68–; Dunlop. Hist. of Fiction (1845) 44–5].

III. *Literature.*

ALZOG. Patrol. (1876) 86–91.

ANGER. Synops. Ev. Proleg. xxxii.

BARBEYRACIUS, J. Praef. vers. gall. operis Pufendorfiani De Jure naturae et gentium. 41–.

BARONIUS. Ann. (1589) 179, 39–49. Cf. Pagi. Crit. 1689) 8–10.

BASNAGE. Ann. Polit. Eccl. 176.

— Hist. de l'Égl. 1105–.

BAUMGARTEN–CRUSIUS. Dogmenges. (1832) 173–4. [v. 1.]

BAUR. Dogmengesch. I. (1865) 257–8, 439–41, 511–2, 713–4.

BAYLE. Dict. crit. (1741) I. 369–72.

ΒΑΦΕΙΔΗΣ. Ἐκκλ. ἱστ. I. (1884) 152–3.

BELLARMIN–LABBE. Scr. eccl. (1728) 35.

BERGER, S. In: Lichtenberger. Encycl. (1877–82) I. 688.

BERTHOLDT. Dogmenges. (1822–3) I. 57, etc.

Bibl. des Romans. 1775. (Aug.)

BLACKBURN. Hist. of Church. (1879) 50. [4 ll.]

BRUCKER. Hist. crit. philos. (1766) III. 401–7.

BURTON. Divinity of Christ. (1829) 62–3.

— Trinity. (1831) 28–33.

BUSSE. Chr. Lit. (1828–9) I. 14.

CAILLAU. Introd. in ss. Patr. (1825) 52–4.

CAVE. Scr. eccl. hist. lit. (1740–3) I. 79–81.

CEILLIER. Apol. de la morale des pères de l'egl. ch. I.

— Hist. gén. d. aut. sacr. II. (1730) 112–23 ; I. (1858) 481–7.

CHARTERIS. Canonicity. (1880) 131–2, 146, 162, 181–2, 202, 219, 228, 235, 259, 267, 342.

CHEVALIER. Rép. d. sources hist. (1877–86) 184.

CLARISSE, THEODOR ADOLPH. Commentatio . . . de Athenagorae vita, scriptis et doctrina. *Ludg. Bat.* 1820. 4⁰. [From: Ann. acad. *Lugd. Bat.* (1818–19)].

CLARKE. Sacred lit. (1830–1) I. 108–11.

CLÉMENT. Bibl. curieuse.

CLINTON. Fasti Rom. (1845–50) I. 161; II. 409.

COTTA. Kirchengesch. §305–8.

CREDNER. Beiträge. I.

CUNNINGHAM. Churches of Asia. (1880) pass.

DARLING. Cyclop. bibl. (1854) 126–7.

DODWELL. Diss. de tempore atque inscriptione legationis Ath. In his: Dissertatt. Cyprianicae. (*Ox.* 1684. 8⁰.) XI. § 37–.

— Diss. in Iren. (1689) App. 488–.

DONALDSON. Hist. Chr. Lit. 1864–6. III. 107–78.

DORNER. Person of Christ. I. (1864) 283–5.

DUPIN. Nouv. bibl. d. aut. eccl. (1698–) I. 141.

Encycl. Brit. (9th ed.) II. 831–2.

ENGELHARDT. Dogmenges. I. (1839) 224, etc.

EPIPHANIUS. Haeres. 64. c. 21.

FABRICIUS. Bibl. gr. (1712) V. 85–91, 97–102. (2ᵃ. VII. 95–101, 116–9.)

— De verit. rel. chr. (1725) 51–4.

FLEURY. Hist. eccl. (1691–) I. 440–6.

FÖRSTER, RICH. Ueber d. ält. Herabilder nebst e. Excurs über d. Glaubwürdigkeit d. kunstgeschichtlichen Angaben d. Athenagoras. Progr. *Breslau*, 1868. 4⁰.

GIESELER. Church Hist. (1868–) I. 146.

GOURCY, DE. Analyse étendue de l'Apol. d'Athenagore. In: Anciens Apologistis de la religion chrét. (*Paris*, 1785. 8⁰.)

GUERICKE. De schola quae Alex. floruit catechet. *Halle*, 1824.

HAGENBACH. Hist. of Doct. I. (1850) 59, etc.

HARNACK. Dogmenges. I. (1886) 387–8.

— In: Herzog. Real.-Enc. (1877–) 1, 748–50. (Abr. in: Schaff. Herz. III. 163–4.)

— In: Gebhardt u. H. Texte u. s. w. I. 176–.

HASE. Kirchenges. (1885–) I. 251, 353.

HAUPT, M. Varia. (Athen. leg. 19). In: Hermes IV. (1870); also in his: Opuscula. III. p. 474.

HEFELE. Beiträge. (*Tüb.* 1864.) I. 60–86.

HENKE. Gesch. d. Chr. Kir. 4 Ausg. I. 128.

HERGENROETHER. Kirchenges. (1879–80) I. 89, 104–6; III. 37–8, 41–2.

HILSCHER and STRAUSS. Schola Alex. (1776) 24–6.

HOLTZMANN. Einl. in d. N. T. (1886) 130.

HOVEN, I. DAN. VAN. Disputatio de vera aetate legationis Athenagorae pro Christianis. *Lingae*, 1752. 4⁰.

— Disputatio de inscr. et vera aetate Πρεσβείας Athenagorae pro Christianis. *Lips.* 1754. 4⁰.

— Disquis. de inscriptione et aetate libelli Athenagorae pro Christianis. In: Symbolarum liter. ad incrementum scientiarum omne genus Collect. alt. (*Hal.* 1754. 8⁰.) p. 163–204.

HUBER. Philos. d. K.–V. (1859) 24–6.

ITTIG. Hist. eccl. (1709) II. 34–7, 227–8.

JACKSON. Ap. fath. (1879) 192–203.

KAISER, H. E. De cod. ms. Ath. Laubanensi disseruit eiusque variantes lect. quae vocantur, enotavit. *Brieg.*, 1833. 4⁰.

KEIL. In: Flatt's Magaz. f. Dogm. u. Moral. (1798) 45–.

KIRCHHOFER. Quellensamml.

KORTHOLT, CH. Comment. in Athen., Theoph. et Tatianum. In: Justini opera. *Colon.* 1685 (6). f⁰.

KUHN. Trinitätslehre. (Dogmatik. II.)

KURTZ. Kirchenges. (1885–) I. 114.

LA CROZE, M. V. Epist. ad. J. C. Wolfium de fabula erotica, quae sub Athenagorae nomine prodiit. In: Fabricii Bibl. Gr. T. VI. p. 800–.

LAFORÈT, N. J. In: Rev. cathol. (*Lond.* 1871) B. VI. 198–215.

LANDON. Eccl. Dict. I. 602–.
LANGE, S. G. Ueber Ath. in wie fern er d. Platon. Philos. m. d. Christenth. vereinigte, etc. In his: Ausführl. Gesch. d. Dogmen, etc. (*Lpz.* 1796. 8º.) 190–.
LARDNER. Credibility. I. II. (*Lond.* 1748. 8º.) 404–420; Works. (1831) II. 193–201.
L'AULNAYE, DE. In: Biog. Univ. (Michaud) (1842–65) II. 353–4.
LE MOYNE. Varia sacra. ii. 171.
LESS, GF. In his: Beweis der Wahrh. d. christl. Relig. (*Brünn*, 1776. 8º.) 54–.
LEYSER, ANDREAS POLYCARP. Dissert. de Athenagora, Atheniensi philosopho christiano. *Lips.* 1736. 4º.
LINDENER, J. G. Curae posteriores, etc. 1775. 8º.
LONGUERUE, LUD. DUFOUR DE. . . . Dissertatio de Athenagora. . . . ed. J. D. Winckero. *Lips.* 1750. 4º.
LUMPER. Hist. ss. patr. (1784) III. 50–104.
MACKENZIE, J. M. In: Smith. Gr. and Rom. Biog. (1859) I. 402–3.
M'CLINTOCK and S. Cycl. (1874–) I. 511.
MANSEL, S. In: Smith and Wace. Dict. I. 204–7.
MARANUS. Proleg. Justin Martyr.
MARCH, F. A. Life of A. and an essay on his style and diction. In his ed. (1876) 87–97.
MÄRKEL. De Athenagorae libro apologetico qui Πρεσβεία Περὶ Χριστιανῶν inscribitur. Gymn. Progr. *Königsberg.* i. d. N. 1857. 4º.
MAURICE. Eccl. Hist. (1854) 216.
MICHAELIS, J. G. Progr. de scholae catech. Alexandr. origine. *Hal.* 1739. 4º; also in: Symbol. litterar. Bremens. fasc. III; and in his: Dissertat. Vol. I.
MIRAEUS. Scr. eccl. 13.
MOMMSEN. In: Theol. Jahrbb. (1855) 250.
MOSHEIM, JO. LAUR. De vera aetate libelli ab Ath. pro. Christianis conscripti disquisitio. In: Bibl. hist.-phil.-theol. (*Bremae*, 1719.) II. 853–83.
— Observat. sacr. (1721) 193.
— Diss. ad hist. eccl. pertin. (1733) I. 279.
— Comm. I. 394.
MUENSCHER. Dogmenges. (1817–8) I. 141, etc.
NEALE. Eastern Ch. Alexandria. I. (1847) 18. (6 ll.)
NEANDER. Hist. of dogmas. (1858) 143–4, 173–4. [v. 1.]
— Church Hist. (1872) I. 328, 522, 586, 673 et pass.
NIRSCHL. Patrol. (1881–) I. 164–71.
NITZSCH. Dogmengesch. I. (1870) 119–20, etc.
NODIER. Bib. sacr. (1826) 151–2.
NOLTE. Conjecturae et emend. In: Migne. Patrol. gr. VI. (1857) 1743–60.
— In: Scheiner's Ztschr. (1860) 405–21.
NONNOTE. Les philosophes. (1789).
Nouv. Biog. Gen. (Hoefer) III. (1852) 506–7.
OBERTHÜR, F. 1778. S. u. Tatian.
Obs. et emendatt in Athenagoram. In: "Historia crit. R. L. T. IX."
ORSI. Ist. eccl. (1746–) II. 247–55; (1749–) II. 354–65.
OTTO. In: Ztschr. f. d. hist. Theol. (1856) 637–.
OUDIN. (1722) I. 203–6.
PERMANEDER. Bibl. patrist. (1841–3) I. 416; II. 175–91.
PETRI, G. E. In: Ersch u. Gruber. I. VI. (1821) 176–7.
PHILIPPUS, SID. In: Nicephorus Callistus.
PHOTIUS. Cod. 224, 234.
PRATTEN, B. P. Introd. note. In: Ante-Nic. Lib. III. (1868) 371–4. Ed. Coxe. II. (1885) 123–7.
PRESSENSÉ. Martyrs. (1879) 125–7.
— Heresy. (*N. Y.*) 250–1.
RAU, J. J. S. u. Justin.
RENAN. Marc-Aurèle. 382–386,
REUSS. Gesch. N. T. (1874) II. 17; Tr. Eng. (1884) 300. [v. 2.]
RITTER. Chr. philos. (1841) I. 308–322.
ROSENMÜLLER. Hist. interp. I. (1795) 193–8.

ROESSLER. Bibl. d. K.–V. I. (1776) 182–217.
SANDAY. Gosp. in 2 cent. (1876) 248–51, 308.
SCHAFF. Hist. . . Church. II. (1886) 730–2.
SCHARPFF. In: Wetzer u. W. Kirch-Lex. (1847–54) I. 498–9.
SCHMID. Patrol. (1879) 41–2.
SCHOLTEN. Die ält. Zeugnisse.
SCHRAM. Anal. ss. patr. (1780–) I. 564–637.
SCHROECKH. Kirchenges. (1772–) III. 119–32.
SCHWARZ, J. C. De Ath. loco quodam (Leg. I.) explicato et restituto. In: Miscell. Lips. VIII. 364–.
SEILER, G. F. S. u. Tatian.
SEMLER. Einl. zu Baumgartens Unters. theol. Streitigk. II. 70–.
STRUVE, C. L. Krit. Bemerk. über e. Stellen griech. Schriftsteller. (Progr. II. de locis Athenagorae, Clementis Alexandrini, Apollonii Lexic. Hom.) *Königsberg*, 1815. 8º; also in his: Opuscula selecta. II. (*Lipsiae*, 1854.)
Supernatural Religion. (1875–) II. 191–200, 379–80; III. 24.
TENTZEL, G. E. Exercitatio de Just. Mart., Athenagora, etc. S. u. Just. Mart.
TILLEMONT. Mémoires. II. (1694) 321–3, 631–2.
TISCHENDORF. Wann wurden. u. s. w.
TZSCHIRNER. Gesch. d. Apol. I. 244–.
UEBERWEG. Hist. philos. (1876) 294–7.
VOIGTLÄNDER. In: Beweis d. Glaubens. (1872).
VOLKMAR. Der Ursprung.
WAITE. Hist. Chr. Rel. (1881) 396 et pass.
WALCH. Bibl. patrist. (1834) 29–30, 370, etc.
WESTCOTT. Canon. (1875) 226–7.
WETTE, DE. Einl. N. T. 1852.
WOLFF, G. Krit. Bemerk. (Athenagor. suppl. pro Christ. c. 1, 6, 11, 12, 23, 27.) In: Philologus XIV. (1860) 527–528.
WURM. S. u. Justin M.
Ztschr. f. Hist. Theol. 1856. IV.

V. CLEMENT OF ALEXANDRIA.

I. *Editions.*

(*Works.*)

VICTORIUS, PET. Gr. *Florent.* 1550. fº.
HERVET. Gr. lat. *Basil.* 1556. fº; *Par.* 1572; 1590. fº.
SYLBURGIUS, FRID. Gr. *Heidelb.* 1592. fº.
HEINSIUS, DAN. Gr. lat. *Lugd. Bat.* 1616. fº. Repr. ["excellently"] *Par.* 1629. fº; ["poorly"] *Par.* 1641. fº; *Colon.*, 1688. fº.
DUCAEUS, FR. Gr. lat. *Par.* 1629. fº; *Par.* 1641. fº.
ITTIG, TH. (Op. suppl.) Gr. lat. *Lips.* 1700. 8º.
POTTERUS, J. Gr. lat. *Oxon.* 1715. 2 v. fº; enlarged. *Venet.* 1757. 2 v. fº.
OBERTHÜR. Gr. lat. *Herbipoli* (*Wirceb.*) 1778–9. 3 v. 8º. In his: Patr. gr. [Potter's text.]
KLOTZ, R. S. *Lips.* 1831–34. 4 v. 12º. ["Singularly inaccurate."]
MIGNE. Gr. lat. Patrol. gr. VIII. (1857) 49–1382; IX. (1857) 9–776.
DINDORF. *Oxon.* 1869. 4 v. 8º. [Disappointing. Hastily put together."]

(*Quis dives.*)

GHISLERUS. Gr. lat. In his: Comment. in Jerem. *Lugd.* 1623. fº. III. p. 262–. [Under the name of Origen. Lat. by J. M. Cariophilus.]
CONDEFISIUS, FR. Gr. lat. In his: Auct. nov. Bibl. patr. *Par.* 1672. fº. I. 163–.
FELL, J. *Oxon.* 1683. 12º.
SEGAAR, CAR. Gr. lat. *Traject. ad Rh.* 1816. 8º; also in: Opusc. patr. sel. *Berol.* 1820. 8º. I.

LINDNER. *Lipsiae*, 1861. 8⁰.
OLSHAUSEN, H. Gr. lat. *Regiomon.* 1831. 8⁰. [' In usum scholarum.' Segaar's text nearly.]

(Hymns.)

BRUXELLUS, HIER. ? In: S. Gregorii Nazianzeni Carmena sel. etc. *Romae*, 1590. 8⁰.
In: Metaphrastae iambici Senarii de salutis nostrae mysteriis. *Paris*, 1606. 8⁰.
In: Poetae. gr. christiani. *Par.* 1609. 8⁰.
In: Poetae gr. vett. Gr. lat. *Colon. Allorb.* II. 751–.
BUTLER. In his: Musuei carmen in Platonem. *Cantab. et Lond.* 1797. 8⁰. App.
PIPER, FERD. Gr. lat. *Gotting.* 1835. 8⁰.

(Supplementum Clementinum.)

The increasing collection of fragments which passes under this name has the following history:—

FELL, JO. In ed. of: Quis dives salvus. (1683).
ITTIG. *Lipz.* 1700.
LeNOURRY. In: Appar. (1703) I. 1334–5.
POTTER. (1715) p. 1011–25.
ZAHN. Forsch. z. Gesch. d. N. T. Kanons. III. Erlangen, 1884. 8⁰. [Full collection, and discussion.]
ARMELLINI, TORQUATUS. Lat.? *Romae*, 1878. (?) 8⁰. (12 p.).
In various relations there have also been published sundry

(Fragments.)

FABRICIUS. Gr. lat. In his: Hippolyti opera. (*Hamb.* 1716–18) II. 66–74.
— (Excerpta ex Theod.) Gr. lat. In his: Bibl. gr. 4⁰. V. (1718) 134–. [Lat. tr. and notes of Combefis.]
GALLANDUS. Gr. lat. In his: Bibl. patr. *Venet.* f⁰. II. (1788) 153–.
ROUTH. (Fragment Hypot.) Rel. sacr. (1846–8) I. 385–7 [9].
BUNSEN. (Hypot.) In: Analect. Antenic. (1854) 157–66; (Pref.) 167–323, (Text) 324–90 (Latin fragments).

III. *Translations.*

Latin.

HERVETUS, GENT. *Florent.* 1551. f⁰ [The Stromata *not* tr. by Massonus Strozza]; also: *Basil.* 1556. f⁰; *Paris*, 1566; 8⁰; *Paris*, 1572. f⁰; *Paris*, 1590. f⁰.
ROUS, F. Mella patrum. *Lond.* 1650. 8⁰. p. 149–292.
CAILLAU et GUILLON. (Irenaeus, Minucius F., Hippolytus and.) *Par.* 1829. 8⁰.

English.

WILSON, W. In: Ante-Nic. Lib. IV. (1868) 15–470; XII. (1869) 1–514; XXII. (1871) 185–217; XXIV. (1872) 137–81. Ed. Coxe. II. (1885) 171–604. [The hymns translated by W. L. Alexander.]

French.

COUSIN, D. (Exh. ad gent.) *Par.* 1684. 12⁰.
FONTAINE, NIC. *Par.* 1696. 8⁰.
GENOUDE. In: Pères de l'égl. *Par.* 1838. 8⁰.

German.

ARNOLD, GOTTFR. (Excerpta Theod.) In his: Kirchen. u. Ketzerhist. *Leipz.* 1729. 4⁰.
HOPFENMÜLLER and WIMMER. *Kempten*, 1875–6. 16⁰. [The Reithmayer-Thalhofer Bibl.]

III. *Literature.*

Account of Clement of Alexandria. In: Ecl. R. LXII. (1835) 307–.
ALEXANDER, NATALIS. Hist. eccl. (1778) III. 371–6.
ALZOG. Patrol. (1876) 122–35.

BAILLET, A. Vies des saints. III.; Lat. tr. in: ed. Potter. 1767.
BARONIUS. Ann. (1589) 196, 22–7; 204, 11.
— Martyrol. VI. Maii. p. 777.
BAUMGARTEN–CRUSIUS. Dogmenges. (1832) 174–6. [v. 1.]
BAUR, F. C. Christliche Gnosis. *Tüb.* (1835) 8⁰. 502–40.
— Kirchenges. 3 e. J. (1863) 248–57.
— Dogmengesch. I. (1865) 218–29, etc.
ΒΑΦΕΙΔΗΣ. Ἐκκλ. ἱστ. I. (1884) 156–7.
BELLARMIN–LABBE. (1728) 41.
BENEDICT XIV. Nova martyrol. Rev. ed. § 19–36. In: Opera. *Venet.* 1767. f⁰; also in: Opera (1842) VI. p. 119. [Letter to John V., an omission of Cl. from the Martyrology.]
BERG, FRANZ. De Clemente Alexandrino ejusque morali doctrina. *Wirceb.* 1779. 8⁰.
BERNAYS, J. Zu Aristoteles und Clemens. In: Symbola philol. Bonn. in honorem Frid. Ritschelii collecta. I. (1864) 301–312.
— In Bunsen. Anal. Ant.-Nic. I.
BERNHOLDUS, JO. BALTH. Hypomnemata de Clemente utriusque ecclesiae ornamente. *Altorf*, 1725. 4⁰.
BERTHOLDT. Dogmenges. (1822–3) I. 56, etc.
Bibl. hist. phil. theol. (1719) II. 191–8.
BIELCKE, J. A. F. De Clemente Alexandrino ejusque erroribus. *Jenae*, 1739.
BIGG, C. Christian Platonists of Alexandria. *Oxf.* and *N.Y.* (1886) 8⁰. 36–114. [Bampton Lectures. 1886.]
Bishop of Lincoln's account of the writings of C. In: Theol. Q. XIX. (1836) 100–32.
BLACKBURN. Hist. of Church. (1879) 50–1.
BOEHRINGER. Kirchenges. (1873–) I. v.
BRUCKER. Hist. crit. phil. (1766–7) III. 414–27; VI. 540–2.
BUCHNER, GF. Christianus antiquus, penicillo Clementis Alex. ex Lib. I. Paedag. cap. VI. *Viteb.* 1687. 8⁰.
BUNSEN. Hippolytus. (1854) I. 236–45.
— Anal. Ante-Nic. I. 288–.
BURTON. Divinity of Christ. (1829) 111–180.
— Trinity. (1831) 54–9.
BUSSE. Chr. Lit. (1828–9) I. 20–1.
BYWATER, J. Critical notes on Cl. In: Journal of philol. IV. (1872) 203–218.
CAILLAU. Introd. in ss. Patr. (1825) 65–9.
CASPARI, C. P. In: Ztschr. f. Kirchl. Wiss. u. Leben. (1886) 352–375.
CAVE. De quibusdam Cl. A. dogmatibus. In his: Epistola apologetica adr. iniquas J. Clerici criminationes in epistolis crit. et nupe e editis. *Lond.* 1700. 8⁰.
— Scr. eccl. hist. lit. (174–) I. 88–91.
— Lives. (1840) I. 296–304.
CEILLIER. Hist. gén. d. aut. sac. II. (1730) 242–316; I. (1858) 563–606.
"CENSUR (Fiebig, Corp. diss. th. 1767)."
CHARPENTIER. In: Nouv. Biog. Gen. (Hoefer). X. (1863) 741–8.
CHARTERIS. Canonicity (1880) lxxxi–lxxxiii, 50–1, 74–5, 134, 146–7, 184, 202, 220, 229, 232, 235, 240, 246, 250, 252, 254, 259–60, 263, 267–8, 277–8, 289, 296, 307, 322, 328, 332, 342–3, 452.
CHEVALIER. Rép. d. sources hist. (1877–86) 463–4.
Christ. Anthologia graec. *Lips.* 1871. p. xviii, 37.
"Chronographia Cl. A. coetate cum Euseb. et Syncel." Migne. Patrol. gr. IX. (1857) 1485–96.
CLARKE. Sacred lit. (1830–1) I. 116–27.
Clemens Alex. a nonnullis pro antiquitate punctorum et accentuum heb. in testimonium vocatus, de iis ne vel per somnium cogitasse demonstratur. In: Bibl. Brem. II. 191.
Clement of Alexandria, Hymn to Christ. In: Cong. M. XXIV. (1841) 458–.

Clement of Alexandria. In: Chr. R. XVII.(1852) 321–; Kitto. XXIX. (1862) 317–.

CLERICUS, J. Vie de Cl. A. In: Bibl. Univ. X. 175–245. (Ger.) in: Lebensbeschreibungen einige K.–V. 30–.

CLINTON. Fasti Rom. (1845–50) I. 179, 195, 211, 213; II. 413.

COBET, C. G. Ad. Clem. Alex. In: Mnemosyne. XI. (1862) 334–336, 383–393.

— Διορθωτικὰ εἰς τὰ Κλήμεντος τοῦ Ἀλεξανδρέως. In: Λόγιος Ἑρμῆς. I. (1866) p. 166–197; I. 2. (1867) p. 201–287, 425–534.

COFFIN. Lives of fath. (1846) 347–55.

COGNAT, JOS. Clément d'Al. sa doctrine et sa polém. Paris, 1859. 8°. Cf. Chalambert, V. de. In: Le Correspondant (1859) B, XI. 244–65; Villemain, in: Jour. d. Savants (1859) 525–35, 729–39; (1860) 20–6.

V. CÖLLN. In: Ersch u. Gruber. I. XVIII. (1828) 4–13.

CONDOS, (Κόντος) C. S. Συμμικτὰ κριτικά (Κλήμ. Ἀλεξ. πρὸτρεπτ. I. 96. [σελ. 77 ποττ.]) In: Bullet. de corresp. Hell. II. (1878) p. 229–230.

CORNWALLIS, Miss. In her: Small books on great subjects. VII.

COTTA. Kirchen-Hist. § 298–304.

COWPER, B. H. In: Kitto. X. (1852) 129–.

CUNNINGHAM. Hist. theol. (1870) I. 146–54.

— Churches of Asia. (1880) pass.

D. D. [JOS. WASSIUS.] Obss. in auctorem Titanomachiae ap. Cl. Alex. laudatae. In: Miscellaneae Obss. IV. 1. 72–.

DÄHNE, A. F. De γνώσει Cl. Al. et de vestigiis philosophiae Neoplatonicae in ea obviis. Lipsiae, 1831. 8°.

— Ges. Darst. d. jüd-alex. Rel. Philos. (1834).

DALLAEUS, J. 258.

DARLING. Cyclop. bibl. (1854) 698.

DAVIDSON. Sacred Hermeneutics. Edinb. 1843. 8°.

— In: Smith. Gr. and Rom. Biog. (1859) I. 786–8.

Dict. scien. philos. (1875) 282.

DIETELMAIER, J. A. Vet. in schola alex. doctorum series. Altd. 1746.

Diss. critique sur un endroit de Cl. A. (Strom. II. p. 421 ed. Paris, 1641.) In: Mém. de Trevoux (1716) 1670–.

Diss. sur quelques endroits de Cl. A. In: Mém. de Trevoux (1717) 392–.

DOMMERICH, J. CPH. Progr. de λογω patrum (praecipue Just. M. et Cl. A.). Helmst. 1760. 4°.

DONALDSON, J. In: Encycl. Brit. (9th ed.) V. 819–21.

DORNER. Person of Christ. I. (1864) 182–3, 285–303, 461–2.

DULAURIER, ED. Examen d'un passage des Stromates de St. Clément d' Alex., relatif aux écritures égyptiennes. Paris, 1883. 8°.

DUPERRON. See Hébert-Duperron.

DUPIN. Nouv. bibl. d. aut. eccl. (1698–) I. 187–215.

ENGELHARDT. Animadv. ad nonnulla excerpt. ex Theodoto et doctr. orient. Cl. A. vulgo attrib. Erlangae, 1830. 4°.

— Dogmenges. I. (1839) 70–1, etc.

EPIPHANIUS. Adv. haer.

EUSEBIUS. Hist. Eccl. V. 11; VI. 6, 11, 13.

EYLERT, F. R. Cl. v. Al. als Philosoph und Dichter. Leipzig, 1832. 8°.

FABRICIUS. Bibl. gr. (1712–19) V. 102–33; IX. 409–10. (2ᵃ. VII. 119–49 = Migne. Patrol. gr. VII. 9–26; X. 710–11.)

— De verit. rel. chr. (1725) 58–61, 159–60.

FARRAR. Interpretation. (1886) 183–7.

FESSLER. In: Wetzer u. W. Kirch-Lex. (1847–54) II. 622–8.

FEUERLEIN, J. W. Program. de gratia Sp. S. operante, ad loc. Clem. A. Gött. 1754. 4°.

FLEURY. Hist. eccl. (1691–) I. 567–95.

FLÜGGE. Gesch. d. Theol. Wissenschaft. I. 177–, 343–.

FOERTSCHIUS, MICH. Diss. patrist. theol. de Cl. A. Paed. Strom., etc. In his: Decas dissertat. theolog. (Tubing. 1704. 4°.) 389–426.

FREPPEL. Clément d'Alexandrie. Paris, 1865. 8°; 1873. 8°. Cf. Tailhan, J., in: Etudes relig. hist. litt. (1866) C, X. 366–85; XI. 214–33.

FRIEDLÄNDER, L. Observ. miscellae. (Clemens Alex. Paedag. lib. II. 1. 3. p. 164 Pott, ed. Kl.) Regimonti, 1869–70. 4°.

FUNK. Titus Flavius Clemens Christ. nicht Bischof. In: Theol. Quartalschr. LXI. (1879) 531–536.

GALLAIS. In: Biog. Univ. (Michaud) (1842–65) VIII. 389–91.

GEEL, I. De loco Clementis Alex. Strom. VI. In: Rhein. Mus. N. F. III. (1845) 128–133.

GEORGIADES, B. (Γεωργιάδησ, B.) Τίς ὁ σωζόμενος πλούσιος κατὰ Κλήμεντα τὸν Ἀλεξανδρέα. In: Ἐκκλησιαστικὴ Ἀλήθεια. (1885) 385–396, 443–444.

GIESELER, J. C. L. Cl. A. et Origenis doct. de Corpore Christi expen. Göttingae, 1837.

— Church Hist. (1868–) I. 209–19.

GRABE. Cl. A. vindicated against W. Whiston. In his: Some Instances of the Defects and Omissions in Mr. Whiston's Collection of Testimonies, etc. (Lond., 1712.) p. 8–18.

GROOT, P. HOFSTEDE DE. See Hofstede de Groot, P.

GUERICKE. De Schola quas Alex. floruit catechetica. Halle, 1824–5. 8°.

— Handbuch d. K-gesch. (Halle, 1843.)

HAGENBACH. Hist. of Doct. I. (1850) 62–3, etc.

— Kirchenges. (1885) I. 196–9.

HARNACK. Dogmenges. I. (1886) 267–71, 286–9, 305–7, 501–12.

HASE. Kirchenges. (1885–) I. 256, 335, 353–4.

HAUPT, M. Analecta. (Schol. in Clement Alex. p. 115. 11 Kl. und p. 105, 16. p. 113, 26. p. 135, 9.) In: Hermes I. (1866) 38, 399–400; also in his: Opusc. III. 2. (1876) 332, 353–354.

HÉBERT–DUPERRON, V. Essai sur la polém. et la philos. de St. Cl. d'Al. Caen, 1855. 8°.

HERGENROETHER. Kirchenges. (1879–80) I. 104–6, 162–3; III. 41–2, 71.

HIERONYMᵁˢ. De vir. ill. 38. (Honor. August 1. 39.)

HILGENFELD. Ketzergesch. (1884) 40–3.

HILSCHER and STRAUSS. Schola Alex. (1776) 27.

HÖFLING. Die Lehre d. Cl. v. A. vom Opfer im Leben und Cultus d. Christen. 1842.

HOFSTEDE DE GROOT, PIETER. Disputatio de Clemente Alexandrino. Groningae, 1826. 8°.

HOLTZMANN. Einl. in d. N. T. (1886) 142, etc.

HOLZCLAU, TH. Diss. de Clemente et eius morali doctrina. Wirceb. 1779. 8°.

HUBER. Philos. d. K.–V. (1859) 130–149.

HYPERIUS, A. De ratione stud. theol. III. 1. 396.

ITTIG. Hist. eccl. (1709) II. 57–62, 230–6.

JACOBI. In: Herzog. Real.-Enc. (1877–) III. 269–77. (Abr. in: Schaff-Herz. I. 494.)

JEREMIE. Hist. Church. (1852) 88–90.

JORTIN, J. Remarks on Eccl. Hist. (Lond. 1751. 8°); I. 353; II. (Lond. 1752. 8°.) 378–401.

K: Obs. seu conjectanea in Clementis Alex. stratum librum. I. 105–.

KAYE, JOHN. Some account of the writings and opinions of Clement of Alexandria. Lond. 1835. 8°.

KILLEN. Ancient Church. (1859) 373–4.

KLING. Bedeutung d. Al. Cl. f. d. Entstehung d. chr. Theol. In: Stud. u. Krit. XIV. (1841) 857–908.

KLOTZ, R. Praef. in Clem. Opera. Lips. 1831–4. 12°. 4 v.; also in: Migne. Patrol. gr. VIII. (1857) 29–32.

KONTOGONES. Ἱστ. τῶν πατέρων. (1851).

KURTZ. Kirchenges. (1885–) I. 118–9.

LABBE. De scr. eccl. (1660) I. 230.

LÄMMER, HUGO. Clementis Alexandrini de ΛΟΓΩΙ doctrina. *Lips.* 1885. 8º.

LAMSON, A. In: Chr. Exam. XXIII. (　) 137-.

LARDNER. Credibility. Works. (1831) II. 220-59.

LE CLERC. Biblioth. universelle. X. 178-; tr. Ger. (1721) 22-; tr. Engl. *Lond.* 1698. 8º; also, 1751. 8º.

LELONG. Bibl. sacr. (1723) II. 677.

LE NOURRY. Appar. Bibl. Vet. Patr. (1703) I. 1104-; repr. in: Sprenger. Thes. patr. II. 481-505; III. 116-176.

LENTZEN, J. H. Erkennen und Glauben mit besonderer Berücksichtigung d. Cl. v. A. u. d. Anselmus v. Canterbury. *Bonn,* 1848. 8º.

LETRONNE. Examen du texte de Cl. d'Al. relatif aux divers modes d'écriture chez les Egyptiens. 8º.

LIPSIUS, R. Ueb. d. πρῶτα στοιχεῖα bei Cl. Alex. In: Rhein. Mus. f. Philologie. IV. (1836) 142-148.

LOWTH, G. Notae. In: Ed. Potter. *Oxon.* 1715.

LUMPER. Hist. ss. patrum. (1784) IV. 58-502; V. 1-604.

LUNDBLAD, SVENO. Dissert. theol. de Clémente Alex. *Upsal.* 1817. 8º.

LUTHARDT. St. John the Author of the Fourth Gospel. (1875) 44.

M'CLINTOCK and S. Cycl. (1874-) II. 375-6.

MANSEL. Gnost. Her. XVI.

MATTER. Essai histor. sur l'Ecole d'Alex. *Paris,* 1820. 8º

MAURICE. Eccl. Hist. (1854) 230-9, et pass.

MEIER, G. T. C, X. §14.

MEINEKE, AUG. Miscellanea. (Clemens Alex. Paed. II. 10.) In: Jahrbb. f. class. Philol. LXXXVII. (1863) 370.

MELLICENCIS. (Anon.) Scr. eccl. 5.

MERK, C. Clemens A. in s. Abhängigkeit v. d. griech. Philosophie. *Leipz.* 1879. 8º. Inaug diss.

MICHAELIS, J. G. Progr. de scholae catech. Alexandr. origine. *Hal. Magdeb.* 1739. 4º; repr. in: Symbol. litter. Bremens. III.

MÖHLER, J. A. Patrologia. (1840) 430-86.

— In: E. c. VIII. 116-29.

MÖLLER, J. H. Kosmologie in d. gr. K. (1860) 506-35.

MÜLLER. Idées dogmatiques de Clement d'Alex. *Strasb.* 1861.

MUENSCHER, W. Darstellung d. moralisch. Ideen. d. Cl. v. A. u. d. Tertullian. In: Henke's Magazin für Religionsphilosophie, etc. (*Helmst.* 1796. 8º.)

— Dogmenges. (1817-8) I. 145-7, etc.

NAUCK, A. Kritische Bemerkungen V. (Clemens Alex. Protr. p. 35; Paed. II. p. 185; Strom. VI. p. 745.) In: Bulletin de l'acad. impér. des sciences de St. Pétersbourg. XII. (1868) p. 526-528. = Mélanges Gréco-Romains. III. p. 72-76.

— VI. (Nachweisungen poet. Reminiscenzen d. Cl. Alex. u. Kritisches.) In: Bulletin, etc. XVII. (1872) p. 267-270. = Mél. Gr.-Rom. III. p. 332-336.

— VII. (Cl. Al. Protr. p. 12; Pott. p. 24.) In: Bulletin, etc. XXII. (1877) p. 100. = Mél. Gr.-Rom. IV. p. 232-233.

NEANDER. De fidei gnoseosque ideae ratione. *Heidelb.* 1811. 4º.

— Hist. of dogmas. (1858) 63-6, 68-9, 82-3, 144-5, 174, 188-90, 201-2, 214, 224, 233, 243. 254. [v. 1.]

— Church Hist. (1872) I. 278-82, 528-43, 691-3, etc.

NIRSCHL. Patrol. (1881-) 209-225.

NITZSCH. Dogmengesch. I. (1870) 203, etc.

NODIER. Bib. sacr. (1826) 156-7.

NONNOTE. Les philosophes. (1789).

NORTON. Genuineness of Gosp. I. (1846) 13, 105-8, etc.

ORNSBY, R. Clement of Alexandria, Hortatory Address. In: Month. XIX. (1873) 231-.

ORSI. Ist eccl. (1746-) II. 306-12, 360-71; (1749-) II. 441-9, 518-35.

PERMANEDER. Bibl. patrist. (1841-) I. 417-8; II. 319-416.

PHOTIUS. Cod. 109-111.

PREISCHE, H. De γνώσει Clementis Alex. Diss. inaug *Jenae,* 1871. 8º.

PRESSENSÉ, E. DE. In: Lichtenbergr. Encycl. (1877-82) III. 208-13.

— Hist. d. 3 prem. sièc. III. 311-320; IV. 203, 278; V. 291, 331; tr. Engl. Heresy (*N.Y.*) 255-95; Martyrs. (1879) 272-82, 540-66.

REDEPENNING. Origenes. *Bonn,* 1841. 8º. p. 83-183.

REINKENS, H. J. De Clemente presbytero Alex. *Vratislav.* 1851. 8º.

REUSS. Gesch. N. T. (1874) II. 20-1, 255; tr. Eng. (1884) 303-5, 534-5. [v. 2.]

REUTER, HERM. Clementis A. theol. moralis cap. select. particulae. Dissert. acad. *Vratislaviae,* 1851. 8º; 1854. 8º.

RITTER. Chr. philos. (1841) I. 421-464.

ROSENMÜLLER. Hist. interp. I. (1795) 209-30.

ROESSLER. Bibl. d. K.-V. II. (1776) 3-75.

RULE, W. H. Oriental Records. *Lond.* 186-9.

SANDAY. Gosp. in 2 cent. (1876) 56, 317, 327.

SCHAFF. Hist. . . Church. II. (1886) 781-5.

SCHLIEMANN. Clementinen. (1844) 258-9, etc.

SCHMID. Patrol. (1879) (1886) 49-50.

Scholia vet. in Cl. A. Protrepticum, etc. In: Migne. Patrol. gr. IX. (1857) 777-94.

SCHRAM. Anal. ss. patr. (1780-) II. 403-944.

SCHROECKH. Kirchenges. (1772) III. 251-89.

SCHÜRMANN, H. Die hellenische Bildung u. ihr Verhältniss zur christlichen nach d. Darstellung d. Clemens v. Alex. Gymn.-Progr. *Münster,* 1859. 4º.

SEMLER. Gesch. d. chr. Glaubensl. vor Baumgartens Unters. theol. Streitigk. *Halle,* 1763. 4º. II. 133-156.

SEVESTRE. Dict. patrol. (1851) I. 1101-15.

SEVIN, FR. Conjectures. ("Restitution d'un passage de Clement d'Alex." In: Mém. de l'Acad. des Inscr. III. Hist. p. 133-, ed. 8; II. Hist. p. 210-; tr. Ger. II. 163-.

SHEDD. Hist. of doct. 3d. ed (1865-) I. 130-1, 274-5; II. 31-3.

SINTENIS, C. Plutarch u. Clemens v. Alex. In: Hermes. I. (1866) 143-144.

SPEELMAN, EDM. In: Rev. cathol. (*Lond.* 1855) E, I. 321-33, 385-95, 449-62.

SPOERLEIN, JOH. Einige Grundsätze d. Klemens v. Al. üb. gr. Philos. u. chr. Wissenschaft. Progr. *Bamberg,* 1840.

STÄUDLIN. Grundsätze d. Clem. v. Alex. in Ansehung d. Weissagungen. In his: Beiträge z. Erläut. d. bibl. propheten. *Stuttg.* 1786. 251-.

— Sittenlehre Jesu. II. 127-144.

STÖCKL. Gesch. d. Philos. *Mainz.* (1870) 266-71.

Supernatural Religion. (1875-7) passim.

TAVERNI, R. S. Sopra il Παιδαγωγς di Tito Flavio Clemente Al. discorso. *Roma,* 1885. 4º.

THIENEMANN. Ueb. d. theol. d. Clem. v. Alex. In: Schuderoff. N. Jahrbb. L, II. 175.

THIERBACH. Erkl. d. auf. Schriftwesen d. alten Aegypter bezügl. Stelle in d. Teppichen d. Clemens Alex. *Erfurt,* 1846.

TILLEMONT. Mémoirs. III. (1695) 181-96, 650-4.

TOURNEMINE, R. J. In: Mém. de Trévoux. (1717) 389-92. (= Mém. d'un soc. cél. I. 205-10.)

TRIBBECHOVIUS, JOH. Dissert. hist. de vita et scriptis Clementis Alex. *Halae,* 1706. 4º. ["Contains nothing new." *Hoffmann.*]

— Diss. in Cl. Alex. eaque de philos. defin. *Hal.* 1706. 4º. [" Wichtiger als d. vor." *Hoffmann.*]

TRITHEMIUS. Scr. eccl. 24.

UEBERWEG. Hist. philos. (1876) 311-5.

VACHEROT. Hist. de l'école d'Alex.

Veterum testimonia. In: Migne. Patrol. gr. VIII. (1857) 33-50.

VINCENTIUS BELVAC. Spec. hist. XI. 126.
VITRY, E. In: Mém. de Trévoux. (1716) 1570–85. (= Mém. d'une soc. cél. I. 210–22).
— De T. Flav. Cl. viri consularis et martyris, tumulo. *Urbin.* 1727. 4°. [Not Cl. A. or Cl. R.]
WAITE. Hist. Chr. Rel. (1881) passim.
WALCH, J. G. Dissert. de Clemente Alex. ejusque erroribus. *Jenae*, 1737. 4°; repr. in his Miscel. sacra. II. 510–74.
— Bibl. patr. (1834) 33, 372–3, etc.
WESTCOTT. Canon. (1875) 339–40, 350–4.
— Bible in the church. (1877) 125–7.
— In: Smith and Wace. Dict. I. 559–67.
WILSON, W. Introd. note. In: Ante-Nic. Lib. IV. (1868) 9–14. Ed. Coxe. II. (1885) 163–9. [Add. notes. Ed. Coxe. 567-8, 604-5.]
WINTER, F. J. Du Lehre d. Alex. Clemens v. d. Quellen d. sittlichen Erkenntniss (Luthardt'sche Gratulationsschrift. p. 99–137). [1881?]
— Studien z. Gesch. d. chr. Ethik. I. Die Ethik d. Clemens v. Alex. *Leipzig*, 1882. 8°.
— Zur Ethik des Clemens von Alexandrien. In: Ztschr. f. kirchl. Wissensch. u. kirchl. Leben. I. 130–144.
WOLFF, G. Krit. Bemerkungen. (Clemens Alex. Protrept. 26a.) In: Philologus. XVI. (1860) 528.
WORDSWORTH. Church Hist. (1881) 251–68.
WÖRTER. Gnade u. Freiheit. I. 171–201.
Writings of Clement of Alexandria. In: Chr. Obs. LXIX. (1869) 134–.
ZAHN, TH. Forschungen zur Geschichte d. neutestamentlichen Kanons. III. Supplementum Clementinum. *Erlangen*, 1884. 8°. (iv, 329.) [Cf. rev. Neumann. Theol. Ltznz. 1885.]
ZELLER. Apostegesch. (1854) 70.
Ztschr. f. hist. theol. (1861) III.

VOLUME III.–IV.

I. TERTULLIAN.

I. *Editions.*

(*Works.*)

RHENANUS. *Basil, Tubin.*, 1521. f°; 1525; –1528(?); –1536; –1539. f°. [Improved edition.]
GAGNAEUS. *Par.* 1545. f°.
GELENIUS. *Basil.* 1550. f°; 1562. f°. *Par.* 1566. 2 v. 8°.
LA BARRE, R. L. DE. *Par.* 1580.
PAMELIUS, JAC. Op. *Antv.* 1579. f°; *Par.* 1583. f°. [With additions by Hoyus.] *Antv.* 1584. f°. [With additional collations by Jo. Mercerius.] *Heidelb.* 1596. f°; *Par.* 1598. f°; *Heidelb.* 1599. f°; *Heidelb.* 1601. f°; *Par.* 1608. f°; 1609. f° (1610 (?) f°; *Par.* 1616. f°; *Colon. Agrip.* 1617. f°; *Rothomagi*, 1622. f°.
JUNIUS, FRANC. Op. *Franequerae*, 1597. f°. [Founded on Pamelius. With Novatian.] 1607. f°.
WOWER, J. A. *Franc.* 1603. 8°; *Francf.* 1612.
LA CERDA, J. L. DE. *Par.* 1624–30. 2 v.; *Par.* 1641. f°.
RIGALTIUS, N. *Lutet. Par.* 1628 [9?] 8° (?); 1634. f°; 1641. f°; 1644; 1646; 1650; *Argent.* 1657. 8° (?); 1658. f°; 1675. f°; 1728. 8°; *Venet.* 1746. f°.
GEORGIUS, P. *Par.* 1646-50. 3 v. f°.
ROUS. In: Mella patr. *Lond.* 1650. 8°. 293–468.
BOECLERUS. *Argent.* 1657. 8°. [?]
MOREAU, C. *Par.* 1658. 3 v. f°.
PRIORIUS, PHIL. *Parisiis*, 1664. [Colophon 1663.] f°. [Following Rigaltius]; 1675. f°; 1695. f°.
Venet. 1701. f°.

VIVIEN, M. *Venet.* 1708. 6 v. 4°.
Venet. 1744. f°.
Venet. 1746. f°. [Rigaltius text.]
SEMLER, J. S. *Halae*, 1769–76. 6 v. 8°.
OBERTHÜR. *Wirceb.* 1780. [Vols. I. and II. of Opera omnia patr. lat.]
LEOPOLD. In: Gersdorf. Bibl. patr. lat. sel. *Lips.* 1839–41. parts IV–VII.
OEHLER, F. *Lips.* 1851–3. 3 v. 8°; ed. minor. *Lips.* 1854.
MIGNE. Patrol. Lat. (1866) I.; II.

(*Various.*)

(Apol., Ad Scap.) *Cantab.* 1686. 12°.
(De baptismo, aet poenit.) *Salisb.* 1755. 4°.
CURREY, G. (Cor. mil., de Spect., de Idol.) *Camb.* 1856. 8°.
ROUTH. (De Orat., De praescr., Adv. haer.) In: Scr. eccl. op. (1858) I. 95–172, 173–225.
MARCH, F. A. (Select works.) *N.Y.* 1876. 12°.

(*Apology.*)

Venet. Benalius, s. a. (1483?) f°; do. 1492.
Mediolini, Scinzingeller, 1493. f°.
Venet. 1494. [With Lactantius.]
Par. 1500. 4°. [With Lactantius.]
Venet. 1502. f°. [With Lactantius]; also *Venet.* 1502. f°; *Venet.* 1509. f°; *Par.* 1509. 4°; *Venet.* 1511. f°; *Paris*, 1513. 4°; *Florent, Junta*, 1513. 8°.
EGNATIUS. *Venetiis, Aldus*, 1515; do. 1535. 8°.
HERALDUS, DESID. *Par.* 1613. 4°. [With Minucius Felix.]
GIRY, L. Lat. fr. *Amst.* 1701. 8°. [?]
HAVERCAMPUS, SIGEB. *Lugd. Bat.* 1718. 8°.
WOODHAM, H. A. *Camb.* 1843. 8°; 1850. 8°.
HURTER, H. Opusc. ss. patr. XIX. *Innsb.* 1872. 16°.

(*Prescription against Hœretics.*)

QUINTINUS, J. *Par.* 1561. 4°.
Colon. 1599. 12°. [From Pamelius.]
Colon. Agrip. 1601. 12°.
Cracov. 1605.
Brux. 1675. 4°.
Salisbury, 1752. 8°.
Lat. it. *Assisi.* 1784. 8°.
HURTER, H. Opusc. ss. patr. IX. *Innsb.* 1880. 16°. [2d ed.]

(*On the Pallium.*)

JUNIUS. *Lugd. B.* 1595. 8°.
RICHERIUS, E. Lat. fr. *Par.* 1600. 8°.
MARCELLIUS, T. *Par.* 1614. 8°.
SALMASIUS, C. *Par.* 1622; *Lugd.* 1656. 8°.
Lugd. 1626. f°. [La Cerda's notes.]

(*Other.*)

GOTHOFRIDUS, JAC. *Aureliopoli*, 1625. 4°.
ORIUS. (De patientia.) *Matr.* 1644. f°.
WETSTENIUS. (De orthodoxa fide.) Gr. lat. *Basil.* 1674. 4°.
PAUCIROLI and MURATORI. (De Orat.) *Patau.* 1713. 4°.
WELCHMAN, E. (Adv. Praxeam.) *Cantab.* 1731. 8°.
HURTER, H. (In orat. dom.) Opusc. ss. patr. II. *Innsb.* 1874 [?] 16°.
— (De sacr.) In: Opusc. ss. patr. VII. *Innsb.* 16°.
— (De poen.) In: Opusc. ss. patr. V. *Innsb.* 16°.

RIVINUS, A. (Opera poët.) *Goth.* 1651. 8°.
DAUMIUS, CHR. (De Jona et Nin.) *Lips.* 1681. 8°.

II. *Translations.*

Dutch.

(Praescr.) *Antw.* 1675. 24°.
(Apol.) *Amst.* 1684. 8°.

English.

HOPER, JOHN. (2d book ad uxorem.) *Lond.* 1550. 8⁰.

B[ROWN], H. (Apol.) *Lond.* 1655. 4⁰.

REEVES, W. (Apol.) *Lond.* 1709. 8⁰; *Lond.* 1716. 2 v. 8⁰. 1848. 12⁰.

BETTY, J. (Praescr.) *Oxf.* 1722. 8⁰. ["Incomplete." *Clarke.*]

DALRYMPLE, D. (Ad Scap.) *Edinb.* 1780–2. [1790?]

CHEVALLIER. *Camb.* 1833. 8⁰. 1851.

DODSON, C. In: Library of fathers. X. (1842; 1854).

HOLMES and THELWALL. In: Ante-Nic. Lib. VII. (1868); XI. (1869); XV. (1874); XVIII. (1870). Ed. Coxe. III. (1885) 17–696, 707–17; IV. (1885) 3–125.

French.

MACERÉ, AUB. DE. (Praescr.) *Par.* 1562.

— (Corona milit.) *Par.* 1563.

DANEAU, L. *Par.* 1565. 8⁰; *Gen.* 1580.

RICHEAUME. *Bordeaux*, 1594. 8⁰.

REMONDUS, F. (Corona milit.) *Par.* 1594. 8⁰. [?]

RICHERIUS, E. (De spect.) In his: Opera. *Par.* 1600.

LABROSSE. *Par.* 1612. 8⁰; 1729. 12⁰.

HÉBERT. *Par.* 1612. 8⁰.

TITREVILLE. (De pall.) *Par.* 1640. 12⁰.

HOBIER. (De Orat. de pat.) *Par.* 1640 (2 v.?) 12⁰.

GIRY, L. *Par.* 1636. 8⁰; 1665. 8⁰; *Amst.* 1701. 8⁰.

MANESSIER. (De pallio.) *Par.* 1665. 12⁰.

— (De pat., Ad mart.) *Par.* 1667.

COLOMESIUS, P. (Ad mart.) *Rupell.* 1673. 8⁰.

VASSOULT, J. B. *Par.* 1714. 4⁰; 1715. 8⁰.

BRAÏER. (De praescr.) *Par.* 1725.

(De praescr.) *Par.* 1729. 12⁰.

GAULIÈRE, MATH. (Select works.) *Par.* 1733. 12⁰.

MEUNIER. *Par.* 1822. 12⁰.

GOURCY, DE. (Apol. praescr.) *Lyon*, 1823. 8⁰; *Par.* 1825. 8⁰; *Avign.* 1833. 12⁰.

ALLARD, J. F. *Marseille et Par.* 1827. 8⁰

CAILLAU. (De spect.) *Paris*, 1835. 8⁰.

GENOUDE. In: Pères de l'égl. *Par.* 1841. 3 v. 8⁰; 2d ed. *Besançon et Paris*, 1852. 3 v. 8⁰.

COLLOMBET. (Praescr.) *Par.* 1845. 12⁰.

(Apol., Pres., Bapt.) *Par.* 1845. 12⁰.

BAUDE. In: Coll. aut. lat. 1845. 8⁰.

LALANNE. (Extr.) *Par.* 1853. 12⁰.

German.

HEDION, C. (De pat.) *Strassb.* 1546. 4⁰.

MAIUS, L. (De pat.) *Smalcald.* 1582. 12⁰.

HINCKELMANN, A. (Ad Scap., Ad. mart.) *Luneb.* 1682. 12⁰.

KLEUKER, J. FR. (Apol.) *Frf.* 1797. 8⁰.

(Praescr.) *Wien*, 1797. 8⁰.

LESSING. (Praescr.) In: Werke. XVI. 324–.

BESNARD, F. A. v. *Augsb.* 1837. 2 v. f⁰.

KELLNER, H. *Kempten*, 1869–72. 16⁰. [The Reithmayer-Thalhofer Bibl.]; *Köln*, 1882. 2 v. 8⁰.

Italian.

BORGHINI. *Roma*, 1756. 4⁰.

PACCHI. *Fir.* 1781. 8⁰.

Russian.

ATHANASJ IWANOW. *Mosk.* 1802.

Spanish.

URBANI, E. *Madr.* 1631. 4⁰.

Barcel. 1639. 8⁰.

MANERUS, P. (Apol. ad Scap.) *Caes. Aug.* 1644. 4⁰. *Madr.* 1657. f⁰; 1789. 4⁰.

III. Literature.

ALEXANDER, NATALIS. Hist. eccl. (1778) III. 376–91.

.[ALLIX, PIERRE.] Disse rtatio de Tertulliani vita et scriptis s. l. et a.; 2d ed. *Par.* 1680. 8⁰.

ALZOG. Patrol. (1876) 168–192.

ARBOUSSE–BASTIDE, ANT. FR. Tert. et Cyprien, comparés comme littérateurs. *Strasb.* 1848. 8⁰.

ARCHIMBAUD. Explication des mots "Caligata militia." In: Nouv. Réceuil de pièces fugitiv.

ARTAUD. In: Dict. scien. philos. (1875) 1715–6

AUBÉ, B. In: Nouv. Biog. Gen. (Hoefer) XLIV..(1865) 1019–34.

Aurifodina patr. theol. *Vitemb.* 1664. 4⁰.

AYMERIC, J. Notes sur le vocabulaire de Tertullien. In: Lettres chrét. II. (1881) 446–8.

BÄHR. Gesch. röm. Liter. Sup. (1837) II. 15–38. (IV. 21–7.)

BALLENSTEDT, H. C. T's. Geistesfähigkeiten, Religionskenntnisse u. Theol. *Helmst.* 1785. 8⁰.

[BARBOUR.] Historic Episcopate. (1887) 27–9.

BARONIUS. Ann. (1589) 197, 7–21; 201, 5–19, 27–38; 203, 5–14; 205–19; 209, 1–3; 210, 4–7; 216, 1–19. Cf. Pagi. Crit. (1689) 173, 4; 197, 4; 201, 3, 6; 203, 7; 209, 3.

BARTH, F. Tertullians Auffassung d. Ap. Paulus. u. s. Verhaltnisses zu d. Uraposteln. In: Jahrbb. f. prot. Theol. (1882) 706–756.

BAUMGARTEN–CRUSIUS. Dogmenges. (1832) 188–90. [v. 1.]

BAUR. Kirchenges. 3 e. J. (1863) 253–6, 496–502.

— Dogmengesch. I. (1865) 262–6, etc.

ΒΑΦΕΙΔΗΣ. Ἐκκλ. ἱστ. I. (1884) 160–1.

BELLARMIN–LABBE. Scr. eccl. (1728) 38–41.

BENICKEN, HANS KARL. Zu Tertullianus (de anima 37). In Jahrbb. f. class. Philol. CXV. (1877) 224.

BENTON, A. A. In: Am. Church R. XVIII. (1867) 525–.

BERGK, TH. Philologische Thesen (Tertull. adv. Gent. II. 8). In: Philologus. XIV. (1859) 391.

BERGMANN. Die christl. Geduld nach Tert. de patientia In: Beweis d. Glaubens. (1881) 194–209.

BERTHOLDT. Dogmenges. (1822–3) I. 53, etc.

BEYER, C. A. Quo sensu Tertullianus Deum dixer. corp. *Lipsiae*, 1764. 4⁰.

BINSFELD, J. P. Beitr. z. Krit. u. Erkl. latein. Prosaiker. In: Rhein Mus. N. F. XXVI. (1871) 312–313.

BIRCH, C. CHR. Dissert. quosdam ex Tert. collectos atq. illustratos locos theol. sisteus. *Hannov.* 1790. 4⁰.

BLACKBURN. Hist of Church. (1879) 42–7.

BLUMENBACH, J. H. Liber de senatusconsulto, Q. S. F. Tertull. *Lips.* 1735. 8⁰.

BLUMENSTEIN, J. Talmud u. Tertullian. In: Jüd. Litblt. (1879) 99.

BOEHMER. Dissert. juris eccl. aut. ad Plinium secund. et Tertullianum. *Halae*, 1729. 8⁰.

BOEHRINGER. Kirchenges. (1873–) I. III. (IV. 1–812.)

BONWETSCH, G. N. Die Schriften Tert. nach d. Zeit. ihrer Abfassung untersucht. *Bonn*, 1878. 8⁰.

BOUËDRON, P. Quid senserit de natura animae Tertullianus? Thesis. *Rennes*, 1861. 8⁰.

BRUCKER. Hist. crit. phil. (1766–7) III. 411–4; VI. 539–40.

BUNSEN. Hippolytus. (1854) I. 253–62.

BURCKHARDT, F. A. Die Seelenlehre d. Tert. nach dessen Tractat: de anima, dargestellt. Progr. *Bautzen*, 1857. 4⁰.

BURTON. Divinity of Christ. (1829) 180–241.

— Trinity. (1831) 60–84.

BUSSE. Chr. Lit. (1828–9) I. 21–2.

CACHEUX. In: Mémor. cathol. (1866–8) B, VII. 395–9; VIII. 32–4, 113–6, 237–40, 369–72, 446–9; IX. 140–3, 227–30, 355–9.

CAILLAU. Introd. in ss. Patr. (1825) 69–79.

CANTOVA, CAR. IGN. De Tertulliano et Epiphanio dissert. duae theol. crit. in quibus antromorphismo neutrum laborasse demonstratur. *Mediolani*, 1763. 8°. Cf. Acta erudit. (1774) 235–8; (1775) 423–7.

CASPARI, C. P. Om nogle Steder i Tertullians: de praescriptionibus haeret. In: Forhandlinger i Vedensk. Selsk. i Christiania. (1869) 344–348.

— Om Tertull. graeske Skrifter. In: Forhandlinger i. Vedensk. Selsk. i Christiania. (1875) 403–404.

CAUCANAS, G. Tertullien et le montanisme. *Genève*, 1876. 8°.

CAVE. Scr. eccl. hist. lit. (1740–3) I. 91–4.

— Lives. (1840) I. 305–320.

CEILLIER. Hist. gén. d. aut. sac. II. (1730) 374–529; II. (1865) 1–87.

CENTNER, G. = Hoffmann, J. G.

CHADWICK, J. W. Tertullian and Montanism. In: Chr. Exam. LXXV. (1863) 157–.

CHARPENTIER. Étude hist. et litt. sur Tertullien. Thèse. *Paris*, 1839. 8°.

CHARTERIS. Canonicity. (1880) 46–50, 75–81, 134, 148, 162–3, 184, 203, 220–1, 229, 232, 236, 241, 246, 250, 252, 254, 260, 264, 268, 269, 278–9, 296–7, 307–8, 323, 333, 343.

CHASSANG, A. Ap. de T., sa vie, ses voyages, ses prodiges, etc. *Paris*, 1862.

CHASTEL.. Histoire du Christianisme. (*Paris*, 1881.) I. 270–.

CHEVALIER. Rép. d. sources hist. (1877–86) 2157–9.

CHLADEN, J. M. De stationibus vet. Christianorum ad Tertull. *Lipsiae*, 1744. 4°.

CLARKE. Sacred lit. (1830–1) I. 131–46.

CLINTON. Fasti Rom. (1845–50) I. 215, 217; II. 413–4.

COENEN, J. A. Commentat. de Tertulliano, christianorum et religionis christ. adv. gentes apologeta. In: Ann. acad. Rheno-Traject. (1823–4) *Trajecti ad Rhen.* 1825. 8°.

COFFIN. Lives of fath. (1846) 251–272.

COLEMAN, L. Introduction in: Ed. March. *N. Y.* 1876. 12°.

CONDAMIN, J. P. De Q. S. F. Tertulliano vexatae religionis patrono et praecipuo apud latinos, christianae liguae artifice. Thesis. *Bar-le-Duc*, 1877. 8°. Cf. Olivier, J. H. In: Ann. du monde relig. (1878) II. 390–4.

COTTA. Kirchenges. §318–35.

CROÏ. S. u. Irenaeus.

CUNNINGHAM. Hist. theol. (1870) I. 158–63.

— Churches of Asia. (1880) passim.

CYPRIAN, E. SAL. Diss. de doctrina Tertulliani evangelica. *Erford*, 1797. 4°.

DALLAEUS. De usu. patr. 259–.

DARLING. Cyclop. bibl. (1854) 2921–2, 2979–80.

DEUTINGER. Geist. d. christl. Ueberl. I. 182–7.

DIERINGER. FRC. XAV. Doctrina Tertull. de republ. et de officiis ac iuribus civium Christianor. Progr. *Bonnae*, 1850. 4°.

DITTRICH, FRANC. De Tertulliano Christianae veritatis regulae contra haereticorum licentiam vindice commentatio. *Brusbergae*, 1876–77. 4°.

DORNER. Person of Christ. II. (1866) 49–80, 448–9.

DUPIN. Nouv. bibl. d. aut. eccl. (1698–) I. 222–91.

DUVERDIER. Bibl. Franç. (1773) V. 390.

EBERT, ADOLF. Tertullians Verhältniss zu Minucius Felix, nebst einem Anhang über Commodian's Carmen apologeticum. (From: Abhandl. d. säche Geselbsch. d. Wiss. XII. Bd. [=Philol. hist. Classe V. Bd.] 1870 p. 319–420.) *Leipzig*, 1868. 4°. Cf. Boissier. In: Rev. critique (1869) VIII. 21–4; Literar. Centralbl. (1869, Jan. 16).

— Gesch. Liter. Mittelalt. (1874) I. 31–54.

Ecclesiastical history from the writings of Tertullian. In: Ecl. R. XLIV. (1826) 433–.

EKERMAN, PET. Dissert. de Tertulliano, primo Latinae eccl. patre. *Upsal.* 1761. 4°.

ENGELHARDT. Dogmenges. I. (1839) 70, etc.

— Ueber Tertullians schriftsteller. Charakter. In: Zeitschr. f. histor. Theol. (1852) 316–319.

EUSEBIUS. H. E. II. 2.

FABRICIUS. Bibl. lat. (1722) III. 347–71.

— De verit. rel. chr. (1725) 173, 207–15.

— Bibl. med. aev. (1746) VI. 617–8. (2ª. 220.)

FARRAR. Interpretation (1886) 177–80.

FISCHER, J. M. = Cyprian, E. S.

FISH, H. C. Tertullian and his writings. In: Chr. R. XXI. (1856) 452–.

FLEURY. Hist. eccl. (1691–) I. 602–10; II. 5–26, 41–69, 72–4, 85–7, 91–5, 114–7.

FOSSÉ, PIERRE THOMAS DU [de la Motte]. Histoire de Tert. et d'Origène. *Par.* 1675. 8°; *Lyon*, 1691. 8°; 1701. 8°.

FRANCUS, F. Confutatio animadv. Kercoetii. *Middelb.* 1623.

— Refut. utr. elenchi Cerco. *Par.* 1623.

FREPPEL. Tertullien. Cours d'éloquence sacrée fait à la Sorbonne pendant l'année 1861–1862. 2 éd. *Par.* 1872. 2 v. 8°. Cf. Le Verdier. In: Bibliog. cath. (1865) XXXIII. 69–77; and in: Rev. d. cours littér. (1863) I. 142–4.

— La notion chrétienne du pouvoir d'après Tertullien. In: Rev. du Monde Cath. (1864) VIII. 275–86.

GAMBA. Testi. Ital. (1828) 1767.

GAUDENTIUS, P. In: Salebris Tert. *Florent.* 1639. 4°.

— Opusc. tria. *Pisis*, 1644. 4°.

GEORGIUS. Tertullianus redivivus, scholiis et observationibus illustratus. *Paris*, 1646–50. 3 v. f°.

GERET. J. GE. Pr. in quendam Tertulliani de terrarum motibus locum. *Onoldinii*, 1756. 4°.

GERMON, BARTH. De vet. haeret. eccl. Codie. corruptor. 587–.

GIESELER. Church Hist. (1868–) I. 150–1, 194, 229–31.

GÖRRES, F. Das Christenthum u der röm. Staat zur Zeit d. Severus. I. Friedensenpoche 193–202; Anhang über Tert. ad Scap. e IV. II. Officielle Verfolgung 202–211. In: Jahrbb. f. prot. Theol. (1878) 273–327.

GOTTWALD. PAUL. De montanismo Tertulliani. Diss. inaug. *Vratislaviae*, 1862. 8°. (62 p.)

GRETSERUS, JAC. . . . Vindicatio locorum quorumdam Tertullianicorum a Franc. Junii Calvin. depravationibus. *Ingolstadii*, 1600. 4°. p. 289–376. (= his Opera (1735) V. II. 305–33.)

GREVE, ARN. Tertulliani testimonium de ἀποθεώσει Christo a Tiberio decreta defensum. *Vittemberg.* 1722. 4°.

GROTEMEYER. H. Ueber Tertullians Leben und Schriften. Progr. *Kempen*, 1863–5. 4°.

GUERRIER, MARCEL. Apulée et Tertullien. Thèse. *Rouen*, 1853. 4°.

HAGENBACH. Hist. of Doct. I. (1850) 60–1, etc.

— Kirchenges. (1885) I. 211–7.

HARDOUIN, JEAN. In: Mém. de Trévoux (1724(9?) mai) 842–9.

HARNACK. Dogmenges. I. (1886) 264–7, 304–5, 393–5, 422–500.

— Zur Chronologie der Schriften Tertullian's. In: Ztschr. f. Kirchengesch. II. (1878) 572–583.

HASAEUS, JAC. De Ononychoete, christianis cujusdam verpi nequitia afficto nomine, ad elucidationem eorum quae hac de re apud Tertullianum reperimus. In: Bibl. hist.-phil.-theol. (*Brem.* 1720.) III. 1052–70.

HASE. Kirchenges. (1885–) I. 252–3, 342–8, 367, 389–90, 432.

HASSELBACH, K. F. W. De multimoda idolatr. cuj. Tertullianus ludimagistr. et ceter. professor. literar. arguit. *Sedani.* 8°.

HAUBER, A. T.'s Kampf gegen d. 2te. Ehe. In: Stud. u. Krit. XVIII. (1845) 607–62.

HAUCK, ALB. Tertullian's Leben und Schriften. *Erlangen*, 1877. 8°.

HAUPT, MOR. Analecta (Zu Tertullian, de pallio c. 5 de spectaculis c. 10.) In: Hermes. I. (1866) p. 259–261; and in: Opuscula. III. 2 (1870) p. 349–351.

— Varia. (Tert. ad martyr. init.) In: Hermes. V. (1871) p. 190; and in: Opuscula. III. 2, p. 535.

— Coniectanea. (Anonymi Sodoma V. 14, 81.) In: Hermes. V. (1871) p. 316; and in: Opuscula. III. 2, p. 539.

— Coniectanea. (Tertullianus ad nation. I. 7. de cultu fem. II. 11.) In: Hermes. VIII. (1874) p. 247–248; and in: Opuscula. III. 2, p. 632.

— Adversaria. (Tert. adv. gent. 35.) In his: Opuscula. III. p. 643.

HAUSCHILD, G. R. Die Grundsätze u. Mittel d. Sprachbildung bei Tert. Progr. *Leipzig*, 1876. 4°; *Lpz.* 1881. 4°.

— T.'s Psychologie u. Erkenntnisstheorie. Programm. *Frankfurt a. M.* 1880. 4°. [*Lpz.* 1880?]

HAVERCAMP. In: Migne. Patrol. Lat. I. (1866) 297–304.

HEFELE, C. J. Tertullian als Apologet. In: Theol. Quartalschr. (*Tüb.* 1838) I. 30.

HERGENROETHER. Kirchenges. (1879–80) I. 104–6, 168; III. 41–2, 73.

HESSELBERG, CARL. Tertullian's Lehre aus seinen Schriften entwickelt, etc. *Dorpat.* 1848. 8°; *Hamb. Gotha*, 1851. 8°.

HEUMANN. Emendat. iib. Tert. de praescr. In: Acta Erudit. (1715) 299–; Suppl. VI. v. 196–.

— Obss. crit. ad posteriorem apol. Tert. capp. In: Miscell. Groning. II. III. 470–.

— Emend. atque illustr. Cap. I. Apolog. Tertull. In his: Poicile. I. (1722) 25–33; II. (1723) 195–213.

HIERONYMUS. De vir. ill. 53. (Honor. August. I. 54.)

HOFFMANN, J. G. Q. Sept. Florentis Tertulliani quae supersunt omnia Montanismo scripta videri. *Wittenbergae*, 1738. 4°. (48 p.)

— Geschichte des Kirchenlateins. fascic. I. et II.

HOLMES, P. and THELWALL, S. In: Ante-Nic. Lib. VII. (1868) vii-xviii; XVIII. (1870) vii-xix. Introd. note. Ed. Coxe. III. (1885) 1–15. [Add. notes. Ed. Coxe. 56–60, 76–7, 103–4, 179–80, 239–41, 265–70, 474–5, 542–3, 594–5, 627–32, 679, 717–18.] V. 125–66.

HOLTZMANN. Einl. in d. N. T. (1886) 153–4, etc.

HOOPER, G. Works. (1757) 327–44.

HOVEN, I. D. VAN. Specim. adnotatt. ad Tert. Apol. In: Stosch. Mus. crit. II. (1777) p. 26–31.

HUBER. Philos. d. K.–V. (1859) 100–104.

HÜCKSTÄDT, ERNST. Über das pseudotertullianische Gedicht *adversus Marcionem*. Diss. *Lpz.* 1875. 8°.

ITTIG. Hist. eccl. (1709) II. 62–78, 236–41.

JAEGER, ALD. ANT. Dissert. de Tertulliano duce Anthropomorphitarum. *Innsbr.* 1774. 8°.

JAHN, OTTO. Variarum lectionum fasciculus alter. (Tertull. apolog. 19. ad nat. II. 14.) In: Philologus. XXVIII. (1869) 10.

JEEP, H. T. as Apologet. In: Jahrb. f. deut. Theol. IX. (1864) 649–87.

JEREMIE. Hist. Church. (1852) 104–8.

JORTIN, J. Tracts philol.-crit.-misc. (1790) II.

Journal des Savans. (1719, Dec.) 663–.

KAYE, JOHN. Ecclesiastical History of the Second and Third Centuries, illustrated from the writings of Tertullian. *Camb.* 1826. 8°; *London*, 1845. 8°.

KEIM. Rom und das Christenthum. *Berlin*, 1881.

KELLNER, H. Ueber Tert. Abhandlg. d. pallio. u. d. Jahr seines Uebertrittes z. Christenthum. In: Theol. Quartalschr. LII. (*Tüb.* 1870.) p. 547–566.

— Zur Chronologie Tertullians. 2. Artikel. In: Theol. Quartalschr. LIII. (1871) p. 585–609.

— Ueb. d. sprachlichen Eigenthumlichkeiten Tert. In: Theol. Quartalschr. LVIII. (1876) 229–251.

KELLNER, H. Organischer Zusammenhang u. Chronologie der Schriften Tertullians. In: Der Katholik. (1879) 561–589.

KERCOETIUS, A. Animadv. ad Salmasii not. in Tert. de Pall. *Rhedon.* 1622.

— Mastigophorus secundus. *Par.* 1623.

— Mastigophorus tertius. *Par.* 1623.

KILLEN. Ancient Church. (1859) 370–3, 475–8.

KIPP, J. F. *pseud.* = Semler, J. S.

KLÜPFEL, E. Mens Tert. de indissolubilitate matrimonii in infidelitate contracti, conjuge alterutro ad fid. chr. converto. *Frib.* 1774. 4°; also in: Riegger. Oblectamenta. *Ulm.* 1776. 4°.

KLUSSMAN, ERNST. Die neueste texteskritik Tertullians. I. II. In: Zeitschr. f. wiss. Theol. III. (1860) 82–100, 363–393.

— Adnotationes criticae ad Tertull. lib. de spectaculis. Progr. *Rudolphopoli*, 1876. 8°.

KLUSSMANN, M. Curarum Tertullianearum, part. I. et II. (*Halle*, 1881.)

— Coniectanea critica ad Tertulliani libros ad Nationes. Festschr. *Hamburg*. 1885. 4°.

KOLTUG, J. Verfassung Cultus u. Disciplin der christlichen Kirche nach den Schriften. Tertullians. *Braunsberg, Huye*, 1886.

KURTZ. Kirchenges. (1885–) I. 124–6, 139–40.

LACTANTIUS. Inst. V. I.

LA FAYOLLE, NIC. DE. La génie de Tertullien. *Paris*, 1658. 4°.

LAFORÊT, N. J. Etude philosophique sur Tertullien. In: Rev. cathol. (*Louv.* 1869) B. I. 481–510; II. 147–72.

LAGARDE, P. DE. Tertullianea (Nachrichten . . *Gottingen*, 1878, I, p. 15–18).

LALLEMAND, PAUL. In: Lettres chret. (1881) II. 307–8.

LA MOTTE. Hist. de T. s. u. Fossé.

LANGEN, PET. De usu praepositionum Tutullianeo. Part I.–III. *Monasterii*, 1869–70. 4°.

LARDNER. Credibility. Works. (1831) II. 267–306.

LAUFKÖTHER. In: Wetzer. u. W. Kirch-Lex. (1847–54) X. 745–65.

LEHANNEUR, L. Le traité de Tertullien contre les Valentiniens. *Caen*, 1886. 8°.

LEIMBACH, K. L. T.'s Sacramentsbegriff. In: Stud. u. Krit. XLIV. (1871) 483–502.

— Tertullian als Quelle f. d. christl. Archaeol. In: Kahnis Zeitschr. f. hist. Theol. (1871) 108–157, 430–459.

— Beiträge zur Abendmahlslehre Tertullians. *Gotha*, 1874. 8°.

LELONG. Bib. sac. II. 983.

LE NOURRY. Dissert. in apol. In: Migne. Patrol. Lat. I. (1857) 783–1244.

— Appar. bibl. patr. (1715) II. 1174.

LEONHARDI, G. D. apol. Grundgedanken T. In: Ztschr. f. kirchl. wiss u. Leben. III. (1882) 573–85.

LEOPOLD, E. F. Ueb. d. Ursachen d. verderbt. Latinität u. s. w . . . mit besond Berühsichtigung d. Tertullian. In: Ztschr. f. hist. Theol. (1838) 12–38.

LIPSIUS, R. A. In: Jahrb. f. deut. Theol. XIII. (1868) 701–24. [T. agst. Praxeas.]

[LIRON.] Singul. hist. litt. (1738–40) I. 404–7; III. 319–23; IV. 36–44.

London Quarterly Review. XXXI. (1868) 459–.

LUDWIG, G. Tertullian's Ethik. *Leipzig*, 1885. 8°.

LUMPER. Hist. ss. patr. (1789) VI. 1–768.

LUTHARDT. St. John the Author of the Fourth Gospel. (1875) 38–41.

M'CLINTOCK and S. Cycl. (1874–) X. 288–90.

MAGALLOTTI, LAUR. Sopra un passo di Tert. In: Lettere scient. ed erudite del Conte Magalotti. 192–.

MARGERIE, AM. DE. De Q. S. F Tertulliano Opusculum philosophicum. Thesis. *Paris*. 1855. 8°.

MAURICE. Eccl. Hist. (1854) 271–88.

Mém. de Trevoux. (1703) 133-. [Genuineness of catalogue of heresies at end of the prescription.]

Mém. de Trevoux. (1719) 1202. [" Obs. touchant de traité de l'Oraison."]

MIGNE. Demonstrations evangeliques de Tertullien, Origene, Eusebe, etc. Traduites en francais, annotees et publiees. 1842–1853. 20 v. 8º.

MINER, A. A. In: Univ. Q. XII. (1855) 174-.

Miscell. obss. in auctt. III. I. 45- [T. and Cyprian]; III. II. 208- [De Oratione].

MÖHLER. Patrol. I. (1840) 701–90.

MOREAU, CAR. Tertulliani Omniloquium alphabeticum rationale, tripartitum . . . Paris, 1657–8. 3 v. fº.

MOSHEIM, J. L. Disquisitio chronologico critica de vera aetate Apologetici a Tertulliano conscripti initioque persecutionis Severi. Lugd. Bat. 1720. 8º. Helmst. 1724. 4º. Lugd. Batav. 1740. Also in ed. of Venet. 1746.

— Hist. eccl. 108-.

MOUCHON, H. Exposition critique des opinions de Tertullien sur l'origine et la nature du péché. Strasbourg, 1859. 8º.

MÜLLER, L. Zu Tertullians Gedichten de Sodoma und de Iona. In: Rhein. Mus. N. F. XXII. (1867) p. 329–344 and 464.

— Zu dem Gedicht de Sodoma. In: Rhein. Mus. N. F. 22. XXVII. (1872) 486–488.

MUENSCHER. Dogmenges. (1817–8) I. 159–62, etc.

MUNTER, F. Primordia eccl. Africanae. Havn. 1829. 4º. 128-.

MURALT, ED. DE. In: Bull. acad. sci. St. Pétersburg. (1848) V. 1–4.

NEANDER, J. A. W. Antignostikus. Geist des Tertullianus und Einleitung in dessen Schriften, mit archaologischen und dogmenhistorischen Untersuchungen. Berl. 1825. 8º. 2. Zum Theil. umgearb. Aufl. Berlin, 1849. 8º; Tr. Eng. Ryland, J. E. Lond. 1859. 2 v. 8º.

— Hist. of dogmas. (1858) 54–6, 79–82, 98, 100–1, 155, 175, 182, 184–6, 199–200, 212, 216–7, 221, 225–6, 231–2, 240–1, 252. [v. 1]

— Church Hist. (1872) I. 516–7, 614–20, 683–5, et pass.

NIELSEN, F. Tertullians Ethik. Afhandling. Schonberg. 1879. 8º.

NIRSCHL. Patrol. (1881-) I. 266–95.

NITZSCH. Dogmengesch. I. (1870) 165–6, etc.

NODIER. Bib. sacr. (1826) 160–2.

NÖLDECHEN, E. Tertullian als Mensch und als Bürger. In: Hist. Ztschr. (1885) 225–260.

— Kultus-Stätten u. Reden der Tertullianischen Tage. In: Ztschr. f. kirchl. Wissensch. u. kirchl. Leben. (1885) 202–208.

— Die Situation von Tertullian's Schrift, Ueber die Geduld. In: Ztschr. f. vaterl. Gesch. u. Alterthumsk. XLIII. (1885), I. 178–198.

— In: Ztschr. f. wiss. Theol. XXVIII. (1885) 333–49. [Matt. 11:13. Luke 16:16 in T.]

— T. "Ueb. d. Geduld." In: Ztschr. f. kirchl. wiss. u. Leben. (1885) 577–80.

— In: Ztschr. kirchl. wiss. u. Leben. (1886) 87–98. [Scorpiace.]

— T.'s Geburtsjahr. In: Ztschr. f. wiss. Theol. XXIX. (1886) 207–23.

— Tertullian's Erdkunde. In: Ztschr. f. kirchl. wiss. u. Leben. (1886) 310–325.

— T. u. St. Paul. In: Ztschr. f. wiss. Theol. XXIX. (1886) 473–97.

— Tertullian. In: Jahrbb. f. prot. Theol. (1886) 615–60.

— Tert. vom Fasten. In: Ztschr. f. wiss. Theol. XXX. (1887) 187–219.

NOLTE, J. Verbesserung einiger Stellen in d. Schriften d. Tacitus u. Tertullianus. In: Jahn's Archiv. XVIII. (1852) 623–627.

NONNOTE. Les philosophes. (1789).

NORTON. Genuineness of Gosp. I. (1846) 47–9, etc.

NOESSELT, J. A. Dissert. de vera aetate ac doctrina scriptorum quae supersunt Tertulliani. Halae, 1757–59. 4º. 2. ed. 1768. 4º; = his: Comment. hist. eccles. (1817) 8º.

OEHLER, FRANZ. Probe e. neuen Bearbeitung von Tertull. Apologeticus u. libri. duo Ad nationes. In: Jahn's Archiv. XV. (1849) p. 80–95.

— Zur Berichtigung über die neueste Texteskritik Tertullians. (Klussmann.) In: Hilgenfelds Ztschr. f. wiss. Theol. IV. (1861) p. 204–211.

OEHNINGER. Tertullian und seine Auferstehungslehre. Ausgb. 1878.

OELRICHS. Scr. eccl. lat. (1791) 17–30.

ORSI. Ist. eccl. (1746-) II. 371–414, 432–5, 460–1; III. 6–14; (1749) II. 535–97, 624–8, 665–6; III. 9–20.

OTT. S. u. Cyprian.

OUDIN. (1722) I. 214–21.

PAGENSTECHER, J. A. G. Oratio de jurisprudentia Tertulliani. Harderovici, 1768. 8º.

PAGNANI, PAGANO. Il materialismo di Tertulliano. (Accad. de Lucca, 1869.) In: Annali delle univ. Toscane. Parte I. Scienz. novl. XII. (Pisa, 1872) p. 204–211.

PAMELIUS [and others]. Argumenta et annot. ed Rigaltii respondentia. Par. 1635.

PAMELIUS, J. Vita T. In: Ed. Rigaltius. Par. 1634; also in: Migne. Patrol. lat. I. (1866) 77–126.

— Paradoxa Tert. In: Migne. Patrol. Lat. I. (1866) 225–56.

PERMANEDER. Bibl. patrist. (1844) I. 418–9; II. 706–89.

PETREIUS, THEOD. Confessio Tertulliana et Cypriana. Paris, 1603. 8º.

PHOTIUS. Biblioth.

PRESSENSÉ, EDM. DE. Un grand hérétique chrétien, Tertullien, sa vie et ses écrits. In: Magasin de librair. (1860) XII. 558–81.

— Hist. des trois premiers siècles de l'Église chrétienne. III. 421–64; IV. 426–; V. 465–; VI. 136–; tr. Engl. Chr. life. (1878) 34–5, 53–5, 123–33, 142; Martyrs. (1879) 143–57, 163–5, 374–414, 591–605 ; Heresy (n. d.) 419–56.

— Lichtenberger. Encycl. (1877–82) XII. 29–36.

RAMSAY, W. In: Smith. Gr. and Rom. Biog. (1859) III. 1006–12.

RATHMANN, HERM. Theosophia priscorum patr. Tert. et Cypriani. 1620. 4º; [with changed title] Vitemb. 1636; 1655.

RAYNOUD. In: Journ. d. Savans. (1827) 483–91.

RECHENBERG, A. D. an haereticorum patriarchae philosophi. Lips. 1705. 4º.

RECK. Minucius Felix u. T. In: Theol. Quartalschr. LXVIII. (1886) 64–114.

REUSS. Gesch. N. T. (1874) II. 19, 21, 258; tr. Eng. (1884) 302–3, 304–5, 537. [v. 2.]

RÉVILLE, ALB. Tertullien, le Montanisme et l'église de son temps. In: Rev. d. Deux Mondes. (1864) H, LIV. 166–99.

— In: Nouvelle Rev. de Theol. 1858.

RIGALT, N. Observationes et notae ad libros Tertulliani. Parisiis, 1641. fº.

RINGELBROCH, C. T. De antiquiss. homin. christ. precib. sollemnib. pro mora finis Tertulliani Apolog. c. 39. Tremoniae, 1744. 4º.

RITSCHL. Altkatholische Kirch.

RITTER. Chr. philos. (1841) I. 362–417.

— Darstellung d. erst. chr. Schriftsteller Afrika's. (" Bonner Ztschr. H. 8.")

ROBERTSON. Hist. of Church. (1885-) I. 109–114.

RÖNSCH, HERM. Zwei Stellen des Tertullianus erläutert. In: Ztschr. f. wissenschf. Theol. X. (1867) p. 295–302.

RÖNSCH, HERM. Das Neue Testament Tertullian's. *Leipz.* 1871. 8º.
— In: Ztschr. f. wiss. Theol. XXVI. (1883) 108–11. [Rev. of Hauschild's Wortbildung (1876–81) and Psychologie (1880).]
— (Nachträge zu: Rönsch, Das neue Testament Tertullian's. *Leipzig,* 1871. S. 527.) In: Ztschr. f. wiss. Theol. XXVIII. (1885). S. 104.
ROOY, A. DE. (? ?)
ROSENMÜLLER. Hist. interp. II. (1798) 1–184.
ROESSLER. Bibl. d. K.–V. III. (1777) 32–172.
SANDAY. Gosp. in 2 cent. (1876) 318–9, 327, 333–43.
SCHAFF, P. Life and writings of Tertullian. In: Mercersb. X. (1858) 621–.
— Creeds of Christendom. II. (1877) 16–20.
— In: Herzog. Real.-Enc. (1877–) XV. 343–51. (Abr. in: Schaff-Herz. III. 2318–9.)
— Hist. . . Church. II. (1886) 818–33.
SCHARFFENBERG. s. u. Justin M.
SCHLIEMANN. Clementinen. (1884) 443 et passim.
SCHMID. Patrol. (1879) 56–9.
SCHMIDT, F. J. De Latinitate Tertulliani. *Erlang,* 1877. 8º.
— Commentatio de nominum verbalium in tor et trix desinentium apud Tertullianum copia ac vi. Programm. *Erlangen,* 1878. 8º.
SCHÖNEMANN. Bibl. patr. lat. (1792) 2–13.
SCHRADER, JO. In his: Observatl. liber (1761) 57.
SCHRAM. Anal. ss. patr. (1780–) III. 1–636.
SCHROECKH. Kirchenges. (1772–) III. 317–84, 71–2; VII. 97–8; IX. 97–102.
SCHUMANN, J. D. De interpolationibus quibusdam Cod. N. T. Tert. perperam afficitis conjectura. In his: Obss. in vet. eccl. Scriptoribus III. & IV. *Hannov.* 1776–7. 4º.
SCHÜTZ, CHR. GODOFR. Explicatio loci Tertullianei de Praescr. haereticorum c. XVI., XVII., Progr. *Jenae,* 1780. fº; also in his: Opuscula philol. et philos. *Halae.* (1830) p. 268–279.
— De regula fidei apud Tertullianum. *Jenae,* 1780. 4º.
— Explicatio loci Tertulliani de eversione stomachi aut cerebri ex congressione Scripturarum. *Jenae,* 1780. fº.
SCHWEGLER. D. Montanismus. (*Tüb.* 1841) 302–.
— Nachap. Zeitalt. (1846) I.
SCULTETUS. Medulla theol. patr. 242–.
SEMLER, JAC. SAL. Exam. crit. opp. Macarii (1745) 21–4.
— Dissert. de antiquitatibus hermeneuticis ex Tertulliano, quibus N. T. loca quaedam illustrantur. *Halae Magdeb.* 1765. 4º.
— Comment ad l. Tertulliani de caare Christi c. 19. *Halae Magd.* 1770. 4º.
— S. u. Irenaeus.
SHEDD. Hist. of doct. 3d ed. (1865–) I. 277–81, etc.
SMEDT, CAR. DE. Dissert. sel. hist. eccles. (1876) 173–83, App. 43–5.
SMITH, THOMAS. Conjecturae in quaedam loca Tertulliani de barbara voce Onochoete. In: Hearne. Script. hist. Anglic. XXX. (1733) 720–3.
STEPHINSKY, ED. (Tert. Apol. c. 23.) In: Jahrbb. f. class. Philol. XCV. (1867) p. 882.
STOECKL, ALB. Tertulliani de anim. human. doctrinae. Partes I. et II. Ind. lect. aest. 1863 et hib. 1863–64. *Monasterii,* 1863. 4º.
STÖCKL. Philos d. patrist. Z. 215–249.
Supernatural Religion (1875–7) passim.
TEUFFEL. Hist. Rom. Lit. (1873) II. 275–8.
THOMAS CORBINIUS. In libr.: De bapt. et poenit. In: Migne. Patrol. Lat. II. (1866) 1197–350.
TILLEMONT. Mémoirs. III. (1695) 196–236, 654–71.
TOURNEMINE, RENÉ. In: Mém. de Trévoux. Tr. Ital. in: Zaccaria. Racc. di dissert. (1794) VIII. 123–32.
TRAVASA, GAET. MAR. Stor. crit. eresiarchi (17 . .) 292 (= Zaccaria, Racc. di dissert. (1794) VIII. 143–57.)

TRITHEMIUS. 29.
UEBERWEG. Hist. philos. (1876) 303–6.
UHLHORN, GERARD. Fundamenta chronologiae Tertullianae. Dissert. *Gottingae.* 1851. 8º.
URLICHS, LUDW. (Tertulian Apolog. 16; ad nation. I. 14.) In: Philologus. (1861) 350.
VALESIUS, HENR. Ad Tertullian Apol. c. 18. In his: Emendatt. libri V. et de crit. libri II. ed. Burnannus (1740) p. 156.
VINCENTIUS BELVAC. Spec. hist. XII. 7.
VINCENT LIR. Commonitorium. 24.
VIVIEN, MICH. Tertullianus praedicans. *Par.* 6 v. 4º; *Avignon,* 1856. 6 v. 8º.
VONCK, C. V. In his: Lection. Latin, libri II. (1745) p. 98.
WALCH, C. W. F. De pompis Satanae. *Gött.* 1758. 4º. [Ad Tert. de spectaculis.]
WALCH, JOH. ERN. IM. De Apostolorum litteris authenticis a Tertulliano commemoratis. *Jenae,* 1753. 4º.
WALCH, J. G. Bibl. patrist. (1834) 35–7; 180–1; 244; 379–81, etc.
WEISS. In: Biog. Univ. (Michaud.) (1842–65) XLI. 182–4.
WERNSDORF, E. F. De veste palmata ad Tertul. Apologet. c. 50. *Vitemberg.* 1766. 4º.
WESTCOTT. Canon (1875) 340–3, 367, 369, etc.
— Bible in the Church. (1877) 127–8.
WIESENHAUER, JUST. CAR. Disput. de jureconsulto. et Qu. S. F. Tertullianis. *Hildesheim,* 1743. 4º.
WOLFF, GUST. (Tertull. Apol. 10.) In: Philologus. XVI. (1860) p. 529.
WORDSWORTH. Church Hist. (1881) 74–5, 93–104, 234–50.
ZACCARIA. Racc. di dissert. (1794) VIII, 133–9.
— Thes. Theolog. (1762) II. 71–4; X. 204–6, 243–, 768–9.
ZEIBICH, H. A. Tertulliani sententia de columba in Jes. devol. *Gerae,* 1772. 4º.
ZELLER. Apostelgesch. (1854) 70–1.
ZEUTGRAVIUS, JO. JOACH. De lapsu Tertulliani ad Montanistas, cum auctario dissertationum aliquot ejusdem selectiorum. *Argenter.* 1706. 4º.
ZIMMERMANN, MATTH. Dissert. in Tertulliani dictum "Fiunt, non nascuntur Christia." *Lipsiae,* 1662. 4º.

Compare also especially all histories of Montanism.

Note. For chronological order of Tertullian's works compare Vol. III. of this series. Introd. note, p. 10–12.

II. MINUCIUS FELIX.

I. *Editions.*

SABAEUS, FAUSTUS. (?) (Arnobius. Book VIII.) *Romae,* 1542. fº.
GELENIUS. *Basil,* 1546; 1560. 8º. [With Arnobius.]
BALDUINUS, F. *Heidelb.* 1560. 8º; *Francof.* 1610. 8º.
BARRE, R. L. DE LA. *Par.* 1580. fº. [With Tertullian and Arnobius.]
URSINUS, F. *Rom.* 1583. 4º.
Par. 1589. fº.
MEURSIUS, J. Hypocriticus Minuc. *Lugd.* 1598. 8º. [With Criticus Arnobianus.]
WOWER, J. A. [*Basil.*] 1603. 8º; *Oxon.* 1627. 12º; 1631. 12º; 1662. 12º [With Cyprian De idol. vanit, etc.]; *Lugd.* 1645. 8º.
ELMENHORSTIUS. *Hanov.* 1603. 8º; *Hamb.* 1612. fº. [With Arnobius.]
HERALDUS, D. *Paris,* 1605. 8º; 1613. 4º. [With Arnobius.]
Hamb. 1610. 4º. [With Arnobius.]
Par. 1610. fº.
Bibl. patr. *Par.* 1624. fº. IX. 1–.
JAMES. *Oxon.* 1636. 12º.

RIGALTIUS. *Lutet.* 1643. 4°. [With Cyprian De idol. vanit.]; 1645. 4°; *Oxon.* 1678. 12°.
Rothom. 1648. 12°.
OUZELIUS, J. *Lugd. Bat.* 1652. 4°; 1672. 8°.
PRIORIUS. 1666. f°. [With Cyprian.]
Bibl. max. patr. (1677) III.
BOUCHARD, P. A. *Kiel*, 1685.
Lat. fr *Lips.* 1689. 12°.
DAVISIUS, JO. *Lond.* 1706. 8°; *Cantabr.* 1707. 8°; 1712. 8°; *Glasg.* 1750. 8°.
GRONOVIUS, J. *Lugd. Bat.* 1709. 8°; *Rott.* 1743. 8°.
CELLARIUS, C. *Hal.* 1699. 8°; *Lips.* 1748. 8°. [With Cyprian.]
POLETUS. Lat. ital. *Venet.* 1756. 8°.
LINDNER. *Longos.* 1760. 8° [With Cyprian]; 1773. 8°; *Haf.* 1794. 8°.
GALLAND. In: Bibl. patr. II. (1766) 377–.
OBERTHÜR. *Wirceb.* 1782. 8°. [With Vol. II. of Cyprian.]
LÜBKERT. Lat. ger. *Lpz.* 1836. 8°.
MURALT, ED. DE. *Turici*, 1836. 8°.
OEHLER. In: Gersdorf. Bibl. patr. XIII. (1847. 8°.)
HOLDEN, H. A. *Camb.* 1853. 8°.
KAYSER. *Padeb.* 1863. 8°.
MIGNE. Patrol. Lat. III. (1865) 239–376.
HALM. *Vindoben.* 1867. 8°. [Corp. eccl. lat. II.]
HURTER, H. Opusc. ss. patr. XV. *Innsb.* 1871. 16°.
CORNELISSEN. *Lugd. Bat.* 1882. 8°.
BAEHRENS. *Leipzig*, 1886. 8°.

II. *Translations.*

Dutch.

Amst. en Haarlem. 1684. 8°.
ELSEVIER, M. A. *Amst.* 1699. 8°.
GARGONUS. *Vliessingen*, 1712. 8°.

English.

JAMES, RICHARD. *Oxon.* 1636. 12°.
LORRAIN, P. *Lond.* 1695. 18°.
COMBE, E. *Lond.* 1703. 8°.
Lond. 1708. 8°.
DALYRYMPLE, D. *Edinb.* 1781. 12°. New ed. *Camb.* 1854. 8°.
WALLIS, R. E. In: Ante-Nic. Lib. XIII. (1873) 451–517. Ed. Coxe. IV. (1885) 173–98.

French.

MAS, G. DU. *Par.* 1637. 4°.
D'ABLANCOURT, N. P. *Par.* 1646. 12°; 1660; 1662; 1672; 1677. *Rouen*, 1669. 12°; *Amst.* 1683. 12°; *Berlin*, 1692. 12°.
RYER, PT. DU. *Par.* 1663. 12°.
PÉRICAUD, A. *Lyon*, 1823. 8°. [With De Gourcey's Tertullian.] *Paris et Lyon*, 1843. 8°.
GENOUDE. [? ?] In: Pères de l'égl. *Par.* 1837–43. 8°.

German.

Berlin, 1763. 8°.
RUSSWURM, J. G. *Hamb.* 1824. 8°.
LÜBKERT, J. H. B. *Lips.* 1836. 8°.
ALLEKER. *Treier*, 1865.
BIERINGER, A. *Kempten*, 1871. 16°. [The Reithmayer-Thalhofer Bibl.]
DOMBART, BERNH. *Erlangen*, 1876. 8°; 1881. 8°.

Italian.

POLETI. *Ven.* 1756. 8°.

III. *Literature.*

ALZOG. Patrol. (1876) 162–165.
Animadverss. in Min. F. In: Misc. obss. in auct. vet. et rec. I. 1. 23; II. 1. 54; III. 408; VIII. 1. 19; 2. 177; 3. 322.

AUBÉ. Hist, d. persécut. *Par.* 1878. II.
BADEN, T. Mittheilungen aus dem literarischen Nachlasse meines Vaters (Zu Catull., Tibull., Properz, Virgil, Octavius). In: Jahn's Archiv. 2 Bd. (1833) p. 27–432. (?)
BÄHR. Gesch. Rom. Lit. Sup. (1837) II. 18–21, 39–46.
BÄHRENS, AEMIL. Lectiones latinae. Diss. Inaug. *Bonnae*, 1870. 8°. p. 22–31.
— Kritische Satura. (Including: Zu Minuc. Felix, 22, 2.) In: Jahrbb. f. class. Philol. CV. (1872) p. 632.
BALDUINUS, F. De Octavio. In: Ed. Lindner. *Longos.* 1773; also in: Migne. Patrol. Lat. III. (1865) 207–34.
BARONIUS. Ann. (1589) 211, 1–7.
BAUR. Dogmengesch. I. (1865) 266–7, etc.
BEHR, ERNST. Der Octavius d. M. F. in s. Verhältnisse zu Cicero's Büchern de natura deorum. *Gera.* 1870. 8°. [Diss.]
BELLARMIN–LABBE. (1728) 41–2.
BERTHOLDT. Dogmenges. (1822–3) I. 157, etc.
BONDAM, P. Epistola ad Vestzinck. (Containing: Ad Minucium, Justinum, Sedul. aliisque.) In: Otia literar. ad Isalam. (*Campis*, 1762) p. 53–73.
BONWETSCH. In: Die Schriften Tert. 1878. p. 21.
BOUCHARD, P. A. Dissertatio de vita et scriptis M. Minutii Felicis. *Kilonii*, 1685. 4°.
BURTON. Divinity of Christ. (1829) 242–4.
BUSSE. Chr. Lit. (1828–9) I. 22–3.
CAVE. Scr. eccl. hist. lit. (1740–3) I. 101.
CEILLIER. Hist. gen. aut. sac. II. (1730) 222–34; I. (1858) 550–7.
CHEVALIER. Rép. d. sources hist. (1877) 583.
CLARKE. Sacred lit. (1830–1) I. 155–6.
CLINTON. Fasti Rom. (1845–50) II. 417–8.
CORNELISSEN, J. J. *Daventriae*, 1871. 4°.
COTTA. §338–9.
CRUSIUS, CHR. Minucius Felix emend. 1753. s. u. Cyprian.
DARLING. Cycl. bibl. (1854) 2078.
DOMBART, B. Krit. Beitr. zu Minucius F. In: Jahrbb. f. class. Philol. XCIX. (1869) p. 417–422.
— Zur Erkl. u. Krit. d. Minucius F. In: Blätter f. d bayr. Gymnasialschulw. IX. (1873) 285–300.
DORNER. Person of Christ. II. (1866) 193.
DUPIN. Bibl. d. aut. eccl. (1698–) I. 312–22.
EBERT, A. Tertullians Verhältniss zu Minucius F. 1868. S. u. Tertullian.
— Gesch. Lit. Mittel. (1874) I. 24–31.
ELDIK, E. H. VAN. Ad Minuc. Fel. In his: Schediasma crit. (*Berol.* 1744) 111–.
Encycl. Brit. (9th ed.) XVI. 492.
ERNESTI. In: Opusc. var. arg. (1794) 383–92.
EUSEBIUS. II. 2, 25: III. 20; V. 5.
Evang. R. XIII. (1862) 34–.
FABER, ALB. De M. F. *Nordhausen*, 1872. 4°. (44 p.)
FABRICIUS. De verit. rel. chr. (1725) 174, 215–7.
— Bibl. med. aev. (1734) II. 468–75.
— Bibl. lat. (1772) III. 371–7.
FÉLICE, PAUL DE. Etude sur l'Octavius de Minucius F. Thèse. *Blois*, 1880. 8°.
FLEURY. Hist. eccl. (1691–) II. 77–85.
FUNCCIUS. De ling. lat. vegeta senectute. X. § 10–16.
GIESELER. Church Hist. (1868–) I. 147.
GRUNER, J. F. Ad Octav. Cap. XXI. In: Actis Soc. Ienens. III. 33. Cf. IV. 208.
HAGENBACH. Hist. of Doct. I. (1850) 59–60, etc.
HALM, KARL. Zu Minutius Felix (Aus d. Sitzungber. d. Kais. Akad. d. Wiss. zu Wien. Phil.-hist. bl. (1865). 168–71.) *Wien*, 1865. 8°.
HARNACK. Dogmenges. I. (1886) 393–5.
HARTEL, W. In: Ztschr. f. d. öst. Gymn. (1869) 348–368. [M. F. and Tertullian. Agst. Ebert.]
HASE. Kirchenges. (1885–) I. 253–4.

HAUPT, MOR. Analecta. (Containing: Minucii Felicis Octavius, c. 14, 16, 21, 26.) In: Hermes. II. (1867) p. 334–336; also in his: Opuscula. III. 2 (1876) p. 389–391.

— Conjectanea. (Containing: Minucius Felix, c. 16.) In: Hermes. VIII. (1874) p. 249; also in his: Opuscula. III. 2 (1876) 634.

HERGENROETHER. Kirchenges. (1879–80) I. 105–6; III. 41–2.

HEUMANN, C. A. Emend. in Min F. In: *Misc. Lips.* V. 3, 476.

— Obs. qua num. Jure-Consultorum eximitur Minuc. F. *Gött.* 1736. 8°. I. 208.

HIERONYMUS. De vir. ill. 58. (Honor. August. I. 59.)

Holden's Edition of the Octavius. In: Fraser. XLVII. (1852) 288–; same art. Liv. Age. XXXVII. (1852) 259–.

HOLSTENIUS. De verubus Dianae Eph. In Migne. Patrol. Lat. III. (1865) 375–82.

HOLTZMANN. Einl. in d. N. T. (1886) 132.

HOVEN, J. D. VAN. Dissertatio de vera aetate, dignitate et patria M. Minutii Felicis. *Campis,* 1762. 4°; also in: Lindner's ed. 1773.

— Vindiciae Minucianae. In: Stosch. Mus. crit. (1774) p. 133–152.

— Epist. ad Gerh. Meermann. Ed. d. Lindner.

— S. u. Justin M.

HUBER. Philos. d. K.–V. (1859) 213–216.

JEREMIE. Hist. church. (1852) 109–110.

J[OUBERT], L. In: Nouv. Biog. Gen. (Hoefer) XXXV. (1861) 604–8.

KAYSER, J. B. In: Wiedemann's Quartalschr. (862).

KEIM, TH. Celsus wahres Wort. *Zürich,* 1873. 8°. 158–168.

— In: Rom. und das Christenthum, 1881, 383–, 468–486.

KLOTZ, CHR. AD. In his: Miscell. crit. (Traj. ad Rh. 1763) p. 3–17.

KLUSSMANN, E. Zu Minucius Felix (c. V, 9.) In: Rhein. Mus. N. F. XXIII. (1868) 543.

— Zu Minucius Felix (II. 1. V. 5.) In: Rhein. Mus. N. F. XXIX. (1874) 638. XXX. (1875) p. 144.

— Zu Minucius Felix. In: Philologus. XXXV. (1876) p. 206–209.

— In: Jenaer Lit. Zeitg. 1878.

KOCH, H. A. Zu Minucius Felix. In: Rhein. Mus. N. F. XXVIII. (1873) 615–621.

KÜHN, R. Der Octavius d. Minucius Felix. *Leipzig,* 1882. 8°.

KURTZ. Kirchenges. (1885) I. 127.

LARDNER. Credibility. Works. (1831) II. 386–93.

LE NOURRY. Appar. bibl. patr. 1715. II. 2. In: Migne. Patrol. Lat. III. (1865) 381–672. [On Octavius.]

LINDNER. Analysis logica. In: Migne. Patrol. Lat. III. (1865) 233–40.

LOESCHE, G. Minucius Felix' Verhältniss zu Athenagoras. In: Jahrbb. f. prot. Theol. (1882) 168–174.

LUMPER. Hist. ss. Patr. (1790) VII. 99–251; also in: Migne. Patrol. Lat. III. (1865) 201–8.

MÄHLY, JAC. Krit. Beitr. zu Minucius F. In: Jahrbb. f. class. Philol. XCIX. (1869) 422–437.

MANGOLD. In: Herzog. Real.-Enc. (1877–) X. 12–17. (Abr. in: Schaff-Herz. II. 1521.)

MASSEBIEAU, L. In: Lichtenberger. Encycl. (1877–82) IX. 175–82.

MAURICE. Eccl. Hist. (1854) 254.

MEIER, HENR. Commentatio de Minutio Felice. *Turici,* 1824 (5?) 8°.

MEINER, J. W. Min. F. loci aliq. perperam sollic. a corrup. suspic. vind. *Longosaliss.* 1751. 4°.

MEUCKENIUS, F. O. Ἐπίκρισις modesta eorum, quae ad Min. F. a cel. Heumann observata sunt, Misc. *Lips.* V. 4, 729.

MEURSIUS, JOAN. Hypocriticus Minucianus. *Lugd. Bat.* 1599. 8°.

Min. F. pro se et statu suo episto. apolog. (ad Meuckenium). In: Nova Acta Erudit. (1738) 210–.

MUENSCHER. Dogmenges. (1817–8) I. 186, etc.

NEANDER. Church Hist. (1872) I. 690–1 et pass.

NIRSCHL. Patrol. (1881–) I. 295–301.

NITZSCH. Dogmengesch. (1870) 167–8, etc.

NODIER. Bib. sacr. (1826) 158–9.

NONNOTE. Les philosophes. (1789).

OELRICHS. Scr. eccl. lat. (1791) 15–6.

ORSI. Ist. eccl. (1746–) II. 453–5; (1749–) II. 653–7.

OTT, J. N. In: Ztschr. f. d. öster. Gymn. XXVI. (1875) 900–902.

PERMANEDER. Bibl. patrist. (1841–) I. 418; II. 694–706.

PRESSENSÉ. Martyrs. (1879) 367–8, 589–90.

PRILESZKY. S. u. Theophilus of Ant.

RAMSAY, W. In: Smith. Gr. and Rom. Biog. (1859) II. 144–5.

RECK. M. F. u. Tertullian. In: Theol. Quartalschr. LXVIII. (1886) 64–114.

RENAN. Marc-Aurèle. 1882. p. 389–404.

REUSCH. In: Wetzer u. W. Kirch-Lex. (1847–54) VII. 153–4.

RHOER, JAC. DE. Minuc. Fel. locu quaedam emend. et indicantur. In his: Feriae Daventrienses s. miscell. libri. II. (1758) 11. c. 23, 24.

RÖNSCH. N. T. Tertull.'s. (1871) 25–.

ROEREN, C. Minuciana. *Bedburg (Köln?)* 1859. 265; do. Pt. II. Gymn. Progr. *Brilon,* 1877. 4°. (8 p.)

ROESSLER. Bibl. d. K.–V. III. (1777) 1–31.

SALMON, G. In: Smith and Wace. Dict. III. 920–4.

SCHAFF. Hist. . . Church. II. (1886) 833–41.

SCHMID. Patrol. (1879); (1886) 59–60.

SCHOENEMANN. Bibl. patr. lat. (1792) I. 58–77.

SCHRAM. Anal. ss. patr. (1780–) III. 637–682.

SCHROECKH. Kirchenges. (1772–) III. 417–24.

SCHULTZE, M. Die Abfassungszeit. d. Octavius d. Minucius F. In: Jahrbb. f. prot. Theol. (1881) 485–506.

SCHWENKE, P. Ueb. d. Zeit. d. M. F. In: Jahrb. f. prot. Theol. IX. (1883) 263–94.

SOULET, A. Essai sur l'Octavius de Minucius Felix. *Strasbourg,* 1867. 8°.

STIEBER, G. F. S. Observatt. nonnullae crit. in quaedam P. Virgilii et Minucii F. loca. Progr. *Onoldi,* 1791. 4°.

STRUEHTMEYER, J. J. Ad. Minuc. F. In: Animadv. crit. libri. II. (1755) 55–59.

Supernatural Religion. (1875–7) pass.

TEUFFEL. Hist. Rom. Lit. (1873) II. 272–5.

TILLEMONT. Mémoires. III. (1695) 163–8, 647–8.

TIRABOSCHI. Stor. lett. Ital. (1806) II. 11. 366.

TRITHEMIUS. Scr. eccl. 34.

UEBERWEG. Hist. philos. (1876) 319–22.

VONCK, C. V. Specim. crit. in var. auctor. (1744) p. 19, 20. 136–137, 139–141; and in: Lection. Lat. libri. II. (1745) p. 51–60.

VOREAUX, ÉLISÉE. Octavius de Minucius F. Thèse. *Strasbourg,* 1859. 8°.

WAITE. Hist. Chr. Rel. (1881) 121.

WALCH. Bibl. patrist. (1834) 42–3, 379.

WALLIS, R. E. Introd. note. In: Ante-Nic. Lib. XIII. (1873) 447–50. Ed. Coxe. IV. (1885) 167–71. [Add. note. Ed. Coxe. 19S.]

WEISS. In: Biog. Univ. Michaud. 1842–65. XXVIII. 349.

WESSELINGIUS, PETR. Obss. variar. libri. II. ed. Frotscher. (1832) p. 31.

WOPKENS, THOM. Adversaria crit. in M. Minucii F. Octavium. 1834. In his: Adversaria critica. (1828–34).

WORDSWORTH. Church Hist. (1881) 109–114.

WORMAN, J. H. In: M'Clintock and S. Cycl. (1874-) VI. 305.

Note. Minucius and Tertullian. M. earlier: Rössler, Muralt, van Hoven, Meier, Russwurm, Boren, Bernhardy, EBERT, Ueberweg, Teuffel, Rönsch, Keim, Caspari, Herzog, Alzog, Hauck, Bonwetsch, Mangold, Kühn, Renan. Schwenke. *T. earlier:* Rigalt, Ceillier, Galland and earlier critics generally, Lübkert, Bähr, Möhler, Hartel, Nirschl, Jeep, Klussmann, Schultze, Salmon, Massebieau, Schaff, Coxe.

III. COMMODIAN.

I. *Editions.*

(Instructiones.)

RIGALTIUS. *Tulli Leuc.* (*Toul.*) 1650. 4°.
PRIORIUS. In: Cypr. op. *Par.* 1666. 4°.
SCHURZFLEISCH. *Vitemb.* 1704. 4°; app. 1709. 4°; *Viteb.* 1750.
DAVISIUS. Cantab. 1712. 8°. 193-269. [With the Octavius of Minucius F.]
GALLAND. In: Bibl. patr. III. (1767) 621-.
MIGNE. Patrol. lat. V. (1844) 189-262.
OEHLER, F. *Lips.* 1847. 12°. In: Gersdorf. Bibl. patr. eccl. lat. XIII.
PITRA. In: Spicil. Solesm. IV. (1858).
LUDWIG, ERN. *Lips.* 1878. 8°.

(Carmen apologeticum.)

PITRA, J. B. In: Spicil. Solesm. I. (1852).
RÖNSCH, H. In: Ztschr. f. d. hist. Theol. (1872) 163-302 (1873) 302-4. [Text much improved.]
LUDWIG. *Lips.* 1877. 8°.

II. *Translations.*

English.

WALLIS, R. E. In: Ante-Nic. Lib. XVIII. (1870) 434-74. Ed. Coxe. IV. (1885) 203-18.

III. *Literature.*

ALZOG. Patrologie (1876) 340-2.
AUBÉ, B. Essai d'interpretation d'un fragment du Carmen apologeticum de Commodien. In: Revue archéologique. (1883) 312-320.
BÄHR. Gesch. Röm. Lit. (1872) IV. 27-34, 329.
ΒΑΦΕΙΔΗΣ. Ἐκκλ. ἱστ. I. (1884) 162 [5 ll.]
BUSSE. Chr. Lit. (1828-9) I. 37-8.
CAVE. Scr. eccl. hist. lit. (1740-3) I. 136-8.
CEILLIER. Hist. gén. aut. sac. IV. (1733) 179-81; III. (1865) 148-53.
CHÉSUROLLES, D. In: Biog. Univ. (Michaud.) (1842-65.) VIII. 692.
CHEVALIER. Rép. d. sources hist. (1877-86) 484.
CLARKE. Sacred lit. (1830-1) I. 193-4.
CLINTON. Fasti Rom. (1845-50) II. 450.
COXE, A. C. Introd. note. In: Ante-Nic. Lib. Ed. Coxe. IV. (1885) 199-201. [Add. note, p. 219.]
DODWELL. Diss. de Comm. In: Annal. Quintil.; and in ed. of Schurzfleisch.
DOMBART, B. Commodian-Studien. In: Sitzungsber. d. kaiserl. Ak. d. Wiss. in Wien. C. (1884) 713-802. ["Gebührt . . . ein hoher u. ansehnlicher Rang." *Rönsch.*]
— Ueber d. Bedeutung Commodians f. d. Textkritik d. Testimonia Cyprian's. In: Ztschr. f. wiss. Theol. XXII. (   ) 374-389.
DUPIN. Nouv. bibl. (1698) I. 625.
EBERT. Anhang. üb. Commodian's Carmen ap. In his: Tertullian's Verhältn. z. Minucius F. (1868) 69-102. S. u. Tertullian.
— Gesch. Lit. Mittel. I. (Gesch. der christl. lat. Lit. *Lpz.* 1874) 86-93.
— In: Herzog. Real. Enc. III. (1878) 325-6.

EBERT. In Herzog. Real.-Enc. (1877-) III. 325-6. (Abr. in Schaff-Herz. I. 518.)
FABRICIUS. De verit. rel. Christ. (1725) 227-30.
— Bibl. med. aev. (1734) I. 1139-43.
FLÜGGE. Gesch. d. theol. wiss. II. 98.
FRITZ. In: Wetzer u. W. Kirch-Lex. (1847-54) II. 715-7.
GENNADIUS. De vir. ill. 15. (Honor. August. 11, 15.)
HAUPT, MOR. Conjectanea. (Commodianus. Instr. II. 22, 13.) In: Hermes. V. (1871) 316-317; also in his: Opuscula. III. 2 (1876) 539-540.
HAVET, L. Varia. (Contains: Commodianus. Instr. 17; 20, 1-3.) In: Revue de philologie. N. S. I. (1877) p. 166.
HERGENROETHER. Kirchenges. (1879-80) I. 105-6; III. 41-.
JACOBI. In: Ztschr. f. Wiss u. Leben. (1853) 203-9.
KAELBERLAH, LUD. Curarum in Commodiani instructiones Specimen. Diss. *Halis Sax.* 1877. 8°.
KRAUS. In: Theol. Lit.-Bl. (1871) No. 22.
KURTZ. Kirchenges. (1885-) I. 127.
LARDNER. Credibility. Works. (1831) III. 131-5.
LEIMBACH. Ueber Commodians Carmen apologeticum. Programm. *Schmalcald,* 1871. 4°. (28 p.)
Lichtenberger. Encycl. (1877-82) III. 280-1.
LIPSIUS, R. A. D. redende Löwe bei C. In: Jahrb. f. Prot. Theol. IX. (1883) 192.
LUDWIG, E. Zu Commodianus. In: Philologus. XXXVI. (1877) 285-305.
LUMPER. Hist. ss. patr. XIII. (1799) 390-407.
M'CLINTOCK and S. Cycl. (1874-) II. 437.
MÖHLER. Patrologie. (1840) 903-.
MÜLLER, LUC. Sammelsurien. (Commod. Instr. II. 18.) In: Jahrb. f. class. Philol. XCVII. (1868) p. 435.
MUNROE, H. A. J. In: Trans. Camb. Phil. Soc. X. II. 9.
NEANDER. Hist. of dogmas. (1858) 171. [v. 1.]
— Church Hist. (1872) I. 686-7, 68, 228-9, 237, 280, 288, 303, 329 et pass.
NIRSCHL. Patrol. (1881-) I. 357-60.
Nouv. Biog. Gén. (Hoefer) XI. (1855) 355-6.
OEHLER, S. FR. Commodian's Carmen apol. In: Theol. Stud. u. Krit. XLV. (1872) 180-188.
OUDIN. Comm. de script. eccl. (1722) I. 319-20.
— Suppl. Bellar. (1728) 64.
PERMANEDER. Bibl. patrist. (1841-3) I. 422; II. 897-9.
RAMSAY, W. In: Smith. Gr. and Rom. Biog. (1859) I. 816.
RÖNSCH, H. In: Ztschr. f. wiss. Theol. XXVIII. (1885) 375-8.
ROVERS, M. A. N. Een apocalypse uit de derde eeuw. In: Theol. Tijdschr. (1886) 457-72. [Carmen ap.]
SCHAFF. Hist. Church. II. 1886) 853-6.
SCHRAM. Anal. ss. patr. (1780-) VI. 482-518.
SCHROECKH. Kirchenges. (1772) IV. 438-441.
TEUFFEL. Hist. Rom. Lit. (1873) II. 304-6.
VONCK, C. V. Ad Commodian. In his: Lection. lat. libri. II. 1745) p. 74.
YOUNG, E. M. In: Smith and Wace. Dict. I. 610-1.

Note. Time of Commodian. 3d century : Dodwell, Cave, Busse, Permaneder, Möhler, Pitra, Ebert, Bähr, Teuffel, Fritz, Nirschl, Young, Schaff, Kurtz, Coxe; *4th century :* Rigaltius, Dupin, Ceillier, Clinton. Alzog dates the Apol. c. 411.

IV. ORIGEN.

I. *Editions.*

(Works.)

DE LA RUE. Gr. lat. *Par.* 1733-59. 4 v. f°.
OBERTHÜR, FR. Gr. lat. *Viceburgae,* 1785. 15 v. 8°.
LOMMATZSCH. *Berol.* 1831-48. 25 v. 8°.
MIGNE. Patrol. gr. XI-XVIII. (1857-63).

(Various.)

WETSTENIUS. (Cont. Marc., Ad mart., Susann.) Gr. lat. *Basil.* 1674. 4⁰.

SPENCERUS, GUIL. (Contra Celsum, Philocalia.) Gr. lat. *Cantabr.* 1658. 4⁰; do. 1677. 4⁰.

(Opuscula.) Gr. lat. *Paris,* 1713. 2 v. f⁰.

(De principiis.)

REDEPENNING. *Lips.* 1836. 8⁰.

SCHNITZER, K. F. *Stuttg.* 1836. 8⁰.

(Against Celsus.)

HENSCHELIUS, DAV. Gr. lat. *Aug. Vindel.* 1605. 4⁰. [Latin tr. by Gelenius.]

SELWYN, W. *Lond.* 1876.

(De oratione.)

Gr. lat. *Oxon.* 1686. (?) 12⁰.

WETSTENIUS, J. R. Gr. lat. *Amst.* 1694. 4⁰.

READING, GUIL. Gr. lat. *Lond.* 1728. 4⁰. Prospectus published, *Lond.* 1727. 4⁰. [8 pp.]

(Hexapla.)

Vetus Test. juxta LXX. *Romae,* 1587. f⁰. passim. [The Sixtine LXX. The fragments of the H. scattered through the notes]; also in: Do., latine redd. *Romae,* 1588. f⁰.

DRUSIUS, J. In: Interpr. vet. graec. . . . fragm. *Arnhem.* 1622.

MONTFAUCON, BERN. DE. Hebr. gr. lat. *Par.* 1713. 2 v. f⁰.

BAHRDT, CAR. FRID. Hebr. gr. lat. *Lips.* 1769–70. 2 v. 8⁰.

FIELD, FR. *Oxon.* 1875.

(Other.)

FAQUES, W. Omelia Origenis. Impressu in alma civitate london. In Abkirche lane. 16⁰. ? [Ten leaves without numerals, signatures, or catchwords.]

MORELLUS, FEDER. (Scholia in orat. dem.) Gr. lat. *Lutet.* 1601. 8⁰.

(De Susanna.) With: Adriani Isagoge. 1602. 4⁰. p. 84–7.

TARINUS, JO. (Philocalia.) Gr. lat. *Paris,* 1618. [" Not 1619 "] 4⁰; with new title. *Paris,* 1624. 4⁰; 1629. 4⁰.

GHISLERIUS, MICH. (Homiliae.) Gr. lat. In his: Comment. in Jeremiam. *Lugd.* 1623. f⁰.

ALLATIUS, LEO. (Comment. on 1 Kings. 28 v.) Gr. lat. In: S. Eustathii Commentarius in Hexaemeron. *Lugd.* 1629. 4⁰. p. 328–344; also in: Critica sacra Anglia. *Lond.* . . f⁰. VIII. (1660) 407–418.

HUET, DAN. (Commentaria.) Gr. lat. *Rothom.* 1668. 2 v. f⁰; with new title. *Par.,* 1679. f⁰; also, *Colon.* 1685. f⁰.

MARTINAEUS, J. (Interpretatio, etc.) Gr. lat. In: Hieronymi Opera. *Paris,* f⁰. II. (1699).

(Lexicon.) In: Hieronymi opera. Veron. f⁰. III. (1735) p. 605.

(Scholia.) In: Vet. patr. eccl. scr. Analecta nova. *Venet.* 1781. f⁰. p. 3–109.

(Fragments.)

GALLAND. In: Bibl. patr. XVI.

MAIUS. In: Class. auct. IX. (*Rome,* 1837. 8⁰.) 257; X. 474–82; Scr. vet. nov. coll. (*Rome,* 1825–) I. II. 161–.

TISCHENDORF, C. Gr. *Lips.* 1860. 4⁰.

II. *Translations.*

Latin.

MERLINUS, J., and PAROY, GUIL. *Parhis.* 1512. 4 v. f⁰; *Par.* 1519. 4 v. f⁰; 1522. f⁰.

Venet. 1516. f⁰. [Works before omitted.]

ERASMUS. *Basil.* 1536. f⁰; *Lugd.* 1536. f⁰; *Basil.* 1545. f⁰.

GRINAEUS, JAC. *Basil.* 1571. 2 v. f⁰. [After Erasmus.]

GENEBRARDUS, GILB. *Paris,* 1574. 2 v. f⁰; *Paris,* 1594. 2 v. f⁰ (?); *Paris,* 1604. 2 v. f⁰; *Paris,* 1619. 2 v. f⁰.

———

(Homiliae.) 1475. f⁰.

"CHRISTOPHERUS PERSONA ROMANUS." (Contra Celsum.) *Romae,* 1481. f⁰; *Venet.* 1514. f⁰.

HIERONYMUS. (Homiliae.) *Venet.* 1503. f⁰; 1512. f⁰.

— (Comment. Rom.) *Venet.* 1506. f⁰; *Venet.* 1512. f⁰.

— (Homil. in Cant. Cantic.) In: Opera. II. (*Paris,* 1669) 807–826; V. 603–678.

HIERONYMUS and HILARIUS. (Homiliae.) *Venet.* 1513. f⁰.

(De principiis.) *Venet.* 1514. f⁰.

ERASMUS. (Fragm. in Matt.) *Basil.* 1527. 8⁰; also in: Erasmi Opera. VIII. (*Lugd. Bat.* 1703. f⁰.) 439–484.

FERRARIUS, AMBR. (Comment. in Joh.) *Venet.* 1551. 4⁰.

PICUS, JOH. (De recta fide.) *Par.* 1556. 4⁰.

HUMPHREY. *Basil.* 1557. [Not pub. until 1571.]

ROUS, FR. (Contra Celsum.) In: Mella patr. *Lond.* 1650. 8⁰. p. 759–830.

— (Hom. in Gen.) In: Mella patr. *Lond.* 1699. 407–.

COMBEFIS, FR. (Homiliae, etc.) In: Bibl. patr. *Par.* 1859.

RUFINUS. In: Caspari. Kirchenhist. anecdota. Christiana, 1883. 8⁰. 3–129. [" 5 dialogues against the Gnostics, falsely ascribed to O."]

———

(Homiliae.) *Lond.* n. d. 16⁰.

English.

WOLFE, R. (Homilies of Mary Magdalene and Abraham.) *Lond.* 1565. 16⁰.

BELLAMY, J. (Against Celsus.) *Lond.* 8⁰.

CROMBIE, F. In: Ante-Nic. Lib. X. (1869) 1–478; XXIII. (1872) 1–559. Ed. Coxe. IV. (1885) 237–669.

French.

DELOYAC. (Homileae.) In: Bibl. Sacra. *Par.* 1634. 4⁰.

BONHÉREAU, E. (Contra Celsum.) *Amst.* 1700. 4⁰.

GENOUDE. [? ?] In: Pères de l'égl. *Par.* 1837–43. 8⁰.

German.

MOSHEIM, J. L. (Contra Celsum.) *Hamburg,* 1745. 4⁰.

KOHLHOFER, J. *Kempten,* 1875-7. 16⁰. [The Reithmayer-Thalhofer Bibl.]

Italian.

PASSAVANTI, JACOPO. (Homiliae.) In: Specchio di Penitenza. *Venet.* 1586. 8⁰; *Venet.* 1608. 8⁰; *Fierenze,* (1681) 12⁰; *Fier.* 1723. 8⁰; *Fier.* 1725. 4⁰.

Note. The "Contra Marcionitas" is the same as "De recta in Deum fide" and the work of ADAMANTIUS. (Cf. Hort. in Smith and W.] For editions of the Philosophumena see HIPPOLYTUS.

Several of Origen's works exist only in the Latin versions of Hieronymus, Rufinus, and others. For eds. of these s. u. Latin translations.

III. *Literature.*

ALEXANDER, NATALIS. Histor. Eccl. Secul. III. Dissertat. 16 sq. p. 701.

— In: Zaccaria. Thes. theol. (1762) X. 761–7.

ALZOG. Patrol. (1876) 135–152, § 33, 34.

— Kirchenges. Vol. I.

American Church R. XX. (1868) 401–.

Arch. d. Missions. (1866) B. II. 504–5.

ARTAUD. In: Dict. scien. philos. (1875) 1227–31.

AUBÉ. Hist. des perséc. II. (1876); also in: "Celse," 1878.

[BARBOUR.] Historic Episcopate. (1877) 30.

BARONIUS. Ann. (1589) 204, 9–10; 205, 3–10; 208, 1–3; 220, 6–12; 230, 1–7; 231, 1–9, 64–5; 232, 1–10; 233, 5–6; 237, 13; 242, 1; 243, 3; 248, 1–4; 251, 1; 253, 116–23; 256, 38–47; Cf. Pagi. Crit. (1689) 204, 6; 208, 2; 217, 3; 230, 2, 7; 231, 5–8, 16; 235, 4; 243, 3; 246, 7; 248, 2–4, 6; 249, 12; 251, 2, 5–6; 253, 6–8; 256, 23–5.

BAUER. Uber des Origenes Hexapla. S. his: Einleitung in die schriften des A. T. p. 151–.

BAUMGARTEN–CRUSIUS. Dogmenges. (1832) 211–7. [v. 1.]

BAUR. In: Theol. Jahrb. (1837).

— Kirchenges. 3 e. J. (1863) 51–3, 350–55.

— Dogmengesch. I. (1865) 274–80, etc.

— Lehre v. d. Versönung. 46–.

— Gesch. d. Dreieinigkeitslehre. I. 186–243, 560–66.

ΒΑΦΕΙΔΗΣ. 'Εκκλ. ίστ. I. (1884) 157–8.

BAYLE. Dict. crit. (1741) III. 538–47.

BELLARMIN–LABBE. Scr. eccl. (1728) 44–7.

BERROW, CAPEL. Theol. dissert. (1772).

BERTHOLDT. Dogmenges. (1822–3) I. 56, etc.

BESTMANN, H. J. In: Ztschr. f. kirchl. Wiss. u. Leben. (1883) 169–87.

BIGG, C. Christian Platonists of Alexandria. Oxf. and N.Y. 1886. 8°. 115–268. [Bampton Lectures, 1886.]

BINDEMANN. Celsus u. s. Schriften gegen die Christen. In: Zeitschr. f. hist. Theol. Lpz. (1842) 58–146.

BINET, ESTIENNE. Du salut d'Origène: quest. I. a sçavoir si Origène est sauvé ou damné . . . Paris, 1629. 12°; 1631. 12°.

BLACKBURN. Hist. of Church. (1879) 49–59.

BOCHART, SAM., and HUET, PIER. DAN. Lettres sur le sentiment d'Origène sur l'invocation des anges et sur l'Eucharistie. In: Tilladet. Dissert. s. div. matier. (1714) I. 1–194.

BOCHINGER, JOH. J. De Origenis allegorica S. interpretione. Dissert. hist.-theol. Argentorati, 1829–30. 3 pts. 8°.

BOEHRINGER. Kirchenges. (1873–) I. v. 104–.

BORNEMANN, FR. W. B. In investiganda monachatus origine quibus de causis ratio habenda sit Origenis. Diss. Gottingae, 1884. 8°.

BRUCKER. Hist. crit. phil. (1766–7) III. 427–59; VI. 542–9.

BUCKMANN, R. Origenes, der Vater der theol. Wissensch., der Apologet. u. Bekenner. In: Beweis des Glaubens (1877) 169–179, 225–36.

BUDDEUS, J. F. Isagog. ad theol. univers. Lib. II. cap. 7. p. 1005–.

— Exercitatio hist.-philol. de allegoriis Origenis. Wittebergae, 1689. 4°. (= his Parerg. histor.-theolog. (17.) 139.

BULL, G. Defensio Fid. Nic. chap. IX. In: Migne. Patrol. Gr. XVII. (1857) 1285–330.

BUNSEN. Hippolytus. (1854) I. 279–300.

BURTON. Divinity of Christ. (1829) 280–348.

— Trinity. (1831) 87–107.

BUSSE. Chr. Lit. (1828–9) I. 23–6.

CAILLAU. Introd. in ss. Patr. (1825) 80–92.

CAVE. Scr. eccl. hist. lit. (1740–3) I. 112–22.

— Lives. (1840) I. 321–61.

CEILLIER. Hist. gén. aut. sac. II. (1730) 584–782. II. (1865) 130–256, 645–9.

CHARTERIS. Canonicity. (1880) lxxxiii-lxxxv. 8–9, 51–2, 81–6, 136–7, 163, 185, 205, 211, 221, 241, 264, 269, 280–2, 297–8, 308–9, 316–7, 323–4, 333–4, 344–5, 452–3.

CHASE, I. Origen on Baptism. In: Chr. R. XIX. (1854) 180–.

CHEVALIER. Rép. d. sources hist. (1877–86) 1683–4.

CLARKE. Sacred lit. (1830–1) I. 160–172.

CLERICUS, J. S. u. Le Clerc.

CLINTON. Fasti Rom. (1845–50) I. 183, 209, 213, 215, 239, 241, 243, 245; 275. II. 415, etc. 496–507.

COBET. Fragmenta comicorum apud Origenum contra Celsum latentia. In: Mnemosyne. VIII. (1859) p. 419–420.

v. COELLN. In: Ersch u. Gruber. III. v. (1834) 251–62.

COFFIN. Lives of fath. (1846) 357–75.

CONDOS (Κοντος) C. S. Κριτικὰ καὶ γραμματικὰ. Containing 'Ωριγέν. τόμ. ΙΓ', σελ. 216. In: 'Αθήναιον. V. (1876) p. 498–499.

— Συμμικτὰ κριτικά. Contains: 'Ωριγέν. τόμ. Κ', σελ. 244 and ΙΗ' 49. βερολ. In: Bullet. de corresp. Hell. I. (1877) p. 76; II. (1878) p. 239.

CONE, O. Origen's Hermeneutics. In: Univ. Q. XXXI. (1873) 209–.

CONTESTIN, G. Origène exégète. Arras, 1867. 8°. Extrait de la Rev. d. sci. eccl. (1866–7) B. IV. 155–71, 320–44, 489–502; V. 133–50.

COTTA. § 356–367.

CROIUS, J. Notae ad Contr Celsum. In: Migne. Patrol. gr. XI. (1857) 1689–710.

— Specimen conject. et obs. in quaedam loca Origenis, Iren., Tert. and Epiph. 1632. 8°.

CROMBIE, F. Introd. note. In: Ante-Nic. Lib. X. (1869) vii-ix; XXIII. (1872) xxiii-xxxviii. Ed. Coxe. IV. (1885) 221–35. [Add. notes. Ed. Coxe. 382-4, 394.]

CUNNINGHAM, FR. A dissertation on the books of Origen against Celsus. Cambridge, 1812. 8°.

CUNNINGHAM, WM. Churches of Asia. (1880) pass.

— Hist. theol. (1870) I. 154–8.

DARLING. Cycl. bibl. (1854) 1157, 2239–44.

DATHE, J. A. = Ernesti, J. A.

D'AUBIGNÉ, J. H. MERLE. L'Orient, ou Origène et la science. In: Union chrét. d. jeunes gens. (Genev. 1857.)

De Hexaplis Origenis disseritur. In: Disquisitiones criticae de variis per diversa loca et tempora Bibliorum editionibus. (Lond. 1684. 4°.) cap. XVIII. p. 143–156.

DELARUE. Praef. In: Migne. Patrol. gr. XI. (1857) 13–38.

DELLMARK, J. P. F. Error. Cf. Dettmer.

DENIS, J. De la philosophie d'Origène. Paris, 1884. 8°.

DETTMER, JOHANN PHILIPP. Commentatio historico-critica de theologia Origenis. Francofurti ad Viadr. 1782–90. 5 pts. 4°.

DIESTEL. Gesch. d. A. T. in d. chr. Kirche. (1869) 36–, 53–.

Dissertation sur deux passages d'Origene au sujet des mesures de l'Arche de Noe. In: Mém. de Trévoux (1740, Déc.) 2353–63.

DOEDERLEIN, J. Ch. Ad edit. Montfauc. Hexaplorum Origenis Animadv. In: Eichhorn's Repertorium für bibl. u. morgenländ. Litteratur. I. 217–256; IV. 257–; VI. 195–; VIII. 85–; IX. 157–; X. 58–; XIII. 177–; XIV. 183–; XV. 38–.

DÖLLINGER. Hippolytus and Callistus (1876) 1–2, 235–49, 253–6.

DORNER. Person of Christ. II. (1866) 104–47, 457–66.

DOUCIN, LOUIS. Histoire des mouvements arrivez dans l'Eglise au sujet d'Origène et de sa doctrine. Par. 1700. 12°.

DUGNET. Dissertationes sur Origène. In: Henrion. Hist. ecclés. (1857) XII. 875–916.

DUPIN. Bibl. aut. eccl. (1698) I. 326–418.

EHINGERUS, ELIAS. Origenes labilis seu de Naevis Origenis dissertatio. In: Jac. Bruckeri Vita Eliae Ehingeri. (Aug. Vindel., 1724. 8°.) p. 151–.

EHRENFEUCHTER. De Celso. Gottingen, 1848, 1849.

EMERSON, R. Life, Writings, and Opinions of Origen. In: Am. Bib. Repos. IV. (1834) 33–.

ENGELHARDT, VIT. In: Theol. Stud. u. Krit. XI. (1839) 157.

— Dogmenges. I. (1839) 95–9.

ENGELHARDT, W. D. Lehre d. O. v.-d. Auferstehung d. Todten. In: Ztschr. f. luth. Theol. XXXV. (1874) 608–24.

EPIPHANIUS. Haeres. 64.

ERASMUS, DESID. De vita, phrasi, docendi ratione et operibus Origenis epitome. In: Erasmi Epistolae. (*Lond.*, 1642. f⁰. 1619–; also in: Opera. *Lugd. Bat.* 1703. f⁰.)

ERDMANN. Gesch. d. Philos. I. (*Berlin*, 1878) 217–9.

ERNESTI, J. A. Disputatio de Origene interpretationes librorum s. s. grammaticae auctore. *Lipsiae*, 1756. 4⁰. (Also in his: Opusc. philol.-crit. (1776) 288.)

EUSEBIUS. Hist. Eccles. VI. 1–6 et pass.

FABRICIUS. Bibl. gr. (1712) II. 342–58; IV. 547–8; V. 213–46, 292; IX. 382–3; XIII. 837. (2ᵃ. III. 708–14; VI. 199–201; VII. 201–49, 329; X. 688.)

— De verit. relig. Christ. (1725) 63–4, 162.

FARRAR, A. S. Crit. hist. of free thought. 50–, 285, 404, 457, 460.

FARRAR, F. W. Interpretation. (1886) 187–201.

FENGER. De Celso, Christian. advers. Epicuroeo. *Havn.* 1828.

FERMAUD, ULYSSE. Exposition critique des opinions d'Origène sur la nature et l'origine du péché . . . *Strasbourg*, 1859. 8⁰.

FIEBIG. Corp. diss. theol. (1847) 1681, 4281, 6785, 9055.

FISCHER. Comment. de Orig. theol. et cosmol. 1846.

FLEURY. Hist. eccl. (1691) II. 40–1, 71–2, 87–9, 100–1, 103–12, 118–20, 122–5, 128–31, 140–51, 256–69.

FOSSÉ, PIERRE THOM. DE (= pseud. Motthe de la) S. u. Tertullian.

FOURNIER, ANDRÉ. Exposition critique des idées d'Origène sur la rédemption. *Strasbourg*, 1861. 8⁰. (54 p.)

FREPPEL, CH. E. (R. C.) Origène. Cours d'éloquence sacrée fait à la Sarbonne pendant les années 1866 et 1867. *Paris*, 1868. 2 v. 8⁰; 2 éd. *Paris*, 1875. 2 v. 8⁰.

— In: Le Correspondant. (1853) XXXI. 509–21.

FRITZSCHE. In: Herzog. I. 285–98.

FROUDE, J. A. Origen against Celsus. In: Fraser, XCVII. (1877) 142–.

FUNK. Die Zeit "Wahren Wortes" von Celsus. In: Theol. Quartalschr. (1886) 302–315.

Future State, The : or, a discourse attempting some display of the soul's happiness, (according to the opinion of Origene) in regard to that eternally progressive knowledge, or eternal increase of knowledge and the consequences of it, which is amongst the Blessed in Heaven. By a Country-Gentleman, a Worshiper of God in the way of the Church of England. *London*, 1683. 8⁰.

GAMBA. Testi. Ital. (1828) 593–6, 1224.

GAUDENTIUS, PAGAN. Opus de dogmatum Origenis cum philosophia Platonis comparatione, salebrae Tertullianae, de vita christianorum ante tempora Constantini. *Florentiae*, 1639. f⁰. *Pisis*, 1641. 4⁰.

— Opusc. tria. *Pisis*, 1644. 4⁰.

GAUPP, C. Vindiciae Origenis in doctrina de divinitate Christi. *Jenae*, 1727. 4⁰. (40 p.)

GEORGIADES, B. (Γεωργιαδης, Β.) ' Ο 'Ωριγένης ὡς ἑρμηνευτὴς τῶν ἁγίων Γραφῶν κατὰ τοὺς ἁγίους πατέρας καὶ διδασκάλους, τῆς 'Εκκλησίας Βασίλειον τον μέγαν καὶ Γρηγόριον τὸν θεολόγον. In: 'Εκκλησιαστικὴ 'Αλήθεια. (1885) 97–110, 193–211; 241–256; 529–543; 1–24, 49–62.

GIESELER. Church Hist. (1868–) I. 177, 209–10, 214–23.

— S. u. Clement of A.

GLEY and BRUNET. In: Biog. Univ. (Michaud) (1842–65) XXXI. 345–9.

GREGORIUS, THAUM. Oratio panegyrica in Origenem.

GUERICKE. Ch. Hist. I. 104–.

HAGENBACH, K. R. Observationes historico-hermeneuticae circa Origenis methodum interpretandae S.S. *Basil.* 1823. 8⁰.

— Hist. of Doct. I. (1850) 63–4, etc.

HAGENBACH, K. R. Kirchenges. (1885) I. 199–210.

HALLOIX, PIERRE. Origines defensus, sive Origenis Adamantii presbyteri amatoris Jesu vita, virtutes, documenta libris. IV. *Leodi.* 1648. f⁰.

HARNACK, A. Dogmenges. I. (1886) 227, 271–2, 289, 307–9, 337–9, 511–56, 648–9.

— Encycl. Brit. (9th ed.) XVII. 839–43.

HARRER. Die Trinitälslehre d. Origenes. Prgr. *Regensb.* 1858. 4⁰. (15 s).

HARRIS, A. Origen and his Opinions. In: Mercersb. XVIII (1871) 526–.

HASE. Kirchenges. (1885–) I. 254–5, 354–60, 433–4, 544–5.

HEFELE. In: Wetzer u. Kirch-Lex. (1847–54) VII. 825–44; also in his: Conciliengeschichte, ii, 76–.

HERGENROETHER. Kirchenges. (1879–80) I. 104–6, 163–6; III. 41–2, 71–2.

HIBBERD, S. S. Origen and Universalism. In: Univ. Q. XXXV (1878) 5–.

HIERONYMUS. De vir. ill. 54. (Honor. August. I. 54. App. II. 3.)

— Ep. 84 ad Pammachum de erroribus Orig., also Epp. 29, 41.

HILGENFELD. Ketzergesch. (1884) 43–4.

HILSCHER and STRAUSS. Schola Alex. (1776) 27–8.

HODY, HUM. De Origenis Hexaplis. In his: De Bibliorum textibus originalibus, etc. (*Oxon.* 1705. f⁰.) 599–.

HOEFER, F. In: Nouv. Biog. Gén. (Hoefer) XXXVIII. (1862) 789–97.

HOEFLING, JOAN GUIL. FRID. Origenes doctrinam de sacrificiis Christianorum in examen vocavit. *Erlangae*, 1741. 3 Pts. 4⁰.

HOLTZMANN. Einl. in d. N. T. (1886) 46–7, etc.

HORBIUS, JOHANN HEINRICH. Historia Origeniana. *Francofurti*, 1670. 4⁰.

HORT, F. J. A. Article: Adamantius. In: Smith and Wace. Dict. I. 39–41. [The Contra Marc. or De recta fide.]

HOVEY, A. In: Chr. R. XXI (1856) 83–.

HUBER. Philos. d. K.–V. (1859) 149–152.

HUETIUS, PET. DAN. Origeniana, seu de vita, doctrina et scriptis Origenis libri III. In: Origenis in s. Scripturae comment. *Rothomagi*. (1668) 1–278. (= Origenis opera omnia. (1759) IV. 11, 79–338, and Migne. Patrol. gr. XVII. (1857) 633–1284.)

JACHMANN. De Celso, etc. 1836.

JAHN, A. Des h. Eustathius, . . . Beurtheilung d. Origenes, betreff. d. Auffassung d. Wahrsagerin i Kön. (Sam) 28, etc. (Gebhardt u. Harnack. Texte u. Untersuch. II. IV.) *Leipz.* 1886. 8⁰. [Cf. Overbeck in Theol. Ltzng. (1887) 151–5.]

JEREMIE. Hist. Church. (1852) 92–101.

JOLY, E. Etude sur Origène. 1860. 8⁰.

JORTIN, J. In his: Remarks on Eccl. Hist. (*London*, 1752. 8⁰.) II. 234–246.

KAHNIS. Lehre v. d. h. Geist. I.

KARSTEN, J. A. Dissert. de Origene oratore sacro. *Groningae*, 1824. 8⁰.

KEIM, THEODOR. Celsus' Wahres Wort. *Zürich*, 1873. 8⁰.

— Rom. u. d. Christenthum. *Berlin*, 1881. pp. 391–415.

KILLEN. Ancient Church. (1859) 375–81.

KIND, AUG. Der Kampf d. Origines gegen Celsus um die Stellung des Menschen in der Natur. *Jena*, 1875. 8⁰. (38 p.) Cf. Soury (Jul.) in: Rev. philos. (1876) II. 303–7.

KNITTEL. Orig. Lehre v. d. Merschenwerdung. In: Theol. Quartalschr. (1872).

KÖTHE, F. A. Origenes, e. biog. Skizze. In: Dippold u. Köthe, Allgm. hist. Archiv. I. 6.

KRAUS, J. B. Die Trinitätslehre des Kirchenlehrers Orige. *Stadtamhof*, 1858. 4⁰.

KRAUS, J. B. Die Lehre d. O. über d. Auferstehung d. Todten. *Stadtamhof*, 1859. 4º.

KRÜGER. Verhältn. d. Orig. z. Ammonius Sakkas. In: Ztschr. f. hist. Theol. (1843) I. 46–.

KURTZ. Kirchenges. (1885–) I. 119–21, 140–1.

L., C. Letter of Resolution concerning Origen and the chief of his opinions, by C. L., Esquire. *London*, 1661. 4º; — Repr. in The Phenix. (*Lond.* 1707. 8º.) I. 1–85.

LAFORÉT, N. J. La philosophie des Pères. Origène. In: Rev. cathol. (*Louv.* 1870) B. III. 685–70; IV. 123–39, 255–73, 545–72.

LAGARDE, P. de. Veteris testamenti ab Origine recensiti fragmenta apud Syros servata. *Göttingæ*, 1880. 8º.

LAMSON, A. Life, Writings, and Opinions of Origen. In: Chr. Exam. X. (1830) 306–; XI. (1831) 22–.

LARDNER, Credibility. III. II. (*Lond.* 1750. 8º.) 180–410. Works. (1881) II. 468–577.

LEBEDEFF. Origen's book against Celsus. *Moscow*, 1878. (In Russian.)

LE CLERC. J. Bibl. univ. hist. (168.) VI. 31–55. Also in: Lebensbeschr. Kirchenvater. (1711) 109.

LE LONG. Bibl. sac. (1723) II. 886–7.

Life and Teachings of Origen. In: Dub. R. LVII. (1869) 43–; LVIII. (1870) 377–; LIX. (1870) 332–.

Life of Origen. In: Bib. R. III. (1847) 11–; 103–.

Life, Writings and Opinions of Origen. In: Brit. Q. II. (1844) 491–; same art. Ecl. M. VII. (1845) 81–.

LOESCHE, G. Haben die späteren Neuplatonischen Polemiker gegen das Christenthum das Werk des Celsus benutzt? In: Ztschr. f. wiss. Theol. XXVII. [1884] 257–302.

LUMPER. Hist. ss. patr. IX. (1792) 1–656; X. (1793) 1–513.

LUTHARDT. St. John the Author of the Fourth Gospel. (1875) 38.

MABILLON. Vet. anal. (1676) II. 260.

MAI. Script. vet. coll. (1825) I. 30.

— Class. auct. (1838) X. 474, 600.

MANSI. Conc. III. 1141–.

MARTIN. Origène et la critique textuelle du N. T. In: Rev. des quest. hist. (1885) 5–62; also separately. *Paris*, 1885. 8º.

MAURIAE. Origenis de libertate arbitrii doctrina. *Monspelii*, 1856. 8º.

MEANS, J. C. In: Smith. Gr. and Rom. Biog. (1859) III. 46–55.

MEHLHORN, P. Die Lehre v. d. menschl. Freiheit nach Origines' περὶ ἀρχῶν. In: Ztschr. f. Kirchengesch. II. 234–253.

MEIER. Trinitätslehre.

MEISNERUS, J. De Origene et Origenianis exercit. hist. theol. *Wittebergae*, 1665. 4º; Ed. 2. *Witteb.* 1712. 4º.

MERLIN, CHARL. Examen d'un Raisonnement, que M. Bayle attribue à Origenes dans son Dictionnaire. In: Mém. de Trévoux. (1736, mai.) 1077–95.

MERLINI, Jac. Apol. pro Orig. In: Lat. ed. operum Orig. 1612, 19. fol.

MIGNE. Patrol. gr. XI–XVII.

MÖHLER. Patrologie. I. (1840) 527–568.

MÖLLER, W. In: Herzog. Real.-Enc. (1877–) XI. 92–109. (Abr. in: Schaff-Herz. III. 1702–5).

— Kosmologie in d. griech. Kirche. pp. 536–.

MONTFAUCON, B. DE. Prolegg. of Hexapla. *Par.* 1713. 2 v. fº; also in: Migne. Patrol. gr. XV. (1857) 9–122.

MOSHEIM, J. LOR. De Origene, Allegoriarum patrono. In his: Commentarii. p. 603–, 630–.

MOTTE, DE LA. Hist. de Tert. et d'Orig. s. u. Fossé.

MULDOON, P. J. Was Origen a Heretic? In: Cath. World. XIX. (1874) 109–.

MUENSCHER. Dogmenges (1817-8) I. 148–59, etc.

NARBONE. Bibl. Sicol. (1850–55) III. 278.

NEALE. Eastern Ch. Alexandria. I. (1847) 18–38, 53.

NEANDER. Hist. of dogmas. (1858) 66–72, 96–7, 105–6, 111–2, 119–23, 128–9, 146–8, 174–5, 190–1, 202–6, 214–5, 233–4, 244, 253, 262. [v. 1.]

— Church hist. (1872) I. 129, 543–57, 693–722; II. 386–9, etc., etc.

NEBE. Gesch. d. Predigt. I. (1879) 1–40.

— Origenes Gedanken von der Predigt. In: Mancherlei Gaben u. Ein Geist. (1876).

NEWMAN, F. W., and FROUDE, J. A. Three Letters on Origen against Celsus. In: Fraser. XCVII. (1877) 548–.

NIRSCHL. Patrol. (1881–) I. 225–50.

NITZSCH. Dogmengesch. I. (1870) 134–8, etc.

NODIER. Bib. sacr. (1826) 162–3.

NONNOTE. Les philosophes. (1789).

NORBERG, M. Praef. in ed. Syriaco-Hexapl. *Lond. Goth.* 1787; also in: Migne. Patrol. Gr. XVI. (1863) 2299–302.

NORTON. Genuineness of Gosp. I. (1846) 66–77, etc.

NORUP (NIERUP?), MATTH. JAC. Quaestio de lapsu Origenis. *Hafniae*, 1709. 4º. (1710?)

ORELLI, J. CASP. Origenis loci aliquot selecti. *Turici*, 1825. 8º.

Origen against Celsus. In: Month. XI. (1869) 159–; 377–.

Origen at Caesarea. In: Dub. R. LIX. (1865) 332–; same art. Cath. World. IV. (1866) 772–.

ORNSBY, R. Origen against Celsus. In: Dub. R. LXXXV. (1879) 58–90.

ORSI. Ist. eccl. (1746–) II. 354–9, 440–3; III. 17–8, 26–40, 44–7. (1749–) II. 511–8, 635–9; III. 23–5, 35–51, 57–61, 62–83, 93–5, 99–100, 102–5, 111–4, 127–31, 199–201, 80–106, 120–2, 127–9, 131–5, 143–7, 163–8, 259–60.

OUDIN. Scr. eccl. (1722) I. 231–66.

OVERBECK. In: Theol. Ltzng. (1878) 531–6; (1879) 201–3.

OWEN, H. Crit. disquisitions on Origen's celebrated Hexapla. *London*, 1784. 8º.

PAMPHILUS. Apologia. In: Migne. Patrol. Gr. XVII. (1857) 541–616.

PÉLAGAUD. Étude sur Celse. 1878.

PERMANEDER. Bibl. patrist. I. (1841) 419–21; II. (1843) 473–575.

PETERMANN, J. H. Variae lect. in O. in Matt. In: Migne. Patrol. Gr. XIII. (1862) 1909–46.

PETZHOLDT, J. Comment. hebraeo-palaeographica de quibusdam Origenis et Hieronymi locis. *Lipsiae*, 1837. 8º. (37 p.)

PHILIPPI. De Celsi philosophandi genere. *Berol.* 1836.

PHOTIUS. Biblioth. Cod. 118.

PICUS, J. De salute Origenis disputatio. In his: Opera. *Basil.* 1601. fº.) 131–148.

PITRA. Spicil. Solesm. (185) I. 267–282; III. 395.

PRESSENSÉ, EDM. DE. La philosophie chrétienne au III. s.: Origène, sa vie et ses écrits. In: Le Magas. de libraire. (1860) XI. 344–72.

— In: Lichtenberger. Encycl. (1877–82) X. 64–78.

— Early years of Christianity. Chr. life. (1878) 106–18, 225–6; Martyrs. (1879) 282–340, 566–88; Heresy. (n. d.) 296–355.

PRIDEAUX, HUMPH. Origen's ed. of the versions of the Scr. In his: O. and N. T. connected. (*Lond.* 1719. fº.) II. 41–45.

PROBST, FERD. Origenes über d. Eucharistie. In: Theol. Quartalschr. (*Tüb.* 1864) 449–534.

— Origenes über d. kath. Gottesdienst. In: Theol. Quartalschr. (1864) 647–719.

RAMBOUILLET. Origène et l'infaillibilité . . . *Paris*, 1870. 18º. (34 p.)

RAMERS, C. Des Origines Lehre om d. Auferstehung d. Fleisches. *Trier*, 1851. 8º. (vi, 78 p.)

READING, W. Notae in De Oratione. *Lond.* 1728; also in: Migne. Patrol. gr. XI. (1857) 1631–88.

REDEPENNING. Des Hieronymus wieder-aufgefundenes Verzeichniss d. Schriften d. Origens. In: Ztschr. f. d. hist. Theol. (1851) 66–.

— Origenes. Eine Darstellung s. Lebens u. s. Lehre. *Bonn,* 1841–46. 2 v. 8⁰.

RETTBERG, F. W. Doct. Origenis de Λόγω divino, ex discipl. Neoplatonica illust. In: Ztschr. f. hist. theol. (183–) III. i. 39–.

REUSS. Gesch. N. T. (1874) II. 32–3, 255–8; Tr. Eng. (1884) 314-6, 535–7. [v. 2.]

REYNAUD. Encyclopédie Nouvelle.

RINGBERG, OLAV. Vita Origenis Adamantii. *Lund.* 1792. 8⁰.

RITTER. Chr. philos. (1841) I. 465–564.

RIVIS, DION. DE. Dissertatio de Origenis Hexaplis et Octaplis . . . *Romae,* 1673. 8⁰; *Lugduni,* 1676. 4⁰.

ROBERTSON. Hist. of . . Church. (1875–) I. 138–158.

ROESSLER. Bibl. d. K.–V. II. (1776) 76–287.

ROSENMULLER. Hist. interp. III. (1807) 1–156.

— Uber des Origenes Hexapla. In his: Handbuch. II. 459–.

RUFINUS. De adulteratione libr. Orig. In: Migne. Patrol. Gr. XVII. (1857) 615–32.

— Peroratio. Origen on Romans. In: Migne. Patrol. Gr. XIV. (1862) 1291–4.

— Pref. to O. on Romans: In: Migne. Patrol. Gr. XIV. (1862) 831–2.

[RUST, GEORGE.] A Letter of Resolution concerning Origen and the chief of his opinions. *Lond.* 1661. 4⁰; also in the Phenix. (1707) I. 1–85.

SAGITTARIUS, CASP. Hist. eccl. p. 1113.

SAWYER, T. J. Was Origen a Universalist? In: Univ. Q. XXXII. (1875) 176–.

SCHAFF. Creeds of Christendom. II. (1877) 21–3.

— Hist. ' . . Church. II. (1886) 785–96.

SCHARFENBERG, J. G. Animadv. quibus fragm. vers. graec. V. F. a Montefalconio coll. illustrantur, emendantur. I. *Lips.* 1776; II. *Lips.* 1781. 8⁰.

SCHLIEMANN. Clementinen. (1884) III. et passim.

SCHMID, B. Patrol. (1879); (1886) 50–3.

SCHMID, J. A. Dissertatio de lapsu Origenis. *Helmstadii,* 1704. 4⁰. (D. et L.)

SCHMIDT, H. Origenes u. Augustin als Apologeten. In: Jahrb. f. deut. Theol. VII. (1862) 237–81; VIII. (1863) 261–325.

SCHMIDT, R. T. In: Stud. u. Krit. XV. (1842) 133–68.

SCHNITZER, CARL FR. Origenes über d. Grundlehren der Glaubens-Wissenschaft. *Stuttg.* 1835. 8⁰.

SCHRAM. Anal. ss. patr. (1730–) IV. and V.

SCHROECKH. Kirchenges. (1772–) III. 314; IV. 29–145; IX. 7–9; 102–3, 213, 292–3, 29, 31–3, 108–266; XVIII. 40–60, 179–81.

SCHULTZ, H. Die Christologie d. Origines u. s. w. In: Jahrb. fur Protest. Theol. 1875. p. 193–247, 369–425.

SEARS, B. Life, Writings and Opinions of Origen. In: Bib. Sac. III. (1846) 378–.

SELWYN, WILL. Proposed emendations of the text of Origen against Celsus. Books I., II., III., IV. In: Journal of Philol. V. (1874) 248–251.

SHEDD. Hist. of doct. 3d. ed. (1865–) I. 159–60, 288–304, etc.

SMEDT, CAR. DE. Dissert. sel. hist. eccles. (1876) 106–8.

SOCRATES. Hist. Eccles. VI. 3–18.

SOZOMEN. Hist. Ecclesias. viii, 220.

Supernatural Religion. (1875–7) pass.

TAMBURINI, PET. Ragionamenti sul primo libro di Origene contro Celso. *Pavia.* 1786. 8⁰.

TAYLOR, CHAS. In: Smith and Wace. Dict. III. 14–23. [Hexapla.]

THEODORET. Hist. Eccles. V. 27–.

THOMASINUS, GOTTFR. Origènes. Ein Beitrag z. Dogmenges. d. dritten Jahrh. *Nürnb.* 1837. 8⁰.

TILLADET. Dissert s. div. matier. (1714).

TILLEMONT. Mémoires. III. (1695) 494–595, 753–77.

TRITHEMIUS. Scr. eccl. 30.

UEBERWEG. Hist. philos. (1876) 315–9.

VAUGHAN, R. A. Life and Writings of Orig. In his: Essays. I. (1838).

Veterum testimonia de Hexapla. In: Migne. Patrol. Gr. XV. (1857) 123–40.

VINCENTIUS BELVAC. Spec. hist. XII. 1–2, 8–15; XIX. 11.

VINCENZI, ALOIS. Origenes ab impietatis et haereseos nota in ceteris institutionibus vindicatus. *Romae,* 1864. 8⁰. (xxxiii–545 p.) Cf. Civiltà cattol. (1866) F. VI, 338–44.

WAITE. Hist. Chr. Rel. (1881) 9–10 et pass.

WALCH, C. W. F. Commendatur et illustratur Origenis de diebus Christianorum festis disputatio. *Goettingae,* 1777. 4⁰.

— Hist. d. Kezereien. VII. 362–.

WALCH, J. G. Vindiciae Origenis in doctrina de divinitate Christi. *Jenae,* 1727. 4⁰.

— Bibl. patrist. (1834) 35–40, 186–7, 373.

WALCH, J. G. = Gaupp, C.

WALTHAM, R. C. Origen as a Defender of Christianity. In: Univ. Q. XXVIII. (1871) 82–.

WEICHMANN, J. S. Comment. hist. theol. de schola Orig. sac. ex Greg. Thaum. inf. *Wittemb.* 1744. 4⁰.

WEIGL, J. B. Bericht des Porphyrios über Origines. Programm. *Regensb.* 1835. 4⁰.

WERNSDORF, G. Memor. Hanovii et de cognom. Origenis. *Gedani,* 1773. 4⁰.

WERTHER, J. F. De schola Origenis sacra. *Wittebergae,* 1744. 4⁰.

WESTCOTT. Canon. (1875) 354–61.

— Bible in the Church. (1877) 134–7.

— Origen and the Beginnings of Christian Philosophy. In: Contemp. Rev. XXXV. (1878) 324–; 489–; same art. Liv. Age. CXLI. (1878) 643–; CXLII. (1878) 131–.

WORDSWORTH. Church Hist. (1881) 114–121, 269–283.

WORMAN, J. H. In: M'Clintock and S. Cycl. (1874–) VII. 428–34.

ZELLER. Apostelgesch. (1854) 70.

ZELLER. Gesch. d. philos.

ZÖCKLER. Hieronymus. (*Gotha,* 1865) 238–, 391–.

ZORN, PETER. Dissertatio de eunuchismo Origenis Adamantii. *Giessae,* 1708. 4⁰. (D.)

Note 1. All special literature on the Philosophumena, whether ascribed to H. or O. by title, is put under Hippolytus. Compare especially the names Armellini, Cruice, Jacobi, Lenormant, Maury, Passaglia.

For literature compare also Encyclopaedia, articles on "Celsus," "Origenistic controversy," etc., etc.

Note 2. For compact summary of controverted points, with literature appertaining, compare Hergenröther, III. 71–2.

VOLUME V.

I. HIPPOLYTUS.

I. *Editions.*

(*Works.*)

FABRICIUS, J. A. Gr. lat. *Hamb.* 1716–19. 2 v. f⁰.

GALLANDIUS. In: Bibl. patr. II. (1766) 409–.

MIGNE. Gr. lat. In: Patrol. gr. X. (1857) 583–884, 901–62.

LAGARDE. *Lips.* and *Lond.* 1858.

(*Philosophumena.*)

GRONOVIUS, JAC. (Frgm.) In his: Thes. antiq. gr. *Lugd. Bat.* 1701. f⁰. p. 248–294.

WOLFIUS, J. C. (Fragm.) Gr. lat. *Hamb.* 1706. 8⁰.

DELARUE. (Fragm.) In Origenis Op. 1733–59. f⁰.

MILLER. *Oxon.* 1851. 8⁰. [1 ed. of recovered work. Publ. under name of Origen.]

CRUICE. *Par.* 1860–1. 8⁰.

DUNCKER and SCHNEIDEWURN. *Gotting.* 1856–9. 8⁰. [Best.]

(Chronicon.)

CANISIUS. Gr. lat. In his: Lect. antiq. 1602. II. 580; 1657; *Amst.* 1729. f⁰. I. 17–19.

LABBE. Nov. bibl. I. 298.

DUCANGE. In his ed. of Chron. pasch. 1688.

MOMMSEN. (2d version.) In: Abh. d. K-Sächs Gesells. (1850) I. 585.

(Canon Pasch.)

SCALIGER. In his: De emend. temporum. *Par.* 1583. f⁰; repr. *Lugd. Bat.* 1595 (not '94). 4⁰; *Genev.* 1629. f⁰. p. 152–3.

BIANCHINUS. In his: Diss. duae, etc. *Romae*, 1664 (3?). 4⁰. [Secunda lit.]

BUCHERIUS, AEGID. In his: Liber de doct. temporum. *Antv.* 1664. f⁰.

(Other.)

PICUS, Jo. (Consum. mundi, Antichr., etc.) Gr. lat. *Lut. Par.* 1557(6?). 8⁰.

POSSEVINUS. (Adv. Jud.) *Ven.* 1603.

SIRMONDUS. (De theol. and Incar.) In: Opera. *Par.* 1606. f⁰. p. 583.

COMBEFIS. (XII. apost.) In: Auct. nov. patr. gr. lat. II. (1648. f⁰.) 831–844.

GUDIUS, MARQUARDUS. (Antichr.) Gr. *Lut. Par.* 1660–1. 8⁰.

COMBEFIS. (Various.) Gr. lat. In his: Auct. Bibl. patr. I. (*Paris,* 1672. f⁰.) 26–63.

LAMBECIUS. (De Salomonis libris.) In his: Comment. de Bibl. Vindelur. VIII. (1679. f⁰.) 390–393.

LE MOYNE. (Contra Graeco.) In his: Varia sacra. I. (*Lugd. Bat.* 1685. 4⁰.)

WOOG, C. C. (Fragm. in Prov. IX. 1–5.) Gr. lat. *Lips.* 1762. 4⁰.

Biblia polyglotta (Daniel). *Romae,* 1772.

MAIUS, A. (Fragm. in Prov.) In his: Nov. coll. scr. vet. I. II. (1827. 4⁰.) 223–.

BUNSEN. (Ref. haer.) In: Analect. Antenic (1854) 341–407.

LAGARDE. (Arab. fragm.) In: Anal. Syr. p. 79–91 and Appendix. *Lips.* 1858.

ROUTH. Scr. (Contr. haer. Noeti.) eccl. op. (1858) I. 43–94.

HAMBERG. (Canones S. Hippol. Arabice e codic. Rom. c. vers. Lat. annot. et prolegomenis.) *Munich,* 1870.

BARDENHEWER. (Daniel.) *Freib.* 1877.

II. *Translations.*

Latin.

PICUS, Jo. (Various.) *Lut. Par.* 1557. 8⁰; *Colon.* 1563. 8⁰; in: Justini opera. *Par.* 1575. 16⁰.

TURRIANUS. (De theol. et Incar.) In: Canisii Lectiones antiq. V. (*Ingolst.* 1604. 4⁰.) 154–. [With Greek]; also in: Canisii Lect. antiq. ed. *Basnage,* 1725. f⁰.

VOSSIUS, GER. (Contra Nocti haer.) In: Gregorii Thaum. op. *Mogunt.* 1604. 4⁰. 58–68; also in: Bibl. patr. III. (*Colon.* 1618. f⁰); also in: Suppl. Morell. *Par.* 1639. I. 620–.

(De theol. et Inc.) In: Collectanea Anastasii Bibliothecarii. *Par.* 1620. 8⁰. p. 209.

(Various.) In: Bibl. patr. XII. (*Par.* 1644. f⁰.)

In: Bibl. Max. patr. III. (*Lugd.* 1677. f⁰.) 252–264.

English.

MACMAHON and SALMOND. In: Ante-Nic. Lib. VI. (1868) 25–508; IX. (1869) ii, 1–141. Ed. Coxe. V. (1886) 9–258.

French.

GENOUDE. [?] In: Pères de l'égl. *Par.* 1837–43. 8⁰.

German.

GRÖNE, V. *Kempten,* 1873. 16⁰. [The Reithmayer-Thalhofer Bibl.]

III. *Literature.*

ALLARD, P. L'hagiographie au IVe siècle. Martyris de saint Hippolyte, etc., d'après les poèmes de Prudence. In: Revue des quest. hist. (1885) 353–405.

ALZOG. Patrol. (1876) 112–118.

ARMELLINI, TORQ. De prisca refutatione haereseon, Origenis nomine ac Philosophumenon titulo, recens vulgata, commentarius. *Romae,* 1862. 8⁰. (193 p.) Cf. Civilta cattol. (1863) E, V. 345–51.

BARDENHEWER, O. Des heil. Hippolytus v. Rom. Commentar zum Buche Daniel. Ein literärgeschichte. Versuch. Freiburg. i. Br. *Herder.* 1877. 8⁰.

BARONIUS. Ann. (1589) 224, 10 (add. 3); 229, 3–10.

BASNAGE, JAC. Animadv. de vita, morte et scriptis Hippolyti. In: Canisii Lectiones antiquae (1725) I. p. 3–12.

BAUMGARTEN–CRUSIUS. Dogmenges. (1832) 254. [v. 1.] (4 ll.)

BAUR. In: Theol. Jahrb. (*Tüb.* 1853.)

— Dogmenesch. I. (1865) 282 etc.

ΒΑΦΕΙΔΗΣ. Ἐκκλ. ἱστ. I. (1884) 155–6.

BAXMANN. Die Philosophumena u. d. Peraten. In: Zeitschrift f. d. hist. Theol. (1860).

BELLARMIN–LABBE. Scr. eccl. (1728) 42–3.

BELLESHEIM, A. Zur Hippolytusfrage. In: Der Katholik (1881) 592–606.

BENSON, E. W. On the fragment of a hymn to Aesculapius preserved in the fourth book of Hippolytus. In: Journ. of class. and sacred philol. I. (1854) p. 395–398.

BIANCHINI, FRANC. De kalendario et cyclo Caesaris ac de paschali canone s. Hippolyti martyris dissertationes. XXX. *Romae,* 1703. f⁰. [Quoted often as Blanchini. nus or Branchinus.]

BLACKBURN. Hist. of Church (1879) 38–9.

BRINK, B. Bisschop Hippolytus, αἱρέσεων ἔλεγχος Bl. 144. In: Mnemosyne. II. (1853) p. 383–387.

BUCHERIUS, AEG. Comment. in can. pasch. In: Migne. Patrol. gr. X. (1857) 885–902.

BUNSEN, C. K. J. Hippolytus and his age. *London,* 1852. 4 v. 8⁰; 1854. 2 v. 8⁰. [= Christianity and Mankind; German. *Leipz.* 1852-3. 2 v. 8⁰.] [Cf. Gröber, Ida v. d. Wissenschaft u. Bibel mit Bezieh. auf Dr. Bunsen: Hippolytus u. s. Zeit. . . . u. auf. d. Recension diseses. Werk in Dr. Hengstenberg's Kirchenz. *Stuttg.* 1856. 8⁰.]

BURTON. Divinity of Christ. (1829) 244–280.

— Trinity. (1831) 84–7.

BUSSE. Chr. Lit. (1828–9) I. 29.

Byzant. hist. script. XXI. (1688); XI–, XVIII., XX–II; IV. (   ) X–XIII., XVI–IX.

CAILLAU. Introd. in ss. Patr. (1825) 79–80.

CASPARI. Quellen z. Gesch. d. Taufsymbols. Christiane. III. (1875) 377–.

CAVE. Scr. eccl. hist. lit. (1740–3) I. 162–9; II. IV. 17.

CEILLIER. Hist. gén. aut. sac. (1730) II. 316–74. I. (1858) 607–42.

CHARTERIS. Canonicity. (1880) 147–8, 192–3, 279–80, 296, 345.

CHEVALIER. Rép. d. sources hist. (1877–84) 1067–8.

CHRONICON PASCHALE. Bonn ed. I. p. 12.

CLARKE. Sacred lit. (1830–1) I. 158.

CLINTON. Fasti Rom. (1845–50) I. 235, 241; II. 414–5.

COFFIN. Lives of fath. (1846) 239–240.

COTELIER, Jo. Bapt. In: Monumenta Eccles. graec. II. 639.

CRUICE, PATR. Études sur de nouv. doc. hist. des Philosophumena. *Paris,* 1853.

CRUICE, PATR. Des travaux de la critique allemande sur St. Hippolyte et sur le pape St. Calliste. In: Rev. Contemp. (*Par.* 1856) XXVI. 58–82.

CUNNINGHAM. Churches of Asia. (1880) passim.

CUPERUS. Comment. histor. criticus. In: Acta ss. Bolland. (1739) Aug. IV. 504–13.

DARLING. Cyclop. bibl. (1854) 1488–9.

DE ROSSI, G. B. Elogio Damasiano del celebre Ippolito martire. In: Bulletino di archeologia cristiana. IV. (VI.?) 26–55.

DÖLLINGER. Hippolytus u. Kallistus. *Regensb.* 1853. 8°; Engl. tr. by Plummer. *Edinb.* 1876.

DORNER. Person of Christ. II. (1866) 83–100, 449–57.

DRÄSEKE, J. Zu Pseudo-H. In: Jahrb. f. prot. Theol. X. (1884) 342–6. [Of Κατὰ Βήρωνος, etc.]

— Beron u. Pseudo-Hippol. In: Ztschr. f. wiss. Theol. XXIX. (1886) 291–318.

— Zu Hippolytos' Demonstratio adversus Judaeos. In: Jahrbb. f. prot. Theol. (1886) 456–461.

DUNCKER. In: Gött. Gel. Anz. 1851.

DUPIN. (1698–) I. 295.

EBEDJESU. Catal. scr. eccl. 7. (Assemani. Bibl. orient. III. i. 15).

Eccles. and Theol. Rev. 1853. Jun., Jul.

Encycl. Brit. (9th ed.) XI. 854.

EUSEBIUS. Hist. eccles. VI. 20, 22, 23. Chronic. II.

FABER, TANAQ. Hippolyti Martyris libellus de Antichristo percurritur et saepius emendatur. In his: Epistolae. Edit. alt. (*Salmuri*, 1674. 4°.) 323–.

FABRICIUS. Bib. gr. (1712–19) V. 203–12; IX. 388, 413–8, 446–7. (VII. 183–98; X. 693–4, 714, 739.)

— Opp. Hipp. *Hamb.* 1716–8. 2 v. f°. Praef.; also in: Migne. Patrol. gr. X. (1857) 261–70.

— De verit. rel. Chr. (1725) 61–3, 161–2.

— Bibl. med. aev. (1735) III. 795–6. (2ª. 272.)

FESSLER. In: Oesterr. Vierteljahrsschr. f. kath. Theol. (1863) III. 287–340.

FINK, G. W. In: Ersch. u. Gruber. II. VIII. (1831) 351–2.

FLEURY. Hist. eccl. (1691–) II. 101–3, 247–8.

FORK. In: Ztschr. f. d. hist. Theol. (1847).

FROMMANN, ERN. NICH. Interpretatt. N. T. ex Hippolyto collectae. *Coburgi*, 1765. 4°.

FUNK. In: Theol. Quartalschr. LXIII. (1881) 277–98. [Basilides in the Philosophumena.]

— Ueb. d. Verf. d. Philosophumenen. In: Theol. Quartalschr. LXIII. (1881) 423–64.

— Zur Philosophumenen-Frage. In: Lit. Rundschau, (1881) 33–38.

— S. Zeit d. Hippolytstatue. In: Theol. Quartalschr. LXVI. (1884) 104–6. [3d century.]

— Zur Hippolytfrage. In: Hist.-pol. Blätter. LXXXIX. 889–896.

GALLAND. Bibl. patr. v. II. Prolegomena. c. XVIII.

Γεωργιάδης, Β. Τοῦ ἁγίου Ἱππολίτου ἐπισκόπου καὶ μάρτυρος περὶ ὁράσεως τοῦ Προφήτου Δανιὴλ λόγος Δ. In: Ἐκκλησιαστικὴ Ἀλήθεια (1885) 15 μαΐ, p. 10–24; 31 μαΐ, p. 49–60.

GIESELER, J. C. L. In: Stud. u. Krit. XXVI. (1853) 759–87.

— Church. Hist. (1868–) I. 224–6.

GUNDERT, E. In: Ztschr. f. d. luth. Theol. XVI. (1885) 209–20. [Basilides in the Philosophumena.]

— In: Ztschr. f. luth. Theol. XVII. (1856) 37–74, 443–85. [Basilides and the Philosophumena.]

GRISAR, H. Bedarf die Hippolytus Frage einer Revision? In: Ztschr. f. kathol. Theol. II. (1878) 505–533.

GRUSCHA. In: Wetzer u. W. Kirch.-Lex. (1847–54) V. 210–3.

GUTSCHMID, A. v. Ueber d. Verhältniss d. Hippolytischen liber generationis u. s. w. (1856) s. u. Julius Africanus.

HAGEMANN. Die röm. Kirche. *Freib.* 1864.

HAGENBACH. Hist. of Doct. I. (1850) 229.

HÄNELL, K. W. Commentatio historico-critica de Hippolyto episcopo, tertii saeculi scriptore. *Gottingae*, 1838. 4°.

HARE. Contest with Rome. p. 214.

HARNACK. Zur Quellenkritik d. Gesch. d. Gnosticismus (1873–4).

— In: Ztschr. f. hist. Theol. (1874) 170–. (?) (1875) 38–.

— Dogmenges. I. (1886) 422–500.

HASE. Kirchenges. (1885–) I. 299, 312–3, 338–42, 371.

HERGENRÖTHER. In: Theol. Quartals. (*Tüb.* 1852.)

— In: Vierteljahrsschrift f. kath. Theol. (1863) 287–340.

— Kirchenges. (1879–80) I. 168; III. 73.

HERZOG. Abriss d. Kirchenges. I. 126.

HEUMANN, CHR. A. Dissertatio, in qua docetur, ubi et qualis episcopus fuerit S. Hippolytus. *Goetting.* 1737. 4°; also in his: Primit. Gotting. acad. (1738) 239–.

HIERONYMUS. De vir. ill. 61. (Honor. Aug. I. 62.)

HILGENFELD. In: Ztschr. f. wiss Theol. (1862).

— Der Basilides des Hippolytus, aufs neue geprüft. In: Ztschr. f. wiss. Theol. XXI. (1878) 228–250.

— Ketzergesch. (1884) 9–21, 58–69, 74–9, 450–626.

Hippolytus to Artemis. In: Fraser. LXXIX. (1868) 39–.

Hist. lit. France. (1733) I. i. 361–400; XI. 11.

HOVEY, A. Bunsen's St. Hippolytus and his Age. In: Chr. R. XVIII. (1853) 425–.

HUBER. Philos. d. K.–V. (1859) 93–100.

IMBONATI, JOS. C. In: Biblioth. lat. ebr. p. 74.

JACOBI. In: Ztschr. f. chr. Wissensch. u. Leben (1851) No. 25, (1853) No. 24.

JACOBI, J. S. Origen or Hippolytus. In: Meth. Q. XI. (1851) 645–.

— In: Neander. Hist. of dogmas. (1858) 51–2, 125, 157–9, 162–3, 182–4, 194. [v. 1.]

— In: Herzog. Real.-Enc. (1877–) VI. 139–49. (Abr. in: Schaff-Herz. II. 995–6.)

JACOBS and SCHMID. In: Ersch. u. Gruber. II. IV. (1828) 95.

JEREMIE. Hist. Church. (1852) 91–2.

J[OUBERT], L. In: Nouv. Biog. Gén. (Hoefer) XXIV. (1858) 777–83.

Journal des Débats. Dec., 1852.

JUNGMANN, B. Dissertationes in Hist. Eccl. *Ratisbon.* 1880. 8°. 173–262.

KILLEN. Ancient Church. (1859) 343–50, 374–5.

KIMMEL, EM. JUL. De Hippolyti vita et scriptis. Partie I. Diss. histor.-theolog. *Jena*, 1839. 8°.

KRAUS. In: Oester. Vierteljahrsschr. f. kath. Theol. (1862).

KURTZ. Kirchenges. (1885–) I. 116–8, 140.

LAMY, TH. J. Études sur les écrits de s. Hippolyte. In: Rev. cathol. (*Louv.* 1861.) G, I. 5–15, 80–94.

LANGEN. Gesch. d. röm. Kir. *Bonn*, 1881. p. 229.

LARDNER. Credibility. Works. (1831) II. 409, 421–38.

LE LONG. Bibl. sac. (1723) II. 778–9.

LE MOYNE. Diatribe de Hippol.

LENORMANT. Controverse sur les Phil. d'Origene. In: Le Correspondant. XXXI. (*Paris*, 1853.) 509–550.

LIPSIUS. Quellenkritik der Epiphanios. *Wien*, 1865.

— Quellen d. ältest. Ketzergesch. *Lpz.* 1875. p. 118–.

LORD, D. N. St. Hippolytus and his Age. In: Theo. & Lit. J. VI. (1855) 353–.

LUMPER. Hist. ss. patr. VIII. *Aug. Vind.* 1791. 8°. VIII. 1–191; also in: Migne. Patrol. gr. X. (1857) 271–394.

McCLINTOCK and S. Cycl. (1874–) IV. 268–9.

MACMAHON, J. H. In: Ante-Nic. Lib. VI. (1868) 17–23. Introd. note. Ed. Coxe. V. (1886) 1–7. [Add. notes. Ed. Coxe. 153–62, 241, 259.]

[MAGISTRIS DE.] Acta Mart. ad Ostia. *Romae*, 1795. f°. 139; also in: Migne. Patrol. gr. X. (1857) 545–70, 1603–8.

MAI. Scr. vet. coll. (1825) I. II. 223.

MARTINOV. Ann. eccl. gr.-slav. (1864) 58.

Martyrium Cyriaei, Hippolyti, etc. Gr. lat. In: Migne. Patrol. gr. X. (1857) 551–570.

MAURY, ALF. Études sur les documents mythologiques contenus dans les Philosophumena d'Origène. In: Rev. archéolog. (1851–2) A, VIII. 233–44, 364–72, 635–47; IX. 144–56.

MEANS, J. C. In: Smith. Gr. and Rom. Biog. (1859) II. 490–2.

MILMAN. Lat. Christ. I. 66–.

MÖHLER. Patrologie. I. (1840) 581.

MÖLLER. Gesch. d. Kosmologie. p. 190.

MORETTI. Rom. 1752.

MUENSCHER. Dogmenges. (1817–8) II. 192.

NEANDER. Hist. of Dogmas. I. 51. S. u. Jacobi.

— Church Hist. (1872) I. 681–3 et pass.

NEWMAN. Tracts. (1874) 220–9.

NIRSCHL. Patrol. (1881–) I. 250–66.

NITZSCH. Dogmengesch. I. (1870) 163–5, etc.

NODIER. Bib. Sacr. (1826) 157–8.

NOLTE. In: Theol. Quartalschr. (1861) 163–9; (1862) 467. [Georgius Hamartolus' testimony to H.] 624–70. [Rev. of Cruice.]

Origen's Philosophumena. In: Quar. LXXXIX. (1851) 170–.

ORSI. Ist eccl. (1746) III. 91, 285–7; (1749) III. 116–7, 368–71.

OUDIN. Comm. d. script. eccl. (1722) I. 220–8.

OVERBECK, F. C. Quaestionum Hippolyteanum specimen. Jenae, 1864. 8°. (113 p.)

PASSAGLIA, CAR. Dei Filosofumeni di Origenis. In: Ann. scienze relig. (1851) B. IX. 419–22.

PEABODY, A. P. St. Hippolytus and his Age. In: No. Am. LXXVIII. (1853) 1–.

PERMANEDER. Bibl. patrist. (1841–43) I. 421; II. 426–63.

PHOTIUS. Bibliot. Cod. 48, 121, 202.

PRESSENSÉ, E. DE. In: Lichtenberger. Encycl. (1877–82) VI. 262–6.

— Chr. Life. (1878) 135.

— Martyrs. (1879) 360–6, 588–9, 635–40.

— Heresy. (N. Y.) 405–16.

RAMBOUILLET. In: Rev. d. Sciences Eccl. XLV. (1882) 258–72, 305–21. [Agst. Funk and most. Philosophumena not by H.]

REUSS. Gesch. N. T. (1874) II. 35; tr. Eng. (1884) 317. [v. 2.]

RÉVILLE, ALBERT. St. Hippolyte, le pape Calliste et la société chrétienne de Rome au commencement du III. siècle. In: Rev. d. Deux Mondes (1865) H, LVII. 892–924. Cf. Desjardins, E. C., in: Rev. d. Sciences eccl. (1865) B. II. 229–38.

RITSCHL. In: Theol. Jahrb. (1854).

ROEPER, GOTTLIEB. Emendationsversuche Hippolyti Philosophumena. In: Philologus. VII. (1852) p. 511–553, 606–637, 767.

ROESSLER. Bibl. d. K.–V. II. (1776) 328–332.

ROSENMÜLLER. Hist. interp. III. (1807) 164–71.

RUGGERIUS, CONSTANT. De Portuensi S. Hippolyti, episcopi et martyris, sede dissertatio posth. ab Ach. Ruschio absoluta et annott. aucta. Romae, 1771. 4°; also in: Lumper. Hist. ss. patr. (1791) VIII. 347–612; Migne. Patr. gr. (1857) 395–546.

RUINART. Vita et passio St. Hippol. In: Act. prim. martyrum. p. 168.

St. Hippolytus and his Age. In: Am. Presb. R. II. (1854) 450–; Chr. Rem. XXV. (1852) 213–; Ecl. R. XCVII. (1852) 385–; C. ( ) 690–; Ed. R. XCVII. (1852) 1–; Kitto. X. (1852) 461–; No. Brit. XIX. (1853) 85–; Prosp. R. IX. (1853) 118–.

SALMON, G. Some notes on the chronology of Hippolytus. In: Hermathena. I. 1874. p. 82–128.

SALMON, G. In: Smith and Wace. Dict. III. 85–105.

— Articles, "Chronicon Canisianum" and "Chronica Horosii." In: Smith and Wace. Dict. I. 506–8, 509.

SARDAGHI, JOS. Osservazioni sopra il martirio di s. Ippolito, vescovo di Porto. 1771. (= Zaccaria. Racc. di dissert. VII. 33–55.)

SCHAFF. Hist. . . Church. II. (1886) 757–74.

SCHMID. Patrol. (1879); (1886) 46–7.

SCHRAM. Anal. ss. patr. (1780–) 683–812.

SCHROECKH. Kirchenges. (1772–) IV. 154–62.

SEINECKE. In: Zeitschr. f. hist. Theol. (1842) III.

SEMLER. Gesch. d. Glaubenslehre. I. 212–.

SEVESTRE. Dict. patrol. (1854) III. 318–37.

SHEDD. Hist. of doct. 3d ed (1865–) I. 225–6, 285–7; II. 43–4.

SILVESTRI, B. DE. Considerazioni storico morali sopra sant' Ippolito martire. Prato, 1884. 16°.

SMEDT, CAR. DE. De Auctore Philosophumenon. In: Dissert. Sel. Ghent, 1876. 109–67. pp. 18–39.

Supernatural Religion. Vol. II. (1875) pass.

TAYLER, WILLIAM ELFE. Hippolytus and the Christian Church of the third century. Lond. 1853. 8°.

TEUFFEL. Hist. Rom. Lit. (1873) II. 297.

TILLEMONT. Mémoires. III. (1695) 238–49, 672–9.

TRITHEMIUS. 36.

UEBERWEG. Hist. philos. (1876) 301–3.

Veterum testimonia. In: Migne. Patrol. gr. X. (1857) 569–82.

VIGNOLIUS. De anno primo imperii Severi Alexandri, quem praefert cathedra marmorea S. Hippolyti in biblioth. Vaticana. Romae, 1712. 4°.

VINCENTIUS BELVAC. Spec. hist. XII. 30.

VOLKMAR. In: Theol. Jahrb. (1854).

— Hippolytus und die röm. Zeitgenossen, oder die Philosophumena und die veswandten Schriften nach Ursprung, Composition und Quellen untersucht (Quellen d. Ketzergeschichte. I.) Zürich, 1855. 8°.

WALCH. Bibl. patrist. (1834) 40–1.

WEISS. In: Biog. Univ. (Michaud) (1842–65) XIX. 466–7.

WESTCOTT. Canon. (1875) 374–6.

WIESELER, F. Ueb. d. Statue d. H. In: Stud. u. Krit. XXVIII. (1855) 893–5.

WOOG, C. CH. Hippolyti Fragmentum ad proverb. IX. 1–3. gr. et lat. Lipsiae, 1762. 4°. [This fragment is missing in Fabricius' ed.]

WORDSWORTH, CHR. St. Hippolytus and the church of Rome in the earlier part of the third century, from the new discovered Philosophumena . . . Lond. 1853. 8°; 1880. 8°.

— Remarks on Bunsen. 1855. 8°. (?)

— La doctrina di S. Ippolito intorno alla supremazia Romana ed alla fallibilita dei papi. Napoli, 1872. 12°. (36 p.)

— Church. Hist. (1881) 285–307.

Wordsworth on St. Hippolytus and the Church of Rome. In: Chr. Obs. LIII. (1853) 758–.

Writings of Hippolytus. In: Chr. Obs. LXIX. (1869) 119–.

Compare also literature under Origen.

Note 1. The Philosophumena is ascribed to *Hippolytus* by Jacobi, Duncker, Bunsen, Gieseler, Ritschl, DÖLLINGER, Volkmar, Overbeck, Herzog, and almost universally, but it is doubted by Möller, Lipsius, Newman, Jungmann, and others; ascribed to Caius of R. by Baur, to Novatian by Armellini, to Tertullian by Cruice and De Rossi, and to Origen by Miller, Lenormant, and others.

Note 2. For compact discussion of time and place compare Schaff.

II. CYPRIAN.

I. *Editions.*

(*Works.*)

ANDREAS, J. ("Epist. et Opuscula.") *Romae, Sweyn-heym et Pannartz*, 1471. f⁰. [Does *not* contain (*Brunet*) many passages suppressed by Baluze. *Graesse*]; *Venet. Vind. de Spira*, 1421. f⁰ (13×9½). [Mere reprint of Roman ed.]; *Venet. Lucas Venetus*, 1483. f⁰. [Slight addition and rearrangement.]

[Memmingen. A. Kunne. 1477.] [" Treatises and epistles first separated."]

[Daventriae, R. Paffroet. c. 1477.] [Is it Colon, 1476? Cf. Graesse.]

Par. 1498. f⁰. (?)

Paris, Jodocus Badius, 1500. [Mythical? Cf. Hartel or Schönemann. The ed. quoted as "Paris, J. Petit, 1500," refers to same.]

Par. 1512. 4⁰. *Rembolt and Waterloes.*

Basil. 1519. f⁰. (????)

Coloniae, Henr. Alopecium, 1520. f⁰.

ERASMUS. *Basil.* 1520. f⁰; 1521. f⁰; *Colon.* 1522. 2 v. 8⁰; *Basil.* 1523. f⁰ (?); 1525. f⁰ (*Colon.* 1525. f⁰?); *Lugd.* 1528. 2 v. f⁰; *Basil.* 1530. f⁰; 1535. f⁰; 1537. 2 v.; 1540. f⁰; *Paris, Langler*, 1541. f⁰; *Paris, Oudin Parvum*, 1541. f⁰; *Paris, Reynault*, 1541. f⁰; *Antv.* 1542 (1?); *Lugd.* 1544. 2 v. 8⁰; *Basil.* 1558. f⁰.

GRAEVIUS. *Colon.* 1544. f⁰; 1549. f⁰.

Venet. 1547. 8⁰.

Rom. P. Manutius, 1563. f⁰. [Really by Latino Latini.]

MORELLIUS, W. *Par.* 1564. f⁰.

PAMELIUS, JAC. *Antv.* 1568. f⁰; 1589. f⁰; *Par.* 1574. f⁰; 1593. f⁰; 1603. f⁰; 1607 (8?). f⁰; 1616. f⁰; *Colon.* 1617. f⁰; *Par.* 1623. f⁰; 1632. f⁰ (*Colon. ?*); *Par.* 1633. f⁰; 1643. f⁰; 1644. f⁰.

ROVEROTUS. *Bas.* 1588. f⁰. (??)

GOULART, S. *Genev.* 1593. f⁰.

RIGALTIUS. *Lutet. Par.* 1648. f⁰; 1649. f⁰.

PRIORIUS, P. *Par.* 1666. f⁰. [After Rigalt.] *Par.* 1679. f⁰.

FELL, JO. *Oxon.* 1682. f⁰; *Bremae*, 1690. f⁰; *Amst.* 1699 (1700?). f⁰; *Bremae*, 1690. f⁰.

BALUZIUS, S., and MARANUS. *Par.* 1726. f⁰; *Venet.* 1728. f⁰; *Par.* 1733; *Venet.?* 1736; 1758. f⁰.

OBERTHÜR. *Wirceb.* 1782. 2 v. 8⁰. [On Baluze. Includes Novatian and Minucius Felix.]

CAILLAU. *Par.* 1837. 8⁰. [On Baluzius.]

Besançon, 1837. 8⁰; do. 1837. 12⁰. [On Baluzius.]

GOLDHORN, D. J. H. *Lps.* 1838. 8⁰. In: Gersdorf. v. II. III.

Lugd. et Par. 1847. 8⁰. [After Baluze.]

KRABINGER. (10 Opuscula.) *Tüb.* 1853-9. 8⁰.

ROUTH. (4 Opuscula.) In: Scr. eccl. op. (1858) I. 265-359.

MIGNE. Patrol. Lat. IV. (1865) 193-1312.

HARTEL, GUIL. Vindobon. 1868-71. 3 v. 8⁰. [In the Vienna Corp. Scr. Eccl. Lat.]

HURTER, H. *Innsbruck*, 1870-3. 16⁰. In: Patrum sanctorum opuscula selecta. v. 1 (Opuscula); v. 21, Epistolae.

(*Poems.*)

(De Ligno Cr.) *Mirandulae*, 1496. f⁰. [With works of Picus.]

(De Ligno Crucis.) In: Poetae Christ. *Venet.* 1501. 4⁰.

(Carmina.) *Par.* 1560.

FABRICIUS, S. Poet. Christ. (1564) 295.

RIVENUS. In: Tertulliani Opera. *Lps.* 1653.

MAITTAIRE. (Gen. Sod.) Op. poet. *Lond.* 1713. f⁰. II. 1537.

MARTENE and DUR. Carm. ad Fel. Vet. scr. et mon. coll. IX. (1724) 1.

(*De idolorum vanitate.*)

S. l. 1603. 8⁰.

RIGALT. In: Minucius Felix, Octavius, etc. *Oxon.* 1662. 16⁰.

Par. 1643. 4⁰. [Rigaltius' notes.]

In: Minucius Felix, Octavius, etc. *Lugd. Bat.* 1709. 8⁰.

(*De unitate ecclesiae.*)

Helmst. 1557. 8⁰.

STEPHANUS, J. *Lond.* 1632. 8⁰.

CALIXTUS, G. *Helmst.* 1657. 8⁰.

AZEVEDO. In transl. Port. *Lisb.* 1801.

HYDE, M. F. *Buckington*, 1853.

(*Other.*)

(De XII. abus.) s. l. et a. [Augsburg, Ant. Serg.]

(De XII. abus.) s. l. et a. [Cologne, Urich Zell?] 4⁰.

(De orat. dom.) *Brix.* (1483. c. 1490?) 4⁰.

(De Eucharistia.) *Hagau.* 1527. 8⁰.

(De orat. dom.) s. l. 1528. 12⁰.

(Exh. ad mort.) *Rostoch.* 1565. 8⁰.

(Dispos. coenae.) *Prag.* 1579. 4⁰.

STEPHANUS, J. (De bono patientiae.) *Oxon.* 1633. 8⁰.

(Epistolae?) Reinhart, L. F. *Altd.* 1681. 4⁰.

FRANEUS, BARTH. Lib. de mort. *Jen.* 1682. 12⁰.

(Some Epist.) In: Coustant. Epp. Rom. Pontif. *Par.* 1721. f⁰. 126–.

TROMBELLI, J. C. (Exh. ad poen.) *Bonon.* 1751. 4⁰.

MAI, A. (De poenit.) In: Class. ant. (1838.)

(Epist. sel.) *Par.* 1852. 12⁰.

MIGNE. (Ep. ad Lucum Papam.) In: Patrol. Lat. III. (1865) 1003-14.

II. *Translations.*

English.

EYLOT, TH. A swete and devote Sermon of Holy Saint Ciprian of Mortalitie. *Lond.* 1534. f⁰.

PAYNALL, TH. A sermon of St. Cyprian, made on the Lordes Prayer. *Lond.* 1539. 8⁰.

St. Cyprian's Sermon on the Mortalitye of Man. *Lond.* 1539. 16⁰.

BREND, JOH. (Two sermons.) *Lond.* 1553. 8⁰.

STORY, JOH. ("Certaine Workes.") 1556. 8⁰.

LUPSET, T. (Sermon.) In: Works. 1560. Y. 11. Bb. VII.

POLE. (Sermon.) *Louv.* 1569.

BARKSDALE, CLEMENT. (Virgins, Prayers, Patience.) *Lond.* 1675. 8⁰.

FELL, JOH. (Unity of the Church.) *Oxf.* 1681. 4⁰.

BURNET, G. *Lond.* 1686. 8⁰; 1714. 8⁰.

T(UNSTALL), W(ILLIAM). (JAMES?) St. Cyprian's discourse to Donatus; done into English metre. *Lond.* 1716. 8⁰.

COLLIER, JER. Manners of the pagan world, Consolatory discourse, and on patience. *Lond.* 1716. 8⁰.

MARSHALL, NATH. (Genuine works.) *Lond.* 1717. f⁰.

DALRYMPLE, D. *Edinb.* 1782. 12⁰.

HORSBURGH. (The Unity of the Church.) 1815.

NEWMAN, J. H. (Treatises.) In: Lib. of the fathers. *Oxf.* 1839.

(Unity of the Church.) In: Tracts for the times. II. 1. (1840).

POOLE, G. A. (Works?) *Oxf.* 1840. 3 v. 8⁰.

(Epistles.) In: Library of the fath. XVII. (*Oxf.* 1844.)

WALLIS, R. E. In: Ante-Nic. Lib. VIII. (1868) 1-468; XIII. (1873) 1-198, 221-71. Ed. Coxe. V. (1886) 275-557, 575-95.

———

FLOWER, W. B. (Select treatises.) *Lond.* 8⁰. In: People's Library of the fathers.

READ, J. B. "Tracts of, condensed."

PEARSON, J.

French.

FOREST, D. DE B. (Sermones.) *Par.* 1565. 8⁰.
DANEAU, L. (Du mal qu'apport l'envie.) *Orleans*, 1566. 8⁰.
TIGEON, JAC. *Par.* 1574. f⁰. ["Deux traitez," f⁰, and a translation by S. Goularts, assigned to this year.]
(XII. maniers d'abus.) *Par.* 1577. 8⁰.
LAVAL, D. DE. (De orat. dom. mortalitate.) *Par.* 1664.
LOMBERT. (Oeuvr.) *Par.* 1672. 4⁰; *Rouen*, 1716. 2 v. 4⁰; *Par.* 1722. 2 v. 4⁰.
LENFANT, JAQ. (Lettres choisies.) *Amst.* 1688. 12⁰.
(De la singularité des clercs.) *Par.* 1718. 12⁰.
GUILLON, M. N. S. *Par.* 1837. 2 v. 8⁰.
GENOUDE. [??] In: Pères de l'égl. *Par.* 1837–43. 8⁰.
(Diss. sur la peste.) *Par.* 1849. 12⁰.
JOSSE, O. (Tr. de la mort.) *Par.* 1856. 12⁰.
THIBAUT. (Oeuvr.) *Tours*, 1869. 3 v. 8⁰.
CORDIER. (De l'unit. de l'Égl.) *Par.* 1878. 18⁰.

LENFANT, D. (Epp. ad Conf.) *Amst.* (?) 12⁰.

German.

GRIMM. Ain erkl. ü. d. Vater-Unser. *Augsp.* 1521. 4⁰.
AMBACH, MICH. (Predigten u. Schr.) *Nurnb.* 1553. f⁰.
HOHENBALKEN, C. C. (Aechte Werke.) *Wien*, 1790–. 8⁰.
FEUERABEND. (Echte Werke.) *München*, 1818–20. 4 Thl. 8⁰.
ZIEGLER. In: Werke d. K.–V. V., VI., VII. (*Kempten*, 1832.)
WAITZMANN, J. G. (Echte Werke.) *Kempten*, 1836–39. 3 v. 8⁰.
KRABINGER. (Ausgew. Schr.) *Augsb.* 1848. 8⁰.
REINLEIN, F. F. (V. d. Sterblichkeit.) *Erlangen*, 1869. 16⁰.
UHL, U. *Kempten*, 1869–70. 16⁰. [The Reithmayer-Thalhofer Bibl.]
NIGLUTSCH, EGGER, and UHL. *Kempten*, 1878–80. [The Reithmayer-Thalhofer Bibl.]

AMMAN, N. Ciprianus von den zwölff misbrüchen dieser welt. *Reutlingen.* (?)

Italian.

CASTRUCCI, RAFFAELO. (?) (Tratt. di due sorte di martirio.) *Fir.* 1567. 8⁰.
COTO, GIR. (Trattato contro il lusso delle donne.) *Ven.* 1577. 8⁰; *Rom.* 1684. 12⁰.
CONTARINI, TH. (Orazione sulla Pestilenza.) *Padov.* 1577. 4⁰.
CARO, A. (Sermone sopra l'elemosina.) In: Opere, VII. (1812).

Portuguese.

AZEVEDO, L. ANT. DE. (Tratado sobre a unitade da Igreja.) *Lisboa*, 1801. 8⁰.

Spanish.

Obras de San Cipriano, obispo y martir, traducidas al castellano y esclarecidas con notas y la vida del santo por el Dr. D. Joaquin Antonio del Camino. *Valladolid*, 1807. 2 v. 4⁰.

Swedish.

GROSCH, JO. (De orat domin.) *Rostoch.* 1615. 8⁰.

III. *Literature.*

Acta proconsularia. In: Martene and Durand. Thesaur. III; also in: Migne. Patrol. Lat. III. (1865) 1557–66, etc., etc.
ADO. Martyrol. Sept. IV. In: Migne. CXXIII. p. 355.

ALEXANDER, NATALIS. In: Zaccaria. Thes. theolog. 1762. IX. 110–31.
ALZOG. Patrol. (1876) 192–204.
ARBOUSSE–BASTIDE, ANT. FR. Tertullien et Cyprien comparés comme litterateurs. *Strasb.* 1848. 8⁰.
AUGUSTINUS. Sermones in natali Cyp. In his: Op. V. 869.
BAEHR. Gesch. röm. Lit. Sup. (1837) II. 50–65.
BALLERIUS. De vi ac primata R. Pont.
BALUZE. Lettres au P. Tournemine sur une nouvelle edition de St. Cyprien. In: Mémoires de Trévoux. (1714) 1538–49; (1715) p. 484; in: Journal des Savans (1716) p. 90, p. 231.
BARONIUS. Ann. (1589) 217, 3–7; 250, 1–13; 253, 27–95; 254, 30–41, 51–110; 255, 4–46, 49–54; 256, 2–5, 11–34; 257, 9–11; 258, 2–56; 260, 33–60; 261, 12–46. Cf. Pagi. Crit. (1689) 250, 2–7; 252, 5–6, 8–12; 253, 13–28; 255, 3–11, 16, 19–20, 23; 256, 8–10, 22; 257, 4; 258, 2–14; 259, 2–17; 260, 5; 261, 8–9.
BARRE, L. DE LA. Hist. christ. vet. patr. (1583) 48.
BAUMGARTEN–CRUSIUS. Dogmenges. (1832) 250–2. [v. I.]
BAUR. Dogmengesch. I. (1865) 266, etc.
ΒΑΦΕΙΔΗΣ. Ἐκκλ. ἱστ. I. (1884) 161–2.
BELLARMIN–LABBE. Scr. eccl. (1728) 51–4.
BENSON, E. W. In: Smith and Wace. Dict. I. 739–55.
BENTON, W. A. In: Am. Church R. XIX. (1868) 615–.
BERTHOLDT. Dogmenges. (1822–3) I. 51, etc.
BINGHAM. Origines. IV.
BLACKBURN. Hist. of Church. (1879) 46–9.
BLAMPIGNON, E. A. De Sancto Cypriano et de primaeva Carthaginiensi ecclesia. *Paris*, 1862. 8⁰.
BOEHRINGER. Kirchenges. (1873–) I. IV. (= pp. 118–1039.)
BOSIUS. Opuscul. hist. et aut. eccl.
BOUIX, D. Le célèbre conflit entre St. Etienne et St. Cyprien. In: Rev. d. Sciences eccl. 1863. VII. 211–32, 305–20, 417–37, 513–45.
BURTON. Divinity of Christ (1829) 348–365.
— Trinity. (1881) 107–116.
BUSSE. Chr. Lit. (1828–9) I. 30–1.
CAILLAU. Introd. in ss. Patr. (1825) 92–104.
CAVE. Scr. eccl. hist. lit. (1740–3) I. 126–8.
— Lives. (1840) I. 374–95.
CEILLIER. Hist. gén. aut. sac. III. (1732) 1–224; II. (1865) 257–387.
CHARTERIS. Canonicity. (1880) 282, 309–10, 317, 324–5, 329, 350–1.
CHEVALIER. Rép. d. sources hist. (1877–86) 529–31.
CLARKE. Sacred lit. (1830–1) I. 177–187.
CLINTON. Fasti Rom. (1845–50) I. 265, 271, 273, 275, 281; II. 419.
COFFIN. Lives of fath. (1846) 285–312.
COLLOMBET, F. Z. See Poole.
CONYBEARE. Bampt. Lect. 1839.
COOPER. Free ch. of anc. christendom. (*Lond.* 1844. 18⁰.) 297–.
(CORGNE.) Dissertation théologique sur la célèbre dispute entre le pape S. Etienne et S. Cyprien. *Paris*, 1725. 12⁰. Tr. latin in: Zaccaria, Thes. theolog. (1763) XIII. 381–455.
COTTA, J. F. Exercitatio hist.-crit. qua conjectura R. J. Tourneminii .. examini subjicitur. *Tubingae*, 1740. 4⁰.
CRUSIUS, CHR. Minucius Felix emend. item Cyprianus. In his: Probabilia crit. 1753. (p. 63–71.)
CULLEN, A. H. C. and the Roman See. In: Am. Cath. Q. XI. (1886) 123–40.
CUNNINGHAM. Hist. theol. (1870) I. 163–71.
DALLAEUS. De ver. usu patr.
DARLING. Cyclop. bibl. (1854) 844–6.
D'AUBIGNY, J. H. MERLE. L'Occident, ou Cyprien et la pratique. In: Union Chrétienne des jeunes gens. *Gen.* 1857.

D'AUBIGNY, J. H. M.　Cyprianus el sacerdotalismens uppkomst i den kristna kyrkan. *Sthm.* 1871. 8°. (39 p.)
— St. Cyprian and his Times. In: New Eng. XXXI. (1872) 643–.
DAVIS.　Carthage, etc.
DE ROSSI.　Rom. sotter.
DODWELL.　Diss. Cypr. *Oxon.* 1684. 8°; *Bremae,* 1690. f°; also in: Ed. Fell. *Oxon.* 1682; *Amst.* 1700; in: Migne. Patrol. lat. V. 9–80; cf. III.–IV.
DORNER.　Person of Christ. II. (1866) 100–4.
DUPIN.　Nouv. bibl. aut. eccl. (1698) I. 423–525.
DU VERDIER.　Bibl. Franç. (1772) III. 277–9.
EBERT.　Gesch. Lit. Mittelalt. (1874) I. 54–61.
ENGELHARDT.　Dogmenges. I. (1839) 213, etc.
EUSEBIUS.　H. E. VII. 3.
FABRICIUS.　Bibl. Lat. (1722) III. 377–87.
— De verit. rel. Chr. (1725) 217–23.
— Bibl. med. aev. (1734) 1252–7.
— Bibl. gr. X. 215.
FARRAR.　Interpretation. (1886) 180–2.
FAVRE (FABRE?), TIM.　S. Cyprien et l'église de Carthage. *Angers,* 1847. 12°.
FECHTRUPP, BERNHARD.　Der heil. Cyprian. sein Leben u. seine Lehre. I. Cyprian's Leben. *Münster,* 1878. 8°.
FEHRER, F.　Error. See Freher.
FISCHER, J. M. E.　S. Cypriani diss. de doctrina Tertulliani evangelica. *Erford,* 1797. 4°.
FLEURY.　Hist. eccl. (1691–) II. 152–5, 163–4, 176–81, 196–209, 222–30, 232–5, 237–46, 251–6, 270–3, 276–88, 302–6, 309–14.
FREHER, F.　Num Cyp. sit auct. doct. d. unica chr. rel. et eccl. salv. *Erf.* 1792. 4°; also, Lumper. XII. 685; 685; also, *Francof.* 1812. 4°.
FREPPEL, CH. E.　Saint Cyprien et l'Église d'Afrique au IIIe siècle. Cours d'éloquence sacrée fait à la Sorbonne pendant l'année 1863–64. *Paris,* 1865. 8°; 1873. 8°.
FUNCCIUS.　De veg. senect. C. X. § 19.
GAMBA.　Test. Ital. 1226.
GARY, A.　In: Lichtenberger. Encycl. (1877–82) III. 547–9.
[GERVAISE, FR. ARM.]　La vie de S. Cyprien aveo la critique de ses écrits. *Amst.* 1689. 12°; *Par.* 1717. 4°.
GIBBON.　Decline and Fall. c. 16.
GIESELER.　Church Hist. (1868–) I. 227–8, 179, 231–2.
GREGORIUS, NAZ.　Oratio in laud. S. Cyp. Mart. In: Op. Ed. Colon. p. 274.
GREISINGER, J.　S. Cypriani, epist. Carthag. de Romani pontificis primata atque de juribus et muneribus eidem annexis sententia. *Wittemberg,* 1790. 8°.
GRISAR, H.　C.'s "Oppositionsconcil gegen Papst Stephan." In: Ztschr. f. kath. Theol. V. (1881) 193–221.
GUILLON.　Not. hist. sur la vie . . (Cyprian). In: Pref. to his trans. of Cyprian, 1837.
HACKENSCHMIDT, K.　Die Anfänge d. Katholischen Kirchenbegriffs. Dogmenhistor. Versuch. I. Abschn., die neutestamentl. Lehre v. der Kirche u. die Geschichte d. Dogma's bis auf Cyprian enthaltend. *Strassb.* 1874. 8°.
HAGEMANN.　Die röm. Kirche. p. 50–.
HAGEN, H.　Eine Nachahmung von Cyprian's Gastmahl durch Hrabanus Maurus. In: Ztschr. f. wiss. Theol. XXVII. (1884) 164–187.
HAGENBACH.　Hist. of Doct. I. (1850) 61–2, etc.
— Kirchenges. (1885) I. 222–35.
— S. u. Leimbach.
HARNACK.　Dogmenges. I. (1886) 310–7, 334–7, 350–4.
HASE.　Kirchenges. (1885–) I. 348–52, 416–7.
HAUPT, MOR.　Conjectanea. (Contains Cyprianus ad Donat. c. 4, p. 6, 13 H.) In: Hermes. V. (1871) p. 315; also in his: Opuscula. Th. 2 (1876) p. 538.
HAVET, E.　Cyprien évêque de Carthage. In: Revue des deux mondes. LXXI. (1885) 27–69, 283–311.

HEFELE.　Conciliengesh. I. 122–.
HERGENROETHER.　Kirchenges. (1879–80) I. 104–6, 168, 176–7; III. 41–2, 73, 81–2.
HUSENBETH.　Cyprian vindicated.
HUTHER, JO. ED.　Cyprian's Lehre v. der Kirche. *Hamb.* 1839. 8°.
ITTIG.　Obs. miscel. In: Clem. Al. Op. Suppl. IV.
JAMES, TH.　Cypr. redivivus. *Lond.* 1600. 4°.
JAMIESON.　Cypr. isotimus. *Edinb.* 1705. (Confut. of J. Sage.)
JEREMIE.　Hist. Church. (1852) 110–113.
JUNGMANN, B.　Dissertationes in Hist. eccl. *Ratisbon.* 1880. 8°. 263–357.
KILLEN.　Ancient Church. (1859) 381–3.
KOLBE, A.　C.'s Lehre v. d. Einheit d. Kirche u. s. w. In: Ztschr. f. d. luth. Theol. XXXV. (1874) 25–40.
KURTZ.　Kirchenges. (1885–) I. 126.
LARDNER.　Credibility. Works. (1831) III. 3–74.
LANNOIUS.　Discus. de duob. Dionys. c. V. p. 54.
LE CLERC, J.　La Vie de St. Cyprien, év. de Carthage, avec la critique de ses ouvrages. In his: Bibl. univ. et hist. XII. 207–403. *Amst.* 1689. 12°.
LÉCUY.　In: Biog. Univ. (Michaud) 1842–65. IX. 604–6.
LEIMBACH (HAGENBACH).　In: Herzog. Real.–Enc. (1877) III. 499–415. (Abr. in: I. 591–3.)
LE NOURRY.　Dissert. de libr. Demetr. et de idol. vanitate. Migne. Patrol. Lat. IV. (1865) 1059–114.
Life and Times of St. Cyprian. In: Kitto. XVII. (1856) 279–.
Life of Cyprian. *Lond., Rel. Tr. Soc.* 1842. 18°.
LIPSIUS.　Chron. Rom. Bisch.
(LIRON.)　Singul. histor. (1738–9) I. 489–90; III. 248–9.
Lit. Zeitung f. Kath. Religionslehrer. (1822) Fasc. VII. p. 79, 102; (1823) IV. p. 33.
LONG, J. C.　Study of St. Cyprian's Life. In: Bapt. Q. XI. (1877) 385–.
LUCHINI.　Atti sinceri.　(1778) II. 248–82.
LUMPER.　Hist. ss. patr. XI. (1795) 58–645; XII. (1797) 1–736; XIII. (1799) 796–912; also in: Migne. Patrol. lat. III. (1865) 1537–40; IV. (1865) 835–52.
M'CLINTOCK and S. Cycl. (1874–) II. 624–6.
MALEVILLE.　Religion natur. et révél. (17—) 528. Tr. Ital. in: Zaccaria. Racc. di dissert. (1794) VIII. 158–68.
MARANUS, PRUD.　Vita S. Cyp. In: Opp. Cyp. *Par.* 1726.
— Praef. In: Migne. Patrol. Lat. IV. (1865) 9–194.
— Vita Cyprianae. In: Ed. op. Cypr. p. 37.
MARCHETTI.　Essercitazioni Ciprianiche. Il battesimo degli eretici. *Roma,* 1787. 4°.
MATTES.　Die Ketzertaufr. In: Tüb. Quartalschr. (1849).
MENDEN.　Beitrage z. Gesch. u. z. Lehre d. nordafrikan Kirche aus d. Briefen d. heil. Cyprian. Gymn. Progr. *Münstereifel.* 1878. 4°.
[MEYER, LIV. DE.]　Causam Cypriani non favere, sed obesse causae protestantium ostenditur. *Lovanir.* 1719. 8°. (52 p.) Cf. Backer. Bibl. Jésuites. (1872) II. 1288.
MILMAN.　History of Christianity. II. 246.
MISSORIUS, RAYM.　In duas celeben. epistolas ss. Firmiliani et Cypriani adversus decretum s. Stephani papae I. disputationes criticae. *Venetiis,* 1733. 4°.
MÖHLER.　Patrologie. 422–518.
MOMBRITIUS BONIN.　Sanctuarium. (c. 1479) I. clxxxxviii–iiii.
MORCELLI.　Africa sacra; also in: Migne. Patrol. Lat. III. (1865) 1475–536.
MUELLER, C. G.　Observ. in V loca epist. d. Cypriani. *Ger.* 1777. (?) 4°.
MUENSCHER.　Dogmenges. (1817–8) I. 163, etc.
MÜNTER.　Primordia eccl. Africanae.

NEANDER. Hist. of dogmas. (1858) 56, 82, 186, 222–3, 224–5, 232–3, 241–3, 253. [v. 1.]
— Church Hist. (1872) I. 134–40, 192–3, 222–37, 248, 319–23, 685–6, et pass.
NEVIN, J. W. St. Cyprian and early Christianity. In: Mercersb. IV. (1852) 259–; 513–.
NIRSCHL. Patrol. (1881–) I. 301–22.
NITZSCH. Dogmengesch. I. (1870) 166, etc.
NODIER. Bibl. sacr. (1826) 165–7.
OBERDICK. D. römerfeindl. Bewegungen, etc. 315–.
OELRICHS. Scr. eccl. lat. (1791) 31–43.
ORSI. Ist. eccl. (1746–) III. 116–23, 146–50, 159–62, 165–78, 185–90, 239–46, 254–8, 268–80, 284–5, 290–5, 298–316, 322–8, 343–8; IV. 80–4; (1749–) III. 150–8, 190–5, 207–10, 215–31, 240–7, 309–19, 329–35, 347–63, 367–8, 375–8, 386–409, 416–24, 443–9; IV. 105–11.
OTT, JOH. N. Zu Gellius (XIII. 8, 2) u. Pseudo-Cyprianus (de Sodoma V. 56 ff.) In: Jahrb. f. class. Philol. CIII. (1871) p. 859.
OUDIN. Scr. eccl. (1722) I. 266–81.
PAMELIUS. Antv. 1568.
Passio Cypr. In: Migne. Patrol. Lat. III. (1865) 1565–8.
PEARSON. Annales Cyprianicae. In: Cyprian. Opera. Ed. Fell. Oxon. 1682; Amst. 1700.
PERMANEDER. Bibl. patrist. (1841–4) I. 422; II. 814–81, 920–4.
PETERS, JOH. Die Lehre d. h. Cyprian v. d. Einheit d. Kirche. Luxemburg, 1870. 8º. (62 p.)
— Der h. Cyprian von Carthago, in seinem Leben und Wirken dargestellt. Regensb. 1877.
PETREIUS, THD. Confessio Tert. et Cyp. Par. 1603. 8º.
PHOTIUS. Cod. 184.
PONTIUS. Vita C. In: Acta ss.; also in Migne. Patrol. Lat. 1537–58; also in various eds., etc.; tr. Engl. Marshall. Lond. 1719. fº; also Wallis in Ante-Nic. fath.
POOLE, GEORGE AYLIFFE. The Life and Times of S. Cyprian. Oxf. 1840. 8º; French tr. by Fr. Z. Collombet. Lyon-Paris, 1841. 8º. [Also 1842. 18º. ?]
PRESSENSÉ. Early years of Christianity. Chr. life. (1878) 142–61, 172–4, 178–90, 192–5; Martyrs. (1879) 414–38; Heresy. (n. d.) 456–62.
PREU, G. P. Cypriani ac Firmiliani epistolarum adversus Stephani I. papae decretum de haereticorum baptismo. Jenae, 1738. fº. [Against Missorius.]
PRILESZKY, JOH: B. S. Cypriani, acta et scripta omnia in summam redacta, etc. Tymaviae, 1761. fº.
QUESNEL. Diss. V ad Leonem.
RAMSAY, W. In: Smith. Gr. and Rom. Biog. (1859) I. 912–5.
RATHMANN, H. On Tertullian and Cyprian. 1620. 4º. Vitemb. 1636, 1655, 1664. 4º.
— Prisc. patr. theosophia.
RECCO, GIUS. Epist. intorno alla cel. controversia del battesimo degli eretici fr. S. Stefano e S. Cipriano. In: Zaccaria, Racc. di dissert. (1794) VII. 195–247.
RECEVEUR. In: Nouv. Biog. Gén. (Hoefer) XII. (1855) 705–14.
REINKENS, J. H. Die Lehre d. h. C. v. d. Einheit d. Kirche. Würzburg, 1873. 8º.
REITHMEIER, WOLFGANG. Geschichte des heiligen Cyprian. Augsb. 1848. 8º. [Not Reithmayr, F. X., as some.]
RETTBERG, Fr. W. Thasc. Casc. Cyprianus, dargestellt nach seinem Leben und Wirken. Götting. 1831. 8º.
REUCHLIN, JOH. J. Dissertationes III. de doctrina Cypriani. Argent. 1751–56. 4º.
REUSS. Gesch. N. T. (1874) II. 35; tr. Eng. (1884) 317–8. [v. 2.]
RIESS, FLOR. Der heil. Cyprian und die "Altkatholischen" seiner Zeit. In: Stimmen aus Maria-Laach. (1874) VI. 433–47, 529–44; VII. 262–73.

RITSCHL, O. Cyprian v. Karthago u. die Verfassung die Kirche. Göttingen, 1885. 8º.
ROBERTSON. Hist. of Church. (1875–) I, 161–82.
ROCHE. De la controverse entre St. Étienne et St. Cyprien au sujet du baptême des héretiques. Paris, 1858. 8º.
ROOY, A. de. Ad Cyprianum. In his: Spicileg. crit. (1771) p. 32–34.
ROSENMÜLLER. Hist. interp. II. (1798) 229–58.
ROESSLER. Bibl. d. K.–V. III. (1777) 173–275.
ROST, H. Cyprianus Kerkvater en martelaar. Utrecht, 1870. 8º.
ROUSTAIN, FR. Court exposé de la doctrine ecclésiastique de S. Cyprien, précédé d'une petite biographie de cet évêque et de quelques mots sur ses ouvrages. Strasb. 1847. 8º.
ROUTH. Notae. In: Opusc. (1840) 330–359; also in: Migne. Patrol. Lat. IV. (1865) 1299–312.
RUDELBACH. Christl. Biogr. I.
RUFFET, LOUIS. Thascius Cyprien, et les persécutions de son temps. Toulouse, Paris, 1872. 12º.
RUINART. Acta sinc. (1689) 193–203.
RULE, GILB. The Cyprianick Bishop. Lond. 1696. 4º. [Answer to Sage.]
[SAGE, JOHN.] The principles of the Cyprianic age, with regard to the Episcopal power and jurisdiction. Lond. 1695. 4º. (1 f.–94 p.); Lond. 1717. 8º; Savoy, 1795. 4º; also in: Works. 1846. II.
— Vindication of principles. Lond. 1701. 4º. [Reply to Rule.]
SAINJORE. Bibl. crit. (1707) II. 213–6.
SALIG. De diptychis veterum.
SALMON, G. In: Hermathena. I. (Dubl. 1873.) 85–6, 90–1, 96–7. [The Computus de pascha.]
SCHAFF. Creeds of Christendom. II. (1877) 20–1.
— Hist. . . Church. II. (1886) 842–9.
SCHARFFENBERG. S. u. Justin M.
SCHARPFF. In: Wetzer u. W. Kirch-Lex. (1847–54) II. 965–9.
SCHMID. Patrol. (1879); (1886) 60–2.
SCHMIEDER, H. E. Ueb. Cyp. Schr. v. d. Einheit d. Kirche. In: Stäudlein u. Tzschirner Archiv. f. Kirchengesch. V. 417; also separately. Lips. 1823. 8º.
SCHMITZ. In: Symb. philol. Bonn. p. 540–3. [C. and Notae tironianae.]
SCHÖNEMANN. Bibl. patr. lat. (1792) 77–134.
SCHRAM. Anal. ss. patr. (1780–) VI. 1–268.
SCHROECKH. Kirchenges. (1772) IV. 235–83, 325–36, 217–9; XI. 427–9; XIV. 381; XXVIII. 102; XXXIII. 338, 346–7.
SCHWANE. Contr. de valore bapt. haeret. Monast. 1860.
— Dogmengesch. vornicän. Zeit. Münster, 1862. I. 730–.
SEVESTRE. Dict. patrol. (1851) I. 1159–82.
SHEDD. Hist. of doct. 3d ed. (1865–) II. 47–8, 414.
SHEPHERD, E. J. Hist. Ch. of Rome. (1851) 126–84.
— Letters (1–5) on the genuineness of the writings ascribed to Cyprian. Lond. 1853. 8º.
Shepherd on St. Cyprian. In: Chr. Obs. LIV. (1854) 308–.
SUICER. Sacr. obs. c. iii. p. 65.
Supernatural Religion. I. (1875) 124, 147, 164.
SURIUS. Vitae ss. (1618) IX. 148–52.
SUYSKENIUS. Comment. praec. In: Acta ss. Bolland. (1753) Sept. IV. 191–325, 334–48, 769–78; cf. Mart. I. 750.
TEUFFEL. Hist. Rom. Lit. (1873) II. 299–301.
THÉROND, R. Étude critique sur le De unitate ecclesiae de Cyprien. Thèse. Genève, 1876. 8º.
THIBAUT. Histoire et oeuvres complètes de St. Cyprien, év. de Carthage . . . Tours, 1869. 3 v. 8º. (XVI. 1417 p.)

THIBAUT. Question du baptême des hérétiques, discutée entre le pape St. Etienne I. et St. Cyprien, évêque de Carthage, vers le milieu du III. s. de l'ère chrét. 18 . . . 8⁰.

TILLEMONT. Mémoires. IV. (1696) 45–198, 601–45.

TIZZIANI, VINC. La celebre contesa fra S. Steph. e. S. Cipriano. *Roma*, 1862. 8⁰; Fr. tr. by Ranvier. *Par.* 1866. 8⁰.

Tizziani on St. Cyprian. In: Dub. R. LXII. (1868) 165.

TOURMENINE, R. J. In: Mém. de Trévoux (1734) 2246–62.

TRITHEMIUS. Scr. eccl. 41.

TROMBELLIUS, J. C. Praef. in exhort. ad poen. in: Migne. Patrol. Lat. IV. (1865) 859–64.

TULLOCH, J. In: Encycl. Brit. (9th ed.) VI. 746–7.

VARIEN, A. Nevin on St. Cyprian. In: Mercersb. V. (1853) 555–.

VINCENTIUS BELVAC. Spec. hist. XII. 62–73.

Vita Cypriani. *Par.* 1566. 8⁰.

VONCK, C. V. Ad Cyprianum. In his: Spic. crit. in var. auctor. (1744) p. 99, 125; and Lection. lat. libri. II. (1745) p. 72–77.

WALCH. Bibl. Patrist. (1834) 44–7, 287–90, 382, pass.

WALLIS, E. Introd. note. In: Ante-Nic. Lib. VIII. (1868) ix–xxxi. XIII. (1873) 219–20. Ed. Coxe. V. (1886) 261–74, 573. [Add. notes. Ed. Coxe. 409-20, 557-64, 595-6.]

WEILLER (WEICKER?), C. E. Aphor. üb. Cyp. Schr. v. d. Einheit d. Kirche. In: Illgen. Histor. theol. Abhandel. *Lips.* 1824. 8⁰. p. 111.

WESTCOTT. Canon. (1875) 369–70.

WIRSING, GREG. Dissert. theol., Orthodoxia S. Stephani Rom. pontif. de baptismo haereticorum, 1738, ms. at Fribourg.

WORDSWORTH. Church Hist. (1881) 312–318, 335–51.

For literature see especially all articles or works on Stephen I., Re-baptism, Baptism of heretics, etc.

> *Note.* Besides the large number of works whose ascription to Cyprian is undoubtedly false, the authenticity of (1) *de spectaculis*, (2) *de disciplina et bono pudicitiae*, (3) *de laude martyrii*, (4) *exhortatio ad poenitentiam*, is dubious. Nirschl.

III. CAIUS.

I. *Editions.*

ROUTH. Rel. sacr. (1846–8) II. 123–158.

MIGNE. (Fragments.) Gr. lat. In: Patrol. gr. X. (1857) 25–34.

> *Note.* Only the fragments are authentic. The ascription of various other works to Caius is not maintained.

II. *Translations.*

English.

SALMOND. In: Ante-Nic. Lib. IX. (1869) II. 154–62. Ed. Coxe. V. (1886) 601–4.

III. *Literature.*

ALZOG. Patrol. (1876) 111–2.

BARONIUS. Ann. (1589) 215, 1–4.

BAUMGARTEN–CRUSIUS. Dogmenges. (1832) 195. [v. 1.]

BUNSEN. In: Hippolytus and his times. *Lond.* 1852; 1854. 8⁰.

BUSSE. Chr. Lit. (1828–9) I. 19–20.

CASPARI. Quellen u. s. w. III. 301–, 407–, etc.

CAVE. Scr. eccl. hist. lit. (1740–3) I. 100.

CEILLIER. Hist. gén. aut. sac. (1730) II. 208-10, 239–41; I. (1858) 561–3.

CHARTERIS. Canonicity. (1880) 210, 279, 343–4.

CHEVALIER. Rép. d. sources hist. (1877–86) 374.

CLARKE. Sacred lit. (1830–1) I. 156–7.

CLINTON. Fasti Rom. (1845–50) I. 217; II. 418.

CUNNINGHAM. Churches of Asia. (1880) passim.

DÖLLINGER. Hippolytus and Callistus. (1876) 250–3.

DUPIN. Bibl. aut eccl. (1698–) I. 291.

DURDENT. In: Biog. Univ. (Michaud) (1842–65) VI. 367.

EBED JESU. In: Assemani Bibl. orient. III. 15.

EUSEBIUS. Hist. Eccl. II. 25; III. 28. 31; VI. 20.

FABRICIUS. Bibl. gr. (1712) V. 267 (2ᵃ. VII. 284–6.)

GALLAND. Bibl. patr. *Venet.* 1765. f⁰; II. xxviii–; also in: Migne. Patrol. gr. X. (1857) 17–24.

GIESELER. Church Hist. (1868–) I. 195.

HARNACK, AD. In: Herzog. Real.-Enc. (1877–) III. 63–4. (Abr. in: Schaff-Herz.) I. 358.

HASE. Kirchenges. (1885–) I. 163–4, 337–8, 340–1.

HEINICHEN. Notes on Eusebius, Hist. Eccl. II. 25.

HERGENROETHER. Kirchenges. (1879–80) I. 168; III. 73.

HIERONYMUS. De vir. ill. 59. (Honor. August. I. 60.)

Hist. lit. France. (1733) I. 1. 356–60.

ITTIG. Hist. Eccl. (1709) II. 54–5.

KÖNIG. In: Wetzer u. W. Kirch-Lex. (1847–54) II. 255–6.

KURTZ. Kirchenges. (1885–) I. 122.

LARDNER. Credibility. Works. (1831) II. 394–410.

Lichtenberger. Encycl. (1877–82) II. 506–7.

LIGHTFOOT. In: Jour. of Philol. (1868) I. 98.

LUMPER. Hist. ss. patrum. (1790) VII. 17–43.

M'CLINTOCK and S. Cycl. (1874–) II. 15.

Meth. Qu. Rev. (1851) 646.

MÖHLER. Patrol. (1840) 617–620.

NEANDER. Ch. Hist. (1872) I. 396, 399, 652, 690; III. 184.

NICEPHORUS CALL. Hist. Eccl. IV. 12, 20.

NIRSCHL. Patrol. (1881–) I. 200–1.

Nouv. Biog. Gén. (Hoefer) VIII. (1854) 137.

ORSI. Ist. eccl. (1746–) III. 1–5; (1749–) III. 3–8.

PERMANEDER. Bibl. patrist. II. (1843) 789–94.

PHOTIUS. Bibl. Cod. 48.

PRESSENSÉ. Martyrs. (1879) 366–7.

REUSS. Gesch. N. T. (1874) II. 35; tr. Eng. (1884) 317. [v. 2.]

SALMON, G. In: Smith and Wace. Dict. I. 384–6.

SALMOND, S. D. F. Introd. note. In: Ante-Nic. Lib. IX. (1869) ii, 153–4. Ed. Coxe. V. (1886) 597–600. [Add. notes. Ed. Coxe. 604.]

SAUSSAYE, L. DE LA. In: Rev. du Lyonnais. (1861) B. XXII. 92–5.

SCHAFF. Hist. . . Church. II. (1886) 775–6.

SCHMID. Patrol. (1879); (1886) 46.

SCHNITZ, L. In: Smith. Gr. and Rom. Biog. (1859) I. 558.

SCHROECKH. Kirchenges. (1772–) III. 426–8.

SCHWEGLER. Nachap. Zeitalt. (1846) I. 312–4; II. 218–9.

SMEDT, P. DE. In: Dissert. selectae (1876).

THEODORET. Haer. Fab. II. 3; III. 2.

TILLEMONT. Mémoires. III. (1695) 174–7.

TIRABOSCHI. Stor. let. Ital. (1806) II. II. 369.

VOLKMAR. Hippolytus u. d. röm. Zeitgenoss. (1855) 60–71.

WAITE. Hist. Chr. Rel. (1881) passim.

WALCH. Bibl. Patrist. (1834) 218.

WESTCOTT. Canon. (1875) 374.

WORDSWORTH. Hippolytus. *Lond.* 1880.

For literature, compare under Hippolytus, and works on Euseb., in: Hist. Eccl. II. 25, etc., etc.

IV. NOVATIAN.

I. *Editions.*

GAGNAEUS. *Par.* 1545. [With Tert.] Also in the various editions of Tertullian by Gelenius, Pamelius, Junius, etc.

Rous, Fr. (De Trin. et de cib. jud.) In: Mell. patrum. (*Lond.* 1650) 8°. 456–68.
Whiston. (De trinitate.) In: Sermons and Essays. 1709. 8°.
Welchman, E. *Oxon.* 1724. 8°.
Jackson, J. *Lond.* 1728. 8°.
Gallandius. Bibl. vet. Patr. III. (1765) 287–.
Migne. Patrol. Lat. III. (1865) 911–1000.

II. *Translations.*

English.

Wallis, R. E. In: Ante-Nic. Lib. XIII. (1873) 297–395. Ed. Coxe. V. (1866) 611–50.

III. *Literature.*

Alexander, Natalis. Hist. eccl. (1778) III. 385–8.
Alletz. Hist. des papes. I. p. 41.
Alzog. Patrol. (1876) 204–5.
Ambrosius. De Poen. III. 3.
Baehr. Gesch. Röm. Lit. Sup. (1837) II. 47–50.
Baronius. Ann. (1589) 254, 59–90, 99, 103–6; 255, 2; 261, 50–1.
Baur. Dogmengesch. I. (1865) 268, etc.
Bellarmin–Labbe. Scr. eccl. (1728) 50.
Bertholdt. Dogmenges. (1822–3) I. 62–3, etc.
Bull. Defens. fid. Nicaen. In: Works. V. ( ) 374.
Burton. Divinity of Christ. (1829) 365–377.
— Trinity. (1831) 116–123.
Busse. Chr. Lit. (1828–9) I. 29–30.
Caspari. Quellen z. Gesch. d. Taufsymbols. III. 428–30, 437–9.
Cave. Scr. eccl. hist. lit. (1740–3) I. 129–30.
Ceillier. Hist. gén. aut. sac. III. (1732) 290–6; II. (1865) 426–30.
Chevalier. Rép. d. sources hist. (1877–86) 1657.
Clarke. Sacred lit. (1830–1) I. 189–92.
Clinton. Fasti Rom. (1845–50) I. 271; II. 420–22.
Cyprian. Epist. 44, 45, 49, 50, 55, 68.
Darling. Cyc. bibl. 2220, 3176.
Desodoards, F. Dict. raisonné du gouvernement, des lois et des usages de l'Eglise. IV. 537.
Desportes. In: Biog. Univ. (Michaud) (1842–65) XXXI. 93.
Dorner. Person of Christ. II. (1866) 80–3.
Dupin. Nouv. bibl. aut. eccl. (1698–) I. 530.
Encycl. Brit. (9th ed.) XVII. 603–4.
Engelhardt. Dogmenges. I. (1839) 213, etc.
Eusebius. Hist. eccles. IV. 43.
Fabricius. De verit. rel. Chr. (1725) 174, 223–4.
— Bibl. med. aet. (1734–) V. 426–8 (2ᵃ. 146).
Fleury. Hist. Eccl. (1691–) II. 218–30.
Forsyth, J. Novatianism; or Primitive Puritanism. In: Theo. & Lit. J. VII. (1855) 446–.
F[resse–Montoul], A. In: Nouv. Biog. Gen. (Hoefer) XXXVIII. (1862) 337–8.
Gary, A. In: Lichtenberger. Encycl. (1877–82) IX. 711–12.
Hagemann. Die röm. Kirche. p. 371–411.
Hagenbach. Hist. of Doct. I. (1850) 182.
— Kirchenges. (1885) I. 226–7.
Harnack. Dogmenges. I. (1886) 339–43.
— In: Herzog. Real.-Enc. (1877–) X. 652–670. (Abr. in: Schaff-Herz.) II. 1669–72.
Hase. Kirchenges. (1885–) I. 349, 391–2.
Hefele. Novatianisches Schisma. In: Wetzer u. W. Kirch-Lex. (1847–54) VII. 658–63.
Hergenroether. Kirchenges. (1879–80) I. 182–3; III. 84.

Hieronymus. De vir ill. 70 (Honor. August. I. 71.)
Jaffe. Reg. pont. Rom. (1851) 8°.
Killen. Ancient Church. (1859) 356–7.
Kurtz. Kirchenges. (1885–) I. 127.
Langen, Jos. Gesch. d. röm. Kirche. (*Bonn*, 1881) 289–314.
Langlet–Dufresnoy. Tablettes chronologiques. II. 321.
Lardner. Credibility. CXLVII.
Leclerc. Biblioth. univ. (1689) 274.
Lumper. Hist. ss. patr. XI. (1795) 20–58.
— Hist. ss. patr. XI. (1795) 20–58; also in: Migne. Patrol. Lat. III. (1865) 889–912.
Möhler. Patrol. (1840) 894–899.
Mosheim. De reb. chr. ante Const.
Muenscher. Dogmenges. (1817–8) I. 164, etc.
Neale. Eastern Ch. Alexandria. I. (1847) 48–51.
Neander. Hist. of dogmas. (1858) 163–4, 226–7. [v. 1.]
— Church Hist. (1872) I. 237–48, 560, 581, 690, pass.
Nirschl. Patrol. (1881–) I. 322–6.
Nitzsch. Dogmengesch. I. (1870) 166 et passim.
Orsi. Ist. eccl. (1746–) III. 248–79; (1749) III. 321–61.
Oudin. Scr. eccl. (1722) I. 281–4.
Overbeck. Z. Gesch. d. Kanons. p. 52–.
Pacian. Ep. 3.
Perennes. Dict. de biog. chret. et antichrét.
Permaneder. Bibl. patrist. (1841–3) II. 799–813.
Philostorgius. Hist. eccles. VIII. 15.
Photius. Bibl. Cod. 182, 208, 280.
Pluquet. Dict. des hérésies.
Pressensé. Chr. life. (1878) 163–72, 174–8.
Ramsay, W. In: Smith. Gr. and Rom. Biog. (1859) II. 1210–1.
Reuss. Gesch. N. T. (1874) II. 35; tr. Eng. (1884) 317. [v. 2.]
Ritschl. Altkath. Kirche. (1857).
Robertson. Hist. of Church. (1875–) I. 167–71.
Roessler. Bibl. d. K.–V. (1777) 276–307.
Schaff. Creeds of Christendom. II. (1877) 21.
— Hist. . . Church. II. (1886) 849–53.
Schmid. Patrol. (1879); (1886) 63–4.
Schönemann. Bibl. patr. lat. (1792) 135–42.
Bibl. patr. lat. (1792) I. 135–42.
Bibl. PP. I. 135–143.
Schram. Anal. ss. patr. (1780–) VI. 269–318.
Schroeckh. Kirchenges. (1772–) IV. 303–4.
Schwegler. Nachap. Zeitalt. (1846) II. 220.
Smedt, Car. de. Dissert. sel. hist. eccles. (1876) 184–9.
Socrates. Hist. eccles. IV. 24.
Sozomen. Hist. eccles. VI. 24.
Teuffel. Hist. Rom. Lit. (1873) II. 301–2.
Tillemont. Mémoires. III. (1693–) 435–62, 478–81, 737, 740–2, 746, 752.
Trithemius. Scr. eccl. 44.
Walch. Bibl. patr. (1834) 155, 219.
— Ketzerhistorie. II. 185–288.
Wallis, R. E. Introd. note. In: Ante-Nic. Lib. XIII. (1873) 293–6. Ed. Coxe. V. (1886) 605–9. [Add. notes. Ed. Coxe. 644.]
Whiston. Sermons and essays.
Wordsworth. Church Hist. (1881) 310–317.
Worman, J. H. In: M'Clintock and S. Cycl. (1874–) VII. 208–11.

See also especially works on Cyprian.

V. APPENDIX.

For literature relating to these works see under Cyprian.

VOLUME VI.
I. GREGORY THAUMATURGUS.

I. *Editions.*

(*Works.*)

VOSSIUS, GER. Gr. lat. *Romae*, 1594. f⁰ (?) do. *Moguntiae*, 1604. 4⁰.
DUCAEUS. Gr. lat. *Paris*, 1621. f⁰ (?); 1622. f⁰; 1626. f⁰. (?)
GALLANDIUS. Gr. lat. Bibl. patr. (1788. f⁰.) III. 385–470; XIV. 119–.
MIGNE. Gr. lat. In: Patrol. gr. X. (1857) 983–1206. [Galland's text.]

(*Epistola canonica.*)

Gr. lat. In: Bibl. patr. *Paris*, 1624. f⁰. VII.
Gr. lat. In: Beveridge. Pandectae canon. *Oxon.* 1672. f⁰. II. 24–35.
ROUTH. Rel. sacr. (1846–8) III. 251–283.

(*Metaphrasis.*)

SCHOTT, A. Gr. lat. *Antv.* 1613. 8⁰.
Gr. lat. In: Catena Gr. Patr. *Antv.* 1614. 8⁰.

(*Expositio fidei.*)

GLASERUS, N. Gr. lat. In: Leonis M. ep. ad Flavium. *Hamb.* 1614. 8⁰. 1–5.
CAVE. Gr. Eng. In: Lives of primitive fathers. 1682. f⁰. 267; also in Ger. tr.
FABRICIUS. Gr. lat. In: Bibl. gr. Ed. Harless.
— Gr. lat. In: S. Hippolyti Op. *Hamb.* 1718. f⁰; II. 224.
CANISIUS. Gr. lat. In his: Lectiones antiq. ed. Basnage. *Amst.* 1725 [?]. f⁰. I. 20–6.
ROESSLER. Gr. ger. Bibl. d. K.–V. 1777. 8⁰. II. 288–. [And frequently.]

(*Other.*)

WEGELINUS. (De trin.) In: Cyrilli Alex. liber de Trin. 1604; 1608. 8⁰.
— Gr. lat. 1622. f⁰. [With homilies of Macarius and Basil of Seleverae.]
(De anima.) In: Adparatus ad Bibl. patr. 1715. f⁰; II. 734.
BENGEL, J. A. (Panegyric.) Gr. lat. *Stutgard*, 1722. 8⁰.
CANISIUS. (Athanematismi.) Lectiones antiq. *Amst.* 1725. f⁰. I. 26–34.
— (Anathematismi.) Gr. lat. In: Gretser. Opera. *Ratisb.* 1734. f⁰. XV. 434–9.
MINGARELLIUS. (Oratio.) *Bonon.* 1770. f⁰.
— (Fragments.) In: Vet. patr. Analecta nova. *Venet.* 1781. f⁰. no. 2.
   Note. For account of the two Syriac treatises see Nirschl. Patrologie. I. (1881) 340.

II. *Translations.*

Latin.

(*Epist. canon.*)

OECOLAMPADIUS. (Epist. canon.) In: Micropresbyticum. *Basil*, 127–9.
In: Monumenta patr. orthodoxographa. *Basil.* 1569. f⁰. II. 22–.
In: Bibl. patr. *Paris*, 1575.
In: Canones poenitent. *Venet.* 1584. 4⁰; *Paris*, 1641. f⁰.

(*Metaphrasis.*)

OECOLAMPADIUS. *Lips.* 1520. 4⁰.
— In: Olympiodorus. Scholia in Ecclesiasten. *Basil.* 1536. 8⁰. 225–34.

In: Micropresbyticum. *Basil.* 1550. f⁰. 119–26.
In: Monumenta patr. orthodoxographa. *Basil.* 1569. f⁰. II. 944–52.

(*Other.*)

OECOLAMPADIUS. (Canons.) *Basil.* 1518. 4⁰.
(De anima.) In: Claudianus. Liber de statu animae. *Cigneae.* 1655. 8⁰. 460.
(De anima.) In: Bibl. patr. *Paris*, 1575. f⁰. VIII. 45.
(Epistles.) In: Canones poenitentiales. *Venet.* 1584. 4⁰; *Paris*, 1641. f⁰.
(De anima.) In: Bibl. patr. *Paris*, 1589. f⁰. III.
(Anathematismi.) In: Possevinus. Adparatus sacrus. *Venet.* 1606. f⁰.
COMBEFIS. (4 Homilies.) In: Bibl. concionatoria. *Paris*, 1662. f⁰.

English.

In: Ante-Nic. Lib. XX. (1871) 5–156. Ed. Coxe. VI. (1886) 7–74.

German.

MARGRAF, J. *Kempten*, 1875. 16⁰. [The Reithmayer-Thalhofer Bibl.]

III. *Literature.*

ALEXANDER, NATALIS. Hist. eccl. VI. 79.
ALLATIUS, L. Diatriba de Theodoris. In: Mai. Bibl. nov. VI. *Roma*, 1853. p. 95–; also in: Migne. Patrol. gr. X. (1857) 1205–32.
ALZOG. Patrol. (1876) 152–6.
AUBÉ, B. In: Nouv. biog. gén. (Hoefer) XXI. (1857) 834–7.
BARONIUS. Ann. (1589) 233, 7–20; 245, 3; 253, 129–38; 256, 6–10; 263, 24–9; 266, 13–24. Cf. Pagi. Crit. (1689) 5.
BASILEIS. De spiritu sanctu. ch. 29.
BASNAGE. Thes. monum (1725) I. 24–25.
BAUMGARTEN–CRUSIUS. Dogmenges. (1832) 217–8. [v. 1.] (5 ll.)
BAUR. Dogmengesch. I. (1865) 280–1. (7 ll.)
BELLARMIN–LABBE. Scr. eccl. (1728) 48–50.
BOYE, JOH. LUD. Dissert. hist. de S. Gregorio Thaumaturgo. *Jenae*, 1703. 4⁰.
BULL. Works. V.
BUSSE. Chr. Lit. (1828–9) I. 27–9.
CAILLAU. Introd. in ss. Patr. (1825) 104–10.
CASPARI. Gesch. d. Taufsymbols. (*Christiania*, 1879.) 1–160.
CAVE. Scr. eccl. hist. lit. (1740–3) I. 132.
— Lives (1840) I. 396–416.
CEILLIER. Hist. gén. aut. sac. III. (1732) 307–25; II. (1865, 437–48.)
CHEVALIER. Rép. d. sources hist. (1877–84) 920–1.
CLARKE. Sacred lit. (1830–1) I. 173–5.
CLINTON. Fasti Rom. (1845–50) I. 247, 287, 291; II. 418.
COFFIN. Lives of fath. (1846) 377–381.
COTTA. § 398–404.
DARLING. Cyclop. bibl. (1854) 1319–20.
DORNER. Person of Christ. II. (1866) 172–3[4] 80–2.
DRÄSEKE, J. Zu Victor Ryssel's Schrift: Gregorius Thaumaturgus. In: Jahrbb. f. prot. Theol. (1881) 379–384.
— Zu: V. Ryssel's G. T. In: Jahrbb. f. prot. Theol. IX. (1883) 634–40.
— In: Jahrb. f. prot. Theol. X. (1884) 657–704. [The 4 homilies and the ΧΡΙΣΤΟΣ ΠΑΣΧΩΝ.]
— See under Ep. to Diognetus.
DUPIN. Nouv. bibl. aut. eccl. (1698–) I. 539.
DÜX. In: Wetzer u. W. Kirch-Lex. (1847–54) IV. 746–9.
Encycl. Brit. (9th ed.) XI. 181.

EUSEBIUS. Eccl. hist. VI. 30; VII. 14.
FABRICIUS. Bibl. gr. (17) V. 247–54; VIII. 163. (2ª. VII. 249–60; IX. 125; X. 233.)
[FALCONE, IPPOL.] Compendio della vita del. glor. s. Gregorio Thaumaturgo con la divozione . . . *Palermo*, 1694. 12º; 1700. 24º.
FLEURY. Hist. eccl. (1691–) II. 109–10, 126–8, 131–8, 164–5, 250–1, 353–6.
GALLAND. Vet. patr. bibl. III. (1767) XXV–; also in: Migne. Patrol. gr. X. (1857) 963–72.
GIESELER. Church Hist. (1868–) I. 221–2.
GOLDWITZER. Patrologie. I. 225–.
(GRASSO, GIO. PAOLO.] Il taumaturgo del Ponto o sia delle azioni di s. Gregorio di Neocesarea di Ponto. *Napoli*, 1645. 4º.
GREGORY, NYSS. Oratio de vita G. Thaum. In: Opera. (*Paris*, 1638. III. fº.) III. 479, 536, and often.
HAGENBACH. Hist. of Doct. I. (1850) 261.
HAHN. Bibl. d. Symb. 2 Aufl. 183–.
HARNACK. Dogmenges. I. (1886) 646–8.
HASE. Kirchenges. (1885–) I. 364–5.
HERZOG. Abr. d. Kirchenges. I. 122.
HIERONYMUS. De vir. ill. 65. (Honor. August. I. 66.)
HOOK. Eccl. Biog. V. 390.
HUETIUS. Origeniana. I. c. 2, § 19.
JEREMIE. Hist. Church. (1852) 101–2.
KILLEN. Ancient Church. (1859) 383–4.
KÜLB, P. H. In: Ersch. u. Gruber. I. LXXXIX. (1869) 422–8.
KURTZ. Kirchenges. (1885) I. 121.
LAMBECIUS. Bibl. Vindob. (1669) II. 270–4.
LARDNER. Credibility. Works. (1831) II. 608–43.
LÉCUY. In: Biog. Univ. (Michaud) (1842–65) XVII. 444.
LELONG. Bib. sac. II. 753.
LIRON. Aménit. de la critiq. (17 . .) Tr. Ital. by Stan. Mar. Geraci in: Zaccaria. Racc. di dissert. (1794) VIII. 102–22.
LUMPER. Hist. ss. patr. XIII. (1799) 251–342.
M'CLINTOCK and S. Cycl. (1874–) III. 995–6.
MAÏ. Scr. vet. coll. (1833) VII. 170.
— Spicil. Rom. (1840) III. 696.
MINGARELLUS. Ep. praev. ed. Sermo in omn. sanct. *Bon.* 1770. 4º; also in: Migne. Patrol. gr. X. (1857) 1191–6.
MÖHLER. Patrologie. (1841) 645–.
MÖLLER, W. In: Herzog. Real.-Enc. (1877–) V. 404–5. (Abr. in: Schaff-Herz. II. 906.)
MORINUS. Tract. de administ. sacramenti poenitentiae. VI. (*Bruxell.* 1658) 355.
MOSHEIM. Ch. Hist. I. 170.
MUENSCHER. Dogmenges. (1817–8) I. 451–2.
NEANDER. Church Hist. (1872) I. 287, 701, 706, 716–20.
NEWMAN. Essays on miracles.
NIRSCHL. Patrol. (1881–) I. 336–42.
NITZSCH. Dogmengesch. I. (1870) 145, etc.
NODIER. Bib. sacr. (1826) 164–5.
ORSI. Ist. eccl. (1746) III. 79–83, 107–11, 203–5, 427–9. (1749) III. 102–6, 137–42, 263–6, 552–5.
OUDIN. Scr. eccl. (1722) I. 289–96.
PALLAVICINI, NICCOLÒ MARIA. Vita Gregorii Thaumaturgi. Rom. 1644. 8º; *Roma*, 1649. 12º. (264 p.) *Bologna*, 1649. 12º. (216 p.)
PATRIGNANI, GIUS. ANT. Vita di s. Gregorio Taumaturgo, colle divozione . . . . *Firenze*, 1730. 4º.
PAUMIER, A. In: Lichtenberger. Encycl. (1877–82) V. 714–5.
PERMANEDER. Bibl. patrist. (1841–3) I. 421; II. 576–94.
PITRA. Jur. eccl. Graec. mon. (1864) I. 562.
POSSEVIN. Appar. sac. (1608) I. 672–6.
PRESSENSÉ. Martyrs. (1879) 354–6.
— Heresy. (*N.Y.*) 358–9.
REYNOLDS, H. R. In: Smith and Wace. Dict. II. 730–7.

RITTER. Chr. philos. (1841) II. 14.
ROESSLER. Bibl. d. K.–V. II. (1776) 288–295; IV. (1777) 262–5.
ROMANO, R. Della vita, virtù, e miracoli del glor. s. Greg- oris Taumaturgo. *Napoli*, 1728. 12º.
RYSSEL, VICTOR. Gregorius Thaumaturgus. Sein Leben u. s. Schriften. *Leipzig*, 1880. (160 pp.)
— Zu Gregorius Thaumaturgus. In: Jahrbb. f. prot. Theol. (1881) 565–573.
SALMOND, S. D. F. Introd. note. In: Ante-Nic. Lib. XX. (1871) 1–4. Ed. Coxe. VI. (1886) 1–6. [Add. notes. Ed. Coxe. 8, 20, 39, 47, 49, 53, 57, 71, 73.]
SCHAFF. Creeds of Christendom. II. (1877) 24–5.
— Hist. . . Church. II. (1886) 796–800.
SCHMID. Patrol. (1879); (1886) 53.
SCHRAM. Anal. ss. patr. (1780–) VI. 319–372.
SCHROECKH. Kirchenges. (1722–) IV, 351–68; IX. 388–9; XIII. 123–4.
SCHULTZE, V. In: Stud. u. Krit. LIV. (1881) 197–200. [Rev. of Ryssel.]
SEVESTRE. Dict. de Patrol. II. 1149–.
SMITH, P. In: Smith Gr. and Rom. Biog. (1859) II. 314–5.
STOLBERG, L. v. Gesch. d. Rel. Jesu Christi. VIII. 382–.
SURIUS. Vitae ss. (1618) XI. 390.
TILLEMONT. Mémoires. (1696) IV. 315–41, 668–70.
TRITHEMIUS. Scr. eccl. 39.
Veterum Testimonia. In: Migne. Patrol. gr. X. (1857) 973–82.
VILLEMAIN. In: Le Correspondant (1858) B, VII. 436–52.
VICENTIUS BELVAC. Spec. hist. XXII. 80–82.
WALCH, J. S. In his: Historia ecclesiae N. T. p. 977–.
— Bibl. patr. (1834) 42.
WEICKHMANN, J. S. Schola Origeniana sacra ex Gregorio Thaumaturgo informata. *Wittebergae*, 1744. 4º.
WESTCOTT. Canon. (1875) 381.
WORDSWORTH. Church Hist. (1881) 274, 283–4.
ZOSIMUS. Hist. I. (*Oxon.*, 1679) 28–.

II. DIONYSIUS OF ALEXANDRIA.

I. *Editions.*

GALLANDUS. Gr. lat. 1788. fº. III. XIII.
MAGISTRIS, SIM. DE. Gr. lat. *Romae*, 1796. fº.
MIGNE. Gr. lat. In: Patrol. gr. X. (1857) 1237–1346, 1577–1602.

BERTRANDUS, B. (De situ orbis.) Gr. lat. *Basil.* 1556. 12º.
TURRIANUS, FR. (2 epp.) Gr. lat. *Romae*, 1608. 8º; Repr. in: Bibl. patr. *Paris*. XI.
DUCAEUS, FRONT. (Ep. ad Paulum S.) Gr. lat. *Paris*, 1624. fº. In his: Auct. Bibl. patr.
LABBEUS. (Basilid., Paul. S.) Gr. lat. 1671. fº. In: Acta concil. I. 831–.
BEVERIDGE. (Ep. ad Basilidem.) Gr. lat. In his: Pandects. *Oxon.*, 1672. fº. VII. 1–7.
CONSTANT. *Par.* 1721. fº. In: Epist. rom. pont.
MANSI. (Ep. ad Paulum S.) 1759. fº. In: Concil. coll. I. 1039–.
MAI. (Fragm.) Class. auct. (1838) X. 484.
MIGNE. (4 epp.) Gr. lat. In: Patrol. Lat. V. (1844) 89–100.
ROUTH. Rel. sacr. (1846–8) III. 219–250. [Epist. canon.] IV. 393–437. [Excerpta ex 'De natura.'] 439–454. [Excerpta ex 'Nicetae in Jobum catena.']
PITRA. Spicil. Solesm. (1852) I. XIV–VI.
— Jur. eccl. Gr. mon. (1864) I. 541.

Note. For editions of the epistles, see also the various editions of Eusebius.

II. *Translations.*

Latin.

PELTANUS, THEOD. (Epp., etc.) *Ingolst.* 1580. 8⁰.
HITTOYSIUS. (Ep. ad Fel.) 1610. f⁰; also in: Auct. bibl. patr. II. 444–; also in: Bibl. patr. lat. *Par.* 1654. XI. *Colon.* 1618. III.
TURRIANUS, FR. (2 epp.) 1677. f⁰. In: Bibl. patr. max. III. 339–.

English.

SALMOND, S. D. F. In: Ante-Nic. Lib. XX. (1871) 161–266. Ed. Coxe. VI. (1886) 81–120.
WALLIS, R. E. In: Ante-Nic. Lib. XXXI. (1873) 399–400. [See: Salmond.]

German.

RÖSLER, C. F. (Br. an d. Basilides.) In: Biblioth. d. K. Väter. IV. 258–.

III. *Literature*

ALEXANDER, NATALIS. Hist. Eccl. saec. III. Diss. XIX.
ALZOG. Patrol. (1876) 157.
ATHANASIUS. De sent. Dionysii; De synod. etc.
BARONIUS. Ann. (1589) 248, 5; 253, 99–109; 260, 9–30; 263, 2–5, 13–7, 30–52; 264, 2; 265, 6–8; 266, 10–2. Cf. Pagi. Crit. (1689) 248, 3–4; 260, 4; 264, 2; 265, 3; 266, 4.
BASIL, S. De spiritu sancto. XXXIX. In: Opp. om. (*Paris*, 1721. III. f⁰.)
BASNAGE. Hist. de l'Église. I. II. v.
BAUMGARTEN–CRUSIUS. Dogmenges. (1832) 217. [v. 1.]
BAUR. Dogmengesch. I. (1865) 484–7, etc.
ΒΑΦΕΙΔΟΣ. 'Εκκλ. ἱστ. I. (1884) 159.
BELLARMIN–LABBE. Scr. eccl. (1728) 54.
BURTON. Divinity of Christ. (1829) 377–419.
— Trinity. (1831) 123–6.
BUSSE. Chr. Lit. (1828–9) I. 33–5.
BYEUS. De ss. Dionysio episc. Alexandrino, Fausto Mart., Caio, Petro, Paulo, et IV. aliis Alexandriae et forte alibi in Aegypto, Comment histor. In: Acta ss. Bolland. (1768) Oct. II. 8–130 (2ª. 26–102.)
CAVE. Hist. lit. script. eccl. (1740–3) I. 124–6.
— Lives. (1840) I. 417–37.
CELLIER. Hist. gén. aut. sac. III. (1732) 241–79; II. (1865) 396–419.
CHARTERIS. Canonicity. (1880) 86–7, 282, 345–50.
CHEVALIER. Rép. d. sources hist. (1877–86) 562–3.
CLARKE. Sacred lit. (1830–1) I. 176–7.
CLINTON. Fasti Rom. (1845–50) I. 247, 267, 293; II. 419.
v. COELLN. In: Ersch u. Gruber. I. xxv. (1834) 353–6.
COFFIN. Lives of fath. (1846) 382.
DARLING. Cyclop. bibl. (1854) 920.
DITTRICH. Dionysius d. Gr. von Alexandrien. *Freiburg i. Breisgau*, 1867. 8⁰. [Diss.]
DORNER. Person of Christ. II. (1866) 177–81, 483–4.
DUPIN. Nouv. bibl. aut. eccl. (1698) I. 549–64.
ENGELHARDT. Dogmenges. I. (1839) 100, etc.
EUSEBᵁUS. Hist. Eccl. Lib. III. 28; VI. 41, 45, 46; VII. 2, 4, 7, 9, 11, 22, 24, 26, 27, 28. Praep. ev. VII. 19; XIV. 23–.
FABRICIUS. Bibl. gr. (1712) V. 263–8. (2ª. VII. 278–84; X. 382.)
FARRAR. Interpretation. (1886) 206–7. [11 ll.]
FLEURY. Hist. eccl. (1691–) II. 162–3, 296–302, 342–53.
FÖRSTER, TH. Dion. d. Gr. In: Ztschr. f. hist. Theol. (1871).
— De Doctrina et Sententiis Dionysii Magni Episcopi Alex. *Berol.*, 1865. 8⁰. (47 p.)
FRITZ. In: Wetzer u. W. Kirch-Lex. (1847–54) III. 159–63.

GALLAND. Bibl. vet. patr. III. xxx–; XIV. apx; also in: Migne. Patrol. gr. X. (1857) 1233–6, 1575–6.
GELZER, H. Sextus Julius Africanus u. die Byzantinische Chronographie. II. 1. Die Nachfolger d. Jul. Af. *Leipzig*, 1885. 8⁰.
GIESELER. Church Hist. (1868–) I. 200–1, 209, 220–1, 294.
GUERICKE, F. Comment. hist. et theol. de Schola s. *Halae*, 1824–25. II. 8.
HAGENBACH. Hist. of Doct. I. (1850) 261–2.
HARNACH. Dogmenges. I. (1886) 634–9.
HASE. Kirchenges. (1885–) I. 371–2.
HEFELE. Conciliengeschichte. I. 222–.
HERGENROETHER. Kirchenges. (1879–80) I. 166–7; III. 39, 72.
HIERONYMUS. De vir. ill. 69. (Honor. August. II. 70.)
HILSCHER and STRAUSS. Schola Alex. (1776) 28.
HOLTZMANN. Einl. in d. N. T. (1866) 471, etc.
JORTIN, J. The character of Dionys. of A. In his: Remarks on Eccl. Hist. (*London*, 1752. 8⁰.) II. 292–295.
JOUBERT, M. L. Traicté et reponse sur la question proposée par d'Angernon et Martel. *Paris*, 1581. 8⁰. (?)
KURTZ. Kirchenges. (1885–) I. 121, 141.
LARDNER. Credibility. II. iv. ch. XLIII. p. 558–736; Works. (1831) II. 643–722; also in tr. Ger. II. II. 520–.
LAUNOIUS. Discussione de duobus Dionysius. In: Opera. Col. Allol. 1731.
LICHTENBERGER. Encycl. (1877–82) III. 669.
LUCHINI. Atti. sinceri. (1778) II. 398–436.
LÜCKE. Einl. i. d. Offenbar. Joh.
LUMPER. Hist. ss. patr. XIII. (1799) 52–193.
M'CLINTOCK and S. Cycl. (1874–) II. 810–1.
MAGISTRIS, S. DE. De vita et scr. Dion. A. In ed : 1796. f⁰.
MARTINOV. Ann. eccl. gr. slav. (1864) 240–1.
MÖHLER. Patrol. (1840).
MUENSCHER. Dogmenges. (1817–8) I. 293–4, 448–50.
MYNSTER, JO. PETR. Dissert. de Dionysii Alexandrini circa Apocalypsin sententia, hujusque vi. *Havniae*, 1826. 8⁰. [Quoted often as Mönster or Münster.]
MURDOCK. In: Mosheim's Ch. hist. I. (1832) 208–10.
NEALE. Eastern ch. Alexandria. I. (1847) 39, etc.
NEANDER. Hist. of dogmas. (1858) 168–9, 251. [v. 1.]
— Church Hist. (1872) I. 243, 320–1, 606–8, 652–3, 712–3, passim.
NIRSCHL. Patrol. (1881–) I. 330–36.
NITZSCH. Dogmengesch. I. (1870) 145, etc.
Nouv. Biog. Gen. (Hoefer) XIII. (1855) 675–7.
ORSI. Ist. eccl. (1746–) III. 123–4, 190–2, 264–6, 295–7, 318–20, 328–35, 401–10, 418–21; (1749–) III. 158–60, 247–9, 341–4, 382–4, 412–4, 424–32, 519–31, 541–4.
OSTERMEYER, JOACH. HEINR. Dissertationes histor. II. de Dionysio, Alex. *Rostochii*, 1735–36. (1730?) 4⁰.
IERMANEDER. Bibl. patrist. (1841–3) I. 421; II. 71, 594–617.
PHOTIUS. Bibl. Cod. 232.
PRESSENSÉ. Chr. life. (1878) 195–6.
— Martyrs. (1879) 342–51.
— Heresy. (*N. Y.*) 360–8.
PRILESZKY, J. B. [Ref. by Chevalier. —?]
REUSS. Gesch. N. T. (1874) II. 34. Tr. Eng. (1884) 312, 316, 513. [v. 2.]
RITTER. Chr. philos. (1841) II. 16.
ROBERTSON. Hist. of Church. (1875–) I. 158–61.
ROCH, G. Die Schrift. d. Dionysius d. Grossen Ueb. die Natur. e altchristl. Widerlegg. d. Atomistik Demokrits u. Epikurs. Diss. *Leipzig u. Dresd.* 1882. 8⁰.
ROSENMÜLLER. Hist. interp. III. (1807) 171–7.
ROESSLER. Bibl. d. K.–V. (1777) 258–62.
RUINART. Acta sinc. (1689) 102, 164–79.
SALMOND, S. D. F. Introd. note. In: Ante-Nic. Lib. XX. (1871) 157–61. Ed. Coxe. VI. (1886) 75–9. [Add. notes. Ed. Coxe. 110, 120.]

SCHAFF. Hist. . . Church. II. (1886) 800–3.
SCHMID. Patrol. (1879); (1886) 54–5.
SCHMITZ, L. In: Smith. Gr. and Rom. Biog. (1859) I. 1037.
SCHRAM. Anal. ss. patr. (1780–) VI. 373–414.
SCHROECKH. Kirchenges. (1772–) IV. 170–90, 336–7; XIII. 34–5.
SHEPHERD. Hist. Ch. of Rome. (1851) 189–97.
SURIUS. Vitae ss. (1618) IV. 127–31.
SEVESTRE. Dict. patrol. (1852) II. 96–116.
Supernatural Religion. I. (1875) 447; II. (1875) 389–, 395.
TILLEMONT. Mémoires. (1694) IV. 242–88, 657–63.
TRITHEMIUS. Scr. eccl. 43.
VILLENAVE. In: Biog. Univ. (Michaud) 1842–65. X. 436–7.
VINCENTIUS BELVAC. Spec. hist. XII. 37–40, 56, 84.
WALCH, CH. FR. GU. Progr. de epistolis Patriarch. Alexandr. paschalibus. *Götting.* 1776. 4⁰.
WALCH, J. G. Bibl. patrist. (1834) 41, 163.
WEIZSÄCKER, C. In: Herzog. Real.-Enc. (1877–) III. 615–6. (Abr. in: Schaff-Herz. I. 642–3.)
WESTCOTT, B. F. Canon. (1875) 361–3.
— In: Smith and Wace. Dict. I. 850–2.
WORDSWORTH. Church Hist. (1881) 304–5, 343–45, 397.

III. JULIUS AFRĪCANUS.

I. *Editions.*

(*Works.*)

GALLAND. Bibl. vet. patr. II. (1766) 339–.
ROUTH. Rel. sacr. (1846–8) II. 219–509.
MIGNE. Gr. lat. In: Patrol. gr. X. (1857) 51–108; XI. (1857) 41–8.

(*Cesti.*)

THEVANOT. In: Veteres mathematici. *Par.* 1693. f⁰; *Flor.* 1746. [Military precepts.]
BUSSUS, CASSIANUS (NEEDHAM?). Geoponica. *Camb.* 1704. [Agricultural precepts.]
PSELLUS, MICHAEL. In: Lambecius Cann. de Bibl. Caes. *Vind.* VII. 223. [Medical precepts.]
NICLAS. *Lips.* 1781. In: Geoponicorum, etc.

(*Others.*)

WETSTEIN. (Ep. ad Or.) *Basle*, 1674. 4⁰.
FABRICIUS. (Frgm. on Luke.) Bibl. gr. VIII. 676.
MAI. (Frgm. on Matt.) In: Scr. vet. IX. 724.
SPITTA, FR. (Ep. ad Arist.) *Halle*, 1877.

Note. The correspondence between Origen and A. first printed in Latin translation by *Leo Castrius. Salamanca,* 1570. The letter of A. is found also in the Benedictine editions of Origen.

II. *Translations.*

English.

SALMOND, S. D. F. In: Ante-Nic. Lib. IX. (1869) 164–202. Ed. Coxe. VI. (1886) 123–39.

French.

GUISCHARDT. (Cesti.) In: Mém. militaires des Grecs et des Romains. 1758. 4⁰.

III. *Literature.*

ALZOG. Patrol. (1876) 156–7.
AUGUSTINE. Retract. II. c. 7. § 2.
BARONIUS. Ann. (1589) 222, 1–2.
BASNAGE. Annal. II. 46.
ΒΑΦΕΙΔΗΣ. ’Εκκλ ίστ. I. (1884) 155.
BELLARMIN–LABBE. Scr. eccl. (1728) 43.
BUSSE. Chr. Lit. (1828–9) I. 27.

CAVE. Scr. eccl. hist. lit. (1740–3) I. 110–2.
CEDRENUS. Hist. compend. p. 207.
CEILLIER. Hist. gén. aut. sac. II. (1730) 535–43; II. (1865) 91–6.
CHARTERIS. Canonicity (1880) 137–8.
CHEVALIER. Rép. d. sources hist. (1877–86) 1311.
CLARKE. Sacred lit. (1830–1) I. 159–60.
CLAVIER. In: Biog. Univ. (Michaud) 1842–65. I. 211–2.
CLINTON. Fasti Rom. (1845–50) I. 233, 235; II. 418.
DARLING. Cyclop. bibl. (1854) 1696.
DE LA RUE. In Migne. Patrol. gr. XI. (1857) 37–42.
DIONYSIUS BARSALIBI. In: Assemanni B. O. III. p. 158.
DUPIN. Bibl. des antiq. eccl. (1698–) I. 307.
EBEDJESU. Cat. scr. eccl. 6. In: Assemanni. Bibl. orient. III. 1, 14.
Encycl. Brit. (9th ed.) I. 273.
EUSEBIUS. Hist. eccl. (ed. Zimmerm.) VI. 31. Chronic. an 2237.
FABRICIUS. Bibl. Gr. (1707) II. 595–9; V. 268–71; IX. 386; IV. 240–6 (= Migne. Patrol. gr. X. 35–46), 881; VII. 288; IX. 691.
— Bibl. med. aet. IV. 593.
FARRAR. Interpretation. (1886) 207–8.
FESSLER. Inst. Patrol. I. 325–6.
F[ISQUET?], H. In: Nouv. Biog. Gén. (Hoefer) I. (1852) 354–6.
FLEURY. Hist. eccl. (1691–) II. 122–6.
GALLAND. Bibl. vet. patr. *Venet.* 1765. f⁰.; II. XXXIII.; also in: Migne. Patrol. gr. X. (1857) 45–50.
GELZER, HEIN. Sextus Julius Africanus u. die byzantinische Chronographie. I. Die Chronographie d. Julius Africanus. *Leipzig*, 1880. 8⁰.
— Zu Africanus. In: Jahrbb. f. prot. Theol. (1881) 376–378.
GIESELER. Church Hist. (1868–) I. 223–4.
GUTSCHMID, A. Ueber d. Verhältniss d. Hippolytischen liber generationis z. Chronographie d. Julius Africanus. In: Rhein. Mus. N. F. (1856) 441–444.
H., F. In: Nouv. biog. gén. (Hoefer) (1853) I. 354–6.
HARNACK, AD. In: Herzog. Real.-Enc. (1877–) VII. 296–8. (Abr. in: Schaff-Herz. II. 1214.)
HASE. Kirchenges. (1885–) I. 342.
HERGENROETHER. In: Wetzer u. W. Kirch-Lex. (1847–54) Supp. I. 624–5.
— Kirchenges. (1879–80) I. 15; III. 8.
HIERONYMUS. De vir. ill. 63. (Honor. August. I. 64.)
— Ep. ad Mayn. 84.
KLEIN, J. Zu den Κεστοί des Julius Africanus. In: Rhein. Mus. XXV. (1870) 447–448.
KURTZ. Kirchenges. (1885–) I. 122–3.
LA MALLE, DUREAU DE. Porliocetique des anciens. *Paris*, 1819. 8⁰.
LARDNER. Credibility. Works. (1831) II. 457–68.
LELONG. Bib. sac. (1723) II. 809.
LE QUIEN. Sacra parallel. In: Opera om. II. 463.
LUMPER. Hist. ss. patr. (1790) VII. 76–98.
M'CLINTOCK and S. Cycl. (1874–) IV. 1092–3.
MILL. On the mythical interpretation of the Gospels. p. 201.
MÖHLER. Patrologie. I. 577–80.
NEANDER. Church Hist. (1872) I. 709.
NICEPHORUS CALL. Hist. eccl. V. 21.
NICOLAI. Gr. Lit. Gesch. II. 581–.
NIRSCHL. Patrol. (1881–) I. 327–30.
ORSI. Ist. eccl. (1746–) III. 99–102; (1749–) III. 127–31.
PAULY. Real-Enc. IV. 501–.
PERMANEDER. Bibl. patrist. II. (1843) 276, 463–8.
PHOTIUS. Bibl. cod. 34.
PRESSENSÉ. Heresy. (*N. Y.*) 368–70.
RELAND. Palaestina. pp. 427, 758.
ROSENMÜLLER. Hist. interp. III. (1807) 157–64.

RUINARTUS, THEO. D. Act. prim. mart. (*Paris*, 1689. 4º.) 18.

SALMON, G. In: Smith and Wace. Dict. I. 53-7.

SALMOND, S. D. F. Introd. note. In: Ante-Nic. Lib. IX (1869) 163-4. Ed. Coxe. VI. (1886) 123-4. [Add. notes. Ed. Coxe. 127-8, 139-40.]

SCHAFF. Hist. . . Church. II. (1886) 803-5.

SCHROECKH. Kirchenges. (1772-) IV. 145-54.

SCHÜRER, E. Julius Africanus als Quelle der Pseudo-Justin'schen Cohortatio ad Graecos. In: Ztschr. f. Kirchengesch. II. (1880) 319-331.

SMITH, W. In: Smith. Gr. and Rom. Biog. (1859) I. 56-7.

SOCRATES. Hist. Eccles. II. 35; III.

SOZOMEN. Hist. Eccl. V. 21.

SPITTA, F. Der Brief d. Julius Africanus an Aristides kritisch untersucht u. hergestellt. *Halle*, 1877. 8º.

SUIDAS. S. v. ἀφρικανὸς.

SYNCELLUS, GEORG. Chronographia. (*Par.* 1652. fº.) 17, 19, 21, 57, 307, 322.

TEUFFEL. Hist. Rom. Lit. (1873) II. 66, 296-7.

THEVENOT, MELCHIOR. De Julio Africano quaedam observanda. 1693.

TILLEMONT. Mémoires. III. (1695) 254-8, 682-5.

TRITHEMIUS. Scr. eccl. 38.

Note. — Africanus is found variously in alphabetical lists under Africanus, or Julius, or Sextus.

IV. (*a.*) ANATOLIUS.

I. *Editions.*

(Mathm. fragm.) *Paris*, 1543. In: Θεολογούμενα τῆς ἀριθμητικῆς.

FABRICIUS. (Mathm. fragm.) In: Bibl. gr. ed. Harles. 1793. 4º. III. 462-. [Older ed. II. 275-.]

MIGNE. Patrol. gr. X. (1857) 209-22, 231-6.

Note. The Greek fragments of the Canon Pasch. found in Eusebius Hist. eccl. in its various eds.

II. *Translations.*

Latin.

BUCHERIUS. Doctr. temporum. *Antv.* 1634. (3?) 4º. 439; 1664. fº.

GALLANDIUS. Bibl. patr. III. (1767) 545-.

SCHRAM. In: Anal. ss. patr. VI. (1784).

KRUSCH. In: Studien z. Chron. (1880) 316-327.

Note. Ideler (II. 230) on the basis of Van der Hagen's investigations has declared this supposed translation of A. by Rufinus a work of not earlier than the middle of the seventh century, and has been generally followed; but Zahn (Suppl. Clement. III. (1884) 196) maintains that it is not later than 270 A.D.

English.

SALMOND, S. D. F. In: Ante-Nic. Lib. XIV. (1874) 411-31. Ed. Coxe. VI. (1686) 146-53.

III. *Literature.*

BARONIUS. Ann. (1589) 263, 8-11; 283, 10-3. Cf. Pagi. Crit. (1689) 271, 9-11.

BAUR. In: Ersch u. Gruber. I. III. (1819) 478.

BRUCKER. Hist. crit. phil. (1766) III. 459-62.

BUCHERIUS, AEG. Comment. In: Migne. Patrol. gr. X. (1857) 221-32.

BUSSE. Chr. lit. (1828-9) I. 38-9.

CAVE. Scr. eccl. hist. lit. (1740-3) I. 136; (1688) p. 99.

CEILLIER. Hist. gén. d. aut. sac. III. (1732) 301-4; II. (1865) 432-5

CHEVALIER. Rép. d. sources hist. (1877-86) 111.

CLARKE. Sacred lit. (1830-1) I. 195-6.

CLINTON. Fasti Rom. (1845-50) I. 319; II. 424.

DE LAULNAYE. In: Biog. Univ. (Michaud) 1842-65. I. 631.

DUPIN. Nouv. bibl. aut. eccl. (1698) I. 572.

EUSEBIUS. Hist. Eccles. VII. 32, etc.

FABRICIUS. Bibl. gr. (1707-11-2) II. 274-5; IV. 19-20; V. 277. (2ª. V. 649; VII. 299-300; VIII. 461.) — Bibl. med. aet. (1734) I. 235. (2ª. 90.)

FLEURY. Hist. eccl. (1691) II. 368-70.

FONTANINI. Hist. lit. aquileiae. V. 15.

GALLAND. Vet. patr. bibl. III. xxxvii-; also in : Migne. Patrol. gr. X. (1857) 207-10.

HAGEN, VAN DER. De cyclis paschalibus. 142-.

HEFELE. In: Wetzer u. W. Kirch-Lex. (1847-54) I. 230.

HIERONYMUS. De vir. ill. 73. (Honor. August. I. 74.)

IDELER. Handb. d. Chron. II. (1826) 226-231.

KRUSCH, BRUNO. Studien z. christlichmittelalterlichen Chron. *Lpz.* 1880. p. 311-.

LARDNER. Credibility. Works. (1831) III. 140-5.

LETRONNE. In: Jour. des savants.

LICHTENBERGER. Encycl. (1877-82) I. 292.

LUMPER. Hist. ss. patr. XIII. (1799) 228-35.

M'CLINTOCK and S. Cycl. (1874-) I. 220-.

NEALE. Eastern Ch., Antioch. (1873) 55.

NIRSCHL. Patrol. (1881-) I. 343-4.

Nouv. Biog. Gén. (Hoefer) II. (1852) 483.

ORSI. Ist. eccl. (1746-) III. 432-3; (1749-) III. 558-60.

PERMANEDER. Bibl. patrist. II. (1843) 624-5.

SALMOND. S. D. F. Introd. note. In: Ante-Nic. Lib. XIV. (1874) 410-11. Ed. Coxe. VI. (1886) 141-5.

SCHRAM. Anal. ss. patr. (1780-) VI. 421-429.

SCHROECKH. Kirchenges. (1772-) IV. 441-2.

SMITH, P. In: Smith. Gr. and Rom. Biog. (1859) I. 162.

SOLLERIUS. De s. Anatolio episc. ejusque decessore s. Eusebio Laodiceae in Syria, comment. histor. in : Acta ss. Bolland (1719) Jul. I. 642-4. (3ª. 564-6.)

SURIUS. Vitae ss. (1618) VII. 75-6.

TILLEMONT. Mémoires. III. (1696) 304-8.

TRITHEMIUS. Scr. eccl. 48.

VENABLES, E. In: Smith and Wace. Dict. I. 111.

ZAHN. Liber A. de ratione paschali. In: Forsch. z. Ges. d. N. T. Kanons. III. (1884) 177-96.

IV. (*b.*) ALEXANDER OF CAPPADO-CIA.

I. *Editions.*

GALLANDIUS. Bibl. patr. II. (1776) 201-.

ROUTH. Rel. sacr. (1846-8) II. 159-179.

MIGNE. Patrol. gr. X. (1857) 203-6.

And all editions of Eusebius.

II. *Translations.*

English.

SALMOND. S. D. F. In: Ante-Nic. Lib. IX. (1869) 273-4. Ed. Coxe. VI. (1886) 154.

III. *Literature.*

BARONIUS. Ann. (1589) 213, 12; 253, 124-5.

BINGHAM. Origenes. II. § 4.

BUSSE. Chr. lit. (1828) 26-7.

CAVE. Scr. eccl. hist. lit. (1740-3) I, 100-1.

CEILLER. Hist. gén. aut. sac. II. (1730) 570-3; II. (1865) 122-4.

CHEVALIER. Rép. d. sources hist. (1877-86) 72.

CHRISTIE, A. J. In: Smith. Gr. and Rom. Biog. (1859) I. 115.

CLARKE. Sacred lit. (1830–1) I. 157.
CLINTON. Fasti Rom. (1845–50) I. 221, 269; II. 418.
Comment. histor. In: Acta ss. Bolland. (1668) Mart. II.
　614–7. (3ª. 613–6.)
DUPIN. 3. s. VI. ch. XIX.
EUSEBIUS. Hist. Eccl. VI. 14, 11, 20, etc.
FABRICIUS. Bibl. gr. (1712) V. 268. (2ª. VII. 287.)
GALLAND. Veter. patr. bibl. II. xxvii–; also in: Migne.
　Patrol. gr. X. (1857) 201–4.
HIERONYMUS. De vir. ill. 62. (Honor. August. I. 63.)
LARDNER. Credibility. Works. (1831) II. 414–20.
LUMPER. Hist. ss. patr. (1790) VII. 9–17.
M'CLINTOCK and S. Cycl. (1874–) I. 146.
NEALE. Eastern Ch., Antioch. (1873) 36–7, 41.
NEANDER. Church Hist. 1872. I. 691, 694, 703, 704.
NIRSCHL. Patrol. (1881–) I. 342–3.
Nouv. Biog. Gén. (Hoefer) I. (1852) 905.
ORSI. Ist. eccl. (1746–) II. 445–7; III. 42–4; (1749–)
　II. 643–6; III. 55–7.
PERMANEDER. Bibl. patrist. (1843) II. 471–3, 685.
RUINART. Acta sinc. (1689) 114–9.
SALMOND, S. D. F. Introd. note. In: Ante-Nic. Lib.
　IX. (1869) 275. Ed. Coxe. VI. (1886) 153–4.
SCHROECKH. Kirchenges. (1772–) IV. 207–8.
SOCRATES. Hist. eccl. VII. 36.
SURIUS. Vitae ss. (1618) III. 199.
TABARAUD. In: Biog. Univ. (Michaud) 1842–65. I. 414.
TILLEMONT. Mémoires. III. (1695) 415–20.
TRITHEMIUS. Scr. eccl. 37.
VALESIUS. Not. ad Euseb. Hist. eccl.
VENABLES, E. In: Smith and Wace. Dict. I. 85–6.
VINCENTIUS BELVAC. Spec. hist. XII. 19.

———

IV. (c.) THEOGNOSTUS OF ALEX-ANDRIA.

I. Editions.

GALLAND. Bibl. patr. III. (1767) 662–3.
ROUTH. Rel. sacr. (1846–8) III. 405–422.
MIGNE. Gr. lat. in: Patrol. gr. X. (1857) 239–42.
　And in editions of Athanasius and Photius.

II. Translations.

Latin.

SCHRAM. In: Anal. ss. patr. VI.

English.

SALMOND, S. D. F. In: Ante-Nic. Lib. XIV. (1874)
　397–8. Ed. Coxe. VI. (1886) 155–6.

III. Literature.

ALZOG. Patrol. (1876) 158.
ATHANASIUS. De decretis synodi Nicaenae.
BULL, GEORG. Defens. fidei Nicaenae, etc. (Oxon.
　1685. 4º.) 135–.
BURTON. Trinity. (1831) 133–5.
BUSSE. Chr. lit. (1828–9) I. 35.
CAVE. Scr. eccl. hist. lit. (1740–3) I. 146.
CEILLIER. Hist. gén. aut. sac. III. (1732) 329–32; II.
　(1865) 450–2.
CHEVALIER. Rép. d. sources hist. (1877–86) 2182.
CLARKE. Sacred lit. (1830–1) I. 196–7.
CLINTON. Fasti Rom. (1845–50) I. 327, 329; II. 432.
DODWELL. Dissert. in Ireneum. (Oxon. 1689) 488–.
DORNER. Person of Christ. II. (1866) 173–5.
DUPIN. Nouv. bibl. aut. eccl. (1698–) I. 564.
FABRICIUS. Bibl. gr. (1714) VI. 276; IX. 408. (2ª.
　VII. 298–9; X. 709–10.)

GALLAND. Bibl. vet. patr. III. XLIX.–; also in: Migne.
　Patrol. gr. X. (1857) 235–8.
GREGORY, NYSS. Contra Eunomium. In: Op. omn.
　(Paris, 1638. III. fº.) II.
GUERICKE. De Schola Alex. (Halle, 1824) I. 78; II.
　325–.
HAGENBACH. Hist. of Doct. I. (1850) 261.
HARNACK. Dogmenges. I. (1886) 641–3.
HEFELE. Conciliengesch. Tr. Engl. (1872) 236–7.
HERGENROETHER. Kirchenges. (1879–80) I. 166; III.
　72.
HILSCHER and STRAUSS. Schola Alex. (1776) 30.
HUETIUS. Origeniana. II. II. ii. No. 25, 27. Ed. Migne.
　Patr. gr. XVII. 785–6.
JÖCHER. Gelehrt. Lex. (1750–1).
KERKER. In: Wetzer u. W. Kirch-Lex. (1847–54)
　Supp. 1189–91.
LARDNER. Credibility. Works. (1831) III. 148–52.
LUMPER. Hist. ss. patr. XIII. (1799) 409–25.
MASON, C. P. In: Smith. Gr. and Rom. Biog. (1859)
　III. 1078.
M'CLINTOCK and S. Cycl. (1874–) X. 324.
MÖLLER, W. In: Herzog. Real.-Enc. (1877–) XV. 414.
　[In: Schaff-Herz. 9 ll. only.]
MUENSCHER. Dogmenges. (1817–8) I. 451.
NEANDER. Church Hist. (1872) I. 713.
NIRSCHL. Patrol. (1881–) I. 354–5.
ORSI. Ist. eccl. (1746) III. 502; (1749) III. 646–7.
PERMANEDER. Bibl. patrist. II. (1843) 637–9.
PHILIPPUS SIDETES. Hist. fragm. in H. Dodwelli Dis-
　sertt. in Irenaeum. (Oxon. 1689. 8º.) p. 488.
PHOTIUS. Biblioth. Cod. 106.
PRESSENSÉ. Heresy. (N. Y.) 359–60.
— Martyrs. (1879) 351.
ROESSLER. Bibl. d. K.–V. II. (1776) 333–6.
ROSENMÜLLER. Hist. interp. III. (1807) 177–8.
SALMOND, S. D. F. Introd. note. In: Ante-Nic. Lib.
　XIV. (1874) 396–7. Ed. Coxe. VI. (1886) 155.
SCHAFF. Hist. . . Church. II. (1886) 806. [9 ll.]
SCHRAM. Anal. ss. patr. (1780–) VI. 518–521.
SCHROECKH. Kirchenges. (1772–) IV. 425–6.
TILLEMONT. Mémoires. III. (1695) 585–6.

———

IV. (d.) PIERIUS OF ALEXANDRIA.

I. Editions.

ROUTH. Rel. sacr. (1846–8) III. 423–435.
MIGNE. Gr. lat. In: Patrol. gr. X. (1857) 243–6.

II. Translations.

English.

SALMOND, S. D. F. In: Ante-Nic. Lib. XIV. (1874)
　400–1. Ed. Coxe. VI. (1886) 157.

III. Literature.

ALZOG. Patrol. (1876) 157–8.
BARONIUS. Ann. (1589) 285, 16.
ΒΑΦΕΙΔΗΣ. Ἐκκλ. ἱστ. I. (1884) 159.
CAVE. Scr. eccl. hist. lit. (1740–3) I. 145–6.
CEILLIER. Hist. gén. aut. sac. III. (1732) 348–50; II.
　(1865) 462–3.
CHEVALIER. Rép. d. sources hist. (1877–86) 1796.
CLARKE. Sacred lit. (1830–1) I. 197–8.
CLINTON. Fasti Rom. (1845–50) I. 323; II. 432.
DORNER. Person of Christ. II. (1866) 171–2.
DUPIN. Nouv. bibl. aut. eccl. (1698–) I. 577.
EPIPHANIUS. Haeres. LXIX.
EUSEBIUS. Hist. eccl. VII. 32.
FABRICIUS. Bibl. gr. (1712) V. 277; IX. 412–3. (2ª.
　VII. 301; X. 713.)

GUERICKE. De schola Alex. I. 74–; II. 28, 325.
HAGENBACH. Hist. of Doct. I. (1850) 261.
HARNACK. Dogmenges. I. (1886) 640–1.
HERGENROETHER. Kirchenges. (1879–80) I. 166; III. 72.
HILSCHER and STRAUSS. Schola Alex. (1776) 29.
HIERONYMUS. De scr. eccl. 76. In: Routh. Rel. sacr. II.; also in: Migne. Patrol. gr. X. (1857) 241–4.
JÖCHER. Gehlert. Lex. (1750–51).
LARDNER. Credibility. Works. (1831) III. 155–9.
LELONG. Bib. sac. II. 906.
LICHTENBERGER. Encycl. (1877–82) X. 612–3.
M'CLINTOCK and S. Cycl. (1874–) VIII. 190.
MÖLLER, W. In: Herzog. Real.-Enc. (1877–) XI. 671–2.
NEANDER. Church Hist. (1872) I. 713.
NIRSCHL. Patrol. (1881–) I. 354.
NITZSCH. Dogmengesch. I. (1870) 207 (6 ll.)
ORSI. Ist. eccl. (1746–) III. 501–2; (1749–) III. 644–5.
PERMANEDER. Bibl. patrist. II. (1843) 635–6.
PHOTIUS. Biblioth. Cod. 118, 119.
PRESSENSÉ. Martyrs. (1879) 351–2.
— Heresy. (N.Y.) 357–8.
ROSENMÜLLER. Hist. interpr. III. (1807) 177–8.
SALMOND, S. D. F. Introd. note. In: Ante-Nic. Lib. XIV. (1874) 399. Ed. Coxe. VI. (1886) 156.
SCHAFF. Hist. . . Church. (1886) 806. [5 ll.]
SCHROECKH. Kirchenges. (1772–) IV. 424.
Supernatural Religion. II. (1875) 190.
TILLEMONT. Mémoires. IV.
TRITHEMIUS. Scr. eccl. 51.
WETZER u. W. Kirch-Lex. (1847–54) VIII. 451.

IV. (e.) THEONAS OF ALEXANDRIA.

I. Editions.

DACHERIUS. In: Spicil. vet aliq. script. XII. (Paris, 1675.) 4°; ed. De la Barre. III. (Par. 1723.) 297–9.
GALLANDIUS. Bibl. patr. IV. (1768) 69–.
ROUTH. Rel. sacr. (1846–8) 437–449.
MIGNE. Patrol. gr. X. (1857) 1569–74. [From Dacherius.]

II. Translations.

English.

SALMOND, S. D. F. In: Ante-Nic. Lib. XIV. (1874) 432–9. Ed. Coxe. VI. (1886) 158–61.

III. Literature.

BURTON. Divinity of Christ. (1829) 433–4.
BUSSE. Chr. lit. (1828–9) I. 39.
CAVE. Hist. litt. de Script. eccl. (1740–3) I. 172.
CEILLIER. Hist. gén. aut. sac. II. (1865) 463.
CHEVALIER. Rép. d. sources hist. (1877–86) 2182.
CLARKE. Sacred lit. (1830–1) I. 197.
CUPERUS. Comment. histor. In: Acta ss. Bolland. (1739) Aug. IV. 579–84.
DUPIN. Nouv. bib. aut. eccl. (1698–) I. 727.
EUSEBIUS. Hist. Eccl. VII.
FABRICIUS. Bibl. gr. (2ª. VII. 306.)
— Bibl. med. aet. (1746) VI. 655–6. (2ª. 233.)
GALLAND. Vet. patr. bibl. IV. VIII–; also in: Migne. Patrol. gr. X. (1857) 1567–70.
HEFELE. Conciliengesch. 2. Aufl. I. 317; Eng. tr. I. (1872) 295.
LARDNER. Credibility. Works (1831) III. 153–4.
LECLERC. In: Biog. Univ. (Michaud) (1842–65) XLI. 289–90.
LUMPER. Hist. ss. patr. XIII. (1799) 604–16.
NEALE. Eastern Ch., Alexandria. I. (1847) 86–9.

NEANDER. Church Hist. (1872) I. 143.
NIRSCHL. Patrol. (1881–) I. 353.
PERMANEDER. Bibl. patrist. II. (1843) 639–41.
SALMOND, S. D. F. Introd. note. In: Ante-Nic. Lib. XIV. (1874)431. Ed. Coxe. VI. (1886) 158.
SCHMIDT, H. In: Herzog. Real.-Enc. (1877) XV. 533–4. (Abr. in: Schaff-Herz. III. 2346.)
SCHRAM. Anal. ss. patr. (1780–) VII. 56–64.
TILLEMONT. Mémoires. IV. (1696) 578–83, 771–2.

IV. (f.) PHILEAS.

I. Editions.

MAFFEI, SCIP. (Ad Meletium.) In: Osserv. lett. III. (Veronae, 1738.) 1–18.
GALLANDIUS. Bibl. patr. IV. (1768) 65–.
ROUTH. Rel. sacr. (1846–8) IV. 83–111.
MIGNE. Gr. lat. In: Patrol. gr. X. (1857) 1561–8.
    Note. The *Ad Thmuitas* also in all eds. of Eusebius, Hist. eccl. The *Ad Meletium* is extant only in the Latin version.

II. Translations.

English.

SALMOND, S. D. F. In: Ante-Nic. Lib. XIV. (1874) 440–6. Ed. Coxe. VI. (1886) 162–4.

III. Literature.

BUSSE. Chr. lit. (1828–9) I. 41–2.
CAVE. Scr. eccl. hist. lit. (1740–3) I. 155.
CEILLIER. Hist. gén. aut. sac. IV. (1733) 10–5; III. (1865) 51–4.
CHEVALIER. Rép. d. sources hist. (1877–86) 1772.
CLARKE. Sacred lit. (1830–1) I. 210.
CLINTON. Fasti Rom. (1845–50) II. 432.
DOUHET. Dict. d. lég. 1083.
DUPIN. Nouv. bibl. aut. eccl. (1698–) I. 598.
EUSEBIUS. Hist. eccl. VIII. 10.
FABRICIUS. Bibl. gr. (1712) V. 279. (2ª. VII. 306; X. 312.)
— De verit. rel. chr. 165.
FLEURY. Hist. eccl. (1691–) II. 429–32.
GALLAND. Vet. patr. bibl. IV. vii–; also in: Migne. Patrol. gr. X. (1857) 559–60.
GASS. In: Herzog. Real.-Enc. (1877–) XI. 537. [25 ll. only.]
HENSCHENIUS. De s. Philea episc. Thmuitarum et s. Philoromo tribuno militum aliisque pluribus martl. Alexandriae in Aegypto. Comment. praev. In: Acta ss. Bolland. (1658) Feb. I. 459–62. (3ª. 464–8.)
HIERONYMUS. De vir. ill. 78. (Honor. August. I. 79.)
LARDNER. Credibility. Works. (1831) III. 234–7.
LE SUEUR, NIC. Vies martyrs. (1660).
LUCHINI. Atti sinceri. (1779) IV. 12–4.
LUMPER. Hist. ss. patr. XIII. (1799) 597–604.
M'CLINTOCK and S. Cycl. (1874–) VIII. 82.
MÖHLER. Patrologie. I. 678–9.
NEALE. Eastern Ch., Alexandria. I. (1847) 97, 99–101.
NEANDER. Church Hist. (1872) II. 254.
NIRSCHL. Patrol. (1881–) I. 353–4.
PERMANEDER. Bibl. patrist. II. (1843) 647–9.
RUINART. Acta sinc. (1689) 547–8.
SALMOND, S. D. F. Introd. note. In: Ante-Nic. Lib. XIV. (1874) 439–40. Ed. Coxe. VI. (1886) 161–2.
SMITH. Gr. and Rom. Biog. (1859) III. 262. [5 ll.]
SURIUS. Vitae ss. (1618) II. 38–9.
TILLEMONT. Mémoires. (1698) V. 484–91, 777–82.
TRITHEMIUS. Scr. eccl. 52.
VINCENTIUS BELVAC. Spec. hist. XIII. 24–5.
WETZER u. W. Kirch-Lex. (1847–54) Supp. 965–6.

IV. (g.) PAMPHILUS.

I. *Editions*.

GALLANDIUS. Gr. lat. In: Bibl. patr. IV. (1768) 3-.
ROUTH. Rel. sacr. (1846-8) III. 485-512; IV. 339-392.
MIGNE. In: Patrol. gr. X. (1857) 1549-58. [Montfaucon's latin.] XVII. (1857) 521-616.
   Note. Of the *Apology for Origen* only the first book is extant, and that in defective translation of Rufinus.

(*Expositio*.)

ZACAGNIUS, LAUR. ALEX. Gr. lat. *Rom.* 1698. 4º. In: his: Collect. monum. eccl. gr. et lat. p. 428-41.
MONTFAUCON, BERN. DE. *Paris*, 1715. fº. In his: Biblioth. Coisliniana. p. 78-82.
FABRICIUS, J. A. Gr. lat. *Hamb.* 1718. fº. In his: Hippolyti opera. II. 205-17. [After Zacagnius.]
LA RUE. In: Orig. opera. IV. (*Par.* 1729.)
LOMMATZSCH. In: Opp. Orig. (1833-) XXV.

II. *Translations*.

English.

SALMOND, S. D. F. (Expos.) In: Ante-Nic. Lib. XIV. (1874) 448-55. Ed. Coxe. VI. (1886) 166-8.

III. *Literature*.

Acta passionis S. Pamphili et Sociorum Martyrum, ex Eusebii Caesariensis libris de vita Pamphili, juxta ms. Medicaeum. graece et latine, cum commentario praevio et notis Dan. Papebrochin. In: Acta Sanctorum Antv. Jun. I. 1. p. 62-70. Also in: Hippolyti Opera. *Hamb.* 1718. fº. II. 217-24. Ed Fabricius; Galland. Bibl. patr. IV. (1768) 41-; Migne. Patrol. Gr. X. (1857) 1533-50. Latin in Surius. I. Jun. 1-.
ALZOG. Patrol. (1876) 158-9.
BARONIUS. Ann. (1589-) 308, 2, 9, 15-16.
BAUR. Dogmengesch. I. (1865) 281, etc.
ΒΑΦΕΙΔΗΣ. Ἐκκλ. ἰστ. I. (1884) 160.
BUSSE. Chr. lit. (1828-9) I. 40.
NICEPHORUS CALLISTUS. Hist. Eccl. X. c. 14.
CAVE. Scr. eccl. hist. lit. (1740-3) I. 153-4.
CEILLIER. Hist. gén. aut. sac. III. (1732) 435-48; 468-9; II. (1865) 522-9.
CHARTERIS. Canonicity. (1880) 352.
CHEVALIER. Rép. d. sources hist. (1877-86) 1711.
[CHRISTIE, TH.] Reflexions suggested by the character of Pamphilus of Caesarea. In: Miscell. phil.-med.-mor. (1792) II.
CLARKE. Sacred lit. (1830-1) I. 208-9.
CLINTON. Fasti Rom. (1845-50) I. 325, 353; 355; II. 432.
COFFIN. Lives of fath. (1846) 384-6.
DARLING. Cycl. bibl. 2282.
DORNER. Person of Christ. II. (1866) 196-7.
DUPIN. Nouv. bibl. aut. eccl. (1698-) I. 595.
Encycl. Brit. (9th ed.) XVIII. 203-4.
EUSEBIUS. Hist. eccl. VI. 32, 33; VII. 32; VIII. 11.
FABRICIUS. Bibl. gr. (1712) V. 277-9; IX. 130, 411-2. (2ª VII. 301-3; X. 303, 712; XI. 705-6.)
F[ISQUET], H. In: Nouv. Biog. Gén. (Hoefer) XXXIX. (1865) 122.
GALLAND. Vet. Patr. bibl. IV. iii-; also in: Migne. Patrol. gr. X. (1857) 1529-34.
GIESELER. Church Hist. (1868-) I. 222-3.
GLEY and GEUCE. In: Biog. Univ. (Michaud) 1842-65. XXXII. 58-9.
HAGENBACH. Hist. of doct. I. 230.
HIERONYMUS. De vir. ill. 75. (Honor. August. I. 76.)

JÖCHER. Gelehrt. Lex. (1750-1).
KURTZ. Kirchenges. (1885-) I. 121.
LARDNER. Credibility. Works. (1831) III. 216-33.
LICHTENBERGR. Encycl. (1877-82) X. 156-7.
LUMPER. Hist. ss. patr. XIII. (1799) 536-62.
MARTINOV. Ann. eccl. gr. slav. (1864) 74-5.
MIRAEUS. 23.
MÖHLER. Patrol. (1840) 672-675.
MÖLLER, W. In: Herzog. Real.-Enc. (1877-) XI. 179-80. (Abr. in: Schaff-Herz. III. 1732).
NEALE. Eastern Ch., Antioch. (1873) 68-70.
NEANDER. Church Hist. (1872) I. 711, 721-2, pass.
— Hist. of dogmas. (1858) 72.
NIRSCHL. Patrol. (1881-) I. 355-6.
NITSCH. Dogmengesch. I. (1870) 155, etc.
ORSI. Ist. eccl. (1746-) III. 503-5; IV. 236-40; (1749) III. 647-50; IV. 308-13.
PAPEBROCHIUS. Comment. praev. In: Acta ss. Bolland. (1695) Jun. I. 62-4. (3ª. 60-2.)
PERMANEDER. Bibl. patrist. II. (1843) 642-7.
PHOTIUS. Biblioth. Cod. 108, 119.
PRESSENSÉ. Martyrs. (1879) 357-9.
— Heresy. (*N. Y.*) 371-3.
REUSCH. In: Wetzer. u. W. Kirch-Lex. (1847-54) VIII. 69.
REUSS. Gesch. N. T. Eng. Tr. (1884) 365, 513.
ROSSI. Bull. archeol. crist. (1863) I. 62, 65-8.
RUFINUS. Praef. in Apol. pro Origene. In: Migne. Patrol. Gr. XVII. (1857) 539-42.
SALMOND, S. D. F. Introd. note. In: Ante-Nic. Lib. XIV. (1874) 447-8. Ed. Coxe. VI. (1886) 165.
SCHAFF. Hist. . . Church. II. (1886) 807; III. 872.
SCHMID. Patrol. (1879); (1886) 54.
SCHRAM. Anal. ss. patr. (1780-) VII. 1-23.
SCHROECKH. Kirchenges. (1772-) IV. 431-6; V. 176.
SMITH, P. In: Smith. Gr. and Rom. Biog. (1859) III. 103-4.
SOCRATES. Hist. Eccl. III. c. 7.
Supernatural Religion. I. (1875) 424.
SURIUS. Vitae ss. (1618) VI. 1-5.
TILLEMONT. Mémoires. (1698) V. 418-28, 750-3.
TRITHEMIUS. Scr. eccl. 47.
VINCENTIUS BELVAC. Spec. hist. XIV. 19.
WESTCOTT. Canon. (1875) 389-91.
WETSTENIUS, J. J. In prolegg. ad N. T. graec. (*Amst.* 1752. II. fº.) 45, 76.
WORMAN, J. H. In: M'Clintock and S. Cycl. (1874-) VII. 606.

IV. (h.) MALCHION.

I. *Editions*.

GALLANDIUS. Bibl. Patr. III. (1767) 558-.
MIGNE. Gr. lat. in: Patrol. gr. (1857) 249-60.
   And in the various editions of Eusebius. Hist. eccl. at VII. 30.

II. *Translations*.

English.

SALMOND, S. D. F. In: Ante-Nic. Lib. XIV. (1874) 402-10. Ed. Coxe. VI. (1886) 169-72.

III. *Literature*.

BUSSE. Chr. lit. (1823-9) I. 35-6.
CAVE. Scr. eccl. hist. lit. (1740-3) I. 135.
CEILLIER. Hist. gén. aut. sac. III. (1732) 298-300; II. (1865) 431-2.
CHEVALIER. Rép. d. sources hist. (1877-86) I, 453.
CLARKE. Sacred lit. (1830-1) I. 194-5.

CLINTON. Fasti Rom. (1845–50) I. 301; II. 423.
DARLING. Cyclop. bibl. 1936.
DUPIN. Nouv. bibl. aut. eccl. (1698) I. 571.
EUSEBIUS. Hist. eccl. VII. 30.
FABRICIUS. Bibl. gr. (2ᵃ. XII. 568.)
— B. m. ae. (1736) V. 28. (2ᵃ. 10.)
FREMANTLE, W. H. In: Smith and Wace. Dict. III. 788–9.
GALLAND. Bibl. vet. patr. III. (1767) xxxix–; also in: Migne. Patrol. gr. X. (1857) 247–50.
HERGENROETHER. Kirchenges. (1879–80) I. 168; III. 73.
HIERONYMUS. De vir. ill. 71. (Honor. August. I. 72.)
JÖCHER. Gelehrt. Lex. (1750–1).
LARDNER. Credibility. Works. (1831) IiI. 135–40.
LUMPER. Hist. ss. patr. XIII. (1799) 245–50.
NEANDER. Church Hist. (1872) I. 605.
NIRSCHL. Patrol. (1881–) I. 344.
PERMANEDER. Bibl. patrist. II. (1843) 625–6.
SALMOND, S. D. F. Introd. note. In: Ante-Nic. Lib. XIV. (1874) 401–2. Ed. Coxe. VI. (1886) 168–9, [Add notes. Ed. Coxe. 172.]
TILLEMONT. Mémoires. IV. (1696) 299–.
TRITHEMIUS. Scr. eccl. 45.
ZEISKE, JOHANN GOTTFRIED. Programma de Malchione, scholastico, divinae veritatis vindice. *Witteb.* 1733. f°.

V. ARCHELAUS.

I. *Editions.*

VALESIUS. In ed. Socrates. (*Mogunt.* 1677) 197–203. [Latin only.]
ZACAGNIUS. In: Collect. mon. vet. (*Rom.* 1698. 4°.)
FABRICIUS. In: Hippolyti op. (*Hamb.* 1718.) 134–.
GALLANDIUS. Bibl. patr. III. (1767) 569–.
ROUTH. Rel. sacr. (1846–8) V. 1–206.
MIGNE. Patrol. gr. X. (1857) 1429–528.

Note. According to Jerome the *Acts* were first composed in Syriac. Fragments are extant in the Greek, but the large part exists only in a Latin translation for the Greek.

II. *Translations.*

English.

SALMOND, S. D. F. In: Ante-Nic. Lib. XX. (1871) 272–419. Ed. Coxe. VI. (1886) 179–235.

III. *Literature.*

ALZOG. Patrol. (1876) 119–20.
ASSEMANI. Bibl. orient. I. (1719) 554–6.
BAUR. Das Manich. Religionssystem. pp. 5–9, 413, 459.
BEAUSOBRE, J. Hist. du Manichéisme. (*Amst.* 1734–39. 4°.) I. 191–.
BURTON. Divinity of Christ. (1829) 432–433.
BUSSE. Chr. lit. (1828–9) I. 37.
CAVE. Scr. eccl. hist. lit. (1740–3) I. 144; II. IV. 17.
CEILLIER. Hist. gén. aut. sac. III. (1732) 333–44; II. (1865) 453–9.
CHEVALIER. Rép. d. sources hist. (1877–86) 156–7.
CLARKE. Sacred lit. (1830–1) I. 212.
CLINTON. Fasti Rom. (1845–50) I. 319; II. 431.
COWELL, E. B. In: Smith and Wace. Dict. I. 152–3.
CYRILL HIEROS. Catech. VI. ed. Maur. p. 140.
DUPIN. Nouv. bibl. aut. eccl. (1698) I. 572.
EPIPHANIUS. Haeres. 66.
FABRICIUS. Bibl. gr. (1712) V. 262–3. (2ᵃ. VII. 275–8.)
FLEURY. Hist. eccl. (1691–) II. 382–3.
GALLAND. Vet. patr. bibl. III. xl–; also in: Migne. Patrol. gr. X. (1857) 1405–20.
GEORGIUS, AUG. ANT. Alphabet. Tibet. (*Rom.* 1762. 4°.) 363–.

HASE. Kirchenges. (1885–) I. 328.
HIERONYMUS. De vir. ill. 72. (Honor. August. I. 73.)
LARDNER. Credibility. Works. (1831) III. 252–9.
LUMPER. Hist. ss. patr. XIII. (1799) 343–89.
M'CLINTOCK and S. Cycl. (1874–) I. 371.
NEANDER. Church Hist. (1872) I. 485, pass.
NIRSCHL. Patrol. (1881–) I. 344–6.
Nouv. Biog. Gén. (Hoefer) III. (1852) 44–5.
OUDIN. Scr. eccl. (1722) I. 296–9.
PAGI. Crit. (1689) 282, 3–4.
PERMANEDER. Bibl. patrist. II. (1843) 627–34.
PHOTIUS. Biblioth. 85. p. 349–.
PRESSENSÉ. Heresy. (*N. Y.*) 53–9.
SALMOND, S. D. F. Introd. note. In: Ante-Nic. Lib. XX. (1871) 267–71. Ed. Coxe. VI. (1886) 173–7. [Add. notes. Ed. Coxe. 235–6.]
SCHMID. Patrol. (1879); (1886) 48.
SCHRAM. Anal. ss. patr. (1780–) VI. 430–482.
SMITH, P. In: Smith. Gr. and Rom. Biog. (1859) I. 261.
SOCRATES. Hist. eccl. I. c. II. 22.
TRAVASA, GAET. MAR. In: Zaccaria. Racc. di dissert. (1794) IX. 85–120.
TRITHEMIUS. Scr. eccl. 49.
Veterum testimonia. In: Migne. Patrol. gr. X. (1857) 1421–8.
ZACAGNIUS. Coll. mon. vet. eccl. (1698) III.–XVII.
For literature compare also articles on Manes and Manichaeism.

VI. ALEXANDER OF LYCOPOLIS.

I. *Editions.*

COMBEFISIUS. In: Auct. bibl. patr. II. (1672) 3–.
(Lat. only.) In: Bibl. max. patr. XXVII. (*Ludg.* 1677. f°.)
GALLANDIUS. In: Bibl. patr. IV. (1768) 73–87.
MIGNE. Gr. Lat. In: Patrol. gr. XVIII. (1857) 411–48.

II. *Translations.*

English.

HAWKINS, J. B. H. In: Ante-Nic. Lib. XIV. (1874) 236–66. Ed. Coxe. VI. (1886) 241–52.

III. *Literature.*

ALZOG. Patrol. (1876) 120.
BEAUSAUBRE. Hist. de Manich. I. 235–37.
CAVE. Scr. eccl. hist. lit. (1740–3) II. III. 2.
CHEVALIER. Rép. d. sources hist. (1877–86) 72.
CHRISTIE, A. J. In: Smith. Gr. and Rom. Biog. (1859) I, 118.
COWELL, E. B. In: Smith and Wace. Dict. I. 86.
FABRICIUS. Bibl. gr. (1712) V. 290. (2ᵃ. VII. 323, 324.)
FLEURY. Hist. eccl. (1691–) II. 75–7.
GALLAND. Vet. patr. bibl. IV. ix–; also in: Migne. Patrol. Gr. XVIII. (1857) 409–12.
HAWKINS, J. B. H. Introd. note. In: Ante-Nic. Lib. XIV. (1874) 231–5. Ed. Coxe. VI. (1886) 237–40. [Add. notes. Ed. Coxe. 252–3.]
H. In: Ersch u. Gruber. I. III. (1819) 31–2.
LE QUIEN. Oriens Chr. II. 597.
LUMPER. Hist. ss. patr. XIII. (1799) 616–9.
MOSHEIM. Eccl. hist. Ed. Murdock. I. (1832) 455.
NEANDER. Church Hist. I. 482, 494, 494, 495, 499, 500; II. 767.
PERMANEDER. Bibl. patrist. II. (1843) 634.
PHOTIUS. Contra Man. I. 11. In: Montfaucon. Biblioth. Coislinian. p. 349–.
SCHRAM. Anal. ss. patr. (1780–) VII. 64–82.

VII. PETER OF ALEXANDRIA.

I. *Editions.*

GALLANDIUS. In: Bibl. patr. IV. (1768) 91–.
ROUTH. Rel. sacr. (1846–8) IV. 19–82.
MIGNE. Gr. lat. In: Patrol. Gr. XVIII. (1857) 467–522.

(Canons.)

In: Micropresbyticon. *Basil.* 1550. [Latin only.]
HEROLDUS. In: Orthodoxographa. *Basil.* 1555. [Latin only.]
GRYNAEUS. In: Orthodoxogr. *Basil.* 1569. [Latin only.]
DE LA BIGNE. Bibl. patr. *Par.* 1575; *Par.* 1589; *Colon.* 1618. [Latin only.]
DUCAEUS, FRONTO. *Par.* 1620. f°.
LABBE. Gr. lat. In: Concil. I. (1671) 955.
BEVERIDGE. In: Pandectae canonum. II. (*Oxon.* 1672. f°.) 8.
HARDOUIN. Gr. lat. In: Concil. I. (1715) 225.
SCHRAM. In: Anal. ss. patr. VII. (*Aug. Vind.* 1784. 8°.) [Latin only.]
And in all collections of canons.

(Other.)

PETAVIUS. (1 Frgm.) In: Uranologion. (*Par.* 1630. f°.) 396–.
LABBE. (De div. frgm.) Lat. In: Conc. III. (1671) 508, 836; IV. (1671) 326. (Sermo. frgm.) V. (1671) 652.
HARDOUIN. (De div. frgm.) In: Conc. I. (1715) 1399; II. (1714) 241. (Sermo. frgm.) III. (1714) 256–7.
MAFFEI, SC. (Ep. ad eccl. A.) In: Observ. letter. *Veron.* 1737–40. 6 v. 12°.
MAI. (2 Frgms.) In: Scr. vet. nov. coll. VII. (*Romae*, 1833. 4°.) 85, 96, 134, 306–7.

II. *Translations.*

English.

HAWKINS, J. B. H. In: Ante-Nic. Lib. XIV. (1874) 292–332. Ed. Coxe. VI. (1886) 269–83.

III. *Literature.*

ALEXANDER, NATALIS. Hist. eccl. (1778) IV. 357.
ANASTASIUS BIBLIOTH. Acta s. Petri. In: Mai. Spicil. III. 671–; also in: Migne. Patrol. Gr. XVIII. (1857) 451–66; Tr. Hawkins. In: Ante-Nic. Lib. XIV. (1874) 272–91. Ed. Coxe. VI. (1886) 261–8.
ATHANASIUS. Apolog. contra Arianos. c. 59.
BAILLET. Vies des saints.
BARONIUS. Ann. (1589–) 300, 1–2; 305, 18–38; 310, 2–14; 311, 48. Cf. Pagi. Crit. (1689–) 300, 2; 305, 4; 310, 4.
ΒΑΦΕΙΔΗΣ. Ἐκκλ. ἱστ. I. (1884) 159. [4 ll. only.]
BURTON. Divinity of Christ. (1829) 448–9.
BUSSE. Chr. lit. (1828–9) I. 42–3.
CAVE. Scr. eccl. hist. lit. (1740–3) I. 160.
CEILLIER. Hist. gén. aut. sac. IV. (1733) 17–25; III. (1865) 56–61.
CHEVALIER. Rép. d. sources hist. (1877–86) 1797.
CLARKE. Sacred lit. (1830–1) I. 211.
DARLING. Cycl. bibl. 2342.
DODWELL. Dissert. sing. ad Pears. c. VI. § 21.
DORNER. Person of Christ. Tr. Eng. A, II. 229, 320; B. 95.
DUPIN. Nouv. bibl. aut. eccl.
EUSEBIUS. Hist. eccl. VII. 32; VIII. 13; IX. 6.
FABRICIUS. Bibl. gr. (1705–) VIII. 411; IX. 135. (2ª. IX. 316–7; X. 311.)
F[ISQUET?], H. In: Nouv. Biog. Gén. (Hoefer) XL. (1862) 138.

GALLAND. Vet. patr. bibl. IV. x–; also in: Migne. Patrol. gr. XVIII. (1857) 449–52.
GASS. In: Herzog. Real.-Enc. (1877–) XI. 543–5. (Abr. in: Schaff-Herz. [11 ll. only.] III. 1818.)
GLEY. In: Biog. Univ. (Michaud) 1842–65. XXXIII. 247.
HARNACK. Dogmenges. I. (1886) 644–5.
HAWKINS, J. B. H. Introd. note. In: Ante-Nic. Lib. XIV. (1874) 267–71. Ed. Coxe. VI. (1886) 255–9. [Add. notes. Ed. Coxe. 283–5.]
HEFELE. In: Wetzer u. W. Kirch.-Lex. (1847–54) VIII. 339–42.
— Conciliengesch. I. 327–; Tr. Engl. I. (1872) 237.
HILSCHER and STRAUSS. Schola Alex. (1776) 30–1.
LARDNER. Credibility. Works. (1831) III. 237–43.
LE QUIEN. Oriens christ. II. 397.
LE SUEUR, NIC. Vies martyrs. (1660).
LICHTENBERGER. Encycl. (1877–82) X. 625.
M'CLINTOCK and S. Cycl. (1874–) VIII. 25.
MAI. Spicil. Roman. (1840) III. 671–2. (= Migne. Patrol gr. XVIII. 451–4.)
MEANS, J. C. In: Smith. Gr. and Rom. Biog. (1859) III. 219–20.
MIRAEUS. Scr. eccl. 32.
NEALE. Eastern Ch., Alexandria. I. (1847) 90, etc.
NEANDER. Church Hist. (1872) II. 252–5, 409, 423, 461.
ORSI. Ist. eccl. (1746–) IV. 248–53, 284–5; (1749–) IV. 324–31, 371–3.
PERMANEDER. Bibl. patrist. II. (1843) 11, 641–2.
PITRA. Jur. eccl. grae. mon. (1864) I. 551.
RENAUDOT. Hist. patriarch. Alex. p. 60.
— Rev. d. soc. sav. (1870) E, I. 91.
ROESSLER. Bibl. d. K.–V. IV. (1777) 265–274.
SCHAFF. Hist. . . Church. II. (1886) 807–8.
SCHRAM. Anal. ss. patr. (1780–) VII. 82–90.
SCHROECKH. Kirchenges. (1772–) V. 55–8, 265–9; XII. 41–4, 52–3.
SURIUS. Vitae ss. (1618) XI. 526–8.
TILLEMONT. Mémoires. (1693–) V. 436–65, 755–65.
VINCENTIUS BELVAC. Spec. hist. XIV. 13, 15–6, 57.

VIII. ALEXANDER OF ALEXANDRIA.

I. *Editions.*

FABRICIUS. (Frgm.) In: Bibl. gr. VIII. (341–2).
GALLANDIUS. (De Ar.) In: Bibl. patr. IV. (1768) 441–.
MAI. (De anim.) Syr. lat. In: Bibl. nov. patr. II.
MIGNE. (Fragms.) Gr. lat. In: Patrol. Gr. XVIII. (1857) 547–.
— (De anim.) Syr. lat. In: Patrol. Gr. XVIII. (1857) 585–608.

Note. The *Epistle to Alexander* is from Theodoret. Hist. Eccl. I. c. 4; the *Epistle Catholic* and the *Epistle* from Athanasius; the *Epistle to Eglon* from Maximus. Compare the editions of their works.

II. *Translations.*

English.

HAWKINS, J. B. H. In: Ante-Nic. Lib. XIV. (1874) 334–63. Ed. Coxe. VI. (1886) 291–302.

III. *Literature.*

BARONIUS. Ann. (1589–) 316, 17; 318, 54–87, 90–; 325, 21; 326, 1.
BAUR. Dogmengesch. I. (1865) 487–95.
BRIGHT. Hist. Chr. p. 11.
— In: Smith and Wace. Dict. I. 79–82.
BURTON. Trinity. (1831) 135–6.

BUSSE. Chr. lit. (1828–9) I. 47.
CAVE. Scr. eccl. hist. lit. (1740–3) I. 173–4.
CEILLIER. Hist. gén. aut. sac. IV. (1733) 101–19; III. (1865) 104–15.
CHEVALIER. Rép. d. sources hist. (1877–86) 69.
CLARKE. Sacred lit. (1830–1) I. 236–8.
CHARTERIS. Canonicity. (1880) 329.
CHRISTIE, A. J. In: Smith. Gr. and Rom. Biog. (1859) I. 111–2.
ECHELLENSIS. Eutych. vindic. p. 40, 19.
EPIPHANIUS. Haer. 70, 9.
EUSEBIUS. Vita Const. II. 64 sq.
FABRICIUS. Bibl. gr. (1705) VIII. 340–2. (2ª. 257–9.)
GALLAND. Vet. patr. bibl. IV. xix–; also in: Migne. Patrol. gr. XVIII. (1857) 523–8.
HAGENBACH. Hist. of Doct. I. (1850) 267.
HASE. Kirchenges. (1885–) I. 477–8.
HAWKINS, J. B. H. Introd. note. In: Ante-Nic. Lib. XIV. (1874) 333. Ed. Coxe. VI. (1886) 287–90. [Add. notes. Ed. Coxe. 303–4.]
HENSCHENIUS. Comment. histor. In: Acta ss. Bolland. (1658) Feb. III. 634–9. (3ª. 639–44.)
HOLSTENIUS. Dissert. II. de Conc. Nic.; also in: Migne. Patrol. Gr. XVIII. (1857) 527–46.
LARDNER. Credibility. Works. (1831) III. 566–9.
LE QUIEN. Oriens chr.
LICHTENBERGER. Encycl. (1877–82) I. 155–6.
M'CLINTOCK and S. Cycl. (1874–) I. 146.
MAI. Bibl. nov. patr. II. 529; also in: Migne. Patrol. Gr. XVIII. (1857) 583–6.
MÖHLER. Patrol. V. (1840). ?
MONTFAUCON, BERN. DE. Epistola . . . an vera narratio Rufini de baptisatis pueris ab Athenasio puero? item de tempore mortis Alexandri episcopi Alexandrini, ac de anno obitus Athanasii Magni. *Parisiis*, 1710. fº et 8º.
MERINUS. De sacr. ordin. III. p. 30.
NEALE. Eastern Ch.; Alexandria. I. (1847) 115, etc.
NEANDER. Hist. of dogmas. (1858) 288–9. [v. 1.]
— Church Hist. I. 190, 722; II. 255, 409, 410, 414, 418, 419, 423, 424, 428.
NITZSCH. Dogmengesch. I. (1870) 217. (5 ll.)
Nouv. Biog. Gén. (Hoefer) I. (1852) 905–6.
ORSI. Ist. eccl. (1746) V. 4–6, 8–9, 19–24, 145–6; (1749–) V. 9–11, 13–4, 27–34, 189–91.
RENAUDOT. Lit. orient. I. 381.
SCHAFF. Hist. Ch. III. (1884) 620. (8 ll.)
SCHRAM. Anal. ss. patr. (1780–) VII. 642–658.
SCHROECKH. Kirchenges. (1772–) V. 306–7, 309–10, 325.
SHEDD. Hist of doct. 3d ed. (1865–) I. 307–8.
SOCRATES. Hist. eccl. I. 5, 6, 7.
SOZOMEN. Hist. eccl. I. 15.
TABARAUD. In: Biog. Univ. (Michaud) 1842–65. I. 422.
THEODORET. Hist. eccl. I. 5, 4.
TILLEMONT. Mémoires. (1693–) VI. 213–38, 730–7.
WORDSWORTH. Church Hist. (1881) 423–448.
For literature see especially articles and works on Arianism.

IX. METHODIUS.

I. *Editions.*

COMBEFISIUS, FRANC. Gr. lat. *Par.* 1644. fº. [Includes also Amphilochius.]
GALLANDIUS. Bibl. patr. III. (1767) 670–.
MIGNE. Gr. lat. In: Patrol. gr. XVIII. (1857) 27–408.
JAHN. *Hal.* 1865. 4º.

(*Convivium.*)

ALLATIUS, LEO. Gr. lat. *Romae*, 1655. 8º.

POSSINUS, P. Gr. lat. *Paris*, 1657. fº.
COMBEFIS. Gr. lat. In: Auctuarium noviss. Bibl. patr. gr. *Paris*, 1672. fº. I. 64–162.

(*Other.*)

PANTINUS, P. (Homilies.) Gr. lat. *Antv.* 1598. 8º.
SAVILUS. (In ramos Palm.) *Etonae*, 1612. fº. In: Chrysostomi Hom. V. 882–.
HUMPHREYS. (Frgm. De res.) In: Apologeticks of Athenagoras. *Lond.* 1714. 8º.
MEURSIUS. (Homil.) In: Varia divina. *Lugd.* 1619. 4º; in Opera. *Florent.* 1741. fº. VIII.
(Revelat.) Gr. lat. In: Mon. patr. orthodoxographa. *Basil.* 1669. fº. I. 93–115.
    Note. The *Revelations* published first in Latin s. l. et a. (*August. Vind. ?*) 4º, and then often; 1496. 4º; *Par.* 1498. 4º; *Basil.* 1504. 4º; *Basil.* 1515. 4º; *Basil.* 1569 [Greek], and in German translation, *Memmingen*, 1497. 4º; *Basil.* 1504. 4º; s. l. 1774. 4º, is clearly of later origin. For literature compare Möller in Herzog. IX. 726.

II. *Translations.*

Latin.

COMBEFIS and POSSINUS. In: Bibl. max. patr. *Lugd.* 1677. fº. III. 673–735.

English.

CLARK, W. R. In: Ante-Nic. Lib. XIV. (1874) 1–230. Ed. Coxe. VI. (1886) 309–402.

German.

RÖSSLER. (De res.) Bibl. d. Kirchen–V. II. 296–314.

III. *Literature.*

ALZOG. Patrol. (1876) 159–61.
ALLATIUS. Diatribe de Meth. Script. In his ed. of the Convivium.
BARONIUS. Ann. (1589–) 302, 62. Cf. Pagi. Crit. (1689) 402, 3.
BAUR. Dogmengesch. I. (1865) 281, etc.
BELLARMIN–LABBE. Scr. eccl. (1728) 58–60.
B[RIQUET], AP. In: Bull. du Biblioph. IX. (1849) 182–6.
BURTON. Divinity of Christ. (1829) 438–442.
BUSSE. Chr. lit. (1828–9) I. 39–40.
CAVE. Scr. eccl. hist. lit. (1740–3) I. 150–3; II. IV. 17.
CEILLIER. Hist. gén. aut. sac. IV. (1733) 26–45; III. (1865) 62–73.
CHARTERIS. Canonicity. (1880) 351.
CHEVALIER. Rép. d. sources hist. (1877–86) 1569–70.
CLARK, W. R. Introd. note. In: Ante-Nic. Lib. XIV. (1874) ix–x. Ed. Coxe. VI. (1886) 305–8. [Add. notes. Ed. Coxe. 355, 382, 402.]
CLARKE. Sacred lit. (1830–1) I. 200–206.
CLINTON. Fasti Rom. (1845–50) I. 343, 361; II. 433.
DARLING. Cyclop. bibl. 2048–9.
DEUTINGER. Geist. d. chr. Ueberlief. II.
DORNER. Person of Christ. II. (1866) 175–7.
DUPIN. Nouv. bibl. aut. eccl. (1698–) I. 578–95.
EBEDJESU. Catal. scr. eccl. 17. In: Assemani. Bibl. orient. III. I. 27–8.
ENGELHARDT. Dogmenges. I. (1839) 292–3.
EPIPHANIUS. Haeres. 64.
FABRICIUS. Bibl. gr. (1705–) V. 255–9; IX. 488–9. (2ª. VII. 260–72; X. 758–9.)
FESSLER. In: Wetzer u. W. Kirch-Lex. (1847–54) VII. 132–4.
GALLAND. Vet. patr. bibl. III. li–; also in: Migne. Patrol. Gr. XVIII. (1857) 9–18.
GRETSER, JAC. De Cruce. (*Ingolst.* 1616. III. fº); II. 404. not. (?)
HAGENBACH. Hist. of Doct. I. (1850) 399.
HARNACK. Dogmenges. I. (1886) 649–62.

HENSCHENIUS. Syllog. histor. In: Acta ss. Bolland. (1707) Jun. IV. 5. (3ª. V. 4–5.)
HERGENROETHER. Kirchenges. (1879–80) I. 165–6; III. 72.
HIERONYMUS. De vir. ill. 83. (Honor. August. I. 84.)
HUBER. Philos. d. K.–V. (1859) 183–185.
JAHN, ALB. S. Methodius Platonizans seu Platonismus ss. patrum eccles. graec. s. Methodii exemplo demonstrat. *Halle*, 1865. gr. 4º. (XXIII. 286 p.)
JEREMIE. Hist. Church. (1852) 102–3.
KURTZ. Kirchenges. (1885–) I. 123–4.
LARDNER. Credibility. Works. (1831) III. 181–201.
LELONG. Bib. sac. II. 859.
LE QUIEN. Oriens Christianus. (*Paris*, 1740. III. fº.) I. 976.
LICHTENBERGER. Encycl. (1877–82) IX. 126–7.
LUMPER. Hist. ss. patr. XIII. (1799) 426–536, 912–22.
MAI. Script. vet. nov. coll. VII. 1.
Meth. Qu. Rev. (1871) 164.
MILMAN. Hist. Lat. Christianity.
MÖHLER. Patrologie. I. (1840) 680–700.
MÖLLER, W. In: Herzog. Real.-Enc. (1877–) IX. 724–6. (Abr. in: Schaff-Herz. II. 1494.)
MUENSCHER. Dogmenges. (1817–8) I. 452.
NEANDER. Hist. of dogmas. (1858) 121. [v. 1.]
— Church hist. (1872) I. 569–70, 720–1, passim.
NIRSCHL. Patrol. (1881–) I. 346–53.
NITZSCH. Dogmengesch. I. (1870) 333–4, etc.
NODIER. Bib. sacr. (1826) 168–9.
ORSI. Ist. eccl. (1746–) IV. 288–9, 296–7; (1749–) IV. 377–9, 388–9.
OUDIN. Commentar. de script. eccl. (1722) I. 299–306.
PERMANEDER. Bibl. patrist. (1841–3) II. 651–81.
PHOTIUS. Biblioth. 234–7.
PLATE, W. In: Smith. Gr. and Rom. Biog. (1859) II. 1066–7.
PRESSENSÉ. Martyrs. (1879) 357.
— Heresy. (*N.Y.*) 370–1.
REUSS. Gesch. N. T. Eng. tr. (1884) 312, 513.
RITTER. Chr. philos. (1841) II. 4–14.
ROESSLER. Bibl. d. K.–V. II. (1776–86) 296–327.
ROSENMÜLLER. Hist. interp. III. (1807) 179–90.
SALMON, G. In: Smith and Wace. Dict. III. 909–11.
SCHAFF. Hist. . . Church. II. (1886) 809–12.
SCHMID. Patrol. (1879); (1886) 55–6.
SCHRAM. Anal. ss. patr. (1780–) VI. 521–686.
SCHROECKH. Kirchenges. (1772–) IV. 427–31.
SIXTUS, JOHANN ANDREAS. Dissertatio de Methodio. Tyri quondam episcopo. *Altorf.* 1787. 4º.
SOCRATES. Hist. eccl. VI. c. 13.
STILTING, JO. In: actt. SS. m. Septb. V. 773.
SUIDAS. In ej. lexic. II. 509, 520.
Supernatural Religion. II. (1875) 192.
THEODORET. Dialog. I. in ej. opp. (*Hal.* 1769–74. V. 8º.) IV. 37.
TILLEMONT. Mémoires. (1693–) V. 466–73, 765–9.
TRITHEMIUS. Scr. eccl. 60.
Veterum Testimonia. In: Migne. Patrol. Gr. XVIII. (1857) 17–26.
WEISS. In: Biog. Univ. (Michaud) (1842–65) XXVIII. 123.
WESTCOTT. Canon. (1875) 382–3.
WORMAN, J. H. In: McClintock and S. Cycl. (1874–) VI. 189.
Y. Nouv. Biog. Gén. (Hoefer) XXXV. (1861) 208–9.

X. ARNOBIUS.

I. *Editions.*

SABAEUS, FAUSTUS. *Romae*, 1543(2). fº. [Contains Minucius F.]

GELENIUS, SIGISM. *Basileae*, 1546. 8º.
ERASMUS and GELENIUS. *Basil.* 1560. 8º.
LA BARRE, R. L. DE. *Par.* 1580. fº.
CANTERUS, T. *Antv.* 1582. 8º.
URSINUS, FULVIUS. *Romae*, 1583. 4º. [Contains Minucius Felix.]
STEWECHIUS, G. *Antv.* 1586. 8º. [Rather; not printed until 1604.]
HERALDUS. *Genev.* 1597 (????)
MEURSIUS, JO. *Lugd.* 1598. 8º.
ELMENHORST, G. *Hanon.* 1603. 8º.
HERALDUS, D. *Par.* 1603. 8º. (?)
STEWECHIUS, G. *Antv.* 1604. 8º; *Duae.* 1634. 8º. [With summaries of "Leander de St. Martino (John Jones) added.]
HERALDUS, D. *Par.* 1605. 8º. [Contains Minucius Felix.]
ELMENHORST, G. *Hamb.* 1610. fº.
SALMASIUS and THYSIUS. *Lugd.-Bat.* 1651. 4º. [For long time the best.]
PRIORIUS. *Par.* 1666. fº. [With Cyprian.]
Bibl. max. patr. *Lugd.* 1677. fº.
In: Le Nourry. Appar. ad Bibl. patr. *Par.* 1715. fº. Ed. Lugd. II. 257–570.
ERNSTIUS. *Havre*, 1726. (??)
GALLANDIUS. Bibl. patr. IV. (*Venet.* 1768. fº.) 133–224.
OBERTHÜR. Opera patr. lat. V. (*Wirceb.* 1783. 8º.)
ORELLI, J. C. *Lips.* 1816–17. 3 v. 8º.
MURALTO. *Zürich*, 1856. (?)
Bisontii, 1838. 8º.
HILDEBRAND. *Hal. Sax.* 1844. 8º.
MIGNE. Patrol. lat. V. (1844) 349–1372.
Lyon-Par. 1845. 8º.
OEHLER, F. In: Gersdorf. Bibl. Patr. Eccl. Sel. *Lips.* 1846. 8º.
ROUTH. (Bk. 1.) Scr. eccl. op. (1858) II. 245–297.
REIFFERSCHEID. *Vindob.* 1875. 8º. In: Corp. scr. eccl. lat. [Critical. Best.]

II. *Translations.*

Dutch.

OUDAEN, J. *Harl.* 1677. 8º.

English.

BRYCE and CAMPBELL. In: Ante-Nic. Lib. XIX. (1871) 1–367. Ed. Coxe. VI. (1886) 413–540.

German.

ALLEKER. *Trier*, 1858. 8º.
BESNARD. *Lands.* 1842. 8º. [Compare its full observations.]

III. *Literature.*

ALZOG. Patrol. (1876) 205–10.
BÄHR. Gesch. Röm. Lit. Sup. (1837) II. 65–71.
— Die chr. röm. Theol. p. 65.
BARONIUS. Ann. (1589–) 302, 63–9; Cf. Pagi. Crit. (1689) 14–16.
BAUMGARTEN–CRUSIUS. Dogmenges. (1832) 253–4. [v. 1.]
BAUR. Dogmengesch. I. (1865) 267, 308–9, 354–5, etc.
ΒΑΦΕΙΔΗΣ. Ἐκκλ. ἱστ. I. (1884) 162. [3 ll.]
BAYLE. Dict. crit. (1741) I. 349–50.
BELLARMIN. Scr. eccl. (1728) 60.
BRUCKER. Hist. crit. phil. (1766–) III. 463–5; VI. 549.
BRYCE and CAMPBELL. Introd. note. In: Ante-Nic. Lib. XIX. (1871) IX–XIX. Ed. Coxe. VI. (1886) 403–11. [Add. notes. Ed. Coxe. 540–3.]
BULENGERIUS, J. C. Eclog. ad Arn. *Tolos.* 1612. 8º. ["Ohne Werth." *Petri.*]
BURTON. Divinity of Christ. (1829) 442–448.
BUSSE. Chr. lit. (1828–9) I. 42.
CAILLAU. Introd. in ss. Patr. (1825) 118–9.

CANNEGIETER, HENR. Epist. ad J. D. Hortensium. (On: Tac. u. Arnobius.) In: Otia liter. ad Isalam. (1761) p. 70–76.

CASSEL, PAULUS. Die älteste histor. Erwähnung d. Zigeuner. (Zu Arnobius.) In: Jahrbb. f. Gesellsch. u. Staatswiss. VIII. (1867) p. 317–322.

CAVE. Scr. eccl. hist. lit. (1740–3) I. 161.

CEILLIER. Hist. gén. aut. sac. II. (1732) I. 373–87; II. (1865) 486–94.

CHEVALIER. Rép. d. sources hist. (1877–86) 168.

CLARKE. Sacred lit. (1830–1) I. 212–6.

CLINTON. Fasti Rom. (1845–50) I. 339, 381; II. 433.

DARLING. Cyclop. bibl. (1854) 105.

DORNER. Person of Christ. II. (1866) 191–3.

DUPIN. Nouv. bibl. aut. eccl. (1698) I. 603.

EBERT. Gesch. Lit. Mittelalt. (1874) I. 61–70.

Encycl. Brit. (9th ed.) II. 625.

FABRICIUS. Opera Hippolyti. Hamb. 1716–18. f°; II. 122–.

— Bibl. lat. (1722) III. 388–94.

— Bibl. m. aet. (1734) I. 359–62. (2ª. 137–8.)

FRANCKE, KARL BERNH. Die Psychologie u. Erkenntnisslehre des Arnobius. Leipzig, 1878. 8°. [Inaug. Diss.]

GEORGES, K. E. Vermischte Bemerkungen. (Zu Arnob. II. 38) In: Philologus. XXXI. (1872) 666.

— Kritische Bemerkungen. (Zu Arnob. II. 38.) In: Philologus. XXXIII. (1874) 334.

GERET, SAMUEL LUTHER. Exercitatio historico-litteraria, variorum de Arnobio ejusque theologia judicia exhibens, etc. Witteb. 1752. 4°.

GIESELER. Church Hist. (1868–) I. 228–9.

HAGENBACH. Hist. of Doct. I. (1850) 250, etc.

HASE. Kirchenges. (1885–) I. 255.

HAUPT, MOR. Analecta. (Zu Arnobius. VII. 12 et 18.) In: Hermes. II. (1867) p. 11; also in his: Opuscula. III. 2 (1876) p. 369–370.

— Varia. (Arnobius. I. 45.) In: Hermes. V. (1871) p. 190; also in: Opuscula. III. 2, p. 535.

— Coniectanea. (Arnobius. III. 9.) In: Hermes. VI. (1872) p. 388–389; also in: Opuscula. III. 2, p. 563–564.

HAVET, L. Notes sur divers auteurs. (Arnobius. VII. 151, p. 257, 10 Reifferscheid.) In: Revue de philologie. N. S. I. (1877) p. 281.

— Témoignage d'Arnobe zur l'accent. In: Revue de philologie. N. S. II. (1878) p. 64.

HERGENROETHER. Kirchenges. (1879–80) I. 104–6, 168; III. 41–2, 73.

HERZOG. In: Herzog. Real.-Enc. (1877–) I. 692–3. [Cf. Schaff.-Herz. I. 148.]

HIERONYMUS. De vir. ill. 79. (Honor. August. I. 80.)

HOFFMANN, A. Conjectanea in Arnobium. In: Archiv f. Phil. u. Pädog. XIII. (Lpz. 1847) 149–58.

HUBER. Philos. d. K.-V. (1859) 216–218.

(HUG, TH.) Zu Arnobius. In: Beiträge z. krit. lat. Pros. (1864) p. 21–31.

— In: Pauly. I. 2. 1747–50.

KETTNER, G. Cornelius Labeo. Ein Beitrag zur Quellenkritik des Arnobius. Progr. Naumburg, 1877. 4°.

KLUSSMANN, E. Eine Verbesserungsvorschläge. (Cicero, Arnobius, Festus.) In: Jahn's Archiv. XII. (1846) 134–6.

— Quaestiones Arnobiane criticae. Gymn.-Progr. von Rudolstadt. Leipzig, 1863. 4°.

— Arnobius und Lucrez, oder ein Durchgang durch den Epicuräismus Zum Christenthum. In: Philologus. XXVI. (1867) 362–366.

— Emendationes Arnobianae. In: Philologus. XXVI. (1867) 623–641.

KURTZ. Kirchenges. (1885–) I. 127.

LARDNER. Credibility. Works. (1831) III. 456–88.

LE NOURRY. In: Migne. Patrol. Lat. V. (1844) 365–714.

LICHTENBERGER. Encycl. (1877–82) I. 613.

M'CLINTOCK and S. Cycl. (1874–) I. 430.

MERLIN, CH. In: Mém. de Trévoux. (1736) 933–59, 1050–8.

— In: Mém. d'une société cel. I. 132–62.

MEURSIUS, J. Criticus Arnobianus. Lugd. Bat. 1598. 8°.

MEYER, K. De ratione et argumento Apologetici Arnobii. Hafniae, 1815. 8°.

MÖHLER. Patrol. I. (1840) 906–916.

MOULE, H. C. G. In: Smith and Wace. Dict. I. 167–9.

MUENSCHER. Dogmenges. (1817–8) I. 164–5, etc.

NEANDER. Church Hist. (1872) I. 150, 687–9 et passim.

NIRSCHL. Patrol. (1881–) I. 362–7.

NITZSCH. Dogmengesch. I. (1870) 168, etc.

NODIER. Bib. sacr. (1826) 167–8.

OBBARIUS. TH. Zu Arnobius. In: Jahn's Archiv. XIV. (1850) 588–590.

ORELLI, J. C. In: Migne. Patrol. Lat. V. (1844) 1291–6.

ORSI. Ist. eccl. (1746–) IV. 69–72; (1749–) IV. 91–5.

PETRI, J. E. In: Ersch u. Gruber. I. v. (1820) 381–2.

PERMANEDER. Bibl. patrist. (1841–3) I. 430.

PRESSENSÉ. 3 prem. sièc. de l'Egl. IV. 487–; Tr. Engl. Martyrs. (1879) 438–9, 605–27.

REIFFERSCHEID, A. Analecta crit. et gramm. (ad Arnobium). Ind. lect. hib. 1877/78. Vratislav. 1877. 4°. p. 9–10.

ROESSLER. Bibl. d. K.–V. III. (1777) 308–52.

SCHAFF. Hist. Church. II. (1886) 856–61.

SCHARPFF. In: Wetzer u. W. Kirch-Lex. (1847–54) I. 464–5.

SCHMID. Patrol. (1879); (1886) 64.

SCHMITZ, L. In: Smith. Gr. and Rom. Biog. (1859) I. 348–9.

SCHÖNEMANN. Bibl. patr. lat. I. (1792) 147–76.

SCHRAM. Anal. ss. patr. (1780–) VII. 91–250.

SCHROECKH. Kirchenges. (1772–) IV. 443–65.

STÖCKL. Gesch. d. Philosophie im patrist. Zeitalt. p. 249–.

TABARAUD. In: Biog. Univ. (Michaud) 1842–65. II. 272.

TEUFFEL. Hist. Rom. Lit. (1873) II. 329–30.

TILLEMONT. Mémoires. (1693–) IV. 573–5, 767–8.

TRITHEMIUS. Scr. eccl. 53.

UEBERWEG. Hist. philos. (1873) 322–3.

UNGER, ROB. Emendationes Arnobianae. Halis. 1851. 4°.

VILLEMAIN. In: Nouv. Biog. Gen. (Hoefer) III. (1852) 307–13.

WALCH. Bibl. patr. (1834) 382.

WASSENBERG, FRANC. Quaestiones Arnobianae criticae. Diss. inaug. Monasterii, 1877.

WESSELING, PETR. Ad Arnobium adv. gent. II. c. 69. In his: Observ. libri II. ed. Frotscher (1832) p. 147.

WOODHAM. In: Ed. of Tertullian's Apol. (1850) prel. essays.

WÖRTER. Lehre üb. Gnade. u. Freiheit. p. 488–.

ZINK, MICH. Kritisches zu Arnobius. In: Blätter. f. d. Bayr. Gymn. VII. (1871) 295–312; VIII. (1872) 292–316.

— Zur Kritik und Erklärung des Arnobius. Gymn.-Progr. Bamberg, 1873. 4°.

VOLUME VII.

I. LACTANTIUS.

I. Editions.

In monasterio Sublacensi, 1465. f°. [" First dated book printed in Italy."]

Romae, Sweynheim et Pannartz, 1468. f⁰.

ANDREAS, JO. *Romae, Sweynheyem et Pannartz,* 1470. f⁰. (222 ff.)

Venetiis, 1471. f⁰. (218 ff.) [Roman ed. 1471 fictitious.]

S. l. 1471. f⁰.

Venetiis, Vindel. de Spira, 1472. f⁰.

SABINUS, ANGELUS ENEUS. *Romae, Gallus et de Luca,* 1474. f⁰. (256 ff.)

Rostochii, 1476. f⁰.

Venetiis, Andr. de Paltasichis et Boninus de Boninis, 1478. f⁰.

Venetiis, Joan. de Colon. 1478. f⁰.

Venet. 1483. f⁰. (?)

Venetiis. Theod. de Regazonibus, 1490. f⁰.

Venet. Benolius, 1493. f⁰.

Venet. 1494. f⁰.

Venet. 1497. f⁰.

VALERIANUS. *Venet.* 1500. f⁰. (? ?) *Venet.* 1502. f⁰; *Par.* 1509. 4⁰; 1513. 4⁰.

PARRHASIUS, J. *Venet.* 1509. f⁰. 1521. f⁰.

Venet. 1511. f⁰.

TUCCIUS, MARIANUS. *Florent., Junta,* 1513. 8⁰.

EGNATIUS, JO. BAPT. *Venetiis, Aldus,* 1515. 8⁰.

TULICHIUS, H. *Lips.* 1520. 4⁰.

Basil. 1521. 4⁰.

Basil. Cratander, 1524. 4⁰; 1532. f⁰.

Antv. 1532.

Lugd. 1532. 12⁰.

FASCITELLIUS, HONORATUS. *Venet. Aldus,* 1535. 8⁰; *Lugd. Gryphius,* 1541. 8⁰; 1543. 8⁰; 1558. 8⁰; *Par.* 1560. 12⁰; 1565. 16⁰.

Antv. 1539. 8⁰.

Colon. Quentel. 1544. f⁰.; do. *Antverp.* 1555. 8⁰.

MASURUS. (?) Lat. gr. *Lugd.* 1548. 8⁰; 1553. 8⁰ or 12⁰; 1565. 12⁰.

HEROLDUS. In: Haeresiologia. *Basil.* 1556. f⁰.

BETULEIUS, XISTUS. *Basil.* 1563. f⁰.

Par. 1563. 4⁰.

Antv. 1568. 12⁰.

THOMASIO, MICH. *Antv. Plantin,* 1570. 8⁰; 1587. 8⁰.

Lugd. 1579. 12⁰.

TORNAESIUS-CUIACIUS. *Lugd.* 1587. 8⁰; 1594. 8⁰; *Genev.* 1613. 12⁰; *Colon.* 1613. 12⁰.

Bibl. patr. *Par.* 1589. f⁰. IX. 1–.

Par. 1589. 8⁰.

DRESSER, M. *Lips.* 1593.

Lugd. 1616. 16⁰.

Bibl. magn. patr. *Colon.* 1618. f⁰. II. III. 206–.

ISAEUS, J. *Caeseu.* 1646. f⁰; *Rom.* 1650.

THYSIUS, A. *Lugd.* 1652. 8⁰.

GALLAEUS. *Lugd. Bat.* 1660. 8⁰.

Bibl. max. patr. *Lugd.* 1677. f⁰. III. 514–672.

SPARKE, TH. *Oxonii,* 1684. 8⁰.

Cantab. Hayes. 1685. 8⁰.

CELLARIUS, C. *Lips.* 1698. 8⁰.

WALCH, J. G. *Lips.* 1715. 8⁰; 1735. 8⁰.

HEUMANUS, CHRIST. AUG. (Symposium). *Hannov.* 1722. 8⁰; *Goett.* 1736. 8⁰.

BÜNEMANN, J. L. *Lips.* 1739. 8⁰; *Hal.* 1764-5. 2 v. 12⁰; *Bepont.* 1786. 2 v. 8⁰.

LE BRUN and DU FRESNOY. *Lutet. Par.* 1748. 2 v. 4⁰.

XAVERIUS. *Romae,* 1754–1759. 14 v. 8⁰. [2d edition announced but did not appear.]

GALLAND. Bibl. vet. patr. *Venet.* 1768. f⁰. IV. 229–436.

OBERTHUR. *Wirceb.* 1783-4. 2 v. 8⁰. (Opera polem. s. patrum. VI., VII.)

Bisontii, 1836. 8⁰.

FRITZSCHE, O. F. In: Gersdorf's Bibl. patr. eccles. selecta. (*Lips.* 1842) X., XI.

MIGNE. Patrol. Lat. VI. (1844) 111–822, 1018–94; VII. (1844).

Lyon, 1845. 8⁰.

(*Divine Institutes.*)

Par. 1500.

Venet. 1578. f⁰.

Genev. 1630. 8⁰.

DALRYMPLE, D. (Bk. V.) *Edinb.* 1777. 8⁰.

(*Epitome.*)

PFAFFIUS, C. M. *Par.* 1712. 8⁰.

In: Giornale de Lett. d'Ital. VI. (1712) 458–65.

DAVIS, J. *Cantab.* 1718. 8⁰.

ROUTH. Scr. eccl. op. (1858) II. 299–383.

(*Workmanship of God.*)

Colon. 1506.

ERASMUS. *Par. Colinaeus.* 1529. 8⁰.

WILLICHIUS, J. *Franc.* 1542. 8⁰.

GOLDNER, G. L. *Gera,* 1715. 8⁰.

(*Persecutors.*)

BALUZIUS. In: Misc. *Par.* 1679. 8⁰. II. 1–46, 345–63; also separately. *Par.* 1679. 8⁰.

FELL, J. *Oxon.* 1680. 12⁰.

COLUMBUS, JO. *Aboae,* 1684. 8⁰.

TOINARDUS, N. *Par.* 1690. 4⁰.

BAULDRIOS, PAULUS. *Traj. ad. Rh.* 1692. 8⁰.; and new title-page do. 1693.

LE NOURRY, N. *Par.* 1710. 8⁰.

—In: Appar. ad Bibl. max. *Par.* 1715. f⁰. II.

RYKEWART. *Gaudae.* 1833. In: Opusc. sel. patr. III.

RAM, F. X. DE. *Louvain,* 1835. 8⁰.

GUÉPRATTE, LUD. *Metz,* 1851. 12⁰.

DÜBNER. *Par.* 1863. 8⁰.

HURTER, H. In: Opusc. ss. patr. XXII. *Inusb.* 1874. 16⁰.

_____

MAICHEL. In: De biblioth. Paris. p. 177-.

HALM. Textverbesserungen. Sitzungsberichte der k. k. Akad. *Wien,* 1865.

(*Phoenix.*)

S. l. et a. 4⁰. (8 ff.); s. l. et a. 4⁰. (6 ff.); s. l. et a. (*Zwollis.*) 4⁰. (4 ff.)

Liptzk. Tanner. 1504. 4⁰.

FICHETUS, A. *Lugd.* 1616. 4⁰.

GRYPHIANDER, J. *Jen.* 1618.

MAITTARIUS, M. Vet. poet. Lat. *Lond.* 1713. f⁰. II. 1599–.

HEINSIUS. *Amst.* 1760. 4⁰.

WERNSDORF, JO. CHR. *Altenb.* 1785. (2?) 8⁰. In: Poetae Lat. min. III. p. 281–322, 543; Addenda. IV. 2. p. 838, 839; V. 2. p. 1464.

LENZ, C. G. *Brauns.* 1794. 8⁰. In: Auserlesene Stücke der eleg. Dichter u. Lyriker. p. 211–224; Noten. p. 491–510.

VIAR et DELATOUR. *Paris,* an VI. (1798) 18⁰.

MARTINI, AD. *Lunaeb.* 1825. 8⁰. (?)

WEBER, E. G. In: Corpus poetarum. Lat. Francef. ad M. 1833. 8⁰. App.

LEYSER, H. *Quellenburg,* 1839. 8⁰. (14 p.)

RIESE, A. *Leipz.* 1870. 8⁰. In: Anthologia Lat. Part I. Fasc. 11. Nr. 731.

(*Other.*)

BEROALDUS. (Carminea. De pass. et resur.) Opuscula. *Par.* 1502. 4⁰. 93–6; *Basil.* 1509. 4⁰. p. 93–6; *Basil.* 1513. 4⁰; *Basil.* 1520. 4⁰.

FABRICIUS, G. (De chr. beneficiis.) Poett. vett. chr. op. *Basil.* 1564. 4⁰.

BUCHNER, A. (Carm. de resur.) *Viteb.* 1627. 8⁰.

KIRCHMAIER, G. C. (De vero Dei cult.) *Witteb.* 1690. 4⁰.

(Ep. ad Zenum.) In: Memoirs of Literature. *Lond.* 1712. 4⁰. II. 339–40. (?)

BÜNEMANN, J. L. ("Specimina.") In: Misc. *Lips.* 1716. 8⁰. III. 115–98.

II. *Translations.*

Bohemian.

BOLESLAWJ, W. (?) (Inst.) *Klaudyan.* 1518. 4⁰. ed. Prochaska. *Prag.* 1518. 4⁰.

English.

BURNET, G. (Persecutors.) *Amst.* 1687; also in: Tracts. 1689. 8⁰; also: 1713; tr. Fr. *Ultr.* 1687. 8⁰.

(Epitome.) In: Memoirs of Literature. Vol. II. Nov. 1712. p. 339, 340.

DALRYMPLE, D. (Persecutors.) *Edinb.* 1782. 8⁰.

FLETCHER, W. In: Ante-Nic. Lib. XXI. (1871) 1–487; XXXI. (1871) 1–222. Ed. Coxe. VII. (1886) 9–328.

French.

FAME, R. (Inst.) *Par.* 1542. f⁰; 1547(6?). 8⁰; 1551. 16⁰; 1555. 16⁰; *Lugd.* 1547; 1555; 1563.

MAUCROIX, F. DE. (Persec.) *Par.* 1677. 12⁰; 1680. 8⁰.

BASNAGE. *Utrech.* 1687. 12⁰. [From Engl. of Burnet.]

MAUPERTIUS, D. DE. (Inst.) *Avign.* 1710. 12⁰ (?); 1712. 12⁰.

(Phoenix.) *Paris*, 1798. 18⁰.

GUÉPRATTE, LUD. (Persec.) *Metz.* 1854. 12⁰.

German.

HERGT, C. G. (Inst.) *Quedlinb.* 1787–1818. 8⁰.

JANSEN and STORF. *Kempten*, 1875–6. 16⁰. [The Reithmayer-Thalhofer Bibl.]

Italian.

POLLASTRINO, GUIL. (Phoenix.) *Roma*, 1544. 8⁰.

ZACCHIA. (Phoenix.) *Roma*, 1608. 4⁰.

BRANCADORO, CES. *Fermo, Paccoroné*, 1783. 4⁰.

Swedish.

BJÖRKMAN, TH. (Phoenix.) *Lund.* 1865. 8⁰. [Inaug. diss.]

III. *Literature.*

A . . . . D. In: Dict. scien. philos. (1875) 897–8.

ALT, H. I. De dualismo Lactantiano. Diss. inaug. *Vratislaviae*, 1839. 8⁰.

ALZOG. Patrol. (1876) 210–214.

AMMON, F. W. Lactantii opinio de relig. in systema redig. *Erlangae*. 1820. 8⁰.

AMPÈRE. Hist. lit. France. (1839) I. 212–33.

APIN, J. P. Lactantius de ver. Dei cult. *Wittebergae*, 1691. 4⁰.

AUBÉ, B. In: Nouv. Biog. Gén. (Hoefer) XXVIII. (1859) 611–20.

BAEHR. Gesch. Rom. Lit. Sup. (1837) II. 72–85.

BAEHRENS, E. Kritische Satura. Anthol. II. 731. Riese. [Lactant. de ave Phoen. 46, 103, 109, 123, 125, 139, 161.] In: Jahrbb. f. class. Philol. CV. (1872) 361–362.

— Zu des Lactantius Phoenix. In: Rhein. Mus. N. F. XXIX. (1874) 200–201.

— Zur latein. Anthologie. Darien: II. Zu d. Lact. Gedicht "de ave Phoenice." In: Rhein. Mus. (1875) 308–309.

— Jahresber. üb. d. röm. Epiker. (Lactant. de ave Phoenice.) In: Bursians Jahresber. I. (1875) p. 220–222. III. (1877) p. 227–228.

BALUZIUS. (Notes on mort. pers.) In: Migne. Patrol. Lat. VII. (1844) 297–386.

BARONIUS. Ann. (1589) 302, 44–50, 60–1; 316, 55–6. Cf. Pagi. Crit. (1689) 315, 7.

BAUDRUS, P. (Notae in lib. De Morte pers.) In: Migne. Patrol. Lat. VII. (1844) 587–840.

BAUER, C. L. Ciceronem de N. D. II. 20, 72. Contra Lactantii Institutt. divin. IV. 28, 3–. defendit. *Lauban.* 1764.

BAUER, WOLFG. Oratio de dicto Lactantii "Religio cogi non potest." *Altdorfi*, 1686. 4⁰.

BAUR. Dogmengesch. I. (1865) 267–8.

ΒΑΦΕΙΔΗΣ. Ἐκκλ. ἱστ. I. (1884) 162.

BELLARMIN–LABBE. Scr. eccl. (1728) 61–2.

BECKER, GUST. Kleinigkeiten (Lactantius Phoenix. 137.) In: Rhein. Mus. N. F. XXIX. (1874) p. 499.

BECONUS, THOM. Lactantii Firmiani Anthologia. . . . *Lugduni*, 1588. 8⁰.

BERGERUS, I. W. *Vitemb.* 1722. 4⁰; 1723. 4⁰.

BERTOLD, PAUL. Prolegomena zu Lactantius. Literarhistor. Abhandlung. (I. Einleitung. II. Leben des Lactantius. III. Schriften des Lactantius. IV. Stil desselben.) Progr. *Metten.* 1861. 4⁰. (38 S. u. ein. lith. Tafel.)

BEYSCHLAG, J. B. Lactantius de vero cultu. *Witteb.* 1690. 4⁰.

BRANDT, SAM. Der St. Gallen Palimpsest d. divinae institutiones d. L. *Wien*, 1885. 8⁰. [110 p.]

BRUCKER. Hist. crit. philos. (1766) III. 465–70.

[BUDDEUS.] Obs. sel. lit. (1700) II. 305–27.

BULL. Works. V. II. (1846) 635–.

BULTEAU, LOUIS. Défense des sentiments de Lactance sur le sujet de l'usure. *Paris*, 1671. 12⁰.

BURCKHARDT, CONST. 46, 327–9, 337, etc. (?)

BURTON. Divinity of Christ. (1829) 449–470.

BUSSE. Chr. Lit. (1828–9) I. 44.

CAILLAU. Introd. in ss. Patr. (1825) 119–22.

CAVE. Scr. eccl. hist. lit. (1740–3) I. 161–3.

CEILLIER. Hist. gén. aut. sac. III. (1732) 387–434; II. (1865) 494–521.

CHEVALIER. Rép. d. sources hist. (1877–86) 1338–9.

CLARKE. Sacred lit. (1830–1) I. 216–236.

CLINTON. Fasti Rom. (1845–50) I. 333, 371; II. 433.

COLUMBUS, J. Notae. In: Migne. Patrol. Lat. VII. (1844) 385–434.

CONYBEARE, J. J. Anglo-Saxon Paraphrase of the Phœnix of Lactantius. In: Archaeologia. XVII. (1814) 193–7.

CHARTERIS. Canonicity. (1880) 52, 352.

CUPERUS, GISB. Praef. In: Migne. Patrol. Lat. VII. (1844) 463–586.

DALLAEUS, J. De vero usu patrum. II. 266.

DARLING. Cycl. bibl. 1752–3.

DECHENT, H. Ueber die Echtheit des Phönix von Lactantius. In: Rheinisches Museum. N. F. XXXV. 39–55.

Disquisitiones dogmaticae in L. In: Migne. Patrol. Lat. VII. (1844) 1011–86.

Divine Institutions of Lactantius. In: Chr. R. X. (1845) 415–.

DODWELL and BALUZIUS. Chronol. persecutionum. In: Migne. Patrol. Lat. VII. (1844) 181–90.

DODWELL, H. Dissert. de ripa striga. In: Migne. Patrol. Lat. VII. (1844) 175–82.

DORNER. Person of Christ. II. (1866) 193–6, 205–17.

DRÄGER, A. Zu Lactantius. (Epit. 25, 4.) In Philologus. XXVII. (1868) p. 149.

DUFRESNOY. Praef. In Migne. Patrol. Lat. VI. (1844) 57–76.

DUPIN. Bibl. des aut. eccles. (1698–) I. 293, 610.

DU VERDIER. Bibl. Franç. (1773) IV. 567.

EBERT, AD. Ueber d. Verfasser d. Buches *De mortibus persecutorium*. In: Berichte d. Sächs. Gesellsch. d. Wiss. Phil. Hist. Cl. XXII. (1870) p. 115–138.

— Gesch. Lit. Mittel. (1874) I. 70–86.

— In: Herzog. Real.-Enc. (1877–) VIII. 364–6. (Abr. in: Schaff-Herz. II. 1269.)

ECKHARD, J. F. Einige Nachr. v. eine. selt. Ausg. d. Schrift d. Lactanz. *Eisenach*, 1781. 4°.

EKERMAN, PETER. Dissertatio de Lactantio, Cicerone christiano. *Upsal.* 1754. 4°. (28 p.)

Encycl. Brit. (9th ed.) XIV. 195–6.

ENGELHARDT. Dogmenges. I. (1839) 213–4, etc.

Esprit d. journ. (1780 Juil.) 255–65; Nov. 227–44.

EUSEBIUS. Comm. in Eccles. c. 10; Comm. in Ephes. c. 4; ad Paulin. epist.

FABRICIUS. Bibl. lat. (1722) III. 394–413.

— De verit. rel. Chr. (1725) 174, 230–40.

— Bibl. m. aet. (1734) IV. 666–94. (2ª. 226–35.)

FALSTER, CHR. Brevis conspectus errorum Lact. in theologia. In: Amoenitatt. philolog. I. 111.

FAUTH, JAC. Pr. de Lactantii dicto "Hominem esse animal sociale." *Heidelberg*, 1800. 4°.

FESSLER. Inst. patrol. I. 328.

FFOULKES, E. S. In: Smith and Wace. Dict. III. 613–7.

FLETCHER, W. Introd. note. In: Ante-Nic. Lib. XXI, (1871) ix–xii. Ed. Coxe. III. (1886) 1–7. [Add. notes. Ed. Coxe. 255–8, 280, 300, 322, 328.]

FLEURY. Hist. eccles. I. (*Paris*, 1856. 8°).

FRITZSCHE, O. F. Ed. Lact. *Lips.* 1844. Praef.; also in: Migne. Patrol. Lat. VI. (1844) 1017–8.

GEORGES, K. E. Vermischte Bemerkungen. (Lactant. de mort. persecut. 43, 5.) In: Philologus. XII. (1873) p. 91.

GERET, J. G. De Lactantio eiusque theologia indicia. *Vitebergae*, 1722. 4°.

GIBBON. Decline and Fall. II.

GIESELER. Church. Hist. (1868–) I. 228, 229.

GOLDNER, G. L. Vita Lac. *Ger.* 1714. 8°.

GÖRRES, FRZ. Miscellen zur Krit. einiger. Quellenschriftst. d. später. röm. Kaiserzeit. (Zur Kritik des Eusebius and Lactantius.) In: Philologus. XXXVI. (1877) 597–614.

GOETZ, G. Ad Anthologiam. (Lact. carm. de ave phoenice.) In: Acta soc. phil. V. (*Lips.* 1875.) p. 322–331. Cf. IV. Praef. III.

HAGENBACH. Hist. of Doct. I. (1850) 250, etc.

HALM, K. Zu Lactantius de mortibus persecutorum. A. d. Sitzsgsber. d. k. k. Akad. d. Wiss. zu Wien. Phil. hist. Cl. (1865) p. 161–167. *Wien*, 1865. 8°.

HASE. Kirchenges. (1885–) I. 222, 255.

HERGENROETHER. Kirchenges. (1879–80) I. 104–6, 168; III. 41–2, 73.

HEUSINGER, JO. M. Emendationes ad Lactantium. In: his: Emandatt. libri. II. (1751) p. 1–161.

HIERONYMUS. De vir. ill. 80. (Honor. August. I. 81.)

Hist. lit. France. (1733) I. 11. 65–92; IV. XXXVIII; VI. 1–11; XI. III. (2ª. not. 3–5.)

HONORIUS. De Luminaribus Ecclesiae.

HUBER. Philos. d. K.–V. (1859) 218–333.

HUNZIKER. In: "Büdinger's investigations in Imperial Hist." I. 117–.

Insignium Virorum testimonia. In: Migne. Patrol. Lat. VI. (1844) 77–82.

ISAEUS. Notes on Div. Inst. In: Migne. Patrol. Lat. VI. (1844) 883–1016.

JACOB, CHARLES FRÉDERIC. Lactance, considéré comme apologiste. Thèse. *Strasb.* 1848. 8°.

KEHREIN, VALENT. Quis scripserit libellum qui est Lucii Caecilii de mortibus persecutorum. Diss. inaug. Monaster. *Stuttgarti*, 1877. 8°.

KIRCHMAIER, G. C. Ad Lact. cap. III. de falsa sap. *Viteb.* 1697. 4°.

KORTHOLT, MATTH. NIC. Dissertatio de Cicerone Christiano Lactantio, s. eloquentia Lactantii ciceroniana. *Giessae*, 1711. 4°.

KOTZE. Specimen hist. theol. de Lact. *Ultr.* 1861.

KREBS, JO. A. Dissertatio de stilo Lactantii Firmiani. *Halae*, 1703. 8°; 1706. 4°. (?)

KREYSSIG, I. TH. De Lact. ep. inst. div. c. 29. (1827).

KURTZ. Kirchenges. (1885–) I. 127–8.

LABOUDERIE. In: Biog. Univ. (Michaud) 1842–65. XXII. 416–8.

LAMSON. The church in the first three centuries. 183–.

LARDNER. Credibility. Works. (1831) III. 481–549.

LECKY. Hist. Europ. Morals. I. 493–.

LENGLETIUS. In: Migne. Patrol Lat. VII. (1844) 157–8. [De mort. pers.]

LE NOURRY. In: App. ad bibl. max. *Par.* 1715. f°. II. 571–1172.

— De Lact. libro de Ira Dei. In: Migne. Patrol. Lat. VII. (1844) 147–56.

— Dissert. in lib. De mort. pers. In: Migne. Patrol. Lat. VII. (1844) 839–1012.

— Dissert. de 7 div. inst. libris. In: Migne. Patrol. Lat. VI. (1844) 823–84.

LESTOCQ, N. Disq. de auct. libri de mort. pers. In: Migne. Patrol. Lat. VII. (1844) 157–72.

LEUILLIER, CH. Études zur Lactance. Thèse. *Caen*, 1846. 8°. (67 p.)

— De variis Lactantii, contra philosophiam aggressionibus. *Caen*, 1846. 8°. (38 p.)

[LIRON.] *Singul. histor.* (1738–9) I. 225–55. (=Zaccaria, Racc. di dissert. (17) X. 217–40.) III. 141–3, 319–23.

McCLINTOCK and S. Cycl. (1874–) V. 185–9.

MECCHI, T. E. Lattanzio e la sua patria. *Fermo*, 1875. 8°.

MERLIN, CH. Apol. de L. In: Mém. de Trévoux. (1736) 1220–37, 1400–17. (= Mém. d'une soc. cel. I. 162–7.)

MEYER, PETER. Quaestionum Lactantianarum particula prima. Progr. *Jülich*, 1878. (8 S.)

MÖHLER. Patrologie. I. 917–933.

MONTFAUCON. Diararium Ital. p. 409.

MOUNTAIN, J. H. BR. A summary of the writings of Lactant. *London*, 1839. 8°.

MÜLLER, IOA. GUST. THEOD. Quaestiones Lactantianae. Diss. inaug. *Gottingae*, 1875. 8°.

MUENSCHER. Dogmenges. (1817–8) I. 165-7, etc.

NEANDER. Hist. of Dogmas. (1858) 164, 176, 186. [v. 1.]

— Church Hist. (1872) I. 608; II. 467 et pass.

NIRSCHL. Patrol. (1881–) I. 367–77.

NITZSCH. Dogmengesch. I. (1870) 168–9, etc.

NODIER. Bib. sacr. (1826) 170–3.

Observationes. (Div. inst.) In: Misc. Obss. IV. (1734) I. 20–8; III. 409–30. (De morte pers.) IV. I. 31–71.

OLZENENGUS, R. Commentaria in VIII. Libr. Inst. 1563.

ORSI. Ist. eccl. (1746–) IV. 389–94; (1749–) IV. 512–9.

OUDIN. Comm. de script. eccl. (1722) I. 307–12.

OVERLACH, E. Die Theologie des Lactantius. Gymn.-Progr. *Schwerin*, 1858. 4°. (40 p.)

PERMANEDER. Bibl. patrist. (1841–3) I. 430–1.

PRESSEL. In: Herzog. VIII. 158–61. [1 ed.?]

RAMSAY, W. In: Smith. Gr. and Rom. Biog. (1859) II. 701–3.

RAU, JOACH. JUST. Diatribe historico-philosophica de philosophia L. Caec. Lactantii Firmiani . . . *Jenae*, 1733. 8°.

REUSS. Gesch. N. T. (1874); II. 35–6; tr. Eng. (1884) 303, 313, 318. [v. 2.]

RIDDLE. Christian Antiquities. 160–163.

RIESE, A. Ueb. d. Phönix d. Lactantius. (A. L. 731) u. s. w. 1876.

RITSCHL, F. Zur latein. Anthologie. (De ave phoenice.) In: Rhein. Mus. N. F. XXVIII. (1873) p. 189–192; also in his: Opusc. philol. III. (1877) p. 806–811.

ROESSLER. Bibl. d. K.–V. III. (1777) 353–422.

ROOY, A. DE. De mortibus persecut. c. VII. u. de Phoenice. In his: Spicilegia crit. (1771) 34, 170–171.

ROSENMÜLLER. Hist. interp. III. (1807) 295–300.

ROTHFUCHS, J. Qua historiae fide Lantantius usus sit in libro "De mortibus persecutorum," disputatar. Gymn.-Progr. *Marburg*, 1862. 4°.

RUFFET, L. In: Lichtenbergr. Encycl. (1877–82) VII. 662–8.
SCHAFF. Hist. . . Church. II. (1886) 864–6; II. (1884) 955–8.
SCHARPFF. In: Wetzer u. W. Kirch.-Lex. (1847–54) VI. 311–4.
[SCHELHORN.] Amoen. liter. (1730) I. 312–7; II. 469–96.
SCHMID. Patrol. (1879); (1886) 64–6.
SCHMIDT, M. Zu Lactantius Firmianus. In: Rhein. Mus. N. F. VI. (1848) 318–320.
SCHOELL. Hist. de la littérature romaine. IV. 26.
SCHÖNEMANN. Bibl. patr. lat. I. (1792) 177–264.
SCHRAM. Anal. ss. patr. (1780–) VII. 250–641.
SCHROECKH. Kirchenges. (1772–) V. 68, 72, 220–65.
SCHWEGLER. Nachap. Zeitalt. (1846) I. 315.
SHEDD. Hist. of doct. 3d ed. (1865–) I. 55–6.
SMITH. Hist. of Christian Church. I. (N. Y.) 451.
SPYKER, H. J. Dissertatio de pretio Institutionibus divinis Lactantii statuendo. Lugduni Bat. 1826. 8°. (152 p.)
Supernatural Religion. (1875) I. 132, 133, 136, 164, 325; II. 168.
TEUFFEL. Hist. Rom. Lit. (1873) II. 330–5.
TILLEMONT. Mémoires. (1693–) VI. 203–12, 727–30.
TOINARD, N. Notae in lib. De morte pers. In: Migne. Patrol. Lat. VII. (1844) 433–62.
TRITHEMIUS. Scr. eccl. 56.
UEBERWEG. Hist. philos. (1876) 323–5.
VALESIUS, HENR. Ad Lactant. Div. inst. V. 2 squ. In his: Emendatt. libri V. et de critica libri II. ed. Burmann. (1740) p. 10–11.
VINCENTIUS BELVAC. Spec. hist. XIV. 89.
VOLKMANN, RICH. Observationes miscellae. (Lactant. instit. div. I. 20; II. 16; III. 4, 6, 12, 14, 28; IV. 14, 20, 23, 27, 28; VI. 13, 23; VII. 3; II. 3, 14, 5.) Gymn.-Progr. Ianer, 1872. 4°. p. 13–14.
VONCK, CORN. VAL. Ad Lactantium. In his: Specim. crit. in var. auctor. (1744) p. 73–74.
WAITE. Hist. Chr. Rel. (1881) passim.
WALCH. Bibl. patrist. (1834) 67–8, 181–2, 383–4.
WEHNU. In welchen Punkten zeigen sich bei Lactantius — de mortibus persecutorum — d. durch d. lokalen Standort d. Verfassers bedingten Vorzüge in d. Berichten üb. d. letzten drei Regierungsjahre Diocletians. Progr. Saalfeld. 1885. 4°.
WESSELINGIUS, PETR. Ad Lactantium. In his: Obss. variar. libri II. ed. Frotscher. (1832) 61–.
WINCKLER, JO. DIETR. Philologemata Lactantiana sacra. Braunsvig, 1754. 8°.

II. VENANTIUS FORTUNATUS.

I. *Editions.*

This work is almost always treated under Lactantius. Those who may wish to compare with the other works of Venantius will find in: MIGNE. Patrol. Lat. LXXXVIII. (1862) 9–532, a reprint of Luichi's ed. (*Romae*, 1786–7. 2 v. 4°.) For other editions and translations see especially Busse. Chr. lit., Engelmann, Brunet, and Graesse.

II. *Translations.*

English.

FLETCHER. W. In: Ante-Nic. Lib. XXII. (1871) 223–7. Ed. Coxe. VI. (1886) 329–30. [Poem on Easter only.]

III. *Literature.*

The following references, selected from such as chance to be in hand, and *excluding* all mentioned by Chevalier,

are included simply as a contribution to the literature of V. F. Few if any of the references mention the *Easter* work.

BERGER, S. In: Lichtenberger. Encycl. (1877–82) V. 33–4.
BÖRSCH, FRIEDR. Ueber die Laugona u. Bordaad. V. F. *Hanau*, 1839. 8°. 32 s.
BUSSE. Chr. lit. (1828–9) I. 185–6.
CHEVALIER. Rép. d. sources hist. (1877–86) 758.
CLINTON. Fasti Rom. (1845–50) I. 827, 829; II. 483.
DANIEL. Thesaurus Hymnologicus. *Leipzig*, 1855. I. 159–74.
EBERT. In: Herzog. Real.-Encycl. (1877–) IV. 596–7. (Cf. Schaff-Herz. I. 824.)
GODRON, A. Des animaux sauvages indiqués au 6° sièc. par Fortunatus, etc. *Nancy*, 1874. 8°. (20 p.)
HEFELE. In: Wetzer u. W. Kirch-Lex. (1847–54) IV. 117–8.
HERGENROETHER. Kirchenges. (1879–80) I. 415; III. 160.
LÉCUY. In: Biog.-Univ. (Michaud) 1842–65. XIV. 434–6.
MARCH, F. A. Latin Hymns. N. Y. 1879. 12°. 251–5.
M'CLINTOCK and S. Cycl. (1874–) III. 628.
ORSI. Ist. eccl. (1746–) XIX. 108–9, 183–5; XX. 50; (1749–) XIX. 121–2, 205–8; XX. 63.
SCHAFF. Christ in song. (N. Y. 1869.)
— Hist. Ch. III. (1886) 595–8.
SCHROECKH. Kirchenges. (1772–) XVI. 162–3.
TEUFFEL. Hist. Rom. Lit. (1873) II. 563–7.
WATERLAND. Works. (*Oxford*, 1843.) III. 134–.
YOUNG, E. M. In: Smith and Wace. Dict. II. 552–3.

III. ASTERIUS URBANUS.

I. *Editions.*

GALLANDIUS. Bibl. patr. III. (1767) 273–.
MIGNE. Gr. lat. in: Patrol. gr. X. (1857) 145–56. [Galland's text.]
And in the various editions of Eusebius.

II. *Translations.*

English.

SALMOND, S. D. F. In: Ante-Nic. Lib. IX. (1869) ii. 224–31. Ed. Coxe. VII. (1886) 335–7.

III. *Literature.*

BALUZIUS. In: Nov. coll. concil.
CAVE. Scr. eccl. hist. lit. (1740–3) I. 85.
CEILLIER. Hist. gén. aut. sac. II. (1730) 529–33; (1865) 88–90.
CHEVALIER. Rép. d. sources hist. (1877–86) 180.
CLARKE. Sacred lit. (1830–1) I. 172.
DODWELL. Dissert. 4. Cypr. § 11. [For Asterius U. as author.]
— Diss. Iren. IV. § 38. [Agst. Asterius U.]
EUSEBIUS. Hist. eccl. V. 16, 17.
FABRICIUS. Bibl. Gr. (1717) VIII. 615. (2ª. IX. 522.)
GALLAND. Vet. patr. bibl. III. xi.-; also in: Migne. Patrol. gr. X. (1857) 141–4.
HALLOIX. Ill. eccl. orient. Script. p. 896.
HEINICHEN. Notes on Euseb.
HIERONYMUS. Catal. Script. eccl. c. 37. 4°.
ITTIG. Hist. eccl. (1709) II. 53.
LUMPER. Hist. ss. patr. (1790) VII. 399–411.
LARDNER. Credibility. Works. (1831) II. 410–4.
LONGUERUE. Diss. de Montan. § 14. p. 265.
NICEPHORUS. Hist. eccl. IV. c. 33.
ORSI. Ist. eccl. (1746–) II. 195–6; (1749–) II. 279–80.

PERMANEDER. Bibl. patrist. (1841–3) II. 422–5.
RUFINUS. Interpret. Euseb. Hist. eccl. V. c. 15.
SALMON, G. In: Smith and Wace. Dict. I. 178.
SALMOND, S. D. F. Introd. note. In: Ante-Nic. Lib. IX. (1869) ii. 224. Ed. Coxe. VII. (1886) 331–3. [Add. notes. Ed. Coxe. 337-8.]
TILLEMONT. Mémoires. (1693–) II. 441–3, 670–1.
— Les Montanistes.

> *Note.* Bp. Coxe here follows Valesius, Cave, Tillemont, Lardner, etc., but the Edinburgh editor (Salmond) takes the ground that Asterius is not mentioned as author. G. Salmon holds that the treatise was against Asterius. Baluzius and others, following Rufinus, ascribe to Claudius Apollinaris, while others follow Jerome, ascribing now to Rhodo and now to Apollonius.

IV. VICTORINUS.

I. *Editions.*

MILLANIUS. (Apocal.) *Bologna*, 1588.
CAVE. (De fabr. mundi.) In: Hist. lit. I. 417.
RIVINUS, A. *Goth.* 1652. 8º.
Bibl. Patr. Max. (Apocal.) III. (1677).
GALLANDIUS. Bibl. patr. IV. (1768) 49–.
MIGNE. Patrol. Lat. V. (1844) 281–344.
ROUTH. Rel. sacr. (1846–8) III. 451–483.

II. *Translations.*

English.

WALLIS, R. E. In: Ante-Nic. Lib. XVIII. (1870) 388–433. Ed. Coxe. VII. (1886) 339–60.

III. *Literature.*

BAEHR. Gesch. d. röm. Litterat. Suppl. 1. § 14; 2. § 33.
BARONIUS. Ann. (1589–) 303, 126–7. Cf. Pagi. Crit. (1689) 9.
BASNAGE. Hist. de l'egl. *Rotterd.* 1699. fº.
BELLARMIN–LABBE. Scr. eccl. (1728) 56–8.
BJÖRN. (Carmina.) *Hafn.* 1818. 8º.
BLEEK. Vorles. ü. d. Apok. p. 34–.
BUSSE. Chr. Lit. (1828–9) I. 40–1.
CAILLAU. Introd. in ss. Patr. (1825) 137–9.
CASSIODORUS. Instit. divina, 5, 7, 9.
CAVE. Scr. eccl. hist. lit. (1740–3) I. 147–51.
CEILLIER. Hist. gén. aut. sac. III. (1732) 345–8; II. (1865) 460–2.
CHARTERIS. Canonicity. (1880) 351–2.
CHAMARD, S. Victorin, évêque et martyr, et s. Nectaire, évêque de Poitiers. *Poitiers*, 1876. gr. 8º. (20 p.)
CHEVALIER. Rép. d. sources hist. (1877–86) 2295.
CLARKE. Sacred lit. (1830–1) I. 198–200.
CLINTON. Fasti Rom. (1845–50) II. 431.
DARLING. Cycl. bibl. 3061.
DORNER. Person of Christ. II. (1866) 485–8.
DUPIN. Nouv. Bibl. aut. eccles. (1698–) I. 574.
FESSLER. Patrologia. I. 326.
FABRICIUS. Bibl. m. aet. (1734–) VI. 822–3. (2ª. 295.)
HAUSSLEITER, J. Die Kommentare d. Victorinus, Tichonius, u. Hieronymus zur. Apokalypse. In: Ztschr. f. Kirchl. Wiss. u. Leben. (1886) 239–257.
HIERONYMUS. De vir. ill. 74. (Honor. August. I. 75.)
HOLTZMANN. Einl. in d. N. T. (1886) 427, etc.
JÖCHER. Gelehrt. Lex. (1750–1) (?)
KURTZ. Kirchenges. (1885–) I. 127.
LARDNER. Credibility. Works. (1831) III. 162–80, 297–302.
LAUNOY, JOAN DE. De Victorino, episcopo et martyre, dissertatio. *Parisiis*, 1653. 8º. *Argentorati*, 1659. 8º. Ed. 2. *Paris*, 1664. 8º. Opera omn. (1731) II. 1. 634.

LEIMBACH. In: Herzog. Real.-Enc. (1877–) XVI. 448–9. (Cf. Schaff-Herz. III. 2457.)
LELONG. Bibl. sac. II. 1003.
LICHTENBERGER. Encycl. (1877–82) XII. 364–5.
LÜCKE. Einl. v. d. Offenb. Joh. 972–82.
LUMPER. Hist. ss. patr. XIII. (1799) 563–97.
M'CLINTOCK and S. Cycl. (1874–) X. 775.
MELLICENSIS. (Anon.) 7. (Ed. Fabricius.)
MÖHLER. Patrol. I. (1840) 900.
MUENSCHER. Dogmenges. (1817–8) II. 431–2.
NEANDER. Church Hist. (1872) I. 296; II. 376 et pass.
NIRSCHL. Patrol. (1881–) I. 360–2.
Nouv. Biog. Gén. (Hoefer) XLVI. (1866) 121.
ORSI. Ist. eccl. (1746–) IV. 153–4; (1749–) IV. 198–9.
PERMANEDER. Bibl. patrist. (1841–3) II. 900–7.
PRESSENSÉ. Martyrs. (1879) 368.
PRZILESZKY, JOH. BAPT. Acta et scripta ss. Cornelii, Firmiliani, Ponti et Victorini suo ordine digesta et annotationibus historico-theologicis illustrato. *Cassoviae*, 1765. 8º. (282 p.)
RAMSAY, W. In: Smith. Gr. and Rom. Biog. (1859) III. 1258.
REUSCH. In: Wetzer u. W. Kirch-Lex. (1847–54) XI. 677–8.
REUSS. Gesch. N. T. (1874) III. 35; tr. Eng. (1884) 318. [v. 2.]
SCHAFF. Hist. Church. II. (1886) 861–4.
SCHÖNEMANN. Bibl. patr. lat. (1792) 144–7.
SCHRAM. Anal. ss. patr. (1780–) VII. 24–55.
SCHROECKH. Kirchenges. (1772–) IV. 442–3.
TEUFFEL. Hist. Rom. Lit. (1873) II. 361, 363.
TILLEMONT. Mémoires. (1693–) V. 311–3, 707–9.
TRITHEMIUS. Scr. eccl. 46.
WINTER, VIT. ANT. Vorarbeiten z. Beleuchtungd. baier, u. östreich. K. Gesch. (*Münch.* 1803) I. 165–.

> *Note. Creation* authentic, *Apocalypse* dubious, all others spurious.

V. DIONYSIUS OF ROME.

I. *Editions.*

MANSI. Coll. concil. I. 1009–.
GALLANDIUS. Bibl. patr. III. (1767) 538–.
RÖSSLER. Bibl. d. Kirchen-V. II. (*Lpz.* 1776) 381–3.
COUSTANT. Epist. Rom. Pontif. I. (1796) p. 270–.
Migne. Patrol. lat. V. (1844) 99–136.
ROUTH. Rel. sacr. (1846–8) III. 369–403.
And in all editions of Athanasius.

II. *Translations.*

Latin.

SCHRAM. In: Anal. ss. patr. VI. (*Aug. Vind.* 1784. 8º.)

English.

WALLIS, R. E. (?) In: Ante-Nic. Lib. XVIII. (1870) 385–7. Ed. Coxe. VII. (1886) 365–6.

III. *Literature.*

ALZOG. Patrol. (1876) 215.
ATHANASIUS. Ep. de Sententia Dionysii.
BARONIUS. Ann. (1589–) 261, 11, 53; 270, 17; 272, 21–2. Cf. Pagi. Crit. (1689–) 261, 7; 270, 3; 272, 9–10.
BAUR, F. C. Lehre v. d. Dreieinigkeit. I. (1841) 311–19.
— Dogmengesch. I. (1865) 485–7.
BOWER. Hist. of the Popes. I. (1749) 74–8.
BURTON. Divinity of Christ. (1829) 420–422.
— Trinity. (1831) 127–132.
BUSSE. Chr. Lit. (1828–9) I. 35.

CAVE. Scr. eccl. hist. lit. (1740–3) I. 133.
CEILLIER. Hist .gén. aut. sac. III. (1732) 326–8; II. (1865) 448–50.
CHEVALIER. Rép. d. sources hist. (1877–86) 566.
CLARKE. Sacred lit. (1830–1) I. 193.
COXE, A. C. Introd. note. In: Ante-Nic. Lib. Ed. Coxe. VII. (1886) 361–4, 366–8.
DORNER. Person of Christ. II. (1868) 182–5, 485.
DUPIN. Nouv. bibl. aut. eccl. (1698–) I. 569.
ENGELHARDT. Dogmenges. I. (1839) 86.
FABRICIUS. Bibl. gr. (1705–) V. 275. (2ª. VII. 293–4.)
— Bibl. m. aet. (1734–) II. 93–4. (2ª. 31.)
GIESELER. Church Hist. (1868–) I. 231, 294.
H. In: Ersch u. Gruber. I. xxv̄. (1834) 356.
HAGENBACH. Hist. of Doct. I. (1850) 261–2.
HARNACK. Dogmenges. I. (1886) 634–40.
HASE. Kirchenges. (1885–) I. 371–2.
HEFELE. Conciliengesch. I. 222.
HERGENROETHER. Kirchenges. (1879–80) I. 200; III. 93.
JAFFÉ. Reg. pont. Rom. (1851) 10–1, 926.
KURTZ. Kirchenges. (1885–) I. 141.
LARDNER. Credibility. Works. (1831) III. 127–31.
LICHTENBERGER. Encycl. (1877–82) III. 669.
LIPSIUS. Chronol. d. röm. Bischöfe. Kiel, 1869. p. 224–231.
LUMPER. Hist. ss. patr. XIII. (1799) 194–214, 778.
M'CLINTOCK and S. Cycl. (1874–) II. 811.
MOBERLY, G. H. In: Smith and Wace. Dict. I. 852.
MÖHLER. Patrologie. I. (1840) 641–4.
MÖLLER, W. In: Herzog, Real.-Enc. (1877–) III. 627–8. (Cf. Schaff-Herzog. [13 ll. only.])
MUENSCHER. Dogmenges. (1817–8) I. 452–4.
NEANDER. Church Hist. (1872) I. 606–8, 610; II. 338.
NITZSCH. Dogmenges. I. (1870) 214, etc.
Nouv. Biog. Gén. (Hoefer) XIII. (1855) 675.
ORSI. 1st. eccl. (1746–) III. 395–6, 423; (1749–) III. 511–3, 547–8.
PERMANEDER. Bibl. patrist. (1741–4) II. 890–4.
PRESSENSÉ. Heresy. (N. Y.) 416–8.
SCHAFF. Hist. . . Church. II. (1886) 570–1.
SCHMID. Patrol. (1879); (1866) 62.
SCHMITZ, L. In: Smith. Gr. and Rom. Biog. (1859) I. 1044.
SCHRAM. Anal. ss. patr. (1780–) VI. 415–7.
SHEDD. Hist. of doct. 3d ed. (1865–) I. 304–5.
SHEPHERD. Hist. of Ch. of Rome. (1851) 32–6.
TAFURI. Scritt. Napoli. (1748) II. 1. 146–8.
TEUFFEL. Hist. Rom. Lit. (1873) II. 537.
TILLEMONT. Mémoires (1693–) IV. 341–4, 670–2.
WATERLAND. In: Works. III. 454–9, etc.
WERNER. In: Wetzer u. W. Kirch.-Lex. (1847–54) III. 169–70.
WORDSWORTH. Church Hist. (1881) 304–7.
ZAVARRONI. Bibl. Calabra. (1753) 28.

VI. THE TEACHING OF THE TWELVE APOSTLES.

I. *Editions.*

Βρυέννιος, Φ. (Bryennios, Ph.) Διδαχὴ τῶν δώδεκα 'Αποστόλων. ἐν Κανσταντινοπόλει, 1883. 8⁰. [From the Jerusalem ms. Ed. princeps.]

FRIEDBERG. In: Ztschr. f. Kirchen. (1884) Cf. Lit.
HARNACK. Leipz. 1884. [July.] Cf. Lit. Gebhardt u. H.
HILGENFELD, A. In: N.T. extra canonem receptum. Ed. 2. IV. (Lips. 1884. 8⁰.) 87–121.

LUTHARDT, C. E. In: Ztschr. f. Kirchl. Wiss. u. Leben. (1884) 139–43. [Repr. from Bryn. without comment.]
WÜNSCHE. Gr. Ger. Leipz. 1884. 8⁰. Cf. Lit.

HITCHCOCK and BROWN. N.Y. (Scribners) 1884; 2d ed. revised and enlarged. N.Y. 1885. 8⁰. Cf. Lit.
ORRIS, S. S. New York, 1884. Cf. Lit.
CURRY, D. Gr. Eng. In: Meth. Q. XXXVI. (1884) 704–15.

DE ROMISTIN, H. Gr. Engl. Oxf. and Lond. Oct. 1884. 8⁰.
FITZGERALD. New York, 1884. Cf. Lit.

PRIUS, J. J. Lugd. Bat. 1884. Cf. Lit.

In: Theologisk Tidsskrift for den ev. luth. Kirke i Norge. X. (Christiania, 1884.)

SPENCE. Lond. 1885. 8⁰. Cf. Lit.
SABATIER, P. Gr. Fr. Par. 1885. Cf. Lit.
MAJOCCHI. Milano, 1885. 8⁰. Cf. Lit.
WARFIELD, B. B. (Latin fragment.) In: Schaff. Teaching of the 12. (1886) 219–25.

(*The two ways.*)

BICKELL, J. W. In his: Gesch. d. Kirchenrechts. I. (1843) 107–132.
LAGARDE. In his: Rel. jur. eccl. aut. (1856) 74–79.
PITRA, D. B. In his: Juris eccl. Gr. hist. et mon. I. (1864) 77–86.
HILGENFELD. In his: N. T. extra Canon Rec. fasc. IV. (1866) 95–105.

II. *Translations.*

Danish.

HELVEG. 1884. Cf. Lit.
POULSEN. Kjöbenhavn, 1884. Cf. Lit.
VARMING, C. Kjöbenhavn, 1884. Cf. Lit.

Dutch.

MEYBOOM. Leiden, Sept., 1885. Cf. Lit.

English.

DE ROMESTIN. Oxf. and Lond. 1884. 8⁰. Cf. Lit.
GARDINER and CAMP. N.Y. Mar. 29, 1884, and separately. Cf. Lit.
HALL and NAPIER. In: S. S. Times. (Phila. 1884. Apr. 5 & 12.) Cf. Lit.
— In: Ante-Nic. Lib. Ed. Coxe. VII. (1886) 377–82.
FARRAR. In: Contemp. R. (May, 1884.) Cf. Lit.
Lond. June, 1884. In: For. Church. Chron. and R.
SPENCE. Lond. 1885. 8⁰. Cf. Lit.
HITCHCOCK and BROWN. N.Y. 1884. 8⁰; 1885. 8⁰; also in: Indian Evangelical Rev. (Calcutta, Jan. 1885.) Cf. Lit.
STARBUCK and SMYTH. Andover, 1884. Cf. Lit.
In: Lobb's Theol. Qt. (1884, July.)
ORRIS, S. S. N.Y., 1884. Cf. Lit.
FITZGERALD. New York, 1884. Cf. Lit.

French.

BONET–MAURY, G. Par. 1884. Cf. Lit.
SABATIER. Par. 1885. Cf. Lit.

German.

FUNK. In: Theol. Quartalschr. LXVI. (1884) 383–402.
FRIEDBERG. In: Ztschr. f. Kirchen. XIX. (1884) Cf. Lit.
FUNK. Tüb. 1884. In: Theol. Quartalschr. Cf. Lit.

HARNACK. *Leipz.* 1884. [July.] Cf. Lit. Gebhardt u. H,
— (Chs. 7–16.) In: Theol. Literaturzeitung. IX. (1884.
Feb. 9.)
VOLKMAR. *Lpz. u. Zür.* 1885. Cf. Lit.

Norwegian.

CASPARI. *Lördag.* 1884. Cf. Lit.

Swedish.

BERGGREN, J. E. *Upsala*, 1884. Cf. Lit.
Note. The list of editions and translations must omit
some included in the literature. It is not possible to ana-
lyze some titles without the works themselves.

III. *Literature.*

ABERLE. Die Didache u. ihre Nebenformen. In: Lit.
Rundschau. (1885, p. 225–228; 257–260.)
ADDIS, W. E. In: Dublin Rev. 3 ser. XII. (1884) 442–
50. [Review of Bryennios, Wünsche, Harnack, Hitch-
cock and Brown, Farrar, Hilgenfeld, Bickell, and Words-
worth.]
Allgemeine Zeitg. (*Munich*) Jan. 25, 1884. [First no-
tice of Br. ed. in Germany.]
ARNOLD, C. F. Die neu entdeckte, Lehre der zwölf
Apostel. In: Ztscher. f. Kirchrecht. XX. (1885) 407–
438.
— Die Didache u. die apostolischen Väter. In: Ztschr.
f. Kirchrecht. XX. (1885) 439–454.
B., J. E. In: Teologisk Tidskrift. XXVII. (1887) 58–9.
[Rev. of Harnack.]
BACKHOUSE, E. Early church history to the death of
Constantine. Edited and enlarged by Ch. Tylor. 2d
edit., with an appendix containing "The Teaching of
the Twelve Apostles." *London*, 1885. 8°. (610 p.)·
BALTZER, E. Die wiedergefundene Zwölfapostellehre.
Mit Bemerkgn. *Rudolstadt*, 1886. 8°. (14 p.)
BAPHEIDES, PHIL. In: Ἐκκλησιαστικὴ Ἀλήθεια Con-
stant. (Jan. 17 [29], 1884.)
— Ἐκκλ. ἱστ. I. (1884) 166–7.
BEHM, H. In: Ztschr. Kirchl. Wiss. u. Leben. (1886)
575–8. [Didache IX. 2.]
BERGGREN, J. E. Om den nyligen återfunna skriften.
'De tolf aposttarnes lära.' In: Teologisk Tidsskrift.
XXIV. (*Upsala*, 1884.) 200–6.
BESTMANN, H. J. Gesch. d. Chr. Sitte. II. *Nördlingen.*
(1885) 136–53.
Beweis des Glaubens. (July, 1884.) [Rev. of Harnack.]
BICKELL, G. Die neuentd. "Lehre d. Ap." u. d. Litur-
gie. In: Ztschr. f. Kath. Theol. VIII. (*Innsbr.* 1884)
400–12.
— Liturgie. In: Kraus. Real-Encycl. d. christl. Alterth.
Freib. i. B. 1885. p. 310–.
BIELENSTEIN, A. Warum enthalt d. Διδαχή nichts Lehr-
haftes? *Riga*, 1885. [Repr. from: Mittheil. u. Nachr. f.
d. evang. Kirche i. Russland. (1885, Feb. Mar., p. 131–7.)]
BINNIE, W. In: Brit. & For. R. XXXIV. (1885, Oct.)
640–60.
BIRKS, E. B. Letter. In: Guardian. (1884, July 2.)
— Note on l. 234–. In: The Guardian. (1884, June 11.)
BOASE. In: Academy. (1884, Apr. 19.) [?]
BONET–MAURY, GASTON. La doctrine des douze apôtres.
In: Critique philos. and Crit. religieuse; repr. *Par.*
1884. (36 p.)
BONHÖFFER. Die religiöse Anschauung d. Did. In:
Theol. Stud. aus Württ. VIII. (1887) 151–78.
BONWETSCH, G. N. Prophetie im apost. u. nachap.
Ztalter. In: Zeitschr. f. kirchl. Wiss. u. Leben. (1884)
408–24, 460–477.
BORNEMANN, W. In: Theol. Lit.-Ztng. X. (1885) 413.
BRATKE. In: Jahrb. f. Prot. Theol. (*Lpz.* 1886) 302–11.
BRIGHT, W. Letter against Birks. In: The Guardian.
(1884, June 18.)

BRYENNIOS, PH. (Βρυέννιος, Φ.) [A letter.] In: An-
dover Rev. (1884, June.) 662–3.
— Περὶ τῆς Διδαχῆς τῶν δώδεκα ἀποστόλων. In:΄ Ἐκκλη-
σιαστικὴ Ἀλήθεια. (1884, 10 [22] νοεμ.) 51^b–57^b.
— S. u. editions.
CASPARI, C. P. Den aeldeste Kircheordning. In: Lu-
thersk Ugeskrift. (*Lördag*, 1884.) Ju. 14 and 21.
CASSEL, PAUL. "Notice in 'Sunem.' No. 25. 1884."
Schaff.
CHASE, F. H. Note on the Teaching of the Twelve
Apostles. Ch. XI. In: The Expositor. (1886, April.)
319–320.
CHIAPPELLI, A. Letteratura christiana. Di una recente
scoperta: 'La dottrina de' dodici apostoli.' In: Nouva
Antologia. (1885) p. 209–225.
Church Q. (*Lond.* 1884, Apr.) 213–7.
CHURTON, W. R. Letter. In: The Guardian. (1884,
July 2.)
CRAVEN, E. R. In: Journ. of Chr. Philos.: repr. *N. Y.*
Apr. 1884. Cf. Paine, J. A.
CURRY, D. In: Meth. R. XXXVI. (1884) 697–715.
DELITZSCH, FRZ. Die Bibel u. d. Wein. *Leipz.* 1885;
also in: Expos. (1886) 68–9.
DE ROMESTIN, H. Letter against Birks. In: The Guar-
dian. (1884, June 18.)
— Teaching of the 12 Apostles. *Oxf.* and *Lond.* 1884.
12°. (118 p.)
DOWDEN, J. In: Scottish Church Rev. (1884, June.)
DRUMMOND, R. B. In: Academy. (Jan. 31, 1885.) [Rev.
of Spence.]
DUCHESNE, LOUIS. In: Bulletin Critique. (*Par.* 1884.)
Nos. 5, 17, 19.
Early Christian ministry and the Didaché, The. In:
Church Q. Rev. XXIV. (1887) 115–143.
FARRAR, F. W. In: Expositor. (1884, May.) 374–92;
(Aug.) 81–91.
— In: Contemp. Rev. (May, 1884.) 698–706. [T rans
with notes.]
FIELD, T. Letter. In: The Guardian. (1884, July 2.)
FITZGERALD, J. Teaching of the Twelve Apostles. *New
York*, 1884. (Apr. 2.)
Foreign Church Chronicle and Rev. (1884, June 2) 92–
8, 112–6. [Transl. and notice.]
FRIEDBERG, E. D. älteste Ordnung d. chr. Kirche. In:
Ztschr. f. Kirchenrecht. XIX. (1884)) 408–25. [In-
troduction, text and translation.]
FUNK. In: Theol. Quartalschr. LXVI. (1884) 381–402.
[Transl. w. brief introduction and notes.]
— Z. Literatur üb. d. Doctrina apostolorum. In: Lit.
Rundschau. (1884, Oct.) 577–582.
— In: Theol. Quartalschr. LXVII. (1885) 159–67. [Rev.
of Hilgenfeld, Wünsche, Gebhardt, and Harnack.]
GARDINER, FR., and CAMP, C. C. The recently discov-
ered Apostolic ms. In: Churchman. (*N. Y.* 1884,
March 29); also, *N. Y.* 1884. (26 p.) [Transl.]
GEBHARDT, O. v., u. HARNACK, ADOLF. Texte und
Untersuch. z. Gesch. d. altchr. Lit. II. 2. Lehre d.
zwölf Apostel, nebst Untersuchungen zur ält. Gesch. d.
Kirchenverfass. u. d. Kirchenvechts von A. H. II.
Halfte, nebst Anhung: Ein überschenes Fragment d.
Διδαχή in alter lat. Uebersetzung, mitgetheilt von O.
v. G. *Leipzig*, 1884. (p. 101–294.)
GEBHARDT, O. v. Letter. In: Schaff. Oldest Church
Manual. (1886) 298–9.
GOOSZEN, M. A. In: Geloof en Vrijheid. (1885) 99–108.
GORDON, A. Teaching of the 12 Apostles. In: Modern
Rev. (1884, July) 446–80; (Oct.) 763–769.
GROSVENOR, E. A. In: Independent. XXXVI. (1884,
Oct. 16.) 1314. [Conversation with Bryennios.]
— An interview with Bryennios. In: Andover R. II.
(1884, Nov.) 515–6.
— In: Century. (1885) 167–71.
HALL, E. E. Teaching of the 12 Apostles. In: New
Eng. VII. (1884, July) 544–60.

HALL, I. H., and NAPIER, J. T. In: Sunday School Times. (*Phila.* 1884, Apr. 5 and 12.)
— Phraseology of —. In: Jour. of Chr. Philos.; also repr. *N.Y.* 1884, Apr. Cf. Paine, J. A.
— In: Independent. (Apr. 16, 1885.) [Rev. of Hitchcock and B., and Spence.]
HARNACK. In: Theol. Ltzng. IX. (1884) 44 [Mention of Bryennios ed.], 49–55 [Notice of B., transl. of Ch. 7-16], 342–3. [Rev. of Hilgenfeld.]
— In: Gebhardt u. H. Texte u. Untersuch. II. 1. *Leipz.* 1884. 8°. [Cf. Gebhardt u. H.]
— In: N. Y. Independent. (Feb. 19, 1885.) [Baptismal question]; repr. in Schaff. (1886) 50–1.
— Apostellehre u. d. jüd. beiden Wege. *Leipzig.* (1886). [Enlarged reprint, with text, from Herzog. Real.-Enc.]
— In: Theol. Ltztg. XII. (1887) 32–4.
HARRIS, J. RENDEL. Genuineness, priority, source, and value. In: Jour. of Chr. Philos.; repr. *N.Y.* 1884. Cf. Paine, R. A.
— The Teaching and the Sibylline Books. *Cambr.* 1885. (36 p.)
— Photographs of three pages of the Bryennois ms. *Balt.* 1885.
HASE. Kirchenges. (1885-) I. 212–3, 278–9.
HAYMAN, H. Further remarks . . . In: Dublin Rev. 3 ser. XIII. (1885) 91–106.
HELVEG, F. Fra Kirchens Oldtid. In: Dansk. Kirketidende (1884) Nos. 24 and 25.
H[ICKS], E[DWARD] L[EE]. In: Guardian. (1884, June 25; postscript do. July 9.) [Teaching and Barnabas.]
HILGENFELD, A. In: Ztschr. f. wiss. Theol. XXVII. (1884) 366–71. [Rev. of Krawutzcky's " Zwei wege " and Bryennios.]
— In: N. T. extra Canon Rec. (1884). Cf. Eds.
— In: Ztschr. f. wiss. Theol. XXVIII. (1885) 73–102.
HITCHCOCK, R. D., and BROWN, FR. Teaching of the Twelve Apostles. Ed. Tr., Introd. and Notes. *New York*, Scribners, 1884. 8°; revised and enlarged. 1885. 8°.
HOBSON, W. F. Letter against Birks. In: The Guardian. (1884, June 18.)
HOLTZMANN, H. Die älteste Kirchenordnung. In: Prot. Kirchztg. XXXIII. (1884) 697–708.
— In: Deutsche Lit.-Ztng. (*Berlin*, 1884, Oct. 4.) 1452. [Rev. of Harnack.]
— Die Didache u. ihre Nebenfumen. In: Jahrb. f. prot. Theol. (1885) 154–66.
— Einl. in d. N. T. (1886) 113–4.
HOWARD, G. B. Query. In: The Guardian. (1884, July 9.)
HOWSON, J. S. Letter against Birks. In: The Guardian. 1884, June 18.)
Indian Evangelical Rev. (*Calcutta*) Jan. 1885. [Trans. Hitchcock & B. and Notes.]
JESSUP, H. H. In: N. Y. Independent. (1886, Feb. 18.) [Baptism.]
KRAWUTZCKY. Ueber d. altkirchl. Unterrichtsbuch " Die zwei Wege u. s. w." In: Theol. Quartalschr. LXIV. (1882) 359–445. [The " Two ways."]
— Ueb. d. sog. Zwölfap.-lehre. In: Theol. Quartalschr. LXVI. (1884) 547–606. [Year 200. Heretical patchwork from Barnabas, Hermas, The two ways, and an Ebionitic ' Kirchenordnung.']
— (Extract from letter of.) In: Schaff. Oldest Church Manual. (1886) 300–1.
KURTZ. Kirchenges. (1885-) I. 109–10.
LANGER, J. D. älteste chr. Kirchenbuch. In: Hist. Ztschr. LIII. (1885) 193–214.
LECHLER. Ap. v. Nachap. Z.-A. (1885) 553–9, 574–, 586–92, etc.; Eng. tr. (1886) 293–7, 307–, 332–40, etc.
LIGHTFOOT, J. B. Results of recent research. In: Official Report of Carlisle Church Congress, 1884. 230–2; also, revised, in: Expos. (1885) 1–11.

— Apost. fathers. II. 1. (1885) 739; also in Schaff. Teaching of the 12. (1886) 301–3.
LINCOLN, H. In: Bibliotheca Sacra. (1884, July.) 590–4.
LIPSIUS. (Ψ) In: Deutsche Lit.-Ztg. V. (1884, Oct. 4.) 1449–51. [Rev. of Bryennios.]
— In: Lit. Centralbl. (1885, Jan. 24.) 138–9. [Rev. of Harnack.]
— In: Lit. Centralbl. (1885, Feb. 14) 233–4.
LONG, J. C. In: Bapt. R. VI. (1884) 369–90. [Sources.]
M'GIFFERT, A. C. The 'Didache' viewed in its relations to other writings. In: Andover Rev. (1886, April.) 430–442.
MAJOCCHI, R. La dottrina dei dodici Apostoli; . . . testo originale conversione e commento. *Milano*, 1885. 8°. (83 p.) [" Estr. dal periodico milanese La Scuola cattolica. Anno XIII. vol. XXV. quad. 145–149"]; Ed. seconda, corvetta ed ampliata. *Modena*, 1887. 8°. (288 p.)
MANEN, W. C. VAN. In: Bejblad van de Heroorming. (1884) No. 6.
MASSEBIEAU, L. In: Rev. d. l'Hist. d. Religions. X. (1884, Sept., Oct.) 129–60; repr. *Par.* 1884. 8°. (36 p.)
— In: Rev. d. Hist. d. Religions. XI. (1885) 333–5. [Rev. of Ménégoz.]
— Communications sur la Did. In: Le Témoignage. (1885, Feb. 7.)
MATHIEAU, S. Les origenes de l'episcopat. In: Rev. de Théol. (*Montauban*, 1884, July–Sept.)
MÉNÉGOZ, E. Une découverte importante. In: Le Témoinage. *Par.* 1884, 23 février.
— Les origenes de l'episcopat. In: Do. 1 mars.
— Les parasites dans l'église primitive. In: Do. 8 Mars.
— Le chemin de la vie. In: Do. 15 mars.
— Les choses finales. In: Do. 29 mars.
— L'agape. In: Do. 5 jouillet.
— Une nouvelle étude sur la Didache. In: Le Témoignage. *Par.* 1885, 3 janvier.
— Le caractère de la Did. In: Do. 28 mars. p. 99–101.
— La doctrine relig. de la Did. In: Do. 4 avril. p. 107–8.
— La Did. et l'interpretation du N. T. In: Do. 11 avril. p. 115–6.
— La date de la Did. In: Do. 18 avril. p. 122–3.
— Les indices de la haute antiquité de la Did. In: Do. 25 avril. p. 131–3.
MEYBOOM, H. U. De leer der Twaalf Ap. In: Theologisch Tijdschrift. XIX. (1885, Sept.) 529–51 (Nov.) 596–632.
MÜNCHEN, K. In: Ztschr. f. Kath. Theol. X. (1886) 629–76. [Early original work, although making use of written sources.]
MURALT, E. DE. In: Rev. de théol. et de philos. (1884, May.) 278–91.
Nieuwe Rotterdammer Courant. (1884, Feb. 19.) [First men. in Holland.]
NIRSCHL, J. In: Lit. Handweiser. (*Mainz*, 1884.) No. 13. [Rev. of Br.]
OLSSEN, W. W. In: Am. Ch. Rev. XLVII. (1886) 168–78. [Rev. of Hitchcock and B.]
ORRIS, S. STANHOPE. Text and transl. In: Jour. of Chr. Philos.; repr. *N.Y.* 1884. Cf. Paine, J. A.
PAINE, J. A. Ed. and Publ. Teaching of the Twelve Apostles; repr. from The Jour. of Chr. Philos. *New York*, 1884, Apr. (84 p.) Cf. ORRIS, S. S., HARRIS, J. P., HALL, I. H., and CRAVEN, E. R.
PETERSEN. Die Lehre d. zwölf Apostel. *Flensb.* (*Lpz. Drescher.*) 1884. 8°. (15 p.)
PHORÓPOULOS, I. (Φορόπουλος, 'I.) Ὁι εν Ἀγγλία καὶ Ἀμερικῇ θεολόγοι περὶ τῆς Διδαχῆς τῶν Ιβ' ἀποστόλων.) In: Ἐκκλησιαστικὴ Ἀλήθεια (1884. I. [13] ιουν. p. 500 a–502 a.
PLUMMER, A. In: Churchman. (*London*, 1884, July.) 274–5. [The Teaching and St. John.]

POTWIN, L. S.   Vocabulary of the Teaching.   In: Bibliotheca Sacra. (1884, Oct.) 800–17.
— Philo and the D.   In: Bib. Sac. XLIII. (1886) 174–6.
POTWIN, TH. ST.   In: The Independent. (Ja. 21, 1886.) [Allusion in Origen.]
— The last chapter of 'The Teaching of the Twelve Apostles,' illustrated from passages in the Early Christian Fathers. In: The Andover Rev. (1886, Apr.) 443–444.
POULSEN, A. S.   Et igenfundet Skrift fra Kirkens äldste Tider. In: Theologisk Tidsskrift. (*Kjøbenhavn*, 1884.) 576–89.
— In: Theologisk Tidsskrift. (*Kjøbenh.* 1884.) 130–31. [Reply to Rørdam, do. 127–30.]
PRIUS, J. J.   Διδαχὴ τῶν δώδεκα ἀποστόλων in usum studiosae juventutie repetiit J. J. P. *Lugd. Bat.* 1884. 8°. (16 p.)
RÉVILLE, J.   Une importante découverte.   In: La Renaissance. (1884, Feb. 29.)
RIDDLE, M. B.   Introd. note. Ed. Coxe. VII. (1886) 369–76, 382–3.
ROBERTSON, A.   In: Durham Univ. Journ. (Feb. 1884.) [First notice in England.]
RØRDAM, TH.   Den apostoliske Troesbekjendelse og se tolv Apostels Läre. In: Theologisk Tidsskrift. (*Kjøbenhavn*, 1884.) 127–30.
RÖVERS, M. A. N.   In his: Biblioth. van. Mod. Theol. V. 310–.
SABATIER, P.   In: Église Libre. (1884) nos. 11–18.
— La Didachè ou l'enseignement des douze apôtres. *Paris*, 1885. 8°. (165 p.)
SADLER.   In: Guardian. (June 4, 1884.)
SCHAFF, P.   Philotheos Bryennios. In: Independent. (Apr. 16, 1885.)
— Philotheos Bryennios. In: Harper's Weekly. (Apr. 25, 1885.)
— The idiom and vocabulary of the Teaching of the Twelve Apostles. In: Journal of the Soc. of Bibl. Lit. and Exegesis. (1885, June and Dec.) p. 3–7.
— The Oldest Church Manual. *N. Y.* 1885, May; 2d ed. revised and enlarged. *New York*, 1886. 8°. [Ed. Transl. Full notes, treatises and literature. For best reviews cf. 2d ed. p. 306.]
— Hist. . . Church. II. (1886)184–5.
SCHERER, R. v.   Ist die fog. Lehre der zwölf Apostel, echt? In: Archiv. f. kath. Kirchrecht. (1885) 4. p. 3–9.
SMEND.   Randbemerkungen zu der neuentdeckten, Lehre der zwölf Apostel. In: Ev. Gemeindeblt. f. Rheinland u. Vestfalen. (1885) 4, Sp. 35–37; 5, Sp. 47–50.
SMYTH, E. C.   Baptism in the Teaching and in early Christian Art. In: Andover Rev. (1884, May) 533–47.
SPDNCE.   The Teaching of the Twelve Apostles. Transl. w. Notes, Excursus and Gr. text. *Lond.* 1885. 8°. (183 p.)
SPITTA, F.   D. Abendsmahlsgebete aus —. In: Ztschr. f. prakt. Theol. VIII. (1886) 313–29.
STARBUCK, C. C., and SMYTH, E. C.   Teaching of the Twelve Apostles. Trans., etc. In: Andover Rev. (1884, Apr.)
STOKES, G. T.   In: Contemp. R. (1884, Apr., Aug.) (1885, Jan.)
TAYLOR, C.   Teaching, with illustrations from the Talmud. 2 lectures, 1885. *Lond.* 1886. 8°. (140 p.)
— The Didaché and Barnabas. In: The Expositor. (1886, April) p. 316–317 (June) 401–28.
VARMING, C. (W.?)   De tolv apostles laerdom, u. oversat. *Kjøbenhavn*, 1884. (35 p.)
V[ENABLES], E.   Teachings of the Apostles. In: British Q. Rev. LXXXI. (1885, Apr.) 333–70.
VOLKMAR, G.   Urchristl. Andachtsbuch. *Leipz.* and *Zürich*, 1885. (47 p.)

WARFIELD, B. B.   Some recent apocryphal gospels. In: Southern Presb. Rev. (1884, Oct.) 711–759.
— In: Andover Rev. (1885, Dec.) 593–9.
— In: Presb. Rev. (1886, Jan.) 173–6. [Rev. of Schaff.]
— The Didache and its kindred forms. And. R. (1886) 81–97.
— Text, sources, and contents of "The two ways," or first section of the Didache. In: Bib. Sac. XLIII. (Oberlin, 1886) 100–61.
— Textual criticism of the Two Ways. In: The Expositor. (1886, Feb.) 156–160.
— In: N.Y. Independent. (1886, Mar. 4.)
Westminster Review. (1885, Jan.) 206–9.
WORDSWORTH, J.   Christian Life, Ritual and Discipline at the close of the First Century. In: Guardian. (1884, Mar. 19, Suppl.); a correction. (Mar. 26); a letter (July 2).
WÜNSCHE, A.   Lehre d. zwölf Apost. *Leipz.* 1884. 8°. [Transl. text, etc.]
ZAHN, T.   In: Theol. Lit.-bl. V. (1884, June 27, July 11) 201–4, 217–20.
— Forsch. zr. Gesch. des NTlichen Kanons u. s. w. *Erlang.* 1884. III. 278–319.
— In: Theol. Lit.-blatt. (1885, Apr. 3) 123–. [Rev. of Bielenstein.]
ZÖCKLER, O.   In: Evang. Kirchenztng. (1884, May 3, Aug. 16.) 377–82, 705–8. Cf. (1885) 21–3.
۴. Cf. Lipsius.
For various short articles compare Hitchcock and B. 2d ed. App. p. 74–5.

Note 1. For discussion of the literature up to March, 1886, compare in Schaff's *Oldest Church Manual*—one of the best bibliographico-literary monographs in the patristic field.

Note 2. Compare all the modern literature relating to the Two ways, to Barnabas, Hermas, Apostolical Constitutions, etc.

VII. CONSTITUTIONS OF THE HOLY APOSTLES.

I. *Editions.*

TURRIANUS, FR.   *Venet.* 1563. 4°.
DUCAEUS, FRONTO. Gr. lat. (Turrianus.) *Paris*, 1618. f°.? In: Zonara, Jo. Canones Apost. et conc.
LABBE.   In his: Concilia. T. I. (*Par.* 1672. f°.)
COTELERIUS.   Gr. lat. In his: Patr. apost. 1672. 1698. f°; *Amst.* 1724. 8°.
GRABE. (Fragm.) Gr. lat. Spicil. patr. (1700) I. 40–55.
WHISTON, WM.   Gr. Eng. In his: Primitive Christianity. *Lond.* 1711. 8°. II. III.
RUSSEL, RICH.   Gr. lat. In his: Patres Apost. *Lond.* 1746. 2 v. 8°. (??)
MANSI.   In his: Concil. col. *Florent.* 1759. f°. I.
GALLAND.   Gr. lat. In his: Bibl. patr. *Venet.* f°. III. (1788) 1–248, 249–72.
LAGARDE.   In: Bunsen. Hippolytus. *Lond.* 1852; *Lpz.* 1852; Analect. Antenic. (1854) II. 33–448.
ÜLTZEN, CAND. GUIL. Gr. *Suerin.* 1853. 8°.
MIGNE. Gr. lat. In: Patrol. gr. I. (1857) 555–1156.
LAGARDE. Gr. *Lipsiae*, 1862. 8°.
PITRA. Gr. In: Jur. eccl. Gr. hist. et mon. I. (*Rom.* 1864.)

II. *Translations.*

Coptic.

TATTAM.   Copt. Eng. *Lond.* 1848; also tr. by Lagarde in Bunsen.

Ethiopic.

PLATT, TH. P.   Ethiop. Engl. *Lond.* 1834.

Syriac.

LAGARDE. Didascalia apost. Syr. *Lips.* 1854. 8⁰.

Latin.

CAPELLIUS, C. *Ingolst.* 1546. f⁰; also in: Crabbe, Pt. Concilia ann. ed. II. *Colon.* 1551. f⁰. p. 27.
BOVIUS, J. C. *Paris*, 1564. 8⁰.
SURIUS, LAUR. In: Concilia ann. *Col. Agr.* f⁰. I. (1567) 33–; *Venet.* f⁰. I. (1585) 26–.
TURIANUS, FR. *Antv. Plantin*, 1578. f⁰.
BINIUS. In: Concilia. *Colon.* f⁰. I. (1606); I. (1618. f⁰.) *Par.* 1626. f⁰.

English.

DONALDSON, J. In: Ante-Nic. Lib. XVII. (1870) II. 5–269. Ed. Coxe. VII. (1886) 391–505.

French.

MAISTRE. In: St. Clément. II. (*Paris*, 1884. 8⁰.) 185–504.

German.

BOXLER, F. *Kempten*, 1873. 16⁰. [The Reithmayer-Thalhofer Bibl.]

III. *Literature.*

ALLIX, P. Remarks upon some Places of Mr. Whiston's Books, either printed or Manuscript. *Lond.* 1711. 8⁰.
BAUMGARTEN–CRUSIUS. Dogmenges. (1832) 89. [v. 1.]
BAUR. In: "Tüb. Zeitschr. (1838) 131.
— Dogmengesch. I. (1865) 250.
ΒΑΦΕΙΔΗΣ. 'Εκκλ. ἱστ. I. (1884) 166.
BEVERIDGE, W. The opinion of W. Beveridge concerning the Apostolical Constitutions. 1712. 8⁰.
— Cod. can. Ch. 2. c. IX. See below.
BICKELL. Gesch. des Kirchenrecht's. (*Giessen*, 1543.) 62, etc.
BOETTICHER. = Lagarde, P. de.
BRUCKNER, J. In: Stud. u. Krit. LVI. (1883) 7–32. [" Liturgie im achten Buche."]
BRUNO. Judicium. In Cotel. Patr. Ap. e II. app.
BULL. Def. fid. Nic. 2, c. 3, § 6.
BUNSEN. In: Hippol. u. seine Zeit. (*Leipz.* 1852) I. 418–525; II. 1–26, and in: 2d Engl. ed. Hippol. and his age, or Christianity and mankind. (*Lond.* 1854) V–VII.
— Extracts and Outlines. Hippolytus. (1854) II. 3–92, 395–424.
CHAPIN, A. B. Chase's Apostolic Constitutions. In: Am. Church R. I. (1849) 536–.
CHARTERIS. Canonicity. (1880) 25–6, 205.
CHASE. Constitutions of the Holy Apostles, including the Canons; Whiston's version revised from the Greek; with a prize essay (of Krabbe) upon their origin and contents. *New York*, 1848.
Christian Remembrancer. XXVII. (1854) 253–.
Christian Rev. XIII. (1848) 201–.
COTELERIUS. Patr. ap. *Amst.* 1724. f⁰. I.; also in: Migne. Patrol. gr. I. (1857) 509–20.
COTTA, D. J. F. De constitutionibus apostolicis. *Tub.* 1746. 4⁰.
CREDNER, Z. Gesch. d. Kanons. 220–.
CUNNINGHAM. Churches of Asia. (1880) pass.
DALLAEUS. De pseudepigr. Apost. *Harderv.* 1653.
DONALDSON, J. Introd. note. In: Ante-Nic. Lib. XVII. (1870) II 1–4. Ed. Coxe. VII. (1886) 385–90. [Add. notes. Ed. Coxe. 506-8.]
v. DREY. Ueb. d. Const. In: Theol. Quartalschrift. (1829.)
— Neue Untersuchungen über die Constitutionen u. Kanones der Apostel. Ein histor.-krit. Beitrag zur Litteratur d. Kirchengeschichte u. d. Kirchenrechts. *Tübing.* 1832. 8⁰.

v. DREY. In: Wetzer u. W. Kirch-Lex. (1847–54) II. 855–9.
EDWARDS, J. Some Observations upon the Apostolical Constitutions. In his: Some brief Observations and Reflections on Mr. Whiston's late Writings, falsely entitul'd Primitive Christianity reviv'd. *Lond.* 1712. 8⁰.
EPIPHANIUS. Haer. 70, no. 10, 11, 12; 75, no. 6; 80, no. 7.
FORSYTH, J. In: Princ. XXI. (1849) 42–.
Forty-sixth chapter of the Apostolic Constitutions. In: Am. Church R. XXIV. (1872) 489–.
FUNK. D. Interpolator d. Ign. Br. v. d.. Interpolation d. ap. C. In: Theol. Quartalschr. LXII. (1880) 378–83.
GIESELER. Church Hist. (1868–) I. 233–4, 542.
GRABE, J. E. An Essay upon Two Arabick Manuscripts of the Bodleian Library, and that Ancient Book call'd " The Doctrine of the Apostles," which is said to be extant in them: Wherein Mr. Whiston's Mistakes about both are plainly proved. *Oxford*, 1711. 8⁰. *Lond.* 1712. 8⁰. Cf. Memoirs of Literature. Vol. 1. p. 317–319.
HANEBERG. Canones St. Hippolyti arabic. *München.* 1870.
HARNACK. Quellen d. sogen. ap. Kirchenordnung. *Lpz.* 1886. 8⁰. (106 p.) = Gebhardt u. H. Texte u. Untersuchungen. II. III.
HASE. Kirchenges. (1885–) I. 416.
HEFELE, R. C. Conciliengesch. I. 792–. (2d ed. 1873.)
HILGENFELD. Ketzergesch. (1884) 44–5.
— Nov. Test. extra Canon rec. *Lips.* 1866. IV.
HUG. In: (ält) Freib. Ztschr. V. V. 153.
ITTIG. Hist. eccl. (1709) I. 50–4.
JACKSON. Ap. fath. (1879) 65–6.
JACOBSON. In: Herzog Real-Enc.
JEWELL. Works. I. (1848) 169.
JORTIN, JOHN. The Apostolical Constitutions and Canons considered; the Recognitions of Clemens a wretched romance. A passage in them explained. In his: Remarks on Ecclesiastical History. (*Lond.* 1751. 8⁰.) I. p. 228–283, 338–342.
— Some remarks upon the Apostolical Constitutions. In his: Discourses on the Christian Religion. Discourse VI.
KRABBE. Ueber den Ursprung u. den Inhalt der apost. Constitutionen des Clemens Romanus. *Hamb.* 1829.
LAGARDE. De indole et origine canonum et constitutionum apostolorum. In: Bunsen. (? ?)
— In: Rel. juris eccl. antiq. 1856.
LAMSON, A. In: Chr. Exam. XLIV. (1847) 223–.
LARDNER. The History of the Apostolical Constitutions and Canons. In his: Credibility. VIII. (*Lond.* 1750. 8⁰.) p. 319–407.
LIGHTFOOT. Epist. to Philippians. (*Lond.* 1868) 201–2.
LINDSAY, T. M. In: Encycl. Brit. (9th ed.) II. 195.
LUMPER. Hist. ss. patr. VII. (1790) 297–399.
M'CLINTOCK and S. Cycl. (1874–) II. 383.
[MAGISTRIS, DE.] Acta mart. ad Ostia. *Rom.* 1795. f⁰. 134–; also in: Migne. Patrol. gr. I. (1857) 523–42.
MANSI. Concil. Flor. 1759. f⁰. I. 254–; also in: Migne. Patrol. gr. I. (1857) 521–4.
MARTIN, EDW. The Authority of the Apostolical Constitutions and Canons. In his: Five Letters. (*Lond.* 1662. 8⁰.) Letter 3.
NEANDER. Church Hist. (1872) I. 660.
NEWMAN, J. H. Hist. sketches. I. *Lond.* 1878. 8⁰. 417–42.
NIRSCHL. Patrol. (1881–) I. 73.
NITZSCH. Dogmengesch. I. (1870) 99.
Object of Forging the Apostolic Constitutions. In: Chr. R. XV. (1850) 505–.

OCKLEY, SIMON. An account of the Authority of the Arabick Manuscript, in the Bodleian Library, controverted between Dr. Grabe and Mr. Whiston. In a Letter to Mr. Thirlby. *Lond.* 1712. 8⁰.

PAGAS. Brev. gust. pont. Rom. Vita Clem. § v–. Also in: Migne. Patrol. gr. I. (1857) 519–22.

PEARSON. Vind. Ignat. In: Cotel. Patr. Ap. II. p. 251.

PEZOLD, C. F. De Clements ejusque constitutionibus apostolicis. Dissert. II. *Lips.* 1698. 4⁰.

PRESSENSÉ. Chr. life. (1878) 190–1, 224–5.

REUSS. Gesch. N. T. (1874) I. 285–7, II. 34; tr. Eng. (1884) 283–5 [v. 1], 316 [v. 2].

RITSCHL. Altkath. Kirche. p. 598.

ROESSLER. Bibl. d. K.–V. IV. (1777) 229–257.

ROSENMÜLLER. Hist. interp. I. (1795) 117–47.

ROTHE. Anfänge d. Chr. Kirche. (*Wittenb.* 1837) I. 541.

SCHAFF. Creeds of Christendom. II. (1877) 39–40.
— Hist. . . Church. II. (1886) 185–6.

SCHROEKH. Kirchenges. II. 127.

SCHWEGLER. Nachap. Zeitalt. (1846) I. 406–13.

SHAW, BENJ. In: Smith and Cheetham. Dict. I. (*Bost.* 1875) 119–126.

SMALBROKE, RICH. The pretended Authority of the Clementine Constitutions confuted, by their Inconsistency with the inspired Writings of the Old and New Testament. In Answer to Mr. Whiston. *Lond.* 171.4 8⁰. Cf. Memoirs of Literature. IV. p. 155–158.

TISCHENDORF. Var. Cet. In: Migne Patrol. gr. II. (1857) 1277–80.

TURNER, ROB. A discourse of the pretended Apostolical Constitutions, wherein all the principal evidence, both external and internal, brought by Mr. Whiston in his essay on those books, to prove them genuine, is examined and confuted. *Lond.* 1715. 8⁰.

TURRIANUS, F. Proem, in libr. Clementis Rom. de Const. Apost. *Antv.* 1578.

UELTZEN, C. H. W. Const. Apost. *Suerini*, 1853.
— Zur Einl. in d. —. In: Ztschr. f. luth. Theol. XV. (1854) 674–85.

USSERIUS, JAC. Dissert. de — in his ed. of Polycarp and Ignatius. *Oxon.* 1644 and 1647.
— Diss. de Ign. ep. In: Cotelerius. Pat. Ap. II. (1724) 251.

Veterum testimonia. In: Migne. Patrol. gr. I. (1857) 543–54.

WERNSDORF, GLI. Adversus Whistonem. *Wittenb.* 1739. 4⁰.

WHISTON, W. A Demonstration, that the Apostolical Constitutions were written in the first Century. In his: Essay towards restoring the true Text of the Old Testament. (*Lond.* 1722. 8⁰.) p. cxvi–cxxxviii.
— An essay on the Apostolical Constitutions. In his: Primitive Christianity. *Lond.* 1711. 8⁰.
— Remarks on Dr. Grabe's Essay upon Two Arabick Manuscripts of the Bodleian Library, etc. *Lond.* 1711. 8⁰.
— A reply to Dr. Allix's Remarks on some places of Mr. Whiston's Books, either printed or Manuscript. With an Appendix containing, I. The Preface to the Doctrine of the Apostles. II. Propositions, containing the Primitive Faith of Christians, about the Trinity and Incarnation. III. A letter to the most Reverend Thoma, etc. *Lond.* 1711. 8⁰.
— St. Clement's and St. Irenaeus's Vindication of the Apostolical Constitutions from Several Objections made against them. As also an account of the two ancient rules thereunto belonging for the celebration of Easter. With a Postscript on Occasion of Mr. Turner's Discourse of the Apostolical Constitutions. *Lond.* 1715. 8⁰; repr. *Lond.* 1716. 8⁰.

CANONS.

I. *Editions.*

MERLIN. (Lat. only.) In: Concil. *Par.* 1523. f⁰; *Colon.* 1530; *Par.* 1536. 8⁰.

HALOANDRUS, GREG. Gr. lat. *Norimb.* 1531. f⁰.

CRABBE. Gr. lat. In: Concilia omnia. *Colon.* 1538. f⁰ I. p. V., etc. See above.

GRUTER, LAMB. Gr. lat. In: Opera. *Col. Nygr.* 1570. f⁰.

EBERIGERUS. Gr. lat. *Wittenb.* 1614. 4⁰.

Gr. lat. *Par.* 1620. f⁰.

BEVERIGIUS, GUIL. Gr. lat. In his: Synoodicm. I. (*Ox.* 1672. f⁰) 1–57.

HARDUINUS. Gr. lat. In: Col. concil. I. (*Par.* 1715 f⁰.) 10–.

BERNHOLDUS, J. B. *Altorphis*, 1733. 8⁰.

HARTMANN, J. D. Gr. ger. In his: Beiträge . . *Jen.* 1796. 8⁰. p. 204.

BUNSEN. Analect. Antenic. (1854) II. 1–32.

MacNALLAY, TH. Gr. lat. eng. *Lond.* 1867. 8⁰.

HEFELE. Gr. lat. In: Conciliengesch. I. (1873) 800–827; also in: Tr. Engl. I. (1872) 449.

FULTON, J. D. Gr. Eng. In: Index Canonum. *New York*, 1883. 8⁰. p. 80–109.

Also in most of the editions of the Constitutions, and in various collections of Canons.

II. *Translations.*

Syriac.

LAGARDE. In: Rel. jur. eccl. 1856.

Ethiopic.

FELL, WINAND. *Leipz.* 1871. (??)

SCHODDE, G. H. The Apostolic Canons, translated from the Ethiopic. In: Journ. of bibl. literature and exegesis. (1885, June–Dec.) c. 61–72.

Note. See translations of the Constitutions.

III. *Literature.*

BENZEL, H. *Lund.* 1730.

BEVERIDGE, W. G. (Bishop of St. Asaph, d. 1708.) Συνόδικον, S. Pandectae Canonum S. G. Apostolorum et Conciliorum, ab Ecclesia Gr. recept. *Oxon.* 1672–82. 2 v. f⁰.
— De Canonibus Apostolorum. In: Codex canonum ecclesiae primitivae vindicatus et illustratus. *Lond.* 1678. 4⁰.

BEVEREGIUS. Judicium de Can. Apost. In: Cotel. patr. apost. (1724) I. 432.

BICKELL. Gesch. des Kirchenrechts. p. 138.

BOURIANT, U. Les canons apostoliques de Clément de Rome. Traduction en dialecte copte thebain, d'après un manuscrit de la Bibliothèque du Patriarche Jacobite du Caire. (Suite.) In: Recueil de travaux rel. à la philol. et à l'archeol. égypt et assyr. VI. (1885) p. 97–115.

BUDDEUS. Isag. 659.

Centuriatores Magdeburg. 11. c. 7. 544, etc.

HEBENSTREIT, J. P. De canon. app. *Jena*, 1701.

JANUS, J. G. Disp. de antiquitate canonum apostolicorum. *Witteb.* 1706; reprinted, 1740. 4⁰.

KRABBE. De cod. can. qui apost. dicuntur. *Eitt.* 1829.

LARDNER. Credibility. II. 4. p. 283.

LARROQUANUS, MATT. In: App. obs. ad Pearsonianas Ignatii Vindic. *Rothomag.* 1674.

NELLER, GEO. CHRISTOPH. L. de S. Clemente I. Papa: ad Can. I. VIII. qu. I. *August. Trev.* 1772. 4⁰. (2. ed. *Frf.* 1772. 4⁰.)

Berg, Hyacinthe. Disquisitio critica in George Christophori Neller . . . uti et Pumatum Pontificium S. Clementis I . . . *Col. Aggi.* 1772. 4⁰. (89 p.); Apologia pro puncto historico-chron. . . contra objecta . . Patris Hyacinthe Berg. . . *August. Trev.* 1772. 4⁰.

The discussion was continued in an inaugural dissertation (*August. Trev.* 1773) "proposuit Joannes Henricus Raymundus ab Hentheim," replied to by Berg (1773). Four other tracts (all 1773) were replied to again by Neller (1774). For details and two additional tracts in the controversy see Backer. Bibl. des ecr. de la comp. de Jesu. 3ᵉ ser. (1856) p. 141–142. (??)

PEARSON. Vindic. Ignat. In: Cotelerius. Patr. Apost. II. 251.

REGENBRECHT. Diss. de Can. ap. et cod. ecc. hisp. *Ratisb.* 1828.

SCHAFF. Hist. . . Church. (1882–) II. 186–7.

SPITTLER, LUD. TIM. Ueber d. (85) apostolisch. Canons. In his: Geschichte des Canonisch. Rechts. (*Hal., Gebauer.* 1778. 8⁰.) 65–.

TURRIANUS, FR. Pro Canon. Apost. et Epp. Decret. Pontif. Apost. Adversus. Magd. Centur. Defensio. *Flor.* 1572; *Lutet.* 1573. I.

WHISTON, W. Apostolical Rules for Ecclesiastical Courts: taken out of the Constitutions of the Apostles. With some brief Observations. Humbly recommended to the Consideration of the present Ecclesiastical and Secular Judges; Civil, Canon, and Common Lawyers: of Jurymen, and of all that are any way concern'd in Judicial Proceedings in these kingdoms. *Lond., Robert.* 1729. 8⁰.

Note 1. Add to the above all general treatises on Clement of Rome, to whom these works were formerly ascribed.

Note 2. All the modern discussions regarding the Teaching of the Twelve, The Two Ways, The Apostolical Church Directory, etc., bear on the Constitutions and Canons.

VIII. THE HOMILY ASCRIBED TO CLEMENT.

Generally known as The Second Epistle of Clement.

I. *Editions.*

JUNIUS. *Oxon.* 1633. 4⁰; 1637. 4⁰.
MADER. *Helmst.* 1654. 4⁰.
FELL. *Oxon.* 1677. 12⁰.
LABBE et COSSART. *Par.* 1671. f⁰.
COTELERIUS. *Par.* 1672. f⁰.
COLOMESIUS. *Lond.* 1687. 12⁰; 1694. 12⁰.
CLERICUS–COTELERIUS. *Amst.* 1698. f⁰; 1724. f⁰.
ITTIG. *Lips.* 1699. 8⁰.
WOTTON. *Cantabr.* 1718. 8⁰.
FREY. *Basil.* 1742. 8⁰.
GRABE. (Fragm.) Gr. lat. In: Spicil. patr. (1700) I. 288–9.
RUSSELL. *Lond.* 1746. 8⁰.
GALLANDIUS. *Venet.* 1765. f⁰.
SCHÖNEMANN. *Goetting.* 1796. 8⁰.
HEFELE. *Tüb.* 1834; 1842; 1847; 1855 (p. 134–49.) 8⁰.
JACOBSON. *Oxon.* 1838. (p. 213–242); 1840; 1847; 1853. (p. 228–58.) 8⁰.
REITHMAYR. *Monach.* 1844. 12⁰.
GRENFELL. *Lond.* 1844. 8⁰.
MADDEN. *Lond.* 1856. 4⁰. (?)
DRESSEL. *Lips.* 1856; 1863. 8⁰. (p. 106–17.)
MIGNE. *Paris,* 1857. 4⁰. (p. 329–48.)
HILGENFELD. *Lips.* 1866; 1876. 8⁰.
TISCHENDORF. *Lips.* 1867; 1873. 4⁰.
LIGHTFOOT. *Cantabr.* 1869; 1877. 8⁰.
LAURENT. *Lips.* 1870; 1873. 8⁰.

BRYENNIOS. *Constantinop.* 1875. 8⁰. [On new ms. with missing portions.]

GEBHARDT u. HARNACK. *Lips.* 1876, 8⁰. p. 110–143; 1877. 8⁰.

FUNK. *Tüb.* 1878. 8⁰; 1881. 8⁰.

Note 1. For further details regarding the above editions compare under *Clement of Rome,* to whom it was formerly ascribed, and with the editions of whose epistle the above list nearly coincides.

Note 2. Until the publication of the remaining portions by Bryennios in 1876 only fragments of this work are known.

II. *Translations.*

WAKE. *Lond.* 1693. 8⁰. 124–30, 531–47; *Lond.* 1710. 8⁰ [Greatly improved]; *Lond.* 1719. 8⁰. 85–9, (2) 347–57; 1737. 8⁰; 5th ed. 1818 [7 ?]; *Hartford,* 1834. 8⁰; 263–77; *Lond.* 1842 [3 ?]. 8⁰. [Revised]; *Lond.* 1846. 8⁰; 1860. 8⁰; *Phila.* 1846. 8⁰.

ROBERTS, DONALDSON, and RIDDLE. In: Ante-Nic. Lib. I. (1868) 55–63. Ed. Coxe. VII. (1886) 517–23.

LIGHTFOOT. *Cambr.* 1877. 8⁰. p. 343–90.

French.

MAISTRE. In: St. Clément. II. (*Par.* 1884. 8⁰) 176–184. [Epistle of Clement, tr. do. 130–176.]

Note. In general the translations under Clement of Rome contain the *Homily;* but the English translations of Burton, that of Aberdeen, 1768, and of Chevallier (?), the German of Arnold and Herzog (?), seem to contain only the first epistle.

II. *Literature.*

Apocr. N. T. (1825) 180–6. (Phila. n. d.) 139–144.

CHARTERIS. Canonicity. (1880) xviii–xxiii, 106–8, 171, 216, 223, 233, 238, 243, 256, 274, 303, 313, 336.

COTELERIUS, J. B. Judicium de posteriore epistola S. Clementis. In: Jacobson, P. P. apost. (1838) I. 205–13. (1863) I. 219–27. In: Migne. Patr. gr. I. 69–76.

DIETELMAIER, J. A. See Nerreter.

DORNER. Person of Christ. I. (1864) 101–2, 357–8.

HAGEMANN. Ueber d. II. Brief d. Clem. v. Rom. In: Tüb. Theol. Quartalschr. IV. (1861) 509–531.

HARNACK. Ueber den sog. 2. Brief des Clem. an die Korinth. In: Ztschr. f. Kirch.-Gesch. I. (1876) 2, 3.

HASE. Kirchenges. (1885–) I. 284.

HEFELE. In: Wetzer u. W. Kirch-Lex. (1847–54) II. 585–6.

HILGENFELD. Die 2te Clemensbr. u. s. w. In: Ztschr. f. w. Theol. XIII. (1870) 394–.

HOLTZMANN. Einl. in d. N. T. (1886) 122.

KURTZ. Kirchenges. (1885–) I. 104–5.

LARDNER. Credibility. Works. (1831) II. 55–7.

LECHLER. Ap. v. Nachap. Z.-A. (1885) 599–601. Engl. tr. (1886) II. 348–49.

M'CLINTOCK and S. Cycl. (1874) II. 382.

NERRETER, Cph. Disp. (Praeside J. A. Dietelmaiero) de fragment Clementios Rom., quod sub. nomine epistolae II. ad Corinthios habetus. *Altorfii,* 1749. 4⁰.

NIRSCHL. Patrol. (1881–) I. 71–2.

NORTON. Genuineness of Gosp. I. (1846) ccxliii–ccxliv.

REUSS. Gesch. N. T. (1874) I. 281; tr. Eng. (1884) 279.

ROBERTS and DONALDSON. Introd. note. In: Ante-Nic. Lib. I. (1868) 51–3. Ed. Coxe. VII. (1886) 509–15.

SCHAFF. Hist. . . Church. (1882–) II. 648–9.

SCHRAM. Anal. ss. patr. (1780) I. 72–6.

SCHWEGLER. Nachap. Zeitalt. (1846) I. 448–55.

SKWORZOW. Patrologische Untersuchungen. Ueber Urspr. der problem. Schriften d. apost. VV. (1875).

WESTCOTT. Canon. (1875) 177–183.

ZAHN, TH. Das altest. chr. Gebet. u. d. ältest. chr. Predigt. In: Ztschr. f, Prot. (1876) IV.

ZELLER. Apostelgesch. (1854) 9.
Note. For full literature compare the section on CLEMENT OF ROME.

IX. EARLY LITURGIES.

It is impossible to decide on a method which shall give an exhaustive treatment of the ancient liturgies in the brief time and space and with few books at command. The collection made is omitted, and its place better supplied by the following references: (1.) For general study the Introductory Notice in VII. p. 529–36 of this series. For further study the literature in Schaff. Church Hist. V. 3. pp. 517–8, and the very full list at the end of the article Liturgy, in Smith and Cheetham. Dict. of Christian Antiquities. I. (*Hartford*, 1881.) 1036–8. Note, however, the following suggestion of a practical working apparatus.

ASSEMANI, JOS. ALOYS. Codex liturgicus eccl. univ. *Rom.* 1746–66. 13 v.
BERSIER, E. In: Lichtenberger. Encycl. (1877–82) VIII. 304–10.
* BRETT, TH. A collection of the principal liturgies . . . with a dissertation upon them. *Lond.* 1720; repr. 1838. 8º. [Engl. translations.]
* CHEETHAM. Liturgy. In: Smith and Cheetham. Dictionary of Christian Antiquities. *Hartford*, 1880. 8º. I. 1018–38.
DANIEL. Codex Liturgicus. *Lips.* 1847. 4 v. 8º.
** HAMMOND, C. E. Liturgies, Eastern and Western. *Oxford*, 1878. 8º. Appendix. *London*, 1879. 8º.
KÖSSING. In: Wetzer u. W. Kirch-Lex. (1847–54) VI. 543–555.
NEALE, J. M. Translation of the Anaphorae of St. Chrysostom, S. Basil, S. James, S. Mark, etc. In: History of the Eastern Church. Introd. (*Lond.* 1850.) 525–.
* — The liturgies of S. Mark, S. James, S. Clement, S. Chrysostom, S. Basil. *Lond.* 1859. 16º. [Greek]; do. English. *Lond.* 1859 (?) ; do. *Lond.* 1868. [Greek]; do. English. 1868.
— Tetralogia liturgica; sive S. Chrysostomi, S. Jacobi, S. Marci missae, quibus accedit Ordo Mozarabicus parallelo ordine. *Lond.* 1849.
[RATTRAY, BP.] Liturgia primit. Hierosolomiana; being the Liturgy of St. James. *Lond.* 1744.
RENANDOT, EUSEB. Liturgiarum Orientalium Collectio. *Par.* 1716. 2 v. 4º; repr. 1847.
SCHAFF. The liturgies. Their origin and contents. In: Hist. . . Church. III. 517–535.
SWAINSON, C. D. The Greek liturgies, chiefly from original authorities. *Lond.* 1884. 4º.
TROLLOPE, W. The Greek liturgy of St. James. *Edinb.* 1848.
WARREN, F. E. In: Encycl. Brit. (9th ed.) XIV. 706–7.
WALKER, C. In: M'Clintock and S. Cyclop. (1874–) V. 456–64. [Very convenient tables.]
ZEZSCHWITZ, G. v. In: Herzog. Real-Enc. IX. (1881) 769–801.
The asterisks indicate simply such things as the author has found most convenient in his own use. Add perhaps Renaudot and Schaff. See also list of works which Bp. Coxe has found especially useful in his studies, v. VII. of this series, p. 536.
The following is the authorship of the translations in this series.
MERRY, G. R. (Liturgy of Mark.) In: Ante-Nic. Lib. XXIV. (1872) 47–71. Ed. Coxe. VII. (1886) 551–60.
MCDONALD, W. (Liturgy of James.) In: Ante-Nic. Lib. XXIV. (1872) 11–45. Ed. Coxe. VII. (1886) 537–50.
DONALDSON, J. (Liturgy of the Blessed Apostles.) In: Ante-Nic. Lib. XXIV. (1872) 73–92. Ed. Coxe. VII. (1886) 561–8.

VOLUME VIII.

I. THE TESTAMENTS OF THE TWELVE PATRIARCHS.

I. *Editions.*

"Lincoln, Robert, Minister. Testamentum XII Patriarcharum. Gr. lat. Cum notis per Graham. *Oxon.* 1698. 4º." *Watt.* [What is it?]
GRABE. Gr. lat. Spicil. patr. *Oxf.* 1698; (1700) I. 129–253; I. (1714) 145–.
FABRICIUS. *Hamb.* 1722. In: Cod. pseud. V. T. I. 496–748.
GALLANDIUS. Bibl. Patr. I. (1765) 195–.
MIGNE. Patrol. gr. II. (1857) 1037–1150. [From Galland.]
SINKER. Testamenta XII Patriarcharum. *Cambr.* and *Lond.* 1869. Append. 1879.

II. *Translations.*

Latin.

GROSSETESTE, ROB. s. l. et a. 4º; *Hagan.* 1532. 8º. [Often under " Grosthead " or Lincoln, Robert. Bp. of.]

Dutch.

Antw. 1570. [From the Latin.]

English.

GOLDING, ARTHUR. *Lond., John Day*, 1577. 12º; 1581. 8º [From Latin]; 1589; 1590; 1595; 1601; 1606; 1619, 18º; *Edinb.* 1634. 12º; *Lond.* 1647; 1660. 18º; 1670. 18º; 1677. 18º; 1681; 1684; 1690; 1699; *Glasgow*, 1704. 12º; *Lond.* 1706. 12º. [1589 ed. given also under the name of John Day.]
SINKER, R. In: Ante-Nic. Lib. XXII. (1871) 13–79. Ed. Coxe. VIII. (1886) 9–38.

French.

Paris, 1555. 16º. [From the Latin.]
MACÉ, FR. *Paris*, 1713. 12º. [From the Latin.]

German.

Wien, 1544; *Strassb.* 1596; *Hamb.* 1637; *Hamb.* 1713. 12º.
DEUTINGER. (Auszug.) In: Geist. d. chr. Ueberl. I. II. 40–3.
Also Danish translation (1601) and Icelandic translation in Brit. Museum.

III. *Literature.*

ALZOG. Patrol. (1876) 99–100.
BAUR. Dogmengesch. I. (1865) 349.
ΒΑΦΕΙΔΗΣ. Ἐκκλ ίστ. I. (1884) 165.
BULL. Defensio fid. Nicaenae. Works. V. (1827) 176.
CAVE. Scr. eccl. hist. lit. I. (1740) 51–2.
CEILLIER. Hist. gén. aut. sac. I. (1858) 266–7.
CHARTERIS. Canonicity. (1880) 445–6.
CLARKE. Sacred lit. (1830–1) I. 153–4.
CUNNINGHAM. Churches of Asia (1880) pass.
DIESTEL. Das A. T. i. d. chr. Kirche. p. 50.
DILLMANN. In: Herzog. Real-Enc. XII. (1883) 361–2.
DODWELL. Tabula chronol. In: Grabe. Spicil patr. 2 ed. *Oxon.* 1714. 8º. I. 366–; also in: Migne. Patrol. gr. II. (1857) 1151–60.
DORNER. Person of Christ. I. (1864) 154–60, 419–22.
EWALD. Gesch. Israel. 3. Ausg. 1. 289. VII. (328) 363–.
GALLAND. Vet. patr. bibl. *Venet.* 1765. fº. I. li–. Also in: Migne. Patrol. gr. II. (1857) 1029–38.

GEIGER. Judische Zeitschrift für Wissenschaft und Leben. (*Bresl.* 1809.) 116–.

HASE. Kirchenges. (1885–) I. 281.

HENGEL, VAN. De Testamenten d. 12. Patr. *Amst.* 1860.

HILGENFELD, In: Ztschr. f. wiss. Theol. (1858) 395–; (1871) 302–.

ITTIG. Hist. eccl. (1709) II. 42–9.

KAYSER. In: Reuss und Cunitz's Beiträge zu den theol. Wissenschaften. (*Jena*, 1851.) 107–140.

KURTZ. Kirchenges. (1885–) I. 130.

LANGEN. Das Judenthum in Palästina zur Zeit Christi. (*Freiburg*, 1866.) 140–.

LARDNER. Credibility. Works. (1831) II. 345–64.

LE NOURRY. Appar. ad bibl. max. I. 235–; also in: Migne Patrol. gr. II. (1857) 1025–30.

LÜCKE. Offenbar. Job. 2te. Aufl. p. 334.

LUMPER. Hist. ss. patr. I. (1783) 228–44.

MOVERS. In: Wetzer u. W. Kirch-Lex. (1847–54) I. 339.

MUENSCHER. Dogmenges. (1817–8) II. 19.

NITZSCH, C. J. Commentatio Critica de Testamentis XII Patriarcharum, Libro V. T. Pseudepigrapho. *Wittenberg*, 1810. 8°.

— Dogmengesch. I. (1870) 109–11, etc.

— Das Anab. d. Jes. In: Theol. Stud. u. Krit. XXX.

PICK, B. In: M'Clintock and S. Cycl. (1874–) X. 291–4.

PRESSENSÉ. Heresy. (*N.Y.*) 173–5.

RITSCHL. Entsteh. d. Altkath. Kirche. p. 322–.

ROESSLER. Bibl. d. K.–V. IV. (1777) 330–47.

REUSS. Gesch. N. T. (1874) I. 265–6; tr. Eng. (1884) 265–6. [v. 1.]

SCHNAPP, FRIEDR. Die Testamente d. zwölf patriarchen. *Halle*, 1884. 8°. [Analyzes interpolations.]

SIMON, R. Biblioth. crit. II. 224–.

SINKER, R. Introd. note. In: Ante-Nic. Lib. XXII. (1871) ii, 5–12. Ed. Coxe. VIII. (1886) 1–8.

UEBERWEG. Hist. philos. (1876) 277.

Veter. Testim. In: Galland. vet. patr. bibl. I. *Venet.* 1765. f°. I. 241–; also in: Migne. patrol. gr. II. (1857) 1025–6.

VORSTMAN. Disquisitio de Testamentorum XII Patriarcharum Origine et Pretio. *Rotterdam*, 1857.

— In: Godgeleerde Bijdragen (1866) 953–.

WARFIELD, B. B. Apologet. value of —. In: Presb. R. I. (1880) 57–84, 185–; also in: Dickinson Th. Q. VI. (1880) 270–87.

WESTCOTT. Canon. (1875) 399–400.

WHISTON, WM. A dissertation to prove the Testaments of the XII Patriarchs equally canonical. 1727.

WIESELER. Die 70 Wochen und die 63 Jahrwochen des Propheten Daniel. *Götting.* 1839.

II. THEODOTUS.

I. *Editions.*

FABRICIUS. Bibl. Gr. V. 108.

— *Hamb.* 1718. In: Opera Hippolyti. II.

MIGNE. Gr. lat. In: Patrol. gr. IX. (1857) 653–98.

II. *Translations.*

WILSON, W. In: Ante-Nic. Lib. XXIV. (1872) 115–35. Ed. Coxe. VIII. (1886) 43–50.

III. *Literature.*

Augenscheinl. Erweis. dass G. Arnold die Valentinian fragm. T–ti wed. verstaendl. noch trenl. uebersetzt habe. *Ulm*, 1701. 4°.

BARONIUS. Ann. (1589) 196, 1–17; 208, 4–6.

BAUMGARTEN–CRUSIUS. Dogmenges. (1832) 146–7. [v. 1.]

BUSSE. Chr. Lit. (1828–9) I. 13.

CAVE. Scr. eccl. hist. lit. (1740–3) (1741) I. 87.

CHARTERIS. Canonicity. (1880) 426–9.

CHEVALIER. Rép. d. sources hist. (1877–86) 2179.

CLARKE. Sacred lit. (1830–1) I. 196.

CLINTON. Fasti Rom. (1845–50) II. 411.

COXE, A. C. Introd. note. In: Ante-Nic. Fath. Ed. Coxe. VIII. (1886) 39–41.

DUPIN. Bibl. aut. eccl. (1698) 871.

ENGELHARDT (J. G. V.) Animadv. ad nonnulla excerpt. ex T–to et doctr. orient. Clementi. Alex. vulgo attrib. *Erlangae*, 1830. 4°.

FABRICIUS. Bibl. gr. 1705 (1714) VI. 201–2; IX. 272. (2ᵃ. VII. 180–3; X. 515.)

HILGENFELD. Ketzergesch. (1884) 505–516.

JÖCHER. IV. 1113.

JONES, JER. Canon. I. 371–6.

KURTZ. Kirchenges. (1885) I. 138–9.

LABOUDERIE. In: Biog. Univ. (Michaud) (1842–65) XLI. 286.

LARDNER. Credibility. Works. (1831) III. 146–8.

LE NOURRY. In: Patrol. gr. IX. 1459–66.

M'CLINTOCK and S. Cycl. (1874–) X. 323. (?)

ORSI. Ist. eccl. (1746–) IV. 51–66; (1749–) IV. 68–87. (?)

PEARSE. In: Migne. Patrol. gr. IX. (1857) 651–4.

ROBERTSON. Hist. of Church. (1875–) I. 117–8.

TILLEMONT. Mém. hist. eccl. (1695) III. 68–70, 617–8.

Note. The various Theodoti are often confused in notices.

III. TWO EPISTLES CONCERNING VIRGINITY.

I. *Editions.*

WETSTENIUS, J. JAC. *Lugd. Bat.* 1752. f°. [In: N. T. Gr. II. Ad fin.]

GALLAND. Syr. lat. In: Bibl. patr. I. (1765).

BEELEN. Syr. lat. *Louvain*, 1856.

MIGNE. Syr. lat. In: Patrol. gr. I. (1857) 379–452. [Syr. text. Galland. Tr. lat. Villecourt.]

FUNK. Patr. ap. (*Tub.* 1881)II. 1–27.

II. *Translations.*

Latin.

VILLECOURT, CL. Lat. Fr. *Par.* 1853.

English.

PRATTEN, B. P. In: Ante-Nic. Lib. XXV. (1874) 367–95. Ed. Coxe. VIII. (1886) 55–66.

French.

PREMAGNY, ÉT. FR. DE. *Rouen*, 1757. Fr. and lat. *Rouen.* 1763. 8°. (76 p.) [With prolegomena of Wetstein and response to Journalists of Trévoux (8 p.).]

VILLECOURT. *Par.* 1853.

German.

ZINGERLE, P. *Wien*, 1827. 8°.

III. *Literature.*

ALZOG. Patrol. (1876) 23–4.

BRÜCK. Kirchenges. Ed. II. (1877) 74.

CEILLIER. Hist. gén. aut. sac. I. (1729) 605.

CHAMPAGNY. Les Antonins. (1863) I. 198.

CHARTERIS. Canonicity. (1880) xxiii.

Clemens R. and the Syriac ep. of virginity. In: Journ. of S. Lit. & Bibl. Rec. IV. (1857) 86–.

COTTERILL, J. M. Modern criticism and Clement's epistles to virgins, first printed 1752, or their Greek version newly discovered in Antiochus Palaestinensis. With appendix containing newly found versions of fragments attributed to Melito. *Lonaon*, 1884. 8⁰

FESSLER. Patrol. I. (1850) 164.

FREUDENBERGER, J. GLI. Historia recentior. controvers. de Clementis Romanis epistolis. *Lipsiae*, 1755.

GRABE. Spicil. I. 262. 2d 11.

HEFELE. In: Wetzer. u. W. Kirch-Lex. (1847–54) II. 586.

HERBST. (?) In: Theol. Quartalschr. (1829) 539–552.

LAND. J. P. N. Clemens Romanus de virginitate. [Reprinted from Godgeleerde Bijdragen (1856).] *Leyden*, 1856. 8⁰.

LARDNER. The Dissertation upon the two Epistles ascribed to Clement of Rome, lately published by Mr. Wetstein. With large Extracts out of them, and an Argument showing them not to be genuine. *Lond.* 1753. 8⁰. Cf. Appendix to the Monthly Review. VIII. p. 504–507.

LUMPER. Hist. theol. crit. I. (1783) 40–.

M'CLINTOCK and S. Cycl. (1874–) II. 383.

MANSI. Concil. I. 157.

MOEHLER. Patrol. I. (1840) 67–69.

NEANDER. Church Hist. (1872) I. 659.

NIRSCHL. Patrol. (1881–) I. 71–2.

PERMANEDER. Patrol. spec. (1842) 26.

PRATTEN and RIDDLE. Introd. note. In: Ante-Nic. Lib. XIV. (1874) 365–6. Ed. Coxe. VIII. (1886) 51–4.

REUSS. Gesch. N. T. (1874) I. 281; tr. Eng. (1884) 279.

SCHAFF. Hist. . . Church. (1882–) II. 649–50.

Two ep. on virginity ascribed to Clem. R. In: Jour. of S. Lit. & Bibl. Rec. XIV. (1862) 31–.

VENEMA. Ep. ad P. Wesseling. *Harlingae*, 1754. Cf. Beelen.

VILLECOURT. Dissertatio. *Rupell.* 1853. 8⁰. Also in: Migne. Patrol. gr. I. (1857) 349–78.

WELTE. In: Theol. Quartalschr. (1856).

WESTCOTT. Canon. (1875) 183 [Note 3]–185.

Note 1. The above list is mainly supplementary to the list under Clement of Rome.
Note 2. The disposition to doubt the Clementine authorship of these epistles was begun by Lardner and Venema, and has become the general view; but the opposite view has been stoutly maintained by Wetstein, Galland, Möhler, Champagny, Brück, Zingerle, Nirschl, and especially by Villecourt and Beelen.

IV. PSEUDO–CLEMENTINE LITERATURE.

I. and II. *Editions and Translations.*

(a.) RECOGNITIONS.

I. *Editions.*

GRABE. (Fragm.) Gr. lat. In: Spicil. patr. (1700) I. 289–99.

The Greek is lost. The work has come down to us in the Latin translation of Rufinus, and the first part in a Syriac translation.

II. *Translations.*

Syriac.

LAGARDE, P. DE. *Lips.* 1861. 8⁰. [Bks. I.–IV. 1, and fragments of the Homilies.]

Latin.

Par. Imp. Joh. Parvi. 1504. f⁰. (??) "In Catal. Crev. I. p. 90, given as 1503. 8⁰; Panzer. Ann. T. VII. p. 510, no. 85." *Hoffmann.* Cf. Schoenemann

SICHARDUS, JO. *Basil., Bebel.* 1526. f⁰; 1536. f⁰.

Par. 1541. f⁰. (??)

Parisiis, Guillard, 1544. 8⁰. (??)

TURNEBUS. (Extract.) Gr. lat. *Paris*, 1554. 4⁰.

GRUTER, LAMB. *Par.* 1568. 8⁰; *Colon.* 1569. f⁰.

COTELERIUS. In his: Patr. apost. 1672. f⁰. Ed. Clericus. 1698. f⁰; 1724. f⁰.

In: Bibl. Patr. *Lugd.* 1677. f⁰.

GALLANDIUS. Bibl. patr. II. (*Venet.* 1766) 209–.

GERSDORF, E. O. *Lps.* 1838. = Bibl. patr. eccl. v. I.

MIGNE. In: Patrol. gr. I. (1857) 1201–454.

Note. Of the above editions of 1541 and 1544 are quoted on the single authority of Hofmann. That of 1504 is quoted repeatedly, but seems not to be an edition. I have not yet been able to see all the editions mentioned.

English.

WHISTON, WM. In his: Primitive Christianity. V. (*Lond.* 1712.)

SMITH, T. In: Ante-Nic. Lib. XII. (1867) 143–471. Ed. Coxe. VIII. (1886) 77–211.

French.

MAISTRE. In: St. Clément. I. (*Par.* 1884. 8⁰.) 67–593.

German.

ARNOLD, GOTFR. *Berlin*, 1702. 8⁰; (with new title page) *Rostock.* u. *Leipz.* 1708. 8⁰.

Note 1. Bk. III., Chapters 2–11, is omitted in the edition of Sichard, and bracketed by Cotelerius and Gersdorf. Translators have avoided the passage, Whiston and Arnold printing the untranslated Latin, the Edinburgh and American editors of this series giving it up as untranslatable, and Maistre giving a sort of paraphrase. But it is contained in the Syriac (cf. Lagarde's ed. p. vi, Text p. 82, 2–87, 22), and in ten mss. It is omitted by more than thirty mss.
Note 2. The author takes this opportunity to mention that he has examined more than fifty mss. of the Recognitions, and secured some full collations, with enough from all to permit of genealogical tabulation. He hopes in a not very remote future to publish a critical edition, unless some one else supplies in the meantime a better text.

(b.) HOMILIES.

I. *Editions.*

COTELIER. Patr. ap. *Amst.* 1672. f⁰. Ed. Clericus. 1698. f⁰; 1724. f⁰.

GRABE. (Fragm.) Gr. lat. In: Spicil. patr. (1700) I. 300–4.

GALLANDIUS. Bibl. patr. II. (1766) 605–.

SCHWEGLER, ALB. *Stuttg.* 1847.

DRESSEL, A. R. M. *Gött.* 1853. 8⁰.

MIGNE. Gr. lat. In: Patrol. gr. II. (1857) 19–468. [Dressel's text.]

LAGARDE, P. DE. *Lpz.* 1865. 8⁰.

II. *Translations.*

English.

SMITH, PETERSON and DONALDSON. In: Ante-Nic. Lib. XVII. (1870) 1–331. Ed. Coxe. VIII. (1886) 215–346.

French.

MAISTRE. St. Clément. 1883.

III (a), III (b). *Literature.* (R. and H.)

ALZOG. Patrol. (1876) 25–28.

BARONIUS. Ann. I. (*Aug. Vind.* 1738.) 346, etc.

BARTH. Advers. b. XLV. c. 5.

BAUMGARTEN–CRUSIUS. Dogmenges. (1832) 89–90 [v. 1], 783 [v. 2].

BAUR, F. C. Ebionitarum origine et doctrina ab Essenis repetenda. *Tüb.* 1831.

— Die Christuspartei zu Corinth. In: Tüb. Zeitschrift. (1831) p. 110, 114–136, 174–206.

— Das Manichäische Religionsystem. (*Tüb.* 1831.) 342–44, 470–75, 483–86.

— Der Hebräische Sabbath u. d. Nationalfeste d. Mosaischen Cultus. In: Tüb. Zeitschrift. (1832) 188–.

— Über Apollonius von Tyana. In: Tüb. Zeitschrift. (1832) Heft. IV.; also separately. *Tübingen,* 1832. p. 226–35.

— Die Christl. Gnosis. (*Tübingen,* 1835.) 300–405, 760–.

— Die s. g. Pastoralbriefe d. Apostles Paulus. (*Stuttgard u. Tübingen,* 1835.) p. 51, 89–, 101–.

— Über Zweck u. Veranlassung d. Römerbriefes. In: Tüb. Zeitschrift. (1836) III. 118–35.

— Das Leben Jesu von Strauss Geprüft. von Hoffmann. (1836) 202–16.

— Lehre von der Versöhnung. (*Tübingen,* 1838.) ["Hierin nur beiläufig erwähnt."]

— Ueber d. Ursprung d. Episkopats i. d. chr. Kirche. In: Tüb. Zeitschrift. (1838.) III. p. 123–133, 182–.

— In: Berliner Jahrbüchern. (1839) [Rev. of Schenkel.]

— Lehre von d. Dreieinigkeit u. Menschwerdung Gottes u. s. w. I. (*Tüb.* 1841.) 149–63.

— In: Theol. Jahr. (1844) III.

— Kirchenges. 3 e. J. (1863) 217–225.

∼ Dogmengesch. I. (1865) 155–8, etc. [H], 251, etc. [R.]

BEAUSOBRE. Hist. de Manichéisme. *Berlin,* 1734. p. 461 and 593.

BELLARMIN. Catal. an. 390, p. 155.

BLONDEL. Pseud-Isidorus et Turrianus vapulantes. (*Genev.* 1624.) p. 28.

BÖCLERUS. Hist. univ. I. 14.

BOVIUS, CARL. Pref. to Constitut. apost.

CAVE. Scr. eccl. hist. lit. I. (*Genev.* 1705.) 20.

— Lives of the fathers. Tr. Carey. (*Oxf.* 1840.) I. 147–163.

CEILLIER. Hist. gén. d. aut. sacr. I. (*Paris,* 1729.)

CHAMIER, DANIEL. Panstratia catholica. (1626) tom. I. lib. XX. cap. 16.

CHARTERIS. Canonicity. (1880) Hom. lxiii–lxviii, 134–5, 148, 184–5, 203, 236, 241, 438–44; Rec. 204–5.

CLARKE. Sacred lit. (1830–1) I. 154. [14 ll.]

CLERICUS. Historia ecclesiae duorum primorum saeculorum. (*Amstelodami,* 1716.)

v. CÖLLN, D. In: Ersch u. Gruber. I. XVIII. (1828) 36–44.

COTELERIUS. Patr. ap. *Amst.* 1724. f⁰. I. 490–; also in: Migne. Patrol. gr. I. (1857) 1187–8.

COTTA. Kirchenhistorie. Theil II. p. 1169.

CREDNER. Ueb. Essäer u. Ebioniten. In: Winer's Ztschr. f. Wiss. Theol. I. II. (*Sulzbach,* 1827.) 211–64; III. (1829) 277–328.

— Beiträge zur Einl. n. d. bibl. Schr. I. 351.

CUNNINGHAM. Churches of Asia. (1880) passim.

DÄHNE. Die Christuspartei in der Kirche zu Corinth. *Halle,* 1841.

DETMER. De Nazaraeis et Ebionitis. *Halis Saxonum,* 1837. p. 50–.

DÖDERLEIN. Comment. de Ebionaeis. *Butsovii et Wismar,* 1770. p. 277–93, 301–9, etc.

DODWELL. Diss. in Irenaeum. *Oxon.* 1689.

DÖLLINGER. Kirchengeschichte. Band I. *Regensburg und Landshut,* 1836. p. 27–.

DORNER. Person of Christ. I. (1864) 203–17, 437–44, [H]; 444–7, [R].

DRIEDO. De eccl. dogm. V. IV. v. 5 (*Lovan.* 1752.)

DUPIN. Nouv. bibl. aut. eccl. (*Par.* 1695) I. 32.

ENGELHARDT. Handbuch d. Kirchengeschichte. I. (*Erlangen,* 1833.)

— Dogmengeschichte. I. (*Neustadt a. d. Aisch,* 1839.) p. 20–30.

EPIPHANIUS. Cod. CXII.

FABRICIUS. Delectus argumentorum et syllabus scriptorum qui verit. rel. chr. assuerunt. *Hamb.* 1725. 41–.

FLÜGGE. Gesch. d. theol. Wissen. I. (*Halle,* 1796.) 315–26.

FONTANINUS. Hist. litt. Aquileiensi. v. 10. In: Galland. Vet. Patr. bibl. *Venet.* 1765. f⁰. II. xxxiii–; also in: Migne. Patrol. gr. I. (1857) 1187–200.

FROMMENBERGER, G. De Simone Mago. I. Dissert. *Vratislav.* 1886. 8⁰.

GALLAND. Vet. patr. bibl. II. (*Venet.* 1766.) f⁰. LV–; also in: Migne. Patrol. gr. II. (1857) 11–20.

GEFRÖRER. D. Jahrh. d. Heils. I. (1838) 260.

GENNON. De veteribus haereticis ecclesiasticorum codicum corruptoribus. *Parisiis,* 1713.

GERHARD. Confessio catholica. (*Jena,* 1663.) Lib. 1, p. 2, cap. 13.

GIESELER. Ueb. d. Nazaraer u. Ebioniten. In: Stäudlin. Archiv. f. Kirchenges. IV. II. *Lpz.* 1820.

GFRÖRER. Kirchengeschichte. I. (*Stuttgard,* 1840.) 290–300.

GOULD, G. P. In: Theo. R. XV. (1878) 1–.

GRAVESON. Hist. eccl. N. T. *Aug. Vind. et Wirceb.* 1756. p. 43.

HAGENBACH. Hist. of Doct. I. (1850) 170, etc.

HAMBERGER. Nachrichten v. d. vornehmsten Schriftstellern. II. (*Lemgo.* 1758.) 189.

HARNACK. Dogmenges. I. (1886) 236–40.

HASE. Kirchenges. (1885–) I. 276–8, 326–7.

HAUSRATH. NTlichen Zeitgesch. III. 326–.

HEFELE. In: Wetzer u. W. Kirch-Lex. (1847–54) II. 587–90.

HEIMPEL, ADR. Étude sur les homélies clémentines, *Mont.* 1861.

HILGENFELD. Die clementische Recognitionen u. Homilien. *Jena,* 1848. ["Epochmachende Schrift." *Uhlhorn.*]

— Ueb. d. Composition d. klement. Homilien. In: Theol. Jahrbb. (1850) 83–92.

— Krit. Untersuchungen üb. d. Ev. Justins, d. clem. Homil. u. Marcions. *Halle,* 1852.

— Apost. V. (1853) 287–30.

— Urspr. d. pseudocl. Rekogn. u. Hom. In: Theol. Jahrbb. (1854) 483–.

— N. T. Extra Canon. Recept. IV. (1866) 52, et passim.

— Bardesanes. *Leipz.* 1864. 8⁰.

— In: Theol. Jahrbb. 1868. p. 357–.

— Ketzergesch. (1884) 35–8.

HILGERS. Kritische Darstellung d. Häresien u. d. orthodoxen dogma. Hauptrichtungen. I. 1. (*Bonn,* 1837) 105–123, 153–183.

HOLTZMANN. Einl. in d. N. T. (1886) 548, etc.

HUBER. Philos. d. K.–V. (1859) 45–6.

ITTIG. Dissertatio de patribus apostolicis. *Lipsiae,* 1699.

— Hist. eccl. (1709) I. 54–60, 208–19.

JACKSON, G. A. Ap. fath. (1879) 61–5.

JACKSON, S. M. Lipsius on the Roman Peter-legend. In: Princ. R. XLVIII. (1876).

KAYSER. In: Strassb. Rev. de Théol. III. (1851).

— In: Lichtenberger. Encycl. (1877–82) VI. 316–23.

KERN. Brief Jacobi. *Tüb.* 1838. p. 56.

KESLER, ANDR. G. Philosophemata Potiora Recognitionum Clementi Romano falso attributarum-publicae disquisitioni subjiciet. *Altorfii,* 1728. 4⁰. [Jac. W. Feuerlein, Praeses.]

KESTNER. Agape. *Jena,* 1819. p. 27–.

KLEUKER. Ueber die Apokryphen des Neuen Testaments. *Hamburg,* 1798.

KÖSTLIN. In: Hallische Allgem. Lit. Ztng. (1849) nos. 73–7.

LAGARDE, P. DE. Clementina. (1865) Prolegg. 3-. [De scriptis, quae sub Clem. nom. circumferuntur.]
— Symmicta. I. (1877) 2-4, 108-112.
— Einl. zu 'Clementina.' In his: Mittheilungen. *Gött.* (1884) p. 26-54.
LANGE, P. Gesch. d. Kirche. I. i. 41.
LARDNER. Credibility. Works. (1831) II. 364-81.
LECHLER. Ap. u. Nachap. Z-A. (1885) 532-9. Engl. tr. (1886) II. 268-76.
LEHMANN, JOH. Die clementinischen Schriften m. besond. Rücksicht auf ihr literarisches Verhältniss. *Gotha*, 1869. 8⁰.
LE NOURRY, NIC. Diss. de libris Recognitionum S. Clementis. In his: Apparatus ad Bibl. max. PP. (*Paris*, 1703. f⁰.) I. 211-224; also in: Migne. Patrol. gr. I. (1857) 1171-86.
LIGHTFOOT. Commentary on Galatians. 4th ed. p. 316.
LIPSIUS. In: Protestantische K. Z. (1869) 477-82. [Rev. of Lehmann.]
— Röm. Petrus-sage. (*Kiel*, 1872) 13-21.
— Zur Quellenges. Epiphanus. p. 148-.
— Simon Magus. In: Schenkels Bibl.-Lexicon. V. 301-321.
— De Cl. Rom. epist. ad Cor. p. 164.
LUMPER. Hist. ss. patr. VII. (1790) 43-76.
LUTTERBECK, A. B. Die Clementinen und ihr Verh. z. Unfehlbarkeitsdogma. *Giessen*, 1872. 8⁰.
MAURICE. Eccl. hist. (1854) 248.
M'CLINTOCK and S. Cycl. (1874) II. 383.
MARANUS. Divinat. D. N. J. C. II. VII. § 4. p. 250-4.
MASSUET. In his ed. of: Irenäus. (*Paris*, 1710.)
MAUERHOFF. Einl. in d. petrinischen Schriften. *Hamburg*, 1835. p. 317.
MEIER. Dogmengeschichte. *Giessen.* 1840.
MERX. Bardesanes v. Edessa. *Halle*, 1863. 8⁰.
MILL. Proleg. ad. N. T. Gr. § 670.
MÖHLER. Patrologie. I. (*Regensburg*, 1840.) 111.
MONUMENTA. In: Galland. Vet. patr. bibl. *Venet.* 1765. f⁰. II. 322-; also in: Migne. Patrol. gr. I. (1857) 1455-74.
MOSHEIM. Diss. ad H. E. pert. (*Altona et Flensb.* 1743.) I. 85.
MÜNSCHER. Dogmengeschichte. I. (1817-8) 316-7; (2. *Augsb.* 1862) I. 342-.
NEANDER. Genet. Entw. d. gnost. Syst. *Berlin*, 1818. [Lehrbegriff d. Hom.]
— Apost. Zeitalt. I. (*Hamb.* 1841.) 444, etc.
— Hist. of dogmas. (1858) 88-9, 92-3, 178. [v. I.]
— Church Hist. (1872) I. 353-62.
NIRSCHL. Patrol. (1881-) I. 74-6. [H. & R.]
NITZSCH. Dogmengesch. I. (1870) 43-6, etc.
NORTON. Genuineness of Gosp. II. (1848) xxiv-xxxiii., etc.
OLSHAUSEN. Commentar. d. N. T. IV. (*Königsberg*, 1840.) Anm. 43.
OSIANDER. Über d. colossischen Irrlehrer. In: Tübinger Zeitschr. 1834. Heft. III. p. 103.
OUDIN. De scr. eccl. (1722).
PANIEL. Pragmatische Gesch. d. chr. Beredtsamkeit u. d. Homiletik. I. i. (*Leipzig*, 1839.) 107.
PERTCHEN. Kirchenhistorie. *Leipz.* 1736.
PETERSEN. Nubes testium verit. de regno Christi. *Francof. ad M.* 1696. II. 60.
PETAVIUS. De theologicis dogmatibus. (*Antverpiae*, 1700.) V. I. ii. 5.
PHOTIUS. Cod. CXII.
PLANK. Das Princip des Ebionitismus. In: Zeller's Jahrbüchern. (1843) Heft. I.
PRESSENSÉ. Chr. life. (1878) 45-7.
— Heresy. (*N.Y.*) 85-99.
RAUSCHER. Geschichte d. chr. Kirche. I. (*Aulzbach*, 1829.) 230-232.
REDEPENNING. In his: Origenes. I. (*Bonn*, 1841.) p. 4.

REUSS. Gesch. N. T. (1874) I. 261-5; tr. Eng. (1884) 261-5. [v. I.]
RIDDLE, M. B. Introd. note. In: Ed. Coxe. VIII. (1886) 67-71.
RITSCHL. D. Entstel. d. altk. K. (1850) 153-; (1857) 206-70.
— Die Bedeutung d. pseudo-clementinischen Literatur. In: Monatschr. f. Wiss. u. Lit. (1852) 61.
RITTER. Handb. d. Kirchengesch. I. (2te Aufl. *Bonn*, 1836.) p. 158.
ROSENMÜLLER. Hist. interp. I. (1795) 73-114.
ROTHE. Anfänge d. Kirche. *Wittenb.* 1837.
ROUARDS. Compendium hist. eccles. I. (*Trajecti ad Rhenum*, 1840.) 51.
SALMON, G. In: Smith and Wace. Dict. I. 567-78.
SANDAY. Gosp. in 2 cent. (1876) 37-9, 161-87, 287-95.
SANDIUS. Nucleus Hist. Eccl. (*Colon.* 1676.) 15.
SCHAFF. Hist. . . Church. II. (1886) 436-42.
SCHENKEL. De eccl. Corinthia primaeva factunibus turbata. *Basil.* 1838. 8⁰. Excursus de Clem. origene argumentoque. p. 33-74.
SCHLIEMANN. Die Clementinen nebst den verwandten Schriften u. der Ebionitismus. *Hamb.* 1844. 8⁰.
— Die Cl. Recogn. e. Ueberarbeitung d. Clementinen. In: Theol. Mitarbeiten hrsg. Pelt. IV. (*Kiel*, 1844) IV. 1-.
SCHMIDT. Handbuch der Kirchengeschichte. I. (2te Auflage. *Giessen*, 1824.) 443-51.
SCHOENEMANN. Bibl. patr. lat. 633-8. [Recognitions.]
SCHROEKH. Kirchengeschichte. II. (*Leipz.* 1770.) 271-.
SCHULTHESS. Symbolae ad internam crit. lib. can. I. (*Turin*, 1833.)
SCHWEGLER. Montanismus. *Tub.* 1841.
— Nachap. Zeitalt. (1846) I. 383-406 [H], 481-90 [R].
SIXTUS SENENSIS. Biblioth. II. p. 83.
SMITH, T. Introd. note. In: Ante-Nic. Lib. III. (1867) 135-42 [R]. XVII. (1870) IX. Ed. Coxe. VIII. (1886) 73-6 [R]. 213 [H].
STAPIUS, A. Etudes hist. et crit. In his: Origines du Christianisme. *Paris*, 1864.
STARCK. Gesch. d. chr. Kirche d. ersten Jahrh. (1780) II. 543-52.
STEITZ, G. E. In: Theol. Stud. u. Krit. XL. (1867) 545-63. [Rev. of Lagarde's ed.]
STOLLE. Nachr. v. d. Leben. Schr. u. Lehre. d. Kirchenv. (*Jena*, 1673.) CII. § 9, p. 23.
STRAUSS. Leben Jusu. 1 Aufl. I. (*Tübingen*, 1835.) 159-165.
Supernatural Religion. (1875-) II. 1-37, 336-54.
TENZEL. Bibl. curios. Rep. I. 218.
— Exercitt. select. II. 68.
Testimonia veterum de clementinis. In: Cotelerius. Patr. ap. *Amst.* 1724. f⁰. I. 605-; also in: Migne. Patrol. gr. II. (1857) 9-12.
THIERSCH, H. D. Kirche in apost. Zeitalt. (*Frf. a M. et Erlang.* 1852.) 341-.
THOLUCK. Commentar. zum Brief au die Hebräer. *Hamburg*, 1836. p. 451.
TILLEMONT. Mémoires. (1701-) II. 163-.
TISCHENDORF. Var. lect. In: Migne. Patrol. gr. II. (1857) 1279-92.
TZSCHIRNER. Der Fall des Heidenthums, hrsg. Niedner. (*Leipz.* 1829) 378-82.
TWESTEN. Vorlesungen über die Dogmatik. I. (4te Aufl. *Hamburg*, 1838.) 100.
UEBERWEG. Hist. philos. (1876) 276-7.
UHLHORN. Die Homilien und Recognitionen des Clemens Romanus. *Götting.* 1854. 8⁰.
— Art. Clementinen. In: Herzog. Real.-Enc. (1877-) III. 277-86.
Veter. testim. In: Galland. Vet. patr. bibl. *Venet.* 1765. f⁰. I. 211-; also in: Migne. Patrol. gr. I. (1857) 1157-72.

VOLKMAR. Evang. Marcions. p. 186.
— Religion Jesu. p. 337–449, 547.
— D. Ursprung unserer Evangelien. p. 62, 104, 134, 163–4.
Voss, G. De hist. gr. II. c. 15.
WAITE. Hist. Chr. Rel. (1881) 105–11 et passim.
WAKE. Lond. 1693. 149–50; Lond. 1710. 8⁰ [Greatly improved]; Lond. 1719. 8⁰. 102–3; 1737. 8⁰; 5th ed. 1818 [7?]; Hartford, 1834. 441–2; Lond. 1842 [3?]. 8⁰ [Revised]; Phila. 1846. 8⁰. Lond. 1846. 8⁰; 1860. 8⁰.
WALCH. Entwurf einer Historie der Ketzereien. I. (Leipz. 1762) 120.
WEISMANN. Introd. in. memorab. eccl. hist. (Stuttgardiae, 1718.) 98–.
WESTCOTT. Bible in the church. (1877) 105–6.
WETTE, DE. Chr. Sittenlehre. II. (Berlin, 1819.) 257–.
— Lehrb. d. chr. Sittenleh. (Berlin, 1833.) 100–.
WIESELER, FR. Clementinorum epitomae duae. Cura A. R. M. Dressel. Accedunt Frid. Wieseleri adnotationes criticae ad Clements Romani quae feruntur homilias. Leipz. 1859, 1873. 8⁰.
WILCKE. K. gesch. (Leipz. 1828.) p. 31, 34.
WINDISCHMANN. Vindiciae petrinae. (Ratisbonae, 1836.) 75.
ZELLER. Apostelgesch. (1854) 53–64.

>   Note 1. Discussions of the Clementines will be found also in all general works on CLEMENT OF ROME. Compare also the apocryphal Acta Petri et Pauli, and any literature on the Ebionites.
>   Note 2. Schliemann gives full literature of early discussions on the Ebionites. (Cf. especially, pp. 22–6, 32–33.) Uhlhorn and Lehmann also give capital literary-historical treatment of the discussion. Hilgenfeld not at hand.
>   Note 3. A select literature from the above might be: (1) Hilgenfeld, Lehmann, Uhlhorn, Salmon, Schliemann; (2) Lutterbeck, Merx, Schenkel; (3) Lagarde, Ritschl, Rothe, Steitz.
>   Note 4. Compare, of course, the EPITOME and any literature relating to it.

V. APOCRYPHA OF THE NEW TESTAMENT.

I. Editions.

NEANDER, MICH. (Soraviensis.) Apocrypha, h. e. narrationes de Christo, Maria, Joseph, cognatione et familia Christi, extra Biblia, etc. In: Cathechesis Mart. Lutheri parva, graeco-latina. Basel, 1564. [2. ed. 1567.]
>   [Contains: Protevangelium Jacobi, Epist. Pilati, Epist. Lentuli, Prochori de Johanne Theologo et Evangelista historia.]
Apocrypha, paraenetica, philologica cum versione Nicolai Glaseri. Hamb. 1614.
FABRICIUS. Codex apocryphus N. T. Hamburg, 1703. 2 v.; ed. 2. Hamb. 1719; v. 3. 1719; v. 3. ed. 2. Hamb. 1743.
— Bibl. Gr. III. 168; XIV. 270.
JONES, JER. A new and full method of settling the canonical authority of the New Testament. Lond. 1726–7. 3 v. 8⁰; Oxf. 1798. 3 v. 8⁰; new ed. Oxford, 1827. 3 v. 8⁰.
SCHMID, C. C. L. Corpus apocr. extra Biblia. Hadum, 1804.
BIRCH, ANDREAS. Auctarium cod. apocr. N. T. Fabriciani (continens plura inedita, alia ad fidem codd. mss. emendatius expressa). I. (Havniae, 1804.)
THILO, JOAN CAR. Codex apocryphus Nov. Test. I. (Lips. 1832.) [Only one vol. published.]
TISCHENDORF. Acta apostolorum apocrypha. Lips. 1851. 8⁰.
— Evangelia apocrypha. Lips. 1853. 8⁰; ed. alt. 1876. 8⁰.
— Apocalypses Apocryphae. Lips. 1866. 8⁰.

GILES, J. A. Uncanonical Gospels, etc. In the original languages. Lond. 1853. 2 v. 8⁰.
WRIGHT. Contributions to the Apocryphal Literature of the New Testament collected, etc. Lond. 1865; 1871.

———

NAUSEA, FR. Anonymi Philalethi Eusebirani invitas miracula passionesque apostolorum rhapsodiae. Colon. 1531. [Abdias.]
Compare also : —
MOMBRITIUS, BONIN. In : Legendarium. Milan, 1474.
LIPOMANNUS. Vitae sanctorum. Rom. 1551.
SURIUS. Vitae sanctorum. Colon. 1569–.
Acta sanctorum. (Bolland.)
BIGNE, DE LA. In: Bibliotheca patrum. Paris, 1575.

English.

COWPER, B. H. The apocryphal gospels and other documents relating to the history of Christ. Translated, etc. Lond. 1867. 12⁰.
HONE. Apocryphal New Testament. Lond. 1820. 8⁰, and often.
WALKER, A. See analysis below.

French.

BRUNET. Les évangiles apocryphes, traduites et annotés d'après l'édition de Thilo, par Gustav Brunet. Paris, 1845.

German.

VORBERG. Bibliothek der neutestamentlichen Apokryphen. 1 Bd. Stuttg. 1841. [Based on Thilo.]
BORBERG. Bibl. d. neutest. Apokryphen. (Stuttg. 1841.)
BARTHOLMÄ. Uebers. d. Apokr. d. N. T. Dinkelsbühl. 1832.

III. Literature.

AMMON. Leben Jesu. I. 91.
ARENS, F. J. De evv. apocr. usu historico, critico, exegetico. Gött. 1838.
BARING–GOULD, S. The lost and hostile gospels. Lond. 1874.
BARONIUS. Ann. Lucae, 1738–57. 38 v. f⁰.
BEAUSOBRE, I. DE. De N. T. ll. apocr. Berl. 1734; tr. Ger. in : Cramer. Beiträge. I. 251–.
BENZEL. De apocr. N. T. (?) In his : Syntagm. I. 316–.
CAVE. Scr. eccl. hist. lit. 1740–. f⁰.
CHUEDENIUS. Pseudo Novum Testamentum, exhibens Pseudo-Evangelia, Acta Epistolas, Apocalypses. Helmst. 1699. [J. A. Schmid, praeses.]
CORRODI, H. Beleuchtung d. Gesch. d. Kanons.
COTTA, J. F. Kirchenges. II. 1107–.
DALE, A. V. De orig. idol. p. 253–.
DUPIN. Nouv. bibl. aut. eccl. I. (1692) 6–, 26–.
ELLICOTT. Cambridge Essays. 1856.
GELASIUS. (Pope.) Decretum. In : Credner. Gesch. d. Kanon. Halle, 1847, p. 219; and in various editions and works.
HAGEMANN. Hist. Nachricht v. N. T. p. 646–.
HOFFMANN, RUD. Apokryphen des Neuen Testamentes. In : Herzog. Real.-Enc. (1877–) I. 511–529.
ITTIG, TH. Diss. de haeresiarchis aevi apost. Lpz. 1796. 4⁰; 2 ed. 1703. Suppl. De Pseudepigraphis Christi, Virginis Mariae, et apostolorum.
— Dissert. de patr. apost. In : Bibl. patr. apost.
JENICHEN. De libr. N. T. et V. T. apocr. illustratione. Viteb. 1786.
KLEUKER. Ueb. Apokr. d. N. T. Hamb. 1798.
KÖSTLIN, R. Die pseudonym. Liter. d. ältesten Kirche. In : Tüb. Jahrbb. 1851. II.
LAMI, J. De erudit apost. 176–.

LAMSON, A. In: Chr. Exam. XIV. (1832) I.
LARDNER. Works. II. (1831) 330–.
LORSBACH. D. heil. Bücher d. Johannis Jünger. *Marb.* 1807.
LÜCKE. Völlst. Einl. Offenb. Joh. 2ᵃ. Aufl. 1852.
McCLINTOCK and S. Cyclop. (Article "Apocrypha.") I. (1874) 289–96. [Very conveniently arranged table of lost (pp. 294–5) and extant (p. 295) apocryphal N. T. writings.]
MIGNARELLI. Reliquae Aegyptiorum codd. in bibl. Naniana reconditorum. *Bonn,* 1785. II. 302–.
MIGNE. Dict. des Apocryphes. *Par.* 1856. 2 v. 4°.
MILL. Proleg. ad N. T. ed. Kuster. (*Amst.* 1710.) 5–7, 15–16.
MOSHEIM, J. L. De caussis suppositorum librorum inter Christianos, sec. I. et II.
NICHOLSON, E. B. Gospel according to the Hebrews. *Lond.* 1879.
NIEMEYER, H. A. In his: Ztschr. I. 257.
NITZSCH, C. I. De apocr. evv. in explicandis canonicis usu et abusu. *Vit.* 1808.
OUDIN. Comment. de scr. eccl.
PERIONIUS, JOACH. De rebus gestis et vitis apost. *Basil,* 1551.
PONS, JOS. Recherches sur les apocryphes du nouveau Testament. Thèse historique et critique. *Montauban,* 1850.
PRITIUS. Introd. p. 6, 58. ed Hofm.
Quarterly Rev. XXX. (1824) 472–; Chr. Obs. XXII. (1822) 1–; 65–; 129–.
RAYNOLD. Censura apocr. V. et N. T. *Oppenh.* 1611.
REUSS. De N. T. apocr. *Argent.* 1829.
RICHARDSON. Canon. (*Lond.* 1700.) 2.
RÖSSLER. Bibl. d. Kirchen–V. IV. (1777) etc. See below.
ROSE, H. J. In: Quar. XXV. (1821) 348–.
SCHMID, J. A. Pseudo- N. T. *Helmst.* 1699. (6?) 4°.
SCHMIDT, J. E. C. Einl. ins. N. T. 234–.
SIMON, RICH. Hist. crit. du texte du N. T. *Rot.* 1689.
— Novae obs. de textu et versionibus N. T.
SIXTUS SENENSIS. Bibliotheca sancta. *Köln.* 1586. II.
STARK. Gesch. d. ersten Jahrh. II.
TILLEMONT. Mémoires. *Par.* 1693–1712. 4°.
TISCHENDORF. Wann wurden unsere Evangelien verfasst? *Leipz.* 1865. p. 29–.
TOLAND. Collection of pieces. I. 350.
TRECHSEL. Kanon d. Manichaer. p. 60–.
ULLMANN. Zur Characteristik d. kanon. u. apokr.
WEDDERCAMP. Hist. saeculi primi fabulis variorum maculata. *Helmst.* 1700.
WESTCOTT. The disputed books of the Canon. Canon. (1875) 346–92.
ZOEGA. Catal. cod. copticorum. p. 227–.

GOSPELS.

Apocryphal Gospels. In: Ed. R. CXXVIII. (1868) 81–; *Lond.* Q. XXXI. (1869) 427–; Liv. Age. LII. (1856) 449–; Saturday Rev. (1877) Sept. 29; Church Q. XII. (1881) 84–114.
CUNNINGHAM. Churches of Asia. (1880) 18–9.
FROTHINGHAM, O. B. Christ of the Apocryphal Gospels. In: Chr. Exam. LIII. (1852) 21–.
GENTHE, F. W. Die Jungfrau Maria ihre Evangelien und ihre Wunder. *H.* 1852.
GREGERSEN, H. G. De apokryfiske evangelier til Ny Testamente med en efterslaet. *Odense, Milo,* 1886. 8°. (240 p.)
HOFMANN. Leben Jesu nach den Apokryphen. *Leipz.* 1851. 8°.
Inferiority of the Apocryphal Gospels. In: Ed. R. CXXVIII. (1868) 81–; same art. Liv. Age. XCVIII. (1868) 707–.
KURTZ. Kirchenges. (1885–) I. 131–2.

LIPSIUS, R. A. In: Smith and Wace. Dict. II. 700–17.
MOGGRIDGE, M. W. In: Expos. XII. (1881) 325–45.
NICHOLAS, MICH. Etudes sur lés Evangiles Apocryphes. *Paris,* 1866.
SCHMID, J. A. Prolusiones Marianae ed. Mosheim. *Helmst.* 1753.
SCHMIDT. Ueb. d. Evv. d. Kindheit. Bibl. II. 481.
SCHWARZ, F. J. De ev. impartiae Jesu verset ficto. *Lips.* 1785.
STEITZ. In: Herzog. Encycl. Art. Maria.
STOWE. Books of the Bible. (1867) 209–38.
TAPPEHORN, A. Ausserbiblische Nachrichten od. die Apokryphen üb. die Geburt, Kindheit u. das Lebensende Jesu u. Mariä, beleuchtet. *Paderborn,* 1885. 8°.
TAYLOR, J. J. In: Theol. R. IV. (1867) 149–.
TISCHENDORF, C. De evangeliorum apocryphorum origene et usu. Hagae Comit. 1851. 8°.
VARIOT, J. Les évangiles apocryphes, histoire litteraire, forme primitive transformation. *Paris,* 1878. 8°.
VEESENMEYER, G. Beitrag zum Cod. apocr. (Herod's command for murder of the children) in the Kirchenhist. Archiv. II. 1. p. 38.
WAITE. Hist. Chr. Rel. (1881) 56–89 et pass.
WALKER, A. Introd. note. In: Ante-Nic. Lib. XVI. (1873) vii–viii. Ed. Coxe. VIII. (1886) 351.

ACTS.

DALLAEUS, JOH. De pseudoepigraphis Apost. *Harderv.* 1653.
CUNNINGHAM. Churches of Asia. (1880) passim.
FABRICIUS. Cod. apocr. N.T. (1719) 762–5.
FUNK. In: Theol. Quartalschr. LXVI. (1884) 670–3, [Rev. of Lipsius.]
GRABE. Spicil. patr. (1700) I. 37–39.
STEMLER, J. C. De vera fictaque certaminis apost. historia. *L.* 1767.
KNABENBAUR, J. In Ztschr. f. Kath. Theol. VIII. (1884) 799–809. [Rev. of Lipsius. I. 11.]
KURTZ. Kirchenges. (1885–) I. 132–5.
LIPSIUS, R. A. In: Smith and Wace. Dict. I. 17–32.
MALAN, S. C. The Conflicts of the Holy Apostles, translated from an Ethiopic ms. *Lond.* 1871.
LIPSIUS, R. A. Die apokryph Apostelgeschten u. Apostellegenden. Ein Beitrag zur Altchr. Literaturgeschichte I. (*Braunschweig,* 1883.) II. 11. (1884); II. 1. (1887). [A remarkable monograph.]
GÜTSCHMID. Die Könignamen in d. Apocr. Apostelgeschichten. In: Rhein. Mus. f. Philol. N. F. XIX. 161–, 380–.
REUSS. Gesch. N. T. (1874) I. 269–70, 275; tr. Eng. 1884) I. 268–9, 273-4. [v. 1.]
SCHEPFS, G. In: Ztschr. f. Kirchenges. VII. (1886) 449–59. [Würzb. lat. ms.]
WALKER, A. Introd. note. In: Ante-Nic. Lib. XVI. (1873) xiii–xiv. Ed. Coxe. VIII. (1886) 354–5.

APOCALYPSES.

LIPSIUS, R. A. In: Smith and Wace. Dict. I. 130–2.
REUSS. Gesch. N. T. (1874) I. 270–1, 281–3; tr. Eng. (1884) 269–70, 279–81. [v. 1.]

(1.) THE PROTEVANGELIUM OF JAMES.

I. *Editions.*

BIBLIANDER. Lat. *Basil.* 1552. [Postellus.] *Argentorati,* 1570.
HEROLDUS. Lat. *Basil.* 1555. In: Orthodoxogr.
NEANDER. Gr. lat. *Basil.* 1564.
GRYNAEUS. Gr. lat. I. (1569) 71.

FABRICIUS. Cod. apocr. N.T. (1719) 66–126.
JONES. Gr. Eng. In: Canon N.T. 1798. II. 99–129.
BIRCH. *Havniae*, 1804. p. 195–242.
THILO. *Lips.* 1832. p. 159–273.
SUCKOW. *Vratislav.* 1840. [" Uncritical."]
TISCHENDORF. Ev. apocr. 1853. 1–49.

II. *Translations.*

English.

JONES. See under eds.
HONE. Apocr. N. T. (1825) 30–47. (Phila. n. d.) 24–37.
COWPER. Apocr. gosp. (1867) 3–26.
WRIGHT. Syr. apocr. (1865) 1–5. (?)
WALKER, A. In: Ante-Nic. Lib. XVI. (1873) 1–15.
Ed. Coxe. VIII. (1886) 361–7.

III. *Literature.*

CAVE. Scr. eccl. hist. lit. I. (1740) 14.
CHARTERIS. Canonicity. (1880) c-ci, 156, 464.
COWPER. Apocr. gosp. (1867) xlviii-liii, 1–2.
FABRICIUS. Cod. apocr. N. T. (1719) 39–65.
HOFFMANN. In: Herzog. Real.-Enc. (1877–) I. 514–5.
HOLTZMANN. Einl. in d. N. T. (1886) 540.
ITTIG. Hist. eccl. (1709) I. 16–8.
JONES. Canon N. T. 1798. II. 130–165.
LIPSIUS. In: Smith and Wace. Dict. II. 701–2.
NORTON. Genuineness of Gosp. III. (1848) 268–72.
PRESSENSÉ. Heresy. (*N.Y.*) 175–6.
REUSS. Gesch. N. T. (1874) I. 273; tr. Eng. (1884)
272. [v. 1.]
ROESSLER. Bibl. d. K.–V. IV. (1777) 357–8.
SCHOLZ. Einleitung in d. heil. schriften. I. (1845) 187.
STOWE. Books of the Bible. (1867) 205–6.
SUCKOW, C. A. De argumento et indol. Protev. Jac. *Br.*
1830.
TISCHENDORF. Ev. apocr. (1853) xii-xxv.
WAITE. Hist. Chr. Rel. (1881) 129–46 et pass.
WALKER, A. Introd. note. In: Ante-Nic. Lib. XVI.
(1873) viii. Ed. Coxe. VIII. (1886) 351.

(2.) THE GOSPEL OF PSEUDO–MATTHEW.

I. *Editions.*

THILO. *Lips.* 1832. p. 337–400. [24 ch.]
TISCHENDORF. Ev. apocr. 1853. 50–105.

II. *Translations.*

English.

COWPER. Apocr. gosp. (1867) 29–83.
WALKER, A. In: Ante-Nic. Lib. XVI. (1873) 16–52.
Ed. Coxe. VIII. (1886) 368–83.

III. *Literature.*

CREDNER. Z. Gesch. d. Kanons. p. 215–217.
COWPER. Apocr. gosp. (1867) liv-lxi, 27–8.
FABRICIUS. Cod. apocr. N.T. (1719) 355 –71.
HOFFMANN. In: Herzog. Real.-Enc. (1877–) I. 515.
HOLTZMANN. Einl. in d. N. T. (1886) 540.
ITTIG. Hist. eccl. (1709) I. 12–4.
LIPSIUS. In: Smith and Wace. Dict. II. 702.
NORTON. Genuineness of Gosp. III. (1848) 273.
TISCHENDORF. Ev. apocr. (1853) xxv-xxxiv. Apocal.
apocr. Proleg. lvi.
WAITE. Hist. Chr. Rel. (1881) 215.
WALKER, A. Introd. note. In: Ante-Nic. Lib. XVI.
(1873) viii. Ed. Coxe. VIII. (1886) 351–2.

(3.) THE GOSPEL OF THE NATIVITY OF MARY.

I. *Editions.*

VORAGINE. Cf. Apx.
FABRICIUS. Cod. apocr. N.T. (1719) 19–38.
JONES. Lat. eng. In: Canon N.T. 1798. II. 77–93.
THILO. *Lips.* 1832. p. 317–336.
TISCHENDORF. Ev. apocr. (1853) 106–14.

II. *Translations.*

English.

HONE. Apocr. N.T. (1825) 21–30. (Phila. n. d.) 17–24.
COWPER. Apocr. gosp. (1867) 85–98.
WALKER, A. In: Ante-Nic. Lib. XVI. (1873) 53–61.
Ed. Coxe. VIII. (1886) 384–7.

III. *Literature.*

COWPER. Apocr. gosp. (1867) lxi-lxiii, 84.
FABRICIUS. Cod. apocr. N.T. (1719) 1–18.
HOFFMANN. In: Herzog. Real.-Enc. (1877–) I. 515.
HOLTZMANN. Einl. in d. N.T. (1886) 540.
In: Jones. Canon N.T. 1798. II. 130–165.
LIPSIUS. Gospels Apocryphal. In: Smith and Wace.
Dict. II. 702–3.
NORTON. Genuineness of Gosp. III. (1848) 272–3.
REUSS. Gesch. N.T. (1874) I. 273; tr. Eng. (1884)
272. [v. 1.]
SCHOLZ. Einleitung in d. heil. Schriften. I. (1845) 188–.
STOWE. Books of the Bible. (1867) 208.
TISCHENDORF. Ev. apocr. (1853) xxv-xxxiv.
WAITE. Hist. Chr. Rel. (1881) 215–8.
WALKER, A. Introd. note. In: Ante-Nic. Lib. XVI.
(1873) viii-ix. Ed. Coxe. VIII. (1886) 352.

(4.) THE HISTORY OF JOSEPH THE CARPENTER.

I. *Editions.*

WALLIN, GEORG. Arabic-Latin. *Lips.* 1722.
FABRICIUS. II. 309–336.
ZOEGA. (Fragm.) Sahidic lat. 1810.
THILO. Arab. lat. *Lips.* 1832. p. 1–61.
DULAURIER. Fragment des révélations apocr. de S. Bar-
thélemi. *Par.* 1835. p. 23–9. [Sahidic-French.]
TISCHENDORF. Ev. apocr. 1853. 115–33.

II. *Translations.*

English.

COWPER. Apocr. gosp. (1867) 101–27.
WALKER, A. In: Ante-Nic. Lib. XVI. (1873) 62–77.
Ed. Coxe. VIII. (1886) 388–94.

III. *Literature.*

COWPER. Apocr. gosp. (1867) lxiii-lxviii, 99–100.
HOFFMANN. In: Herzog. Real.-Enc. (1877–) I. 515.
HOLTZMANN. Einl. in d. N.T. (1886) 540.
LIPSIUS. In: Smith and Wace. Dict. II.
REUSS. Gesch. N.T. (1874) I. 273; tr. Eng. (1884)
272. [v. 1.]
SCHOLZ. Einleitung in d. heil. Schriften. I. (1845) 187.
STERN, L. In: Ztschr. f. wiss. Theol. XXVI. (1886)
267–94. [Translation from the Coptic.]
STOWE. Books of the Bible. (1867) 208.

TISCHENDORF. Ev. apocr. (1853) xxxiv-xxxviii.
WAITE. Hist. Chr. Rel. (1881) 213-4.
WALKER, A. Introd. note. In: Ante-Nic. Lib. XVI.
  (1873) ix. Ed. Coxe. VIII. (1886) 352.

(5.) THE GOSPEL OF THOMAS.

I. *Editions.*

FABRICIUS. Cod. apocr. N. T. (1719) 159-67.
COTELERIUS. In: Note to Constit. apost. 6, 17. [Fragment from Paris ms. XV. century.]
MINGARELLI. Nuova raccolta d'opuscoli scientifici. XII.
  (*Venet.* 1764.) p. 73-155.
TISCHENDORF. Ev. apocr. 1853. 134-70.
WRIGHT. Syr. apocr. (1865).

II. *Translations.*

English.

HONE. Apocr. N. T. (1825) 75-78 (Phila. n. d.) 60-2.
WRIGHT. Syr. apocr. (1865) 6-11.
COWPER. Apocr. gosp. (1867) 130-69, 449-56.
WALKER, A. In: Ante-Nic. Lib. XVI. (1873) 78-99.
  Ed. Coxe. VIII. (1886) 395-404.

III. *Literature.*

CHARTERIS. Canonicity. (1880) ci.
COWPER. Apocr. gosp. (1867) lxviii-lxxv, cx, 128-9,
  448.
HOFFMANN. In: Herzog. Real.-Enc. (1877-) I. 515-6.
HOLTZMANN. Einl. in d. N. T. (1886) 541.
JONES. Canon N. T. 1798. I. 396-9.
LIPSIUS. Gospels Apocryphal. In: Smith and Wace.
  Dict. II. 703-5.
NORTON. Genuineness of Gosp. III. (1848) 273-6.
ROESSLER. Bibl. d. K.-V. IV. (1777) 358-60.
SCHOLZ. Einleitung in d. heil. Schriften. I. (1845) 188.
STOWE. Books of the Bible. (1867) 206.
TISCHENDORF. Ev. apocr. (1853) xxxviii-xlix.
WALKER, A. Introd. note. In: Ante-Nic. Lib. XVI.
  (1873) ix-x. Ed. Coxe. VIII. (1886) 352.

(6.) THE ARABIC GOSPEL OF THE INFANCY OF THE SAVIOUR.

I. *Editions.*

SIKE, HENR. Ev. inf. vel libre apocryphus de infantia
  Servatoris; ex manuscripto edidit ac latina versione et
  notis illustravit. *Traj. ad Rhenum,* 1697. [Arabic,
  Latin.]
FABRICIUS. Lat. In: Cod. apocr. N. T. (1719) 168-212.
JONES. Lat. Eng. In: Canon N. T. 1798. II. 168-226.
SCHMID. Lat. *Hadam.* 1804. [Latin only.]
THILO. Arab. lat. *Lips.* 1832. p. 63-158.
TISCHENDORF. Lat. In: Ev. apocr. 1853. 171-202.

II. *Translations.*

English.

HONE. Apocr. N. T. (1825) 47-75 (Phila. n. d.) 38-59.
WALKER, A. In: Ante-Nic. Lib. XVI. (1873) 100-24.
  Ed Coxe. VIII. (1886) 405-15.
COWPER. Apocr. gosp. (1867) 172-216.

III. *Literature.*

COWPER. Apocr. gosp. (1867) lxxvi-lxxx, 170-1.
FABRICIUS. Cod. apocr. N. T. (1719) 127-58.

HOFFMANN. In: Herzog. Real.-Enc. (1877-) I. 516.
HOLTZMANN. Einl. in d. N. T. (1886) 541.
JONES. Canon N. T. 1798. II. 166-261.
LIPSIUS. Gospels Apocryphal. In: Smith and Wace.
  Dict. II. 705-6.
NORTON. Genuineness of Gosp. III. (1848) 274-5.
PRESSENSÉ. Heresy. (*N.Y.*) 161-4.
REINSCH, R. Die Pseudo-Evangelien v. Jesu u. Maria's
  Kindheit in der romanischen u. germanischen Literatur.
  Mit. Mittheilgn. aus Pariser u. Londoner Handschriften versehen. *Halle,* 1879. 8°.
REUSS. Gesch. N. T. (1874) I. 273; tr. Eng. (1884)
  272. [v. 1.]
ROESSLER. Bibl. d. K.-V. IV. (1777) 358-60.
SCHOLZ. Einleitung in d. heil. Schriften. I. (1845)
  187-8.
STOWE. Books of the Bible. (1867) 208-9.
TISCHENDORF. Ev. apocr. (1853) xlix-liv.
WAITE. Hist. Chr. Rel. (1881) 147-76.
WALKER, A. Introd. note. In: Ante-Nic. Lib. XVI.
  (1873) x-xi. Ed. Coxe. VIII. (1886) 352-3.

(7.) THE GOSPEL OF NICODEMUS.

I. *Editions.*

VINCENTIUS BELVAC. Spec. hist. VII. 40-. [1st part.]
VORAGINE. Hist. Lomb. ch. LII. [2d part.]
HEROLDUS, JOAN. In: Orthodoxographa. *Bas.* 1555.
GRYNAEUS, J. J. In: Monumenta S. Patrum orthodoxographa. *Basil.* 1569.
FABRICIUS. Lat. In: Cod. apocr. N. T. (1719) 238-98.
JONES. Lat. Eng. In: Canon N. T. 1798. II. 262-
  328.
BIRCH. Gr. (*Havn.* 1804) 1-154.
THILO. Gr. *Lips.* 1832-. Proleg. and p. 487-795. ["Contains a full account of the English, French, Italian and German translations." *Walker.*]
TISCHENDORF. Gr. lat. Ev. apocr. 1853. 203-410.

II. *Translations.*

Anglo-Saxon.

In: Heptateuch. *Oxf.* 1698.

English.

HONE. Apocr. N. T. (1825) (79-116.) (Phila. n. d.) 63-
  91. [22 chapters.]
COWPER. Apocr. gosp. (1867) 229-388.
WALKER, A. In: Ante-Nic. Lib. XVI. (1873) 125-
  222. Ed. Coxe. VIII. (1886) 416-58.

German.

Berleburger Bibel, and often.

III. *Literature.*

AMERSBACH, K. Ueber die Identität des Verfassers des
  gereimten Evangeliums Nicodemi mit Heinrich Hesler,
  dem Verfasser du gereimten Paraphrase der Apokalypse. Progr. *Konstanz,* 1884. 4°.
BRAUN, J. W. J. De Tiberii Christum in deorum numerum referendi consilio. *Bonn,* 1834.
BRUNN. Disq. de indole aetate et usu Evang. Nicod. *B.*
  1794.
CHARTERIS. Canonicity. (1880) ci, 173-4, 464-5.
COWPER. Apocr. gosp. (1867) lxxxv-cii, 227-8.
DALE, A. v. De oracc. p. 608.
FABRICIUS. Cod. apocr. N. T. (1719) 213-37.
Gött. Bibl. I. 762.
GREVIUS, A. Apoth. Christo a Tib. decreta. *Vet.* 1722.

HASAEUS, T. De decreto Tib. *Erf.* 1715.
HASE. Kirchenges. (1885–) I. 275.
HENKE. De Pontii Pilati actis in causa J. C. missis. 1784.
HESS. Bibl. d. Heil. Gesch. I. 433–.
HOFFMANN. In: Herzog. Real.-Enc. (1877–) I. 517–8.
— Leben Jesu. p. 264, 379, 386, 396 u. a.
HOLTZMANN. Einl. in d. N. T. (1886) 541–2.
HORSTMANN, C. Gregorius auf dem Steine aus Ms. Cotton. Cleop. DIX, nebst Beiträgen zum Evangelium Nicodemi. In: Archiv. f. d. Studium d. neuer. Sprachen. u. Lit. LVII. 59–83.
ITTIG. Hist. eccl. (1709) I. 19–20.
JONES. Canon N. T. 1798. II. 262–353.
LACROZE. Thesaur. epist. III. 129.
LILIENTHAL. Gute Sache d. Offenb. XVI.
LIPSIUS, R. A. Krit. Untersuchung d. Pilatus-Akten. *Kiel,* 1871. 4°. Neue verm. Aufl. 1886. 8°.
— Gospels Apocryphal. In: Smith and Wace. Dict. II. 708–9.
LORSBACH, G. W. De vetusta Evang. Nic. interpr. germ. *Herb.* 1802.
MAURY, ALFRED. Nouvelles recherches sur l'époque à laquelle a été composé l'ouvrage connu sous le titre d'évangile Nicodème. 1832. [Places later than Eusebius Alexandrius.]
— Mém. de la Soc. des Antiq. de France. XX.
— Croyances et légendes de l'antiquité. p. 289–.
MEYER. Vertheid. d. Gesch. Jesu. p. 35–.
MÜNTER, F. Probabilien zur Leidensgesch. aus d. Evang. Nicod. In: Stäudlin's Archiv. V. 317–.
NORTON. Genuineness of Gosp. III. (1848) 284–7.
PAULUS. Ueb. d. Entsteh. d. Nic. Evang. In his: Conservat. I. 181.
PRESSENSÉ. Heresy. (*N. Y.*) 177–8.
Quarterly Review. CXVI.
RENAN. Études d'Hist. Rel. p. 177.
REUSS. Gesch. N. T. (1874) I. 267–8; tr. Eng. (1884) 266–8. [v. I.]
— Gesch. N. T. (1874) I. 266–7; tr. Eng. (1884) 266. [v. I.] [Acts of Pilate.]
ROESSLER. Bibl. d. K.–V. IV. (1777) 363–4.
SCHMIDT. Exeg. Bibl. II. 508.
SCHOLZ. Einleitung in d. heil. Schriften. I. (1845) 189.
SMITH. Bibl. Dict. Pilate.
STOWE. Books of the Bible. (1867) 206–8.
TISCHENDORF. Ev. apocr. (1853) liv–lxxvi.
— Pilati circa Christum judicio quid lucis offeratur ex actis Pilati. *Lips.* 1855.
WAITE. Hist. Chr. Rel. (1881) 177–212 et pass.
WALKER, A. Introd. note. In: Ante-Nic. Lib. XVI. (1873) xi–xii. Ed. Coxe. VIII. (1886) 353.

(8.) THE LETTER OF PONTIUS PILATE CONCERNING OUR LORD JESUS CHRIST.

I. *Editions.*

BIRCH. *Havn.* 1804. p. 154.
FABRICIUS. Cod. apocr. N. T. (1719) 298–301.
THILO. *Lips.* 1832. p. 796–.
TISCHENDORF. Ev. apocr. (1853) 411–2.
WRIGHT. Syra. apocr. (1865) 13–.
FLECK. In: Anecdot. p. 141.

II. *Translations.*

English.

WRIGHT. Syr. apocr. (1865) 12–7.
COWPER. Apocr. gosp. (1867) 390–9.
WALKER, A. In: Ante-Nic. Lib. XVI. (1873) 223. Ed. Coxe. VIII. (1886) 459.

III. *Literature.*

ALTMANN, J. S. De ep. P. ad Tib. *Br.* 1755.
COWPER. Apocr. gosp. (1867) cii–cv, 389–90.
HOFFMANN. In: Herzog. Real-Enc. (1877) I. 518.
TISCHENDORF. Ev. apocr. (1853) lxxvi–lxxvii.
WALKER, A. Introd. note. In: Ante-Nic. Lib. XVI. (1873) xii. Ed. Coxe. VIII. (1886) 353.
and the literature of the Gospel of Nicodemus.

(9.) THE REPORT OF PILATE THE PROCURATOR CONCERNING OUR LORD JESUS CHRIST.

(10.) THE REPORT OF PONTIUS PILATE.

I. *Editions.*

FABRICIUS. Gr. lat. In: Cod.-Apocr. III. 456–. [1st form.]
BIRCH. Gr. lat. *Havn.* 1804. [Both forms.]
THILO. *Lips.* 1832. [Both.]
TISCHENDORF. Ev. apocr. (1853) 413–25. [Both.]

II. *Translations.*

English.

COWPER. Apocr. gosp. (1867) 400–9.
WALKER, A. In: Ante-Nic. Lib. XVI. (1873) 224–30. Ed. Coxe. VIII. (1886) 460–3.

III. *Literature.*

COWPER. Apocr. gosp. (1867) cv–cvi.
HOFFMANN. In: Herzog. Real.-Enc. (1877–) I. 518–9.
TISCHENDORF. Ev. apocr. (1853) lxxvii–lxxviii.
WAITE. Hist. Chr. Rel. (1881) 177–9, 218.
WALKER, A. Introd. note. In: Ante-Nic. Lib. XVI. (1873) xii. Ed. Coxe. VIII. (1886) 353–4.
and the literature of the Gospel of Nicodemus.

(11.) THE GIVING UP OF PONTIUS PILATE.

I. *Editions.*

BIRCH. *Havn.* 1804.
THILO. *Lips.* 1832.
TISCHENDORF. Ev. apocr. (1853) 426–31.

II. *Translations.*

English.

COWPER. Apocr. gosp. (1867) 410–4.
WALKER, A. In: Ante-Nic. Lib. XVI. (1873) 231–4. Ed. Coxe. VIII. (1886) 464–5.

III. *Literature.*

COWPER. Apocr. gosp. (1867) cvi–cvii.
HOFFMANN. In: Herzog. Real.-Enc. (1877–) I. 519.
TISCHENDORF. Ev. apocr. (1853) lxxviii–lxxix.
WAITE. Hist. Chr. Rel. (1881) 219.
WALKER, A. Introd. note. In: Ante-Nic. Lib. XVI. (1878) iii. Ed. Coxe. VIII. (1886) 354.
and the literature of the Gospel of Nicodemus.

(12.) THE DEATH OF PILATE.

I. Editions.

VORAGINE. Legenda Aurea. Cf. Apx.
TISCHENDORF. Latin. In: Ev. apocr. (1853) 432–5.

II. Translations.

English.

COWPER. Apocr. gosp. (1867) 415–9.
WALKER, A. In: Ante-Nic. Lib. XVI. (1873) 234–6.
Ed. Coxe. VIII. (1886) 466–7.

III. Literature.

COWPER. Apocr. gosp. (1867) cvii-cviii.
HAHN, R. A. Das alte Passional. Frf. a. M. 1845. p. 88.
HOFFMANN. In: Herzog. Real.-Enc. (1877–) I. 519.
TISCHENDORF. Ev. apocr. (1853) lxxix-lxxx.
WAITE. Hist. Chr. Rel. (1881) 219.
WALKER, A. Introd. note. In: Ante-Nic. Lib. XVI. (1873) xii-xiii. Ed. Coxe. VIII. (1886) 354.
and the literature of the Gospel of Nicodemus.

(13.) THE NARRATIVE OF JOSEPH.

I. Editions.

BIRCH. Havn. 1804.
THILO. Lips. 1832.
TISCHENDORF. Ev. apocr. (1853) 436–47.

II. Translations.

English.

COWPER. Apocr. gosp. (1867) 420–31.
WALKER, A. In: Ante-Nic. Lib. XVI. (1873) 237–44.
Ed. Coxe. VIII. (1886) 468–71.

III. Literature.

COWPER. Apocr. gosp. (1867) CVIII.
HOFFMANN. In: Herzog. Real.-Enc. (1876–) I. 519.
TISCHENDORF. Ev. apoc. (1853) lxxx-lxxxi.
WAITE. Hist. Chr. Rel. (1881) 214–5.
WALKER, A. Introd. note. In: Ante-Nic. Lib. XVI. (1873) XIII. Ed. Coxe. VIII. (1886) 354.
and the Pilate literature in general.

(14.) THE AVENGING OF THE SAVIOUR.

I. Editions.

TISCHENDORF. Ev. apocr. (1853) 448–63.

II. Translations.

Anglo-Saxon.

GOODWIN, C. W. (Ed.) Angl. Sax. Engl. Cambr. 1851.

English.

COWPER. Apocr. gosp. (1867) 432–47.
WALKER, A. In: Ante-Nic. Lib. XVI. (1873) 245–55.
Ed. Coxe. VIII. (1886) 472–6.

Note. Substantial translations or versions of the story of Veronica are found in every language and in multitudinous editions.

III. Literature.

COWPER. Apocr. gosp. (1867) CIX–CX.
HOFFMANN. In: Herzog. Real.-Enc. (1877–) I 519.
TISCHENDORF. Ev. apocr. (1853) lxxxi-lxxxiii.
WAITE. Hist. Chr. Rel. (1881) 220.
WALKER, A. Introd. note. In: Ante-Nic. Lib. XVI. (1873) XIII. 245. Ed. Coxe. VIII. (1886) 354, 472.
Note. See also all works on Veronica, especially works on Christian Iconography. The literature is large and curiously interesting.

(15.) ACTS OF THE HOLY APOSTLES PETER AND PAUL.

I. Editions.

VITALIS, ORDERICUS. Lat. In: Hist. eccl. II. p. 392. In: Duchesne. Scr. Norm.
LASCARIS, CONST. (1490) Lat. In: Abela, J. F. Melita illustrata. (1647) II. VII. 179 [Extracts from chs. 1–6]; also in Reina [Chs. 1–6 complete]. Cf. below.
NAUSEA, FR. Lat. In: Anon. Philalethi, etc. (1531) 1–8.
FLORENTINI, FR. MAR. Lat. In: Mart. Hieron. (Luccae, 1668.) 103–111.
REINA (or REYNA), PLACIDO. Gr. lat. In: Delle Notizie ist. della citta di Messina. II. (Messina, 1668. f°.) 166–8. [Chs. 1–6. Latin of Lascaris]; also in do. tr. Lat. in: Graevius, J. G. Thesaurus antiq. et hist Siciliae. Lugd. Bat. 1723–5. 15 v. f°. v. IX.
COTELERIUS. Notae in Const. Apost., Lib. VI. c. 9. II. (1672) 269. [Quotes fragment from Greek ms. (the same quoted by Du Cange, acc. to Tischendorf.)]
FABRICIUS. Lat. In: Cod. apocr. III. 632–653.
THILO. Acta Petri et Pauli. I. Halle, 1837. 4° (p. 28); II. 1838. 4° (p. 30).
TISCHENDORF. Acta apocr. (1851) 1–39.
LIPSIUS, R. A. Passiones Petri et Pauli graece ex codice Patmensi primum edidit. In: Jahrbb. f. prot. Theol. (1886) 86–106, 175–176. (?)

II. Translations.

English.

WALKER, A. In: Ante-Nic. Lib. XVI. (1873) 256–78.
Ed. Coxe. VIII. (1886) 477–86.

III. Literature.

ABELA, JO. Franc. (1647) Melita illustrata lib. II. notit. VII. cod. 179. In: Graevius F, XV. [Cf. art. Melite in Winer. Bibl. Realwörterb.]
CIANTAR, J. A. Dissert. apol. Pauli. apostoli in Melitam, etc. Venetiis, 1738.
DUCANGE. Gloss med. et inf. graec. s. v. Βούλλα, καστέλλιν, ’ορδινεύειν, etc.
FABRICIUS. Cod. apocr. N. T. (1719) 775–6.
GEORGIUS, IGN. D. Paulus apostolus in mari quodnunc Venetus, etc. Venet. 1720. [Cf. Baumgarten. Nachrichten von Merkwurdigen Büchern. VIII. (Halle, 1755.) 157–74.]
HOFFMANN. In: Herzog. Real.-Enc. (1877–) I. 523–4.
HOLTZMANN. Einl. in d. N. T. (1886) 546.
ITTIG. Hist. eccl. (1709) I. 45–6.
KURTZ. Kirchenges. (1885–) I. 133–4.
LIPSIUS. Röm. Petrus-sage. (1872) 47–163.
— Gospels Apocryphal. In: Smith and Wace. Dict. II. 708–9.
— Apokr. apostelleg. II. 1. (1887) 1–423.
LUMPER. Hist. ss. patr. I. (1783) 466–70.
PRESSENSÉ. Heresy. (N.Y.) 178–9.

ROESSLER. Bibl. d. K.–V. IV. (1777) 368. [Mention.]
TISCHENDORF. Acta apocr. (1851) xiv-xxi.
WAITE. Hist. Chr. Rel. (1881) 111–3, etc.
WALKER, A. Introd. note. In: Ante-Nic. Lib. XVI. (1873) xiv. Ed. Coxe. VIII. (1886) 355.

(16.) ACTS OF PAUL AND THECLA.

I. *Editions.*

GRABE. Gr. lat. In: Spicil. patr. I. (1698) 93–128; (1700) I. 81–128.
HEARNE, THOM. In: App. ad Joannis Lelandi anti-quarii collectanea, parte secunda. VI. (*Oxf.* 1715.) 67–69. [Supplies lacuna in Grabis ed. sect. 27, post Κατέκρινεν usque sect. 32. Τῶν δὲ λεγουσων.]
JONES. Canon N. T. (1726); (1798) II. 353–386.
TISCHENDORF. Acta apocr. (1851) 40–63.

II. *Translations.*

Latin.

GRABE. In: Spicil. patr. I. (1698) 120–.
GALLANDIUS. Bibl. patr. I. 177–.
Bibl. Casin. III. Florileg. p. 271–6. gr. Bibl. Casin. III. 266–.

Syriac.

WRIGHT. Syr. Engl. 1871.

English.

HONE. Apocr. N. T. (1825) 126–142. (Phila. n. d.) 99–111.
WALKER, A. In: Ante-Nic. Lib. XVI. (1873) 279–92. Ed. Coxe. VIII. (1886) 487–92.

III. *Literature.*

Acta sanctorum. Sept. VI. p. 546.
BASILIUS SELEUC. De vita ac mir. S. Theclae. Ed. Pantinus. V. *Antv.* 1608.
CHARTERIS. Canonicity. (1880) 180, 199, 236.
CLARKE. Sacred lit. (1830–1) I. 152. [7 ll.]
FABRICIUS. Cod. apocr. N. T. (1719) 794–6.
GRABE, ERN. Spicil. SS. Patr. I. (1700) 87.
GUTSCHMID. Königsnamen. Ed. above.
HASE. Kirchenges. (1885–) I. 275–6.
HILGENFELD. N. T. extra canon rec. IV. p. 69.
HOFFMANN. In: Herzog. Real.-Enc. (1877) I. 524.
HOLTZMANN. Einl. in d. N. T. (1886) 546.
ITTIG. De bibl. et cat. patr. (*Lips.* 1707) 700–705.
— Hist. eccl. (1709) I. 10–11.
JONES. Canon N. T. 1798. I. 311–313, 387–411.
KURTZ. Kirchenges. (1885–) I. 134–5.
LARDNER. Credibility. Works. (1831) II. 331–3.
LIPSIUS. Acts, Apocryphal. In: Smith and Wace. Dict. I. 30–31.
— Apokr. Apostelgesch. II. 1. (1887) 424–67.
LUMPER. Hist. ss. patr. I. (1799) 452–64.
LUTHARDT. St. John the Author of the Fourth Gospel. (1875) 68.
METHODIUS. Conviv. virgin. in psalmo, quem ipsa Thecla dicit. In: Galland. III. p. 742.
ORSI. Ist. eccl. (1746–) 78–80; (1749–) I. 111–3.
PANTINUS, PETR. Basilii Seleuciae in Isauria episcopi de vita ac miraculis D. Theclae virginis martyris Iconiensis. *Antv.* 1608. [" Adj. est Simeonis Metaphrasti Logothetae de eadem martyre tractati sinulari."]
PRESSENSÉ. Heresy. (*N.Y.*) 179–80.
RITSCHL. Altkatl. Kirche. 2. Aufl. p. 292–4.
ROESSLER. Bibl. d. K.–V. IV. (1777) 369. [2½ ll.]
SCHLAU, C. Die Acten d. Paulus u. der Thecla, u. die ältere Thecla-Legende. Ein Beitrag zur christl. Literaturgesch. *Leipzig*, 1877. 8°.

SCHLIEMANN. Clementinen. (1844) 431–3.
SIMEON METAPHRASTES. Acta Pauli et Theclae. See all eds. of S. M.
STILTING, JO. In: Acta sanctorum.
STOWE. Books of the Bible. (1867) 318–27.
TISCHENDORF. Acta apocr. (1851) xxi-xxvi.
Unschuldigen Nachrichten. (*Leipz.* 1702) 136–.
WAITE. Hist. Chr. Rel. (1881) 23 et pass.
WALKER, A. Introd. note. In Ante-Nic. Lib. XVI. (1873) xiv. Ed. Coxe. VIII. (1886) 355.
ZAHN. Acta Johannis. p. lxix.
ZENO VERON. De timo re. 1. I. Tract. 8. In: Galland. V. 122.

Note 1. Ancient allusions to this work are numerous, among others allusions by Ambrose, Chrysostom, Cyprian of Ant., Epiphanius, Gelasius, Gregory Naz., Gregory Nyss., Jerome, and Tertullian.
Note 2. Literature of the Thecla legend is abundant.

(17.) THE ACTS OF BARNABAS.

I. *Editions.*

PAPEBROCHIUS. Gr. lat. In: Acta S.S. mensis Junii. II. (*Antv.* 1698) p. 431–436.
TISCHENDORF. Acta apocr. (1851) 64–74.

II. *Translations.*

Latin.

MOMBRITIUS. Passio S. Barnabae. 1479.
MAZOCCHI. Comment. in vet. marmoreum. S. Neap., etc. II. (   ) 540–544.

English.

WALKER, A. In: Ante-Nic. Lib. XVI. (1873) 293–300. Ed. Coxe. VIII. (1886) 493–6.

III. *Literature.*

BARONIUS. Annal. ad an. Chr. 51. num. 51.
BRAUNSBERGER. Der Apost. Barnabas. *Mainz.* 1876.
FABRICIUS. Cod. apocr. N. T. (1719) 781–2.
HARNACK. In: Theol. Literaturztng. (1876) 487–.
HOFFMANN. In: Herzog. Real.-Enc. (1877–) I. 524.
LIPSIUS. Acts, Apocryphal. In: Smith and Wace. Dict. I. 31.
— Apokr. Apostelleg. II. 11. (1884) 270–320.
SIEGEBERT GEMBL. Catal. script. eccl.
TILLEMONT. Mem. hist. eccl. (I. p. 1189; II. p. 413.)
TISCHENDORF. Acta apocr. (1851) xxvi-xxxi.
VITALIS, ODER. Hist. eccl. Cf. Apx.
VORAGINE. Legenda aurea. Cf. Apx.
WALKER, A. Introd. note. In: Ante-Nic. Lib. XVI. (1873) XV. Ed. Coxe. VIII. (1886) 355.
Note. Compare also general works on Barnabas.

(18.) THE ACTS OF PHILIP.

I. *Editions.*

TISCHENDORF. Acta apocr. (1851) 75–104.

II. *Translations.*

English.

WALKER, A. In: Ante-Nic. Lib. XVI. (1873) 301–34. Ed. Coxe. VIII. (1886) 497–510.

III. *Literature.*

ANASTASIUS SINAITA. De tribus quadragesimis. Contains an epitome, printed in Cotelerius, Monum. Eccl. Gr. I. 3. p. 428–430. Fabricius. Cod. apocr. II. p. 806–810 and Beausaubre. Hist. Manich. I. p. 346 seq.

FABRICIUS. Cod. apocr. N. T. (1719) 806–10.
HOFFMANN. In: Herzog. Real.-Enc. (1877–) I. 524.
HOLTZMANN. Einl. in d. N. T. (1886) 548.
JONES. Canon N. T. 1798. I. 381.
LIPSIUS. Apokr. Apostelgesch. II. II. (1884) 1–53.
— Acts, Apocryphal. In: Smith and Wace. Dict. I. 30.
ROESSLER. Bibl. d. K.–V. IV. (1777) 369. [2½ ll.]
TISCHENDORF. Acta apocr. (1851) xxxi-xl. 141–56.
WAITE. Hist. Chr. Rel. (1881) 125.
WALKER, A. Introd. note. In: Ante-Nic. Lib. XVI.
(1886) xv. Ed. Coxe. VIII. (1886) 355.

(19.) PHILIP IN HELLAS.

Literature.

LIPSIUS. Apokr. Apostelgesch. II. II. (1884) 27–31.
HOFFMANN. In: Herzog. Real.-Enc. (1877–) I. 524.
TISCHENDORF. Acta. p. xxxviii-xl.
WALKER, A. Introd. note. In: Ante-Nic. Lib. XVI.
(1873) xv-xvi. Ed. Coxe. VIII. (1886) 355.

I. Editions.

WOOG, KARL CHRIST. Epist. . . . de martyrio S. An-
dreae. Lips. 1747.
TISCHENDORF. Acta apocr. (1851) 105–31.
MIGNE. Patrol. gr. II. (1827) 1215–48. [Tischendorf.]

II. Translations.

English.

WALKER, A. In: Ante-Nic. Lib. XVI. (1873) 335–47.
Ed. Coxe. VIII. (1886) 511–6.

III. Literature.

FABRICIUS. Cod. apocr. N. T. (1719) 747–59, 767–8.
GALLAND. Vet. patr. bibl. Venet. 1765. f°. I. xxxviii–;
also in: Migne. Patrol. gr. II. (1857) 1199–1216.
HOFFMANN. In: Herzog. Real.-Enc. (1877–) I. 524–5.
HOLTZMANN. Einl. in d. N. T. (1886) 547.
KURTZ. Kirchenges. (1885–) I. 134.
LIPSIUS. Acts, Apocryphal. In: Smith and Wace. Dict.
I. 30.
— Apokr. Apostelleg. I. (1883) 563–7.
LUMPER. Hist. ss. patr. I. (1783) 202–27.
PRESSENSÉ. Heresy. (N.Y.) 180–1.
ROESSLER. Bibl. d. K.–V. IV. (1777) 367.
TISCHENDORF. Acta apocr. (1851) xl-xlvii.
Veterum Testim. In: Galland. Vet. patr. bibl. Ven. 1765.
f°. I. 145–. Also in: Migne. Patrol. gr. II. (1857)
1187–98.
WAITE. Hist. Chr. Rel. (1881) 125.
WAKE. Lond. 1693. 152–3; Lond. 1710. 8°; Lond.
1719. 8°. 104–5; 1737. 8°; 5th ed. 1818 [7?]; Hart-
ford, 1834. 444; Lond. 1842 [3?]. 8°; Phila. 1846.
8°; Lond. 1846. 8°; 1860. 8°.
WALKER, A. Introd. note. In: Ante-Nic. Lib. XVI.
(1873) xvi. Ed. Coxe. VIII. (1886) 356.

(20.) ACTS OF ANDREW AND MATTHIAS.

I. Editions.

THILO. Acta Andreae et Matthiae. Halle, 1846.
TISCHENDORF. Acta apocr. (1851) 132–66.
WRIGHT. Gr. Syr. Eng. In: Apocr. Acts. 93–115.

II. Translations.

Ethiopic.

MALAN. In: Certamen. apost. 147–63.

Anglo-Saxon.

GRIMM, JAKOB. Andreas u. Elena. Kassel. 1840. [Con-
tains the Anglo-Saxon form of the Acts of Andrew and
Matthew.]

English.

WALKER, A. In: Ante-Nic. Lib. XVI. (1873) 348–68.
Ed. Coxe. VIII. (1886) 517–25.

III. Literature.

HOFFMANN. In: Herzog. Real.-Enc. (1877) I. 525.
HOLTZMANN. Einl. in d. N. T. (1886) 547.
PRESSENSÉ. Heresy. (N.Y.) 164–5.
STOWE. Books of the Bible. (1867) 327–34.
TISCHENDORF. Acta apocr. (1851) xlvii-lix.
— Apocal. apocr. (1866) 139–41.
WALKER, A. Introd. note. In: Ante-Nic. Lib. XVI.
(1873) xvi-xvii. Ed. Coxe. VII. (1886) 356.

———

(21.) ACTS OF PETER AND ANDREW.

I. Editions.

WOOG. p. 401–.
THILO. Acta Andr. et Matt. (1846) 30–.
TISCHENDORF. Apocal. Apocr. (1866) 161–.

II. Translations.

Ethiopic.

MALAN. Certam. ap. 221–9.

Old Slavic.

TICHONRAWOW. Denkmäler d. apokr. Lit. II.

English.

WALKER, A. In: Ante-Nic. Lib. XVI. (1873) 368–72.
Ed. Coxe. VIII. (1886) 526–7.

III. Literature.

BONWETSCH, N. Ein Beitrag zu den Akten des Petrus
u. Andreas. In: Ztschr. f. Kirchengesch. V. (1882)
506–509.
LIPSIUS. Apokr. Apostelgesch. I. (1883) 554–7.
— Zu den Acten des Petrus und Andreas. In: Jahrbb. f.
prot. theol. (1883) 191.
TISCHENDORF. Apocal. apocr. (1866) 161–7.
WAITE. Hist. Chr. Rel. (1881) 31 et pass.

———

(22.) ACTS AND MARTYRDOM OF ST. MAT-
THEW THE APOSTLE.

I. Editions.

TISCHENDORF. Acta apocr. (1851) 167–89.

II. Translations.

English.

WALKER, A. In: Ante-Nic. Lib. XVI. (1873) 373–88.
Ed. Coxe. VIII. (1886) 528–34.

III. Literature.

HOFFMANN. In: Herzog. Real.-Enc. (1877) I. 525.
TISCHENDORF. Acta apocr. (1851) lx-lxiii.
WALKER, A. Introd. note. In: Ante-Nic. Lib. XVI.
(1873) xvii. Ed. Coxe. VIII. (1886) 356.

(23.) ACTS OF THE HOLY APOSTLE THOMAS.

I. *Editions.*

THILO. Leipz. 1823. 8⁰.
TISCHENDORF. Acta apocr. (1851) 190–234.
BONNET, MAX. Suppl. ad. apocr. 1883 (?) [Supplies hitherto missing fragments.]

II. *Translations.*

Syriac.

WRIGHT. Syr. Engl. In: Apocr. Acts. *Lond.* 1871.

English.

WALKER, A. •In: Ante-Nic. Lib. XVI. (1873) 389–422. Efl. Coxe. VIII. (1886) 535–49.

III. *Literature.*

FABRICIUS. Cod. apocr. N. T. (1719) 819–28.
HILGENFELD, A. In: Ztschr. f. wiss. Theol. XXVII. (1883) 383–4. [Rev. of Bonnet, (1883).]
LIPSIUS. Acts, Apocryphal. In: Smith and Wace. Dict. I. 30.
HOFFMANN. In: Herzog. Real.-Enc. (1877–) I. 525.
HOLTZMANN. Einl. in d. N. T. (1886) 547.
JONES. Canon N. T. (1798) I. 394–6.
KURTZ. Kirchenges. (1885–) I. 134.
LIPSIUS. Apokr. Apostelleg. I. (1883) 225–347.
PRESSENSÉ. Heresy. (*N.Y.*) 166–71.
SIMON. Nov. obs. de textu, etc. p. 7–.
TISCHENDORF. Acta apocr. (1851) lxiii-lxviii.
— Apocal. apocr. (1866) 156–61.
WALKER, A. Introd. note. In: Ante-Nic. Lib. XVI. (1886) xvii-xviii. Ed. Coxe. VIII. (1886) 357.

(24.) CONSUMMATION OF THOMAS THE APOSTLE.

I. *Editions.*

TISCHENDORF. Acta apocr. (1851) 235–42.

II. *Translations.*

English.

WALKER, A. In: Ante-Nic. Lib. XVI. (1873) 423–8. Ed. Coxe. VIII. (1886) 550–2.

III. *Literature.*

HOFFMANN. In: Herzog. Real.-Enc. (1877) I. 525.
TISCHENDORF. Acta apocr. (1851) lxviii-lxix.
WALKER, A. Introd. note. In: Ante-Nic. Lib. XVI. (1873) xviii. Ed. Coxe. VIII. (1886) 357.

(25.) MARTYRDOM OF THE HOLY AND GLORIOUS APOSTLE BARTHOLOMEW.

I. *Editions.*

TISCHENDORF. Acta apocr. (1851) 243–60.
MIGNE. Gr. lat. In: Patrol. gr. II. (1857) 785–6.

II. *Translations.*

Armenian.

MÖSINGER. Vita et martyrium S. Bartholomaei. *Innsbruck,* 1877. [Latin transl. from the Armenian.]

English.

WALKER, A. In: Ante-Nic. Lib. XVI. (1873) 429–39. Ed. Coxe. VIII. (1886) 553–7.

III. *Literature.*

HOFFMANN. In: Herzog. Real.-Enc. (1877–) I. 525.
LIPSIUS. Acts, Apocryphal. In: Smith and Wace. Dict. I. 30.
— Apokr. Apostelgesch. II. II. (1884) 54–108.
MOESINGER, G. Vita et martyrium sancti Bartholomaei apostoli, ex sinceris fontibus armeniacis in linguam latinam conversa. *Salsburgi,* 1877. 8⁰.
WALKER, A. Introd. note. In: Ante-Nic. Lib. XVI. (1873) xviii-xix. Ed. Coxe. VIII. (1886) 357.
    Note. Perhaps identical with the Pseudo-Abdias Latin. Cf. especially Mösinger.

(26.) ACTS OF THE HOLY APOSTLE THADDAEUS.

I. *Editions.*

TISCHENDORF. Acta. p. 261–265.

II. *Translations.*

English.

WALKER, A. In: Ante-Nic. Lib. XVI. (1873) 440–3. Ed. Coxe. VIII. (1886) 558–9.

III. *Literature.*

HOFFMANN. In: Herzog. Real.-Enc. (1877–) I. 525–6.
TISCHENDORF. Acta. p. lxxi-lxxiii.
WALKER, A. Introd. note. In: Ante-Nic. Lib. XVI. (1873) xix. Ed. Coxe. VIII. (1886) 357.
    Note. See literature under Ancient Syriac Documents.

(27.) ACTS OF THE HOLY APOSTLE AND EVANGELIST JOHN THE THEOLOGIAN.

I. *Editions.*

TISCHENDORF. Acta apocr. (1851) 266–76.
ZAHN. *Erlangen,* 1880. p. 238–.

II. *Translations.*

English.

WALKER, A. In: Ante-Nic. Lib. XVI. (1873) 444–53. Ed. Coxe. VIII. (1886) 560–4.

III. *Literature.*

FABRICIUS. Cod. apocr. N. T. (1719) 765–7, 788–91, 815–8.
HOFFMANN. In: Herzog. Real.-Enc. (1877–) I. 526.
KURTZ. Kirchenges. (1885–) I. 134.
LIPSIUS. Acts, Apocryphal. In: Smith and Wace. Dict. I. 29–30.
— Apokr. Apostelleg. I. (1883) 490–2.
LUMPER. Hist. ss. patr. I. (1783) 464–6.
PRESSENSÉ. Heresy. (*N.Y.*) 181–2.
ROESSLER. Bibl. d. K.-V. IV. (1777) 367. [2 ll.]
TISCHENDORF. Acta apocr. (1851) lxxiii-lxxvi.
WALKER, A. Introd. note. In: Ante-Nic. Lib. XVI. (1873) xix-xx. Ed. Coxe. VIII. (1886) 357–8.
ZAHN, PROF. DR. THDR. Acta Joannis, unter Benutzung von C. v. Tischendorf's Nachlass bearbeiter. *Erlangen,* 1880. 8⁰.
    Note. Much of the above literature relates to other Acts of John. For the editions and thorough treatment of various Acts, and recensions, translations, etc., not included in this series, compare Lipsius's admirable monograph.

(28.) REVELATION OF MOSES.

I. Editions.

TISCHENDORF. Apocal. apocr. (1866) 1–23.

II. Translations.

English.

WALKER, A. In: Ante-Nic. Lib. XVI. (1873) 454–67. Ed. Coxe. VIII. (1886) 565–70.

III. Literature.

DILLMANN. In: Herzog. Real.-Enc. VII. (1860) 317–.
LÜCKE. Offenb. Joh. (1848) 232–.
PRESSENSÉ. Heresy. (N.Y.) 183–5.
TISCHENDORF. In: Heidelb. Studien u. Krit. (1851) 432–.

(29.) REVELATION OF ESDRAS.

TISCHENDORF. Apocal. apocr. (1866) x–xii.
WALKER, A. Introd. note. In: Ante-Nic. Lib. XVI. (1873) xx–xxi. Ed. Coxe. VIII. (1886) 358.
DILLMANN. In: Herzog. Real.-Enc. XII. (1883) 356. [Lit. 7 ll. only.]
WALKER, A. In: Ante-Nic. Lib. XVI. (1873) xxi. 468–76. Ed. Coxe. VIII. (1886) 358, 571–4. [Eng.]
TISCHENDORF. Apocal. apocr. (1866) xii–xiv. 24–33. [Gr.]

(30.) REVELATION OF PAUL.

I. Editions.

TISCHENDORF. Gr. Apocal. apocr. (1866) 34–69. [English transl. of the Syriac added.]

II. Translations.

Syriac.

PERKINS. Syr. Eng. In: Jour. of the Am. Oriental Soc. VIII. (1864); repr. in: Jour. of Sacred Lit. ed. Cowper. (Lond. 1866.) 372–.

English.

WALKER, A. In: Ante-Nic. Lib. XVI. (1873) 477–92. Ed. Coxe. VIII. (1886) 575–81.

III. Literature.

ASSEMANI. Catal. Bibl. Orient. Clem. Vat. III. I. 282.
DUPIN. Bibl. proleg. II. 94.
FABRICIUS. Cod. apocr. N. T. (1719) 943–53.
HÄVERNICK. Lucubr. crit. in Apoc. p. 14.
HOFFMANN. In: Herzog. Real.-Enc. (1877–) I. 528.
HOLTZMANN. Einl. in d. N. T. (1886) 551. [5 ll.]
JONES. Canon N. T. 1798. I. 317–324.
LÜCKE. Einl. in d. Offenb. d. Joh. I. (1848) 232–.
ROESSLER. Bibl. d. K.–V. IV. (1777) 383. [5 ll.]
SCHOLZ. Einleitung in d. heil. Schriften. I. (1845) 192.
STOWE. Books of the Bible. (1867) 499–508.
TISCHENDORF. Apocal. apocr. (1866) xiv–xviii.
— In: Studien. (1851) II.
WALKER, A. Introd. note. In: Ante-Nic. Lib. XVI. (1873) xxi. Ed. Coxe. VIII. (1886) 358–9.

(31.) REVELATION OF JOHN.

I. Editions.

BIRCH. Auct. cod. apocr. Fabr. Havn. 1804.
TISCHENDORF. Apocal. apocr. (1866) 70–94.

II. Translations.

English.

WALKER, A. In: Ante-Nic. Lib. XVI. (1873) 493–503. Ed. Coxe. VIII. (1886) 582–6.

III. Literature.

FABRICIUS. Cod. apocr. N. T. (1719) 953–5.
HOFFMANN. In: Herzog. Real.-Enc. (1877–) I. 528.
PRESSENSÉ. Heresy. (N.Y.) 187–8.
ROESSLER. Bibl. d. K.–V. IV. (1777) 383. [3 ll.]
TISCHENDORF. Apocal. apocr. (1866) xviii–xix.
WALKER, A. Introd. note. In: Ante-Nic. Lib. XVI. (1873) xxi–xxii. Ed. Coxe. VIII. (1886) 359.

(32). THE BOOK OF JOHN CONCERNING THE FALLING ASLEEP OF MARY.

I. Editions.

BERGER, FR. XAV. In: Aretin, J. C. v. Beitr. z. Gesch. u. Lit. V. (1805) 629–.
TISCHENDORF. Apocal. apocr. (1866) 95–112.

II. Translations.

English.

WALKER, A. In: Ante-Nic. Lib. XVI. (1873) 504–14. Ed. Coxe. VIII. (1886) 587–91.

III. Literature.

BONNET, M. In: Ztschr. f. wiss. Theol. XXIII. (1880) 222–47. ["Die ältesten Schriften v. d. —."]
HOLTZMANN. Einl. in d. N. T. (1886) 540–1.
ROESSLER. Bibl. d. K.–V. IV. (1777) 361. [2 ll.]
TISCHENDORF. Apocal. apocr. (1866) xxxiv–xlvi.
Compare below.

(33.) THE PASSING OF MARY.

I. Editions.

Bibl. patr. max. Lugd. II. II. 212–6.
MIGNE. Patrol. gr. V. (1857) 1231–40.
TISCHENDORF. Apocal. apocr. (1866) 113–36.
BICKELL. In: Theol. Quartalschr. (1866) 469–.

II. Translations.

Syriac.

WRIGHT. Syr. Engl. In: Jour. of Sacr. Lit. 1865; Jan. 417–; Apr. 129–.
— Syr. Engl. Syr. apocr. (1865).

Arabic.

ENGER. Arab. Lat. Elb. 1854.

English.

WALKER, A. In: Ante-Nic. Lib. XVI. (1873) 515–30. Ed. Coxe. VIII. (1886) 592–8.

III. Literature.

BONNET. See above.
FABRICIUS. Cod. apocr. N. T. (1719) 352–.
LIPSIUS. Gospels, Apocryphal. In: Smith and Wace. Dict. II. 706–7.
REUSS, E. In: Strassb. theol. Beitr. VI. 119.
— Gesch. N. T. (1874) I. 273; tr. Eng. (1884) 272. [v. 1.]

TISCHENDORF. Apocal. apocr. (1866) xxxiv-xlvi.
WALKER, A. Introd. note. In: Ante-Nic. Lib. XVI. (1873) xxii-xxiii. Ed. Coxe. VIII. (1886) 359–60. Compare above.

VI. THE DECRETALS.

The purpose and limits of this *Synopsis* compel, as a question of relative value, the omission of almost all the references gathered on this topic, leaving only the following suggestions.

I. *Editions.*

MIGNE. Patrol. gr. X. (1857) 9–18, 109–142, 155–202.
And in all editions of Pseudo-Isidore, various collections of councils, etc.

II. *Translations.*

SALMOND, S. D. F. In: Ante-Nic. Lib. IX. (1869) 145–52, 203–23, 232–274. Ed. Coxe. VIII. (1886) 599–644.

III. *Literature.*

COXE, A. C. Note. In: Ante-Nic. Fath. Ed. Coxe. VIII. (1886) 641–4.
And the abundant literature on the Pseudo-Isidor. Compare Encyclopædias under Pseudo-Isidor, Decretals, etc. A fairly full literary apparatus for general study will be found in SCHAFF. *Hist.* . . . *Church.* IV. (1885) 266–7. For accounts of the nominal authors compare the various *Lives of the Popes* and the literature in CHEVALIER. *Répertoire des sources hist. du Moyen Age. Par.* 1877–86.
Space is taken, however, on account of his relation to Hippolytus, for the following supplementary titles on Callistus, which, with two exceptions, *exclude* all titles given in CHEVALIER.

CALLISTUS.

BAUR. Dogmengesch. I. (1865) 472–3.
BERGER, S. In: Lichtenberger. Encycl. (1877–82) II. 524–6.
BOWER. Hist. of the Popes. I. (1749) 42–4.
BUNSEN. Hippolytus. (1854) I. 390–6.
Callistus and his accuser. In: Dub. R. XXXV. (1853) 447.
CHÉVALIER. Rép. d. sources hist. (1877–86) 377–8.
HARNACK. Dogmenges. I. (1886) 310–1.
HASE. Kirchenges. (1885–) I. 370–1, 387, 429–31.
HERGENROETHER. Kirchenges. (1879–80) I. 198–9; III. 92.
HERZOG. In: Herzog. Real.-Enc. (1877–) III. 64–5. (Abr. in: Schaff-Herz. I. 363.)
HIR, A. LE. Le pape St. Calliste et les " Philosophumena." In: Etudes relig., hist. et lit. C. VIII. (1866) 163–87, 277–98.
History of Callistus. In: Month. VIII. (1867) 1; 181–; 285–.
LUMPER. Hist. ss. patr. XIII. (1799) 736–40.
M'CLINTOCK and S. Cycl. (1874) II. 29.
MARX. In: Wetzer u. W. Kirch-Lex. (1847–54) II. 259–60.
MOBERLY, G. H. In: Smith and Wace. Dict. I. 390–2.
MORRIS, J. Lives of Callistus and Hippolytus. In: Month. XXXIII. (1877) 214; 321–.
NITZSCH. Dogmengesch. I. (1870) 201, etc.
ORSI. Ist. eccl. (1746–) III. 52–3; (1749–) III. 68–9.
PRESSENSÉ. Chr. life. (1878) 125–7, 134–9. Martyrs. (1879) 369–73.

ROSSI, G. B. DE. Esame archeologico e critico della storia di s. Callisto narrata del libro IX. dei Filosofumeni. In his: Bull. archeol. crist. A. IV. (1866) 1–14, 17–33, 65–72, 77–99.
SCHROECKH. Kirchenges. (1772–) XXXV. 67.

VII. MEMOIRS OF EDESSA AND ANCIENT SYRIAC DOCUMENTS.

I. *Editions.*

CURETON, WM. Spicilegium Syriacum. Containing remains of Bardesan, Meliton, Ambrose, and Mara. *Lond.* 1855. [Introduction, Text, Translation, Notes.]
— Ancient Syriac Documents. With Preface by W. Wright. *Lond.* 1864. 4°. [King of Edessa, Doctrine of Addaeus, Doctrine of the Apostles, Doctrine of Simon, Acts of Sharbil, Mart. of Barsamya, of Habib, etc. Hom. on Habib, on Guria, Extracts relating to Abgar, all Syr.-Engl. Mart. of Shamuna, Surius' lat. tr. from Simeon Metaphrastes, and Extract from Moses of Chorene, tr. Fr. by Le Vaillant de Florival.]

LAGARDE. Rel. jur. eccl. ant. gr. *Lpz.* 1856. p. 89–95.
PHILLIPS. The Doctrine of Addai the Apostle, with an English translation and notes. *Lond.* 1876.

II. *Translations.*

English.

CURETON. See editions.
PRATTEN, P. B. In: Ante-Nic. Lib. XX. (1871) 11. Ed. Coxe. VIII. (1886) 651–743.

The correspondence of CHRIST AND ABGAR is found in : —

GRABE. Gr. lat. Spicil. patr. (1700) I. 6–12.
FABRICIUS. Cod. apocr. N. T. (1719) 317–9.
BAYER. Gr. lat. In: Hist. Osrh. (1734).
And translated.

(*English.*)

WAKE. *Lond.* 1693. 8°. 134–9; *Lond.* 1710. 8°. [Greatly improved]; *Lond.* 1719. 8°. 91–4; 1737. 8°; 5th ed. 1818[7?]; *Hartford*, 1834. 8°. 430–4; *Lond.* 1842[3?]. 8° [Revised]; *Lond.* 1846. 8°; 1860. 8°; *Phila.* 1846. 8°.
HONE. Apocr. N. T. (1825) 78. (*Phila.* n. d.) 62–3.
COWPER. Apocr. gosp. (1867) 219–20.

(*German.*)

Berleburger Bibel. VIII. 413.
GRYNAEUS. In: Apost. Männer. *Bas.* 1772. 8°.
HESS, J. J. In: Erst. Jugendgesch. Jesu. (*Zürich*, 1774) 142–. [Grynaeus.]
In: Christl. Magaz. (Pfenninger). III. (1780).
ROSEGARTEN, L. TH. Legenden. II. (*Berl.* 1802) 37–.
STOLBERG. In: Gesch. u. s. w. XI. (*Hamb.* 1816) 427–8.
Partial or complete translations are frequent.

III. *Literature.*

ABGAR.

ALBINUS, M. T. De epistola Christi ad Abgarum. *Witteberg.* 1694. 8°.
ALEXANDER, NATAL. Hist. eccl. (1778) III. 84–6.
ASSEMANI. Biblioth. orientalis. I. 554–; II. 393–; III. 2, 8–.
BARONIUS. Ann. (1589–) 31, 57–61. Cf. Pagi. Crit. (1689–) 8.
BASNAGE. Annal. polit.-eccl. contr. Baronium. p. 431–.
BAUMGARTEN, S. J. Ausz. d. Kirchenges. *Halle*, 1743–6. I. 226–32.

BAYER, GOTTLIEB SIEGFRIED.   Historia Osrhoena et
    Edessana. (1734) 358–; 94–125.
BOURGET, L.   In : Biblioth. Ital. XIII. 124–.
BÜSCHING, J. J.   Wöchentl. Nachr. u. s. w. II. (Bresl.
    1817) 57– (67–8).
CARRIÈRE, A.   In : Lichtenberger. Encycl. (1877–82) I.
    20–1.
CASPARI, C. P.   In : Theol. Tidssk. f. d. Kirke i. Norge.
    III. (1886) 427–8.
CAVE.   Scr. eccl. hist. lit. (1740–3) I. 2–3; II. IV. 16.
CEILLIER.   Hist. gén. aut. sac. I. (1729) 474–9; I.
    (1858) 268–71.
CHEVALIER.   Rép. d. sources hist. (1877–86) 5.
COFFIN.   Lives of fath. (1846) 176–9.
CONSTANTIUS PORPHYR.   De Edessena Christi imagine,
    ed. Combefisius.   In : Manip. rer. Constantinop. p. 81.
COWPER.   Apocr. gosp. (1867) lxxxi-lxxxii, 217.
DALHUSIUS, ENE.   De Epist. quae vulgo Servatori
    tribuitur, responsoria ad Abg. Edes. principem.   Hafn.
    1699. 4°.
DUPIN.   Bibl. aut. eccl.
DURDENT.   In : Biog. Univ. (Michaud) (1842–65) I.
    69–70.
Encycl. Brit. (9th ed.) I. 48.
EUSEBIUS.   Hist. eccl. I. 13.
EVAGRIUS.   Hist. eccl. IV. 27.
FABRICIUS.   Cod. apocr. N. T. (1719) 317–20.
FRAUENDORFF, J. C.   De epist. Christi ad Abgarum,
    speciat, contra G. Cave.   Lipsiae, 1693. 8°.
GIACHETTI, JEAN.   Iconologia Salvatoris, de imagine
    Christi ad Abgarum missa.   Romae, 1628. 8°.
GIESELER.   Church. Hist. (1868–) I. 68–9.
GOETZIUS, G. H.   De Christi scriptis.   Vit. 1687.
GRABE, E.   Spicil. P. P. Sec. I. p. 1–, 399–.
GRAVESON, I. H. DE.   Fr. de mysteriis et annis Chr. Serva-
    toris nostri.   (Rom. 1711. 4°.) 263–.
GREGORIUS BARHEBR.   Chronic. ed. Bruno. p. 51.
GRIMM, W.   Die Sage v. Ursprung d. Christusbildes.
    Berlin, 1843.
GUTSCHMID.   Die Königsnamen in den apokryphen
    Apostelgeschichten.   In : Rhein. Mus. N. F. XIX. 171.
HALL, I. H.   Syriac version of Epistle of King Abgar to
    Jesus.   In : Hebraica. (1885) 232–235.
HARTMANN, J. D.   In his : Beitrr. z. christl. Kirchen-u.
    Rel. Gesch.   (Jena, 1796.) 188–.
HASE.   Kirchenges. (1885–) I. 191.
HEINE, J. E. C.   De Christi ad Abgarum epist. edit. 2.
    Halae, 1768. 8°   [J. S. Semler, praeses.]
HILGENFELD, A.   In : Ztschr. f. wiss. Theol. XXVI.
    (1883) 124–8.
HOFMANN.   Leben Jesu. (Lips. 1851) 307–.
HOLTZMANN.   Einl. in d. N. T. (1886) 213.
ITTIG.   Hist. eccl. (1709) I. 1–2.
— In : Hept. diss. I. c. 1–2.
JACOB OF SARUG.   In : Grimm. Syr. Chrest. p. 102.
JIBBEN, U.   De imagine Christi Jesu Abgarena s. Edes-
    sena.   Jenae, 1671. 8°.
JOHANNES DAMASC.   De imagin. Ed Lequien. p. 320.
JONES, W.   Canon. N. T. (1798) II. 1–26.
KLEUKER.   In : Christl. Magaz. (Pfenninger) III. (1780)
    1–.
— Apokr. d. N. T.   Hamb. 1798.
LAGARDE.   Abhandlungen. p. 6.
LARDNER.   Works. VI. (1831) 596–605.
LIPSIUS, R. A.   Die edessenische Abgar-Sage kritisch
    untersucht.   Braunschweig, 1880. 8°. 92 p.
— Zur edesseinschen Abgarsage.   In : Jahrbb. f. prot.
    Theol. (1882) 190–192.
MATTHES, K. C. D.   Die edessenische Abgarsage, auf
    ihre Fortbildungs untersucht.   Leipzig, 1882. 8°. 77 p.
M'CLINTOCK and S. Cycl. (1874–) I. 14.
MOHINKE.   In : Ersch u. Gruber. I. I. (1818) 110–3.
MOSHEIM.   Canon. I. 95.

NEANDER.   Church Hist. (1872) III. 201, 240, 241.
Nouv. Biog. Gén. (Hoefer) I. (1852) 120.
PIANELLO, J. B.   Portrait de Jesus Christ, ferit par luy-
    même âgé de 32 ans et envoyé à Abgare roi d'Edesse.
    Histoire et dissertation.   Lyon, 1691, 12°.
PRATTEN, B. P.   Introd. note.   In : Ante-Nic. Lib. XX.
    (1871) ii. 1–4.   Ed. Coxe. VIII. (1886) 645–9.
PROCOPIUS.   De bello pers. II. c. 12.
REISKE, J.   De imag. J. C. Abgarena.   Jenae, 1671. 8°.
REUSS.   Gesch. N. T. (1874) I. 274; tr. Eng. (1884)
    273. [v. 1.]
RINCK, W. F.   Ueb. d. Brief d. Kgs. Abgar. au J. Chr.
    etc.   In : Morgenblatt. (1819) Nr. 110.
— In : Illgen's Zeitschrift. (1843) ii.
RÖHR.   Krit. pred. biblioth. I. 161–.
RONI, PELLEGR.   Le Gesù Cristo scrivesse ad Abgaro
    principe di Edessa e se gl' inviasse la propria immagine.
    In : Zaccaria. Racc. di dissert. (1792) II. 116–54.
RULE, W. H.   Oriental Records.   Lond. 173–6.
SARTORIUS, C. F.   Caus. cur Christ. scripti nihil relig.
    Disq. hist. th.   Lips. 1815. 4°.
SCHMIDT, K.   In : Herzog. Real.-Enc. (1877–) I. 81–2.
    (Abr. in : Schaff-Herz. I. 14.)
SCHROECKH.   Kirchenges. (1772–) II. 32–3.
SCHULTZE, GE.   D. de Epist. Christ. ad Abg.   Regiom.
    1706. 4°.
SEMLER, J. S.   S. u. Heine.
SERPOS, GIOV, DE.   Sulle lettere del re Abgars a Gesù
    Cristo e di questo a quel re.   In : Zaccaria. Racc. di dis-
    sert. (1792) II. 155–66.
SIMON, R.   Hist. crit. d. N. T. I. c. 3.
SPANHEIM.   A. L. T.   I. 578, 794.
STOLBERG.   Gesch. d. Rel. J. Chr. II. 427.
Supernatural Religion. I. (1875) 264–.
THILO.   Proleg. ad. Acta Thomae. (Lipz. 1832. 8°.) p. 85.
TILLEMONT.   Mémoires. (1693–) I. 399–404, 659–62; I.
    (1732) 55, 261, 361–3.
THIERSCH.   Kirchenges. I. 106.
WAITE.   Hist. Chr. Rel. (1881) passim.
WELTE, B.   In : Theol. Quartalschr. (1842) 336.
Wetzer u. W. Kirch-Lex. (1847–54) I. 36–7.
WISE, T.   Hist. de Nummo Abgari Regis.
WRIGHT, W. A.   In : Smith and Wace. Dict. I. 6.
ZELLER, J. E.   (praef. J. Ph. Dettmers), Ep. Jesus ad
    Abg.   Frof. 1798. 8°.

ADDAEUS.

BICKELL.   In : Ztschr. f. kath. Theol. (1877) 296–304.
— Conspectus rei lit. Syr. p. 15–.
CHEVALIER.   Rép. d. sources hist. (1877–86) 2161.
FABRICIUS.   Cod. apocr. N. T. (1719) 379.
HARNACK.   In : Ztschr. f. Kirchenges. II. 93.
HASE.   Kirchenges. (1885–) I. 191.
HECKE.   Comment. praev.   In : Acta ss. Bolland (1867)
    28 Oct. XII. 450–8.
KURTZ.   Kirchenges. (1885–) I. 135.
LIGHTFOOT.   In : Contemp. Rev. (1877) May. p. 1137.
LIPSIUS.   Acts, Apocryphal.   In : Smith and Wace. Dict.
    I. p. 31.
— Apokr. Apostelgesch. I. (1883) 217.
MÖSINGER.   Acta mart Edessen.
NEALE.   Eastern Ch. Antioch. (1873) 7–8.
NEANDER.   Church Hist. (1872) I. 180.
NESTLE.   In : Theol. Ltzng. (1876) 643–.
— Zur Altersbestimmung der Doctrina Addaei.   In :
    Ztschr. f. Kirchengesch. III. 194–5.
NÖLDECHE.   In : Lit. Centralbl. (1876) 937–.
PICK, B.   In : M'Clintock and S. Cycl. (1874–) X. 299.
PRESSENSÉ.   Heresy.   (N.Y.) 182–3.
SIEFFERT.   Judas Lebbäus.   In : Herzog. Real.-Enc.
    (1877–) VII. 276–7.   (Abr. in Schaff-Herz. II. 1206.)
TILLEMONT.   Mémoires. (1693–) I. 360–5, 613–7.

TISCHENDORF. Acta apocr. (1851) 261–5. [Later Acta Thaddaei.]

ZAHN. In: Gött. Gel. Anz. (1877) 161–84.

— Die Lehre d. Addai. In: Forschungen. I. Tatian's Diatessaron (1881) 350–82.

Note. The teaching of Addaeus is treated usually under Abgar. Compare literature above. For the Armenian translation, the Tischendorf Greek Acta Thaddaei and later recensions compare Lipsius, Matthes, and Zahn.

JACOB OF SARUG.

ABBELOOS (JOA. BAPT.) De vita et scriptis s. Jacobi. Batnarum Sarugi in Mesopotamia episcopi. dissertatio historico-theologica. *Lovanii.* 1867. 8°. (xx–322 p.) Cf. A. V. W. In: Ann. de philos. chrét. (1867) E. XVI. 235–42.

— In: Rev. Cathol. (*Louv.* 1875) B. XIV. 620–1.

ASSEMANI. Bibl. orient. Clem.-Vatic. (1719) I. 283–340.

BALL, C. J. In: Smith and Wace. Dict. III. 327–8.

BARHEBRAEUS. Chron. eccl. I. 189–.

BICKELL, G. Consp. Syr. 25, 26.

— *Kempten,* 1872. 16°. [The Reithmayer-Thalhofer Bibl.]

CAVE. Scr. eccl. hist. lit. (1744) II. IV. 34–5.

CEILLIER. H. a. e. (1748) XV. 545–51 (2ª. X. 639–43.)

CHEVALIER. Rép. d. sources hist. (1877–86) 1148.

HERGENROETHER. Kirchenges. (1879–80) I. 415; III. 160.

HOFFMANN, A. G. In: Ersch u. Gruber. II. XIII. (1836) ii. 175–6.

JÖCHER. Gelehrt. Lex. II. col. 1816–17.

LAMY. S. Jacques de Sarug. Extr. de la Rev. Cath. (?) LELONG. Bib. sac. II. 751.

M'CLINTOCK and S. Cycl. (1874–) IV. 737.

MARTIN [PAUL]. Un évêque-poète au Vᵉ et au VIᵉ siècles, ou Jacques de Saroug, sa vie, son temps, ses oeuvres, ses croyances. In: Rev. d. scien. eccles. (1876) D. IV. 309–52, 385–419.

MATAGNE (H.) Comment. praev. In: Acta ss. Bolland. (1867) octb. XII. 824–30, 927–9.

MEANS, J. C. In: Smith. Gr. and Rom. Biog. (1859) II. 545–6.

NESTLE, E. In Herzog. Real.-Enc. (1877–) VI. 450–2. (Abr. in: Schaff-Herz. II. 1136.)

PAUMIER, A. In: Lichtenberger. encycl. (1877–82) VII. 134.

RENAUDOT. Liturg. Orient. II.

WENIG. Schl. syr.

ZINGERLE, Pius. In: Wetzer u. W. Kirch-Lex. (1847–54) V. 457.

— Leben d. heil. Simeon Stylite. *Innsbr.* 1855.

— In: Zeitschr. deutsch. Morgenländ. Ges. (1858–60) XII. 115; XIII. 44; XIV. 679; XX. 511.

— Sechs Homilien d. heil. Jacob v. Sarug. *Bonn,* 1867.

ZINGERLE, J. In: Ztschr. f. kath. Theol. (1887) 92–108.

HABIB.

ASSEMANI. Bibl. Orient. I. 331.

BARONIUS. Ann. (1588–) 316, 48–52.

CHEVALIER. Rép. d. sources hist. (1877–86) 5.

FABRICIUS. Bibl. gr. (1705) IX. 49. (2ª. X. 186–7.)

HOLE, C. In: Smith and Wace. Dict. II. 833–4.

LE QUIEN. Oriens chr. II. 955.

Nouv. Biog. Gén. (Hoefer) I. (1852) 121.

SIMEON METAPHRASTES. In: Surius: Hist. ss. 15 Nov. p. 342 [Latin]; Migne. Patrol. Gr. CXVI. 141 [Gr. lat.]

WRIGHT. In: Jour. Sacr. Lit. (1866) 429.

GURIA.

ASSEMANI. Mart. orient. I. 226.

BASIL. Menol.

CEILLIER. Hist. gén. aut. sac. IV. (1733) 97–8; III. (1865) 102–3.

CHEVALIER. Rép. d. sources hist. (1877–86) 986.

FABRICIUS. Bibl. gr. (1705–) IX. 82 (2ª. X. 233–4.)

MARTINOV. Ann. eccl. gr.-slav. (1864) 280.

STOKES, G. T. In: Smith and Wace. Dict. II. 822.

SURIUS. Vitae ss. XI. (1618) 339–49.

SYMEMON METAPHR. In: Migne. Patrol. gr. CXVI. 127–62.

TILLEMONT. Mémoires. (1693–) V. 395–9, 743–4.

WRIGHT. Syr. mart.

MOSES OF CHORENE. (HISTORY.)

(*Editions.*)

Amst. 1695.

BRENNER, H. 1723. [Extract.]

WHISTON. Arm. lat. *London,* 1736.

SARGIS of Const. *Venet.* 1752.

Venet. 1827. 18°. [Mechitarite Fathers.]

LE VAILLANT DE FLORIVAL. Arm. Fr. 1836; 1849.

Venet. 1843. 8°. [Mechitarite. Improved.]

Venet. 1865. 8°.

(*Translations.*)
English.

PRATTEN. See above.

French.

LE VAILLANT DE FLORIVAL. *Venet.* 1841. 2 v. 8°.

LANGLOIS, V. Historiens de l'Arménie. *Par.* 1867. II. 47–175.

Italian.

FANTI, GER. *Venez.* 1841. [By Mechitarite Fathers.]

Russian.

JOHANNES, Jos. *St. Petersb.* 1809. 2 v. 8°. ["Very poor." *Emin.*]

EMIN, J. B. *Moscow,* 1858.

(*Literature.*)

CHEVALIER. Rép. d. sources hist. (1877–86) 1601–2.

DULAURIER. Études sur les Chants historiques. . . . de l'ancienne Arménie. In: Journal Asiatique. (1852) 5–58.

— In: Rev. d. deux Mondes. XIV. (1852) 224.

DWIGHT. In: Jour. Am. Orient. Soc. III. 248.

EMIN, J. B. *Moscow,* 1850. 8°. (98 p.)

GARINIAN, AGEP. *Tiflis,* 1858. 4°. [Collations of mss.]

v. GUTSCHMID. Ueb. d. Glaubwürdigkeit d. Arm. Gesch. d. M. von Khoren. In: Ber. d. phil.-hist. Classe d. Königee. Sächs. Gesellsch. d. Wiss. (1876) 1–.

— In: Encycl. Brit. (9th ed.) XVI. 861–3.

HERGENROETHER. Kirchenges. (1879–80) I. 16, 221; III. 97–8.

LANGLOIS, VICTOR. Etude sur les sources de l'historie d' Arménie de Moïse de Kohren. In: Bull. acad. scier. *St. Petersb.* (1861) III. 51–383.

— Coll. hist. Armén. (1867) I. 3–11.

LE VAILLANT DE FLORIVAL. Cf. Bibl. éc. Chartes. (1842) A. III. 585–9.

M'CLINTOCK and S. Cycl. (1874–) VI. 688.

NEANDER. Church Hist. (1872) II. 138.

NEUMANN. In: Jour. Asiatique. (1829) p. 56. (??)

— Armen. Liter. (1836) 45–57.

NICARD, POL. In: Mém. soc. antiq. France. (1877) D. VIII. 177–97.

PATCANIAN. Catal. lit. Arm. (1860) 83–4.

PETERMANN. In: Ztschr. d. deut. Morgenl. Gesellch. V. (1851) 366.

— See v. Spiegel.

PICHARD, C. E. Essai sur Moyse de Khoren, historien Arménien du V. siècle du Christ et analyse succincte de son ouvrage sur l'historie d'Arménie. . . . *Paris*, 1866. 8⁰. (99 p.) [100 copies only. "No critical value." *Stokes.*]
QUATREMÈRE. In: Jour. des Savants. (1850) p. 364.
ST. MARTIN, J. DE. Mém. hist.-géog. Arménie. (1819) II. 301–17.
— Notice sur la vie et les écrits de Moyse de Khoren, historien armenien. In: Journ. Asiatiq. A. II. (1823) 321–44. (??).
— In: Biog. Univ. (Michaud) (1842–65) XXVIII. 500–2.
SCHROECKH. Kirchenges. (1772–) XVI. 175.
SOMAL. Letter Armen. (1829) 23–8.
SUKIAS DE SOMAL. Storia di M. C. *Venez.* 1850. [Tr. ?]
SPIEGEL, v. (Petermann). In: Herzog. Real.-Enc. (1877–) X. 325–8. (Abr. in: Schaff-Herz. II. 1886.)
STOKES, G. T. In: Smith and Wace. Dict. III. 949–50.
STRUVE. Bibl. hist. (1782–) II. i. 47–9.
TESSIER, F. X. In: Nouv. biog. gén. (Hoefer) XXVIII. (1859) 84–6.

BARDESAN.

Arch. d. missions. (1851) II. 556.
ASSEMANI. Bibl. orient. I. 389, etc.
AUGUSTI. De hymn. Syr.
BARHEBRAEUS. Chron. Eccl.
BARONIUS. Ann. (1589) 175, 16–21.
BAUMGARTEN–CRUSIUS. Dogmenges. (1832) 159–61. [v. 1.]
BAUR. Dogmengesch. I. (1865) 539.
BAYER. Hist. Osrh. 169–80.
BEAUSOBRE. Histoire de Manichée, etc. II. 128–.
BUDDÆUS. Diss. de haeres. Valentin. § XVIII.
BURTON. Lectures upon Ecclesiastical History. Lect. XX. Vol. II. p. 182–185.
BUSSE. Chr. lit. (1828–9) I. 13–4.
CAVE. Scr. eccl. hist. lit. (1741) I. 77–8.
CEILLIER. Hist. gén. aut. sac. II. 1730) 86–9; I. (1858) 465–7.
CHEVALIER. Rép. d. sources hist. (1877–86) 220.
Christian Remembrancer. (Jan. 1856.) p. 201.
CHWOLSOHN. Sabier. I. 170.
CLINTON. Fasti Hel. III. 370.
DODWELL. Diss. ad Irenaeum. IV. 35.
DUPIN. Bibl. aut. eccl. (1698) I. 850.
Encycl. Brit. (9th ed.) III. 370–1.
ENGELHARDT. Dogmenges. II. (1839) 47–8.
EUSEBIUS. Hist. Eccl. IV. 30.
EWALD. In: Gött. gel. Anz. (1854) 529–.
FABRICIUS. Bibl. gr. 1705. (1712) V. 198 (2ᵃ. 172–5.)
FÉTIS. Biog. music. (1860) I. 245.
GIESELER. Church Hist. (1868–) I. 118.
GALLANDIUS. Bibl. vet. patr. I. p. cxxii.
GRABE. Spicil. I. 317.
HAGENBACH. Hist. of Doct. I. (1850) 137–8, etc.
HAHN, AUG. Bardesanes gnosticus. Syrorum primus hymnolgous. commentatio historico-theologica. *Lipsiae*, 1819. 8⁰. (94 p.)
HASE. Kirchenges. (1885–) I. 323–4.
HÄUSLE. In: Wetzer u. W. Kirch-Lex. (1847–54) I. 611–2.
HEEREN. Stobaei Eclog. P. ii.
HERGENROETHER. Kirchenges. (1879–80) I. 135; III. 58.
HEUMANN. Armen. Liter. (1836) 4.
HIERONYMUS. De vir. ill. 33 (Honor. August 1. 34.)
HILGENFELD, A. Bardesanes der letzte Gnostiker. *Leipz.* 1864. 8⁰. Cf. Rev. crit. (1866) I. 141–2.
— In: Theol. Jahrb. (1854) 529–.
HORT, F. J. A. In: Smith and Wace. Dict. I. 250–60.
ITTIG. Append. Diss. de Haeresiarch. Sect. 11. 6. § 85.
JEREMIE. Church History. p. 125.

— Jour. Sac. Lit. Jan. 1856. p. 256.
KUEHNER. Bardesanis gnostici numina astralia. *Hildburghausen*, 1833. 4⁰.
LAND, J. P. N. Bardesanes de fato. *Leyden*, 1857. 8⁰. [Reprinted from Godgeleerde Bijdragen. (1857).]
— Anelet. Syr. p. 32.
LANGLOIS, V. Coll. histor. Armén. (1867) I. 55–62.
LARDNER. Credibility. Works. (1831) II. 316–23.
LICHTENBERGER. Encycl. (1877–82) II. 81.
LIPSIUS. Gnosticismus. In: Ersch. u. Gruber.
— Ueb. d. Ophit. Syst. In: Hilgenfeld. Ztschr. (1863) 435–.
LUMPER. Hist. ss. patr. III. (1784) 38–49.
MACKENZIE, J. M. In: Smith. Gr. and Rom. Biog. (1859) I. 462–3.
M'CLINTOCK and S. Cycl. (1874–) I. 665–6.
MERX, A. Bardesanes von Edessa. nebst e. Untersuchg. üb. das Verhältniss d. Clement. Recognitionen zu dem Buche d. Gesetze der Länder. *Halle*, 1863. 8⁰.
MOSES OF CHORENE. ii. 66.
MOSHEIM. De reb. Chr. pp. 395–7.
NEANDER. Church Hist. (1872) I. 80, 304, 375, 377, 440–2.
— Genet. Entw. d. Gnost. Syst.
NITZSCH. Dogmengesch. I. (1870) 89-90, etc.
North British Review. (Aug. 1853.) Art. VI.
Nouv. Biog. Gén. (Hoefer) IV. (1853) 480.
ORSI. Ist. eccl. (1746–) II. 184–7; (1749–) II. 262–7.
PERMANEDER. Bibl. patr. (1842) II. 159–61.
PETRI, G. E. In: Ersch u. Gruber. I. VII. (1821) 375–8.
PHOTIUS. Bibl. cod. 223.
PRATTEN, P. B. Introd. note. In: Ante-Nic. Lib. XXII. (1871) ii. 83–4; XXIV. (1872) 95. Ed. Coxe. VIII. (1886) 721–2.
PRIAULX. In: Jour. of Asiatic Soc. (1862).
RITSCHL. Entsth. d. altk. Kir. ed. 1. 186–.
RITTER. Erdkunde. X. 552.
SCHROECKH. Kirchenges. (1772–) III. 169.
SCOTT. Royal coins of M.
SOMAL. Letter. Armen. (1829) 3.
STRONZIUS, FR. Historia Bardesanis ac Bardesanistratum ex veterum doctorum monumentis erua. *Witteb.* 1710. 4⁰.
Supernatural Religion. II. (1875) 70, 222, 223.
TABERAUD. In: Biog. Univ. (Michaud) (1842–65) III. 81.
TILLEMONT. Mém. hist. eccl. (1694) II. 454–7, 676.
WAITE. Hist. Chr. Rel. (1881) 397.
WALCH, C. W. F. Ketzerhistorie. I. 415–422.

Note. See also encyclopaedia articles and general literature on Gnosticism, Valentinian, and on the Clementine literature.

AMBROSE (OF ALEXANDRIA?).

CAVE. Scr. eccl. hist. lit. (1741) I. 288.
CHEVALIER. Rép. d. sources hist. (1877–86) 96.
CHRISTIE, A. J. In: Smith. Gr. and Rom. Biog. (1859) I. 139.
CLINTON. Fasti Rom. (1845–50) I. 249, 265; II. 417.
DUPIN. Nouv. bibl. aut. eccl. (1701) II. 897.
Encycl. Brit. (9th. ed.) I. 662.
EUSEBIUS. Ch. Hist. VI. 18.
FABRICIUS. Bibl. gr. (1717) VIII. 342–3. (2ᵃ. IX. 259–60.)
FARRAR. Interpretation. (1886) 205–6.
HERZOG. In his: Real.-Enc. (1877) I. 331. (Abr. in: Schaff-Herz. I. 70.)
HIERONYMUS. De vir. ill. 126. (Honor. August. 1. 127.)
LANDON. Eccl. Dict. I. 302.
LICHTENBERGER. Encycl. (1877–82) XII. 563.
LUMPER. Hist. ss. patr. XIII. (1799) 12–4.
M'CLINTOCK and S. Cycl. (1874–) I. 191.
NEALE. Eastern Ch., Alexandria. I. (1847) 25–6.

NEANDER. Church Hist. (1872) I. 163, 367, 682, 700-2, 707-9.
ORSI. Ist. eccl. (1746-) III. 28-30, 62-3, 93-5, 129-30; (1749-) III. 38-41, 80-1, 120-2, 167-8.
ROUTH. Rel. sacr. (1846-8) III. 1-9.
SCHROECKH. Kirchenges. (1772-) IV. 34, 47, 96, 126-7.
Supernatural Religion. I. (1875) 170.
TRITHEMIUS. Scr. eccl. 87.
WESTCOTT, B. F. In: Smith and Wace. Dict. I. 90-1.
WETZER U. W. Kirch-Lex. (1847-54) I. 198.

> *Note.* "Nor is there the least ground for identifying with Ambrose of Alexandria." *Westcott.*

VIII. REMAINS OF THE SECOND AND THIRD CENTURIES.

(1.) QUADRATUS.

I. *Editions.*

GRABE. Gr. lat. Spicil. patr (1700) II. 119-25.
GALLANDIUS. Bibl. patr. I.
ROUTH. Rel. sacr. (1846-8) I. 69-90.
In: Migne. Patrol. gr. V. (1857) 1265-6.
and in all editions of Eusebius.

II. *Translations.*

English.

PRATTEN, P. B. In: Ante-Nic. Lib. XXII. (1871) ii. 139. Ed. Coxe. VIII. (1886) 749.

III. *Literature.*

BARONIUS. Ann. (1589) 128, 1.
BAUMGARTEN–CRUSIUS. Dogmenges. (1832) 92. [v. 1.]
BAUR. Dogmengesch. I. (1865) 352. [5 ll.]
BERTHOLDT. Dogmenges. (1822-3) I. 57, etc.
BUSSE. Chr. Lit. (1828-9) I. 6.
CAVE. Scr. eccl. hist. lit. (1741) I. 52.
— Lives. (1840) I. 219-27.
CEILLIER. Hist. gén. aut. sac. (1729) I. 688-90; I. (1858) 401-3.
CHARTERIS. Canonicity. (1880) 66.
CHEVALIER. Rép. d. sources hist. (1877-86) 1887.
CLARKE. Sacred lit. (1830-1) I. 147. [8 ll.]
CLINTON. Fasti Rom. (1845-50) I. 110; II. 402.
COXE, A. C. Introd. note. In: Ed. Coxe. VIII. (1886) 749.
DALLAEUS, Jo. De script. Dion. Areop. I. ch. 13. p. 83, 123.
DONALDSON. Hist. Chr. Lit. (1864-6) II. 51-4.
DORNER. Person of Christ. I. (1864) 119-20, 374-7.
DUPIN. Bibl. aut. eccl. (1698) I. 95.
EUSEBIUS. Hist. eccles. IV. 3.
FABRICIUS. Bibl. gr. (1712) V. 186. (2ª. VII. 154-5.)
— Verit. relig. Christ. (1725) 156.
FLEURY. Hist. eccl. (1691-) I. 388-9.
GALLAND. Vet. patr. bibl. *Venet.* 1765. fº. I. lxxii.; also in: Migne. Patrol. gr. V. (1857) 1261-6.
HALLOIX. Eccl. orient. script. (1633) I. 668-701.
HARNACK. Ueberlieferung d. gr. Apol. (1882) 100-.
HASE. Kirchenges. (1885-) I. 246-7.
HAUCK. (Herzog †) In: Herzog. Real.-Enc. (1877-) XII. 425. (Abr. in; Schaff-Herzog. III. 1986.)
HENSCHENIUS. Sylloge histor. In: Acta ss. Bolland. (1688) maii. VI. 357-9. (3ª. 355-7.)
HERGENROETHER. Kirchenges. (1879-80) I. 86, III. 37.
HIERONYMUS. De vir. ill. 19. (Honor. August. I. 20.)
HOOK. Eccles. Biog. VIII. 173.
ITTIG. Hist. eccl. (1709) II. 49-51, 244.

KURTZ. Kirchenges. (1885-) I. 110.
LABOUDERIE. In: Biog. Univ. (Michaud) (1842-65) XXXIV. 595-596.
LARDNER. Credibility. Works. (1831) II. 307-8.
LICHTENBERGER. Encycl. (1877-82) XI. 47.
LUMPER. Hist. ss. patr. I. (1783) 374-82.
M'CLINTOCK and S. Cycl. (1874-) VIII. 831.
MAURICE. Eccl. Hist. (1854) 206-7.
MEANS, J. C. In: Smith. Gr. and Rom. Biog. (1859) III. 630-1.
NEANDER. Church Hist. (1872) I. 661.
NIRSCHL. Patrol. (1881-) I. 201. [7 l.]
Nouv. Biog. Gén. (Hoefer) XLI. (1862) 268.
ORSI. Ist. eccl. (1746-) II. 63-4; (1749-) II. 92-4.
OTTO. Corp. apol. chr. IX. 333-.
PERMANEDER. Bibl. patrist. (1812) II. 62-3.
PHOTIUS. Cod. 162. p. 343.
PRATTEN, P. B. Introd. note. In: Ante-Nic. Lib. XXII. (1871) ii. 83-4. Ed. Coxe. VIII. (1886) 747-8.
PRESSENSÉ. Martyrs. (1879) 236.
SCHAFF. Hist. . . Church. II. (1886) 708-9.
SCHMID. Patrol. (1879) (1886) 43. [9 ll.]
SCHROECKH. Kirchenges. (1772-) II. 372-4.
SURIUS. Vitae ss. (1618) V. 311.
TILLEMONT. Mém. hist. eccl. (1694) II. 232-7, 588-90.
TRITHEMIUS. Scr. eccl. 12.
VINCENT BELVAC. Spec. hist. XI. 72.
WAITE. Hist. Chr. Rel. (1881) 225-6 et pass.
WESTCOTT. Canon. (1875) 83-4.
YONGE. Pupils of St. John. (1878) 169-78.

(2.) ARISTO OF PELLA.

I. *Editions.*

GRABE. Gr. lat. Spicil. patr. (1700) II. 127-33.
Cyprian. Works. (Edit. Oberthür. *Wirceb.* 1782.)
ROUTH. Rel. sacr. (1846-8) I. 91-109.
In: Migne. patrol. gr. V. (1857) 1277-86.

> *Note.* Fragments gathered from Hieronymus, Eusebius, Maximus, and Origen. See eds.

II. *Translations.*

English.

PRATTEN, P. B. In: Ante-Nic. Lib. XXII. (1871) ii. 139-40. Ed. Coxe. VIII. (1886) 749-50.

III. *Literature.*

BUSSE. Chr. Lit. (1828-9) I. 8.
CAVE. Scr. eccl. hist. lit. (1741) I. 88.
CEILLIER. Hist. gén. aut. sac. (1729) I. 692-5; I. (1858) 404-5.
CHEVALIER. Rép. d. sources hist. (1877-86) 164.
CLARKE. Sacred lit. (1830-1) I. 148. [10 ll.]
COXE, A. C. Introd. note. In: Ed. Coxe. VIII. (1886) 749.
DONALDSON. Hist. Chr. Lit. 1864-6, II. 56-61.
DORNER. Person of Christ. I. (1864) 121-2, 378-9.
EUSEBIUS. Hist. Eccles. IV. c. 6.
FABRICIUS. Bibl. gr. (1712-5) V. 187-8; VII. 96. (2 . VI. 745-6; VII. 156-8.)
— De Verit. Chr. Rel. p. 153.
GALLAND. Vet. patr. bibl. *Venet.* 1765. fº. I. lxxiv.; also in: Migne. Patrol. gr. V. (1857) 1271-8.
GIESELER. Church Hist. (1868-) I. 148.
GRABE. Spicileg. PP. Sec. II. 1, 131.
HARNACK. Ueberl. d. gr. Apol. (*Lpz.* 1882) 115-30.
HIERONYMUS. Epist. ad Galat. III. 13, etc.
ITTIG. Hist. eccl. (1709) II. 56.
KURTZ. Kirchenges. (1885-) I. 111.
LARDNER. Credibility. Works. (1831) II. 310-11.

LUMPER. Hist. ss. patr. I. (1783) 385-95.
MANSEL, S. In: Smith and Wace. Dict. I. 160-1.
Nouv. Biog. Gén. (Hoefer) III. (1852) 187-8.
ORSI. Ist. eccl. (1746) I. 87-8; (1749-) II. 126-8.
PERMANEDER. Bibl. patrist. (1842) II. 97.
SCHAFF. Hist. . . . Church. II. (1886) 107, 710.
SCHMITZ, L. In: Smith. Gr. and Rom. Biog. (1859) I. 310.
TILLEMONT. Mém. hist. eccl. (1694) II. 137-9.
UEBERWEG. Hist. philos. (1876) 295.
WAITE. Hist. Chr. Rel. (1881) 393-4.
WESTCOTT. Canon. (1875) 93-4.
YONGE. Pupils of St. John. (1878) 166-7.

(3.) MELITO.

I. *Editions.*

ROUTH. Rel. sacr. (1846-8) I. 111-153.
MIGNE. Gr. lat. In: Patrol. gr. V. (1857) 1207-32.
OTTO. Corp. Ap. I. (1872) 375-478.

CURETON. (2d Apol.) Syr. Engl. In: Spicil. syr. *Lond.* 1855.
PITRA. (2d Apol.) In: Spicil. Solesmense. II.
KITTO. (Fragm.) Jour. sac. lit. XV.

II. *Translations.*

English.

PRATTEN, P. B. In: Ante-Nic. Lib. XXII. (1871) ii. 112-39. Ed. Coxe. VIII. (1886) 751-62.

German.

WELTE. In: Theol. Quartalschr. (1862) 302-.
GRÖNE, V. *Kempten*, 1873. 16°. [The Reithmayer-Thalhofer Bibl.]

III. *Literature.*

Acta, ss. Bolland. (1675) apr. I. 10-2.
Ann. de phil. Chrét. (1872) F. IV. 432-5.
Arch. d. Missions. (1851) A. II. 558.
BARONIUS. Ann. (1589-) 172, 1-7. Cf. Pagi. Crit. (1689) 347, 3.
BAUMGARTEN-CRUSIUS. Dogmenges. (1832) 166-7. [v. 1.]
BAUR. Dogmengesch. I. (1865) 337-8. (6 ll.)
BELLARMIN-LABBE. Scr. eccl. (1748) 34.
BURTON. Divinity of Christ. (1829) 63-7.
BUSSE. Chr. lit. (1828-9) I. 11-12.
CAVE. Scr. eccl. hist. lit. (1741) I. 71-2.
— Lives. (1840) I. 280-6.
CEILLIER. Hist. gén. aut. sac. (1730) II. 75-9; I. (1858) 449-61.
CHARTERIS. Canonicity. (1880) 43-4, 314, 339-40.
CHEVALIER. Rép. d. sources hist. (1877-86) 1559.
CLARKE. Sacred lit. (1830-1) I. 103-4.
CLINTON. Fasti Rom. (1845-50) I. 167; II. 409.
COXE, A. C. Introd. note. In: Ed. Coxe. VIII. (1886) 750-1.
CUNNINGHAM. Churches of Asia. (1880) passim.
DONALDSON. Hist. Chr. lit. 1864-6. III. 221-39.
DUPIN. Bibl. aut. eccl. (1698) I. 133.
Encycl. Brit. (9th ed.) XV. 840.
EUSEBIUS. Hist. eccles. IV. ch. 26.
FABRICIUS. Bibl. gr. (1712) V. 184-5. (2ª. VII. 1495-1.) B. m. ae. (1736) V. 204-5. (2ª. '68.)
FLEURY. Hist. eccl. (1691-) I. 485-7, 488-90.
GALLAND. Bibl. patr. I. n. 24.
GIESELER. Church Hist. (1868-) I. 143, 167.
HAGENBACH. Hist. of Doct. I. (1850) 105-6.
HALLOIX. Eccl. orient. script. (1636) II. 817-39.

HARNACK. In: Gebhardt. u. H. Texte, etc. I. 240-278.
HASE. Kirchenges. (1885-) I. 251.
HEFELE. In: Wetzer u. W. Kirch-Lex. (1847-54) VII. 46-50.
HERGENROETHER. Kirchenges. (1879-80) I. 88; III. 37.
HIERONYMUS. Vir. ill. 54. (Honor. August. I. 25.)
HOFFMAN. Lex. bibl. gr. (1836) III. 87.
HOLTZMANN. Einl. in d. N. T. (1886) 129-30, etc.
ITTIG. Hist. eccl. (1709) II. 37-9, 223-5.
JACKSON. Ap. fath. (1879) 189-191.
Journal Sac. Lit. XV., XVI., XVII.
KURTZ. Kirchenges. (1885-) I. 111-2.
LARDNER. Credibility. Works. (1831) II. 157-160.
LE CLERC. Hist. eccles. duorum prim. saeculor.
LEDRAIN, E. In: Le Correspondant. (1871) B. XLIX. 370-9.
LELONG. Bibl. sac. II. 857.
LICHTENBERGER. Encycl. (1877-82) IX. 59.
LIGHTFOOT. In: Contemp. Rev. (Feb. 1876.)
LUMPER. Hist. ss. patr. III. (1784) 11-25.
LUTHARDT. St. John the author of the Fourth Gospel. (1875) 49.
MEANS, J. C. In: Smith. Gr. and Rom. Biog. (1859) II. 1023-5.
Melito of Sardis and his remains. In: Kitto. XV. (1855) 121-; XVI. (1855) 434-; XVII. (1856) 121-.
MUENSCHER. Dogmenges. (1817-8) I. 245-7, etc.
NEALE. Hist. East. Ch. Introd. I. 38.
NEANDER. Church Hist. (1872) I. 104-5, 299, 676.
— Hist of dogmas. (1858) 103. [v. I.]
NIRSCHL. Patrol. (1881-) I. 178-81.
NITZSCH. Dogmengesch. I. (1870) 123, etc.
Nouv. biog. gén. (Hoefer.)
ORSI. Ist. eccl. (1746-) II. 203-6; 255-60, (1749-) II. 290-5, 365-72.
PERMANEDER. Bibl. patrist. (1842) II. 149-53, 943.
PIPER, F. In: Stud. u. Krit. XI. (1838) 54-154.
PITRA. Spicil. Solesm. (1855) II. ivxxxvij-lxv-j.
PRESSENSÉ. Hist. des trois prem. sièc. II. 2, 166; tr. Engl. Martyrs. (1879) 124-5, 241-2, 530-1.
RENAN. L'égl. chrêt. p. 436.
— Marc.-Aurèle. 172-.
REUSS. Gesch. N. T. (1874) II. 16; tr. Eng. (1884) 300. [v. 2.]
SALMON, G. In: Smith and Wace. Dict. III. 894-900.
SANDAY. Gosp. in 2d cent. (1876) 244-5.
SCHAFF. Hist. Church. II. (1886) 736-9.
SCHMID. Patrol. (1879); (1886) 43. [12 ll.]
SCHROECKH. Kirchenges (1772-) III. 115-8.
SEMLER. Hist. eccles. select. capita saec. II. c. 5.
STEITZ. In: Theol. Stud. u. Krit. (1857) 584-96.
— Jour. Sac. Lit. 1856, 1857.
— In: Herzog. Real.-Enc. (1877) IX, 537-9. (Abr. in: Schaff-Herz. II. 1464.)
Supernatural Religion. II. (1875) 172-85, 392; III. (1877) 24.
TILLEMONT. Mem. hist. eccl. (1694) II. 407-9, 663-5.
TRITHEMIUS. Scr. eccl. 14.
UEBERWEG. Hist. philos. (1876) 295.
UHLHORN. In: Ztschr. f. hist. Theol. (1866).
WAITE. Hist. Chr. Rel. (1881) 395.
WEISS. In: Biog. Univ. (Michaud) (1842-65) XXVII. 577-8.
WELTE. In: Theol. Quartalschrift. (1862) 302-.
WESTCOTT. Bible in the Church. (1877) 124.
— Canon. (1875) 218-23.
WOOG, CARL CHRISTIAN. Dissertationes II. de Melitone, Sardium in Asia episcops. *Lips.* 1744-51. 4°.
— De scriptis s. Melitonis. *Lips.* 1751. 4°.; also in: Migne. Patrol. gr. V. (1857) 1183-208.
— De vita et meritis s. Melitonis. *Lips.* 1744. 4°; also in: Migne. Patrol. gr. V. (1857) 1145-84.

WORMAN, J. H. In: M'Clintock and S. Cycl. (1874-) VI. 64-5.

Y. In: Nouv. Biog. Gen. (Hoefer) XXXIV. (1861) 842-3.

YONGE. Pupils of St. John. (1878) 205-10.

ZAHN, T. In: Ztschr. f. kirchl. wiss. u. Lebens. (1884) 628-30.

(4.) HEGESIPPUS.

I. *Editions.*

HALLOIX. *Duaci,* 1633. In: Scr. eccl. orient. II. 697—.

GRABE. Gr. lat. Spicil. patr. (1700) II. 203-14.

GALLANDIUS. Bibl. patr. II. (1766) 59-.

FLORIS, FR. Opusc. posthuma. *Bonon.* 1793-. 4º.

SCHULTHESS. In: Symb. crit. I. (Tur. 1833.)

ROUTH. Rel. sacr. (1846-8) I. 203-284.

BUNSEN. Analect. Antenic. (1854) 123-35 (Pref.) 137-55.

MIGNE. Gr. lat. In: Patrol. gr. V. (1857) 1307-28.

HILGENFELD. In: Ztschr. f. wiss. Theol. (1876) 179-; (1878) 194.

and in editions of Eusebius.

II. *Translations.*

English.

PRATTEN, P. B. In: Ante-Nic. Lib. XXII. (1871) ii. 142-7. Ed. Coxe. VIII. (1886) 762-5.

III. *Literature.*

Acta ss. Bolland. (1675) apr. 1. 656-7. (3ª. 654-5.)

ALLEMAND–LAVIGERIE, CAR. De Hegesippo disquisitio historica. *Par.-Lugduni,* 1850. 8º. 61 p.

ALZOG. Patrol. (1876) 162.

ARNAULD. Diss. sur ce qui raconte Hégésippe, etc. In: Tillemont. Hist. eccl. I. (*Ven.* 1732. 4º.)

BARONIUS. Ann. (1589) 167, 11-5.

BAUR. In: Tüb. Zeitschrift. 1831. IV. 171.

— Dogmengesch. I. (1865) 209-10.

— Kirchenges. I. 84.

ΒΑΦΕΙΔΗΣ. '*Εκκλ. ίστ.* I. (1884) 153.

BELLARMIN–LABBE. Scr. eccl. (1728) 36.

BULL, G. Primit. et apost. traditio. 1703. c. 3.

BUSSE. Chr. lit. (1828-9) I. 9.

CASPARI. Quellen z. Gesch. u. s. w. III. 345-8.

CAVE. Scr. eccl. hist. lit. (1740-3); (1741) I. 73.

CEILLIER. Hist. gén. aut. sac. (1730) II. 100-2; I. (1858) 473-5.

CHARTERIS. Canonicity. (1880) lxxvii-lxxix. 127-8, 199, 227, 258.

CHEVALIER. Rép. d. sources hist. (1877-86) 1006.

CLARKE. Sacred lit. (1830-1) I. 103.

CLINTON. Fasti Rom. (1845-50) I. 141, 169; II. 409.

COXE, A. C. Introd. note. In: Ed. Coxe. VIII. (1886) 762.

CREDNER. Gesch. d. N. T. Kan. 77-.

CUNNINGHAM. Churches of Asia. (1880) pass.

DANNREUTHER, H. In: Lichtenberger. Encycl. (1877-82) VI. 126-9.

— Du témoignage d'Hégésippe sur l'église chrétienne aux deux premiers siècles. *Nancy,* 1878. 8º. (69 p.)

DANZ. De Eusebio Caes. (*Jen.* 1815) 117-.

DONALDSON. Hist. Chr. lit. 1864-6. III. 182-213.

DORNER. Person of Christ. I. (1864) 137-42, 400-6.

DOWLING. Study of Eccl. Hist. pp. 8-9.

DUPIN. Bibl. aut. eccl. (1698) I. 99.

ENS, JO. In: Hegesippi test. de ecclesia origine. *Traj. ad Rh.* 1721.

EUSEBIUS. Hist. eccl. II. 23; III. 19, 20, 32; IV. 8, 22.

FABRICIUS. Bibl. gr. 1705. (1712) V. 188-9. (2ª. VII. 158-60.)

FLEURY. Hist. eccl. (1691-)I. 434-5.

FLORIUS (FRANC.) De quodam Hegesippi fragmento, etc. *Bononiae,* 1793. 4º.

FLÜGGE. Gesch. d. theol. Wissensch. I. 407-20.

GALLAND. Vet. patr. bibl. *Venet.* 1765. fº. II. vii-; also in: Migne. Patrol. gr. V. (1857) 1303-8.

GAMS. In: Wetzer u. W. Kirch.-Lex. (1847-54) IV. 927-8.

GUDENUS. Gesch. d. 2ten. chr. Jahrh. p. 264-9.

HAAR, B. TER. Historiographie der Kerkgeschedenis. I. (*Utrecht,* 1870. 8º.) 11-12.

HALLOIX. Eccl. orient. script. (1636) II. 695-734.

HARNACK. Z. Quellenkr. d. Ges. d. Gnost. (1873) 36-.

HASE. Kirchenges. (1885-) I. 117-8, 175.

HENSCHIUS. In: Acta sanctorum.

HERGENROETHER. Kirchenges. (1879-80) I. 15; III. 8.

HIERONYMUS. De vir. ill. 22. (Honor. August. I. 23.)

HILGENFELD. Apost. Vät. p. 102.

— Hegesippus. In: Ztschr. f. wissensch. Theol. (1876).

— Hegesippus u. die Apostelgeschichte. I. Noch einmal Heges. II. Die Kirchenpolitik der Apostelgesch. In: Ztschr. f. wissen. Theo. XXI. (1878) 297-330. Cf.. p. 424.

— Ketzergesch. (1884)30-5.

HOLTZMANN. Einl. in d. N. T. (1886) 125-6, etc.

HOLTZMANN u. HILGENFELD. In: Ztschr. f. wiss. Theol. XX. 290-294. ["Ueber Hegesipp, gegen Nösgen."]

ITTIG. Hist. eccl. (1709) II. 40-1, 242.

JACOBS, F., and SCHMID, HEINR. In: Ersch u. Gruber. II. IV. (1828) 95.

JESS. Die kirchengeschichtl. Bedeutung des Hegesippus. In: Zeitschr. f. histor. Theolog. (1865) 1-95.

KURTZ. Kirchenges. (1885-) I. 122.

LARDNER. Credibility. Works. (1831) II. 152-157.

LECHLER. Ap. u. Nachap. Z.-A. (1885) 539-42; Engl. tr. (1886) II. 276-80.

LUMPER. Hist. ss. patr. III. (1784) 105-21.

LUTHARDT. St. John the Author of the Fourth Gospel. (1875) 140.

M'CLINTOCK and S. Cycl. (1874-) IV. 158.

MILLIGAN, W. In: Smith and Wace. Dict. II. 875-8.

MUENSCHER. Dogmenges. (1817-8) I. 275-6.

NEANDER. Church hist. (1872) I. 675-6.

NIRSCHL. Patrol. (1881-) I. 181-2.

NÖSGEN, K. F. Der Kirchliche Standpundt Hegesipp. In: Ztschr. f. Kirchengesch. II. 2, S. 193-233. [Agst. Hilgenfeld.]

ORSI. Ist. eccl. (1746-) I. 213-9; II. 124-6; (1749-) I. 300-9; II. 180-3.

OUDIN. Scr. eccl. (1722) II. 1026.

PERMANEDER. Bibl. patrist. (1842) II. 161-3, 278-82, 943-4.

PHOTIUS. Bibliotheca. No. 32, p. 288. Ed. Bekker.

PLITT, G. L. In: Ztschr. f. luth. Theol. XXV. (1864) 28-33. [H. on James the Just.]

PRESSENSÉ. Martyrs. (1879) 237-9.

— Heresy. (*N. Y.*) 99-100.

PRIESTLEY. Gesch. d. Verfälsch. (1785.)

REUSS. Gesch. N. T. (1874) II. 16, 17; tr. Eng. (1884) 300, 301. [v. 2.]

RITSCHL. Entst. d. Altk. Kirche. p. 267.

RÖNSCH, H. Ein frühes citat aus d. lat. H. In: Ztschr. f. wiss. Theol. XXVI. (1883) 239-41.

SANDAY. Gosp. in 2 cent. (1876) 138-45.

SCALIGER. Animadv. ad Euseb. Chron. p. 193-.

SCHAFF. Hist. . . Church. II. (1886) 742-4.

SCHLIEMANN. Clementinen. (1844) 428-31.

SCHMID, HEINR. See Jacobs, F.
SCHMIDT. Kirchenges. I. 215–6, 524–6.
SCHROECKH. Kirchenges. (1772–) I. 143–4; III. 165–6.
SCHULTHESS, J. Heg. prin. auct. rerum Christ, etc. *Turic.* 1833.
SCHWEGLER. Nachap. Zeitalt. (1846) I. 342–59.
Supernatural Religion. (1875–) I. 429–43; II. 316–20; III. xviii–xx. 18.
SURIUS. Vitae ss. (1618) IV. 125–6.
TILLEMONT. Mem. hist. eccl. (1695) III. 47–8, 610–1.
TRITHEMIUS. Scr. eccl. 10.
VINCENT BELVAC. Spec. hist. XI. 112.
VOGEL, F. De Hegesippo, qui dicitur, Josephi interpréte. *Erlangen*, 1881. 8°. (62 p.)
WAITE. Hist. Chr. Rel. (1881) 398–9, 406–9, et pass.
WEISS. In: Biog. Univ. (Michaud) (1842–65) XIX. 45.
WEIZSÄCKER, C. In: Herzog. Real.-Enc. (1877–) V. 695–700. (Abr. in: Schaff-Herz. II. 959.)
WESTCOTT. Canon. (1875) 202–8.
— Bible in the Church. (1877) 107.
Y. In: Nouv. Biog. Gén. (Hoefer) XXIII. (1858) 759–60.
ZAHN. Dei griech. Irenaeus u. d. ganze Hegesippus im. 16ter Jahr. In: Ztschr. f. Kirchenges. (1877) 288–91.
ZWICKER. Irenicum Irenicorum. 1658.

Note. Confusion with later Hegesippus is frequent.

(5.) DIONYSIUS, BISHOP OF CORINTH.

I. *Editions.*

GRABE. Gr. lat. Spicil. patr. (1700) II. 214–8.
GALLANDIUS. Bibl. patr. I. (1765) 675–.
ROUTH. Rel. sacr. (1846–8) I. 175–201.

II. *Translations.*

English.

PRATTEN, P. B. In: Ante-Nic. Lib. XXII. (1871) 167–8. Ed. Coxe. VIII. (1886) 765–.

III. *Literature.*

BARONIUS. Ann. (1589) 175, 8, 11–5.
BERTHOLDT. Dogmenges. (1822–3) I. 52, etc.
BLACKBURN. Hist. of Church. (1879) 33.
BUSSE. Chr. lit. (1828–9) I. 8–9.
CAVE. Scr. eccl. hist. lit. (1741) I. 73.
CEILLIER. Hist. gén. aut. sac. II. (1730) 80–3; I. (1858) 461–3.
CHARTERIS. Canonicity. (1880) 44–5, 197.
CHEVALIER. Rép. d. sources hist. (1877–86) 566.
CLARKE. Sacred lit. (1830–1) I. 101.
CLINTON. Fasti Rom. (1845–50) I. 167, 169; II. 410.
v. COELLN. In: Ersch u. Gruber. I. xxv. (1834) 356.
COFFIN. Lives of fath. (1846) 203–4.
COXE, A. C. Introd. note. In: Ed. Coxe. VIII. (1886) 765.
DONALDSON. Hist. Chr. Lit. (1864–6) III. 214–20.
DORNER. Person of Christ. I. (1864) 119–20.
DUPIN. Bibl. aut. eccl. (1698) I. 152.
EUSEBIUS. Hist. eccl. II. 25; III. 4; IV. 21, 23, 35.
FABRICIUS. Bibl. gr. 1705. (1712) V. 191. (2ª. VII. 162–3.)
FLEURY. Hist. eccl. (1691) I. 480–3.
FRITZ. In: Wetzer u. W. Kirch-Lex. (1847–54) III. 167–8.
HALLOIX. Eccl. orient. script. (1636) II. 767–85.
HASE. Kirchenges. (1885–) I. 163.
HENSCHENIUS. In: Acta ss. Bolland. (1675) Apr. I. 742–5. (3ª. 739–41.)

HERZOG. In his: Real.-Enc. (1877–) III. 627. Cf. Schaff-Herz. [7 ll. only.]
HIERONYMUS. De vir. ill. 27. (Honor. August. 1. 28.)
HOLTZMANN. Einl. in d. N. T. (1886) 214, etc.
ITTIG. Hist. eccl. (1709) II. 53, 243.
LARDNER. Credibility. Works. (1831) II. 144–147.
LICHTENBERGER. Encycl. (1877–82) III. 669.
LUMPER. Hist. ss. patr. III. (1784) 1–11.
M'CLINTOCK and S. Cycl. (1874–) II. 811.
MAURICE. Eccl. Hist. (1854) 205, 216–8.
MÖHLER. Patrologie. (1840) 320–.
NEANDER. Ch. Hist. (1872) III. 467; IV. 382.
NIRSCHL. Patrol. (1881–) I. 204. [7 ll.]
NORTON. Genuineness of Gosp. I. (1846) 61–3, etc.
Nouv. Biog. Gén. (Hoefer) XIII. (1855) 675.
ORSI. Ist. eccl. (1746–) II. 198–203; (1749–) II. 284–90.
PERMANEDER. Bibl. patr. (1842) II. 153–5.
PRESSENSÉ. Martyrs. (1879) 239–40.
REUSS. Gesch. N. T. (1874) II. 16–7; tr. Eng. (1884) 300. [v. 2.]
SALMON, G. In: Smith and Wace. Dict. I. 849–50.
SANDAY. Gosp. in 2 cent. (1876) 242–3.
SCHAFF. Hist. . . Church. II. (1886) 745.
SCHMITZ, L. In: Smith. Gr. and Rom. Biog. (1859) I. 1039.
SCHROECKH. Kirchenges. (1772–) III. 166–7.
SCHWEGLER. Nachap. Zeitalt. (1846) I. 307–12.
STOLBERG. Gesch. d. Rel. J. VIII. 89–.
Supernatural Religion. (1875–) I. 218, 295; II. 163–71.
TILLEMONT. Mém. hist. eccl. (1694) II. 448–51, 674–5.
TRITHEMIUS. Scr. eccl. 17.
VILLENAVE. In: Biog. Univ. (Michaud) (1842–65) X. 435–6.
WAITE. Hist. Chr. Rel. (1881) 394.
WESTCOTT. Canon. (1855) 185–190.

(6.) RHODON.

I. *Editions.*

OLSHAUSEN. Monumenta. I.
GALLANDIUS. Bibl. patr. II. (1766) 144–.
ROUTH. Rel. sacr. (1814) I. 347–; (1846–8) I. 435–446.
MIGNE. Patrol. gr. V. (1857) 1331–8.
and in editions of Eusebius.

II. *Translations.*

English.

PRATTEN, P. B. In: Ante-Nic. Lib. XXII. (1871) ii. 149–50. Ed. Coxe. VIII. (1886) 766.

III. *Literature.*

BUSSE. Chr. lit. (1828–9) I. 18.
CAVE. Scr. eccl. hist. lit. (1741) I. 85.
CEILLIER. Hist. gén. aut. sac. II. (1730) 133–5; 1. (1858) 494–5.
CHEVALIER. Rép. d. sources hist. (1877–86) 1933.
CLARKE. Sacred lit. (1830–1) I. 150 [7 ll.]
CLINTON. Fasti Rom. (1845–50) I. 199; II. 413.
COXE, A. C. Introd. note. In: Ed. Coxe. VIII. (1886) 766.
DARLING. Cypl. bibliog. 2542.
DUPIN. Bibl. aut. eccl. (1698) I. 183.
EUSEBIUS. Hist. eccl. v. 13.
FABRICIUS. Bibl. gr. 1705. (1712) V. 195. (2ª. VII. 168.)
HIERONYMUS. De vir. ill. 37. (Honor. August. I. 38.)
HILSCHER and STRAUSS. Schola Alex. (1776) 32.
LARDNER. Credibility. Works. (1831) II. 324.

LUMPER. Hist. ss. patr. IV. (1785) 9–11.
MEANS, J. C. In: Smith. Gr. and Rom. Biog. (1859) III. 651–2.
NEANDER. Ch. Hist. (1872) I. 467, 474, 475.
NIRSCHL. Patrol. (1881–) I. 203–4. [10 ll.]
PERMANEDER. Bibl. patrist. (1842) II. 213–4.
ROUTH. Reliquiae sac. (1846) I. 347; Patrol. gr. V. 1331–2.
TILLEMONT. Mém. hist. eccl. (1695) III. 64–5.
TRITHEMIUS. Scr. eccl. 23.

(7.) MAXIMUS, BISHOP OF JERUSALEM.

I. *Editions.*

GALLANDIUS. Bibl. patr. II. (1766) 146–.
ROUTH. Rel. sacr. I. (1874) 347–; II. (1846) 77–107, 108–21.
MIGNE. Patrol. gr. V. (1857) 1339–56.

II. *Translations.*

English.

PRATTEN, P. B. In: Ante-Nic. Lib. XXII. (1871) ii. 150–62. Ed. Coxe. VIII. (1886) 767–72.

III. *Literature.*

BUSSE. Chr. lit. (1828–9) I. 15.
CAVE. Scr. eccl. hist. lit. (1740–3); (1741) I. 95.
CEILLIER. Hist. gén. aut. sac. II. (1730) 206; I. (1858) 537.
CHEVALIER. Rép. d. sources hist. (1877–86) 1545.
COXE, A. C. Introd. note. In: Ed. Coxe. VIII. (1886) 766–7.
EUSEBIUS. Chron. Hist. Eccles. V. 27.
FABRICIUS. Bibl. gr. 1705 (1712) V. 199. (2ᵃ. VII. 175; IX. 680.) Verit. Relig. Christ. (1725) 162.
GALLAND. Vet. patr. bibl. *Venet.* 1765. fᵒ. I. XVII.; also in: Migne. Patrol. gr. V. (1857) 1337–40.
HIERONYMUS. De vir. ill. 47. (Honor. August. I. 48.)
LUMPER. Hist. ss. patr. IV. (1785) 13) 13–5.
M'CLINTOCK and S. Cycl. (1874–) V. 918–9.
MEANS, J. C. In: Smith. Gr. and Rom. Biog. (1859) II. 995–6.
NEANDER. Church hist. (1872) I. 721.
PERMANEDER. Bibl. patrist. (1842) II. 214–5
VENABLES, E. In: Smith and Wace. Dict. III. 877–8. (?)
WAITE. Hist. Chr. Rel. (1881) 394. [4 ll.]

(8.) CLAUDIUS APOLLINARIS, BISHOP OF HIERAPOLIS, AND APOLOGIST.

I. *Editions.*

ROUTH. Rel. sacr. I. (1814) 149–. (1846–8) I. 155–174.
MIGNE. Patrol. gr. V. (1857) 1293–302.

II. *Translations.*

English.

PRATTEN, P. B. In: Ante-Nic. Lib. XXII. (1871) ii, 140–1. Ed. Coxe. VIII. (1886) 772–3.

III. *Literature.*

BARONIUS. Ann. (1589) 172–7.
BAUR. Dogmengesch. I. (1865) 259.
BIRLO, J. A. Das Leben u. Wirken des h. Apollinaris. *Bonn.* 1857. 12ᵒ.
BOLLANDUS. Comment. histor. In: Acta ss. (1658) Feb. 11, 4–8.

BUSSE. Chr. Lit. (1828–9) I. 18–9.
CAVE. Scr. eccl. hist. lit. (1740–3); (1741) I. 72.
CEILLIER. Hist. gén. aut. sac. II. (1730) II. 83–5; I. (1858) 463–5.
CHEVALIER. Rép. d. sources hist. (1877–86) 461.
CLARKE. Sacred lit. (1830–1) I. 149–50. [8 ll.]
CLINTON. Fasti Rom. (1845–50) I. 167; II. 410.
COXE, A. C. Introd. note. In: Ed. Coxe. VIII. (1886) 772.
CUNNINGHAM. Churches of Asia. (1880) passim.
DONALDSON. Hist. Chr. Lit. 1864–6. III. 240–9.
DUPIN. Bibl. aut. eccl. (1698) I. 150.
EUSEBIUS. Hist. eccl. IV. 27; V. 5, 19, 16.
FABRICIUS. Bibl. gr. 1705. (1712) V. 189–90. (2ᵃ. VI. 746; VII. 160–2; VIII. 586; X. 688.) Verit. relig. Christ. (1725) 160.
FLEURY. Hist. eccl. (1691–) I. 490.
HALLOIX. Eccl. orient. script. (1636) II. 793–817.
HARNACK. In: Herzog. Real-Enc. (1877–) I. 529. [Abr. In: Schaff-Herz. I. 109.]
HASE. Kirchenges. (1885–) I. 488.
HERGENROETHER. Kirchenges. (1879–80) I. 89; III. 37–8.
HIERONYMUS. De vir. ill. 26. (Honor. August. 1. 27.)
HOLTZMANN. Einl. in d. N. T. (1886) 130.
ITTIG. Hist. eccl. (1709) II. 53.
LARDNER. Credibility. Works. (1831) II. 313–6.
LICHTENBERGER. Encycl. (1877–82) I. 423.
LUMPER. Hist. crit. patr. Aug. Vind. 1784. 8ᵒ. III. 26–34; also in: Migne. Patrol. gr. V. (1857) 1285–94.
M'CLINTOCK and S. Cycl. (1874–) I. 296.
NEANDER. Church Hist. (1872) I. 117, 298, 635, 677.
NIRSCHL. Patrol. (1881–) I. 202–3. [8 ll.]
— Nouv. Biog. Gén. (Hoefer) II. (1852) 888.
ORSI. Ist. eccl. (1746–) II. 260–1; (1749–) II. 372–4.
PERMANEDER. Bibl. patrist. (1842) II. 156–8.
PHOTIUS. Cod. 14.
PRESSENSÉ. Martyrs. (1879) 240–.
REUSS. Gesch. N. T. (1874) II. 16; tr. Eng. (1884) 300. [v. 2.]
SALMON, G. In: Smith and Wace. Dict. I. 132–3.
SANDAY. Gosp. in 2 cent. (1876) 246–8, 307–8.
SCHMID. Patrol. (1879); (1886) 43. [7 ll.]
SCHROECKH. Kirchenges. (1772) III. 118–9.
SMITH, P. In: Smith. Gr. and Rom. Biog. (1859) I. 229.
SOCRATES. Hist. Eccl. III. 7.
Supernatural Religion. II. (1875–) 185–91; III. (1877) 24.
TABARAUD. In: Biog. Univ. (Michaud) (1842–65) II. 107.
TILLEMONT. Mém. hist. eccl. (1694); II. 452–4, 675–6.
TRITHEMIUS. Scr. eccl. 17.
WAITE. Hist. Chr. Rel. (1881) 396–7.
WESTCOTT. Canon. (1875) 224–5.
WETZER u. W. Kirch-Lex. (1847–54) I. 356–7.

(9.) POLYCRATES.

I. *Editions.*

GALLANDIUS. Bibl. patr. II. (1766) 160–.
OLSHAUSEN. Monumenta. I.
ROUTH. Rel. sacr. (1846–8) II. 9–36.
MIGNE. Gr. lat. In: Patrol. gr. (1857) 1357–62.

II. *Translations.*

English.

PRATTEN, P. B. In: Ante-Nic. Lib. XXII. (1871) II. 162–3. Ed. Coxe. VIII. (1886) 773–4.

III. *Literature.*

BUSSE. Chr. lit. (1828–9) I. 15–6.
CAVE. Scr. eccl. hist. lit. (1740–3); (1741) I. 94.
CEILLIER. Hist. gén. aut. sac. II. (1730) 203–5; I. (1858) 535–6.
CHARTERIS. Canonicity. (1880) 183.
CHEVALIER. Rép. d. sources hist. (1877–80) 1858.
CLARKE. Sacred lit. (1830–1) I. 127–8.
CLINTON. Fasti Rom. (1845–50) I. 189, 199; II. 413–.
COXE, A. C. Introd. note. In: Ed. Coxe. VIII. (1886) 773.
CUNNINGHAM. Churches of Asia. (1880) pass.
FABRICIUS. Bibl. gr. 1705. (1712) V. 194–5. (2ᵃ. VII. 169–70.)
FLEURY. Hist. eccl. (1691–) I. 597–9.
GALLAND. Vet. patr. bibl. *Venet.* 1765. f⁰. II. xix–; also in: Migne. Patrol. gr. V. (1857) 1355–8.
HASE. Kirchenges. (1885–) I. 185–394.
HIERONYMUS. De vir. ill. 45. (Honor. August. I. 46.)
ITTIG. Hist. eccl. (1709) II. 41–2.
LARDNER. Credibility. Works. (1831) II. 259–61.
LICHTENBERGER. Encycl. (1877–82) X. 676.
LUMPER. Hist. ss. patr. IV. (1785) 26–31.
LUTHARDT. St. John the Author of the Fourth Gospel. (1875) 48–9.
MAURICE. Eccl. hist. (1854) 252–3.
NEANDER. Church Hist. (1872) I. 194, 298–9.
ORSI. Ist. eccl. (1749–) II. 319–20; (1749–) II. 460–1.
PERMANEDER. Bibl. patrist. (1842) II. 215–6.
PRESSENSÉ. Chr. life. (1878) 96–7.
— Martyrs. (1879) 342–3.
SCHROECKH. Kirchenges. (1772–) III. 238–9.
SIGEBERT GEMBL. Scr. eccl. 3.
Supernatural Religion. II. (1875) 189, 406, 473.
VINCENT BELVAC. Spec. hist. XII. 16.
WAITE. Hist. Chr. Rel. (1881) 415.

(10.) THEOPHILUS, BISHOP OF CAESAREA IN PALESTINE.

I. *Editions.*

MIGNE. Gr. lat. In: Patrol. gr. V. (1857) 1369–72.

II. *Translations.*

English.

PRATTEN, P. B. In: Ante-Nic. Lib. XXII. (1871) ii. 163. Ed. Coxe. VIII. (1886) 774.

III. *Literature.*

BUSSE. Chr. lit. (1828–9) I. 16.
CAVE. Scr. eccl. hist. lit. (1741) I. 87.
CEILLIER. Hist. gén. aut. sac. II. (1730) 202; I. (1858) 534–5.
CHEVALIER. Rép. d. sources hist. (1877–86) 2185.
CLARKE. Sacred lit. (1830–1) I. 151. [4 ll.]
CLINTON. Fasti Rom. (1845–50) I. 189, 199; II. 413.
Comment. histor. In: Acta ss. Bolland. (1668) Mart. I. 361–2. (3ᵃ. 359–60.)
COXE, A. C. Introd. note. In: Ed. Coxe. VIII. (1886) 774.
DUPIN. Bibl. aut. eccl. (1698) I. 178.
FABRICIUS. Bibl. gr. 1712. V. 95, 194; XII. 655. (2ᵃ. VII. 107, 169.)
GALLAND. Vet. patr. bibl. *Venet.* 1765. f⁰. I. xx; also in: Migne. Patrol. gr. V. (1857) 1363–70.
HARNACK. Dogmenges. I. (1886) 391–2. (?)
HIERONYMUS. De vir. ill. 43. (Honor. August. I. 44.)
JÖCHER. Gel. Lex. (1750–).
LARDNER. Credibility. Works. (1831) II. 325.
LUMPER. Hist. ss. patr. IV. (1785) 31–7.

M'CLINTOCK and S. Cycl. (1874) X. 335.
NEALE. Eastern Ch., Antioch. (1873) 31–4.
NEANDER. Church Hist. (1872) III. 347.
PERMANEDER. Bibl. patrist. (1842) II. 217–8.
SMITH, P. In: Smith. Gr. and Rom. Biog. (1859) III. 1085.

(11.) SERAPION, BISHOP OF ANTIOCH.

I. *Editions.*

GALLANDIUS. Bibl. patr. II. (1766) 163–.
ROUTH. Rel. sacr. (1846–8) I. 447–462.
MIGNE. Gr. lat. In: Patrol. gr. V. (1857) 1373–6.

II. *Translations.*

English.

PRATTEN, P. B. In: Ante-Nic. Lib. XXII. (1871) ii. 164–5. Ed. Coxe. VIII. (1886) 775.

III. *Literature.*

BARONIUS. Ann. (1589) 191, 1–4.
BERTHOLDT. Dogmenges. (1822–3) I. 54, etc.
BUSSE. Chr. lit. (1828–9) I. 19.
CAVE. Scr. eccl. hist. lit. (1740–3); (1741) I. 86.
CEILLIER. Hist. gén. aut. sac. II. (1730) 235–7. I. (1851) 558–9.
CHEVALIER. Rép. d. sources hist. (1877–86) 2065.
CLARKE. Sacred. lit. (1830–1) I. 130–1.
CLINTON. Fasti Rom. (1845–50) I. 178–211; II. 413.
COXE, A. C. Introd. note. In: Ed. Coxe. VIII. (1886) 744–5.
DUPIN. Bibl. aut. eccl. (1698) I. 181, 730.
EUSEBIUS. Hist. eccl. VI. c. 12.
FABRICIUS. Bibl. gr. 1705. (1712) V. 193. (2ᵃ. VII. 166–7.)
FLEURY. Hist. eccl. (1691–) I. 558–9.
GALLAND. Vet. patr. bibl. *Venet.* 1765. f⁰. I. xxii–; also in: Migne. Patrol. gr. V. (1857) 1371–4.
GAMS. In: Wetzer u. W. Kirch.-Lex. (1847–54) X. 87–.
GASS. In: Herzog. Real. Enc. (1877–) XIV. 146.
HALLOIX. Eccl. orient. script. (1636) II. 825–63.
HARNACK. Dogmenges. I. (1886) 284.
HIERONYMUS. De vir. ill. 41. (Honor. August. I. 42.)
HILSCHER and STRAUSS. Schola Alex. (1776) 30.
JÖCHER. Gelehrt. Lex. (1750–).
LARDNER. Credibility. Works. (1831) II. 264–6.
LICHTENBERGER. Encycl. (1877–82) XI. 559.
LUMPER. Hist. ss. patr. IV. (1785) 48–55.
M'CLINTOCK and S. Cycl. (1874–) IX. 568–9.
MÖHLER. Patrologie (1840).
NEALE. Eastern Ch., Antioch. (1873) 35–6.
NIRSCHL. Patrol. (1881–) I. 203. [6 ll.]
Nouv. Biog. Gén. (Hoefer) XLIII. (1864) 775.
ORSI. Ist. eccl. (1746–) II. 443–5; (1749–) II. 639–42.
PERMANEDER. Bibl. patrist. (1842) II. 269–70.
PHILBERT. In: Biog. Univ. (Michaud) (1842–65) XXXIX. 87–8.
Supernatural Religion. (1875–) I. 419–; II. 160–167.
TILLEMONT. Mém. hist. eccl. (1695) III. 168–9.
TRITHEMIUS. Scr. eccl. 27.
WAITE. Hist. Chr. Rel. (1881) 409 et pass.
WESTCOTT. Canon. (1875) 385–7.
— Bible in the Church. (1877) 131.

(12.) APOLLONIUS.

I. *Editions.*

GALLANDIUS. Bibl. patr. II. (1766) 199–.
OLSHAUSEN. Monumenta. I.

ROUTH. Rel. sacr. (1846–8) I. 463–485.
MIGNE. Gr. lat. In: Patrol. gr. V. (1857) 1381–6.

II. *Translations.*

English.

PRATTEN, P. B. In: Ante-Nic. Lib. XXII. (1871) 11. Ed. Coxe. VIII. (1886) 775–6.

III. *Literature.*

ACTA. In: Ruinart. 73–.
Acta ss. Bolland. (1675) Apr. II. 539–40. (3ᵃ. 536–7.)
BARONIUS. Ann. (1589) 189, 1–5; cf. Pagi. Crit. (1689) 3–4.
BUSSE. Chr. lit. (1828–9) I. 22.
CAVE. Scr. eccl. hist. lit. I. 86.
CEILLIER. Hist. gén. aut. sac. II. (1730) 132–3; I. (1858) 493–4.
CHARTERIS. Canonicity. (1880) 340.
CHEVALIER. Rép. d. sources hist. (1877–86) 151.
CLARKE. Sacred lit. (1830–1) I. 156.
CLINTON. Fasti Rom. (1845–50) I. 221; II. 413.
COXE, A. C. Introd. note. In: Ed. Coxe. VIII. (1886) 775.
DRÄSEKE, J. Zur Apologie des Apollonios. In: Jahrbb. f. prot. Theol. (1885) 144–153.
DUPIN. Nouv. bibl. aut. eccl. I.
EUSEBIUS. Hist. eccl. V. 18–21.
FABRICIUS. Bibl. gr. 1705. (1712) V. 191. (2ᵃ. VII. 163–4.)
FLEURY. Hist. eccl. (1691–) I. 557–8. (?)
GALLAND. Vet. patr. bibl. *Venet.* 1765. (fᵒ. I. xxv–.; also in: Migne. Patrol. gr. V. (1857) 1375–8.
HERZOG. Real.-Enc. (1877–) I. 536. [Cf. Schaff-Herz. I. 110.]
HIERONYMUS. De vir. ill. 42. (Honor. August. I. 43.)
ITTIG. Hist. eccl. (1709–) II. 52–3.
LANDON. Eccl. Dict. I. 452.
LARDNER. Credibility. Works. (1831) II. 323–4.
LICHTENBERGER. Encycl. (1877–82) I. 425.
LUCHINI. Atti. sinceri. (1777) I. 396–400.
LUMPER. Hist. ss. patr. (1785) IV. 1–3.
— Hist. ss. Patr. VII. (1790) 1–8.
LUTHARDT. St. John the Author of the Fourth Gospel. (1875) 140.
MUELLER (L.) De eloquent. Apollonis. *Schleusingae.* 1717.
MUZZECHELLI. Scr. Ital. (1753) I. 11. 879–80.
NEANDER. Church Hist. (1872) I. 118.
NIRSCHL. Patrol. (1881–) I. 203. [8 ll.]
Nouv. Biog. Gén. (Hoefer) II. (1852) 910.
ORSI. Ist. eccl. (1746–) III. 5–6; (1749–) III. 8–9.
PERMANEDER. Bibl. patrist. (1842) II. 208–9.
RUINART. Acta sinc. (1689) 73–4 (83–4?)
SCHAFF. Hist. . . II. (1886) 740–41.
SCHMITZ, L. In: Smith. Gr. and Rom. Biog. (1859) I. 239.
SCHROECKH. Kirchenges. (1772–) III. 168.
SURIUS. Vitae ss. (1618) IV. 184.
TILLEMONT. Mém. hist. eccl. (1695) III. 55–9, 613–5.
TRITHEMIUS. Scr. eccl. 28.
VENABLES, E. In: Smith and Wace. Dict. I. 135.

(13.) PANTAENUS, THE ALEXANDRIAN PHILOSOPHER.

I. *Editions.*

HALLOIX. Ill. eccl. orient. scr. *Duaci,* 1633.
ROUTH. Rel. sacr. I. (1814) 337–. (1846–8) I. 373–383.

MIGNE. Patrol. gr. V. (1857) 1327–32.
and in eds. of Theodotus.

II. *Translations.*

English.

PRATTEN, P. B. In: Ante-Nic. Lib. XXII. (1871) 147–8. Ed. Coxe. VIII. (1886) 777.

III. *Literature.*

ALZOG. Kirchenges. I. 194.
BARONIUS. Ann. (1589) 185, 1–4.
BAUR. Dogmengesch. I. (1865) 218. (8 ll.)
ΒΑΦΕΙΔΗΣ. 'Εκκλ ἱστ. I. (1884) 156.
BERTHOLDT. Dogmenges. (1822–3) I. 56, etc.
BLACKBURN. Hist. of Church. (1879) 50–1.
BRUCKER. Hist. crit. phil. (1766) III. 417–20.
BUNSEN. Hippolytus. (1854) I. 235–6.
BUSSE. Chr. lit. (1828–9) I. 20.
CAVE. Scr. eccl. hist. lit. I. (1740–3); (1741) I. 83–5.
— Lives. (1840) I. 287–95.
CEILLIER. Hist. gén. aut. sac. II. (1730) 237–8; I. (1858) 559–61.
CHARTERIS. Canonicity. (1880) 133.
CHEVALIER. Rép. d. sources hist. (1877–86) 1715.
CLARKE. Sacred lit. (1830–1) I. 115.
CLINTON. Fasti Rom. (1845–50) I. 179, 187, 195; II. 412.
COXE, A. C. Introd. note. In: Ed. Coxe. VIII. (1886) 776–7.
DUPIN. Bibl. aut. eccl. (1698) I. 184.
Encycl. Brit. (9th ed.) XVIII. 214.
EUSEBIUS. Hist. eccl. V. 10.
FABRICIUS. Bibl. gr. 1705. (1712) V. 193–4. (2ᵃ. VII. 167–8.)
F[ISQUET?], H. In: Nouv. Biog. Gén. (Hoefer) XXXIX. (1865) 144.
FLEURY. Hist. eccl. (1691–) I. 559–60.
GENCE. In: Biog. Univ. (Michaud) (1842–65) XXXII. 80.
GUERICKE. De schola Alexandr. I.
GUNN, W. M. In: Smith. Gr. and Rom. Biog. (1859) III. 113.
HALLOIX. Eccl. orient. script. (1636) II. 839–51.
HERGENROETHER. Kirchenges. (1879–80) I. 162; III. 71.
HIERONYMUS. De vir. ill. 36. (Honor. August. I. 37.)
HILSCHER and STRAUSS. Schola Alex. (1776) 26–7.
HUBER. Philos. d. K.–V. (1859) 129–130.
ITTIG. Hist. eccl. (1709) II. 54.
JÖCHER. Gelehrt.-Lex. (1750–).
KURTZ. Kirchenges. (1885–) I. 118.
LARDNER. Credibility. Works. (1831) II. 215–9.
LELONG. Bib. Sacr. II. 892.
LICHTENBERGER. Encycl. (1877–82) X. 158.
LUMPER. Hist. ss. patr. IV. (1785) 42–8.
MAURICE. Eccl. Hist. (1854) 230.
MÖLLER, W. In: Herzog. Real.-Enc. (1877–) XI. 182. (Abr: in: Schaff-Herz. III. 1733.)
MONGITORE. Bibl. Sicula (1714) II. 116–8.
NARBONE. Bibl. Sicola. I. 80, 402.
NEALE. Eastern Ch., Alexandria. I. (1847) 18–20.
— Eastern Ch., Antioch. (1873) 40.
NEANDER. Church Hist. (1872) I. 529, 691, 694.
NITZSCH. Dogmengesch. I. (1870) 132 et passim.
ORSI. Ist. eccl. (1746–) II. 303–6; (1749–) II. 434–41.
PERMANEDER. Bibl. patrist. (1842) II. 270–1.
PRESSENSÉ. Martyrs. (1879) 270–2.
REDEPENNING. Origenes. I. 63–.
REUSCH. In: Wetzer u. W. Kirch-Lex. (1847–54) VIII. 75.
RITTER. Gesch. der christ. philos. I. 421–.
SCHAFF. Hist. . . Church. II. (1886) 778.

SCHMID. Patrol. (1879); (1886) 48–9.
SCHROECKH. Kirchenges. (1772-) III. 191–2.
SOLLERIUS. Comment. In: Acta ss. Bolland. (1721) Jul. II. 457–61.
Supernatural Religion. (1875–) I. 471; II. 191.
TILLEMONT. Mém. hist. eccl. (1695) III. 170–4, 649–50.
TIRABOSCHI. Stor. lett. Ital. II. 365.
WAITE. Hist. Chr. Rel. (1881) 368 et pass.
WESTCOTT. Canon. (1875) 338–9.
WORMAN, J. H. In: M'Clintock and S. Cycl. (1874–) VII. 615.
ZAHN. Forsch. z. Gesch. d. N. T. Kanons. III. (1884) 159-.

> *Note.* Compare Encyclopaedia articles and other literature on the Alexandrian School.

(14.) PSEUD.-IRENAEUS. (LETTER OF THE CHURCHES OF VIENNA AND LUGDUNUM.)

I. *Editions.*

OLSHAUSEN. In: Monumenta. *Berol.* 1820.
ROUTH. Rel. sacr. (1846–8) I. 285–371.
MIGNE. Gr. lat. In: Patrol. gr. V. (1857) 1405–54.
and in all editions of Eusebius.

II. *Translations.*

English.

LARDNER. Works. VII. (1831) 156–176.
DALRYMPLE, D. (Lord Hailes.) Account of the martyrs at Smyrna and Lyons. *Edinb.* 1776.
DONALDSON. Hist. Chr. Lit. 1864–6. III. 263–79.

PRATTEN, P. B. In: Ante-Nic. Lib. XXII. (1871) ii. 168–83. Ed. Coxe. VIII. (1886) 778–84.

III. *Literature.*

CHARTERIS Canonicity. (1880) 158–9, 180, 198–9, 218, 245, 257–8, 306, 321, 340.
CLARKE. Sacred lit. (1830–1) 104.
COXE, A. C. Introd. note. In: Ed. Coxe. VIII. (1886) 777–8.
CUNNINGHAM. Churches of Asia. (1880) 273–92.
DONALDSON. Hist. Chr. Lit. 1864–6. III. 250–85.
FLEURY. Hist. eccl. (1691–) I. 511–28.
GALLAND. Vet. patr. bibl. *Venet.* 1765. f°. I. cxxv-; also in: Migne. Patrol. gr. V. (1857) 1401–6.
HERGENROETHER. Kirchenges. (1879–80) I. 90; III. 38.
ITTIG. Hist. eccl. (1709) II. 47–8.
KILLEN. Ancient Church. (1859) 294–6.
LARDNER. Credibility. Works. (1831) II. 160–165.
LIGHTFOOT. Apost. fath. II. i. (1885) 499–500.
LUMPER. Hist. ss. patr. II. (1784) 482–504; X. (1793) 541–67.
LUTHARDT. St. John the Author of the Fourth Gospel. (1875) 48.
MAURICE. Eccl. Hist. (1854) 254–60.
NEANDER. Church Hist. (1872) I. 111–4.
ORSI. Ist. eccl. (1746–) II. 211–31; (1749) II. 302–32.
ROBERTSON. Hist. of Church. (1875–) I. 44–5.
SANDAY. Gospel. in 2 cent. (1876) 251–3, 306.
Supernatural Religion. (1875) II. 200–4, 380–1; III. 24–6.
WAITE. Hist. Chr. Rel. (1881) 395. [6 ll.]
WORDSWORTH. Church. Hist. (1881) 171–7.
YONGE. Pupils of St. John. (1878) 219–34.

> *Note.* The above work is a favorite and its literature abundant. Supplement this meagre list by works on Irenaeus, commentaries on Eusebius, all works on Martyrs, and especially works on the history of Lyons.

APPENDIX

APPENDIX

I. PATROLOGIES.

(a.) Ancient and Mediæval.

PETRUS SUFFRIDUS. (R. C.) De illustribus ecclesiasticis scriptoribus auctores praecipui veteres. *Coloniae*, 1580. 8º; *Antv.* 1630. 8º.

> Contains: Hieronymus, Gennadius, Isidorus, Honorius, Sigebertus, Henricus Gandavensis, but omits Ildefonsus.

MIRAEUS, AUBERTUS. (R. C.) Bibliotheca ecclesiastica; sive Nomenclatoribus septem veteribus, auctariis et scholiis illustratis. *Antverpiae*, 1639. fº.

> Contains: Hieronymus, Gennadius, Isidorus, Ildefonsus, Honorius, Sigebertus, Henricus Gandavensis.

FABRICIUS, JO. ALBERTUS. Bibliotheca ecclesiastica in qua continentur de scriptoribus ecclesiasticis, S. HIE-RONYMUS cum veteri versione Graeca quam vocant Sophronii, et nunc primum vulgatis editoris notis, Hieronymum cum Eusebio accurate conferentibus; adjunctis praeterea castigationibus Suffridi Petri et Jo. Marcianaei, nec non integris Erasmi, Mariani Victorii, Henr. Gravii, Aub. Miraei, Wilh. Ernesti Tentzelii et Ern. Salomonis Cypriani annotationibus. Appendix de vitis evangelistarum et apostolorum, Graece et Latine. Appendix altera, quae fertur jam sub titulo Hieronimi De duodecim doctoribus, jam sub nomine Bedae, De luminaribus ecclesiae [pp. 228], GENNADIUS MASSILIEN-SIS, annotatus lectionibus codicis antiquiss. Corbejensis, et subjunctis variorum notis Suffridi Petri, Aub. Miraei, E. Gal. Cypriani [p. 1-46], S. ISIDORUS HISPALENSIS [p. 47-58], ILDEFONSUS TOLETANUS [p. 59-65], HONO-RIUS AUGUSTODUNENSIS [p. 73-92], SIGEBERTUS GEM-BLACENSIS [p. 93-116]. Appendices. JULIANI [p. 65-66] ac FELICIS [p. 66-67] et tertia, ANONYMI AD ISIDORUM ET ILDEFONSUM [p. 68-72], HENRICUS GANDAVENSIS [p. 117-140 (pp. 132-139 omitted in paging)], ANONYMUS MELLICENSIS a R. P. Bernando Pez nuper vulgatus [p. 141-160], PETRUS CASINENSIS De viris illustribus monasterii Casinensis, cum supplemento PLACIDI RO-MANI et Jo. Baptiste Marie annotationibus [p. 161-202], Jo. TRITHEMII Abbatis Spanhemensis, Liber de s. e. cum notis editoris [p. 1 -270], AUB. MIRAEI Auctarium de s. e. et a tempore, quo desinit Trithemius, De scripti-bus saeculi XVI et XVII libri duo [p. 1-356]. Curante Jo. Alberto Fabricio, ss. Theol. D. et Professore in Gymnasio Hamburgensi. *Hamburgi*, 1718. fº. [pp. [4] [1-8] 9-228, 202, 270, 356 in 1 v.]

EUSEBIUS. († 340.) Historia ecclesiastica. Compare especially the editions of Valesius, *Par.* 1659, and Heinichen. *Lps.* 1827-8. 8º; 2. 1868(-70). [Largely patrological. Extends to year 324.]

HIERONYMUS. († 419.) Hieronymi de viris illustribus liber. Accedit Gennadii catalogus virorum illustrium. Ex recensione Guil. Herdingae. *Leipzig*, 1879. 8º. (xliv. 112 p.) [To the year 393. 135 writers, beginning with the apostles. The work is also quoted as *Catalogus scriptorum ecclesiasticorum* or *De scriptoribus ecclesiasticis*.]

GENNADIUS. († c. 495.) Catalogus virorum illustrium. Ed. Herding. *Lpz.* 1879. s. u. Hieronymus. [Continuation of Hieronymus to year 495.]

ISIDORUS. (Hispalensis I. of Seville, † 636.) De viris illustribus. Compare the editions in Fabricius and Migne. [47 chapters. Extends to c. 610.]

ILDEPHONSUS (of Toledo, † 667). De scriptoribus eccle-siasticis. Compare eds. above. [Adds 14 chapters to Isidore.]

PHOTIUS. († 890.) Bibliotheca [Μυριοβίβλιον ἡ Βιβλιο-θήκη]. Ed. Auch. Schott. Gr. lat. *Genev.* 1613; Ed. Bekker. Gr. *Berol.* 1824. 2 v. 4º; and after Hirschel and Schott. (*Rothemagi.* 1653) in Migne. Patrol. Gr. CIII-IV. [Includes 280 writers and has many extracts preserved here only.]

HONORIUS (of Autun, † c. 1110). De illuminationibus ec-clesiae libri. IV. [Taken without addition from Hierony-mus, Gennadius, and Isidorus.]

SIGEBERTUS GEMBLACENSIS. († 1112.) Des scriptoribus ecclesiasticis. See above. [170 chapters.]

ANONYMUS MELLICENSIS. Compare Fabricius. Bibl. Eccl., above. [From 500-112. 117 chapters.]

PETRUS CASINENSIS DIACONUS OSTIENSIS. (c. 1158.) Opusculum de viris illustribus Casinensibus. Cf. above and Migne. CLXXIII. 1003-1050. [With continuation by Placidus in all eds.]

HENRICUS GANDAVIENSIS. († 1293.) De scriptoribus ec-clesiasticis. [About 70 authors.]

TRITHEMIUS, JOAN. (R. C. † 1516.) De scriptoribus ecclesiasticis. *Par.* 1512. 4º; *Colon.* 1531. 4º; *Colon.* 1546. 4º, and as above, etc. [Continued by Miraeus († 1640.) De scr. eccl., to his time.]

(b.) Modern.

ANNEGARN, JO. A. (R. C.) Handbuch der Patrologie. *Münster*, 1839. 8º. ["Unimportant."]

ALZOG, J. (R. C.) Grundriss der Patrologie, oder der ältern christlichen Literärgeschichte. *Freiberg im Br.* 1866. 8º. (xi. 420 p.) 2te umgearb. u. verb. Aufl. 1869. 8º. (x. 452 p.); 3. Aufl. "Handbuch d. Patrol." 1876. 8º. (xiii. (3) 572 p.) French translation by Bélet. *Par.* 1867. 8º (viii. 524 p.) [Patrological and patristical. A capital handbook.]

BÄHR, JOHANN CHRISTIAN FELIX. Geschichte der römi-schen Literatur. *Carlsruhe*, 1868-73. 8º. Bds. 1-3, 4te verb. u. verm. Aufl. 1868-70. [1. Aufl. 1828. 2te 1832; 3te 1844-45]; Bd. 4. Die christlich-römische Literatur. 1. Die christliche Dichter und Geschrichtsschreiber. 2. verb. u. verm. Aufl. 1873 (X. 339. S.) [1. Aufl. Supple-mentband 1-111 Abth. 1836-1840. 8º. Abth. 11, 111, treat of the latin theology and latin literature in the Carolingian age.] [From the literary-historical rather than the theological standpoint.]

BARECROFT. Ars concionandi. 1715. 8º. [Centuries 1-3. Brief. Unimportant.]

BELLARMIN, ROBERT. (R. C. Cardinal. Jesuit. 1542-1621.) De scriptoribus ecclesiasticis liber. Cum adjunctis indicibus undecim, et brevi chronologia ab orbe condita usque ad annum 1612. *Romae*, 1613. 4⁰; Also : *Coloniae Agrippinae*, 1613. 8⁰ [pp. 44S, 117]; 1617. 8⁰; 1622. 8⁰; 1624. 4⁰; 1645. 8⁰; 1657. 8⁰ [pp. 333, 127]; 1663. 4⁰ (?); 1684. 4⁰; *Lugdunum* (*Colon. ?*), 1613. 4⁰ (ed. Maresius); *Parisiis*, 1617. 8⁰ (ed. Sirmond. One of the most correct); 1630. 8⁰; 1631. 8⁰ ; cum appendice philologica et chronologica Philippi Labbe. *Parisiis*, 1658 and 1660. 8⁰; *Lugduni*, 1663. 8⁰; 1675. 8⁰; Editio sexta. *Lovani*, 1678. 8⁰ [w. cont. of Saussay. pp. 317 without the chronology]; editio . . auctior . . ad ann. 1718. *Bruxelles*, 1719. 8⁰. [pp. 346, without the chronology] 1728 (??) [" By some considered best of all . . . but overlooks many things . . . makes no mention of many illustrious writers . . . shows his ignorance of Greek . . . is often mistaken." *Walch*.] Continued by : Labbe. Diss. philol., q. v.; Oudin. Suppl. de scr., q. v. and Andreas de Saussay. Insignis libri de scriptoribus ecclesiasticis cardinalis Bellarmini continuatio ab anno MD. in quo desinit, ad annum MDC. *Tulli Leucorum*, 1665. 4⁰; also : *Coloniae*, 1684. 4⁰.

BERNHARDY. Grundriss der römischen Literatur. 4 Aufl. *Braunschw.* 1865. (5ᵗᵉ. Aufl. 1872) p. 896–921 Ueberblick der latein. Kirchenväter. [An estimate from the literary stand-point.]

BLAKEY, R. Lives of the primitive fathers, with copious lists of their writings, etc. 1842. 8⁰.

Book of the fathers of the Christian Church, and the spirit of their writings. *Lond.*, 1837. 8⁰; 1846. 8⁰. [Unimportant. Few Ante-Nicene names.]

BÖHRINGER, FRDR. Die Kirche Christi und ihre Zeugen oder die Kirchengeschichte in Biographien. s. u. Church Histories. [Reaches to the 16th century. Strongly rationalistic.]

BOSIUS, JO. ANDR. Introductio in notitiam scriptorum ecclesiasticorum. *Jenae*, 1673. 8⁰; 1676. 8⁰ [= Schediasma de comparanda notitia scriptorum ecclesiasticorum] ; in : Crenius, Th. De comparanda eruditione. *Lugd. Bat.* 1699. 4⁰; ed. J. G. Meuscherius. *Kilonii*, 1704; ed. J. G. Walch. *Jenae*, 1723. 8⁰.

BOTTON, F. Les pères de l'eglise latine, extraits de leurs principaux ouvrages; avec des notices biographiques et des notes. *Paris*, 1884. 8⁰.

BOTTSACUS, JO. (?) (Prot.) Patrologia. *Stettin*, 1664. 8⁰.

BOUCAT, ANTON. Dissertatio ultima de sanctis patribus et doctoribus, quorum consensus est fidei regula. In his : Theologia patrum schol.-dogm.-pos. 2 ed. accur. et emend. (*Venet.* 1765–6. 8 v. 4⁰.) V. 165–215. [Clement R— Bonaventura (1274). Notice and list of works.]

BUSSE, J. B. J. (R. C.) Grundriss der christlichen Literatur. *Münster*, 1828–9. 2 Bd. 8⁰. (xxiv. 368, 407 [1] xvi.) [Centuries 1–15. " Of permanent value."— *Alzog*. Convenient.]

Biographia ecclesiastica; or, the lives of the most eminent fathers of the Christian Church who flourished in the first four centuries. *Lond.* 1704. 2 v. 8⁰. [" Worthless."]

CAILLAU. Introductio ad ss. patrum lectionem. *Parisiis*, 1825. 8⁰ (496 p.); *Mediol.* 1830–31. 2 v. 8⁰.

CAVE, W. (Anglican. d. 1713.) Tabulae, quib. doctores et scriptores ecles. . . . a epochae christ. 1–1519 exhibenten. *Lond.* 1674. f⁰; cur. Rdf. Capellus. *Hamb.* 1676. f⁰.

— Apostolici; or the History of the lives . . of the fathers for the first 300 years. *Lond.* 1677. f⁰; 2d ed. corrected. 1682. f⁰; 3d. 1687. f⁰; also 1716. f⁰; and 1733. f⁰.

— Ecclesiastici; or, the history of the . . . fathers in the 4th century . . . *Lond.* 1683. f⁰.

— Lives of the most eminent fathers of the church that flourished in the first four centuries. . . New edition carefully revised by Henry Cary. *Oxford*, 1840. 3 v. 8⁰. [" Apostolici " and " Ecclesiastici " combined.]

— Chartophylax Ecclesiasticus quo prope 1500 scriptores eccl. . . . indicantur. *Londini*, 1685. 8⁰. [" Dr. Cave's own abridgment of the Historia Literaria."]

Colomesius, P. Ad Gul. Cave Chartophylacem Ecclesiasticum paralipomena. *Lond.* 1686. 8⁰.

— Scriptorum Ecclesiasticorum Historia Literaria a Christo nato usque ad saecul. XIV. *Lond.* 1688–98. 2 v. f⁰; best ed. *Oxonii*, 1740–43. 2 v. f⁰; and repr. 1749. 2 v. f⁰; also repr. *Basil.* 1741–45. 2 v. f⁰. Other editions, *Colon.* 1720. f⁰; *Geneva*, 1693–99; 1708; 1720. f⁰. Includes App. Wharton, H. De scriptoribus eccl. ab a 1300–1517; and Gere, Rob. De concil. secular. 14 et 15.

[" Characterized by . . marked individuality, . . earnest desire for the truth and by extraordinary erudition . . . . does not go critically . . cannot be relied on." *Donaldson*.]

CEILLIER, REMY. (R. C.) Histoire générale des auteurs sacrés et ecclésiastiques. *Paris*, 1729–63. 23 v. 4⁰; Table génerale, par L. E. Rondet. *Par.* 1782. 2 v. 4⁰; 2. éd. *Paris*, 1858–69. 17 v. 4⁰. [14 t. in 15. 1858–63. Index. 2 t. 1868-9 (also 1870. 2 t.).] [Extends to Guillaume d'Auvergne (1248). Special attention is paid to the doctrine of the Fathers. The work is more complete than that of Dupin, but more strictly Roman Catholic in its stand-point.]

CHARPENTIER, J. P. Études sur les Pères de l'Église. 1853. 2 v. 8⁰; German tr. Bittner. *Mainz*, 1855. [Rhetorical and superficial (cf. Alzog).]

CLARKE, ADAM. Concise view of the succession of sacred literature. New ed. with continuation to 1300 by J. B. B. Clarke. *Lond.* 1830–1. 2 v. 8⁰; 1st ed. 1807. 12⁰. [Brief. Unimportant, but convenient.]

CLINTON, H. FYNES. Fasti Romani. Vol. II. Appendix. (*Oxford*, 1850. 4⁰.) Ch. VIII. Ecclesiastical Authors. pp. 395–495, etc.

COCUS, ROBERT (COOKE). Censura quorundam scriptorum quae sub nominibus Sanctorum et veterum auctorum pontificiis citari solent. *Lond.* 1614. 4⁰; 1623. 4⁰; *Helmst.* 1641. 8⁰; 1655. 8⁰; 1683. 8⁰. [Brief. Formerly much quoted, now seldom or never.]

COFFIN, WILLIAM H. The lives and times of the most distinguished Christian fathers to the close of the third century. *Baltimore*, 1846. 8⁰. [Popular, general, uncritical.]

COLLINSON, JOHN. Key to the writings of the principal fathers who flourished during the first three centuries. *Lond.* 1813. 8⁰.

CONTOGONES, CONSTANTINUS R. (Greek Ch.) Φιλολογικὴ καὶ κριτικὴ ἱστορία τῶν ἀπὸ τῆς ά μέχρι τῆς ἡ ἑκατονταετηρίδος 'ακμασάντων ἁγίων τῆς ἐκκλησίας πατέρων καὶ τῶν συγγραμμάτων. 1851–3. 2 v.

COX, ROBERT. (Prot.) Narratives of the lives of the more eminent fathers of the first three centuries. *Lond.* 1817. 8⁰. [Uncritical. " One of the best of its kind." *Donaldson*.]

DEUTINGER. Geist der christlichen Ueberlieferung. Versuch die werke der vorzüglichsten Schriftsteller der Kirche in ihrem Zusammenhange und durch übersichtliche Auszüge zu veranschaulichen. *Regensb.* 1850–51. 2 bks. [To Athanasius.]

DODWELL, HENRY. (Non-juror. 1641–1711.) Two letters of advice: I. for the susception of the holy orders; II. for studies theological, with a catalogue of the Christian writers, and genuine works of the first three centuries, with a discourse concerning Sanchoniathon's Phœnician history. *London*, 1691. 8⁰. 1 ed.; 1672. 8⁰. 2 ed.; 1680. 8⁰.

DONALDSON, JAMES. A critical history of Christian literature and doctrines, from the death of the apostles to the Nicene Council. *London*, 1864–66. 3 v. 8⁰. 1. Apost. Fathers; 2 and 3. The Apologists. [" Very valuable, but unfinished ed."]

DUPIN, LOUIS ELLIES. (1657–1719. Prof. Dr. of the Sorbonne-Jansenist.) Nouvelle bibliothèque des auteurs ecclésiastiques, contenant l'histoire de la vie ; la catalogue, la critique, et la chronologie des leurs ouvra-

ges; le sommaire de ce qu'ils contiennent; un juge-
ment sur leur stile, et sur leur doctrine; et le dénom-
brement des differents editions. *Paris.* 8⁰.

The work is variously quoted as 3e éd. 1698–1704, 61 **v.**; 9e éd.
1698 sq. 61 v.; 1688 sq. 43 v.; as 58 v., as 47, as 32, and as 16.
The confusion is in the various editions of the early volumes
and the various works included or omitted. The following is
its history:—

T. 1. [3 prem. s.] *Par.* 1686. 8⁰; 2e éd. *Par.* 1688. 8⁰ [not
much changed]; 3. éd. *Par.* 1698. 2 v. 8⁰. [Prel. diss. on the
Bible omitted. Succession of bishops, Histories of persecu-
tions, of councils, and of heresies added.]
T. 2. [4. siècle.] *Par.* 1689. 2 v. 8⁰; 3 éd. *Paris*, 1702. 3 v. 8⁰ [re-
vised and enlarged.]
T. 3. [5. siécle. 1. Partie, commencement.] *Par.* 1688. 8⁰; 2. éd.
Par. 1690. 2 v. 8⁰. [2. partie. 430–500.] *Par.* 1690. 8⁰; 2. éd.
Par. 1702. 3 v. 8⁰.
T. 4. [6. siècle.] *Par.* 1690. 8⁰. [Reprinted substantially.]
T. 5. [7. and 8. sièc.] av. réponse . . . Petitdidier. *Par.* 1691.
8⁰ (repr.).
Supplement contenant les principaux points de l'histoire eccle-
siastique des 4, 5, 6, 7, and 8 siècles, etc. *Par.* 1711. 8⁰.
Hist. des controverses . . . dans le 9. siècle. *Par.* 1694. 8⁰. 2. éd.
1698. 8⁰.
Hist. des controverses . . . dans le 10. siècle. *Paris*, 1696. 8⁰; do.
11. siècle. *Par.* 1696. 8⁰; do. 12. siècle. *Par.* 1696. 2 v. 8⁰; do.
13. siècle. *Par.* 1698. 8⁰; do. 14. siècle. *Par.* 1698. 8⁰; do. 15.
siècle. *Par.* 1698. 2 v. 8⁰.
Hist. de l'égl. et des aut. eccl. du 17. siècle. *Par.* 1708. 7 v. 8⁰.
Hist. eccl. du 18. sièc. *Par.* 1714. 4 v. 8⁰.
Bibl. des aut. eccl. du 18. sièc. 1700–1710. *Par.* 1711. 2 v. 8⁰.
Discours prél. sur l'Anc. & le Nouv. Test. *Par.* 1699. 3 v. 8⁰.
Table universelle des Aut. eccl. *Par.* 1704. 5 v. 8⁰. [Very defective. Cf. Niceron, Memoirs. T. 2. pp. 31–37.] The often-
quoted "edition in 61 v." consists of: Prolég. 3 v.; 3 prem.
sièc. 2 v.; IV. s. 3 v.; V. s. 4 v.; VI. s. 1 v.; VII. et VIII. s.
1 v.; suppl. IV–VIII. s. 1 v.; IX. s. 1 v.; X, XI, et XII s.
4 v.; XIII, XIV, XV s. 4 v.; XVI s. 5 v.; Auteurs séparés
de l'Égl. 4 v.; XVII. s. 7 v.; Hist. eccl. du 17. s. 4 v.; XVIII
s. 2 v.; continuation par Goujet. 3 v.; Tables. 5 v.; Remarques
par Petit-Didier. 3 v.; Critique par R. Simon, et rem. par Est.
Souciet. 4 v.
Other editions are: *Amst.* 1690–1713. 19 v. 4⁰. [Incomplete, and
also imperfect, being reprinted from the unrevised edition.]
Latin translation. *Paris*, 1692–93. 3 v. [Only to 9th century.]
English translation. *Dublin*, 1722–24 [Best Eng. ed., but
only 16 centuries]; *Lond.* 1693 (v. 1, 3d ed. 1696)–1725. 14 v. f⁰.
[17 centuries.]
SIMON, RICH. Critique de la bibliothèque de M. Du Pin. *Par.*
1730. 4 t. [Very bitter. Before this he published under the
name of "Jo. Reuchlin" a "Dissertation critique sur la nou-
velle bibl. des aut. eccl. *Frf.* 1688. 12⁰.|
PETITDIDIER, MATTHIEU. Remarques sur les premiers tomes
de la bibl. eccl. de M. Du Pin. *Par.* 1691–6. 3 v. 8⁰.

DU SAUSSAY, A. Insignis liber de scriptoribus ecclesiasticis eminent. card. Bellarmini continuatio ab anno 1500
. . . ad annum 1600. . . *Tulli Leuc.* 1665. 4⁰.
EBERL, J. W. (R. C.) Leitfaden zu den Vorlesungen
und zum Studium der Patrologie. Zunächst fur seine
Zuhörer in den Druck gegeben. *Augsb.* 1854. 8⁰. (vi,
40 p.)
EBERT, A. Allgemeine Geschichte der Literatur des
Mittelalters in Abendlande. *Lpz.* 1874–1880. 8⁰.
Bd. 1. Geschichte der christlich lateinischen Literatur
von ihren Aufängen bis zum Zeitalter Karls des Grossen.
1874. (XII. 624 p.) Bd. 2. Geschichte der lateinischen Literatur vom Zeitalter Karls des Grossen bis
zum Tode Karls des Kahlen. 1880. (VIII. 404 S.)
[Accurate and exhaustive literary treatment. Not full bibliographically.]

ENGELHARDT, J. G. V. (Prot.) Literar. Leitfaden zu patrist. Vorlesungen. *Erlangen*, 1823. 8⁰. [Unimportant.]
EVANS, ROBERT WILSON. (Prot.) Biography of the
early church, containing lives of Clement of Rome,
Symeon, Ignatius, Polycarp, Marcion, Justin Martyr,
Tatian, Dionysius of Corinth, Irenaeus, Victor, Appo-
lonius, Clement, Alex., Tertullian, Alexander of Jerus,
Origen, Cyprian, Novatian, Dionysius of Alexander,
etc. *Lond.* 1837–39. 2 v. 8⁰. [Uncritical.]
FABRICIUS, JOHANN ALBRECHT. Bibliotheca latina, sive,
notitia auctorum veterum latinorum. *Venetiis*, 1728.
2 v. 8⁰. ((14) 676, (2) 687); 1 ed. *Hamb.* 1697. 8⁰;
Suppl. *Hamb.* (?) 8⁰; 5(?) ed. *Hamb.* 1721–2. 3 v. 8⁰.
[Much esteemed because it contains considerable matter

omitted in the ed. of Ven. 1728, which is yet preferred for
use because it incorporates in the text the inconvenient sup-
plements of the former.]
CONSTANTIS A FERRIS.] (Bernard Heinrich Reinold.) Epistola ad sincerum amicum, continens monita quaedam, ad
Joannis Alb. Fabricii. *Supplementa Bibliothecae latinae*,
lib. iv. cix. *Traj. ad Rhen.* 1722. 8⁰.

— Bib. lat.; nenc melius delecta, rectius digesta et aucta
diligentia J. A. Ernesti. *Lipsiae*, 1773–74. 3 v. 8⁰.
["Omissions not compensated for by the additions. A promised fourth volume of Christian authors did not appear."]
— Bibliotheca latina mediae et infiniae aetatis, cum supplemento Christiani Schoettgenii . . a P. Joanne Dom-
inico Mansi . . correcta, illustrata, aucta. *Patavii*, 1754.
6 v. 4⁰; 1 ed. 1734–46. 6 v. 8⁰ [v. 6 by Schoettgen]; enlarged edition. *Florent.* 1858. 6 v. 8⁰.
— Bibliotheca Graeca, sive Notitia scriptorum vet.
graecorum quorumcumque monumenta integra aut
fragmenta edita extant. Ed. III. *Hamb.* 1718–28.
14 v. 4⁰; Ed. IV. curante Th. Cph. Harless. *Hamb.*
1790–1809. [12 v. et Index. (1838) 4⁰. T. 1. 1 ed. 1705; 2
ed. 1708; 3 ed. 1718. T. 2–10. 1 ed. 1707–21; 2 ed. 1716–37. T.
11–14. 1 ed. 1721–28. T. 1–11. [p. 544.] 4 ed. (unfinished)
1790–1806 as above.]
[Invaluable collection of fragments, but leaves much to be
desired bibliographically, and this is not supplied by Harless. Includes centuries 1–17.]

FESSLER, JOS. Institutiones patrologiae. *Oeniponte*, 1850–
51. 2 t. 8⁰. (XXX. 762; XII. 1071 S.) [Extends to
Gregory I. "Excellent."]
FREPPEL, CHARLES EMIL. Cours d'éloquence sacrée.
1857–68. 12 v. 8⁰. [Includes Apologistes chrétiens au 11
siècle, Clément d'Alexandrie, Origene, Péres apostoliques,
Cyprien, Irenée, Tertullien.]
GERHARD, JOHANN. (Prot.) Patrologia, s. de primitivae
ecclesiae christ. doctor. vita ac lucubrationibus . . .
Ed. ab. Ern. Gerhardi fil. *Jenae*, 1653. 8⁰; 3. ed. cura
J. G. Olearii. *Jena*, 1673. 8⁰.
GOLDWITZER. Patrologie verbunden mit Patristik bearbeitet für Theologen. *Nüremb.* 1833–34. 2 v. 8⁰. [To
9th century. Uncritical. "Useless." Cf. also Bibliographies.]
HALLOIX, PETRUS. (Jesuit. 1572–1656.) Illustrium ecclesiae orientalis scriptorum, qui sanctitate juxta et
eruditione primo christi saeculo floruerunt, et apostolis,
convixerunt. *Duaci*, 1633. f⁰ [pp. xxvi, 730]; do.
secundo saeculo . . *Duaci*, 1636. f⁰. [pp. xxvi, 863.]
[He intended to publish other volumes, and prepared vol. 3,
but all that appeared of it was his "Origenes defensus."]

HAUMER, JONATHAN. (†1677.) View of antiquity, pre-
sented in a short but sufficient account of some of the
Fathers who lived within or near the first three hundred
years after Christ. *Lond.* 1677. 8⁰.
HEDERICHE, BENJ. Notitia auctorum antiqua et media
oder Leben, Schriften, *Editiones*, und Censuren d.
Biblischen u. entweder noch gantz, oder auch nur in
considerablen *Fragmentis* vorhanden fürnehmsten.
Gr. u. Lat. Kirchen-Scholastischen-u. Profan Scriben-
ten u. s. w. *Wittenberg*, 1714. 8⁰.
HEUNISCHIUS, CASP. (Prot.) Aetates patrum praecipuo-
rum, ex certis fundamentis historicis atque chronologicis
accurate demonstratae. *Rotenburgi*, 1677. 8⁰.
Histoire litteraire de la France par des religieux Bénédic-
tins de la congregation de S. Maur (D. Rivet, D. Tail-
landier et D. Clémencet). *Paris*, 1733–1763. 12 v. 4⁰;
continuation par des Membres de l'Institut. v. 13–26.
Paris, 1813–1873. 4⁰; reprinted *Paris*, 1865–. 4⁰.
HÜLSEMANN, JO. (Prot.) Patrologia. ed. ab. Jo. Ad.
Scherzer. *Lips.* 1670. 4⁰.
ITTIG, TH. Schediasma de auctorib., qui de scriptorib.
ecclesiasticis egerunt. (ed. Ludovici.) *Lpz.* 1711. 8⁰.
JACKSON, GEORGE A. Early Christian literature primers.
Edited by Prof. George P. Fisher. *New York*, D. Ap-
pleton & Co. 1879–84. 4 v. 16⁰. V. 1. Apostolical
fathers and apologists of the second century; v. 2.
Fathers of the third century. [Popular, with extracts.
Well planned and executed.]

JEREMIE. History of the Christian Church. (1852.) See under Church Histories.

KAUFMANN, MELCH. (R. C.) Ueber die göttliche Erblehre in den Schriften der heil. Väter, oder Grundriss der Patrologie. *Luzern.* 1832. 8⁰. ["Unimportant."]

KURTZ. Kirchengeschichte. See under Church Histories.

LABBE, PHILLIP. Dissertation philologica et historica de scriptoribus ecclesiasticis, quos attigit Bellarminus. *Parisiis,* 1660. 2 v. 8⁰.

LANG, JOHANN BA. (R. C.) Patrologia. *Budae,* 1809. 8⁰. ["Unimportant."]

LARDNER, N. The credibility of the gospel history. *Lond.* 1727–55. 17 v. 8⁰; also in Works. *Lond.* 1788. 11 v. 8⁰; 1815. 5 v. 4⁰; 1827. 10 v. 8⁰; 1831. 10 v. 8⁰; 1838. 10 v. 8⁰. [Not strictly a Patrology; but so complete and in such method that it belongs here.]

LARKIN (E.) Speculum Patrum; a Looking-glass of the Fathers, wherein you may see each of them drawn, characterized, and displayed in their true colours. *Lond.* 1659. 12⁰.

LE CLERC (JOHN). Lives of Clemens Alexandrinus, Eusebius, Gregory Nazienzus, and Prudentius, with a History of Pelagianism, translated from the French. *Lond.* 1696. 8⁰.

— Unpartheiische Lebensbeschr. einiger Kirchenväter u. Ketzer, namentlich Justini Martyris, Clementis Alex., Origenis, Cypriani, Prudentii, Gregorii Naz., Eusebii, Pelagii, u Coelestii, a. Dessen. Bibliotheque universelle ubersetzt. *Hal.* 1721. 8⁰. [From the "Bibl. universelle." Pref. by Chr. Thomasius. "Worth reading." *Walch.*]

LE NOURRY, DENIS-NICOLAS. (Benedictin. 1647–1724.) Apparatus ad bibliothecam maximam patrum veterum et scriptorum ecclesiasticorum Lugduni editam. . . . *Parisiis,* 1703–15. 2 v. f⁰. First published *Paris,* 1694–97. 2 v. 8⁰. [Very learned and valuable discussions of the works of the Fathers. Extends only to beginning of the fourth century. It is usually joined to the Bibliotheca Max. vet. patrum of Despont as vols. 28 and 29.]

LOCHERER, JO. NEP. (R. C.) Lehrbuch der Patrologie fur akad. Vorlesungen. *Mainz,* 1837. 8⁰. ["Unimportant."]

LOESCHER, CASP. (Prot.) De patribus africanis libri duo. *Rochlitz,* 1722–4. 2 v. 8⁰.

LUMPER, GOTTFRIED. (Benedictin.) Historia theologica critica de vita, scriptis, atque doctrina Sanctorum Patrum, aliorumque Scriptorum eccl. trium priorum seculorum et virorum doctissimum literariis monumentis collecta. *Aug. Vind.* 1783–99. 13 v. 8⁰. [Centuries 1–3. "Remarkably learned." Constantly used and referred to.]

MAGON, FR. CARL. (R. C.) Handbuch der Patrologie und der kirchlichen Litteraturgeschichte. *Regensburg,* 1864. 2 v. 8⁰. (vi, 1014 p.) ["Very faulty."]

MAKARIUS, of St. Elias. (R. C.) Institutiones patrologicae. *Graecii,* 1781. 8⁰. ["Unimportant."]

MARCEL and SCHMIDT. Cours élémentaire de patrologie, à l'usage des seminaires et des colléges. *Par.* 1848. 8⁰.

MEELFÜHRER, JO. CHPH. (Prot.) Corona centum patrum et doctorum ecclesiae. *Giessae,* 1760. 4⁰.

MELANCTHON, PH. (Prot.) Libellus de scriptoribus ecclesiasticis. *Viteb.* 1539. 8⁰; access. ejusd. orat. de vitis Ambrosii Augustini et Hieronymi; rec. et praef. est G. Thd. Strobel. *Nur.* 1780. 8⁰.

MIRAEUS, AUB. Bibliotheca ecclesiastica sive de scriptoribus eccl. qui ab anno Chr. 1494, quo Joannes Trithemius desinit, ad usque tempora nostra floruerunt. Pars altera. *Antv.* 1649. f⁰. [Posthumous. Ed. A. van d. Eede.]

MÖHLER, JOH. ADAM. (R. C.) Patrologie, oder christliche Literärgeschichte; hrsg. v. Fr. X. Reithmayr. *Regensb.* 1840. 8⁰. Bd. 1. Die ersten drei Jahrb. [Unfinished. Especially valuable.] French translation by Jean Cohen. *Louvain,* 1844. 8⁰.

NAGEOTTE, E. Histoire de la littérature latine depuis ses orignes jusqu'an VIe siècle de notre ère. *Paris,* 1884. 18⁰. (559 p.)

NIRSCHL, JOSEPH. (R. C.) Lehrbuch der Patrologie und Patristik. *Mainz,* 1881–. 8⁰.[Very convenient and useful manual, especially for its *Patristical* method.]

NODIER, CH. Bibliothéque sacrée grecque-latine. *Paris,* 1826. 8⁰. ["From Moses to St. Thomas Aquinas." Of some use for synopsis and description of editions.]

NOURRISSON, J. F. Les Pères de l'Église latine. Leur vie, leurs écrits, leur temps. 1858. 2 v. 12⁰.

OEHLRICHS, J. G. ARN. (Prot.) Commentarii de scriptoribus ecclesiae latinae priorum sex saeculorum cur. Arn. Hm. L. Heeren. *Lips.* 1791. 8⁰.

OLEARIUS, JO. GOTTFR. (Prot.) Abacus patrologicus . . eccl. chr. patrum atque doctorum . . *Jen.* 1673. 8⁰; ed. auct. s. t. Bibliotheca script. eccl. Ed. J. G. Olearius cum Praef. J. Fr. Buchter. *Jenae,* 1711. 4⁰. [2d part dated 1710.]

OUDIN, CASIMIR. Supplementum de scriptoribus ecclesiasticis a Bellarmino omissis ad annum 1460. *Parisiis,* 1686. 8⁰.

— (ex-monk. Librarian of Leyden Univ. b. 1638; d. 1717.) (Prot.) Commentarius de scriptoribus ecclesiae antiquis, illorumque scriptis, tam impressis; quam manuscriptis . . . a Bellarmino . . et aliis omissis, ad annum MCCCCLX. vel ad artem typographicam inventam, etc. *Lipsiae,* 1722. 3 t. f⁰. [v. 1 Centuries 1–8; v. 2. Cent. 9–12; v. 3. Cent. 13–15.] [Recast because of criticisms of Cave. Of considerable value.]

PERMANEDER. Bibliotheca Patristica. *Landishuti,* 1841–3. 2 v. in 3. 8⁰. T. 1. Patrologia generalis. 1841; T. 2. Patrologia specialis; pt. 1. 1. et II. s. 1842; pt. 2. III. s. 1843. [Valuable.]

PESTOLOZZI, H. J. (Prot.) Grundlinien der Geschichte der kirchlichen Literatur der ersten VI. Jahrhunderte. *Göttingen,* 1811. 8⁰. [Unimportant.]

POSSEVIN, ANTONIUS. (R. C.) Apparatus sacer ad scriptores V. et N. T., eorum interpretes . . . . *Venet.* 1603–; auct. et emend. *Col. Agripp.* 1708. 2 v. f⁰.

REITHMAYR, F. X. (R. C.) Ed. See Möhler.

RÖSSLER. (Prot.) Bibliothek der Kirchenväter. *Leipzig,* 1776–86. 10 v. 8⁰. [Brief accounts, with large extracts in German translation. "Valuable in its time." *Alzog.*]

RUEFF, JOS. LEONAR. (R. C.) Kurze Patrologie. *Sulzbach,* 1828. 8⁰. ["Unimportant."]

RUGGIERI, E. Storia dei santi padri e dell' antica litteratura della chiesa: opera postuma. Vol. V. *Roma,* 1885. 16⁰. (VIII. 388 p.)

SANDIUS, CHRPH. Tractatus de veteribus scriptoribus ecclesiasticis. *Cosmopoli (Amstelodami),* 1668. 8⁰; *Coloniae (Amst.)* 1676. 8⁰. [Canonical and apocryphal N. T. and Ante-Nicene writers. "Nec sine notis pravae doctrinae arianae." *Walch,*]

SARDAGNA, CAROLUS. (Jesuit.) Indicibus patrum ac veterum scriptorum eccl. ordine alphabetico. *Ratisb.* 1772. 8⁰. [Compend.]

SAUSSAY, AND. DU. Insignis libri d. script. eccles. continuatio ab a 1500, in quo desinit B. ad a. 1600. *Toul.* 1665. 4⁰; *Col.* 1684. 4⁰. [Continuation of Bellarmin, q. v.]

SCHAFF. History of the Church. See Church Histories. [Best handbook of Patrology in English.]

SCHLEICHERT, BONIF. (R. C.) Institutiones patrol. *Prag.* 1777. ["Unimportant."]

SCHMID, BERNH. (R. C.) Grundlinien d. Patrologie. *Freib. i. Br.* 1879. 8⁰ (100 p.); 2te verm. Aufl. *Freib.* 1886. 8⁰. (XI. 155 p.) [Clement of Rome to Gregory the Great. Very condensed, but good sketch.]

SCHOPF, JOANNES. (Prot.) Academia J. Chr. s. brevis descriptio patrum ac doctrorum ecclesiae. *Tub.* 1593. 4⁰; ed. auct. c. Hammel. *Speier.* 1616.

SCHRAM, DOMINICUS. (Benedictin.) Analysis operum ss. patrum et scriptorum ecclesiasticorum. *Aug. Vind.*

1780–1796. 18 v. 8⁰. [Contains extracts, with biographical notices. Extends to Epiphanius among the Greek, Ambrose among the Latin, fathers.]

SCULTET, ABR. (Prot.) Medullae theologiae patrum syntagma. . . . *Frkf.* 1634. 4⁰. [Earlier eds. 1. Thl. *Amberg*, 1598; Ed. 4. 1613. 4⁰; 2 Thl. *Neust. a. d. H.* 1605; *Amberg*, 1615. 4⁰; 3 Thl. *Neust. a. d. H.* 1609. 4⁰; Thl. 4. *Heidelb.* 1613. 4⁰.]

SCHÖNEMANN, KARL TRAUGOTT GOTTLOB. (Prot.) Bibliotheca historico-literaria Patrum latinorum a Tertulliano principe usque ad Gregorium M. et Isidorum Hispal.; ad bibliothecum Fabricii latinum accommodato. *Lipz.* 1792–94. 2 v. 8⁰. (XXII. (2) 672; XII. 1064.) [A remarkable and standard literary-historical account of editions.]

SIXTUS SENENSIS. (R. C.) Bibliotheca sancta. *Francof.* 1575. f⁰.

SPRENGER, PLACIDUS. (Benedictin.) Thesaurus rei patristicae. *Wirceb.* 1782 (4?)–. 3 v. 4⁰; *Stuttg.* 1784–92. (?) 3 v. 4⁰. [Contains the dissertations of Le Nourry and Galland, with editions. Ends with Clement of Alexandria.]

STEPHANUS LUSIGNANUS. (R. C.) Catalogus virorum illustrium V. et N. T. nec non omnium primitivae ecclesiae. . . *Paris*, 1580. 8⁰. [" Rare, but of very moderate value." *Walch.*]

STOLLE, G. (Prot.) Aufrichtige Nachricht von den Leben Schriften u. Lehren der Kirchen-Väter d. ersten vier Hundert Jahre . . . *Jenae*, 1733. 4⁰.

TENTZELIUS, GUIL. ERN. Exercitationes selectae. *Lipsiae*, 1692. 4⁰. [Clemens R., Ignatius, Polycarp, Justin M., Athenagoras, Theophilus Ant., Tatian, Hermiae, Jacobus Nisib., and Ephraim Syrus.]

TEUFFEL, W. S. Geschichte der römischen Literatur. 3 Aufl. *Lpz.* 1875. gr. 8⁰. (XVI. 1216 S.) 1 : Aufl. 1870. 2ᵗᵉ 1872; English translation by Wilh. Wagner. *Lond.* 1873. 2 v. 8⁰. [Chronologically arranged, heathen and Christian together. Critical. Excellent method. Good bibliographical treatment.]

TILLEMONT, LOUIS-SEBASTIEN LE NAIN DE. (R. C. 1637–1698.) Mémoires pour servir a l'histoire ecclésiastique des six premiers siécles justifiés par les citations des auteurs originaux : avec une chronologie et des notes. *Laris*, 1693–1712. 16 v. 4⁰; Sec. éd., rev. et cor. *Paris*, 1700–1713. 16 v. 4⁰. [Enlarged from notes left by author]; *Bruxelles*, 1694 sq. 24 v. 12⁰. [Elsewhere quoted 30 t. in 10 v. Unfinished. Stops at v. 13 of 4⁰ ed.] *Brux.* 1734–60. 16 t. in 10 v. f⁰; *Ven.* 1732 sq. 16 v. 4⁰; tr. English. *Lond.* 1733–35. 2 v. f⁰. [Only to year 177.] [Extends to year 513. Monumental. Standard. Of constant usefulness.]

TOBENZ, DANIEL. (R. C.) Institutiones usus et doctrina Patr. *Vindobon.* 1779. 8⁰; Ed. emend et auct. 1819. 8⁰. [" Insignificant."]

TRICALET, PIERRE JOSEPH. (R. C. 1696–1761.) Bibliothéque portative des pères de l'Église, qui renferme l'histoire abrégée de leur vie, l'analyse de leurs principaux écrits . . . *Paris*, 1758–62. 9 v. 8⁰; Nouv. éd. revue, corr. et augm. par Laurent-Étienne Rondet. *Paris*, 1787. 8 (9?) v. 8⁰.

— Bibliotheca manualis ecclesiae patrum. *Bassani*, 1783. 9 t. 8⁰. [Lat. transl. of the above.]

VARENIUS, AUG. (Prot.) Rationarum theologicum de scriptoribus ecclesiasticis seculi primi . . . et secundi. *Rostochii*, 1669, 1673. 4⁰.

VILLEMAIN. Tableau de l'eloquence chrétienne au IV. siécle. *Par.* 1851; German tr. by Köhler. *Regensb.* 1855. [Rhetorical, but not useless.]

VOYON, SIMON DE. (R. C.) Catalogue des docteurs de l'église de Dieu . . . *Rupell*, 1607. 8⁰. [O. and N. T. and to modern times.]

WALCH, J. G. Bibliotheca patristica litterariis annotationibus instructa. Ed. nov. emend. et multum auct. ab. Jo. Trang. Lehr. Danzio. *Jenae*, 1834. 8⁰. (XVI., XVIII. 806 p.); also *Jenae*, 1757–65 and 1770. 8⁰.

More additions by : Danz. Initia doctrinae patristicae. *Jenae*, 1839. 8⁰. [This Walch-Danz Bibliotheca is still of first usefulness.]

WERNER, KARL. (R. C.) Geschichte der apologetischen und polemischen Literatur der christlichen Theologie. *Schaffhausen*, 1861–67. 5 v.

WIEST, STEPH. (R. C.) Institutiones patrologie in usum academ. *Ingolst.* 1795. 8⁰. [" Good compend."]

WILHELM, WILHELM. (R. C.) Patrologia ad usus academicos. *Frib. i. Breisg.* 1775. 8⁰. [" Inadequate."]

WINTER, VITUS ANTON. (R. C.) Kritische Geschichte d. ältesten Zengen u. Lehrer des Christenthums oder Patrologie. *Münch.* 1813 (5?) 8⁰. [" Hypercritical." " The special part includes only the Apostolical Fathers Justin Martyr and Irenaeus."]

Note 1. Among other literary-historical works referred to in the Synopsis are the histories of philosophy of BRUCKER, ERDMANN, HUBER, JANET, RITTER, STÖCKL, TENNEMANN, UEBERWEG, and ZELLER; also, AMPÈRE. *Hist. lit. de France* (1839) ; ARISIUS. *Cremona literaria* (*Parmae*, 1702) ; COLLOMBET. *Scr. disc. Lyon.* (1835) ; COLONIA. *Hist. lit. de Lyon.* (1728–30) ; GAMBA. *Test. Ital.* (1828) ; LE LONG. *Bibliotheca sacra* (*Paris*, 1723) ; NARBONE. *Bibliog. Sicola.* (*Palerm.* 1850–5) ; NEUMANN. *Armen. lit.* (1836) ; NICOLAI. *Gr. lit. Gesch.* ; PATCANIAN. *Catal. litter. Armén.* (1860) ; SCHÖLL. *Hist. lit. romaine;* SOMAL. *Letter. Armén.* (1829) ; TAFURI. *Scritt. Napoli.* (1748) ; TIRABOSCHI. *Storia lett. Ital.;* ZOLA. *Diz. biog. Sardegna* (*Torino*, 1837) ; ZAVARRONI. *Bibliotheca calabra.* (*Neap.* 1753).

Note 2. For further literary discussion of the above works compare the introductions to Alzog and Nirschl, and the various articles in Herzog, Ersch u. Gruber, etc.

Note 3. The three most convenient modern manuals of Patrology are those of Alzog, Nirschl, and Schmid, all Roman Catholic. The best manual in English is Dr. Schaff's History of the Church.

II. VARIOUS WORKS.

Being a selected list of such works mentioned or used in this *Synopsis* as seem to require further description or explanation.

I. *Bibliographies.*

CHEVALIER, ULYSSE. Répertoire des sources historiques du Moyen Age. Bio-Bibliographie. *Paris*, 1877–86. 8⁰. [" Answers the question, What are the sources to consult on such and such a historical personage?" Its author's plan contemplates a similar volume on places and events, and another of mss. editions and translations. A marvellously full and useful work, indispensable to every student of Church History. Least strong in modern German, and especially in periodical literature.]

DARLING, J. Cyclopaedia Bibliographica : a library manual of theological and general literature. *London*, 1854. 8⁰ (Authors) ; 1859 (Subjects v. I.). [A careful and very useful collection of titles with descriptions. Especially valuable for the numerous Tables of Contents given.]

ENGELMANN, WM. Bibliotheca scriptorum classicorum. Achte Auflage, umfassund die Literatur von 1700 bis 1878, neu bearbeitet von Dr. E. Preuss. *Leipzig*, 1880–2. 2 v. 8⁰. I. Scriptores Graeci, 1880; II. Scriptores Latini, 1882. [Editions, Translations, and Literature. On the whole less full on ecclesiastical than on secular writers, but a model work, of the greatest value to the student of Patrology.]

HOFMANN, S. F. W. Bibliographisches Lexicon der gesammten Litteratur der Griechen. Zweite umgearbeitete, durchaus vermehrte, verbesserte und fortgesetzte Ausgabe. *Leipzig*, 1838–45. 3 v. 8⁰. [Editions, Translations, and Literature. E. and T. very full and satisfactory; L. is less so.]

OETTINGER, E. M. Bibliographique biographique universelle. Dictionnaire des ouvrages relatifs à l'histoire de la vie publique et privée des personnages célèbres de tous les temps et de toutes les nations. *Bruxelles*. 1854. 2 v. 4⁰; *Paris*, 1866. 2 v. 8⁰. [1st ed. Brux. 1850. 2 v. 4⁰.]

GOLDWITZER, F. WENZESL. (R. C.) Bibliographie der Kirchenväter und Kirchenlehrer. *Landsh.* 1828(9). 8⁰. [Centuries 1–12. "Not valuable."]

STEWART, C. J. Catalogue of works in patristic and mediæval literature. *London*, n. d. 12⁰. [A booksellers' catalogue, but careful and of some, though not great, value.]

Note. For bibliographies of theological literature compare PETZHOLDT. *Bibliotheca Bibliographica. Leipz.* 1866. 8⁰. pp. 475–519 (514–5, *Patristik*), and VALLÉE. *Bibliographie des Bibliographies. Paris*, 1883. 8⁰. p. 727 (*Patristique* and *Patrologie*), p. 761–2 (*Theologie*).

The general works on the Bibliography of Theology add very little to the bibliography in the Patrologies, but those of NÖSSELT, NIEMEYER, ERSCH, DANZ, LOWNDES (*British Librarian*), ZUCHOLD, BALDAMUS, and especially of WINER and of MÜLDENER, are of more or less use for various purposes.

Of works on general bibliography the subject indexes of WATT, the ENGLISH and the AMERICAN CATALOGUES, of LORENZ and KAYSER [to 1832], and HINRICH's "Wissenschaftliche Uebersicht," in his semi-annual "Verzeichniss," with the quinquennial Repertorium by BALDAMUS founded on it, are especially valuable.

One who does not have a full range of Bibliographies will find the following the most direct apparatus for the majority of questions. Of general bibliographies, GRAESSE is, on the whole, much the best for first reference, although of course BRUNET is invaluable for its descriptions, while EBERT seldom yields much additional information. WATT is more particularly English, is brief title, and not very accurate; but has a vast amount of information and an invaluable subject-index. LOWNDES' *Bibliographers' Manual* is a bibliographical standard, but is select rather than exhaustive. ALLIBONE's *Dictionary of English and American authors* is an invaluable companion to Watt and Lowndes. For later English and American titles compare the respective catalogues published by Low and Leypoldt-Bowker.

For French titles the works of QUERARD and LORENZ form a series intended to cover all works in French, but especially those from the year 1700 to the present time. So in Germany HEINSIUS begins at 1700 and KAYSER at 1750. Either of these, with HINRICH's semi-annual *Verzeichniss* and BALDAMUS' *Repertorium*, furnish a sufficient apparatus, although HINRICH's *Fünfjähriger Bücher-Catalog* is an excellently convenient book.

For older titles, especially in Latin, German, and French, compare the wonderfully inaccurate, but invaluable, GEORGIUS. For incunabula compare, of course, PANZER and HAIN. For best bibliographies of various languages other than the above compare the *Hand list of bibliographies . . . placed in the Reading Room of the British Museum for Reference.*

For select bibliographies introductory to the Patrology and Church History of this period compare, besides the Patrologies and Church Histories, the various works on Theological Encyclopaedia, especially ZÖCKLER. *Handbuch d. theol. Wissenschaften. Nordlingen*, 1883–. 8⁰, and HAGENBACH. *Encyclopädie und Methodologie. 11te Aufl. hrsg. Kautzsch-Leipz.* 1884. 8⁰; translated with somewhat heterogeneous bibliographical additions by Drs. Crooks and Hurst. *New York*, 1884. 8⁰.

II. *Encyclopædias.*

HERZOG, J. J. Real-Encyklopädie für protestant. Theologie und Kirche. *Gotha*, 1854–68. 22 v. 8⁰; 2te durchgängig verb. und vermehrte Aufl. von J. J. Herzog, G. L. Plitt und A. Hauck. *Leipzig*, 1877–86. 17 v. 8⁰. [A – Z and Nachträge A – Hamburger. Patrological articles full, and all by first-class writers.]

LICHTENBERGER, F. Encyclopédie des sciences religieuses. *Paris*, 1877–82. 13 v. 8⁰. ["In vielen seiner Mitarbeiter mehr (als Herzog) zum Latitudinarismus hinneigend." *Zöckler.* v. 13 contains, besides Tables, a valuable *Dictionaire des contemporains.*]

M'CLINTOCK, JOH., and STRONG, JAS. Cyclopaedia of Biblical, Theological, and Ecclesiastical Literature. *New York*, 1874–81. 10 v. 8⁰, and two supplementary volumes. [Largely compiled, and not over-critical or exact, but has been and is of great practical pioneer value.]

MIGNE. Encyclopédie théologique, ou série de Dictionnaires sur toutes les parties de la science religieuse. 1. série. *Paris*, 1844–59. 52 v. 8⁰; 2. série, 1851–9. 53 v. 8⁰; 3. série, 1855–75. 65 v. 8⁰. [A most uncritical, but provokingly necessary mass of matter. Includes SEVESTRE. *Dictionnaire de patrologie. Paris*, 1855. 5 v. 8⁰; DOUHET. *Dictionnaire des legendes* (1855) and *Dict. des mystéries* (1854), and other works referred to in the *Synopsis.*]

SCHAFF, PH. A religious encyclopaedia; or Dictionary of Biblical, Historical, Doctrinal, and Practical Theology. Based on the Real-Encyklopädie of Herzog, Plitt and Hauck. *New York, Funk & W.* 1882–4. 3 v. 4⁰; new ed., slightly revised and enlarged by a supplementary volume containing an "Encyclopaedia of living divines and Christian workers." *New York*, 1887. [Rev. S. M. Jackson, M.A., and Rev. D. S. Schaff, Associate Editors. The abridged articles from Herzog have considerable bibliographical additions by Mr. Jackson. The valuable *Encyclopaedia of Living Divines* especially valuable biographically.]

WETZER, H. J. u. WELTE, BENED. Kirchen-Lexikon oder Encyklopädie d. kathol. Theologie und ihrer Hilfswissenschaften. *Freiburg i. Br.*, 1846–60. 13 v. 8⁰. [A.–Z. 11 v. Supplement IV. Index IV.]; 2te Aufl. v. Hergenröther u. Kaulen. 1881–. ["Much improved." Even the old ed. is especially useful.]

Note. The briefer general theological dictionaries, such as Aschbach, the Elberfeld Theol. Universal-Lexikon, Bergier, Glaire, etc., hardly repay consulting if any of the others are at hand.

KRAUS, F. X. Real-encyclopädie der christlichen Alterthümer. 1880–86. 2 v.

SCHENKEL, DANIEL. Bibel-Lexicon. Realwörterbuch zum Handgebrauch für Geistliche und Gemeindeglieder. *Leipzig*, 1869–75. 5 v. 8⁰.

SMITH, WM. Dictionary of Greek and Roman biography and mythology. *London*, 1843–8. 3 v. 8⁰; *Boston*, 1859. 3 v. 8⁰. [Compare for literary history of editions. Excellent, though largely superseded for Patrology by Smith and Wace.]

— Dictionary of the Bible. *Lond.* 1860–3. 3 v. 8⁰; revised and edited by Prof. H. B. Hackett, D.D., with the coöperation of Ezra Abbott, LL.D. *Boston*, 1868. 4 v. 8⁰; do. 1879. 4 v. 8⁰.

SMITH, W., and CHEETHAM, SAM. Dictionary of Christian Antiquities, being a continuation of the Dictionary of the Bible. *Lona.* 1876–80. 2 v. 8⁰; reprinted, *Hartford*, 1880. 8⁰. ["Durch grosse Gründlichkeit ausgezeichnet." *Zöckler.*]

SMITH, WM., and WACE, HENRY. A dictionary of Christian biography, literature, sects and doctrines: being a continuation of "The dictionary of the Bible." *London*, –82. vols. 1–3. 8⁰; reprinted from same plates. *Boston*, 1877–. [V. 1–3. A–Myensis.]

[The above series edited by Dr. Smith is marked for thoroughness both in the collection of topics and in the treatment.]

Encyclopaedia Britannica. A dictionary of Arts, Sciences, and General Literature. Ninth edition. *London*, 1875–; reprinted *New York*, 1878–1887–. [Vols. 1–21, A–Siam. In progress. Patrological articles are by such men as Harnack, Donaldson, etc.]

ERSCH and GRUBER. Allgemeine Encyclopädie der Wissenschaften u. Künste. *Leipzig*, 1818–1887–. 4⁰. [About three-fourths finished, containing now not far from 75,000 pages.]

MICHAUD, LOUIS GABRIEL. Biographie universelle ancienne et moderne. Nouv. éd. *Paris*, 1842–65. 45 v. 8⁰. [1 éd. 1811–1828. 52 v. 8⁰; Supplément. 1832–62. v. 53–85. 8⁰. In general articles more extended than in Hoefer.]

HOEFER, J. C. F. Nouvelle biographie générale. *Paris*, 1852–66. 46 v. 8⁰. [Vols. 1–8 have "universelle" for générale. The portion A–M. "exceeds in completeness every other publication of the kind." *Thomas.*]

Note. General encyclopaedias such as Brockhaus, Larousse, the Encyclopaedia Popolare, Chambers, Appleton, Johnson, etc., usually add nothing excepting an occasional bibliographical fact. Even the usually indispensable Zedler is not of sufficient patrological value to justify analysis. The same is true of various general and special Dictionaries which are mentioned occasionally in the *Synopsis;* and especially of the briefer biographical dictionaries like Thomas.

III. Collections.

ASSEMANI, JOS. SIM. Bibliotheca orientalis Clementino Vaticana. *Rom.* 1719–28. 3 v. in 4. 8⁰.

BICKERSTETH, EDWARD. (Prot. 1786–1850.) The Christian fathers of the first and second centuries, their principal remains at large, with selections from their other writings . . *Lond.* 1838.

BÖHL, G. Opuscula patrum selecta. Praef. Neander. *Berol.* 1826–7. 2 v. 8⁰.

CAILLAU, A. B., and GUILLON, M. N. S. Collectio selecta ss. eccl. patrum. *Paris,* 1829–42. 130 v. 8⁰; repr. *Mediol.* 1830–. 8⁰.

CASPARI, C. P. Ungedruckte unbeachtete und wenig beachtete Quellen zur Geschichte des Taufsymbols und der Glaubensregel, herausgegeben und in Abhandlungen erläutert. *Christiana,* I. 1866; II. 1869; III. 1875. 3 v. 8⁰.
— Alte und neue Quellen zur Geschichte des Taufsymbols und der Glaubensregel. 1879.

Corpus scriptorum ecclesiasticorum latinorum. Editum consilio et impensis academiae litterarum caesareae Vindobonensis. *Wien,* 1867–1886. 9 v. 8⁰. [In progress.]

COUSTANTIUS, PETR. Epistolae romanorum Pontificum usque ad annum 440. *Par.* 1721. f⁰; ed. Schönemann. *Götting.* 1796. 8⁰; continued to 523 by A. Thiel. *Braunsb.* 1868. 8⁰.

FABRICIUS, GEO. Poetarum veterum ecclesiasticorum opera christiana et operum reliquiae atque fragmenta. *Basil.* 1564. 4⁰.

FUNK, FRANC. XAV. Opera patrum apostolicorum. Edit. post Hefelianam quartum V. *Tübing,* 1878–81. 2 v. 8⁰; 1881. 2 v. in 1. 8⁰. [Good account of the literature.]

GALLANDIUS, A. Bibliotheca veterum patrum antiquorumque scriptorum ecclesiasticorum. *venet.* 1765–81. 14 v. et Appendix. f⁰.

GEBHARDT, O., and HARNACK, AD. Texte und Untersuchungen zur Geschichte der altchristlichen Literatur. *Leipzig,* 1882–. 8⁰.

GEBHARDT, OSC. DE, HARNACK, AD., and ZAHN, TH. Patrum apostolicorum opera. Edit. post Dresselianam alteram III. *Leipzig,* 1875–7. 8⁰; ed. 2. 1876–8. 8⁰; ed. minor. 1877. 8⁰. [Capital bibliographical monographs.]

GENOUDE, ANTOINE EUGÈNE DE. Les Péres de l'Église des trois premiers siècles de l'ère chrétienne. Traduit en français. *Paris,* 1837–1843. 9 v. 8⁰.

GERSDORF, E. G. Bibliotheca patrum ecclesiasticorum latinorum selecta. 1838–47. 13 v. 8⁰.

GRABE, J. E. Spicilegium ss. patrum. *Oxon.* 1698–9. 2 v. 8⁰; 1700. 8⁰; 1714. 8⁰; and (Lowndes) 1724 8⁰ (?).

[GRYNAEUS, J. J.] Monumenta ss. patrum orthodoxographa. *Basil.* 1569. 2 v. f⁰.

[HEROLDUS.] Orthodoxographa theologiae sacro sanctae ac syncerioris fidei doctores numero LXXVI ecclesiae columina luminaque clarissima authores partim Graeci, partim Latini . . . . *Basileae,* 1555. f⁰.

HURTER, H. Opuscula selecta ss. patrum ad usum praesertim studiosorum theologiae. 1868–85. 48 v.; 2d series. 1884–.

JACOBSON, GUIL. S. Clementis Romani, S. Ignatii, S. Polycarpi, patrum apostolicorum quae supersunt accedunt S. Ignatii, et S. Polycarpi martyria ad fidem codicum recensuit, annotationibus variorum et suis illustravit indicibus instruxit. *Oxonii,* 1838. 8⁰; 1840. 8⁰; 1847. 8⁰; 1863. 8⁰. [Notable prolegomena. Good synopsis of editions and translations.]

JONES, JEREMIAH. A new and full method of settling the canonical authority of the New Testament. 1726–7. 8⁰; 1798; *Oxford,* 1827. 8⁰.

LA BIGNE, MARGARIN DE. Bibliotheca ss. patrum supra 200 . . . *Paris,* 1575–9. 9 v. f⁰; 1589. 9 v. f⁰;

1609–10. 10 v. f⁰; 1624. 9 v. f⁰; ed. Schott and others under the name Magna bibliotheca veterum patrum. *Colon.* 1618–22. 15 v. f⁰; *Paris,* 1654. 17 v. f⁰.

LAGARDE, P. Analecta syriaca. *Leipzig,* 1858. 8⁰.

LE MOYNE, ST. Varia sacra, s. sylloge variorum opusculorum graecorum. Gr. et lat. *Lugd. Bat.* 1685–94. 2 v. 4⁰.

LE QUIEN, MICH. Oriens christianus, in quatuor patriarchatus digestus; quo exhibentur ecclesiae, patriarchae, ceterique praesules totius Orientis. *Paris,* 1740. 3 v. f⁰.

LIGHTFOOT, J. B. The apostolic fathers. I. S. Clement of Rome. *London,* 1869–77. 2 v. 8⁰; II. S. Ignatius, S. Polycarp. *London,* 1885. 2 v. in 3. 8⁰.

LINDNER, W. B. Bibliotheca patrum ecclesiast. selecta. *Lips.* 1857–61. 8⁰.

MATTAIRE. Opera et fragmenta veterum poetarum Latinorum profanor. et ecclesiast. duob. voll. comprehensa. *Londini,* 1713. 2 v. f⁰; with new title page. *Lond.* 1721.

Maxima bibliotheca veterum patrum et antiquorum scriptorum ecclesiasticorum. *Lugd.* 1677. 27 v. f⁰. [Adds more than 100 authors to the Magna bibliotheca. Latin only. "Editor is usually considered to have been Ph. Despont (Dupont), but the real editors were John and James Arvison." *Darling.*]; in epist. redacta Ph. a S. Jacobo. *August.* *Vind.* 1719. 2 v. f⁰.

MIGNE. Cursus patrologiæ completus. *Paris,* 1844–66. 8⁰. Patrologia latina 1844–55. 221 v. Patrologia graeca, 1857–66. 116 v. Continued by HOROY (Abbé). Bibliotheca Patristica ab anno MCCXVI, usque ad Concilii Tridentini Tempora. *Paris,* 1879–.

[Migne's editions, like his Encyclopaedia, are not to be used when there are better. The Abbé Horoy's continuation will add one hundred or more volumes.]

Mikropresbytikon. Veterum quorundam brevium Theologorum, sive Episcoporum sive presbyterorum . . . elenchus. *Basil.* 1550. f⁰.

MÜNTER, FR. Fragmenta patrum graecorum. *Hafniae,* 1788. 8⁰.

NICLAS, JO. NIC. Γεωπονικά. Geoponicorum seu de re rustica libri XX. *Lips.* 1781. 4 v. 8⁰.

NOURRISSON, J. F. Morceaux choisis des pères de l'eglise latine. *Paris,* 1874. 16⁰.

OBERTHÜR, FR. Sanctorum patrum opera polemica, etc. Opera patrum Graecorum, Graece et Latine. *Wirceb.* 1777–94. 21 v. 8⁰.
— Opera omnia patrum latinorum. *Wirceb.* 1780–91. 13 v. 8⁰.

OLSHAUSEN, HERRM. Historiae ecclesiast. veteris monumenta praecipua. *Berol.* 1822.

OTTO, JOH. K. TH. Corpus apologetarum Christianorum saeculi secundi. *Jena,* 1842–72(81). 9 v. 8⁰. [Justin M., Tatian, Athenagoras, Theophilus of Ant., Hermias, Quadratus, Aristides, Ariosto, Miltiades, Melito, Apollinaris.]

PITRA, J. B. Spicilegium Solesmense, complectens Sanct. patrum scriptorumque eccl. anecdota. *Par.* 1852–8. 4 v. 8⁰.
— Juris ecclesiastici Graecorum historia et monumenta. I. A primo p. C. n. ad VI. saec. *Rom.* 1864. 4⁰.

REITHMAYR, FR. X. and THALHOFER, VAL. Bibliothek der Kirchenväter. Auswahl der vorzüglichsten patristischen Werke in deutscher Uebersetzung. *Kempten,* 1869–1886. 410 v. 8⁰. [V. 410 extends to p. 480 of the Index.]

ROBERTS, ALEXANDER, and DONALDSON, JAMES. The Ante-Nicene Christian Library. *Edinburgh,* 1867–72. 24 v. 8⁰; ed. A. Cleveland Coxe, D.D. *Buffalo,* 1884–6. 8 v. 8⁰, and with original supplement, 1887. 8⁰.

ROUS, FRAN. Mella Patrum omnium, usque ad Pacem sub Constantino scripta prodierunt. 1650. 8⁰.

ROUTH, JOS. Reliquæ sacrae. *Oxon.* 1814–18. 4 v. 8⁰; 2. ed. 1846–8. 5 v. 8⁰. [V. 5 supplementary to both editions.

Compare also supplemental sheets for private circulation, 1853.]

— Scriptorum ecclesiasticorum opuscula. *Oxonii,* 1832. 2 v. 8º; 1840. 2 v. 8º; 1848. 2 v. 8º.

SAILER, J. M. Briefe aus alle Jahrh. d. christl. Zeitrechn. *München,* 1804. 8º.

SCHAFF, P. Bibliotheca symbolica ecclesiae universalis, The creeds of christendom, with a history and critical notes. *New York* and *London,* 1877. 3 v. 8º; 4th ed. 1884. 8º.

THEVENOT, MELCHIOR. Mathematicorum Veterum Athenaei, Apollodori, Philonis, Betonis Heronis et aliorum opera, gr. et lat. pleraque nunc primum edita ex. mss. codd. bibl. regiae. *Parisiis,* 1693. fº.

WEBER. Corpus poetarum latinorum uno volumine absolutum. Cum selectis varietate lectionis et explicatione brevissima ed. Guil. Em. Weber. *Francof. ad M.* 1833. lex. 8º.

Werke d. Kirchenväter (Die sämmtl.) a. d. Urtexte i. d. Deutsche übersetzt mit Vorrede von ZIEGLER. *Kempten,* 1831–1851. 38 v. 8º.

WERNSDORF. Poetae latinae minores. Curavit Joa. Chsti Wernsdorf. *Altenbruge* (v. I–V. po. I.) 1780–88, and *Helmstadii* (v. V. 2, 3 u. VI. 1, 2) 1791–1799. 6 v. 8º.

WHISTON, W. Primitive Christianity Revived, containing the Epistles of Ignatius, Apostolic Constitutions, Recognition of St. Clement, etc. 1711–12. 5 v. 8º.

ZAHN, THEOD. Forschungen zur Geschichte des neutestamentlichen Kanons und der altkirchlichen Literatur. *Erlangen,* 1881–3. 3 v. 8º.

ZINGERLE. Monumenta Syriaca ex Romanis codicibus collecta. Praefatus est P. Pius Zingerle, Ordin. S. Benedicti. Vol. I. *Oeniponti,* 1869. gr. 8º. (vi, 44 u. 132 p. syr. Text); — edita a Dr. Georgio Mösinger, Vol. II. *Oeniponti,* 1878. gr. 8º. (xv, 20 v. 174 S.)

(Councils.)

MERLINUS, JACOBUS. Tomus primus (et secundus) quatuor conciliorum generalium. *Parrhis.* 1523-4. 2 v. fº; *Colon.* 1530. 2 v. fº. [Bulls of Charles IV. and Pius II. added]; *Par.* 1535 (6?). 2 v. 8º. [" With corrections and omissions." *Graesse.* "No additions." *Hefele.*]

CRABBE, P. (PIERRE GRABLE?) (Franciscan.) Concilia omnia tam generalia quam particularia ab apost. tempore celebrata. *Colon.* 1538. 2 v. fº; 1551. 3 v. fº.

SURIUS, L. (Carthusian.) Concilia omnia tum generalia tum provincialia atque particularia, quae iam inde ab Apostolis usque in praesens habita, obtineri potuerunt, magna insignium synodor. *Cöln.* 1567. 4 v. fº. [" Somewhat more complete." *Hefele.*]

NICOLINI and BOLLANUS. (Dominican.) Concilia omnia, tam generalia, quam provincialia. *Vened.* 1585. 5 v. fº. [New impression of Surius.]

BINIUS, LEO. Concilia generalia et provincialia, graeca et latina, quotquot reperiri potuerunt, item epistolae decretales. *Cöln.* 1606. 4 v. fº; do. 1618, fº; *Paris,* 9 v. in 10. fº. [Improved.]

SIRMONDUS. (Jesuit.) Concilia generalia ecclesiae cathol. Pauli V. auctoritate ed. *Romae,* 1608–12, 1628. 4 (3) v. fº. [" Gives for first time the Greek text of many of the synodal acts."]

Concilior. omnium generalium et provincialium collectio regia. *Paris,* 1644. 37 v. fº. [" Printing magnificent." "Faults of Roman ed. . . . uncorrected." "One fourth less complete than . . . Labbe." *Hefele.*]

LABBEUS et COSSARTUS. (Jesuit.) Sacrosancta concilia ad reg. ed. exacta a — cum duobus apparatibus. *Paris,* 1671–72. fº; continued by Baluzius. *Par.* 1683. fº; with new title-page, 1707. fº. [1 vol. only appeared.]

HARDUINUS, Jo. (Jesuit.) Collectio regia max. conciliorum ab anno 34 ad a. 1714 ad P. Labbei et G. Cossartii labores accessionibus, emendationibus et indicibus locupl. *Paris,* 1715. 12 v. fº. [As offset to the Ultramontanism of

H. a volume of corrections was ordered printed with it— *Addition ordonnée par arrêt du parlement, pour etre joint à la collection des conciles. Paris,* 1722. fº, which was suppressed, but reprinted by the Jansenists under the title *Avis des censeurs, etc. Utrecht,* 1730. 4º; 1751. 4º.] "The favorite . . recommended on account of . . type, and . . . tables." *Hefele.*]

COLETUS, N. Sacrosancta concilia ad regiam editionum exacta. *Ven.* 1728-33. 23 v. fº. [" Reprint not wholly correct of Hardouin"]; continued by MANSI. *Lucae,* 1748-52. 6 v. fº. [Extends to 1727.]

MANSI, J. D. (Dominican.) Sacros. concil. nova et amplissima collectio. *Flor.* 1759–98. 31 v. fº. [Extends to 1509.]

(Lives of Saints and Martyrs.)

Acta Sanctorum quotquot tote orbe coluntur, vel à Catholicis scriptoribus celebrantur, quae ex Latinis et Graecis, aliarumque gentium antiquis monumentis, collegit, digessit, notis illustravit Joannes Bollandus, Societatis Jesu theologus, servata primigenia scriptorum phrasi. Operam et studium contulit Godefridus Henschenius, ejusdem Societatis theologus. *Antv.* 1643–1794. 54 v. f. ??? Reprinted *Venet.* 1734 sq. 42 v. fº. (Incorrect and stops at Sept. 15.) The work interrupted in 1794 was taken up in 1838 by the new Bollandists, who published enlarged editions of certain volumes, seven additional volumes 1845–1883 (?), and 1 vol. of Supplement, and the whole reprinted, edited by G. J. Camadet. *Paris* and *Rome,* 1863–1883. 61 v. and Supplem. fº.

LIPOMANNUS, ALO. Vitae sanctorum. *Rom.* 1551–60. 8 v. 4º.

MOMBRITIUS, BONINUS. Sanctuarium s. vitae sanctorum s. l. et a. 2 v. fº.

PETRUS DE NATALIBUS. Catalogus sanctorum et gestorum eorum ex diversis voluminibus collectus. *Vincentiae,* 1493. fº; *Venet.* 1506. fº; *Lugd.* 1543. fº. and often.

ROSWEYD. Vitae patrum. *Antv.* 1615; *Lugd.* 1617; *Antv.* 1628. fº.

— Vitae sanctorum. *Antv.* 1619. fº; 1629. 2 v. fº.

— Vitae sanctor. virginum. *Antv.* 1626; 1642. 8º.

SURIUS, LAM. Vitae sanctorum, ex probatis authoribus et mss. codicibus edit. *Colon.* 1569. 6 v. fº; 1581, 2 v. fº; *Venet.* 1581. 6 v. fº; and enlarged and improved. *Colon.* 1617. 4 v. fº.

VINCENTIUS BELVACENSIS. Speculum quadruplex, naturale, doctrinale, morale, et historiale. [*Argent.*] 1473-6. 7 v. fº. [" Edition originale et la seule complete." *Graesse;* but various editions more or less complete, e.g. *Duaci.* 1624. 4 v. fº.]

VORAGINE, JACOBUS DE. Legenda aurea, vulgo Historia lombardica dicta, ad oppt. libr. fidem recensuit Dr. Th. Graesse. *Dresdae* et *Lips.* 1846. 8º. [This is the most convenient edition, and the French of Gust. Brunet (*Paris,* 1843. 2 v. 12º.) the best translation. Written originally as Historia longobardica it was published variously under this title, or as "Legendae sanctorum," "De vitis sanctorum," or, on account of its great popularity, generally, "Legenda aurea." A list gathered (probably not exhaustive) of editions of text and translations numbers more than one hundred.]

———

RUINART, TH. Acta primorum martyrum sincera et selecta. *Par.* 1689. 4º; *Amst.* 1713. fº; repr. with additions. *Veronae,* 1731. fº; *Aug. V.* 1802–3. 3 v. 8º; tr. French by Drouet de Maupertuy. *Par.* 1708. 8º; 1739. 2 v. 12º; tr. Italian by Luchini. *Roma,* 1774. 4 v. 4º; tr. German by F. W. Fraaz. *Klagenfurt,* 1785. 2 v. 8º.

IV. *Church Histories.*

DOWLING, JOHN GOULTER. An introduction to the critical study of ecclesiastical history, attempted in an account of the progress, and a short notice of the sources, of the history of the Church. *London,* 1838. 8º.

HAAR, B. TER. Die Historiographie der Kerkgeschied-enis. *Utrecht*, 1870–71. 8°.

ALEXANDER, NATALIS. Selecta hist. eccl. capita et diss. hist., chron. et dogm. *Par.*, 1676–89. 24 v. (26?) 8°; 1699. 8 v. in 7. f°; ed. C. Roncaglia. *Lucca*, 1734. 9 v. in 8. f°; ed. Mansi. *Lucca*, 1749. 9 v. f°; *Ferrara*, 1758-62. 9 v. f°; *Bassano*, 1778. 12 v. f°; *Bingen*, 1785–90 ('86–91?) 20 v. 4°.

BAPHEIDES, PHILAR. Εκκλησιαστικη ιστορια, απο του κυριου ημων Ιησου Χριστου μεχρι των καθ' ημας χρονων, υπο Φιλαρετου Βαφειδου. I. (1–700.) Εν Κωνσταντινουπολει, 1884. 8°. [Good little compend., but brief and mainly from secondary sources. Value of its insertion doubtful.]

BARONIUS, CAES. Annales ecclesiastici a Chr. nato ad an. 1198. *Rom.* 1588–1607. 12 v. f°; continued (v. 13-20) by Bzovius (ab an. 1198– usque ad an. 1565); *Rom.*, 1616–. f°; *Colon.* 1621–30. f°; also by Spondanus (1197–1646); *Paris*, 1640–1. 2 v. f°; 1647. 2 v. f°; *Lyon*, 1678. 3 v. f°; by Raynaldus (1198–1565, vols. 13–21); *Rom.* 1646–77. f°; *Colon.* 1693–1727. f°; by Laderchius (1566–1571, vols. 22–24); *Rom.* 1728-37. f°; by Theiner (–1584); *Paris*, 1856. 3 v. f°. Among various editions of Baronius compare ed. Mansi. *Lucca*, 1738–57. 38 v. f°, and ed., with continuations of Raynaldus and Laderchius, by Aug. Theiner, *Bar-le-Duc (Paris)*, 1864–. 4°. [" To form 45 to 50 volumes," vol. 36 (1568–9), 1882.]

BASNAGE, JAC. Hist. de l'église depuis J. Chr. jusq' à present, divisée en 4 parties. *Rotterd.* 1699. 2 v. f°, etc.

— Annales politico-ecclesiast. ann. 645 a Caesare Auguste ad Phocam usque. *Rotterdam*, 1706. 3 v. f°.

BAUR, F. C. Kirchengeschichte der drei ersten Jahrhunderte. *Tübingen*, 1853. 8°; 3 Aufl. 1863. 8°; tr. English by Allan Menzies. *London*, 1878. 8°.

BLACKBURN, W. M. History of the Christian Church, from its origin to the present time. *Cincinnati*, Hitchcock & Walden, 1879. 8°. (719 p.) *N. Y.*, Phillips and H. 1880. 8°. [Not full or critical on Ante-Nicene period. Better on Hist. of American Church.]

BÖHRINGER, F. Die Kirche Christi und ihre Zeuger, oder die Kirchengesch. in Biographien. *Zurich*, 1842-58. 12 v. 8°; 2 Auf. *Stuttg.* 1861–; 3 Ausg. 1873–.

COTTA, J. F. Vers. eine. ausfuhrl. Kirchenhist. des N. T. *Tübingen*, 1768–73. 3 v. 8°. [" Unvoll., noch nicht bis auf Constant."]

DANZ, J. T. L. Lehrbuch der christl. Kirchengesch. zum gebrauch akad. Vorlesungen. *Jena*, 1818–26. 2 v. 8°.

FLACIUS ILLYRICUS, MATT. Ecclesiastica historia, integram ecelesiae Christi ideam . . . . . secundum singulas centurias perspicuo ordine complectens. *Basil.* 1559-74. 8 v. f°; repr. deterioriated ed. Lucius. *Basil.* 1624. 3 v. f°. [The " Centuriae Magdeburgenses." The collaborators were J. Wigandus, Matt Judex, and Basil Faber.]

FLEURY, CLAUDE. Histoire ecclésiastique. *Paris*, 1691-1720. 20 v. 4°; and often. [Extends to year 1414.]

GFRÖRER, A. F. Allgem. Kirchengesch. *Stuttg.* 1841-46. 4 v. [To 1056.]

GIESELER, J. K. L. Lehrbuch der Kirchengesch. *Bonn*, 1824-53. 8°. 3 v. I., 4 Aufl., 1844–. II., 4 Aufl., 1847–. III., 2 Aufl., 1849–; also, posthumous, ed. Redepenning, IV. Kirchengesch. des 18 Jahrh. von 1648–1814. *Bonn*, 1857. V. Kircheng. der neuesten Zeit. *Bonn*, 1855; tr. English by Davidson and Hull, revised by H. B. Smith. *N. Y.* 1868–79. 5 v. 8°.

GUERICKE, H. E. F. Handbuch der Kirchengesch. *Halle*, 1833. 2 v. 9 Aufl. *Lpz.* 1866–. 3 v. 8°; tr. English by W. G. T. Shedd. *Andover*, 1857–70. 2 v. 8°.

HAGENBACH, K. R. Kirchengeschichte von der ältesten Zeit bis zum 19 Jahrhundert. Neue (4), durchgänzig

überarbeitete Gesamtausgabe. *Leipzig*, 1885. 8°. [pp. 660–712 a good literary-historical (Litterarisch-kritischer Anhang) survey.]

HASE, K. Lehrbuch der Kirchengesch. *Lpz.* 1834. 8°. 10 Aufl. 1877. 8°; tr. English by C. E. Blumenthal and C. P. King. *New York*, 1855. 8°.

— Kirchengeschichte auf der Grundlage akademischer Vorlesungen. *Leipzig*, 1885. 8°.

HENKE, H. P. C. Allgem. gesch. des christlichen Kirche. *Braunschw*, 1788–1823. 9 v. 8°.

HEPP, F. Gesch. der christl. Kirche in Lebensbeschreib. *Mainz*, 1850–. 2 v.

HERGENRÖTHER, F. Handbuch de allg. Kirchengesch. *Freiburg*, 1876–78. 2 v. 8°; 2 Aufl. 1879–80. 3 v. 8°. 3 verb. Aufl. 1884–. 8°. [V. 3 (634 close pages of 2 Aufl.) is entirely taken up with a condensed synopsis of authorities and literature, forming a useful handbook of reference. As handbook of Patrology of less value than Kurtz, Schaff, and others.]

ITTIG, TH. Historiae ecclesiast. 1 (et 2) a Chr. n. saeculi selecta capita. *Lpz.* 1709–11. 4°.

JEREMIE, JAMES AMIRAUX. History of the Christian Church in the second and third centuries. *London*, 1852. 12°. [First published in the Encyclopaedia Metropolitana. Very accessible patrological method. Select rather than exhaustive.]

JORTIN, J. Remarks on ecclesiastical history. *London*, 1751–73. 5 v. 8°; tr. German by J. P. Cassell. *Bremen*, 1755–6. 3 v. 8°.

KILLEN, W. D. The ancient Church: its history, doctrine, worship, and constitution, traced for the first three hundred years. *New York*, 1859. 8°.

KURTZ, J. H. Lehrbuch der Kirchengeschichte für Studierende. *Leipzig*, 1st ed., 1849; 2d, 1850; 3d, 1857; 4th, 1860; 5th, 1863; 6th, 1868; 7th, 1874; 8th, 1880–81; 9th, 1885. 8°; tr. English by Edersheim. *Edinb.* 1860. 8°; tr. C. F. Schaeffer. *Philadelphia*, 1868. 8°; 14 ed. 1875. 8°. [Patrological method of this capital handbook is like the rest, sensible though brief.]

LECHLER, G. V. Das apostolische und das nachapostolische Zeitalter, mit Rücksicht auf unterscheid und Einheit in Lehre und Leben. *Stuttgart*, 1851. 8°; 2. Aufl. 1857. 8°; 3 Aufl. (thoroughly rewritten) 1885. 8°; tr. English by A. J. K. Davidson. *Edinb.* and *New York*, 1886. 2 v. 8°.

MATTER, M. J. Histoire universelle de l'église chrétienne. *Strasb.* 1829-35. 4 v. 8°; ed. 2. *Paris*, 1838. 4 v.; *Strasb.* 1843. 4 v. 8°.

MAURICE, F. D. Lectures on the Ecclesiastical History of the first and second centuries. *Cambridge*, 1854. 8°.

MILMAN, HENRY H. History of Latin Christianity; including that of the Popes to the Pontificate of Nicholas V. *Lond.* and *New York*. 2d ed. 1860. 8 v. 8°; *New York*, 1881. 8 v. 12°.

— The History of Christianity from the birth of Christ to the abolition of Paganism in the Roman Empire. *Lond.* 1840. 3 v. 1866; *New York*, 1881. 3 v. 12°.

MOSHEIM, J. LR. V. De rebus christianorum ante Constantinum M. commentarii. *Helmst.* 1753. 4°; tr. English. *New York*, 1851. 2 v. 8°.

MOSHEIM, L. Institutionum historiae ecclesiasticae libri IV. *Helmst.* 1755; ed. 2. 1764. 4°; tr. English by Maclaine. *Lond.* 1765–1806. 6 v. 8°; do. tr. by Murdock and Soames (often), and ed. W. Stubbs. *Lond.* 1863. 3 v. 8°.

NAEBE, F. A. A. Compend historiae eccles. ac sacrorum christianorum in usum studiosae juventutis compositum. *Lips.* 1832.

NEANDER, A. Allgem. geschichte der christl. Religion und Kirche. *Hamb.* 1825-52. 6 v. 8°; v. 6, posthumous ed. R. F. T. Schneider (bis 1431) 4 Aufl. 9 Bde. *Gotha*, 1864-65. 9 v. 8°; Neue Ausg. ed. Nippold. *Leipz.* 1885–. 8°; tr. English. tr. Torry. *Edinb.* 1851–

55. 9 v. 8°; *London, Bohn.* 10 v. 12°; *Boston,* 1859. 5 v. 8°; and 1872. 6 v. 8°. [With Index vol.]

NIEDNER, C. W. Lehrbuch der christlichen Kirchengeschichte von der ältesten Zeit bis auf die Gegenwart. Neueste von dem Verfasser kurz vor seinem Tode ausgearbeitete Auflage. (*Berlin,* 1846); 2 Aufl. 1866. 8°.

ORSI, GIUSEPPE AGOSTINO. Storia ecclesiastica. *Roma,* 1748–62. 21 v. 4°; 1754–62. 21 v. 4°; with continuation by Becchetti to A.D. 1377. *Roma,* 1749–88. 38 v. 8° (16°).

PERTSCH, J. G. Versuch einer Kirchenhistorie. *Wolfenbüttel,* 1736–40. 5 v. 4°.

PRESSENSÉ, E. D. DE. Histoire des trois premiers siécles de l'Eglise chrétienne. 1858–77. 4 v.; tr. English by Annie Harwood. *N.Y.* 1873–8, etc. 4 v. 12°.

RENAN, ERNEST. L'histoire des origines du Christianisme. *Paris,* 1863–82. 7 v.

RITSCHL, ALBRECHT. Die Entstehung der altkatholischen Kirche. Eine Kirchen- und dogmengeschichtliche Monographie. *Bonn,* 1850. 8°; 2 Aufl. 1857. 8°. [" 2d ed. partly reconstructed."]

ROBERTSON, J. C. History of the Christian Church from the apostolic age to the reformation. (A.D. 64–1517.) *London,* 1858–73. 4 v. 8°; new ed. 1875. 8 v. 8°.

ROHRBACHER. Histoire universelle de l'église catholique. *Par.* 1842–. 29 v.; nouv. ed. par Fêvre. *Par.* 1875–; tr. German by Rump, Toppehorn u. Neteler. *Münster,* 1858–.

ROTHE, R. Die Anfänge der Christlichen Kirche und ihrer Verfassung. *Wittenberg,* 1837. 8°.
— Vorlesungen ueber Kirchengeschichte und Geschichte des christlich-kirchlichen Lebens. Hrsg. v. H. Weingarten. *Heidelb.* 1875. 2 v. 8°.

SCHAFF, PHILIP. History of the Christian Church. *New York,* 1858–. A.D. 1–600. 3 v. (German ed. *Leipzig,* 1867; 2d ed. 1869. 3 v.) entirely rewritten in English. *New York* and *Edinburgh,* 1882–84. 3 v. Vol. IV. A.D. 590–1073. *New York* and *Edinburgh,* 1885; 3d revision. 1886–. [At the end of each volume is a brief patrology of the period with well selected and arranged bibliography, forming by far the best handbook in English.]

SCHMIDT, J. E. C. Handbuch der christl. Kirchengesch. *Giessen,* 1801–20. 6 v.; 2. Aufl. (of vols. 1–4) 1824–27; continued by F. W. Rettberg. Bd. 7. (to Boniface VIII.). *Giessen,* 1834.

SCHRÖCKH, JOH. MATT. Christliche Kirchengeschichte. *Leipzig,* 1768–1802. 35 v. 8°; Kirchenges. seit. d. Reformation. 1804–11. 10 v. 8°.

SCHWEGLER, A. Das nachapostoliche Zeitalter in den Hauptmomenten seiner Entwicklung. *Tübingen,* 1846. 2 v. 8°.

STARKE, J. A. Geschichte d. christl. kirche d. in Jahrh. *Berlin,* 1779–80. 6 v. 8°.

STOLBERG, F. L. v. Gesch. der Rel. Jesu Christi. *Hamb.* 1806–18. 15 Bde. (to 430) fortges. von F. V. Kerz, 16–45 v. (to 12 century). *Mainz,* 1824–48. Neue Folge von J. N. Brischar. 46–53 v. (to 13 Jahrh.). *Mainz,* 1851–.

THIERSCH, H. W. J. Die Kirche im apostolischen Zeitalter. *Frankfurt-am-Main,* 1852. 8°; 3. ed. 1879. 8°; tr. English by Carlyle. *Lond.* 1852.

WAITE, C. B. History of the Christian Religion to the year two hundred. Third edition, revised. *Chicago,* 1881. 8°. [Introduced into the *Synopsis* on account of extensive, though crude and mal-critical, treatment of Apocryphal literature. The author's modest belief " that this will be found to be the most complete record of the events connected with the Christian religion during the first two centuries " is hardly justified.]

WEIZÄCKER, CARL. Das apostolische Zeitalter der christlichen kirche. *Freiburg,* 1886. 8°.

WORDSWORTH, CHR. A church history to the council of Nicaea. *New York,* 1881. 8°.

V.   Miscellaneous.

[BARBOUR, J. H.] The beginnings of the Historic Episcopate exhibited in the words of Holy Scripture and ancient authors. *N.Y.* 1887. 12°. [A popular chronological exhibition of the argument.]

BAUMGARTEN–CRUSIUS, L. F. O. Lehrbuch der christlichen Dogmengeschichte. *Jena,* 1832. 2 v. 8°.

BAUR, F. C. Vorlesungen über de Christliche Dogmengeschichte. *Leipzig,* 1865–67. 3 v. 8°.

BEAUSOBRE, ISAAC DE. Histoire critique de Manichée et du Manichéisme. *Amst.* 1734–39. 2 v. 4°.

BERTHOLDT, L. Handbuch der Dogmengeschichte. *Erlangen,* 1822. 8°.

BURTON, EDWARD. Testimony of the Ante-Nicene fathers as to the divinity of Christ. *Oxford,* 1829. 8°.
— Testimonies of the Ante-Nicene fathers to the doctrine of the trinity and of the divinity of the Holy Ghost. *Oxford,* 1831. 8°.

CHARTERIS, A. H. Canonicity, a collection of early testimonies to the canonical books of the New Testament, based on Kirchofer's ' Quellensammlung.' *Edinburgh* and *London,* 1880. 8°.

COLEMAN, L. Ancient Christianity, exemplified in the private, domestic, social, and civil life of the primitive Christians and the original institutions, officers, ordinances and rites of the church. *Philadelphia,* 1852. 8°; new ed. 1853. 8°.

CREDNER, C. A. Geschichte des neutestamentlichen Kanon. Ed. Volkmar. *Berlin,* 1860. 8°.

CUNNINGHAM, WM. Historical Theology. 2 v. 1st ed. *Edinburgh,* 1862. 8°; 2d ed. 1864. 8°; 3d ed. 1870. 8°.
— The Churches of Asia: A methodical sketch of the second century. *London,* 1880. 8°.

DONALDSON, JAMES. The apostolical fathers: a critical account of their genuine writings and of their doctrines. *London,* 1874. 8°. [Substantially reprint from his History of Christian Literature.]

EICHHORN, J. G. Einleitung in das A. T. *Leipzig,* 1780–83. 3 v.; 4 Aufl. 1823–4. 5 v.

ENGELHARDT, J. G. B. Dogmengeschichte. 2 v. *Neustadt a. d. Aisch.* 1839. 8°.

EWALD, H. Gesch. des Volkes Israel. *Gott.* 1843–52. 3 v.; 3. Ausgabe, 1864–68. 7 v. 8°.

FARRAR, F. W. History of interpretation. Eight lectures preached before the University of Oxford in the year 1885. *New York,* 1886. 8°.
— The early days of Christianity. *London,* 1882. 8°.

GILSE, J. VAN. Comment. de patrum apostolicorum doctrina morali. *Lugduni Batav.* 1833.

HARNACK, ADOLF. Lehrbuch der Dogmengeschichte. I. Die Entstehung des Kirchlichen Dogmas. *Freiburg i. B.* 1886. 8°.

HAUSRATH, A. Neutestamentliche Zeitgeschichte. 1868–73. 4 parts; 2d ed. 1873–77; 3d ed. 1st part. Die Zeit Jesu, 1879.

HEFELE, C. J. Conciliengeschichte. (bis 16 Jahrh.). *Freiburg,* 1855–74. 7 v. 8°; 2 Aufl. 1873–. Tr. English to year 325 by Clark and Oxenham. *Edinburgh,* 1871–6. 2 v. 8°.

HEYNS, S. P. Comment. praemio ornata de patrum apostolicor. doctrina morali. *Lugd. Bat.* 1833.

HILGENFELD, A. Die apostolischen Väter, Untersuchungen über Inhalt und Ursprung der unter ihrem Namen erhaltenen Schriften. *Halle,* 1853. 8°.
— Der Kanon und die Kritik des Neuen Testaments in ihrer geschichtlichen Ausbildung und Gestaltung, nebst Herstellung und Beleuchtung des Muratorischen Bruchstücks. *Halle,* 1863. 8°.
— Die Ketzergeschichte des Urchristenthums. *Leipzig,* 1884. 8°.

HOLTZMANN, H. J. Lehrbuch der Historisch-Kritischen Einleitung in das Neue Testament. *Freiburg i. B.* 1886. 8°.

JAFFÉ, PHIL. Regesta pontificorum romanor. a cond. ecclesia usque ad ann. 1198; ed. alt. cur. F. Kaltenbrunner, T. Ewald, S. Loewenfeld. *Lipsiae*, 1881-4. [1 ed. *Berol.* 1851. 4⁰.]

JUNIUS, F. Comment. praemio ornata de patrum apostolicor. doctrina morali. *Lugduni Batav.* 1833.

KEIM, THDR. Celsus' wahres wort. Aelteste Streitschrift antiker Weltanschauung gegen das Christenthum vom J. 178 n. Chr. wiedergestellt, aus dem Greich. übersetzt, untersucht und erläut.., mit Lucian und Minucius Felix verglichen. *Zurich*, 1873. 8⁰.
— Aus dem Urchristenthum. Geschichtliche Untersuchungen in zwangloser Folge. *Zurich*, 1878. 8⁰.
— Rom und das Christenthum. Ed. H. Ziegler. *Berlin*, 1881.

KESTNER, A. Die Agape, oder der geheime Weltbund der Christen, von Clemens in Rom unter Domitians Regierung gestiftet. *Jena*, 1819. 8⁰.

KRAUS, F. X. Roma sotteranea. *Freiburg*, 1873. 2d ed. 1879.

LAURENT, J. C. M. Clementis Romani ad Corinthios Epistula. Insunt et altera quam ferunt Clementis epistula et fragmenta. *Lipsiae*, 1870. 8⁰.

LIPSIUS, R. A. Chronologie der römischen Bischofe bis zur mitte des 4 Jahrh. *Kiel*, 1869. 8⁰.

LÜCKE, F. Commentar über das Evangelium des Johannes. *Bonn*. v. I. 1840. 8⁰.; v. II. 1843. 8⁰.

LUTHARDT, C. E. Der johannische Ursprung des vierten Evangeliums untersucht. *Ebendas.* 1874; tr. English by C. R. Gregory. *Edinb.* 1875. 8⁰.

MAYERHOFF, E. T. Historisch-critische Einleitung in die petreinischen Schriften. *Hamburg*, 1835. 8⁰.

MICHAELIS, JOH. DAV. Einleitung in die gottlichen Schrifter d. Alten Bundes. *Hamburg*, 1787. 4⁰.

MÖHLER, J. A. Gesammelte Schriften u. Aufsätze. *Regensburg*, 1839. 8⁰.

MÜNSCHER, WM. Handbuch der christlichen Dogmengeschichte. *Marburg*, 1817–18. 3 v. 8⁰.

NITZSCH, FRIED. Grundriss der christlichen Dogmengeschichte. *Berlin*, 1870. 8⁰.

OVERBECK, F. Studien zur geschichte der alten Kirche. *Schloss-Chemnitz*, 1875. 8⁰.

REUSS, E. (W. E.) Geschichte der heiligen Schriften, Neuen Testaments. *Halle*, 1842. 5th ed. *Braunschweig*, 1874. Eng. trans. by Edward L. Houghton, *Boston*, 1884. 2 v.
— Histoire de la théologie chrétienne, au siècle apostolique *Paris* et *Genève*. 2 v. 1852. 8⁰. 3d ed. 1864. 8⁰.

ROSENMÜLLER, J. G. Historia interpretationes librorum sacrorum in ecclesia. christiana. 3 v. I. and II. Ab apostolorum aetate usque ad Origenem. *Heidburghusae*, 1795. 16⁰. III. Ab Origene ad Io. Chrysostomum et Cypriano ad Agustinum. *Lipsiae*, 1807. 16⁰.

SANDAY, W. The Gospels in the second century. *London*, 1876. 8⁰.

SCHILLER, HERM. Geschichte des römischen Kaiserreichs unter der Regierung des Nero. *Berlin*, 1872. 8⁰.

SCHOLTEN, J. H. Het Evangelie naar Johannes. Kritisch historisch onderzoek. *Leiden*, 1864. 8⁰.
— Die ältesten Zeugnisse betr. die Schriften des Neuen Testaments. Historisch untersucht. Mit Bewilling des Verf. aus dem Holländ übers von Carl Manchot. *Bremen*, 1867. 8⁰.

SCHOLZ, F. M. A. Einleitung in die heiligen Schriften. *Köln*, 1845. 8⁰.

SCHUERER, ÉMIL. Lehrbuch der neutestamentlichen Zeitgeschichte. *Leipzig*, 1873. 8⁰.

SIMON, R. Histoire critique du Vieux Testament. *Paris*, 1678. 4⁰ [Confiscated]; *Rotterdam*, 1685. 4⁰. ["Best ed."]

SIXTUS SENENSIS. Bibliotheca sancta . . . ex prae cipuis catholicae ecclesiae auctoribus collecta. *Venet.* 1566· f⁰; *Colon.* 1626. 4⁰; *Neap.* 1742.

SKWORZOW, CONST. Patrologische Untersuchungen. Ueber Ursprung der problemat. Schriften der apostol. Väter. *Leipzig*, 1875. 8⁰.

STOWE, C. E. Origin and history of the books of the Bible, both canonical and apocyrphal. *Hartford*, 1867. 8⁰. [Popular. Uncritical.]

TISCHENDORF, CONST. Wann wurden unsere Evv. verfaszt? *Lpz.* 1865; 4 Aufl. 1866.

TZSCHIRNER, H. G. Der Fall Heidenthum. *Leipzig*, 1829. 8⁰.

UHLHORN, GERH. Der Kampf des Christenthums mit dem Heidenthum. 3 Aufl. *Stuttg.* 1879; tr. Engl. by E. C. Smyth and C. J. H. Ropes. *N.Y.* 1879. 8⁰.

VOLKMAR, G. Das Evangelium Marcions. *Leipzig*, 1852.
— Die Religion Jesu und ihre Entwickelung. *Leipzig*, 1857.
— Der Ursprung unserer Evangelien nach den Urkunden, laut den neuern Entdeckungen und Verhandlungen. *Zurich*, 1866. 8⁰.

WEIZSÄCKER, KARL. Untersuchungen üeber die evangelische Geschichte. *Gotha*, 1864.

WERNER, CARL. Geschichte der apologetischen und polemischen Literatur der Christlichen Theologie. *Schaffhausen*, 1861. 8⁰.

WESTCOTT, B. F. A general survey of the history of the canon of the New Testament. 4th ed. *London*, 1875. 8⁰; 5th ed. 1881. 8⁰.
— The Bible in the church: a popular account of the collection and reception of the Holy Scriptures in the Christian churches. *London*, 1877.

WIESELER, KARL. Die Christenverfolgungen der Cäsaren bis zum 3. Jahrh. historisch und chronologisch untersucht. *Gutersloh*, 1878. 8⁰.

YONGE, CHARLOTTE M. The pupils of St. John the divine. *London*, 1868. 8⁰; new ed. 1878. 8⁰. [Popular.]

ZELLER, EDUARD. Die Apostelgeschichte nach ihrem Inhalt und Ursprung Kritisch untersucht. *Stuttgart*, 1854. 8⁰.

III. PERIODICALS.

In the following list the method has been followed of giving only what there seemed to be actual authority for, even when a conjecture seemed perfectly safe. Bracketed dates indicate that only these data are at hand. Where a periodical was still in progress at date of latest information, it is indicated by a short following dash. The abbreviations in parenthesis following some are those of Poole's Index to Periodical Literature. *Boston*, 1882.

Abhandlungen für d. Kunde des Morgenlandes, hrsg. v. d. Deutschen Morgenländ. Gesellschaft (at present E. Windisch). *Leipzig*, 1859 (?) –1886. 9 v. 8⁰.

Abhandlungen d. königl. Gessellschaft d. Wissenschaften zu Göttingen. *Gottingen*, — 1885. 32 v. 8⁰.

Abhandlungen d. königl. sächsischen Gesellschaft d. Wissenschaften. *Leipzig*, — 1884. 21 v. 8⁰. (v. 21 = Philol. hist. Classe. v. 9.)

Academy (The). *London*, 1869–1886-. 30 v. 4⁰.

Acta eruditorum. *Lipsiae*, 1682–1731. 50 v.; Nova Acta erud. 1732–76. 43 v. [1764-7 = 2 v.]; Actorum erud. Suppl. 1692–1724. 10 v.; Ad nov. Act. erud. Suppl. 1735–57. 8 v.; Indices. 1692–1745. 6 v. 4⁰.

Allgemeine evang. luther. Kirchenzeitung. (Luthardt.) *Leipzig*, 1868–87. 4⁰.

Allgemeine Literatur-Zeitung. *Halle.* 1804–1849. 4⁰. [Continuation of the " Jenaische."]

Allgemeine Monatschrift für Wissenschaft u. Literatur. [Halle] Braunschweig, 1851–4. 4⁰.

Allgem. Repertorium für die theolog. Literatur und kirchl. Statistik. 28 Jahrgg. *Berlin*, 1833–60 (5?) 111 v. and Index. 8⁰. [Jahrg. 1-12, 47 v. hrsg. G. F. H. Reinwald; 12-28 hrsg. H. Reuter.]

Allgemeine Zeitung. *Augsburg.* [1847–62. 17 v. 4º.]
Allgemeine Zeitg. *München.* [1884.]
American Bible Repository. (Am. Bib. Repos.) *New York*, 1831–50. 30 v. 8º.
American Catholic Quarterly. (Am. Cath. Q.) *Philadelphia*, 1876–87. 12 v. 8º.
American Church Review. (Am. Church R.) (*New Haven* and) *New York*, and *Boston*, 1849–87. 50 v. 8º. [Now " Church Review."]
American Presbyterian Review. (Am. Presb. R.) *New York*, 1853–71. 20 v. 8º.
Analecta Juris Pontificii. (*Rome, Paris, Brux.*) *Genève*, — 1886. 26 sèrie. sm. fº.
Andover Review (The). *Boston*, 1884–7. 7 v. 8º.
Annales de Philosophie chrétienne. *Paris*, 1830–1887. 57 An. 8º.
Annales du Monde Relig. [1878.] II.
Annali delle scienze religiose. *Roma*, 1835. [Still in progress in 1859.]
Annali delle università Toscane. *Pisa*, 1846–. [Parte I. Scienz, novl. XII. (*Pisa*, 1872.).]
Archaeologia. (Arch.) *London*, 1770–1879–. 45 v.
Archaeologische Zeitung. Hrsg. v. Archäol. Institut d. Deutschen Reichs (Fränkel). *Berlin*, 1843–1884–. 42 Jg. 4º.
Arch. d. Missions. [1866. B.] [=Archives des missions scientifique et litteraires. *Paris*, 1850–. 8º. ?)
Archiv für das Studium der neueren Sprachen u. Literaturen. (L. Herrig.) *Braunschweig*, — 1886. 78 v. 8º.
Archif f. kath. Kirchenrecht. *Innsbr.* (now *Mainz*) 1857–86–. 56 v. (N. F. 50 v.)
Archiv fur theol. Literatur. *Regensburg*, 1842–3. 2. Jg. 8º.
Archiv für Philologie u. Pädagogik. *Lpz.* 18 . — 53. 18 v. 8º. [Suppl. to Neue Jahrbücher für Philolgie u. Pädagogik.]
Archiv für Slavische Philologie. *Berlin*, — 1886–. 9 v. 8º.
Archiv für alte und neue Kirchengeschichte; (K. F. Stäudlin u. H. G. Tzschirner.) *Lpz.* 1813–22. 5 v.
'Αθήναιον. [1872–1876–. 5 v.]
Augsb. allg. Ztng. (1857.) See Allgemeine Zeitung.
Augusti's Neue theol. Bibl. I. See Theol. Blätter, etc.
Axil, L', cathol. [II. (1845-6.)]
Baptist Quarterly Review (The). *New York*, –1887. 9 v. 8º.
Beiträge zu den theologischen Wissenschaften in Verbindung mit der theolog. Gesellschaft zu Strassburg hrsg. Ed. Reuss u. Ed. Cunitz. *Jena*, 1847–55. 6 v. 8º.
Bejblad van de Heroorming. [1884.]
Berichte über die Verhandl. d. königl. Sächs. Gesellsch. d. Wissenschaften. (Phil. Hist. Class.) *Leipzig*, 1849–1886–. 38 v. 8º.
Beweis des Glaubens, Der. Monatsschr. zur Begründ. u. Vertheid. der christl. Wahrh. für Gebildete, hrsg. von O. Andreä u. C. Brachmann. *Gütersl.* 1865–87. 22 v. (N.F. 7 v.) 8º.
Biblical Review. (Bib. R.) *London*, 1846–50. 6 v.
Bibliographie Catholique. *Paris*, 1841–. 8º. [To 1865. 33 v.]
Bibliotheca hist.-philolog. theol. Bremensis Cl. *Bremae*, 1719–. 8º; Nova bibl. Bremensis VI. Classes. *Bremae*, 1760–66. 8º.
Bibliotheca Sacra. (Bib. Sac.) (*Andover* and) *Oberlin*, 1844–87. 44 v. 8º.
Blätter für das bayerische Gymnasialschulwesen. *München*, 1865–86–. 22 v. 8º.
Bremisch. und Verdische Bibl. *Hamburg.* [1753.]
British and Foreign Evangelical Review, The. *London*, –1887. 36 v. 8º.
British and Foreign Review. (Brit. & For. R.) *London*, 1835–44. 18 v.
British Quarterly Review. (Brit. Q.) *London*, 1844–86. 83 v. 8º.

Brownson's Quarterly Review. (Brownson.) *Boston* and *New York*, 1844–75. 24 v.
Bulletin de l'acad. impér. des scienœs de St. Petersbourg. *St. Petersb.*, Avril, 1886. v. 31.
Bulletin critique. –1887.
Bulletin de Correspondence Hellenique. 1877–. v. 1–.
Bulletin Theologique. [1869.] 8º.
Bulletino di archaeologia cristiana del de Rossi. *Roma*, –87. 8º. [1884= an. 2 ser. 4.]
Catholic World. (Cath. World.) *New York*, 1865–86. 44 v.
Century, The. (Cent.) *New York*, 1870–1887. 1–34 v. 8º. [Vols. 1–22 under name Scribner's Magazine.]
Christian Examiner. (Chr. Ex.) *Boston*, 1824–69. 87 v. 8º.
Christian Observer. (Chr. Obs.) *London*, 1802–77. 77 v.
Christian Remembrancer. (Chr. Rem.) *London* (1819?), 1841–68. 56 v.
Christian Review. (Chr. R.) *Boston*, 1836–63. 28 v. 8º.
Christijanskoje Tchtenije. *Petrop.* [1825, 1842.]
Churchman, The. *New York*, –1887. 44 years. sm. fº.
Church Quarterly Review. (Church Q.) *London*, –1886. 22 v. 8º.
Civita Cattolica. *Napoli*, 1850–87. 8º. [12 v. to a series, and Indexes.]
Congregational Magazine. (Cong. M.) *London*, 1818–45. 28 v.
Contemporary Review. (Contemp.) *London*, 1866–87. 52 v. 8º.
Correspondent, Le. 1 sér. *Paris*, 1843–55. 36 v. 8º; 2 sér. 1856–1864. 1–18. 8º; — 1886–.
Dansk Kirketidende. [1884.]
Δελτίον τῆς ἱστορικῆς και ἐθν. ἑταιρ. τῆς Ἑλλάδος. *Athens.* [1883.]
Deutsche Kirchenfreund, Der. Organ für d. gemeinsamen Interessen dea amerikanisch-deutschen Kirche. Hrsg. Ph. Schaff. *Mercersburg* (*Philadelphia*), 1848–53. 6 v. 8º.
Deutsche Literaturzeitung. (*Roediger*) *Berlin*, 1880–86. 7 v. 4º.
Dublin Review. (Dub. R.) *London* and *Dublin*, 1836–86–. 99 v. (N. S. 16.) 8º.
Dublin University Magazine. (Dub. Univ.) *Dublin* and *London*, 1833–80. 96 v. [78– under title University Magazine.]
Durham University Journal. [1884.]
Ecclesiastical and Theological Review. [1853.]
Eclectic Magazine. (Ecl. M.) *New York*, 1844–86. 107 v.
Eclectic Review. (Ecl. R.) *London*, 1805–67. 125 v.
Edinburgh Review. (Ed. R.) *Edinb.* 1802–86–. 164 v. 8º.
Eichhorn's Repertorium für Bibl. u. Morgenländ. See Repertorium, etc.
'Εκκλησιαστική 'Αλήθεια. [1884–5.]
English Review. [1845.]
Evangelische Kirchenzeitung, Begründet von E. W. Hengstenberg. (Now by Zöckler.) *Berlin*, 1827–1886–. 119 v. 4º.
Evangelical Review. (Evang. R.) *Gettysburg, Pa.*, 1850–70. 21 v.
Evangelisches Gemeindeblett f. Rhinland u. Vestfalen. —1885–.
Expositor (The). *London*, 1875–1887. 3 s. v. 8º.
Flatt's Magazin f. Christl. Moral, etc. See Magazin, etc.
Foreign Church Chronicle and Review. 1884–.
Fraser's Magazine. (Fraser.) *London*, 1830–81. 104 v. 8º.
Frazer. See Fraser.
Freiburger Ztschr. See Ztschr. f. d. Geistl. d. Erzb. Frieb. (?)
Geloof en Vrijheid. [1885.]
Gentleman's Magazine. *London* [1731–1858–. 205 v. 8º; N. S. *London*, 1868–81–. 27 v. 8º.]

Gersdorf's Repertorium.   See Leipziger Repertorium, etc.

Good Words. *London*, 1860–86. 27 v.

Göttingesche gelehrte Anzeigen, unter der Aufsicht d. königl. Gesellschaft d. Wissenschaften. *Gött.* 1886–. 8⁰.

Guardian. *London*, — 1886–.

Gymnasialschulw. See Blätter f. d. bayerische, etc.

Haller Litt. Zeitung. See Allgemeine Literatur-zeitung.

Hallische Allgem. Lit. Ztng. (1849.) See Allgem., etc.

" Halte was du hast." See Ztschr. f. Pastoral-Theol.

Hamburgische Vermischte Bibliothek. *Hamb.* 1743-5. 3 v. 8⁰.

Harper's Weekly. A Journal of Civilization. *New York*, — 1887. 31 v. sm. f⁰.

Hebraica. A quarterly journal in the interests of Semitic study. (Harper, Haupt, and Strack.) *Chicago* (Now *New Haven*), 1885-7. 3 v. 8⁰.

Heidelb. Studien u. Krit. (1851.) [? Perhaps intended for Hamburg. S. u. K. = Theol. Stud. u. Krit.]

Hengstenberg's Kirchenz. See Evangelisch. Kirchenz.

Henke's Magazin f. Religionsphilosophie. See Magazin, etc.

Hermathena. A series of papers on literature, science, and philosophy. By members of Trinity College, Dublin. *Dublin* and *London*, 1873–86–. 5 v. 8⁰.

Hermes. Zeitschrift für classische Philologie. *Berlin*, 1866–86–. 21 v. 8⁰.

Historische politische Blätter für das kathol. Deutschland, redig. von J. E. Jörg. *München.* 1838 ff.

Historische Zeitschrift. (Sybel.) *München* und *Leipzig*, — 1887–. 58(22)– v. 8⁰.

Illgen's Ztschr. See Zeitschr. f.

Independent (The). *New York*, — 1887. 39 v. f⁰.

Indian Evangelical Review. *Calcutta.* [1885.]

Jahn's Archiv. See Archiv, etc.

Jahrbücher der bibl. Wissenschaft von H. Ewald. *Gött.* 1849–65. 12 v.

Jahrbücher für classische philologie. *Lpz.* — 1886–. 134 v. 8⁰.

Jahrbücher für deutsch Theologie (herausg. von Liebner, Dorner, Ehrenfeuchter, Landerer, Palmer, Weizsäcker.) *Gotha*, 1856–78. 23 v. 8⁰.

Jahrbücher für Gesellschafts und Staatwissenschaften. *Berlin*, 1864-9. 12 v. 8⁰.

Jahrbücher für protestantische Theologie begründet unter Mitwirkung von mitgliedern der theologischen Facultäten zu Bern, Bonn, Giessen, Heidelberg, Jena, Kiel, Leiden, Strassburg, Wien, und Zürich, etc. *Leipzig*, 1875–1887. 13 v. 8⁰.

Jahrbücher, Neueste, für Religion-Kirchen u. Schulwesen. Hrsg. Schuderoff. *Neustadt a. d. O.* — 1831. 61 v. 8⁰. [For the various series published at Leipzig and at Neustadt a. d. O. from 1802 to 1831, cf. Zuchold I. (1864) 607.]

Jenaer Literaturzeitung (Klette). *Jena*, 1874-9. 6 v. 8⁰.

Journal Asiatique. *Paris*, 1822–1887. 8 sér. v. 9–. 8⁰.

Journal des Débats, politiques et littéraires. 1814–64–.

Journal des Savans. *Laris*, 1665-1792. 111 v. 4⁰; continued 1816–1887.

Journal of Classical and Sacred Philology. 1854–.

Journal of Philology. *London* and *Cambridge*, 1868–83–. 12 v. 8⁰.

Journal of S. Lit. & Bibl. Rec. 1856 (5)–. [= Kitto's Journal. 3d series. Ed. Burgess. 1855– ?]

Journal of the American Oriental Society. *Boston*, 1849–. 8⁰.

Journal of the Society of Biblical Literature and Exegesis. (*Middletown*) *Boston*, 1880–1886. 8⁰.

Jüdische Zeitschrift für Wissenshaft und Leben. *Breslau*, 1809.

Der Katholik. Zeitschrift. f. kathol. Wissenschaft u. kirchl. Leben. *Mainz*, 1821–1886–. 66 v. Jg. (N. F. 22 Jg.) 8⁰.

Kath. Monatsschr. [III. (1828.)] [? = Theol. prakt. Monatsschr. zunächst f. Seelsorger. 2te Aufl. *Linz*.1810; 4te Aufl. *Prag.*, 1827-32. 30 v. 8⁰.]

Kirchenhistorisches Archiv (herausgeg. von Stäudlin, Tzschirner und I. S. Bater). *Halle*, 1823–26. 4 v.

Kitto's Journal of Sacred Literature. (Kitto.) *London*, 1848–68. 40 v.

Krit. Prediger. bibliothek (Röhr). *Neust. a. d. O.* 1820–. [Following: Predigerliterat. *Zeitz*. 1810-14. 3 v. 8⁰; Neue P—. do. 1815-17. 4 v. 8⁰; neueste P—. do. 1818-19. 2 v. 8⁰.]

Le Lien. Journal des Eglises réformées de la France. *Paris*, 1840–1866–. f⁰.

Literarisches Centralblatt f. Deutschland. (Zarncke.) — 1887. 4⁰.

Literarischer Handweiser. zunächst für das katholische Deutschland. *Münster*, — 1886–. 25 Jg. 8⁰. [? *Mainz*.]

Littell's Living Age. (Liv. Age.) *Boston*, 1844–86–. 171 v. 8⁰.

Literatur Zeitung für d. Kathol. Religionslehrer. (hrsg. Felder. 16-25 v. 8–, followed by Mastraux and then by Besnard). *Landshut*, 1816–34. 25 v.

Literarische Rundschau. *Freiburg i. Br.* 1875–. 4⁰.

Lobb's Theological Quarterly. *London*, 1884. 4⁰. [Continuation of Dickinson's Theol. Qt.]

London Quarterly Review. (Lond. Q.) *London*, 1853–81–. 57 v. 8⁰.

Leipziger Repertorium der deutschen u. ausländischen Literatur. (Gersdorf.) *Leipzig*, 1843–60. 18 v.

Luthersk Ugeskrift. — 1887. 21 v.

Magasin de libraire, Le. [1860. XI., XII.]

Magazin f. d. christlichen Dogmatik u. Moral. *Tübing.* 1796–1811. 10 v. 8⁰. [V. 13–16 by Särskind.]

Magazin für Religions, Moral u. Kirchengesch. (Stäudlin.) *Hannover*, 1802-5. 4 v. (?)

Magazin für Religionsphilosophie, Exeg., u. Kirchengesch. *Helmst.* 1794–6. 6 v. 8⁰; Neues Magazin, etc. *Helmst.* 1719–1802. v. 7–12. 8⁰.

Mancherlei Gaben u. Ein Geist. Homilit. Vierteljahrsschr. f. d. ev. Deutschland (Ohly). 1864–.

Museum criticum ed Stosch. *Lemgo*, 1774-8. 3 v. 8⁰.

Neues kritisches Journal d. theol. Literatur. (Winer u. Engelhardt.) *Sulzbach*, 1824–30. 9 v. 8⁰. [Preceded by the Krit. Journal d. neuest. theol. Lit. hrsg. Ammon u. Bertholdt. I. 1-3. *Nürnberg*, 1813. 1–xv. *Sulzbach*, 1814-23].

Mémoires de l'Académie des Inscriptions et Belles-Lettres. *Paris*, 1717–1809. 50 v. 4⁰; — 1874–. 28 v. 4⁰.

Mémoires de l'Institut. de la France. *Paris.* 4⁰. [References are to the section; Acad. des Inscr., etc. See Mémoires de l'Acad., etc.]

Mémoires de la Société des Antiquaires de France. *Paris*, 1807–12. 5 v. 8⁰ (l'Acad. celtique), 1817–34. 10 v. 8⁰ (antiq. nationale et étrang.), Nouv. sér. 1835-50. 10 v. 8⁰; 3 série. 1852-9. 4 v. 8⁰.

Mémoires de Trévoux. See Mém. pour servir à l'hist., etc.

Mémoires pour servir à l'histoire des sciences et des arts recueillis par l'ordre de S. A. S. Monseigneur le prince souverain de Bourbes. *Trévoux* et *Paris*, 1701–67. 878 pt. in 265 v. 12⁰. [Generally known as Mémoires de Trévoux.]

Memoirs of Literature. *London*, 1712. 4⁰.

Mémorial Catholique. 1860–68–. 9 v. [1841. 8⁰.]

Mercersburg Review. (Mercersb.) 1849–78. 25 v.

Methodist Magazine. (Meth. M.) *London*, 1798–1836. 39 v. 8⁰.

Methodist Quarterly. (Meth. Q.) *New York*, 1841–81. 41 v. 8⁰.

Methodist Review. *New York*, — 1887–. 69 v. (46?) 8⁰. Cf. Meth. Q.

Mnemosyne. Bibliotheca philologica Batava. *Lugd. Bat.* — 1886–. n. s. 15 v. 8⁰.

Modern Review. (Mod. R.) *London*, 1880-4–. 5 v.

Monatsschr. f. Wiss. u. Lit. See Allgemeine Monatsschr., etc.
Month. *London*, 1864–86. 58 v.
Morgenblatt. für gebildete Stände. (*Tübing*) *Stuttgart*, 1807–65. 59 Jg. 4º.
Neueste theolog. Annalen u. theol. Nachrichten. *Zurich*, 1826–9. 4 v. 8º; Neue Folge. do. 1830. 8º.
New Englander. *New Haven*, 1843–87. 46 v. 8º.
New Jerusalem Magazine. *Boston*, — 1887. 11 v. 8º.
New York Review. (New York R.) *New York*, 1837–42.
Niemeyer's Zeitschr. See Zeitschr. f. prot. Geistl.
Nieuwe Rotterdamer Courant. [1884.]
Nineteenth Century. (19th Cent.) *London*, 1877–86. 20 v. 8º.
North American Review. (No. Am.) *Boston* and *New York*, 1815–87. 145 v. 8º.
North British Review. (No. Brit.) *Edinburgh*, 1844–71. 53 v. 8º.
Nouv. Rev. de Theol. See Rev. de Theol.
Nova Acta Erudit. See Acta Erud.
Nuova Antologia di sienze lettere ed arte. *Roma*, — 1884. 19 an. 2 ser. 43 v. 8º.
Oesterrichische Vierteljahrsschrift für Katholische Theologie. *Wien*, 1862–63. 12 v. 8º.
Otia literar. ad Isalam. *Campis*. [1761–2.] (?)
Phillips u. Görres. Hist. polit. Bl. See Historische-politische Bl.
Philologus. Zeitschr. f. d. klass. Alterthum. (v. Leutsch) 1846–1886-. 45 v. 8º.
Presbyterian Quarterly Review. (Presb. Q.) *New York*, 1872–77. 6 v.
Presbyterian Review. *New York*, 1880–87. 8 v. 8º.
Princeton Review. *Princeton* and *New York*. (*Princ.*) 1829–71. 43 v. New series, 1886-. 62 year. n. s. v. 4. 8º.
Prospective Review. (Prosp. R.) *London*, 1845–54. 10 v. 8º.
Protestant. Kirchenzeitung für das evang. Deutschland. (Websky.) *Berl.* 1854–86-. 4º.
Quarterly Review. (Quar.) *London*, 1809–86-. 163 v. 8º.
Radical. (Radical.) *Boston*, 1866–72. 10 v.
Renaissance, La, revue du progrès moral et social. *Paris.* 4º. [Continuation of "La Vie humaine." 1855–9. 5 v.; L'Initiation anc. et mod. 1860-; La R. in 1866.]
Repertorium für bibel. u. morgenl. Literat. *Leipzig*, 1777–86. 18 pts. 8º.
Reuss und Cunitz's Beiträge zu den theol. Wissenschaften. See Beiträge, etc.
Reuter's Repertorium. See Allgem. Rep. f. d. theol. Lit.
Revue archéologique. *Paris*, 1844–1886. (= 3 sér. vii.) 8º.
Revue Catholique. *Louvain*. [1830-, 1835-, 1837-?]
Revue Contemporaine. *Paris*. (— 1863 = 2 sér. v. XXXI–VI.)
Revue critique d'histoire et de litterature. *Paris*, 1867–86-. 20 an. 8º. (?)
Revue de l'Histoires des Religions. *Paris*, — 1887. 7 an. Nouv. ser. (14 v. ?) 8º.
Revue de philologie. Littérature et d' histoire anciennes. Nouv. sér. (Chatelain et Riemann) 1877–86-. 10 v. 8º.
Revue de Théologie et de Philosophie Chrétienne, publiée sous la direction de T. Colani. *Strasbourg*, 1857-. 8º. [Rev. de Théol. XIII. 1851?]
Revue des études Juives. 1880–1887. 8 an. 8º. [1884 = v. 7.]
Revue des questions historiques. *Paris*, 1867–1887. 21 an. (42 v. ?) 8º.
Revue des sciences ecclésiastiques. *Paris*, 1860–86. 54 v. (6 ser. v. 4) 1887. 8º.
Revue des cours litteraires. *Paris*, 1863. 4º.
Revue des deux mondes. *Paris*, 1829–87. 57 an. 8º.
Revue du Lyonnais. *Lyon*, —1887. [1861 = B. xxii.]

Revue du Monde Catholique. 1859(?)–1887.
Revue philosophique de la France et de l'étranger (Ribot). *Paris*, 1879–87. 12 an. (24 v.?) 8º.
Rheinisches Museum für philologie (Ribbeck u. Bücheler). *Frankfort*, —1886-. N. F. 41 v. 8º.
Röhr's Krit. Prediger-Biblioth. See Krit. Prediger. Bibl., etc.
Saturday Review. [1877.]
Scheiner's Ztschr. See Zeitschr. f. d. gesammt. Kath. Theol.
Schuderhoff. See Jahrbücher fur Religions-, Kirchen-, u. Schulwesen.
Schulthess. Neuest. Theol. Annal. See Neuest. Theol. An., etc.
Scottish Church Review. —1886-.
Sitzungberichte der Kaiserl. Akademie des Wissenschaften zu Wien. Phil.-Hist. Bl. *Wien*, —1886. 110 v. 8º.
Stäudlein u. Tzschirner Archiv f. Kirchengesch. See Archiv., etc.
Stimmen aus Maria Laach. Katholische Monatschrift. *Freib. i. Br.* 1869–84-. 28 v. 8º.
Stirm's Studien d. ev. Geistlichkeit Würtemburgs. See Studien, etc.
Stosch Mus. crit. See Museum crit.
Strassb. theol. Beitr. See Beitrage zu den theol. Wiss.
Studia Biblica. *Oxford*. [1885.]
Studien d. evangel. Geistlichkeit. Würtemburgs. Ed. Klaiber. (1–82) ; Stirm, (82–); *Stuttg.* 1827–48. 20 v. 8º.
Stud. u. Krit. See Theologische Studien u. Krit.
Sunday School Times. *Philadelphia*, — 1887. 29 v. sm. fº.
Sybel. Histor. Zeitschr. See Hist. Ztschr.
Témoignage, Le. *Paris*. — 1885-.
Theol. Blätter oder Nachrichter, Aufragen, u. Bemerkungen theol. Inhalts. *Gotha*, 1796–8. 2 v. 8º; Neue theol. Blätter, etc. *Gotha*, 1799–1800. 3 v. 8º.
Theological and Literary Journal. (Theo. and Lit. J.) *New York*, 1849–61. 13 v.
Theological Critic. [1852.]
Theological Eclectic Review. (Theol. Ecl.) *Cincinnati*, 1864–70. 7 v. 8º.
Theological Review. (Theo. R.) *London*, 1864–79. 16 v.
Theologisch Tijdschrift. *Leiden*, 1867–1886. 20 v. 8º.
Theologische Jahrbücher ("herausg. von E. Zeller, seit 1847 von F. C. Baur u. E. Zeller"). *Tüb.* 1842–57. 16 Jg. 8º.
Theologische Monatschrift. (Alzog, etc.) *Mainz*, 1850–1. 2 v. 8º.
Theologische Literaturzeitung. *Leipzig*, 1876–87. 12 v. 4º.
Theologische Quartalschrift. In: Verbind. mit mehr. Gelehrten herausg. von Drey u. a. *Tüb.* 1819–1887. 69 v. 8º.
Theologisches Literaturblatt. (Luthardt) *Leipzig*, 1883–1886. 4º.
Theologisches Literatur-Blatt. (Ed. Reusch.) *Bonn*, 1866–77. 12 Jg. 4º.
Theolog. Mitarbeiten hrsg. Pelt. u. a. *Kiel.* 1838–41. 4 v. 8º.
Theol. Studien und Kritiken. Eine Zeitschrift für das gesammte Gebiet der Theologie, begründet von C. Ullmann u. F. W. C. Umbreit, etc. *Gotha.* 1828–1887. 60 v. 8º.
Theologische Studien aus Würtemberg. *Ludwigsburg*, 1880–7. 8 v. 8º.
Theologische Tidskrift. grundad af A. F. Beckman. . . . *Upsala*, — 1887. 27 v. 8º.
Theologisk Tidsskrift. for den danske Folkekirke. *Kjøbenhavn*, — 1887. 8º.
Theol. Tidssk. f. d. Kirke i. Norge. [III. (1886.)]
Transactions of the Cambridge Philological **Society.** (Postgate.) *London, Trübner*, — 1886-.

Tüb. Theol. Jahrbb. See Theol. Jahrbb.
Tüb. Theol. Quartalschr. See Theolog. Quartalschr.
Tübinger Zeitschr. See Zeitschr. f. Theol.
Universalist Quarterly Review. (Univ. Q.) *Boston,* 1844–
86. 43 v.
Vierteljahrsschrift f. Kath. Theol. See Oesterreichische.
Vierteljahrschr. etc.
Vierteljahrsschrift für Theologie u. Kirche. (Lücke u.
Wiseler.) 1845–53. 8⁰. [In 3 series. Series 2. = Monat-
schrift instead of Vierteljschr, etc.]
Westminster Review. (Westm.) *Lond.* 1824–86. 126
v. 8⁰.
Winer's n. kr. Journal. See Neues krit. Journal, etc.
Wöchentl. Hallische. Anz. [1751.]
Woskresnoe Tschenie. [(1849) No. 33-.]
Zeitschrift der deutschen. morgenländischen Gesellschaft.
Leipzig, — 1887-. 41 v. 8⁰.
Zeitschrift. für christl. wissenschaft. u. christl. Leben.
1850–1861. 12 Jg. 8⁰.
Zeitschrift für die gesammte kathol. Theologie, (red. von
J. Scheiner u. J. M. Häusle). *Wien,* 1850–6. 8 v. 8⁰.
Zeitschrift für Geistlichkeit des Erzbisth. Freiburg.
Freib. 1828–34. 7 v. 8⁰. (?)
Zeitschrift für die gesammte lutherische Theologie und
Kirche, herausg. von A. G. Rudelbach und H. E. F.
Guericke, fortgeführt von F. Z. Delitzsch und Gue-
ricke. *Leipzig,* 1840–78. 39 v. 8⁰.
Zeitschrift für die historische Theologie; herausgeg. v.
Ch. F. Illgen; (1846) von Ch. W. Niedner; (1867-)
von Kahnis. *Lpz.* 1832–74. (5?) 8⁰.
Zeitschrift. für die österreichischen Gymnasien. *Wien,*
— 1884. 35 Jg. 8⁰.
Zeitschrift für Katholische Theologie. *Innsbruck,* 1877–
1887. 11 v. 8⁰.

Zeitschrift für Kirchengesch. in Verbind. mit W. Gass,
H. Reuter u. A. Ritschl, hersg. von Th. Brieger. *Gotha,*
1876–87. 8 v. 8⁰. [" Bringt jahrlich auch gediegene Ueber-
sichten über die neueste kirchengesch. Literatur."]
Zeitschrift für Kirchenrecht. *Freiburg i. Br.* — 1887.
22 v. (N. F. 7 v.) 8⁰.
Zeitschrift für kirchl. Wissenschaft u. kirchl. Leben.
(Luthardt.) *Leipzig,* 1880–87. 8 Jg. 8⁰.
Zeitschrift für Pastoral-Theologie. (Oehler.) *Heilbronn,*
1878–87. 10 v. 8⁰.
Zeitschrift für Philosophie u. Kathol. Theol. *Köln,* 1832–
9. 8 v. 8⁰; Neue Folge, 1842–8. 9 v. 8⁰.
Zeitschrift für praktische Theologie. *Frankfurt a. M.*
1879–87. 9 Jg. 8⁰.
Zeitschrift für protestantische Geistliche. (Franke u.
Niemeyer.) *Halle,* 1844–5. 3 v. 8⁰.
Zeitschrift für Protestantismus und Kirche. (" Herausg.
von Harless, seit 1847 in verb. mit G. Thomasius und
v. Hofmann, dann von letzterem, Heinr. Schmid u.
Ad. von Scheurl.") *Erl.* 1839–76. 8⁰.
Zeitschrift für Theologie. *Tübing.* 1828–30. 3 pts. 8⁰;
1830–40. 11 v. and Index. 8⁰.
Zeitschrift für Wissenschaftliche Theologie, in Verbindung
mit mehreren Gelehrten, hersg. von A. Hilgenfeld.
Jena, 1858–87. 30 Jg. 8⁰.
Zeitschrift f. wissenschaftl. Theologie, hrsg. Winer. *Sulzb.*
1826–32. 8⁰.
Zeitschr. f. wiss. u. Leben. (1853.) See Der Katho-
lik. (?)
Zeitschr. v. Lücke u. Wieseler. N. F. II. (1850.) See
Vierteljahrsschrift für Theol.
Zeller's Jahrbüchern. See Theologische Jahrbücher.
Zeitschrift für vaterlandische Geschichte und Alterthums-
kunde. *Münster,* — 1885-. 43 v. 8⁰.

INDEX OF SUBJECTS

INDEX OF SUBJECTS.

COMPREHENSIVE GENERAL INDEX

TO

The Ante-Nicene Fathers

BY

REV. BERNHARD PICK, PH.D.,

Author of Index to " Lange's Commentary on the Old Testament."

THE ANTE-NICENE FATHERS

INDEX OF SUBJECTS

Aaron, i, 6, 60; an example of circumspect behavior, viii, 65; anointed, 89; and Miriam, their sin against Moses, i, 573.

Abbanes, a merchant, buys the Apostle Thomas from the Lord, to be a carpenter for Gundaphoros, an Indian king, viii, 535; thrown into prison by Gundaphoros, 539; released, 540.

Abbot, Ezra, referred to, ii, 522.

Abdera, proverbial for stupidity, vi, 494.

Abeddadan, i, 60.

Abel, i, 6, 81, 89, 119; ii, 105; name and nature of, viii, 243; the offering of, i, 485; ii, 105; killed by Cain, viii, 565; buried by angels, 570.

Abgar, reign of, viii, 702; trouble between Herod and, 702; builds Edessa, 702; arranges between Ardachès and his brothers, 703; helps Aretas against Herod, the Tetrarch, 703; sends deputies to Marinus, 703; hears from them of Jesus Christ, 703; suffering from a disease, writes a letter to Jesus, 558, 651, 704; copy of the letter sent by, 652, 704; reply of Jesus to, 652, 704, who sends an image of himself on a towel, which heals him, 558; Thaddeus visits and heals, 558, 652, 653, 704; Abgar is converted, and intends to destroy the Jews for crucifying Christ, 656, 662; writes to Tiberius, 656, 662, 705; answer from Tiberius to, 705; writes to Narses of Assyria concerning Addæus, 662, 705, and to Ardachès concerning Simon, 706; is made bishop of Edessa, 663.

Abiathar, the high priest, wishes to obtain Mary as wife for his son, viii, 371; proclaims that a protector should be sought for Mary, 372; gives to Mary and Joseph "the water of drinking of the Lord" to drink, 373, 374.

Abiding city, not here, ii, 31.

Abiram, i, 6, 60.

Abominations practised by the Valentinians, i, 324.

Abortion, a heathen crime, iv, 192.

Abraham, i, 7, 9, 13, 81, 84, 142, 178; ii, 107; viii, 186; elect, ii, 445; saw the day of Christ, i, 467, 469; waited for the promises of God, 561; had faith identical with ours, 492; both covenants prefigured in, 495, 496; vain attempt of Marcion to exclude him from Christ's salvation, 470; meaning of the sacrifice of, vi, 325; the posterity of, viii, 186.

Abram, i, 7; meaning of, ii, 446.

Abraxas, Bassilides' doctrine of, i, 350; iii, 649.

Absalom, i, 60.

Absolution, form of, iii, 668.

Abstraction from material things necessary to the knowledge of divine truth, ii, 460.

Absurdity of the heretics concerning the creation, i, 362 seq.

Abudem, viii, 447.

Abusive language, punished by law, vi, 487.

Abyss, what is meant by, viii, 43.

Academics, vii, 15, 71; confused teaching of, v, 21.

Acantho, mother of the fourth Sun, vi, 480.

Acceptable year of the Lord, i, 391.

Access, Prayer of, vii, 559, 567.

Accius Navius and Tarquinius Priscus, vii, 51.

Accommodation, unknown to Christ and his apostles, i, 417.

Accused, the, on, viii, 637.

Accusers, false, to be punished, vii, 416, 418; qualification of, viii, 616; how to be treated, 617; disqualification of, 637.

Acdestis, birth of, vi, 491; a hermaphrodite, 491; self-mutilated by the craft of Bacchus, 491; love of Attis, 492; fatal consequences of this fury, 492.

Achaia, Christianity attested by miracles in, vi, 438.

Achamoth, account of, i, 320; origin of the visible world from, 321;

iii, 513; shall at last enter the Pleroma, i, 325; iii, 518; asserted to be referred to in Scripture, i, 326.

Acharneis quoted, ii, 506.

Acheron, vi, 439, 500.

Acherusian Lake, the, viii, 578.

Achilles, vi, 485; and Polyxena, Peleus and Thetis, Prometheus, viii, 265.

Acinetos, i, 316; iii, 507.

Acorns and chestnuts, the food of primitive men, vi, 442, 459.

Acrisius, buried in temple of Minerva at Larissa, vi, 508.

Acta Pauli et Theclæ, referred to, iii, 677.

Actaeon, the horned hunter, vi, 473.

Action better than speech, ii, 310.

Actions, involuntary and voluntary, ii, 361, 362; wicked, to be avoided, viii, 336.

Actors, freed from taxes, vi, 488.

Acts, the genuine, of Peter of Alexandria, vi, 261 seq.

Acts of the Apostles, Pamphilus' summary of contents, vi, 166-168.

Acts of the Apostles, Apocryphal, viii, 354.

    Andrew and Matthias, viii, 356, 517 seq.

    Barnabas, viii, 355, 493 seq.

    John, viii, 357, 560 seq.

    Paul and Thecla, viii, 355, 487 seq.

    Peter and Paul, viii, 355, 477 seq.

    Peter and Andrew, viii, 526 seq.

    Philip, viii, 355, 497 seq.

    Pilate, i, 175; viii, 416-434, 439-447.

    Sharbil, viii, 676 seq.

    Thaddæus, viii, 357, 558 seq.

    Thomas, viii, 535 seq.

Acts and Martyrdom of Andrew, viii, 356, 511 seq.

Acts and Martyrdom of St. Matthew, viii, 528 seq.

Adæus and Maris, Liturgy of, vii, 561–571.

Adam, i, 6, 71, 89, 114; ii, 105; called

rative of the ministry of Jesus, and of the opposition of men to him, 519, 520; carried by the angels from the boat to the city of the man-eaters, 520; vision of his disciples, 521; Jesus appears to, as a child, 521; enters the city of the man-eaters, and visits Matthew in prison, 521; lays his hands on the men deprived of sight in prison, and heals them, 521, 522; walks about the city, and beholds its abominations, 522; by prayer stays the hand of inhuman executioners, 523; rebukes the devil, 523; sought for by the man-eaters, he shows himself to them. 523; dragged repeatedly by ropes through the city, till his hair and flesh are torn off, 523; causes an alabaster statue to send forth water, and flood the city, and drown the inhabitants, 524; sends down certain bad men into the abyss, 525; brings to life the men that were drowned, 525; when he is leaving the city Jesus appears to him as a child, and sends him back, 525; caught up in a luminous cloud, and conveyed to a mountain, where were Peter and others, 526; Jesus appears to, and sends him to a city of the barbarians, 526; what befell him there, 526 seq.

Andromeda, viii, 199.

Anemurium, the city of, Barnabas preached at, viii, 494.

Angel of the covenant, the Son of God, v, 627, 631.

Angel guardian, office and benefits of, vi, 24; of infants, viii, 48; of generation, 49; of the sun, 50.

Angel, an, appears to Anna, viii, 362, 369; to Mary, 363; to Joseph, 364, 373; to Joachim, 370; shows to the people the vile demon that dwelt in the temple at Astaruth, 556.

Angels, i, 68, 88, 118, 148; nature of, iv, 241, 256; the world not made by, i, 361; could not be ignorant of the supreme God, 365; not essentially (inherently) good, iv, 257; how they transgressed, i, 190, 238; vi, 370; vii, 64, 231; unawares, viii, 192; appearance of, how caused, viii, 49; their freedom, i, 250, 269, 301; ii, 142; are spiritual beings, ii, 493; number of, viii, 585; ministry of, ii, 517, 518, 575; various offices, iv, 264; souls of, iv, 287; the fall of and its cause, viii, 272; incite to good and evil, iv, 332; how superior to men, iv, 509; ministering spirits, iv, 544, 650, 664; not to be invoked, iv, 544, 650–652, 661; not worshipped by Jews, iv, 545; inferior given to Gentiles, ii, 524; bear sway over nations, viii, 178; guardian. ii, 533; viii, 108;

give in to God at sun-setting their report of the conduct of men, viii, 575; the two, ii, 24, attend men at their death, viii, 576; fallen, evil seducers, viii, 140; discoveries made by, 273; taught idolatry, iii, 62, astrology, 65, astronomy, divination, and other arts, viii, 49; the giant offspring of, 273; demons sprung from the fallen, 274; the metamorphoses of, 272; the names of, used as incantations, vi, 425; called days, viii, 50; different orders of, 50; of human flesh, unborn, iii, 328.

Anger, i, 17, 35, 54; ii, 49; defined, vii, 274; necessary to punishment, 274; of God, against sin, 273; unlike man's, 277; witnessed to by the sibyls, 278, and by the oracle of Apollo, 279; the mischief of, viii, 25; righteous, 153, 205; of God, a treatise by Lactantius, vii, 259 seq.

Anicetus, i, 416, 569; iii, 630.

Animal men, the, of the Valentinians, i, 324; pass into the intermediate habitation, 326.

Animals, creation of, vii, 60, 382; noxious, 199; figure of, 286; theories of Epicurus, 287; man closely allied to the other, vi, 440, 441, 443, 444; man not morally superior to the other, 520, 521; deified and worshipped, 420; viii, 148; cloven-footed, i, 144; ruminant, 143; forbidden or allowed as food to Israel, spiritual significance of, 143; clean and unclean, a figure of the gift of the Holy Spirit, 533; a figure of the church, Jews and heretics, ii, 555; and plants, illustrating the providence of God, viii, 172.

Animosity of the Jews, viii, 91.

Anna, type of the Gentiles, vi, 391.

Anna, the wife of Joachim, bewails her barrenness, viii, 361, 369; is visited by an angel, and promised a child, 362, 369; gives birth to Mary—her song of praise; 362, 371; married to Cleophas after the death of Joachim, 382.

Annas, the son of, killed by the child Jesus, viii, 378, 395.

Annas and Caiaphas, various references to, viii, 416, 423, 425, 433, 447 seq., 512; inherit Levi's curse, v, 164.

Annubion (also Anubion), and Appion, viii, 205, 207, 252, 342, 344; explains the design of Simon Magus' transformation of Faustinianus, 207, and of Faustus, 344; persuades Matthidia to go to Antioch with Faustinianus, 207, 208.

Annunciation, the, homilies on, vi, 58–71.

Anointing, viii, 89; in baptism, v, 376; vii, 431, 469, 476; thanksgiving at, 476.

Anonymous writers quoted, ii, 288, 291, 337, 385, 473, 475.

Ansus appointed bishop of Rome by Peter, viii, 675.

Answer to the Jews, a treatise by Tertullian, iii, 151 seq.; date of, 151 occasion of writing, 151.

Ant, Jupiter's conversion into an, vi, 485.

Antaradus, viii, 292.

Ante-Nicene theology, its freedom from errors, iv, 223; reliance on Holy Scripture, 223; its understanding of church teaching, 240, 382, 383.

Anterus, Epistle of, viii, 626 seq.

Anthem, the, vii, 553.

Anthrobians, the, vii, 133.

Anthropopathism of God, how explained, ii, 362; v, 611, 615, 644.

Anthropos, meaning of the term, vii, 41.

Antichrist, i, 34, 138; vii, 215, 354; prophecy of, v, 190, 204–206, 214, 216, 217, 242 seq.; springs from the tribe of Dan, 207; his two advents, 217; coming of, iv, 211; at hand, v, 346, 349; how prefigured, i, 558; his reign and death, 558; different names answering, 559; the fraud, pride, and tyranny of the kingdom of, 553; concentrates in himself the apostasy, 557; the ideal evil, iv, 594; the number of the name of, i, 558, 559; the man of sin 453, 463; seen by Esdras in Tartarus, a description of, viii, 572, 573; seen and described by John, 582; time of the continuance of, 583.

Antichrist and Christ, a treatise of Hippolytus on, v, 204 seq., 243.

Antidoron, the, vii, 356.

Antimachus quoted, ii, 483.

Antinoites, epistle of Alexander of Cappadocia to the, vi, 154.

Antioch, church at, i, 48, 85, 91, 96, 100, 129; epistle of Alexander of Cappadocia, to, vi, 154; seat of early Christians, ii, 87; see of Theophilus, 88; excitement at, caused by Simon Magus, viii, 206.

Antiochians, genuine and supposed epistle of Ignatius to them, wherein he speaks of his bonds, of the true doctrine concerning Christ against the views of early heretics, and exhorts them to certain duties, i, 110–112.

Antiochus, v, 184, 214.

Antiochus of Cyzicum, sacrilege of, vi, 515.

Antipas, martyr, iii, 646.

Antiphanes, the theogony of, i, 376; quoted, ii, 272.

Antipho quoted, ii, 483.

Antipodes, theory of, incredible, vii, 94.

Antiquity, the most fertile source of errors, vi, 429.

Antisthenes, testifies to the unity of God, vii, 14; quoted, ii, 193, 470.

Antonianus, epistle of Cyprian to, v, 327.

German reformation, iii, 3; referred to, iii, 39; viii, 35, 37, 44.

Augustus, Emperor, refused divine honors, iii, 43; ordered a census, viii, 365, 374.

Aulus, capitol named from, vi, 509.

Aurelian, persecutor, vii, 303.

Aurelius, confessor, v, 311; ordained reader, 311.

Aurelius of Chullabi, on baptism, v, 572.

Aurelius of Utica, on baptism, v, 569.

Aurelius Marcus, i, 187; Lightfoot on, viii, 778.

Aurora's love of Tithonus, vi, 485.

Ausès, viii, 87.

Authority, apostolic, vii, 106.

Authors, profane, ii, 111; their ignorance, 111; their contradictions, 111.

Authors quoted; *see* Quoted authors.

Autogenes, i, 353.

Autolycus, an idolater and scorner of Christians, ii, 89; address of Theophilus to, 94–121; misled by false accusations, 112; concluding advice to, 121.

Autun inscription, vii, 536.

Avarice, effects of, viii, 220.

Ave Maria, vii, 546.

Aventine, Jupiter drawn down to the, vi, 459.

Avenging of the Saviour, the, viii, 354, 472 seq.

Aves quoted, ii, 96.

Aviricius Marcellus, vii, 335, 338.

Axe, the, made to float by means of wood, i, 572; laid at the root, 573; v, 595.

Axionicus, opinion of, concerning the body of Jesus, v, 89.

Azarias, i, 17, 178; proof of resurrection, 531; his persecution, 558.

Babai, sister of Sharbil, killed on the spot where she caught the blood of her brother, viii, 684; is buried, 684.

Babel, the tower of, ii, 106; raised to Zoroaster, viii, 141.

Babylon, identified with Rome, v, 211; symbol of the Roman State, vii, 352; judgment of, in Apocalypse, v, 212.

Babylonians, invention of the, ii, 65; system of the, v, 40.

Bacchanalia, two kinds of, vi, 496, 497.

Bacchus, son of Semele, vi, 473, 483; dashed by lightning from his mother's womb, 422; born again from his father's thigh, 483; giver of a good vintage, 459; represented as effeminate, 511; and as bearing a drinking-cup, 517; *phalli* displayed at rites of, 500; identified with the sun, 473; goats sacrificed to, 525 (note); called Evius, 500, Nysius, 500, Zagreus, 497, Bromius, 483; torn in pieces by Titans, 424, 497; destruction of temple at Athens of, 516; character of, vii, 226;

fable about invented by the devil, i, 233.

Bacchylides quoted, ii, 470, 483.

Bacchylus, viii, 477.

Bacis, the soothsayer, vi, 431.

Backbiting, ii, 49.

Bacon referred to, iv, 73.

Bactrian, Zoroaster a, vi, 428.

Bactrians, war of Assyrians with, vi, 415; laws of the, viii, 731.

Baebulus, the Magian, vi, 428.

Baehr, referred to, vi, 339.

Balaam, i, 571; forbidden to curse Israel, 572; is slain, 573; his ass a type, 572.

Bald Venus, the, vii, 33.

Balsamon, commentary on Peter of Alexandria's canons, vi, 269–278.

Bancroft referred to, i, 552.

Banquet, the, of the ten virgins, by Methodius, vi, 309–355, 382.

Banquet, the, of the gods, vi, 531; viii, 203.

Baptism, prefigured in the Old Testament, i, 144; of Jesus not a type of the thirty æons, 390; of Christ, iii, 675; why, viii, 44 (homily on, vi, 68–71), example to Christians, v, 236; effect of, ii, 215; Christian, i, 183, 201; names and effects, ii, 215, 216; directions regarding, vii, 379, 382; grace in, v, 276, 388 seq.; called illumination, i, 183; ii, 126; with faith and repentance, ii, 217; iii, 661, 662; for the remission of sins, ii, 222, 361; iii, 293, 669; v, 354; viii, 269; in good works, viii, 275; extinguishes the fire of sin, 185; removes the unclean spirits from men, 116; the seal, ii, 349, 462; a birth into Christ, ii, 439; typified in the Apocalypse, vi, 337; the wedding garment, viii, 142, 274; first of Christian mysteries, ii, 461; the sign of regeneration, viii, 43; not to be repeated, ii, 361; v, 360; vii, 456; must be preceded by fasting, viii, 164; renunciation in, ii, 73; iii, 85; vii 476; promises made in, viii, 621; consecration of water for, vii, 477; chrism in, v, 376; vii, 431, 469, 476; iii, 672; imposition of hands necessary after, iii, 672; viii, 621; requisite to communion, vii, 414; not to be hastily given, iii, 662; reservation of, 361, 426; not to be refused, vii, 456; sin after, iii, 438; vii, 398; why possible, vi, 365; of water, v, 360, 670; of the Spirit, v, 669, 671; of fire, v, 676; with Spirit and fire, meaning of, viii, 46; of blood, iii, 677; v, 676; compared to a stream, viii, 43; substituted for sacrifices, viii, 88; is imitated by demons, i, 183; outward simplicity of, a stumbling-block to unbelief, but a motive to faith, iii, 669; contrasted with heathen ceremonial, 669; formula implies the church, 672; none out of the church, v,

375, 385, 565 seq.; necessity of, viii, 154, 290; objection to its necessity, iii, 674, 676; received by the apostles, ii, 578; iii, 675; oneness of, iii, 676; use of, viii, 155, 290; fruits of, vii, 477; rites of, vii, 431; customs of, iii, 94, 103; seasons for, iii, 678; preparation for, 679; Lord's Prayer at, vii, 431; candidates for, to be examined, vii, 494, 495; office of, vii, 469; invitation to, viii, 132; multitudes receive, viii, 133; types of, iii, 673; clinic, valid, v, 401, 419; heretical baptism invalid, iii, 676; v, 377; 456; and disallowed by African councils, vi, 102; and council of Carthage on, v, 565–572; may be given by laymen, not by women, iii, 677 (by neither, vii, 429); of infants to be deferred, iii, 678 (not to be delayed, v, 353 seq.); of the eunuch, iii, 678; of the unmarried, iii, 678; of the Samaritan converts, v, 381; true immersion in, vii, 502; by Peter, viii, 251; of John, not celestial, iii, 674; not administered by Christ, 674, nor by St. Paul, 676; of St. Paul, 676; not received by Abraham, 676; Cainite heresy concerning, iii, 669; for the dead, how understood, iii, 449, 581; a treatise by Tertullian on, iii, 669 seq., introduction to, 669.

Baptized, the, eucharistic prayer for, vii, 484; privileges of the, viii, 278.

Barabbas preferred to Jesus, viii, 420, 442.

Barbarians, their rites of worship, vii, 229.

Barbeliotes, doctrines of, i, 353.

Barcochebas, i, 173.

Bardesanes, life of, viii, 722; dialogue of, with Avida, 723 seq.; opinion of, concerning the body of Jesus, v, 89; referred to, viii, 87.

Barjesus met by Barnabas and Mark, viii, 495; opposes Barnabas, 495.

Bark, used in ancient times for clothing, vi, 459.

Barnabas, i, 133; ii, 354, 579; vii, 453; comes to Rome, viii, 78; preaches Christ there, 78, 79; Clement's interposition in his behalf, 79; Clement's intercourse with, 79; departure of, from Rome, 80; addresses the Jews at Jerusalem, 93; preaches at Alexandria, 225; is interrupted by the crowd, 225; defended by Clement, 225, 226; instructs Clement, 226; departs from Alexandria, 226; the Acts of, 355. 493 seq.; the contention between Paul and, 493, 494; with Mark, 494; comes to Anemurium, and preaches there, 494; ordains Heracleides bishop of Cyprus, 495; visits Lapithus and Lampadistus, 494, 495; reaches Paphos

27; ii, 115; iii, 51, and love of enemies, i, 27; ii, 115; are lovers of truth, ii, 116; live under God's eye, i, 166, who protects them, iv, 467; look for the kingdom with God, i, 166; contemn death, i, 192; hope in death, iv, 197; their true hope, vii, 243, 255; glory in persecution, vii, 148; increase under persecution, 148, 160; glory in martyrdom, iv, 196; triumph in martyrdom, iii, 54, 50; their patience, vii, 159; their fortitude, 149; surpassing the heathen in heroism, iii, 55; vindicated by martyrdom, 18, their blood the seed of the church, 55, 60; they believe in a resurrection, ii, 67; iii, 545. Though they are the preservers of the world, i, 27; pray for the Emperor in martyrdom, iii, 42; more loyal than the heathen, 44; obey rulers, iv, 664; because exhorted to obedience, v, 284; and not seditious, iv, 640; not a cause of calamity to the State, iii, 117, but a value, 49, 59, because their doctrine is opposed to dissensions and fitted for all, ii, 78; yet they are accused of atheism, i, 164; heathen practices were imputed to them, iii, 25; blamed for not observing the law, i, 199, 203; branded by the Valentinians as simple persons, iii, 504, though excelling in wisdom, iv, 482, in virtue, 484, in purity, iii, 107, iv, 192, to which they were exhorted, v, 285, and which they attained, iv, 631, and not teaching philosophical theories of the soul, nor of good and evil, vi, 454, 455; are called the third race, iii, 117, 643; ill-treated by the Jews, i, 203, 214, 246, 247, 256, for whom they pray, i, 266, because as the true spiritual Israel, 200, 258, 259, 261, 267, they are the heirs of the covenant, 145, have the true circumcision, 206, 208, 256, and possess the true righteousness, 209, as has been predicted, 256, 257, and the absolute truth, iii, 127. The Gentiles, too, ill-treated the, i, 169, 182, 188, 191, 253, 254; unjustly accused them, iii, 18, 110, crimes were imputed to, 21, 23, 24, 115, though they were free from crime, iii, 105; iv, 195, and defamed by rumor only, iii, 114; calumnies were brought against the, i, 570; ii, 117; iv, 178, 190. 191, 585, 627, who were accused of public calamities, iii, 47, 59, accused by Galerius, vii, 306, persecuted only for the name of Christ, iii, 109, in the profession of whom they gloried, 109. Autolycus scorned them, ii, 89, yet they were protected by good rulers, iii, 22, 57, and Roman emperors testified in

their behalf, i, 186, 187. Because unjustly hated, ii, 76; vii, 144, 243, the Christians were defended, ii, 115; viii, 688, by Justin Martyr in his Apologies, i, 164–193, who demanded justice for the, 162–165; a plea was addressed in their behalf to Marcus Aurelius and Commodus, ii, 129, showing the injustice towards the, 129, who have a claim to legal protection, 130, on account of the false charges against the, 130; the philosophy of the, is older than that of Greece, 77, and theirs is superior, 132; they worship the Trinity, 133; the teachings of the, are full of morality, 134; enjoining duties, v, 500, humility, 283, perseverance, 284, prayer, 286, temperance, 287; confutation of the calumnies against the, ii, 145, by showing the inconsistency of their accusers, 135, the elevated morality of the, 146, their conjugal chastity, 146, which is in contrast with the accusers of the, 147, when their lives compared with those of the heathen, iv, 506, so that the censures on, more applicable to philosophers, iv, 510; cruelty is condemned by the, ii, 147, who abolish gladiatorial shows, 147, abhor fœticide, 147, and refuse worship to the emperors, 148; they are sons of God, 191; their increase in the Empire, iii, 45, 58, 107, is a proof of Christianity, vi, 429; they decline public office, iv, 668, cannot keep heathen feasts, 647, are known by their character, iii, 112, number and union of, iv, 468, in spite of heresies among, 469; have not corrupted the Gospel, iv, 443; character of the teachers of vindicated, 486, 487, by the power of their teaching, 491, Christians have right and duty in this life, iv, 660; though pleasures of public shows, theatres, race-courses and amphitheatres are forbidden to, iii, 79, yet they know how to conduct themselves among heathens, viii, 63, and how to receive each other, vii, 381; they had to flee to Jericho, viii, 97, and must expect suffering in this life, v, 472, for they are like passengers in a troubled sea, viii, 221, but are exhorted to faithfulness, vii, 222, in order to get the rewards of their faith, v, 465. Though illegally tried and punished, iii, 110, they know that their prayers are answered, 107; they submit to injuries, vii, 159, are subject to evil, 160, are poor and oppressed, 165, endured persecutions under Demetrianus, v, 461; but God's vengeance comes on their persecutors, iii, 106; v,

462–465; vii, 161; it is therefore folly and cruelty of persecuting the, vii, 147.
Christmas Day to be honored, vii, 443, 495.
Christophorus, i, 130; *see also* Ignatius.
Chronography of Julius Africanus, fragments of, vi, 130 seq.
Chronological history in the time of Tertullian, iii, 17.
Chronology, biblical, ii, 325–334, 346; from Adam to Saul, 118; from Saul to captivity, 119; Theophilus founder of, 87, 106, 118; Roman, to the death of Aurelius, 119; leading epochs, 120; Jewish v, 148.
Chronos, vii, 25.
Chrysippus, on Good and Evil, iv, 526; *Subjugation of the Passions*, 658; asserted that the world would be destroyed by fire, vi, 437; object of Jupiter's lust, 485; on the unity of God, vii, 14.
Chrysis, Juno's priestess, burned at Argos, vi, 516.
Chrysostom referred to, i, 127; ii, 69, 70.
Church, the Catholic, vii, 133, 134; 545, 555, 562–565, ante-Nicene theory of, vi, 304, and Apostolic, 545, 556; prayer for, 553, 555, 556; in what sense equivalent to the Holy Spirit, iv, 99; existing, proof of the Divinity of Christ, 476; the body of Christ, 595; vii, 521; spiritual Temple of God, iv, 646; the bride of Christ, vi, 319; meaning of the word, 381; apostrophe to, 392; typified by the Ark, v, 394, by the Sun, 423, by Jacob's marriage, i, 266, by the Bride and Coat of Christ, v, 423, by Rahab and by the Passover, 424, by the woman of the Apocalypse, vi, 336, 355; the minister of the Lord's power, viii, 45; of whom composed, vii, 391, not to be forsaken, 413, 501, nor divided, v, 322, 423; no Christian apart from, 333; necessity of communion with, 318; order in the, i, 16, 17, 90; order of ministers in the, 16; her officers appointed by the Apostles, viii, 668; their duties in the, 250; duties of members in the, 251; the regard Moses had for order in the, i, 17; the regard the Apostles had for order in, 18; this order is disturbed by the wicked, 17–20; her creed, 330; her gifts, 409; has one baptism, v, 382; performs nothing by incantations or curious arts, i, 409; is the depository of truth, 416, 458; the true expounder of the Scriptures, 496; earthly is the image of the heavenly, ii, 421; the union of the, 555; unity of, in the episcopate, v, 318, 376, 421; how to go to, ii, 290, 297;

how to live outside of the, 290; mysteries in the building of the triumphant, 12, 43, and of militant, 43; implied in the baptismal formula, iii, 672; harmony between the Scriptures and the, 261; teaching of the, iv, 240, 382; faith of the, 347, 383; keys given through St. Peter to, iii, 643; a ship, viii, 220; shape, direction, and various parts of a, vii, 420; like a ship, 420; of Rome, founded by Peter and Paul, i, 415.

Church, unity of the, a treatise by Cyprian on, v, 421 seq.

Churton referred to, iv, 386.

Cicero, on the unity of God, vii, 14; Jupiter, 22; De Natura Deorum, 27, and mutilations of, vi, 465; the gods mere men, vii, 28, 29; fears to testify against idolatry, 43; on the authority of ancestors, 50; on creation, 53; on philosophy, 81; on wisdom, 81, 83; on the character of philosophers, 84; why men were born, 89; on the immortality of the soul, 90; on future rewards and punishments, 90; on life and death, 90; on philosophy as adverse to the multitude, 95; on fortune, 98; on the divine law, 170; on justice, 184; why God made noxious animals, 199; on the origin of souls, 267; quoted, viz.: —

Academ., vii, 190.
De Finibus, vii, 49.
De Leg., iv, 509; vii, 61.
De Nat. Deor., iii, 141; iv, 587; vi, 455, 467, 468, 486, 515; vii, 25, 29, 44, 47, 50, 131, 226.
De Officiis, vii, 29, 81, 99, 176, 183, 192.
De Republ., vii, 146, 148, 154, 170.
De Senectute, iii, 70.
Epist. ad Attic., vi, 494.
Pro Archia, iii, 65.
Pro Ligario, vii, 185.
Tusc. Disp., vii, 28, 207.

Cincian law against gifts to advocates, vi, 460.

Cincius, regards the Novensiles as the gods of conquered states, deities brought from abroad, vi, 474.

Cinxia, a name of Juno, vi, 472; presides over the loosening of the zone, 470; the Thespians worship a branch as, 510.

Cinyras, king of Cyprus, vi, 484; king of Paphos, 509; deified Venus, a courtesan, 484; was buried in temple of Venus, 509; founder of the mysteries of Cyprian Venus, 496.

Circe, mother of the fifth Sun, vi, 480.

Circensian games, evils of, vii, 188.

Circumcision, vii, 118; spiritual meaning of, i, 142, 143; a sign, 202; to distinguish Israel only before Christ, iii, 154; unknown before Abraham, i, 203; not derived

from the Egyptians, iv, 405; probable origin of, 564; of the Christians, i, 206, 256; of wealth, ii, 15, 53.

Circus, idolatrous in name and origin, iii, 83; combats in, evil customs of, 86; martyrdoms in, 643; story of recelebration of the games of the, vi, 425.

City, no abiding, here, ii, 31; the holy, of the Apocalypse, symbolical meaning of, vii, 359; the of God, viii, 578.

Clarus of Mascula, on baptism, v, 572.

Claudia, alleged miracle of, vii, 51.

Claudius Cæsar, the letter of Pilate to, respecting Jesus, viii, 454.

Claudius Ephebus, i, 21.

Clean and unclean, i, 534.

Cleansing, inward and outward, viii, 155.

Cleanthes on the unity of God, vii, 14; quoted, ii, 192, 448, 470.

Clemens, i, 155; ii, 12.

Clement of Alexandria, a reformer, ii, 165; teacher of Origen, 166, 167; of Alexander, bishop of Jerusalem, and of Hippolytus, 167; successor of Pantænus, 166; his life and works, 167, 168, 169; teacher of philosophic Christianity, 380; exhorts to abandon the mysteries of idolatry, 171, 205; answers the objections against doing so, 197; fragments of, 571–587; his knowledge of Hebrew questioned, 439, 443, 446, 476; referred to, i, 7, 134, 140, 143; viii, 13, 390; quotes Tatian, ii, 82. (See Comments.)

Clement, of Rome, i, 122, 466; called an apostle, ii, 428; First Epistle of, i, 1–21, 416; introductory note to, 1; literature on, 3; referred to, 505; ii, 308, 428, 495; iv, 273; homily ascribed to, vii, 517–523; text and editions of, 572; date and authority of, 573; contents and version, 514; introductory note to, 511; not the author of the epistle concerning Virginity, viii, 53; Epistle of, to James, 218; ordained by Peter his successor, 218 seq.; installation of, 221; his early history, 77, 223; his mental distress, 77, 223; his dissatisfaction with the schools, and increasing disquiet, 77, 78; his design to test the immortality of the soul, 78, 224; hears of Christ, 78, 224; meets with Barnabas at Rome, 78; interposes in behalf of Barnabas, 79; intercourse with Barnabas, 79; sets out for Judæa, but is driven to Alexandria, 225; hears Barnabas, 125; interposes in his behalf, 225, 226; his intercourse with Barnabas, 226; arrives at Cæsarea, and is introduced to Peter, 80, 227; cordial reception of, by Peter, 80, 227; his account of himself to Peter, 80; instruc-

tions given to, by Peter, 81, 227; requested to be Peter's attendant, i, 69; viii, 81; profits by Peter's instruction, and Peter's satisfaction with, 82, 228; repetition of Peter's instruction to, 83, 84; convinced of the truth of Christianity, 228; Peter's thanksgiving on account of, 228; sent by Peter to Tyre, 251, 252; meets his friend Appion, and holds a discussion with him, 253; relates his previous acquaintance with Appion, 256; the trick he played on Appion, 257; result of the trick, 261; meets Appion again for discussion, 262; not as yet baptized, he is not admitted to unite with the disciples in prayer, 143; his joy at remaining with Peter, 157, 293; his affection for Peter, 157, 293; his family history: disappearance of his mother and brothers, 158, 294, and father, 159, 294; his mother found at Aradus as a beggar-woman, 159–161, 294, 295; recapitulation of her story by Peter, 162, 296; recognition of his brothers, 162, 163; his mother requests to be baptized, 163, 301, 302; his mother receives baptism, 165, 305; discussion with the old workman about genesis, 183–190, 308; recognition of his father in the old workman, 190, 191; his father recognized by his mother, 191, 307; a suggestion made by, to Peter, 193; discussion with his father respecting good and evil, 194 seq.; Niceta's admonition to, 196; his discourse on the heathen cosmogony and mythology, 197–200; happy ending of his family history, 210, 307; baptism of his father, 210.

Clementina, meaning of, viii, 69; discussions of, 69, 70; introductory notice to, 69, 70.

Clementine, Homilies referred to, viii, 15; Recognition referred to, viii, 15.

Cleobius, heretic, vii, 453.

Cleochus (or Clearchus), buried in the Didymaeon at Miletus, vi, 508.

Cleomenes, disciple of Noetus, v, 125, 128.

Cleopas, the mother of, and her rival, viii, 410.

Cleophas marries Anna after the death of Joachim, viii, 382.

Clepsydra, an imperfect measure of time, v, 216.

Clergy, ii, 16; orders and duties of, vii, 493, 494, 501, 502; subordination of orders of, 499, 500.

Cleronomus, an Irenarch, i, 40.

Cletus, bishop of Rome, viii, 76.

Climacteric periods, viii, 185.

"Climates" in astrology, viii, 189; the doctrine of, untenable, 189.

Clinton referred to, iii, 6.

Felicitas, martyrdom of, iii, 697, 703, 704.

Felicissimus, and his followers excommunicated, v, 316; his crimes, 338; authors of schism, 415.

Felix, epistle of, to Cyprian, v, 406.

Felix of Amaccora, on baptism, v, 569.
of Bagai, " " v, 567.
of Bussacene, " " v, 571.
of Gurgites, " " v, 571.
of Marazana, " " v, 570.
of Uthina, " " v, 568.

Felix Subscribonius, Epistle of Pontianus to, viii, 622.

Female prophetess, the, viii, 242; a deceiver, 242.

Fenelon referred to, iii, 239.

Fescennine verses, sung at marriages, vi, 482.

Festivals and fasts, Christian, iv, 112.

Fetiales, the forms of the, neglected, vi, 460.

Fever, a child cured by a bandage from the child Jesus, viii, 410.

Few shall be saved, viii, 239.

Fidus, epistle of, to Cyprian, v, 353.

Fifth day, the, of creation, ii, 101.

Figurative teaching of Scripture and philosophy, ii, 449.

Figure, of the Apostles, i, 215; of the Eucharist, 215.

Fillets, worn by suppliants, vi, 498.

Filthy speaking and acts, reproved, ii, 250.

Fire, principle of life, vii, 58; a primal principle, according to Simon Magus, v, 79; the origin of all things, vi, 437; the power of, viii, 46.

Fire-worship, the origin of, viii, 276; of the Persians, 141.

Firmilian, epistle of, to Cyprian, v, 406.

First-fruits, how to be offered and used, vii, 494, 497.

Fish, Israel may not eat, spiritual significance of, i, 143.

Fisher referred to, iv, 595.

Five, the number, the frequent use of in Scripture, i, 394, 395.

Flattery, on, i, 58; or magic, which the more potent, viii, 257.

Flesh, the, as nourished by the body of the Lord, incorruptible, i, 486; in the resurrection, our, capable of bearing the conditions of eternal life or eternal death, iii, 591; made capable of salvation, i, 527, 528; iii, 524; quickened, i, 537; saved by the Word taking flesh, 541; the saints having suffered, shall receive their rewards in, 561, 562; works of the, 536 seq.; iii, 578; we shall be judged in the, vii, 519; desires of the, to be subdued, viii, 144; persons, who first ate, the, 273; and blood, i, 534, 535; of Christ, as real, denied by certain heretics, iii, 521, who therefore deny his true nativity, 522, and attribute falsehood to him, 523, shown by the appearance of angels in human

body, and of the dove, 523, 542; really suffered and rose again, 525-6; not sidereal and unborn, 526; recognizes human relations, 527, 543; pure, yet natural and human, not angelic, 530, 533, 535; distinct from soul, not spiritual, 533, 534; born by miracle, as Adam, 536; proved by gospel history of his birth, presentation, and prophecies, 538-41; a treatise by Tertullian on the flesh of Christ, 521 seq., also on the resurrection of, 545 seq.

Flesh of man, exalted by Christ's incarnation, and by his love of man, iii, 523.

Fleury referred to, v, 155.

Flint, people of Pessinus worship a, vi, 510.

Flocks, ii, 54.

Flood, history of the, ii, 106; viii, 85; tradition of, vii, 59; brought as a punishment of evil-doers, viii, 178, 273; the world after the, 86.

Flora, watches over the blossoming of plants, vi, 470; a harlot, 470; shameful actions done openly at games of, 531.

Floralia, the, vi, 531.

Florentinus Pupianus, epistle of Cyprian to, v, 373.

Florinus, i, 568.

Flowers, right use of, taught by nature, iii, 96; Christian use of, iv, 197.

Flute-girl, the Hebrew, and the Apostle Thomas, viii, 536.

Fluonia (or Fluvionia), a name of Juno, vi, 472.

Folly, ii, 49; of arguments derived from numbers, letters, and syllables, i, 393; of idolatry, viii, 139, 146.

Fons, son of Janus, vi, 471.

Food, all kinds to be received with thanksgiving, vii, 469.

Foods, spiritual significance of Mosaic precepts respecting different kinds of, i, 143 seq.

Foot-baths, ii, 92.

Foreknowledge, viii, 240; of God, i, 178; viii, 246; not the cause of events, iv, 440; no proof of divinity, 539; of Moses, viii, 247.

Forewarned, forearmed, viii, 229.

Forgiveness, of sin, i, 200; of injuries, duty of, vii, 417.

Forks, Caudine, overthrow of Romans at, vi, 477.

Form of sound words, the, viii, 175.

Forms and types, viii, 176.

Fornication, viii, 219; what constitutes, ii, 581; its effects, viii, 10, 12.

Forswearing, how to be treated, viii, 640.

Fortitude, religious duty of, vii, 250.

Fortuna Virginalis, maidens' garments offered to, vi, 460.

Fortunatus, i, 21; schismatic bishop, v, 342, 415; epistle of Cyprian to, 335; a treatise addressed to,

496; a poem on Easter by, vii, 329.

Fortunatus of Tuccaboris, on baptism, v, 567.

Fortune, a deity, vi, 459; no goddess, vii, 97; one of the Penates, according to Caesius, vi, 474, 475; represented with a horn filled with fruit, 517; not man's adversary, vii, 99.

Forty days before the passion of Christ should be a fast day, viii, 668.

Foulkes referred to, iv, 383.

Fountains, ii, 51.

Four, number, mystical meaning of, vii, 341; gospels, why? i, 428; covenants, 429.

Four living creatures of the Apocalypse, symbols of the four Evangelists and of the life and works of our Lord, vii, 348.

Fourth day, of the week, kept as a fast, or " Stationary Day," vii, 341; of creation, ii, 100.

Fraction of the Bread, vii, 535, 536, 544, 548, 557, 566, into parts for the faithful, 559, 567.

Fragments, from Justin's lost writings, i, 300-2; of Clement Alexandrinus, ii, 571-87; from commentaries of Hippolytus, v, 163.

Frauds, pious, singular illustrations of, viii, 206-9; of the Decretals as demonstrated by Dupin, 605 seq.

Free choice is given to the soul, viii, 45.

Free schools of the Christians, ii, 78.

Free-will, ii, 581; possessed by all, iv, 240, 265, 267, 290; condition of all obedience, iv, 51; vi, 362; in angels, i, 250, 270; in man, 250, 270, 518, 519; ii, 69, 105; vi, 204; viii, 144, 183; God's gift to man, vi, 342, 362, necessary to man's nature, vi, 458; baffles astrology, viii, 195; the origin of sin, ii, 319, 362, 363; iv, 51, 292; necessary to faith and repentance, ii, 349; condition of judgment, 353; proofs of, 424, 426, 437, 502, 524; power of choosing salvation, 441; source of obedience, 519, 527, 528; iii, 302, and of faith, 525, 527, 528; choice of virtue, 525; man's likeness to God in, 301; error of Basilides, 444; illustrated by Plato, 475; controlled not by desire but by reason, iv, 303; Scripture proofs of, 305; instance of Pharaoh answered, 309; illustrated from nature, 310, and from the parable of the Sower, 314; proof of God's justice, 320; implies man's co-working with God, 321, 328; objections answered, 324; definition of, 347, 383; Methodius concerning, vi, 356 seq.

Freedom and nature, on, viii, 726.

Freedom, of the will, viii, 119; of man, 286.

Friday-evening, service appointed by the Apostles, viii, 668.

Friends of the Son of God, the, viii, 183.

Friendship, how threefold, ii, 369; with God, how secured, viii, 84; and philanthropy, 297.

Frontispicists (physiognomy), art of the, v, 32.

Fronto, i, 50.

Frugality, a mark of Christian living, ii, 280; examples of, 281.

Frugifer, a god with lion's face called, vi, 510.

Fruit of the belly and of the loins, i, 453.

Fruits worthy of repentance, ii, 38.

"*Fuga, De, in persecutione*," a treatise by Tertullian, iv, 116 seq.

Fuller, referred to, iv, 13.

Fulvius, censor, story of, vii, 52.

Fulvana, Fulvanus, and Erva, demoniac nobles, are healed by Matthew, viii, 529; are baptized, 529; the king is enraged with, 529.

Funeral pomp reproved, iv, 217.

Funeral rites, heathen, iii, 545.

Funerals, Christian rites at, vii, 464.

Furies, the, vi, 471, 500; the three, vii, 185.

Furni, epistle of Cyprian to the people of, v, 367.

Fürst referred to, iii, 331; iv, 329, 380.

Future and the present, viii, 310.

Future judgment, testimonies to, v, 291.

Gabinius, the consul, vi, 462.

Gabriel, v, 180, 181; sent to Mary to announce the birth of Jesus, viii, 364; sent to Joseph, 389; receives the soul of Joseph, 392; pleads for men, 580.

Gad, the brother of King Gundaphoros, his sickness and death, viii, 539, 540; caught away by angels, he is shown the heavenly palace built for his brother by the Apostle Thomas, 540; is allowed to return to the earth to obtain the heavenly palace for the king, 540; is permitted by the king to occupy the palace, 540; is sealed by Thomas, 541.

Gad, the patriarch, speaks of his youth, viii, 29, of his hatred against Joseph, 29, of his punishment, 30; warns his children against hatred, 29, and envy, 30; his death and burial, 30.

Gaetuli, afflicted with droughts because of the Christians, vi, 417.

Gain, gods of, vi, 478.

Gaius, i, 85, 91.

Galatians, Christianity attested by mighty works among the, vi, 438.

Galaticism, charge of, refuted, iv, 111.

Galerius, persecutor, stirred up by his mother against the Christians, vii, 305; edict against them, 306; his cruelty and oppression, 309, 314; recognizes Constantine as emperor, 311; invasion of Italy and retreat, 312; stricken

with incurable disease, 314; edict in favor of Christians, and death, 315.

Gallandi referred to, vi, 120.

Galli, priests of the Great mother, vi, 424; beat their breasts, wailing for Attis, 496.

Gallicanism, extinguished by , Pope Pius ix, viii, 643.

Gallus, emperor, persecutor of Christians, vi, 106; mutilation of a daughter of, 492, 495.

Gamaliel, stills a tumult raised against the apostles, viii, 94; his speech, 94, 95.

Games, Greek, in Africa, iii, 638.

Gams referred to, ii, 4.

Ganymede, vii, 21; carried off to satisfy Jupiter's lust, vi, 506; represented on the stage in ballets, 531.

Garamantes, the tawny, vi, 508.

Garment of baptism, the, how it may be spotted, viii, 142.

Gate, guardians of the, Roman superstition, iii, 643.

Gaudomeleta, viii, 477.

Gaul, innumerable Christians in, vi, 417; laws in, viii, 731; bishops of, Epistle of Callistus to, viii, 614.

Gauls, why called Galatians, vii, 323.

Geese, the guardians of the Capitol, vi, 515.

Gehazi, an example of circumspect behavior, viii, 65.

Gehenna, meaning of, iv, 584; punishments of, v, 584.

Geli, laws of the, viii, 730.

Gellius quoted, vii, 232.

Gelones, customs of the, viii, 188.

Gemini, types of those born under, v, 33.

Geminius of Furni, on baptism, v, 571.

Genealogies, fabulous heathen, ii, 96; of Christ, vi, 126, 139; of St. Matthew and Luke, both of Joseph, vii, 360.

Generation, of man, in what sense God's work, vi, 312; proof of the resurrection of the body, 368; not spontaneous, vii, 60; an illustration of divine providence, viii, 173; the angel of, 49.

Genesis, viii, 234, 254; discussion about, 166; does and regulates all things, 166, 167, 305; prayer inconsistent with, 168, 305; further discussions about, 176 seq., 182 seq., 306, 308; not it, but free-will, determines the history of men, 188; divided into seven parts or *climates*, 189; the Gospel more powerful than, 189; inconsistent with the justice of God, 189; stubborn facts in support of, 190; the difficulties cleared up by recognitions, 190.

Genesis, the truth of its testimony, ii, 103; a poem, iv, 132, 166; commentaries on, v, 163; beginning of in Hebrew according to some, iii, 600.

Genii, of husbands, invoked at marriages, vi, 460; of states, 420.

Genius Jovialis, said to be one of the Penates, vi, 474, 475.

Gentile cosmogony, viii, 197.

Gentile nations, their universal acceptance of sacrifice, vii, 530.

Gentiles, the call of, viii, 88, 145; expectation of, 145; invitation to, 146; conversion of, i, 253, 260, 264, 265; more difficult than that of the Jews, 495; counsel to the, iv, 209.

Gentilism, buttress of, viii, 200.

Geometry, ii, 65; mystery of, 499–501.

German critics, strictures on, ii, 126.

Germanicus, his constancy, i, 39.

Germans, irruptions of the, regarded as special calamities caused by the Christians, vi, 415.

Germanus, epistle of Dionysius of Alexandria, against, vi, 103.

Germination of seeds, illustrating divine providence, viii, 172.

Gesenius referred to, iii, 331; iv, 329, 380; viii, 10.

Ghosts, the Lares said to be, vi, 475.

Giants, viii, 85; their progeny, ii, 142; origin of, viii, 273.

Gibbon, on Lactantius, vii, 300; referred to, i, 187; ii, 57, 92, 147; iii, 58; iv, 468.

Gideon, a type, i, 445, 571.

Gieseler referred to, iv, 495, 504, 542, 579.

Gifts, the, of the Holy Spirit, i, 533; miraculous and prophetic object of, vii, 480, 481.

Girdle, the, of Adam, a sign of repentance, i, 457.

Girl, a, cured of the leprosy by the water in which the infant Jesus was washed, viii, 407.

Gladiatorial shows, wickedness of, v, 277, 576, 577.

Gladiators, ii, 75.

Gloria in Excelsis, vii, 490, 542.

Gnidus, statue of Venus at, loved by a young man, vi, 516.

Gnosis, true wisdom, revealed by God, ii, 494.

Gnostic, speculation, fundamental object of, i, 311; true (Christian), as defined by Clement of Alexandria, ii, 342, 358, 369, 370; his contempt for pain and poverty, 412; divine contemplation, 414; object of life, 418; trained by Christian knowledge, 433, 438; perfected by martyrdom, 433; seeks good for itself, 434–7, and knowledge, 495; philosophic testimony to, 436; how regards earthly things, 439; an imitator of God, 440; freed from passion and perturbation, 496; uses all knowledge, 498; conjectures things future, 501, 521; alone attains perfection, 502; represses sensual desire, 503; worshipper of God, 523; attains likeness to Christ, 526; knowledge, 527; content, self-control, 528; his

130; testimony of the prophets, 133; distinguished from matter, 135; how revealed in the Old Testament, iii, 32; acknowledged in various ways, 176, though his gifts are perverted by man, 80; known by science only as manifested in Christ, ii, 438; knowledge of, a divine gift, 464; excellent, viii, 245; his best gift to man, iii, 299, because necessary to self-knowledge, iv, 181, as proved by order of nature, 182, and by nature of man, 182; this shown by philosophers, ii, 464, 465; how far revealed to the heathen, 474, 475; knowledge of, in Greek philosophy, 489; the true doctrine of God, the creator, iii, 297 seq.; he elects and rejects according to desert, 315, is the Father of mercies as creator, 452; eternal as God, but not as Lord, 498; a body (corporeal soul) as well as spirit, 602; is not to be confounded with the world, vii, 265; ruler of nations, iv, 666; government of the Jews, 193; how to be glorified, viii, 48; how to be conceived, 45; belief in him intuitive, vi, 421; shall be seen by the pure in heart, 122; the ways of, 231; he begets the Son, one with himself, vii, 105, 109, 132; the honor of, vindicated in the incarnation, iii, 524; why incarnate, vii, 242; why he reveals himself to man, iv, 500; because his Saviour, viii, 44; is to be loved more than parents, 154; he will be all in all, iv, 345; seen with the spiritual body, 624; manifested by the Word, 603, 604; knowledge of, in a future life, 298; endowed man with freedom of will, viii, 724; why he has made vile creatures, 176; the folly of sitting in judgment on, 181; fore-knowledge of, 246; decrees of, 246; disparagements of, 247; the, of the Jews, 254; indicated as blameless, 272; neither the world nor any part of it to be considered as being, 283; creatures avenge the cause of, 286; is philanthropic, 298; the shape of, in man, 316; the character of, 317; man in the shape of, 319; the figure of, 320; the centre or heart of the universe, 320; the nature and shape of, 320; the fear and love of, 321; misconceptions respecting, in the Old Testament, 329; not blamable for permitting the existence of the devil, 322; produced the evil one, but not evil, 334; the maker of the devil, 334; his power of changing himself, 341; not the author of the evil one, in the manner as he is of the good one, 341; why he appoints the evil one over the wicked, 342; of

Simon Magus, unjust, 113; unrevealed, 325; defects ascribed to, by Simon Magus, 245, refuted by Peter, 246.

God, of this world, the, i, 420, 575.

God, the Son of, viii, 315.

God, what is not, viii, 297.

Gods, the execrable, of the heathen, a fragment concerning, iii, 149, 150.

Gods, the so-called, in the Old Testament, i, 419; false, their vain pretensions, 292; abandoned by Christians, 171; of the heathen, ii, 68, 91, many so-called, viii, 108; human origin of, iii, 26, 142; men, as shown by Ennius and Euhemerus, vii, 26; possess sex, 28; human passions attributed to, vi, 417; not underrated, 420, 422; absurdities concerning, i, 69; iv, 203 seq., 184–186; how interpreted, iii, 140, 141; not justified by allegorical interpretation, vi, 502–506; their immoralities, i, 91; their vile character, iii, 28, unworthy character, 138; examples of vice, 143, 148; vices of, and patrons of vice, vii, 30, 146, 227; their wickedness, i, 113, 174–185; absurdities and cruelty of their worship, i, 92, 183; iii, 29, 39; impious rites of worship, iv, 187, 188, 191; their temples, tombs, i, 184; their worship a late invention, iii, 40; origin of their worship, vii, 32, 63; worshipped for their crimes, vi, 432; why they are worshipped being so vile, viii, 200, 254; adulterers, 259, evil influence of the example of the, 255; attempted explanation of the bad actions ascribed to, 200 seq., 256; cannot give blessings, iii, 49; impotent to help, 146; despicable when made, i, 94; valuable when purchased, 94; despised by heathen as well as by Christians, iii, 118, 119, 120; Varro's threefold division of, 129; their number and officers, 139, 144; recognized by Romans, iv, 176; Roman, how classified, iii, 137, their rites, vii, 32, speculations of philosophers on, iii, 131; cannot include the elements, 131; called elements by Zeno, iv, 184; name not from verb of motion, iii, 132; stars regarded as, vii, 32; heavenly bodies not gods, nor subject to change, iii, 134; attributes given by poets to heroes, 135; objects deified by different nations, 136; divers doctrines concerning, i, 112; Homer and Herod concerning, 95; their genealogy, 96; not really gods, viii, 260; imitation of, 260; really wicked magicians, 266; their existence not proved, vi, 465; the contemporaries of, did not look on them as being gods, viii, 266, 267; those which are made by hands are

not, 281; of the worshippers, like the worshippers, 202; the, which have not made the heavens, 289; of the Egyptians, 282; how consecrated, instances of Ceres and Liber, vii, 30; their rites vain, 33, 203, and depraving, 64; things sacred to, viii, 199; kinds of sacrifice offered to them, vii, 32; demons, 64, 130; vainly worshipped by images, 67; religion of, 203; supper of the, viii, 203; graves of the, 266; vilely represented in heathen mythology, vi, 466, 469, 470–2, 482–8; proved false by its contradictory fables, 473–82; tutelary, belief in, absurd, 477–82, crimes and vices attributed to, 482–99, 539, 540; deities not honored by temples and images, 508–10, nor by sacrifices, 518, nor by incense and wine, 528, nor by other heathen rites, 530; anthropomorphic ideas of false, 532; what has become of them, i, 94; have no power over Christians, vi, 418; why not acknowledged by Christians, 464, 507; witness to Christianity, iii, 38.

Golden age fabled under Saturn, vii, 142, 230; exists in obedience to God, 143.

Golden rule, the, viii, 268, 285, 299.

Good and evil, viii, 129, 193.

Good one, the, and the evil one, the different origins of, viii, 341.

Good out of evil, viii, 223.

Good, the sufferings of the, viii, 298.

Good, the, is to be done, ii, 25; the chief, opinions on, 374, 375; vii, 74, 76, 234; nature of, 77; in immortality alone, 80, 235; not in bodily life, 74, 80; not without evil, 75.

Good works, necessity of, viii, 155.

Goodness, divine, not inconsistent with justice, ii, 225; none without liberty, viii, 121; and justice defined, 324; essential to God, not to any created being, iv, 260; instance of St. Peter, 265; identical (in God) with his justice, 278; goodness of rational beings destroyed through free will, 292.

Gospel, the, the success of, viii, 89; preached at Rome, 225, and at Alexandria, 225; gives power over demons, 133; more powerful than genesis, 189; the objections to, apply yet more to heathen mythology, vi, 429; its language defended, 430; its effects shown in the lives of Christians, 435; read by the deacon, vii, 535, 553; salutation of, 562; reading of the, should be heard standing, viii, 668; of Peter, Serapion on the, 775.

Gospels, apocryphal, list of, viii, 351–354.

Government, civil, of God, to be obeyed, i, 552; iii, 647.

Hemerobaptists, Jewish heretics, vii, 452.

Henna, grove of, whence Proserpine was carried off, vi, 503.

Henotes, i, 332.

Hephaestus, shortcomings of, viii, 740.

Hera and Pallas, viii, 264.

Heracleius, or Heracleides, ordained bishop of Cyprus, viii, 495.

Heracleon, agrees in substance with Valentinus, iii, 652; opinion of, concerning the body of Jesus, v, 89.

Heraclides quoted, ii, 182.

Heraclitus, i, 178, 191, 274; ii, 66, 403; philosophy of, v, 13, 126, 157; origin of Noetian heresy, 126, 158; referred the origin of all things to fire, vi, 437; quoted, ii, 181, 446, 470, 471, 476, 484.

Herculanus, epistle of Cyprian to, v, 315.

Hercules, i, 170, 172, 192; ii, 66, 69; viii, 265; life and death, vii, 18, 31; vices, 226; rites in honor of, 36; fable about, invented by the devil, i, 233; his unworthiness in fable, iii, 143; an inferior character, 143; burned alive after punishment, vi, 422, 424; son of Jupiter and Alcmena, 460, 485; this the Theban defended by his club and hide, 483; worshipped as divine, 462, 465; a mortal, deified, 474; wounded by Hippocoon's children, 484; entangled in robe of Nessus, 488; violated the fifty daughters of Thestius, 485; wounded Dis and Juno, 484; put an end to human sacrifices in Italy, 460; was a slave at Sardis, 484; burned on Mount Œta after an attack of epilepsy, 484; the Theban, burned on Mount Œta, 422; the Phoenician, buried in Spain, 422; six gods named, 480; deified because he subdued robbers, wild beasts, and serpents, 423.

Heresies, origin of, i, 410; ii, 554; iii, 257, 477, 598; iv, 469; vii, 133; foretold, iii, 243; vi, 338; how originated, vi, 241; originate in heathen philosophy, v, 10; offspring of heathen philosophy, iii, 246; characteristics of, v, 47, 100; proceed from self-will, iii, 245; never rest in truth, 248; how regarded by Christians, iv, 570; contemporaneous, v, 125, 155; no argument against Christian belief, ii, 549, 550; aid in discovering the truth, 508; tested by Scripture, 551; founded on opinion, 555; vi, 241; authors of, ii, 555; their analogy with bodily disease, iii, 243; condemned by St. Paul, 245; their false pretence of St. Paul's authority, 254; have no succession from Apostles, 258; a mockery of Christian truth, 264; warnings against, 245; epitome of, v, 140; twelve *heresies,*

anathemized, vi, 50–53; treatise of Irenaeus against, i, 309–567; by Tertullian against, iii, 648 seq., and heretics, to be avoided, vii, 450, 451, 457, 458, 461; forbidding marriage, meat, and wine, 453.

Heresy, Adam's sin, iii, 298.

Heretical baptism, acts and records of, noted, v, 653; not to be repeated, 667, but completed by imposition of hands, 668, 673, but valid without such complement, 669, 673; note from Eusebius on, 678.

Heretics, views of early, i, 34, 56, 62, 63, 68, 71, 80, 82, 87, 88, 89, 138; confirm the Catholics in the faith, 212; resort to Scripture to support their opinions, 319, 343, 344; iii, 250; have no right to Scripture, 251; modes of initiation practised by, i, 346; their inconsistency, 322; style themselves spiritual, 403; their perverse interpretation of Scripture, 369; iii, 251, 261; their irregularity of conduct and discipline, 263; their women teachers, 263; feign three kinds of men, i, 323; have fallen into an abyss of error, 370; fabric idols with words, iii, 613; their Christology, 623; cannot give true baptism, v, 376–385, 425, 565–572, nor attain true martyrdom, 384, 426; appoint bishops without ordination, 424; have not Christ's presence, 425; types of, in the Old Testament, 427; compared with the lapsed, 427; why favored by certain confessors, 427; the first order of productions maintained by (viz., aeons) indefensible, i, 373; borrow their system from the heathen, 376; miracles claimed to be wrought by, 407; blasphemous doctrine of, further exposed, 408; follow neither Scripture nor tradition, 415; refutation of, from the orderly succession of bishops in the churches, 415; tossed about by every wind of doctrine, 458; unlearned, ignorant, and divided in opinion, 547; their pretexts for licentiousness, ii, 385; claim all carnal things as lawful, 388, 404; condemn marriage, 389, 392, 404; character of, 555; first heretics post-apostolic, 555, 556; St. John's course regarding, 577; to be avoided, i, 547; to be shunned, viii, 630; how to be treated, 631; work to pull down, iii, 243; prefer loose company, 264; ungodliness the effect of the teaching of, 264; the prescription against, a treatise by Tertullian, 243; the peculiar place assigned to, in the region of the damned, viii, 579.

Hermae at Athens like Alcibiades, vi, 511.

Hermammon, epistle of Dionysius of Alexandria to, vi, 106.

Hermas, of St. Paul, ii, 4, 56; brother of Pius, 4, 56; the pastor of, 7, 9–55; date of, 7; apocryphal and erroneous, iv, 85, 101; called "angelic," 156; known to the East, but little in the West, ii, 7; question of authorship, 7; versions and manuscripts of, 7; written in Italy, 7; the morals of, 6; introductory note to, 3–8; elucidation on, 56–58; on creation of matter, iv, 252; on interpretation of Scripture, 359; quoted by Irenaeus, 6; referred to, i, 341, 348, 357, 360, 422, 488, 510.

Hermes Trismegistus, his opinion concerning God, i, 289; vii, 15; on immortality, 210; on the last days, 215.

Hermippus, on the Jews, iv, 402; quoted, ii, 317.

Hermogenes, origin of his heresy, iii, 259; his character, 477, 629; maintains eternity of matter, 479; making matter divine, yet not equal to God, 480, and God the author of evil, 482; makes matter neither corporeal nor incorporeal, and neither good nor evil, 498; opinion of, v, 122, 148; his theory of the soul refuted, iii, 191; a treatise of Tertullian against, 477 seq.

Hermotimus, story by, iii, 223.

Hero, deacon of Antioch, Epistle of Ignatius to him, wherein he is exhorted, cautioned, instructed, and pointed out as the future bishop of Antioch, i, 113–115, 123.

Hero-worship, viii, 141, 276.

Herod, an Irenarch, i, 40, 43; a roaring lion, 250.

Herod, mocked by the Magi, seeks to kill Jesus, viii, 389, 406; slaughters the infants in Bethlehem, 366, 376, 420; Jesus sent to, by Pilate, 429; the death of, 389; in Tartarus, 572; wishes to have his statue in the temple of Armenia, 702; is refused by Abgar, 702; indignant, sends his nephew against Abgar, is killed, 702.

Herodians maintained Herod to be Christ, iii, 649.

Herodotus, v, 69; referred to, i, 12, 410; ii, 92, 112, 144, 279, 285, 484, 485, 521; iii, 37, 138, 146, 225, 686; iv, 6, 198, 433, 453, 474, 558, 559, 561, 590, 636, 642; v, 44, 69; viii, 19.

Heroes of immense and huge bodies, vi, 462.

Heroic ages, incense unknown in the, vi, 528.

Hesiod, poetical origin of the muses, v, 22; on the gods, ii, 95; on the generation of the gods, vii, 14; cosmogony of, viii, 200; referred to, i, 389; ii, 95, 96, 142, 144, 182, 192, 277, 279, 282, 304, 307,

Homilies, fragments of, iv, 238; the, of Clement, introductory notice thereto, viii, 213; relation to the Recognitions, 70, 73, 213; editions of, 213; contents of, 223–346.

Homily, or sermon, at Holy Communion, vii, 535; on the fall of idols, viii, 656; on Habib, the martyr, 708 seq.; on Guria and Shamuna, 714 seq.

Honesty enjoined, viii, 220.

Honoratus of Thucca, on baptism, v, 571.

Honor deified and worshipped, vi, 476.

Hooker referred to, iii, 70, 689; iv, 58.

Hope, i, 35; vain, of the Jews, 269; Christian, witnessed to by philosophers, ii, 447; objects of, how perceived, 448.

Horace, vii, 45; referred to, i, 403; iii, 71, 176, 177, 178; iv, 112; vi, 261; vii, 45, 149, 153.

Horos, an aeon, i, 317; different names of, 318; iii, 508; faculty of i, 320.

Horoscope, the foundation of astrology, v, 21; impossibility of fixing the, 25, 26.

Horses of the Apocalypse, symbolical meaning of, vii, 350, 351.

Hortensianus of Lares, on baptism, v, 568.

Hosanna, the, vii, 544.

Hosea, prophecy of last days, v, 243.

Hospitality, viii, 295; true principle of, vii, 176; reward of, i, 8; a contest about, viii, 174.

Host, the, not a primitive word, vii, 566.

Hosthanes, grandfather of the Armenian Zoroaster, vi, 428.

Hours, canonical, ii, 12; of prayer, iii, 689, 690, origin of, iv, 108, 109.

Household life, habits of, 251.

Huet referred to, iii, 372, 426.

Human, form, whence attributed to God, i, 278; flesh, not the proper food of man, ii, 153; life, the inequalities of lot in, viii, 338; race, how dispersed, ii, 107; sacrifices, offered to Dis and Saturn, vi, 460.

Humanity, Christian doctrine of, ii, 114; of Christ, iii, 624.

Humility, enjoined, i, 8, 9, 11, 15, 53; of Christ, 9; of saints, 9, 10, 20; Christian, iv, 580.

Husbands, duty of, i, 95, 111.

Huss, i, 188; ii, 62.

Hyacinthus, vi, 485; viii, 199.

Hyginus, bishop of Rome, i, 416, 569; ii, 56.

Hylas, vi, 485.

Hymn, the Cherubic, vii, 540, 554; of the Naasseni, v, 58; of Gnostics, 91; a primitive, based on Isaiah, 218; of the virgins, vi, 351, 352.

Hymnology, early Hebrew, vii, 531.

Hymns, primitive, in the New Testament, vii, 507; to Christ, ii, 295; to the Paedagogus, 296; evening, of Greek Christians, 79, 298; German, vii, 570.

Hyperboreans, vi, 508.

Hyperiona, mother by Jupiter of the second Sun, vi, 480, 483.

Hyperoche, buried in the shrine of Diana, vi, 508.

Hyperides quoted, ii, 484.

Hypocrisy, sin of, vii, 468.

Hypocrites, ii, 50; how regarded, viii, 221; counsel to, iv, 216.

Hypotyposes, or outlines, fragments from, of Theognostus of Alexandria, vi, 155 seq.

Hypsipyle, loved by Apollo, vi, 485.

Hyssop, i, 142.

Hystaspes, i, 169.

I am that I am, i, 419.

Ia, bride of Attis, vi, 492; her blood turned into violets, 492.

Iachus, nursed (or loved) by Ceres, vi, 466.

Ialdabaoth, i, 355; primary aeon of the Ophites, iii, 650.

Ialysus, son of the fourth Sun, vi, 480.

Iambus of Germaniciana, on baptism, v, 570.

Iao, i, 321.

Icarians, the, worship an unhewn log, vi, 510.

"Icthus," iii, 669.

Idaci Dactyli, Greek name of Digiti Samothracii, vi, 475.

Idleness, perniciousness of, viii, 58.

Idol, meaning of the word, iii, 62.

Idolatry, absurdities of, ii, 92; folly of, viii, 139, 146, 284; in wider sense includes all sin, iii, 61; not confined to acts of worship, 62; origin of the name, 62; origin of, viii, 137; originated in Egypt, vii, 63; includes idol-

his parents to Jerusalem, and tarries after them, 398, 414; makes a dried fish live, 400; feat of, in the dyer's shop, 412; turns three boys into kids, 413; crowned king by boys, 413; heals a boy of a serpent's bite, 413, 414; the priests and scribes conspire against, and accuse before Pilate, 416 seq., 426 seq., 468; Judas betrays, 468, 469; the standards of the soldiers bend down before, 417, 440; message of Pilate's wife respecting, 417, 428, 440; Pilate desires to release, 417 seq., 427; Nicodemus and others appear as witnesses for, 419, 428, 442; is sentenced to death, 420, 429, 443; is led forth to crucifixion, 429; the accusation of, placed over his cross, 420, 443; crucified between two malefactors, 420, 430, 443; wonderful events which occurred at his crucifixion. 421, 430, 431, 443, 461; Joseph of Arimathæa begs and takes down the body of, 421, 431, 443; the guard placed at the tomb of, report his resurrection, and are bribed by the Jews to lie, 422, 433, 444; other witnesses of his resurrection are also persuaded and bribed to be silent, 422, 433, 444, 445; Nicodemus proposes to the council that search be made for, which is accordingly done, but in vain, 422, 433, 445; lamentation of Mary and the other women for, 431; raised others when he rose himself, 435; testimony of those raised by, 435 seq.; the descent of, into Hades, 435 seq., 456 seq.; triumphs over Satan in Hades, 437, 457; delivers Adam and his posterity from Hades, 437, 451, 557; sets up his cross in Hades, 458; the miracles of, reported by Pilate, 460 seq., 462 seq.; at the mention of the name of, the gods fall in the senate-house in Rome, 464; Veronica's portrait of, 466; seamless tunic of, worn by Pilate in the presence of Tiberius: its strange effect, 466; the wonderful works wrought by, related by Nathan to Titus, 472, and by Velosianus to Tiberius, 475.

Jesus, meets Peter departing from Rome to avoid persecution, and tells him he is coming to be crucified for him, 485; appears to Philip at Ophioryma, and rebukes his revengeful spirit, 501, 509; Philip's prayer to, 502 seq.; appears to Andrew to send him to the country of the man-eaters, 517; appears again to Andrew as a pilot, and conducts him by the sea to the place of his destination, 518; Andrew's narrative of the ministry and works of, 519 seq.; appears to Andrew as a beautiful little child, 521; appears again to

Andrew in prison, 524; appears to Andrew and Peter as a child, 527; appears as a child to Matthew on the mountains, 528; Abgarus' letter to, 558, 651, 652; reply of Jesus, 652; sends his picture to Abgarus, 558; appears at the burial of Mary, 598; raises Mary from the tomb, and brings her to paradise, 598.

Jewell quoted, iii, 266, 267; iv, 170.
Jewelry, Christian use of, ii, 267.
Jewish sacrifices abolished, i, 137; institutions and laws older than Greek philosophy, ii, 324–333; customs, viii, 189, and Marcionite error, community of, iii, 324; Christians, two classes of, iii, 433.

Jews, history of, vii, 108, allegorical, iv, 517, 518–21; their true origin, 512, not Egyptian rebels, 467; the chosen people, iii, 34, why, iv, 556; in favor with God, 565; examples of prayer to Christians, vii, 423; prophets of, iv, 412; charged with removing passages from the Scriptures, i, 234, 235; system of the religion of, v, 138; animosity of, viii, 91; observances of, i, 62, 82; superstitions of, 26; rites of, vii, 118; neglect mercy and charity, v, 530–33; humility and patience, 534, trust in God, 535; fear of God, 539, forgiveness, 541; exacting usury, 546; accuse Christ, i, 253; persecute him, v, 220, and reject him, v, 509; viii, 90, and the prophets, 508; by rejecting Christ reject God, i, 267, are punished, iv, 433, 506, and conquered, iii, 40, and rejected by God, v, 510; vii, 241; blame Christians for not observing the law, i, 199, 203; hate Christians, 214, 247, who pray for the, 266; obstinacy of, 232, 266; especially in disputations, 256, and in interpreting 'the Scriptures, 261; they violate the eternal law, and interpret ill that of Moses, 200; they still expect the Messiah, v, 138; not understanding why circumcision, i, 202, which differs from the Christian, 256, the law, 203, choice of meats was given, 204; nor why the Sabbath, sacrifices and oblations were instituted, 205, they do injury to God by their opinion of the law, 206; excellent as were their laws, iv, 510, and rites, 511, their customs, iii, 95, and ceremonies not binding on Christians, vii, 462, their law and priesthood abrogated and the temple destroyed, v, 511; they boast in vain that they are the sons of Abraham, i, 206, 269, and are apostate through idolatry, iii, 151; v, 508; forsake God before forsaken by him, iv, 193, and are not heirs of the covenant, i, 138, 139; their history a

witness of Christ, iii, 34; verifies prophecy, iv, 465, and miracles, 466; dispersion of, vii, 123; prophecies of the rejection of, 451, 452; why taken captive, 461; they were divinely taught, iv, 562, their learning acknowledged by heathen authors, iv, 402, yet not understanding the Scripture, v, 509; their unbelief unreasonable, iv, 446, 452, 461, but a means to the calling of the Gentiles, 463, who take their place, v, 512, 513; and Gentiles, relative position of, illustrated, iii, 151; error of the, clue to the, 172 seq.; heresies of, vii, 452; sects of, v, 134; viii, 91, Esseni, v, 134, Pharisees, 137, Sadducees, 137, chronology of, 148–149; discussion with the apostles, viii, 92–93; counsel to the, iv, 210; admonished to accept Christ as the Saviour, v, 518; viii, 94, as salvation for them is only in Christ, i, 207, 216, 217, which they can obtain by repentance and conversion, 258, 268; his Baptism and Cup replaces the rites of the, v, 514; he is the acknowledged God of, viii, 110, the wisdom and Word of God, v, 515, 516, divine, 517, incarnate, 519, born in Bethlehem, 520, of low estate, 520, the Lamb slain, 521, the Stone, 522, the Bridegroom, 523, crucified, 524, risen and exalted, 525, revealing the Father, 526, Judge and King, 527; an answer to the, by Tertullian, iii, 151 seq.; treatise by Hippolytus concerning the, v, 219.

Jezebel, her eyes painted, v, 193.
Joachim, his wealth, charity, and offerings, viii, 361, 369; taunted by the high-priest on account of his childlessness — grieved, he goes away to the mountains, 361, 369, 384; his wife Anna, 361 seq., 369; visited by an angel, who announces the birth of a child to him, 362, 370, 384; his offerings of gratitude, 362; feast of, 361.

Job, 1, 9, 81, 89, 111, 119; an example of patience, iii, 716, of offerings, v, 481; faith of, vi, 401; book of, by Moses, 381.

John, the Baptist, i, 81; ii, 62; saved by his mother from Herod's wrath, viii, 366; precursor of Christ, i, 220, 221; pretypified by Samson's boy, 572; his birth, 575; a voice of the Word, ii, 174; baptism of, iii, 674; Christ's message to, 375, 427; the link between the old and new dispensation, 404; in Hades, announces the coming thither of Jesus, viii, 435, 449, 456; the disciples of, 92; refuted, 93; Simon Magus formerly a disciple of, 233.

of the week, vii, 417; by the bishop, in presence of presbyters and deacons, 417; sentences to be in proportion to sin, 418; instances from the story of Susanna and from heathen tribunals, 419.

Judith, i, 20; Anna's handmaid, viii, 361.

Julian referred to, i, 195.

Julian, a Magian, vi, 428.

Julian, of Apamea, vi, 336.

Julianus, of Marcelliana, on baptism, v, 572.

Julianus, of Telepte, on baptism, v, 570.

Julius Africanus, life and works, vi, 123, 124, 140; on the genealogies of Christ, 125, 126 seq., 139; narrative of events in Persia, at the birth of Christ, 127 seq.; fragments of the chronography of, 130 seq.; on the passion of Symphorosa and her seven sons, 138 seq.

Junius referred to, i, 20.

Junius, of Neapolis, on baptism, v, 572.

Juno, vi, 459, 465, 483; viii, 107; daughter of Saturn and Ops, vi, 460; queen of the gods, 483; wounded by Hercules, 484; named Lucina, and aiding women in childbirth, 466, 469; said to be the air, 472 (note); destruction of the temple and priestess of, 516, and in the capitol, of the statue of, 516; named Caprotina, Cinxia, Februtis, Fluonia, 472; Ossipagina, Pomona, Populonia, 472; the cestus of, 517 (note); as Cinxia, a branch worshipped for, 510; Samians worship a plank instead of, 510 (note); one of the Penates, 475.

Jupiter, i, 164, 170, 192; the greatest and best, vi, 421; is not God, 421, 422, but both human and immortal, iii, 142; his history, 149, 150; origin, life, name, and death, vii, 20; tomb, 23; his and his sons' sepulchres, viii, 199; had father and mother, vi, 422; his birth, viii, 197; his father, vii, 23; the Saturnian king, vi, 483; son of Aether, 480; son of Coelus, 480; son of Saturn, 480, of Saturn and Ops, 460, 461, 472, 482; the Cretan, vii, 23, born in Crete, vi, 480; nursed by the Curetes, vii, 23, and his life saved by the Curetes, vi, 484; concealed in Crete, 472; buried in Crete, 480, 484, his cries concealed, 475; temples to, vii, 23; his actions, vi, 465, as related by Euhemerus, vii, 24; his licentious life, 227, and wicked deeds, viii, 740; overthrew his father, vi, 484, by going to war with him, viii, 198, 254; made a meal unwittingly on Lycaon's son, vi, 484; incests of, viii, 197, 198, 254; married his sister, vi, 484; attempted to violate the

mother of the gods, 491; adulteries and vile transformations of, viii, 198, 199, 258; lusted after Alcmena, Danae, Electra, Europa, and matrons and maidens without number, vi, 460, 461, 498; even after the boys, Catamitus, 485, 498, and Fabius, 485; ravished his daughter Proserpine, 498; for lustful purposes became an ant, a golden shower, a satyr, 506, a swan, 483, 506, and a bull, 483, 541; spoken of as recounting his amours to his wife, 487; said to be the sun, 472, and by others to be the ether, 472; three gods named, 480; vii, 23; father of Apollo, Diana, Castor and Pollux, Hercules, Liber, Mercury, vi, 460, 483, of the Muses, 473, of the Sun, 480, of Hercules, 485, 488; Diespiter, 460, 461, 482; fall at Dodona of the temple of, 516; destruction of the statue of Capitoline, 516, 534; termed Capitoline, 427, 516, the Thunderer, 516, the Olympian, 512, 513, the Supreme, 460, the Stygian, i.e., Pluto, 460, Verveceus, 497 (note); of Dodona, 419, 516; bulls sacrificed to, 526; represented with a thunderbolt in his right hand, 517, and as driving in a winged chariot, 472; gave power to the Novensiles to wield his thunder, 474; Pales, the steward of, 474; the counsellors of, 474, 475; one of the Penates, 475; represented as an adulterer, 488, and as easily overreached, 489, 490; forced to leave heaven by Numa, 489; statues of, dishonored, 515; descent of rain signified by the embraces of Ceres, 502, 505; the feast of, 531; ludi circenses celebrated in honor of 534; allegory of, viii, 201.

Just one, the, v, 221.

Just man, character of, vii, 183; Cicero's error, 184.

Just, the place of the, viii, 576, 577 seq.

Just and unjust, cannot be distinguished in this world, ii, 32; but will differ in the world to come, 33.

Justa, the Syro-Phoenician woman, viii, 232; becomes a proselyte, 232; adopts two boys whom she educates with Simon Magus, 232.

Justice, demanded for Christians, i, 163; of God, 459; and goodness unite in God, iii, 307, 308, 309; reveal him as father and master, 308; case of the Ninevites, 315; of Adam, of Cain, and of Sodom, 317; their union refutes Marcion's dualism, 320; banished by Jupiter and restored by Christ, vii, 142; made known to all, but embraced by few, 143; argument of Carneades for and against, 158; nature of, 150, 154; source

in piety and equity, 150; answers to objections, 153; of the Christians, 151; violated by persecution, 145, 147; duties of, 151, 247; man's birthright, 225; the worship of God, and true wisdom, 245.

Justification, i, 13, 63, 64; ii, 12, 23; according to Clement, ii, 345, 346.

Justin Martyr, life of, i, 159, 160; studies philosophy, 195; is converted, 195; defends Christianity against Judaism, 194–270; writes two apologies for the Christians, 163–193; his dialogue with Trypho, the Jew, 194–270; discourse to the Greeks, 271, 272; hortatory address to the Greeks, 273–289; on the sole government of God, 290–293; on the resurrection, 294–299; fragments from his lost writings, 300–302; is examined and condemned by Rusticus, 305, 306; adversary of heresy, iii, 506; on the resurrection of the body, vi, 374; order of the divine liturgy given by him, vii, 507; his account of Christian worship, 532; testimony to the Clementine liturgy, 572; concurrence of Irenaeus with, 572; quoted by Anastasius, i, 302, Antonius Melissa, 302, Irenaeus, 300, 468, John of Antioch, 300, John of Damascus, 301, 302, Leontius, 301, Tatian, 300 — relation of Tatian to, ii, 61 — Methodius, vi, 374; referred to, i, 8, 41, 348, 468, 555; viii, 365, 390.

Justinian referred to, iv, 288, 289.

Justinians, oath of the, v, 73.

Justinus, heresy of, origin of the Ophites, v, 69; essentially heathen, 69; his allegory of Herodotus' legend of Hercules, 69–73; summary of his teaching, 145.

Justus, i, 154.

Juturna, wife of Janus, vi, 471.

Juvenal, referred to, i, 341; iii, 53, 87; v, 98; vii, 99.

Juvenalius, Bishop, viii, 478.

Kahnis, referred to, i, 397; iii, 266.

Karinus and Leucius, sons of Simeon, who were raised from the dead when Jesus rose, their narrative of the descent of Christ into Hades, and the deliverance he wrought there, viii, 445–452, 454–458.

Kaye, classification of Tertullian's works, iii, 11, 12; referred to, viz.: —

(Eccles. Hist.) i, 311; ii, 3; iii, 5, 9, 76, 91, 181, 239, 270, 274, 429, 604, 629; iv, 73.

(Illustr.) i, 234, 236, 239, 241, 242, 258, 262, 268, 270.

(Just.) ii, 66, 67, 70, 72, 74, 90, 97, 100, 101, 103, 105, 132, 133, 135, 137, 139, 142,

archs, 486–489; obedience drawn from, iii, 708; union with faith, 711, 717; under worldly loss, 711; violence, 712; bereavement, 713; pleasure of, 713; connection with the Beatitudes, 714; ministers to repentance, 714; connected with charity, 714; bodily, 715; power of spiritual over body, 716; of Job, 716; virtues of, 716; pictures of, 716, 717; of heathen, 717; Tertullian on, 707 seq.; the world's misusage of, 718; sin and result of impatience, v, 489.

Patmos, John sent to, by Domitian, viii, 562.

Patriarch, or *Papa*, prayer for, vii, 551, 553, 556; title, applied to Hippolytus, v, 258.

Patriarchate, the, viii, 642.

Patriarchs, the types of the Holy Trinity, vi, 403; and prophets, foretold the advent of Christ, i, 494, types of evangelists and apostles, iv, 151.

Patrimus, place in the ceremonies of the body called, vi, 486.

Patripassianism, synonym for Monarchianism, iii, 597, 598, 605, 612, 625, 626.

Paul, i, 6, 18, 35, 52, 55, 63, 69, 75, 81, 103, 107, 111, 122, 130; imprisoned seven times, 6, 495; preached no new God, iii, 286, 429; typified in the blessing of Benjamin, and in Saul, 430; Benjamin's blessing applied to, v, 168; enlightened by Christ Himself, therefore an original evangelist, viii, 532; his witness to the Creator, iii, 430; agreement with other apostles in doctrine, 433; teaches the Creator revealed in Christ, 440, 466, and as final Judge, 457; his precepts those of the Old Testament, 468; his Christology, 625; delivers the ordinances, and prescribes order and decorum, vii, 532; calls himself a liturge and hierurge, 552; his norm of the divine liturgy, 506; ministers the Gospel in sacrifice, 532; his teaching in regard to spiritual gifts, iv, 255; is caught up into the third heavens, i, 405; and Peter, founders of the Church of Rome, 415; sometimes uses words not in their grammatical sequence, 420; knew no mysteries unrevealed to the other apostles, 437; refutation of the Ebionites, who disparaged the writings of, 439; his description of anti-Christ, 553; result of his preaching on Mars Hill, ii, 125; late witness of Old Testament truth, 434, 442; persecutor, persecuted and martyr, iii, 647, with Peter, i, 11; beheaded at Rome, viii, 675; canon of, vii, 494; *Acts* of, iv, 246; *Apocalypse of*, viii, 358, 575 seq.; his coming to

Rome opposed by the Jews, 477; invited by the Christians, he sets out for Rome and reaches Syracuse, 477; the Jews kill Dioscorus, mistaking him for, 477; his journey towards Rome, 478; his vision at Tribus Tabernes, 478; reaches Rome, 478; the Jews strive to incite him to speak against Peter — his reply, 478; appeases the contentions between Jews and Gentiles, 479; with Peter opposes Simon Magus, 481; by prayer arrests the flight of Simon, so that he falls and is killed, 484; ordered to be put in irons, 484; sentenced to be beheaded, 484; meets Perpetua on his way to execution, and obtains a handkerchief from her, which is miraculously returned, and restores her sight, 485; the conversion and martyrdom of his executioners, 486; received as he is going to Iconium by Onesiphorus — his personal appearance described, 487; converts Thecla, 487; Acts of, and Thecla, 355, 487 seq.; cast into prison by the governor of Lystra, 489; visited in prison by Thecla, 489; cast out of the city, 489; fasts with Onesiphorus, 489; goes with Thecla to Antioch, 489; contention with Barnabas, 493; the "Revelation" of, found under the foundation of his house at Tarsus, 575; conducted to the "place of the just," 577; conducted to the "place of the wicked," 578; conducted to paradise, 580.

Paul of Samosata, his character and heresies, vi, 169; deposed, 170; epistle by Malchion against, 169, 172; other matters pertaining to, 171, 172.

Paulus of Obba, on baptism, v, 570.

Pausi, vi, 420.

Payne-Smith referred to, vii, 530, 531.

Peace, i, 10; of the universe, 10; of the Church, 19; deified, vi, 476; on earth at the first coming of Christ, iv, 444; given to the lapsed by certain martyrs, v, 299; and strife, proclaimed by Christ, viii, 105; to the sons of, 105; and war, 106; and the sword, 153, 288.

Pearl, parable of, interpreted, ii, 578.

Pearls not to be cast before swine, viii, 117, interpreted, vi, 379.

Pearson referred to, his (*Creed*), i, 176; ii, 71, 474; iv, 383, 582, 608; v, 229, 259. (*Vindic.*), i, 47, 128; ii, 6.

Pelagianus of Luperciana, on baptism, v, 570.

Peleus, father of Achilles, loved by Thetis, vi, 485; and Thetis, Prometheus, Achilles, and Polyxena, viii, 265.

Pellonia, a goddess who repels enemies, vi, 477.

Peloponnese, Apis born in the, vi, 422.

Pelops, vi, 485; the Palladium formed from the remains of, vi, 484.

Penance, early Christian, iv, 86, 101; remedial, 87, 101; Roman doctrine of, iii, 425; for sin, degrees of, vii, 402; required in order to communion, 414.

Penates, said to be Neptune and Apollo, vi, 474, 475; gods of the recesses of heaven, 474; said to be of four kinds, 474; said to be Fortune, Ceres, the genius Jovialis, and Pales, 474, 475; and by the Etruscans to be the Consentes and Complices, 474.

Penitent thief (robber), the, his first meeting with Jesus, viii, 409; character and deeds of, 468; on the cross, rebukes his companion, and confesses Jesus, 469; Jesus promises paradise to, and writes respecting him to his "archangelic powers," 470; with Jesus in Galilee, seen transformed by John, 470; entrance of, into Hades, 457; entrance of, into paradise, 438, 452.

Penitential discipline, ii, 15, 22.

Penitents, proper conduct of, iii, 664; counsel to, iv, 212; place and privileges of, vi, 20; to be mercifully received, vii, 400; admitted to prayers, but not to communion, till after penance, 414; eucharistic prayer for, 485.

Pentateuch, purpose of, iv, 161.

Pentecost, the Christian, iv, 112; feast of, to be honored, vii, 449; Christian observance of, iii, 70.

Peratae, heresy of, v, 58; not generally known, 67; derived from astrology, 50; their system, 60; doctrine, 63, 142; name of, 62.

Perfect, why man was not made, i, 521.

Perfection, distinct from completeness, ii, 459; 478; may be shared by men and women, 431; possible to human nature, 502; attained by the true Gnostic alone, 502; true, in what it consists, 438.

Perfica, goddess of filthy pleasures, vi, 478.

Period, the seventh, v, 179.

Periodicity, Celsus' theory of, destroys free will, iv, 528.

Peripatetics, i, 195; ii, 191; Aristotle the father of, vi, 437.

Perowne referred to, iii, 270, 299.

Perpetua, martyr, the story of, viii, 485, 486; imprisoned, iii, 699, 700; her visions, 700; trial, 700, 701; courage, 701 seq., martyrdom, 697, 702, 703; and Felicitas, 697 seq.

Persecution, foretold, i, 509; how understood, ii, 598; duty in, vii, 439; those fleeing from, to be received, 498; tortures of, iii, 634; its cruelty and irrationality, vii, 147, 243; of the righteous, throughout history, iii, 640; God's discipline, iv, 116; Satan the instrument of, 117; not to be shunned as evil, 118; instance of Rutilius, 119; only Apostles commanded to flee, 119; Greek proverb on, answered, 121; instance of Jonah, 122; duty of clergy in, 122; not to be bought off, 122; table of persecutions of Christians, 125; in Lyons and Vienne, description of, viii, 778 seq.

Persecutions, how endured, v, 461–465; divine judgments for, 462–464; reward of faith and patience under, 465; the ten, iv, 125.

Persecutors of the church and their punishments, vii, 301 seq.

Persephone, viii, 197.

Perseus, son of Danae, i, 170.

Perseverance in faith better than attainment, v, 284.

Persians, inventions of, ii, 65; system of the, v, 40; laws of the, viii, 730; overcome because of the Christians, vi, 417; Christianity attested by mighty works among, 438; worshipped rivers, 510; skilled in secret arts, 480; the fire-worship of, viii, 141, 276; incest practised among the, 187.

Persius, on the vanity of idols, vii, 45; quoted, vii, 42, 85, 163.

Person, applied to the *hypostasis* in the divine nature, iii, 613, 615, 621; of Jesus Christ, 624.

Pertunda, a goddess presiding over the marriage court, vi, 478.

Pessinuntic Dindymene, vi, 488.

Pessinus, people of, worshipped a flint for the mother of the gods, vii, 510; Great Mother brought from, 538; Midas king of, 492.

Pestilence, sent to punish pollution of the circus, vi, 534; abated when deities were brought from abroad, 534; put to flight by Aesculapius, 536.

Peta, presiding over prayers, vi, 478.

Petavius, charges Tertullian with quasi-Arianism, iii, 630.

Peter, St., i, 6, 63, 69, 75, 81, 87, 103, 107, 111, 122, 153; tradition of his wife's martyrdom, ii, 541; imprisoned and released by Herod, 579; why change of name of, iii, 365, 426; modern claims from, iii, 266; receives the keys of the kingdom of heaven, 643; why given the power of the keys, iv, 99; Christ's charge to, refers to the whole episcopate, v, 305; the church built on him answering for all, 341, 374, 377, 382, 394, 422; does not claim supremacy, 377; meaning of " the Rock," 561; his office and work at Rome, vi, 47; and Paul, martyrdom of, i, 11; vii, 302; victory over Simon Magus, vi, 438; canon of, vii, 495.

Peter *according to the Clementines:* his cordial reception of the Clement, viii, 80, 227; instructions given by, to Clement, 81, 82, 83,

84, 227, 235, 236; his satisfaction with Clement, 82, 228; requests Clement to be his attendant, 81, 293; names of the attendants of, 229; postponement of his discussion with Simon Magus, 82, 83, 235; tactics of, in regard to Simon Magus, 236; exposes the design and object of Simon Magus, 239; sent to Caesarea, 96; is welcomed by Zacchaeus, 96; is challenged by Simon Magus, 96; his discussion with Simon Magus begins, 102, 243; lays down the principles on which the discussion should be conducted, 104; interrupted by Simon, 104, 105 seq.; his experience of the fallacy of imagination, 114, 115; his reverie, 114; rebuked by Andrew, 115; adjournment of his discussion with Simon Magus, 116, 249; his discussion with Simon Magus resumed, 117 seq.; accessibility of, 127; resolves to follow Simon Magus to Rome, 131; appoints Zacchaeus bishop of Caesarea, 131, 250, and ordains elders and deacons there, 131; sends twelve persons before him, 132; follows Simon to Tyre, 249; addresses the people at Tyre, 268; departs to Sidon, 269; proceeds to Tripolis, 133, 270; his thoughtfulness, 270; addresses the people, 271 seq.; halts at Dora, 134; addresses the people, 135; heals the sick, 136, 275, 276; arrangements made by, at Tripolis, 156; his third day at Tripolis, 280; leaves Tripolis for Antioch, 157, 292; at Antaradus, 292; sends Nicetus and Aquila to Laodicea, 292; his simplicity of life, 157, 293; his humility, 157, 293; his excursion to Aradus, 159, 294, where he finds the mother of Clement as a beggar-woman, 159, 160, 295; his reflection on the story told by the beggar-woman, 160, 296; brings her to Clement, 161, 296; leaves Aradus, 161, 297; proceeds to Laodicea, 300; recapitulates the story of Clement's mother, 162, 300, which leads to the discovery that Niceta and Aquila are her sons, 162–163, 300, 301; requires that their mother shall fast before receiving baptism, 164–165, 300; baptizes Mattihida, 165, 305; finds an old workman at the harbor, who accosts him, 165, 305; his discussion with the old man, 306, 307; arranges for a friendly conference with the old workman, 166; states the question for discussion, 166; has a contest of hospitality with the chief man of the city, 174; arranges for another conference at the house of the chief

man, 175; renews the conference, 182; discovers the old workman to be the father of Clement, 190, 307, wishes to convert him, 308 seq.; heals a demoniac daughter of the chief man by his presence in the house, 192; shows Clement the necessity of probation in the case of his father, 192; is appointed umpire in the further discussion with the old man, 194; his words about the true Prophet, his Master, 196; Clement's discourse before, 196 seq.; remarks of, on Clement's speech, 199 seq.; his discussion with Simon respecting the unity of God, 312; the mode of the discussion, 312; his reply to Simon's appeal to the Old Testament, and other objections, 313 seq.; close of the first day's discussion, 317; second day's discussion with Simon, 318 seq.; third day's discussion with Simon, 324; fourth day's discussion with Simon, 330 seq.; Simon is confounded by, rebuked by Faustus (Faustinianus), and retires, 338; reply to the questions of Sophonias and others, 339 seq.; Clement's father requests his permission to visit Appion and Annubion, 206, 342; Simon Magus excites the people at Antioch against, 206, 345; stratagem suggested to, by Cornelius, against Simon Magus, 206, 343; a counter-plot of, against Simon Magus, 207, 208, 345; success of his plot, 209, 342; the old man goes to Antioch, 609, 345; Peter's entry into Antioch, 209, 346; his thanksgiving, 210; miracles of, 210; baptizes Faustinianus, 210; ordains Clement his successor, 218; his charge to Clement, 219, 220; martyrdom of, 218; epistle of, to James, 215 seq.

Peter and Andrew, Acts of, viii, 526 seq.; and Paul, Acts of, 355, 477 seq.; hears with joy of Paul's coming to Rome, 478; the Jews strive to stir up Paul to speak against, 478; comes to Paul, 479; assailed by the Jews, he defends himself, 479; Simon Magus speaks against, 480; Simon excites Nero against, 480; disputes with Simon, before Nero, 480; by prayer causes Simon, who attempts to fly, to fall and be killed, 484; sentenced to be crucified, 484; curious story of the Lord's meeting him when he was escaping from Rome, 485; the burial of, 485; on a mountain with Matthew and Alexander, 526; Christ appears to, and salutes as bishop of the whole church, 526; asks an old husbandman for bread, and ploughs and sows for him, 526; ill-treated by one Onesiphorus,

Queen, a certain, v, 240; of the South, the, viii, 291; of Virgins, Mary, the, 373.

Questions, many, must be left in the hand of God, i, 399.

Quicunque vult, the hymn, vii, 366.

Quietus of Baruch, on baptism, v, 568.

Quindecemviri, the, wore wreaths of laurel, vi, 488.

Quinet referred to, v, 162.

Quintus, the apostate, i, 40.

Quintus, epistle of Cyprian to, v, 377.

Quintus of Aggya, on baptism, v, 571.

Quirinus, Cyprian's address to, v, 528; precepts and teachings to, 528–557, 562, 563.

Quirinus, excelled all in throwing the javelin, vi, 476.

Quirinus Martius, Romulus torn in pieces by the senators, called, vi, 424.

Quirites, vi, 477; the fathers of Rome, vii, 50.

Quotations in the New Testament, source of the, i, 452.

Quoted or referred authors and authorities, see under:—

Abbot.
Acta Pauli et Theclae.
Aeschylus.
Agatho.
Alcmaeon.
Alexis.
Alford.
Alzog.
Anacreon.
Anastasius Sinaita.
Antimachus.
Antiphanes.
Antipho.
Apollodorus.
Aquila.
Aquinas.
Aratus.
Archilochus.
Archinus.
Aretas.
Ariston.
Aristophanes.
Aristotle.
Ascension of Moses
Assemani.
Athamas.
Athanasius.
Auberlen.
Augias.
Augustine.
Bacon.
Baehr.
Bancroft.
Bardesanes.
Barnabas.
Beausobre.
Bede.
Bellarmine.
Bernard.
Bethune.
Bingham.
Black.
Bledsoe.
Boehl.
Bossuet.

Bryce.
Bull.
Bunsen.
Burgon.
Burton.
Buttler.
Caesar.
Callias.
Callimachus.
Calmet.
Calvin.
Canning.
Cary.
Casaubon.
Cassius.
Cave.
Chevallier.
Chilo.
Chrysostom.
Churton.
Cicero.
Cleanthes.
Clement of Alexandria.
Clementine Homilies.
Clementine Recognitions.
Clinton.
Coleridge.
Conybeare and Howson.
Cook.
Cooke.
Cotelerius.
Cowper, H.
Cowper, W.
Cox.
Coxe.
Cratinus.
Critias.
Cureton.
Cyprian.
Cyril.
Daillé or Dallaeus.
Dante.
Davidson.
Delitzsch.
De Maistre.
De Montor.
Demosthenes.
Deodati.
Diodorus.
Diogenes.
Diognetus, Epistle to.
Dionysius.
Dionysius Jambus.
Dionysius Thrax.
Dion Thytes.
Diphilus.
Doddridge.
Dodwell.
Döllinger.
Donaldson.
Dorner.
Dressel.
Dupin.
Edersheim.
Eldad and Modat, book of.
Empedocles.
Encylop. Britannica.
Ennius.
Epiphanius.
Eubulus.
Eudemus.
Eumelus.
Euphorion.

Eupolemus.
Euripides.
Eusebius.
Evans.
Ezekiel, the poet.
Faber.
Farrar.
Fenelon.
Fisher.
Fleury.
Foulkes.
Fuller.
Fürst.
Gallandi.
Gams.
Gellius.
Gesenius.
Gibbon.
Gieseler.
Grabe.
Griesbach.
Grosseteste.
Grotius.
Guettee.
Guillon.
Haag.
Hagenbach.
Hardwick.
Hartley of Winwick.
Harvey.
Hefele.
Heraclides.
Heraclitus.
Hermas.
Hermippus.
Herodotus.
Hesiod.
Hessey.
Hilgenfeld.
Hippias.
Hippo.
Hippocrates.
Hoffmann.
Hofman.
Homer.
Hooker.
Horace.
Huet.
Hyperides.
Iophon.
Irenaeus.
Isidore.
Isocrates.
Jacobson.
Janus.
Jarvis.
Jason and Papiscus.
Jerome.
Jewell.
Jones.
Jones of Nayland.
Jortin.
Josephus.
Jowett.
Jubilees, Book of.
Julian.
Junius.
Justin Martyr.
Justinian.
Juvenal.
Kahnis.
Kaye.
Kayser.

Rabbinical education, vii, 531.

Racami, laws of, the, viii, 731.

Race, an abominable, performed at Paphos, viii, 495.

Race-course, the, why not to be visited by Christians, iii, 87; injuries in, not redressed by law, 638.

Races, guilt contracted if the music stopped at the, vi, 486; in the games of Jupiter, 534, 535; seven rounds of the course in, 534.

Rahab, her example, i, 8.

Raiment, yellow, ii, 36; white, 36, 40.

Rainbow, the, viii, 176.

Ram, the, a type of Christ, viii, 759.

Rational creatures, capable of good and evil, iv, 256; term includes evil spirits, 257; final judgment of, 293; existed from the beginning, 342; fallen through free will, 342; of one nature, 342, 381; restored in the incarnation

183; the second advent of the Son of Man, viii, 584.

Song, the new, symbolizes the confession of the faith, vii, 350.

Sons, of the devil, i, 525.

Sonship of Christ, v, 229.

Sophia, the aeon, so called, i, 317; iii, 507; her passion, i, 317; iii, 508; her shapeless offspring, i, 317; iii, 508; restored by Horos, i, 318; iii, 508, 509; another name of Achamoth, i, 320; could have produced nothing apart from her consort, 372; exposure of the absurdity of the whole Valentinian theory respecting, 383 seq.

Sophists, foolishness of, ii, 304, 308; pretentious show of the, vi, 430.

Sophocles, on unity of God, i, 290; on future judgment, 291; quoted, i, 280, 290, 291; ii, 110, 131, 192, 197, 244, 284, 410, 447, 450, 470, 472, 473; also his —
Ajax, ii, 362, 482.
Aleades, ii, 482.
Antigone, ii, 482, 484.
Eriphyle, ii, 482.
Hipponos, ii, 482.
Minos, ii, 482.
Oedipus, ii, 97.
Peleus, ii, 484.
Philoctetes, i, 293.

Sophonias, his questions, and Peter's replies to, viii, 338, 339.

Sorcery, charged upon Christ, iv, 399.

Sorrow, ii, 49.

Soter, i, 393; bishop of Rome, 416, 569.

Sotio, i, 59.

Soul, the, of itself cannot see God, i, 196; not immortal in its own nature, 197; these things unknown to Plato and other philosophers, 198; how apprehended, vi, 54, 57; existence and nature of, 55; immortal, 55; viii, 124; immortality of, taught by philosophers, vii, 205; proofs of, 206, 253; and from the success of the wicked in this life, viii, 124; and because partaking of the divine nature, iv, 381; Clement's perplexities about, viii, 223, 224; the belief of, necessary to correct views of God, 231; denied by Simon Magus, 234; asserted by Peter, 286; the conscious witness to God, iii, 176. 179, to Christian truth, 178, and against heathen living, 179; its nature and functions, 532; its nature revealed in Holy Scripture, 184; birth of, 184; corporeal, 184, 557, 570, 587; not properly incorporeal, vi, 377; this shown by the parable of the rich man and Lazarus, 187; philosophical objections refuted, 187; revealed to a Montanist sister, 188; has free choice, viii, 45; not originated from matter, iii, 191; how revealed to the mind, 191; distinguished from the mind, vii,

298; its supremacy over mind, iii, 192; undivided, with various functions, 193; its office, vii, 162; its affections, 298; the seat of, as held by philosophers, 297; a better temple than any edifice, ii, 530; its vitality in the heart, iii, 194; rational, vi, 56, 57; rational in nature, irrational only in sin, iii, 194; the gift of God, vii, 298; the true man, 43; has perception through the intellect and senses, iii, 198; implies knowledge (instinct) as well as vitality, 199, illustrated, 200; one in nature, but subject to various development and changes, 201; defined, 202; heretical theories of its origin derived from Plato, 203; his theory of self-existence inconsistent, 204; existence of the soul before birth shown from physiology, 206, from Holy Scripture, 207; of one formation with the body, 208, 217; theories of transmigration refuted, 209–15; grows with growth of body, 218; corrupted by sin, 219, and the source of sin to the body, but not totally depraved, 220; regenerated by water and the Holy Spirit, 221; wholly separated from the body by death, 230, not unconscious in Hades, 235; extinction of the, held by Lucian, 547; and body, views of heretics relating to the future destruction of, refuted, i, 402; judgment of, and body, ii, 158; Tertullian on the soul, iii, 181 seq., and on the testimony of the, 175 seq.; Melito, on body and, viii, 756.

Soul of *man*, the image of Christ, vi, 329; origin of, undetermined, iv, 240; formed without the body, 264; theories on the final condition of, 273–375; (*anima*) in all beings, 286; distinct from spirit, iii, 463, 474; iv, 287; separated from the spirit by sin, 296; God's care of, 313; philosophical speculations on, 337; not tripartite, 337; whether intermediate between flesh and spirit, 338; subject to temptations of the flesh, 340; not of different natures, 340; souls of *angels*, 287; soul of *Christ*, intermediate between God and flesh, 282; soul of *God*, anthropomorphic term, 289; the *animal*, does not partake of the divine nature, vi, 444; philosophical theories of its immortality uncertain and contradictory, 446; made immortal only by God's gift, 447, 454, 457.

Souls, absurdity of the doctrine of the transmigration of, i, 409; existence of, after death, 410; immortal, although they had a beginning, 411; ii, 580; borne aloft, i, 572; ii, 580; said to pass into cattle, vi,

440; of the righteous and the wicked how they go out of the body, viii, 576.

Sound mind, a, in a sound body, viii, 229.

Southey referred to, ii, 62.

Sower, parable of the, an illustration of free-will, iv, 314.

Spain, vi, 417; Hercules buried in, 422; epistle of Cyprian to the people in, v, 369.

Sparrows made of clay by the child Jesus, viii, 378, 414.

Sparta and Lacedaemon, Castor and Pollux buried in, vi, 485.

Spartanus, Mars identified with, vi, 484.

Speaking, filthy, on, ii, 250.

Spear, a, worshipped by the Romans for Mars, vi, 510.

Spectacles, public, ii, 289; Tertullian on, iii, 79–61.

Speech, subordinate to action, ii, 310.

Spencer referred to, iv, 418.

Spermatic word, i, 193.

Speusippus quoted, ii, 351.

Sphinx, a, in a heathen temple, rebukes the unbelief of men in relation to Jesus, viii, 520; the testimony of, to Jesus, 520.

Spies, in the enemy's camp, viii, 236.

Spirit, definition of, ii, 584; in the sense of breath (or life) identical with soul, iii, 190; but more probably the spirit of God or of evil, coming upon the soul, not born with it, 191; the Holy, i, 164, 167, 177, 243; gifts of, 533; necessity of a union with, in, 71; prophetic, 28; of divinity how manifest, 28; not to be grieved, 26; to be tried by his works, 27.

Spirits, ii, 49; two kinds, 24, 27, 70; in man, viii, 9; of error, 9; in prison, preached to, ii, 490.

Spiritual, absurdity of heretics, claiming to be, while they declare the Demiurge to be animal, i, 403; men, 506, 533; enter the Pleroma, 325, 326.

Spiritus, used of the Divine Nature of Christ, iii, 630.

Spoiling the Egyptians, the act examined and vindicated, i, 502.

Spurious epistles of Ignatius, i, 107–126; introductory note to, 105, 106; pieces, v, 242.

Stachys, viii, 497; receives Philip to his house, appointed bishop of Ophioryma, 503, 510.

Stage, gods brought on, vi, 487, 488.

Standards, the Roman, miraculously bow down to Jesus, viii, 440.

Stanley referred to, iv, 418; vi, v, vi.

Stans, Simon Magus so-called, viii, 96, 99, 100, 233.

Star in the east, the, iv, 422; seen at the birth of Christ, viii, 375.

Stars, astronomical theories of, influence on life, v, 43; worshipped as gods, vii, 47, 231; ordered by God, 48; the motions of, viii, 171; what they are, 49.

Stasius quoted, ii, 484.

States, genii of, vi, 420.

Station, ii, 33.

Stationary days, vii, 445; fasts of, ii, 544; iv, 103, 109; observance of, vi, 278.

Stations, iv, 103, 108.

Statius Quadratus, proconsul, i, 43.

Statues of the Greeks ridiculed, ii, 79.

Stauros and Horos, i, 318, 319.

Stellar influence, futility of the theory of, v, 34.

Stentors, vi, 462.

Stephanus, epistle of Cyprian to, v, 367, 378, 418.

Stephen, i, 69, 107, 113; bishop of Rome, position in regard to heretical baptism, v, 376–379; breaks the unity of the church, 396; epistle of Dionysius of Alexandria to, vi, 101; deacon and martyr, feast of, to be honored, vii, 442.

Steps, the fifteen, of the temple, viii, 385.

Sterope, loved by Apollo, vi, 485.

Stesichorus, the story of, i, 348.

Stoic theory, of a future life, iv, 552; of the world, vi, 455; that souls survived death for a little, 455; dilemma quoted, iv, 616.

Stoics, i, 169, 190, 191; probable view of the, concerning the soul, iii, 184; theory of fate, v, 20; of soul and body, 20; their physical interpretation of mythology, vii, 24; called the elements gods, 24, 29; make all the world to be God, 196; take away human affections, 237; errors respecting God and nature, 196; their further views of God, 197, 261.

Stone, the, cut out without hands, i, 453; the Arabians worshipped an unhewn, vi, 510; a, sent from Phrygia as the great mother, 538.

Stones, ii, 14, 44, 46, 50; after the deluge men sprung from, 491; anointed with oil, and worshipped, 423.

Strangers, the church's care for, v, 314; to be received in church with honor, vii, 422.

Stratocles, brother of Aegeates, viii, 516.

Strife, its effects, i, 5, 6, 17.

Stromata, the, of Clement of Alexandria, object and character of, ii, 168, 342, 347, 480; meaning of the term, 408; why written, 299; objections to the many extracts, answered, 303.

Study, necessary for teachers, viii, 48; diligence in, recommended, 122, 152.

Stygian Jupiter, i.e., Pluto, vi, 460.

Styx, a river in the infernal regions, vi, 439, 500.

Sub-deacons, vii, 400; ordination of, 492.

Submission, viii, 292; to Christ, i, 90; to one another, 15; of authors of sedition, 11.

Substance, how distinct from qualities, iv, 379.

Suburbicarian Sees, v, 159.

Successus, Cyprian to, v, 408.

Successus of Abbir Germaniciana, on baptism, v, 567.

Sueton referred to, i, 163; iii, 135; viii, 484.

Sufferings, objection to, answered, ii, 423; of Christ, i, 76; of men, 6, 39, 129; why desired by the ancients, viii, 44; sin the cause of, 137, 143; salutary, 137; different effects of, upon heathens and Christians, 159.

Suggestions of the old serpent, viii, 147–149.

Suicer referred to, viii, 16.

Suicide, taught by Pythagoreans and Stoics, vii, 89.

Suidas referred to, iii, 136.

Sulla, the proscription of, spoken of as the battle of Cannae, vi, 504.

Summanus, i.e., Pluto, vi, 476, 503.

Sumptuary laws, not observed in time of Arnobius, vi, 460.

Sun, the, all things vivified by the heat of, vi, 413; said to be only a foot in breadth, 457; identified with Bacchus and Apollo, 473, and with Attis, 505; five gods said to be, 480; represented with rays of light, 511; father of Phaethon, 505; worship of, retorted on the heathen, iii, 123; and moon, the, bear testimony against the sins of men, viii, 575; moon and stars, motions of, 177; ministers of good and evil, 177.

Sunday, i, 186; its observance not worship of the sun, iii, 123; service appointed by the apostles, viii, 668.

Sunsetting, the time when the angels give in to God their report of the conduct of men, viii, 575.

Supererogation, ii, 34, 52.

Superstition, not reasonable, vii, 157; origin of, ii, 528; of the Jews, i, 26.

Supper, the, of the gods, viii, 202, 203.

Supreme Jupiter, the, in opposition to the Stygian, vi, 460.

Sura, consul, i, 131.

Sursum Corda, vii, 535, 543, 555, 563; in the Holy Communion, 486; verse and response in Cyprian's time, v, 455, 559.

Susanna, an argument for the veiling of women, iii, 95; conduct of, viii, 64; story of, warning against false judgment, vii, 417; book of, interpreted, v, 191–194; history of, question of Africanus, iv, 385; Origen's answer, 386; play of Hebrew and Greek words in, 388; why not in the Hebrew of Daniel, 388; other objections answered, 390.

Susidae, customs of the, viii, 188.

Swan, Jupiter changed into a, vi, 483, 506.

Swearing, i, 168.

Swift referred to, iii, 239.

Swine, not allowed as food to Israel, i, 143; casting pearls before, viii, 117.

Sword, not peace, but a, viii, 153, 288.

Sylburg referred to, i, 29.

Syllables, absurdity of arguments derived from, i, 393.

Symbolism of the letters, i, 337–341.

Symbols, of the cross, i, 181; of the four evangelists, 428; Pythagorean, in philosophic proverbs, ii, 450; Egyytian, 454; of philosophical language, 455; of the Mosaic law, 456; reasons for, 457; apostolic opinion of, 459; Jewish, do not sanction image worship, 453, 477.

Symeon, the son of Clopas, bishop of Jerusalem, is martyred under Trajan, viii, 764.

Symmachus quoted, v, 164.

Symphorosa, St., and her seven sons, passion of, vi, 138–139.

Synagogue, worship of, provided for villages, a preparation for Christian worship, vii, 531.

Synaxis, term applied to the Holy Communion, v, 257, 259; succeeds the synagogue, vii, 532, 544.

Synchronisms of the luminaries, viii, 734.

Syneisactae, ii, 58.

Synod, a primitive, under Dionysius, vi, 82; African, decree of, on giving peace to the lapsed, v, 336.

Syracuse, Paul at, viii, 477.

Syria, plagued with locusts because of the Christians, vi, 417.

Syriac, Calendar, viii, 666; documents, introductory notice to, viii, 647 seq., 721; language, viii, 742; its importance, 742, 743; version of the Ignatian epistles, i, 99–104; introductory note to, 97.

Syro-Phoenician woman, the story of, amplified, viii, 232.

Systems, various, of the heretics, i, 332–333.

Tabernacle, and its furniture, symbolic meaning of, ii, 452; the, type of the church and of heaven, vi, 328.

"Tabernacle in the Sun," meaning of, viii, 49.

Tabernacles, Feast of, spiritually interpreted, vi, 344, 347; type of the resurrection, 368.

Tacitus referred to, iii, 65.

Tactics, the, of Peter against Simon Magus, viii, 236.

Tages, the Etruscan, vi, 460.

Talkative wife, ii, 11.

Talmud, the, referred to, i, 63.

Vulcan, explained as fire, vi, 472; lame, 484; wrought as a smith in Lemnos, 480, 484; son of the Nile, 480, loved by Ceres, 485; father of the third Sun, 480, and of Apollo by the first Minerva, 480; four gods named, 480; lord of fire, 460, 469, 470; represented in workman's dress, 511, with cap and hammer, 511.

Vulturnus, the father-in-law of Ja , vi, 471.

Wake referred to, i, 6, 43, 133, 134; ii, 27; viii, 647.

Walk, how to, ii, 288.

Walpole referred to, v, 266.

Wantonness, ii, 49.

War and strife, proclaimed by Christ, viii, 105, 106.

Warburton referred to, i, 277, 292; ii, 520; vii, 138.

Warren referred to, ii, 298.

Watch, the, who were placed at the tomb of Jesus, bribed by the Jews to give lying testimony, viii, 422, 432, 444.

Watchers, the, viii, 10, 27.

Watches of the night, spiritually interpreted, vi, 326.

Water, a symbol of Christ, v, 234; made wine, spiritual meaning of, 362; the power of, illustrating divine providence, viii, 172; of baptism prefigured in the Old Testament, i, 144; iii, 672, 673; why used in baptism, 670; first brought forth life in the Creation, 670; sanctified by the brooding of the Holy Spirit, 670; cleanses flesh and spirit, 671; blessed at the pool of Bethesda, 671; born of, viii, 155, 289; baptized with, 290; regeneration by, 155, 184; heathen uses of, iii, 671; the medicine of temperance, ii, 243; in the Eucharist, vii, 486; blessing of, 494.

Waterland referred to, ii, 20; iv, 409, 480.

Watts referred to, ii, 77.

Waverers, worship idols, ii, 51.

Way of salvation, the, viii, 270.

Ways, the two, i, 148, 149, of life and death, vii, 164, 246, 465; of God, opposed to man's ways, viii, 231.

Weaving, analogue of the Incarnation v, 205.

Wedding garment, baptism, the, viii, 142.

Wednesday-service appointed by the apostles, viii, 668.

Weekly worship of the Christians, i, 185.

Weitzäcker referred to, i, 137.

Wells of the patriarchs, iv, 517.

Westcott referred to, i, 155; ii, 3, 6, 7; iv, 437; viii, 3, 5.

Westropp referred to, iii, 477.

Wheat, introduced into Attica by Ceres, vi, 504.

Whiston referred to, i, 47.

"Who is the rich man, that shall be saved," a treatise by Clement of Alexandria, ii, 169, 591–605.

Wicked, their punishment, i, 164, 165, 168; viii, 543, 547, 572 seq., to be separated from the righteous, i, 556; souls of the, pass into beasts, vi, 440; the success of, in this life a proof of immortality, viii, 124; and righteous, chastisement of, 178; actions to be avoided, 336; One, the, why appointed over the wicked by a righteous God, 342; why entrusted with power, 335.

Wickedness, ii, 49.

Wiclif, i, 497; ii, 62.

Widowhood, highly honored, iv, 43; advantages of, 56.

Widows, i, 34, 82, 94; ii, 52; concerning, vii, 426, 427; character of, falsely so called, 428; duty of, 429, 430; not to marry again, iv, 43; examples in Holy Scripture, v, 480.

Wieseler referred to, iii, 378.

Wife, character of a good, ii, 432; Tertullian's treatise to his, iv, 39 seq.; design of the treatise, 39, 44.

Wiles of the devil, viii, 240.

Will, the freedom of, in man, i, 518; viii, 119; of God irresistible, viii, 120; how to be done, v, 451; divine and human in Christ, vi, 114, 117; free, in salvation, vi, 458.

Williams referred to, i, 21; vii, 571.

Willing, definition of, ii, 580.

Willow, the, why a type of chastity, vi, 324, 346.

Willows, ii, 39.

Winds, the, represented as blowing trumpets, vi, 510.

Wine jars, ii, 29.

Wine, in the Eucharist, mixed with water, i, 185, 527; and bread in the Eucharist, 528; how used by Christians, ii, 242; how abused to drunkenness, 243 seq.; Christ's example in, 246; in Holy Scripture, true and spurious, vi, 327, 349; in the rites of Bona Dea, vi, 496; sanctuary of Attis not entered by those who had drunk, 492; Roman matrons not allowed to drink, 460.

Wisdom, Christ the, i, 227; object of true philosophy, ii, 492; manifold, 518; the word of God, iii, 487, 601, 614, 629; in Proverbs, interpreted, v, 175; the artificer of all things, vi, 369, 381; why not found by the Greeks, 401; cannot be separated from religion, vii, 10, 11, 51, 100, 103, 238; divine, its power over life, 96; freely given to all, 96; errors of Lucretius and Cicero respecting its origin, 85; where to be found, 100; false, 233; a name of Christ, iv, 247; three-

fold, 334; divinely taught in Old and New Testaments, 482–485; does not mislead, 492; divine and human distinguished, 579; Christian, distinguishes between knowledge and sense, 630.

Wisdom of Solomon, book of, not canonical, iv, 379, 384.

Wise men of Greece, the Seven, vii, 101.

Wise, the, divine things justly hidden from, viii, 335.

Within, the Penates said to be those, vi, 474.

Witness, qualification of a, viii, 616.

Witnesses, the two, v, 213, 249.

Witnesses, the three, ii, 576; v, 380, 382, 418; spurious text of, iii, 631.

Witnesses, the, who appeared for Jesus before Pilate, viii, 419, 428, 440 seq.

Witnesses of the resurrection of Jesus, viii, 422, 424, 432.

Wives, duties of, i, 34, 81, 86, 95, 100, of clergy, not to be cast off, vii, 500.

Woman, meaning of the word, iii, 687, 688; generic name not for the married only, iv, 30, 38; applied to the Blessed Virgin, 31; the, with the issue of blood, not a type of the suffering aeon, i, 392, healed by Christ, viii, 460, 462; is Veronica, 428, 442; of the Apocalypse, a symbol of church, v, 217; vi, 336; her child typifies not Christ, but Christians, 337, 355; the, of sorrowful spirit, viii, 294; her story, 295.

Womanhood, self-evident, not to be concealed, iv, 35.

Womb, the, viii, 173.

Women, not to be despised, i, 114; Christian, ii, 78; counsel to, iv, 214 seq.; heathen, ii, 78, 79; right adorning of, 287; chaste habits in, 288; behavior at church, 290; example of perfection in, 431; dress of, iii, 687; veiling of, 687, 689; why to be veiled, iv, 31 seq.; ought not to teach, vii, 427.

Wood referred to, iii, 270.

Word, the, in the world before Christ, i, 178, 192; foretold in the Psalms, iii, 299; called the Logos, vii, 107; a divine person, i, 166, 264; how divine, vi, 41; Christ, the, i, 164, 170, 190, 191, 272; the eternal generation of, v, 227; vi, 92, 120; eternal and incarnate, ii, 234; how incarnate, iii, 623; incarnate in Christ, v, 229, 231–232; the spermatic, i, 193; the world made through, i, 361; ii, 97; has the names of the seven spirits in Isaiah, vii, 342; reveals the Father, i, 467, 468; always with the Father, 487; consubstantial with the Father, vi, 45, 120; all things created by, i, 487, 488; declares God, 489; truly man, v, 230; takes flesh to save the flesh,

THE ANTE-NICENE FATHERS

INDEX OF TEXTS